The Last Dance

FOURTH EDITION

Encountering Death and Dying

L Y N N E   A N N   D E S P E L D E R
Cabrillo College

A L B E R T   L E E   S T R I C K L A N D

Mayfield Publishing Company
Mountain View, California
London • Toronto

To our parents Bruce Erwin DeSpelder & Dorothy Roediger DeSpelder and Luther Leander Strickland (1896–1966) & Bertha Wittenburg Strickland (1905–1985), who gave us our first "Golden Books" and shared with us the joys of reading.

Library of Congress Cataloging-in-Publication Data

DeSpelder, Lynne Ann
    The last dance : encountering death and dying / Lynne Ann
DeSpelder, Albert Lee Strickland. — 4th ed.
        p.   cm.
    Includes bibliographical references and indexes.
    ISBN 1-55934-458-X
    1. Death—Psychological aspects.   2. Death—Social aspects.
I. Strickland, Albert Lee.   II. Title.
BF789.D4D53   1995
155.9′37— dc20   95-35005
                                                                                                          CIP

Manufactured in the United States of America
10   9   8   7   6   5   4

Mayfield Publishing Company
1280 Villa Street
Mountain View, California 94041

Sponsoring editor, Franklin C. Graham; *production editor,* Merlyn Holmes; *copy editor,* Carol Dondrea; *text designer,* Albert Burkhardt; *cover designer and art manager,* Susan Breitbard; *art and photo research,* Lynne Ann DeSpelder and Albert Lee Strickland; *computer illustrator,* Joan Carol; *manufacturing manager,* Amy Folden. The text was set in 10/12 Baskerville by Graphic World, Inc. and printed on 50# Saybrook Opaque, an acid-free paper, by Quebecor Printing Book Group.

Credits and sources are listed on a continuation of the copyright page, p. 671.

Contents

CHAPTER 4

CHAPTER 5

C H A P T E R 6

C H A P T E R 7

CHAPTER *8*

Last Rites: Funerals and Body Disposition   287

C H A P T E R   9

The Law and Death   327

C H A P T E R   I 2

CHAPTER 13

CHAPTER 14

CHAPTER 15

Preface

*T*he study of death is concerned with questions that are rooted at the center of human experience, the most important of which are not fully answerable in terms of a standard textbook definition. Thus, the person who sets out to increase his or her knowledge of death and dying is embarking on an exploration that is partly a journey of personal and experiential discovery. In writing *The Last Dance: Encountering Death and Dying,* our aim has been to offer a comprehensive and readable introduction to the study of death and dying, one that highlights the main issues and questions as well as the most interesting problems. We are sensitive to the reader's need for a text that balances intensity with relief, detailed investigation of specific issues with general discussion of broader topics. There is a sense of genuine collaboration between author and reader in exploring the sometimes difficult, perhaps painful, issues and questions relative to dying and death. The text embodies an approach to the study of death and dying that combines the intellectual and the emotional, the social and the individual, the experiential and the scholarly. It emphasizes the positive values of compassion, listening, and tolerance for the views of others and encourages the reader to engage in a constructive process of self-discovery.

This book presents a comprehensive survey of an area of study that is still in its formative stage. It is not an indoctrination to any one point of view, but an introduction to diverse points of view. The reader is invited to participate in discovering the assumptions and predispositions that have inhibited open discussion about death and dying for much of the twentieth century. Readers may well form their own opinions, but, when they do, it is to be hoped that this is done only after considering other possibilities in a spirit of tolerance and open-mindedness. Unbiased investigation makes available choices that might otherwise be neglected because of ignorance or prejudice.

The Last Dance: Encountering Death and Dying provides readers with a solid grounding in theory and research as well as methods for applying what is learned to their own situations, personal and professional. For individuals who wish to pursue further study of particular topics, a list of recommended readings is provided at the end of each chapter, and citations given in the chapter notes can be used as a guide to additional sources, including pertinent selections in the companion volume to this text, *The Path Ahead: Readings in Death and Dying* (Mayfield, 1995). Thus, readers are introduced to a broad range of topics in death studies while being encouraged to investigate more deeply particular topics that evoke special interest.

The study of death is necessarily interdisciplinary. Accordingly, contributions from medicine, the humanities, and the social sciences can all be found here in their relevant contexts. Throughout the book, principles and concepts are made more meaningful by extensive use of examples and anecdotes. Boxed material and other illustrative materials expand upon and provide counterpoint to the textual presentation. We urge readers to make use of these materials. Excessive technicalities and jargon are avoided; specialized terms, when needed, are clearly defined. Although topics are organized in a way that we believe will meet the needs of most readers, the book has been written to allow for flexibility in sequencing the chapters for those who prefer a different approach.

While retaining all of the features that instructors and students have found beneficial in earlier editions, the fourth edition reflects ongoing evolution in the study of death and dying. For example, Chapter 3 focuses attention on how forces of socialization influence the way people relate to dying and death in a given society. This material builds on the examination of American attitudes toward death in Chapter 1 and the discussion of historical and cross-cultural perspectives on death in Chapter 2. We believe the emphasis on sociocultural factors in the first three chapters will give readers a solid basis for appreciating how specific issues in death, dying, and bereavement affect individuals, families, and social groups. In addition, throughout the text, we discuss the role of ethnic traditions in modern, culturally diverse societies.

Chapters 4 and 5 deal, first, with the modern health care system, including options for delivering medical care to terminally ill patients, and, then, with the experience of life-threatening illness and patterns of coping with it. The issues discussed in these two chapters lead naturally to a concern with the ethical questions that arise in the context of dying in a technological age. Chapter 6 is devoted to an exploration of such concerns, including informed consent, euthanasia, and the definition of death. Taken together, these three chapters provide a comprehensive investigation of issues related to medical care at the end of life.

In the next three chapters, attention is given to the experience of bereavement and its aftermath. Chapter 7 deals with grief and how its expression is influenced by a variety of psychosocial factors. Chapter 8 examines how rites and ceremonies for the dead create opportunities for expressing grief. It also includes detailed coverage of the elements and costs associated with contemporary funeral rituals. Chapter 9 looks at ways in which the legal system influences our understanding and practices relative to dying and death. This influence is evident in the evolving nature of advance directives, organ donation, death certification, and the procedures and processes associated with wills and probate.

A lifespan perspective on dying and death is presented in Chapters 10 and 11. The kinds of death-related issues likely to be encountered at different stages of life are placed within a developmental context that draws upon both theoretical work and clinical findings. Building on this discussion of normative patterns through the life cycle, Chapter 12 examines suicide as a mode of death that relates to a variety of risk factors, many of which are subject to alleviation through timely application of techniques of prevention and intervention. New to the fourth edition is an expanded discussion of the psychological autopsy as a means of investigating the antecedents of suicidal behavior. Continuing the examination of issues that are crucial to a comprehensive view of death and dying, Chapter 13 provides detailed discussion about various risks of death that have a particular impact in contemporary societies. Addressed are issues relating to risk-taking, accidents, disasters, violence and homicide, war and the nuclear threat, AIDS and other emerging diseases, and stress.

Questions about the meaning that human beings ascribe to mortality come to the fore in Chapters 14 and 15. Chapter 14 presents a wide range of concepts and beliefs regarding questions of immortality and the afterlife, drawing from religious and secular traditions as well as modern research into near-death experiences. Chapter 15 reviews the topics discussed throughout the text and provides a summary of the personal values and societal applications that can be gained through education about death. In bringing together many of the topics covered in the text, the chapter concludes with a discussion about how the "good death" might be defined.

Many people have assisted us in the making of this book. Over the course of its four editions, *The Last Dance* has been reviewed by instructors in a broad range of academic disciplines who have provided suggestions for making it a better teaching tool. Formal reviews have been provided by Thomas Attig, Bowling Green State University; Michael Beechem, University of West Florida, Pensacola; John B. Bond, The University of Manitoba; Sandor B. Brent, Wayne State University; Tom Bruce, Sacramento City College; Charles A. Corr, Southern Illinois University; Gerry R. Cox, Fort Hays State University; Steven A. Dennis, Utah State University; Kenneth J. Doka, College of New Rochelle; Audrey K. Gordon, Oakton Community College; Debra Bence Grow, Pennsylvania State University; John Harvey, Western Illinois University; Russell G. Henke, Towson State University; David D. Karnos, Eastern Montana College; Linda C. Kinrade, California State University, Hayward; Anthony Lenzer, University of Hawaii at Manoa; J. Davis Mannino, Santa Rosa Junior College; Wendy Martyna, University of California, Santa Cruz; Marsha McGee, Northeast Louisiana University; Walter L. Moore, Florida State University, Tallahassee; Vincent M. Rolletta, Erie Community College; Rita S. Santanello, Belleville Area College, Illinois; Thomas W. Satre, Sam Houston State University; Edwin S. Shneidman, University of California, Los Angeles; Judith M. Stillion, Western Carolina University; Jeffrey S. Turner, Mitchell College; Hannelore Wass, University of Florida, Gainesville; John B. Williamson, Boston College; C. Ray Wingrove, University of Richmond; Joseph M. Yonder, Villa Maria College of Buffalo; and Andrew Scott Ziner, University of North Dakota. Other colleagues have informally shared their ideas for enhancing particular aspects of the text. To all of these educators who have taken time to comment on the book through its successive incarnations, we extend our appreciation.

In addition, a debt of gratitude is owed to the scholars whose work is represented in these pages.

Assistance in gathering both text and art materials was willingly provided by staff members at a number of museums, libraries, and governmental institutions. Other individuals helped with research, clerical, and production tasks. Our collaborators on successive editions of the *Instructor's Guide* that accompanies this text deserve special thanks, and we express our gratitude to Barbara Jade Sironen, Patrick Vernon Dean, and Robert James Baugher. In our association with Mayfield Publishing Company, we have had the pleasure of working with a host of people who exemplify excellence in publishing. Particular thanks is due to Robert C. Erhart, who nurtured this book during its early development; Franklin C. Graham, whose editorial vision and warm friendship inspires and sustains us when the going gets rough; Albert Burkhardt and Nancy Sears, who initially set the tone for the book's design and art direction; Linda Toy, who, as head of the production department, somehow displays uncommon (though welcome) calm and cheerfulness despite pressing deadlines. For this new edition, we also thank Merlyn Holmes, who kept manuscript, galleys, and proofs on track, and Julie Wildhaber, who provided timely editorial assistance. Finally, we are grateful to Matt Strickland, whose generous and expert help in completing both the textbook and its ancillaries came in the nick of time. To all whose help was instrumental in bringing this edition of *The Last Dance* to readers, our sincere thanks.

L. A. D.
A. L. S.

I don't know how much time I have left. I've spent my life dispensing salves and purgatives, potions and incantations—miracles of nature (though I admit that some were pure medicine-show snake oil). Actually, half the time all I offered was just plain common sense. Over the years, every kind of suffering person has made his or her way here. Some had broken limbs or broken bodies . . . or hearts. Often their sorrow was an ailing son or daughter. It was always so hard when they'd lose a child. I never did get used to that. And then there were the young lovers. Obtaining their heart's desire was so important to them. I had to smile. I always made them sweat and beg for their handful of bark, and for those willful tortures I'll probably go to hell . . . if there is one. My God, how long has it been since I had those feelings myself? The fever, the lump in the throat, the yearning. I can't remember. A long time . . . maybe never. Well, there have been other passions for me. There's my dusty legion of jars. Each one holds its little secret. Barks, roots, soils, leaves, flowers, mushrooms, bugs—magic dust, every bit of it. There's my book—my "rudder," a ship's pilot would call it. That's a good name for it. Every salve, every purgative . . . they're all in there. (Everything, that is, except my stained beard, scraggly hair, and flowing robes—they'll have to figure those out on their own.) And then there's my walking stick (always faithful) . . . and the ballerina. And ten thousand mornings, ten thousand afternoons, ten thousand nights. And the stars. Oh, I have had my loves.

It hurts to move. My shelf and jars seem so far away, though I know that if I tried I could reach them. But no. It's enough and it's time . . . almost. I hope he makes it back in time. He burst through my door only two days ago. A young man, well spoken. Tears were streaming down his face. He looked so bent and beaten that I could not refuse him. He told me that his wife had died over a month ago and that he had been inconsolable since.

I

"Please help me," he pleaded, "or kill me." He covered his face with his hands. "Perhaps they're the same thing. I don't know anymore."

I let him cry awhile so I could watch him, gauge him. When at last he looked up, with my good hand I motioned him to take a seat. Then, between coughing fits, I went to work. "Do you see that toy there?" I said. "The little ballerina . . . Yes, that's it. Pick it up."

"Pick it up?"

"It won't bite. Pick it up." (He probably thought it was a trick—that's what they expect.) He grasped it carefully, with one hand, then wiped his eyes with the other. "That's better," I continued. "That's just a toy to you. You don't know what meaning to put to it, yet. So I want you to look at that ballerina."

He was hesitant, but I waited, stubbornly, until he looked down and fixed his attention on the little toy dancer. I went on: "I knew a young man once who was very handsome—always had been. He not only turned every head, he was strong and smart, and his family was wealthy. His main concern each day was which girl he should court that evening. He had planned that after several seasons of playing at love he would marry a beautiful girl, have beautiful children, and settle down to spend the money his father had promised him. And he had plans for that money. He had already purchased the land he wanted to live on and was having built there the biggest house in the area. He was going to raise and race horses, I think. One morning he got on his favorite horse and went for a ride. He whipped that horse into a gallop; it stepped in a whole and threw him. The young man broke his neck, and died." I stared at my guest and waited.

"That's a tragedy," he finally croaked.

"For whom? For those he left behind, perhaps. But was it for him? When he opened his eyes that morning, he didn't know he would die that day. He had no intention of dying for another sixty years—if then. None of us does." The young man looked confused. "His mistake was that he forgot that he could die that day."

"That's a morbid thought," he replied, and he looked as though he had just smelled something putrid.

"Is it? A moment ago you asked me to end your grieving by ending your own life. Suppose I oblige?" I stared at him for a few moments with my most practiced penetrating glare. "Suppose I did agree to kill you. How would you spend your last few minutes?"

He was still a little wary of me, but relieved that I seemed to be suggesting a hypothetical situation, rather than a serious course of action. He considered the possibilities for a while, then straightened in his chair. "Well, I guess I would step outside and take a last, best look at the sky, the clouds, the trees."

"Suppose you lived that way all the time?" He stared at me, then looked down at his hands, searching them. "That young man I told you about . . . perhaps the tragedy for him was not that he died, but that he failed to use the eventual certainty of his death to make him live! Did he woo each of those ladies as though it might be his last romance? Did he build that house as though it might be his last creation? Did he ride that horse as though it would be his last ride? I don't know; I hope so." My

young guest nodded, but he was still sad. I pointed to the toy ballerina he was holding. "That was given to me by a young lady who understood these things."

He looked at the figure closely. "Is she a dancer?"

"Yes, she is, and she is dead." The young man looked up, once again off balance. "She has been dead for, oh, a very long time." After all these years, a tear fell onto my cheek. I let it go. "She was many things. A child, a woman, a cook and a gardener, a friend, lover, daughter . . . But what she really was—who she was—was a dancer. When she was dying, she gave that doll to me, smiled, and whispered, 'At the moment of my death, I will take all of my dancing and put it in there, so my dancing can live on.'"

Tears welled in my guest's eyes.

"I can help you," I said, "but first there is something that you must do." He became very attentive. "Go to town and knock on the door of the first house you come to. Ask the people inside if their family has ever been touched by death. If so, go to the next house. When you find a family that has not *been touched by death, bring them to me. Do you understand?" He nodded, and I sighed. "I'm tired now."*

He got up, set the ballerina back on the table, and started for the door. I stopped him. "Young man!" He faced me from the doorway. "Come back as soon as you can."

David Gordon

In a Spanish village, neighbors and relatives peer through a doorway onto the deathbed scene of a villager.

CHAPTER I

Attitudes Toward Death: A Climate of Change

*O*f all human experiences, none is more overwhelming in its implications than death. Yet, for most of us, death remains a shadowy figure whose presence is only vaguely acknowledged. The predominant outlook and social customs of American society still reflect a queasy uncertainty that some observers characterize as a denial of death.[1] Anxiety in the face of death is not new, of course. Death has always been the central question of human experience, although it is one that, for the greater part of the twentieth century, most Americans have tried in various ways to avoid. Recently, however, this attitude of avoidance has become somewhat balanced, as increasing numbers of people find it appropriate to engage in a more open investigation of death. When death touches our lives, the experience goes beyond the merely academic or theoretical. Thus, our inquiry into the issues that pertain to dying, death, and bereavement must, in the end, be practical.

To provide a context for the journey that follows, we begin by casting a glance backward in time. Looking to the past can provide clues about how and why present attitudes evolved. By acquiring a sense of the way that people believed, behaved, and felt about death in an earlier time, we can appreciate more fully how our attitudes are influenced by social forces that tend to lessen our familiarity with dying and death. With this understanding in mind, we then look at how attitudes toward death are revealed in the cultural artifacts of language, music, literature, and the visual arts, as well as by the mass media in the form of news

You can feel the silence pass over the community as all activity is stopped and the number of rings is counted. One, two, three—it must be the Myer's baby that has the fever. No, it's still tolling—four, five, six. There is another pause at twenty—could that be Molly Shields? Her baby is due at any time now—no, it's still tolling. Will it never stop? Thirty-eight, thirty-nine, another pause—who? It couldn't be Ben; he was here just yesterday; said he was feeling fit as a fiddle—no, it's starting again. Seventy, seventy-one, seventy-two. Silence. You listen, but there is no sound—only silence. Isaac Tipton. He has been ailing for two weeks now. It must be Isaac.

Figure *1-1*   *Tolling the Bell*

and entertainment. Before closing the chapter with a section devoted to the process of examining assumptions, we survey the present milieu as it has been shaped by pioneering contributions to the field of death studies and by the impact of AIDS.

Patterns of Death and Dying: Then and Now

The predominant attitude toward death today is dramatically different from what it was even as recently as a hundred years ago.[2] In contrast to the death-related experiences of most Americans today, consider those that were commonplace to someone living before the turn of the century. Death usually took place in the home, with all family members present, down to the youngest child. Friends and relatives gathered for the death watch, maintaining a vigil at the bedside of the dying person. Following the death, the family washed and prepared the body for burial. A neighbor or local carpenter, or family members themselves, built a coffin that was set up in the parlor of the home. Within close-knit communities, a death bell tolled the age of the deceased, notifying people of the death so they could participate in the final rites marking the life of the deceased (see Figure 1-1).

Friends and acquaintances, along with other relatives, came to the family's home to hold a wake, with the body of the deceased in an open coffin, and to share in the ritual of mourning. Children kept vigil along with adults, sometimes sleeping in the same room as the corpse. Later, the body would be carried to the gravesite, perhaps a family plot on the home property or at a nearby churchyard cemetery. There, a local parson would read a few appropriate verses from the Bible as the coffin was lowered and the grave filled in by relatives. From caring for the dying family member through disposition of the corpse, death was within the realm of the family.

If you were a person of the nineteenth century suddenly transported through time to the present, you would find a rich source of information about current attitudes toward death by observing modern funeral practices. Walking into the "slumber room" of a typical mortuary, you would experience

Gordon Parks, FSA Collection, Library of Congress

Five generations of the Machado family form an extended family network rarely seen today. Firsthand experiences of death in such a family come through the closeness of multigenerational living.

culture shock. The familiar coffin has been replaced by a more elaborate "casket," and the corpse shows the mortician's skill in cosmetic "restoration."

At the funeral, you would observe as family and friends eulogize the deceased. Ah, that's familiar, you say—but where is the dear departed? Off to the side a bit, the casket remains closed, death tastefully concealed.

When the service at the grave concludes, you look on with amazement as the mourners begin to leave although the casket lies yet unburied. The cemetery crew will complete the actual burial. As a nineteenth-century onlooker at a twentieth-century funeral, you are perhaps most struck by a sense that the family and friends of the deceased are observers rather than participants: The tasks of preparing the dead for burial are handled by hired professionals who are paid to perform these services. Compared to a time when skills for dealing with a dead body were an ordinary aspect of domestic life, our present participation in the rituals surrounding the dead is minimal.

Factors Affecting Familiarity with Death

The size, shape, and distribution of the population—that is, its demographics—have changed dramatically since the turn of the century. Increased life expectancy and lower mortality rates have significantly influenced our attitudes and expectations about life and death. The extended family, composed of several generations of adults and children, has been replaced by smaller family units, including the nuclear family and single-parent family. The typical nineteenth-century household included parents, uncles, aunts, and aged grandparents, as well as children of varying ages. In this setting, the chance of experiencing the deaths of loved ones firsthand was greater than in today's smaller families. Our increased geographical mobility also makes it less likely that we will be present when aged family members die. Advances in medical technology and health care also exert a strong influence that shapes the course of dying, not to mention the setting where it occurs.

Social and technological forces affect the manner in which we deal with death and dying. It is in the interplay between individuals and social forces that society assumes a particular shape. Over the course of the twentieth century, this dynamism between individuals and society has created a social milieu in which the care of our dying and dead is no longer part of the common experience. Instead, we call upon professionals—from the cardiologist to the coroner to the cremator. The net result is that death and dying are unfamiliar to most of us.

Life Expectancy and Mortality Rates

Since the turn of the century, the average life expectancy for people born in the United States has increased from forty-seven years to seventy-six years.[3] Figure 1-2 shows changes in life expectancy by sex and race during this period. In 1900, over half of reported deaths involved persons fourteen years of age and younger. Today, less than 3 percent of all deaths occur among this age group.[4] This shift has important implications for how we think about death and dying.

Imagine a time when death at an early age was common. Today, we would characterize such people as having been "struck down in their prime." It is taken for granted that a newborn child will live into his or her seventh or eighth decade, perhaps longer. Of course, the expectation that babies

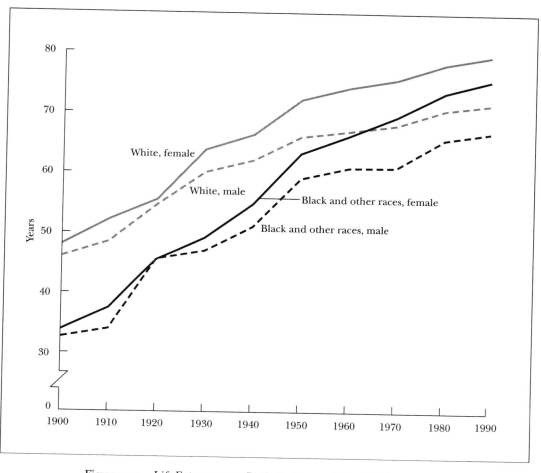

Figure *1-2*   *Life Expectancy at Birth, by Race and Sex, 1900–1990*
Source: National Center for Health Statistics, *Health, United States, 1993,* p. 91; and Bureau of the Census, *Statistical Abstract of the United States 1994,* p. 87.

survive and mature into old age is not shared equally by all Americans, nor by people elsewhere who live where poverty and unhealthy conditions contribute to high rates of mortality during infancy and childhood. For most North Americans and Europeans, however, long life is assumed to be a birthright.

At the beginning of the twentieth century, the death rate in America was about 17 per 1000; today, it is about 8.6 per 1000 (see Figure 1-3).[5] Comparing these figures suggests how different the experience of death and dying was for our ancestors. Frequent encounters with the deaths of loved ones meant that both young and old knew death as a natural and inevitable part of the human condition. Mothers died in childbirth; babies were stillborn; one or both

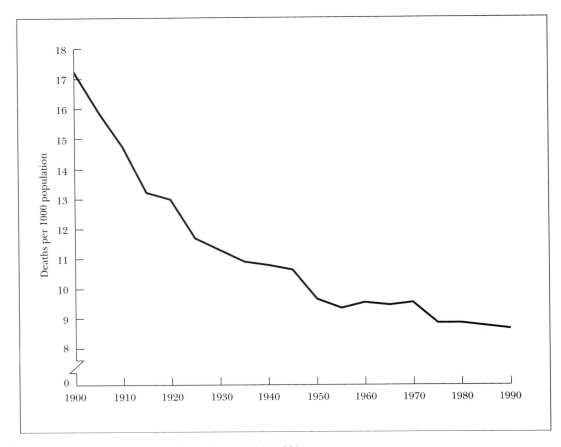

Figure *1-3*   *Death Rates, 1900–1990*
Source: Bureau of the Census, *Historical Statistics of the United States, Colonial Times to 1970* (Washington, D.C.: Government Printing Office, 1975), p. 59; and *Statistical Abstract of the United States 1994*, p. 89.

parents might die before their children had grown to adolescence. Given a high mortality rate, much of it attributable to deaths occurring in infancy, people could not deny the fact of death.

Causes of Death

Our experience also differs from that of our forebears because death now generally results from other causes. At the turn of the twentieth century, death was usually rapid and sudden, typically caused by acute infectious diseases such as tuberculosis, typhoid fever, syphilis, diphtheria, streptococcal septicemia, and pneumonia. Microbial diseases accounted for 40 percent of all deaths in 1900; today, they account for about 5 percent.[6] Now death most often follows

TABLE *1-1*   *Ten Leading Causes of Death, 1992*

Cause of Death	Death Rate per 100,000	% of Total
All causes	852.9	100.0
Heart disease	281.4	33.0
Cancer	204.1	23.9
Stroke	56.4	6.6
Lung disease	36.0	4.2
Accidents	34.0	4.0
Pneumonia and influenza	29.7	3.5
Diabetes	19.6	2.3
HIV infection (AIDS)	13.2	1.5
Suicide	12.0	1.4
Homicide	10.0	1.2

Source: National Center for Health Statistics, "Advance Report of Final Mortality Statistics, 1992"; *Monthly Vital Statistics Report* 43, no. 6, Supplement (March 22, 1995), p. 5.

a slow, progressive course resulting from such chronic maladies as heart disease and cancer (see Table 1-1). These changes in the cause and manner of dying promote the assumption that death happens in old age.

The shift in disease patterns is termed an *epidemiologic transition.*[7] (Epidemiology can be defined as the study of the patterns of disease.) Simply stated, this transition involves the redistribution of deaths from the young to the old. With a reduced risk of dying at a young age from infectious diseases, people are surviving into older ages, where they tend to die from degenerative diseases. The result is a larger and steadily increasing proportion of aged people in the population. In 1900, people sixty-five or older made up 4 percent of the population in the United States; today they comprise 13 percent, or about 32 million persons. In 1900, people sixty-five or older accounted for about 17 percent of all deaths; today, nearly three-quarters of the 2 million deaths each year in the United States occur among people in this age group.[8]

Geographical Mobility

Geographical mobility also tends to lessen our experience with death. Each year, nearly one-fifth of the American population is on the move. Although most of these moves involve changes of residences within the same county, each year nearly 15 million people pull up stakes, say goodbye to friends, neighbors, and relatives, and move to a different county; half of them move to a different state.[9] Historically, relationships have been closely tied to place and kinship; now they depend more on present function than on a lifetime of shared experiences. Children, once grown, rarely live in the same house with their parents or, even more rarely, with their brothers and sisters in an extended family. How many college friendships continue through marriage and the childrearing years into retirement, with corresponding participation in death rituals?

I often wonder what it would be like to be born and raised and live one's whole life in the same zip code. I wonder what it would be like to be able to dial all of one's family and friends without an area code. What it would be like not to always be missing one person or the other, one place or the other. What it would be like to return to a family home in which one grew up and still had things stored in the attic.

My family is in area code 405 and my best friend's in 415 and I'm living in 212. The in-laws are in 203. And there are other friends in 213 and 202, in 412 and 214.

Beverly Stephen, "A Mobile Generation in Search of Roots"

Distance separates family and friends as changes in life style and employment require moving on. In such circumstances, people are less likely to be present at the deaths of relatives or friends. Even with the economic resources to travel by airplane to care for the dying or attend funerals, most people cannot take time off from work or other responsibilities for long periods of time; thus, they are unable to participate in death-related experiences to the extent possible in less geographically diverse populations.

This mobile pattern of living is, of course, variable. Some families maintain a high degree of intimacy even when they no longer share the same dwelling. This is especially the case among ethnic groups who place a high value on family ties. Nevertheless, as a social force influencing the lives of Americans in the late twentieth century, geographical mobility is yet another factor that contributes to making death less familiar.

Displacement of Death from the Home

In 1900, most Americans died in their own beds. About 80 percent of deaths occurred at home, even in cities. The combination of more aged people in the population, fewer deaths among the young, smaller family units, and increased geographical mobility has created a situation such that people are less likely to be present when friends or relatives die.

Although most older people prefer to live in their own homes located in typical residential neighborhoods, the trend toward creating senior citizen subdivisions and age-segregated mobile-home parks is one that discourages close intermingling of the generations. Consider the experience of two small children on a Halloween trek, going door to door. After knocking on several well-lighted doors in a large mobile-home park, their cries of "Trick or treat!" were answered by a woman who said, "You'll not get any Halloween treats in this place. Only old people live here, and they leave their lights on for security and safety, not to welcome children on Halloween!"

Failing health or illness usually results in the confinement of the sick and the aged in hospitals or nursing homes. Even for those elderly who are able to live independently, the onset of a final illness usually brings admittance to a medical facility. Death, when it comes, is not likely to occur amid familiar

Grandmother, When Your Child Died

Grandmother, when your child died
hot beside you
in your narrow bed,
his labored breathing kept
you restless
and woke you when
it sighed,
and stopped.

You held him through the bitter dawn
and in the morning
dressed him, combed his hair,
your tears welled, but you didn't weep
until at last he lay
among the wild iris in the sod,
his soul gone inexplicably to God. Amen.

But grandmother, when my child died
sweet Jesus, he died hard.
A motor beside
his sterile cot
groaned, and hissed, and whirred
while he sang his pain—
low notes and high notes
in slow measures
slipping through the drug-cloud.
My tears, redundant,
dropped slow
like glucose or blood
from a bottle.
And when he died
my eyes were dry
and gods wearing white coats
turned away.

Joan Neet George

surroundings. The present pattern of death in our society is such that, regardless of age, about 80 percent of all deaths occur in institutional settings. Given over to professional caretakers, death is kept apart from most of us. A long-distance phone call announcing the passing of grandpa or grandma substitutes for the intimate experience of a loved one's death.

Life-Extending Technologies

Striking advances in modern medicine have brought about immense changes in how we relate to death. The dying are often surrounded by an astonishing array of machinery designed to monitor life until the last impulse fades. Biological malfunctions that were once lethal are now restored to proper functioning with the aid of innovative medical devices. Replacement or repair of dysfunctional organs is an accepted, and expected, part of modern medical practice. Sophisticated machines monitor biological functions such as brain wave activity, heart rate, body temperature, respiration, blood pressure, pulse, and blood chemistry. Signaling changes in body function by light, sound, and computer printout, such devices often make the crucial difference in situations of life or death.

But the medical technology that seems to one person a godsend, extending life, may seem to another a curse that only prolongs dying. The dignity of death may be devalued amid an overarching emphasis on technology focused exclusively on the biological organism. The marriage of medicine and technology alters our understanding of death and dying. The highly publicized case of Karen Ann Quinlan, whose death in 1985 came nearly a decade after she was removed from a respirator, exemplifies the moral and legal complexities that accompany the use of life-sustaining technologies. What trade-offs do we incur in applying medical technologies to the end stage of life? Does the preservation of human dignity imply limits to their use? New medical technologies quickly become part of the therapeutic norm, causing some people to question whether it would be more prudent to decide in advance *not* to develop certain technologies.[10]

Biomedical technologies have even altered the way death is defined. The conventional definition of death as "the cessation of life, the total and permanent cessation of all vital functions" has been augmented by a complex medicolegal definition that embraces the reality that life can be artificially sustained. The modern definition of death is not as simple as the statement, "When you're dead, you're dead."

Our technological genius becomes yet another factor in lessening our familiarity with death and dying. Family and friends may be distanced from the patient who is dying. The pervasive attitude that "what can be done, should be done" increases the likelihood that technological fixes will be tried even in cases where success is unlikely. The deathbed scene may occur in the context of a decision to "pull the plug" on a hopelessly comatose patient. Medical technology creates thorny ethical dilemmas that are difficult to resolve. In considering the influence of such technologies on our expectations of medical success, Willard Gaylin reminds us that "*All* medical technologies are halfway technologies; they sustain the human being in the terminal condition we call life."[11]

Expressions of Attitudes Toward Death

Attitudes develop out of assessing past experiences and projecting our imaginations into the future. Such assessment and projection are vital human activities, giving us a range of responses to the varied situations we encounter. In effect, "Attitude is what 'fits' us for what we are, and do, in the world."[12] Even though direct contact with death is uncommon for people in modern societies, death nevertheless occupies a significant, even if mostly unacknowledged, place in our cultural environment. Prevailing attitudes toward death are evident in many facets of social interaction, including the language people use when talking about death and the kinds of humor employed in response to it, as well as in the ways that death is portrayed by the mass media and in music, literature, and the visual arts.

Language

The language used to discuss the process of dying or the fact of death is rarely direct. People avoid speaking the words *dead* or *dying;* instead, loved ones "pass away" or "were called home." The dead person is "laid to rest," and burial becomes "interment," while the undertaker changes his or her title to "funeral director"—all terms that suggest a well-choreographed

TABLE *1-2* *Death Talk: Metaphors, Euphemisms, and Slang*

Passed on	Made the change
Croaked	Taking the dirt nap
Kicked the bucket	On the other side
Gone to heaven	God took him/her
Gone home	Asleep in Christ
Expired	Departed
Breathed the last	Transcended
Succumbed	Bought the farm
Left us	With the angels
Went to his/her eternal reward	Feeling no pain
Lost	Offed himself/herself
Met his/her Maker	His/her time was up
Wasted	Cashed in
Checked out	Crossed over Jordan
Eternal rest	Perished
Laid to rest	Ate it
Pushing up daisies	Was done in
Called home	Translated into glory
Was a goner	Returned to dust
Came to an end	Withered away
Bit the dust	In the arms of the Father
Annihilated	Gave it up
Liquidated	It was curtains
Terminated	A long sleep
Gave up the ghost	On the heavenly shores
Left this world	Out of his/her misery
Rubbed out	Ended it all
Snuffed	Angels carried him/her away
Six feet under	Resting in peace
Passing	Changed form
Found everlasting peace	Dropped the body
Went to a new life	Returned to the source
In the great beyond	That was all she wrote
No longer with us	Passed away

production for disposing of the dead. Euphemisms, metaphors, and slang form a large part of "death talk" (see Table 1-2).

Sympathy cards allow us to express our condolences without explicitly mentioning the event of death. Death is a metaphor in such sentiments as "What is death but a long sleep?" and is apparently denied in verses like James Whitcomb Riley's "He is not dead, he is just away." Sympathy cards include images of sunsets or fields with grain or flowers, all of which convey an impression of "peace, quiet, and perhaps a return to nature."[13] The deceased is referred to indirectly, usually within the context of the survivor's memories or the healing process of time. Metaphors provide a way to acknowledge the fact of death and express our condolences while being sensitive to the bereaved's feelings of loss.

Euphemisms—substitutions of indirect or vague expressions for ones considered harsh or blunt—are used by political and military leaders to place death at a distance by masking its reality. Plain talk about death is subverted by a lexicon of substitutions that cite "body counts" or "KIAs" (killed in action). Soldiers who are killed in battle are described as "being wasted," while civilian deaths are termed "collateral damage." Military briefings depict the ability of weapons to inflict "megadeath" on the enemy. Terms such as "pacification" and "peace-keeping" provide cover for hostile actions. In short, euphemisms replace words that would accurately describe the harsh reality of death in battle and the horrors of mass destruction. Used in this way, euphemisms depersonalize and devalue death.

When rock musician Kurt Cobain, lead singer of the group Nirvana, committed suicide, stunned fans said: "Can you believe it? Cobain offed himself. He actually blew himself away." Whereas slang was typically used in casual conversations, news articles used more formal language in describing Cobain's death by "suicide" from "gunshot."

Although metaphors and euphemisms tend to blunt the reality of death, their use does not always involve an attempt to deny or avoid death. Such language is also employed more subtly. Among the members of some religious and ethnic traditions, for example, the term "passing" or "passing on" refers to an understanding of death as a spiritual transition. Thus, we should not automatically conclude that the use of such terms implies avoidance or denial of the fact of death. They may reflect an understanding of death within a context that acknowledges its reality while suggesting additional meanings.

The way language is used also can reveal the intensity and immediacy of a person's encounter with death. In "danger of death" narratives—stories about close calls with death—a tense shift typically occurs when the narrator comes to the crucial point in his or her story, the point when death seems unavoidable and imminent. In one instance, a man who had experienced a frightening incident some years earlier while driving in a snowstorm began his story in the past tense as he described the circumstances surrounding the incident. But as he came to the point in the story when his car went out of control on an icy curve and slid into the opposing lane of traffic, he switched to the present tense. It was as if he were *reliving* the experience of watching the oncoming car heading straight for him and believing in that moment that he was about to die.[14]

As with such tense shifts, shifts in word choice can also reveal changes in the way death is experienced at different times. In the aftermath of the disastrous car bombing of the federal building in Oklahoma City, as the focus of rescue efforts changed, so did the language used to describe the work of emergency personnel and search-and-rescue teams. As hours stretched into days, *rescue* work became *recovery* work.

Look again at the words and phrases used in death talk (see Table 1-2). Notice how the language people use provides clues about the manner of death and how it is experienced by the speaker. Language about death sometimes relates to a spiritual or cultural framework. Small distinctions may embody

The Undertakers

Old Pops had been stone cold dead for two days. He was rigid, gruesome and had turned slightly green and now he lay on a slab at the undertakers, about to be embalmed by two lovable old morticians.

"At least he lived to a ripe age," said one.

"Yep," said the other. "Well, let's get to 'er."

Suddenly, Old Pops bolted upright and without opening his eyes, began to utter this story:

"In 1743, Captain Rice set sail from England with an unreliable and mutinous crew. After three days at sea, the mast of the mainsail splintered, and then broke completely in half. The ship tossed about at sea for two days; the men mutinied, and the ship tossed about for another two days. At the end of the third day, a ship appeared on the horizon and rescued them and good Captain Rice failed to mention to the admiral the incident of mutiny, and his crew became faithful and hard-working and devoted themselves to their captain."

Old Pops laid back down on the marble.

"Well," said one mortician, "there goes the old saying, 'dead men tell no tales'!"

Steve Martin, *Cruel Shoes*

rather different understandings, as, for instance, in the difference between "passed away" and "passed on."

Paying attention to language reveals a great deal about personal as well as cultural attitudes toward death. By becoming aware of the metaphors, euphemisms, slang, and other linguistic patterns that are used when talking about death, we appreciate more completely the range of attitudes and responses that death elicits.

Humor

Humor is yet another way in which attitudes toward death held by individuals and groups are expressed. Laughter can defuse some of the anxiety about death. Serious and somber matters become easier to deal with when there is comedic relief. In this way, humor puts frightening possibilities into manageable perspective.

In California, passing motorists are taken aback by a gleaming white hearse with the cryptic license plates, "Not Yett." Caskets have been pressed into use for comic relief at birthday parties and mock wakes.[15] Death-related humor comes in many different forms, from funny epitaphs to so-called black or gallows humor.

There are constraints on the kind of humor that a particular person or group finds acceptable. A joke that is shared gleefully among the members of one group may be shockingly unacceptable to others, who have a different set of assumptions about what is funny. When a newspaper columnist wrote a parody of "USA for Africa" that poked fun at efforts to alleviate famine, even some loyal readers reacted with disgust. The heartrending facts of famine and

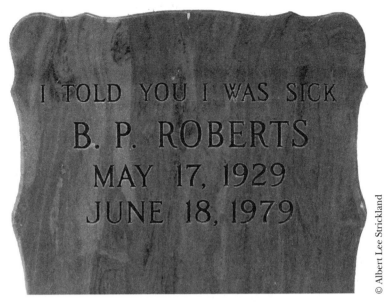

I TOLD YOU I WAS SICK
B. P. ROBERTS
MAY 17, 1929
JUNE 18, 1979

© Albert Lee Strickland

In place of the conventional sentiment usually engraved on tombstones, a touch of whimsy adorns this memorial to B. P. Roberts at a cemetery in Key West, Florida.

the positive image of the relief efforts outweighed what seemed by comparison a feeble and unfeeling attempt at humor.[16]

Mary Hall observes that "what is humorous to each of us depends on our particular cultural set, our own experience, and our personal inclination."[17] She outlines several ways that humor functions relative to death. First, it raises our consciousness about a taboo subject and allows us to talk about the indescribable. Second, it presents an opportunity to rise above immediate sadness, thus giving momentary release from pain and promoting a sense of control over the situation even if we cannot change it. Third, humor is a great leveler; it treats us all alike and conveys the message that there are no exemptions from the human predicament. In doing so, it binds us together and encourages the closeness we need to feel in confronting the fearful unknown. Finally, after death has occurred, humor is comforting to survivors as they recall the funny as well as painful events of a loved one's life.

For people with life-threatening illness, the use of humor is a way of coping with the debilitating effects of a shattering diagnosis and its attendant pain and anxiety. Humor can give us a different perspective on a painful situation, as in the jest, "Halitosis is better than no breath at all." Humor also gives relief to caregivers who have frequent contact with dying or death. Mary Hall and Paula Rappe describe how emergency personnel use humor to distance themselves from horror as well as to "rebond" following traumatic incidents.[18] A firm that provides instructional materials for emergency medical technicians includes in its catalog a musical recording entitled "You

Respond to Everyone But Me." In another example, doctors at a teaching hospital avoided using the word "death" when a patient died because of their concern that other patients might become alarmed. One day, as a medical team was examining a patient, an intern came to the door with information about the death of a patient. Knowing that the word "death" was taboo and finding no ready substitute, she stood in the doorway and announced, "Guess who's not going to shop at Woolworth's any more?" This phrase quickly became the standard way for staff members to convey the news of a patient's death.

The things we find funny about death can reveal a good deal about our attitudes. As a means of coping with painful situations, humor helps us confront our fears and gain a sense of mastery over the unknown. Finding humorous aspects to death, casting it in an unconventional light, reduces the anxiety that accompanies awareness of one's own mortality.

Mass Media

Communications technology now has the potential to make us all instantaneous survivors. News about disasters, terrorist attacks, wars, and political assassinations can be flashed around the world almost instantaneously.[19] Stunned television viewers watch in disbelief as news footage is broadcast showing the terrible event. Because most of us no longer experience death firsthand, the way we think about death is influenced by vicarious experiences provided by the mass media. What do we learn about death and dying from these secondhand sources?

In the News

As you read the daily newspaper, what kinds of encounters with death vie for your attention? Perhaps, scanning the day's news, you find an assortment of accidents, murders, suicides, and disasters involving violent deaths. A jetliner crashes, and the newspaper announces the fact with banner headlines. Here you see a story about a family perishing when trapped inside their burning home; in another, a family's vacation comes to an untimely end when they become the victims of a fatal collision on the interstate.

And there are the deaths of the famous. Most deaths are reported in *death notices*—brief, standardized statements, usually printed in small type and listed alphabetically in a column of vital statistics "as uniform as a row of tiny grave plots."[20] The deaths of the famous, however, are announced by lengthy *obituaries*. Prefaced by individual headlines and set in the same size type used in other newspaper stories, obituaries show the degree of newsworthiness that editors attribute to the deaths of famous people. Files of pending obituaries on people whose deaths would be considered newsworthy are maintained by most media organizations—wire services, metropolitan newspapers, and network news bureaus. These obituaries are updated periodically so they are ready to be printed or aired when the occasion demands.

The death of a neighbor or someone working alongside you on the job is not likely to be reported with such emphasis. On the contrary, efforts by ordinary people to obtain an obituary rather than a death notice for a loved one may meet with resistance, as illustrated by the following account. The family of a young woman who died of Hodgkin's disease brought a brief account of her life and her photo to the local newspaper, along with a request that these items be used in announcing her death. Despite their efforts, and the efforts of others in the community who knew of the young woman's accomplishments in the face of serious illness, a spokesperson for the newspaper maintained that it was against policy to run obituaries instead of death notices in such cases; neither the photograph nor the biographical sketch was printed. Ordinary deaths—the kind most of us can expect to experience—

tend to be neglected or mentioned only in routine fashion. The spectacular obscures the ordinary.

Whether routine or extraordinary, our encounters with death in the news influence the way we think about and respond to death. Journalism now seeks to go beyond merely providing information to sharing experience. Thus, the news may have less to do with an *event* than with how that event is *perceived.*[21] Jack Lule illustrates this point by citing the manner in which Huey Newton's death was reported in newspapers across the country.[22] As cofounder of the Black Panther Party, Newton's public career spanned two decades and he occupied many roles; yet, with few exceptions, his death in 1989 was reported in ways that disavowed and debased his accomplishments as well as his standing as a political figure. Most news reports focused on the violent nature of Newton's demise while ignoring other aspects of his life or the tragedy of his death. The implicit message seemed to be: "He who lives by the sword dies by the sword."

A quite different illustration of the distinction between event and perception in news reporting occurred with the explosion of the space shuttle *Challenger.* This event, which caused the deaths of seven crew members (including the first private citizen slated for space flight, Christa McAuliffe, a schoolteacher), received detailed coverage. Perceived as a tragedy on a national scale, it evoked a sense of shared grief. Some commentators likened the role of television during this event to a "national hearth" around which Americans symbolically gathered. Others, however, said that television fulfilled its function no better and no worse than would be expected of any household appliance. The repeated showings of the shuttle exploding were criticized by some as evidence of the media's macabre fascination with the "pornography of grief."

Whether television is perceived as a national hearth or simply as an appliance, most people expect the media to not only provide information about events but also convey some sense of their meaning. When the news involves death, questions arise about the propriety of the media's focus on those most affected. During the memorial service for the *Challenger* crew, for example, the astronauts' grieving families were shown close up. Was such coverage of the bereaved an intrusion on their private sorrow or was it legitimate news? The distinction between *public* event and *private* loss sometimes blurs.

When a Canadian newspaper ran a photograph showing a distraught mother at the moment she learned about her daughter's fatal injuries in an accident, many readers were outraged. Some called the photograph "a blatant example of morbid ludicrousness" and "the highest order of poor taste and insensitivity."[23] The mother did not share these feelings. She said that seeing the photo helped her to comprehend what had happened. Indeed, many people who are bereaved by sudden, unexpected deaths want to reconstruct, in as much detail as possible, the events surrounding the death; it helps them cope with the reality of the loss. John Huffman, commenting on this incident, suggests that, because most people are unfamiliar with death and the emotions it elicits, they may "ascribe emotions to the grief-stricken that are not really present."[24] Were the outraged readers defending the prerogatives of a grief-stricken mother who was the victim of a too-intrusive press? Or were these volatile emotions related to their own uncomfortable feelings about death, feelings that were triggered by the photograph's publication? Such questions are not amenable to simple answers.

Television, with its visual power and intimacy, has heightened the privacy question. When Pan Am flight 103 crashed at Lockerbie, Scotland, en route from London to New York, television crews were on hand at JFK Airport to cover the reactions of grief-stricken relatives and friends. The image of one mother's grief became a symbol of the "grief-torn passenger lounge."[25]

Although there is an undeniable community interest in such events, such coverage can be intrusive. For the victims of disaster, the media may unwittingly stimulate a "second trauma" following the initial trauma of the horrible event itself. Opportunistic journalists may seek to capture the experience of a tragedy at the expense of its victims.[26] The sensational "if it bleeds, it leads" stance dominates much of television journalism.

Recall from your experience both the types of death reported on television and the commentator's manner of presenting this information. The "detached and captionlike quality" of network news coverage, observes Michael Arlen, results in "snippets of information" about the deaths that are reported.[27] News of the bus crash or mine disaster is interposed between reports about stock market prices and factory layoffs. Robert Fulton and Greg Owen point out that such reports "characteristically submerge the human meaning of death while depersonalizing the event further by sandwiching actual reports of loss of life between commercials or other mundane items."[28] Television, they add, "portrays grief and the ruptured lives that death can leave in its wake only superficially." Michael Arlen contrasts media messages about death with experiences of death in our own lives, where it evokes "myriad expressions of grief, incomprehension, and deep human response."[29]

Entertaining Death

Television's pervasive influence is indicated by the fact that over 98 percent of American homes have at least one television set.[30] The average American child has seen between 13,000 and 18,000 deaths on television by the age of twenty-one. Far from being ignored, death is a central theme of much television programming. In a typical week of listings in *TV Guide*, about one-third describe programs in which death or dying is a featured theme. Out of a possible total of 168 hours of weekly viewing time, an avid television viewer could spend more than two-thirds of those hours watching programs that feature death in some way.

These figures are even more striking when it is considered that they take into account only such programs as talk shows, crime and adventure series, and movies. Not included are newscasts (which typically feature several stories

Herbert Johnson, Library of Congress

about death in each broadcast); nature programs (which often depict death in the animal kingdom); children's cartoons (which often present caricatures of death); soap operas (which seem always to have some character dying or recently deceased); sports programs (which give us descriptions such as "the ball is dead" and "the other team is killing them today"), or religious programming (which includes theological as well as anecdotal discussions of death).[31]

Despite this massive volume of programming in which death is prominent, televised images of death seldom add to our knowledge of its reality. Few programs deal with such real-life topics as how people actually cope with a loved one's death or how they confront their own dying. Instead, television presents a depersonalized image of death, an image characterized most often by violence.

Consider, for example, the western or detective story, which glazes over the reality of death by describing the bad guy as "kicking the bucket" or as having "croaked"—relegated, no doubt, to Boot Hill at the edge of town, where the deceased "pushes up daisies." Think about the last death you saw portrayed in a television entertainment or movie. Perhaps the camera panned from the dying person's face and torso to a close-up of hands twitching—then all movement ceases as the person's breathing fades away in perfect harmony with the musical score. Or, more likely, the death was violent: the cowboy gunfight at the OK Corral; high noon. The gent with the slower draw is hit, reels, falls, his body convulsing into cold silence.

Recall the Saturday morning cartoon depiction of death. Daffy Duck is pressed to a thin sheet by a steamroller, only to pop up again a moment later. Elmer Fudd aims his shotgun at Bugs Bunny, pulls the trigger, bang! Bugs, unmarked by the rifle blast, clutches his throat, spins around several times, and mutters, "It's all getting dark now, Elmer. . . . I'm going. . . . " Bugs falls to the ground, both feet still in the air. As his eyes close, his feet finally hit the dirt. But wait! Now Bugs pops up, good as new. Reversible death!

Realistic portrayals of death are not the media's standard bill of fare. When told of his grandfather's death, one modern seven-year-old asked, "Who did it to him?" The understanding of death offered by the media is that it comes from outside, often violently. Such notions of death reinforce the belief that dying is something that *happens* to us, rather than something we *do*. Such portrayals affect our attitudes. Death is seen as an accidental rather than a natural process.

People who have been present at a death describe a very different picture. Many recall the gurgling, gasping sounds as the last breath rattles through the lungs; the changes in body color as flesh tones tinge blue; the feeling of a once warm and flexible body growing cold and flaccid. They often say, "Death is not at all what I thought it would be like; it doesn't look or sound or feel like anything I see on television or in movies!"

Television portrayals of death are embedded in a structure of violence that George Gerbner characterizes as a "ritualistic demonstration of power" from which viewers derive "a heightened sense of danger, insecurity, and mistrust."[32] They reflect a "mean world" syndrome in which the symbolic use of death contributes "to the irrational dread of dying and thus to diminished vitality and self-direction in life." These conclusions are based on a study that has been ongoing at the Annenberg School of Communications since 1967.[33] Researchers conclude that "our children are born into a home in which—for the first time in human history—not the parents, church, or school, but a centralized commercial institution tells most of the stories most of the time."

And what is the content of this story? "For most viewers," Gerbner says, "television's mean and dangerous world tends to cultivate a sense of relative danger, mistrust, dependence, and—despite its supposedly 'entertaining' nature—alienation and gloom." In Gerbner's view, television's portrayal of a mean world

invites not only aggression but also exploitation and repression. Fearful people are more dependent, more easily manipulated and controlled, more susceptible to deceptively simple, strong, tough measures and hard-line postures—both political and religious. They may accept and even welcome repression if it promises to relieve their insecurities and other anxieties.[34]

Turning our attention to the cinema, we find that death is also a major theme here, but fantasy generally replaces reality to enhance the story line. Films often exhibit what critic Roger Ebert calls "Ali McGraw Disease" (alluding to her character in *Love Story*), in which characters with terminal illness are depicted as becoming more and more beautiful until ultimately "they're so great that they die."[35] The message that we live in a violent society is promoted by such contemporary films as the "Terminator" series and Oliver Stone's *Natural Born Killers*. About *Natural Born Killers,* AP film critic Bob Thomas commented that Stone and his technicians did "everything possible to jazz up the bloody narrative," with one killing following another "until they appear to be bloodless child's play."[36] Although Stone claimed that the film was meant to be a "satire on the nation's violence and the media that thrive on it," Thomas raised a nagging question: "Is it satire, or another exploitation of the violence that seems to both repel and fascinate Americans?"

Fascination with death can sometimes turn bizarre, as in the "blood and gore" movies released at Halloween and in pseudo-documentaries like *Faces of Death,* which depict graphic scenes of animal and human death, including suicide and autopsies. The lack of firsthand experience with death may cause people to exhibit a fascination with *anything* related to death. Rather than a lack of death symbolism in the media, we find what Frederic Tate characterizes as "a lack of symbols that represent rebirth, continuation, and the positive aspects of death and dying."[37]

Realistic portrayals of dying and death do occur in the media, though they represent exceptions. Documentaries as well as fictional dramas have depicted individuals and families coping with terminal illness and bereavement. In the aftermath of the Vietnam war, several films portrayed the experience of combat and its devastating effects on warriors, as in the film *Born on the Fourth of July,* which was based on an account by Vietnam veteran Ron Kovic. Set during the genocide of an earlier war, Steven Spielberg's *Schindler's List* captured public attention and several Oscars for its heartrending look at a hero of the Nazi Holocaust. Although the media can, and occasionally do, produce positive contributions toward our understanding of death and dying, these positive messages unfortunately tend to be nearly buried under an avalanche of messages about death that bear slight resemblance to its reality.

Music

Themes of death and loss are frequently heard in music. Indeed, such themes form the *raison d'être* for some music. Leonard Bernstein's *Symphony No. 3* (Kaddish) is based on the Jewish prayer for the dead. The Requiem Mass (Mass for the Dead) has attracted composers like Mozart, Berlioz, and Verdi, to name a few. One section of the Requiem Mass, the *Dies irae* ("Day of Wrath"), has become a musical symbol for death in works by many composers.

One Tree Hill

We turn away to face the cold, enduring chill
As the day begs the night for mercy
Your sun so bright it leaves no shadows, only scars
Carved into stone on the face of earth
The moon is up and over One Tree Hill
We see the sun go down in your eyes
You ran like river to the sea
Like a river to the sea
And in our world a heart of darkness, a firezone
Where poets speak their hearts, then bleed for it
Jara sang, his song a weapon, in the hands of love
You know his blood still cries from the ground
It runs like a river to the sea
Like a river to the sea
I don't believe in painted roses or bleeding hearts
While bullets rape the night of the merciful
I'll see you again when the stars fall from the sky
And the moon has turned red over One Tree Hill
We run like a river to the sea
Like a river to the sea

Bono, U2. For the funeral of Greg Carroll
(1960–1986), Wanganui, New Zealand,
July 10, 1986.

In Berlioz's *Symphonie Fantastique* (1830), this theme is heard, first following the ominous tolling of bells and then, as the music reaches its climax, in counterpoint to the frenzied dancing of witches at a *sabbat*. The *Symphonie* tells the story of a young musician who, spurned by his beloved, attempts suicide with an overdose of opium. In a narcotic coma, he experiences fantastic dreams, including a nightmarish march to the gallows. The *Dies irae* is also heard in Saint-Saëns' *Danse Macabre* (1874) and Liszt's *Totentanz* (1849), two of the best known musical renditions of the Dance of Death. Opera, of course, frequently includes themes relating to violent death and suicide.[38]

Traditional American folk music includes ballads describing visions and premonitions of death, deathbed scenes, last wishes expressed by the dying, mental states of soldiers entering the battlefield and of condemned prisoners awaiting execution, the sorrow and grief of mourners, admonitions about caring for the gravesite, and expectations about the afterlife.[39] Themes describing suicide and murder are commonly expressed in song, especially when they conjoin love and death. Many folk songs describe the horror of war or death resulting from mining and railroad disasters. Examples include "Where Have All the Flowers Gone" (war), "Long Black Veil" (mourning), "The Wreck of the Old 97" (accidental death), "The School House Fire" (disaster),

"The TB Is Whipping Me" (life-threatening illness), and "John Henry" (occupational hazards). Murder, mayhem, and misery have long been staples of American music.

Death themes are standard in rock and other forms of contemporary popular music. Some observers believe that the presence of death imagery in rock played an important role in breaking the taboo against public mention of death. A survey of "Top 40" rock songs from 1955 through 1991 provides evidence supporting this thesis.[40] Death-related songs comprise a distinct subset of popular music. Lyricists have written songs covering a wide range of death-related themes, from the humorous to the poetic (see Table 1-3). In 1994, Mitch Ryder, perhaps best known for his 1967 hit "Devil with a Blue Dress On," showed support for Dr. Jack Kevorkian's campaign to legalize assisted suicide by writing a song entitled "Mercy," which includes the lyrics "Won't you help me Dr. Jack, help me with this suicide."[41]

The lyrics in so-called heavy metal rock often convey stark images of homicide and suicide. The sometimes bizarre manifestations of dying and death in heavy metal lyrics have caused some listeners to express concern about their possible effects on young people.[42] At issue is the glorification of death in heavy metal that is hinted at in titles like "Skeleton on Your Shoulder," a song performed by a group that calls itself Coroner. Other groups that will be familiar to listeners of this music include Napalm Death, Carcass, Morbid Angel, Megadeath, Suicidal Tendencies, Slayer, Nuclear Assault, and Dead Kennedys. Are the lyrics of heavy metal "destructive," or do they simply provide an outlet for confronting death-as-bogeyman? As its evolving forms make clear, rock music continues to give considerable attention to the subject of death.

In religious music we find another rich source of themes related to dying and death, much of it centering on the passion of Jesus Christ, his suffering and death. Gospel music is replete with images of loss and mourning. Examples include songs like "Will the Circle Be Unbroken" (death of family members), "Oh, Mary Don't You Weep" (mourning), "This May Be the Last Time" (impermanence of life), "Known Only to Him" (facing death), "When the Saints Go Marching In" (vision of afterlife), "If I Could Hear My Mother Pray Again" (parent death), and "Precious Memories" (integration of loss).

The *dirge* is a musical form associated with funeral processions and burials. Beethoven, Schubert, Schumann, Strauss, Brahms, Mahler, and Stravinsky all wrote dirges. The jazz funeral, associated with New Orleans, is probably the best-known example of a popular interpretation. Related to the dirge are *elegies* and *laments*—musical settings for poems marking the loss of a person. The lament is a musical expression of ritual leave-taking that is found in many cultural settings, as in the case of bagpipes played at Scottish clan funerals. In vocal form, the characteristic lament is an expression of mourning called "keening," a dramatic and emotionally moving expression of loss and longing.

In pre-Christian Hawaii, chants known as *mele kanikau* were the traditional lament for commemorating a person's death.[43] Some *kanikau* were carefully

TABLE *1-3*   *Death Themes in Contemporary Popular Music*

Performer	Song	Theme
Alice in Chains	Dirt	Suicidal thoughts
Tori Amos	Little Earthquakes	Multiple losses
Rubén Blades	El padre Antonio y el Monaguillo Andres	Assassination of Archbishop Romero and altar boy
Boyz II Men	Say Goodbye to Yesterday	Loss and grief
Garth Brooks	One Night a Day	Coping with grief
Jackson Browne	For a Dancer	Eulogy
Eric Clapton	Tears in Heaven	Death of young son
Elvis Costello	Waiting for the End of the World	Threat of death
Rodney Crowell	Things I Wish I'd Said	Cherishing memories
Joe Diffie	Almost Home	Death in old age
Dion	Abraham, Martin, and John	Political assassination
Doors	The End	Murder
Doors	Ship of Fools	Environmental disaster
Bob Dylan	Knockin' on Heaven's Door	Last words/Death scene
Marvin Gaye	What's Going On	War and brutality
Gettovettes	Gangster Lean	Grief over death of fellow gang member
Grateful Dead	Black Peter	Social support in dying
Jimi Hendrix	Mother Earth	Inevitability of death
Indigo Girls	Pushing the Needle Too Far	Drug-related death
Elton John	Candle in the Wind	Death of Marilyn Monroe
Elton John	The Last Song	AIDS/Deathbed resolution
The Judds	Guardian Angels	Ancestors
Kenny Loggins	My Father's House	A father's death
Patty Loveless	How Can I Help You to Say Goodbye?	A mother's dying
Madonna	Promise to Try	Friend's suicide
Metallica	Disposable Heros	Death in war
Metallica	Fight Fire with Fire	Nuclear catastrophe
Mike and the Mechanics	The Living Years	Father's death
Morrissey	Angel, Angel, Down We Go	Suicide intervention
Holly Near	The Letter	Friend dying of AIDS
Sinead O'Connor	I Am Stretched on Your Grave	Mourning behavior
Oingo Boingo	No One Lives Forever	Facing death stoically
Jimmy Page and David Coverdale	Whisper a Prayer for the Dying	Death in war
Pink Floyd	Dogs of War	War-related death
Pink Floyd	The Great Gig in the Sky	Acceptance of mortality
Poison	Something to Believe In	Post-traumatic stress disorder

TABLE *1-3*   (*continued*)

Performer	Song	Theme
The Police	Murder by Numbers	Political killings
Porno for Pyros	Sadness	Grief
Queen	Another One Bites the Dust	Violent death
Lou Reed	No Chance/Regret	Unfinished business
Lou Reed	Sword of Damocles	Coping with terminal illness
Henry Rollins	Drive-by Shooting	Satire on death by random violence
Carly Simon	Life Is Eternal	Desire for immortality
Snoop Doggy Dog	Murder Was the Case	Urban homicide and justice system
Bruce Springsteen	Streets of Philadelphia	Dying of AIDS
James Taylor	Fire and Rain	Suicide
Toad the Wet Sprocket	Corporal Brown	Spousal killing
UB40	Your Eyes Were Open Together	Terminal illness
Stevie Wonder	My Love Is with You	Violent death of a child

composed; others were chanted spontaneously during the funeral procession. In *kanikau*, subtlety and levels of meaning are important, with imagery of the natural world used to portray the writer's experience of loss.[44] Memories of times spent amid natural surroundings with the deceased are mentioned: "My companion in the chill of Manoa" or "My companion in the forest of Makiki." Such chants recall with special fondness the things that lovingly bind together the deceased and his or her survivors. The message in the Hawaiian lament was not "I am bereft without you," but rather "These are the things I cherish about you."

As you listen to music, notice the references to death and dying. What themes or images are being conveyed? What attitudes are being expressed? Whether your musical taste tends toward rock, folk, country, gospel, or classical—or all of the above—you will find a rich source of information about cultural and individual attitudes to death in music.

Literature

Death is an enduring theme in literature. From classic drama like Sophocles' *Oedipus the King* and Shakespeare's *King Lear,* through modern works like Leo Tolstoy's "The Death of Ivan Ilych" and James Agee's *Death in the Family,* to such recent novels as Ernest J. Gaines's *A Lesson Before Dying,* writers treat death as significant and meaningful to human experience. Recall for a moment a favorite literary work. Was death an element of the plot? How did the author portray dying or death in the story? In many works of literature, the meaning of death is explored as it relates to society as well as the individual.

Buffalo Bill's
defunct
      who used to
      ride a watersmooth-silver
                     stallion
and break onetwothreefourfive pigeonsjustlikethat
                                     Jesus
he was a handsome man
                   and what i want to know is
how do you like your blueeyed boy
Mister Death

     e.e. cummings

Expressing the human dimensions of death and portraying the range and subtlety in experiences of loss, literature balances a diet of factual and technical information.

Literature has been applied in just this way as a teaching tool within the medical profession and in medical schools. Plays like Marsha Norman's *'night, Mother,* which dramatizes factors behind suicide, and Laurence Housman's *Victoria Regina,* which focuses on issues of aging, are presented to audiences made up of physicians and other medical personnel. These programs aim to foster insight into human behaviors and problems that generally receive little discussion during formal medical training.

Since the end of the Vietnam war, numerous literary accounts have contributed to a distinct genre that depicts the trauma of combat as well as the quest to restore meaning following shattering experiences of loss. The best of these accounts are not merely war stories. Rather, an author's experiences form a basis for confronting and coping with the overwhelming grief that affects both individuals and societies.[45]

Holocaust literature is of special interest to the student of death and dying. Experiences of incarceration and extermination are expressed through victims' diaries as well as persecutors' memoirs, in novels and psychological studies. Notable examples include Chaim Kaplan's *Warsaw Diary,* Charlotte Delbo's *None of Us Will Return,* Elie Wiesel's *Night,* and Anne Frank's *Diary of a Young Girl* (which was published in a new "definitive" edition in 1995). This literature forces the reader to contemplate fundamental aspects of human nature. As one writer says, "The human imagination after Auschwitz is simply not the same as it was before."[46] Also explored is the syndrome of the observer-victim whose familiar self, by means of radical detachment bordering on schizophrenia, deteriorates to the point that it finally accepts "business as usual" amid unspeakable horror. The victim becomes indistinguishable from the violence.

Increasingly, literature is focusing on what Frederic K. Hoffman calls the "landscape of violence" that seems to pervade life in the twentieth century.[47] Reflecting human experience in a century that has seen the mass deaths of two world wars and innumerable smaller conflicts, the modern fictional hero tries to come to terms with sudden and violent death in situations that allow no time for survivors to express their grief or mourn the dead.[48] Whatever meaning death has is no longer clear. Violence reduces individuals to the status of *things*.

Modern literature includes many attempts to delineate and explore the meaning of death in situations that are apparently absurd and ultimately incomprehensible. In the "vigilante" stories that characterize detective novels, the hero sets out to avenge evil but is often corrupted by a self-justifying morality that perpetuates violence.[49] Modern writers try to deal with death in a variety of ways: by creating a mythology or metaphor significant enough to account for evil; by portraying violence within an ideological melodrama or showing it as a farce, alternating between the trivial and the grotesque; or by presenting experiences in a manner as impersonal as the events themselves seem to be, letting the bare violence speak for itself.[50]

Turning to the elegy as a literary form, Jahan Ramazani says, "The poetry of mourning for the dead assumes in the modern period an extraordinary diversity and range, incorporating more anger and skepticism, more conflict and anxiety than ever before."[51] Examples include Wilfred Owen's poems of moral objection to the pain wrought by modern industrialized warfare; Langston Hughes's "blues poems," which express the soul-weariness of African Americans in their encounters with racial injustice; Allen Ginsberg's *Kaddish* after the death of his mother; Seamus Heaney's memorials to suffering caused by political violence in Ireland; and the "parental elegies" in the poetry of Sylvia Plath, Anne Sexton, and Adrienne Rich. Poetry, says Ramazani, has become an important "cultural space for mourning the dead" as writers and artists search for "credible responses to loss in the modern world."[52] For modern writers, death often elicits less a contemplation of judgment or concern for immortality than a deep anxiety about annihilation and loss of identity.

Visual Arts

Death themes in art are revealed through symbols, signs, and images. Richard Pacholski says that "to declare an interest in death themes as expressed in the visual arts is to declare an interest in iconography," which is defined as "that branch of the history of art which concerns itself with the subject matter or meaning of works of art."[53] Artworks embody something of the attitudes and beliefs about death that are present in the artist's culture. In Western European societies, art often contains themes from classical mythology and the Judeo-Christian tradition. Comparable sources inspire artists of other cultures. The scenes inscribed in relief on the limestone sarcophagi of ancient Egypt, for example, attest to that culture's beliefs about what follows upon death, beliefs that are also portrayed in the illustrations that accompany Egyptian religious texts. Graphically portrayed is the expectation that, after

Of the modern artists who have expressed death themes in art, few have done so more frequently or more powerfully than German artist Käthe Kollwitz—as in this 1925 woodcut, Proletariat—Child's Coffin.

death, a person will be judged according to his or her deeds during earthly life. Artistic themes that draw upon the processes observed in nature—life, growth, decay, and death—transcend cultural boundaries.

When we view a work like the thirteenth-century French sepulchral effigy of Jean d'Alluye, which depicts a recumbent knight in chain mail, sword girded and shield at his side, feet resting on the image of a lion, it conveys to us a vivid expression of the intellectual and social milieu characteristic of medieval Europe and the age of chivalry, the tension between faith and heroism that influenced the way people of that era perceived and responded to death.

In the fifteenth and sixteenth centuries, there arose in Western Europe one of the most arresting expressions of death ever to emerge in the graphic arts: the Dance of Death. Growing out of widespread fears about the spread of bubonic plague, known as the Black Death, these images proclaim a society's preoccupation with mortality and the possibility of sudden, unexpected death. As an artistic theme, the Dance of Death continues to fascinate artists even in our own time. Fritz Eichenberg's twentieth-century woodcuts reveal the frightening possibilities of our era: humankind facing the prospect of universal annihilation resulting from total war, environmental catastrophe, or epidemic diseases like AIDS.[54]

Franco José de Goya's *Self-Portrait with Dr. Arieta* is an example of a genre in art that depicts deathbed scenes and persons *in extremis.* Goya painted this work for the doctor who aided his recovery from life-threatening illness. It shows the doctor holding medicine to Goya's lips and includes the figure of Death next to people who are thought to be Goya's priest and his housekeeper. Another painting by Goya, "The Third of May 1808," is his response to mass executions that took place in Madrid during the Napoleonic occupation of Spain. About this painting, Paul Johnson observes that "Goya makes no attempt to conceal the horror of violent death, or to redeem it by hints of heroism and redemption."[55] Besides death from illness or war, artists have also dealt with themes relating to suicide. In *The Death of Lucretia,* Rembrandt portrays Lucretia with a tear in her eye, moments after she has stabbed herself with a dagger. In this work, painted shortly after the death of his wife and one of his sons, the artist's saddened mental state is evident.

Attitudes toward death during the American colonial and early republican period are evident in Charles Wilson Peale's *Rachel Weeping* (1772 and 1776). The customs and beliefs of the time are illustrated in this painting, which shows a mother mourning her dead child. In her deathbed, the child's jaw is wrapped with a fabric strap to keep it closed and her arms are bound with cord to keep them at her sides. Medicines, all of which have proved ineffective, sit on a bedside table. The mother gazes heavenward and holds a handkerchief to wipe away the tears streaming down her face, a marked contrast to the dead child's peaceful countenance.

In modern art, death themes are found in the works of many artists, including Edvard Munch, Ernst Barlach, Käthe Kollwitz, and American sculptor Richard Shaw. For artists like Kollwitz, art is a vehicle for expressing the painful impact of personal loss. In contrast, Shaw's *Walking Skeleton* (1908) expresses a whimsical attitude toward death: The skeleton is composed of twigs, bottles, player cards, and similar found objects.

Although some modern artists have taken on the mission of communicating the impact of the Nazi Holocaust to ensure that the slaughter of 6 million people will not be forgotten, others are addressing the tragedy of AIDS.[56] Before his death in 1989, Robert Mapplethorpe had begun making portraits "filled with gaunt men and hollow-eyed skulls."[57] A similar sense of futility is expressed in Joseph Beuy's "The End of the 20th Century," a scattering of toppled stone pillars that suggests a fragile civilization giving way to decay.

The artistic community's response to AIDS has been expressed through both activist art with a political edge and mourning art that seeks to convey the magnitude of loss. Michael Franklin points out that "the social construction of the AIDS crisis is deeply rooted in the wide range of fabricated images that permeate all sectors of society."[58] Responding to a society in which people with AIDS have been objectified, stereotyped, and stigmatized, artists are calling attention to what they perceive to be a diseased society calling the kettle black. One artist stated, "When I was told that I'd contracted this virus, it didn't take me long to realize that I'd contracted a diseased society as well." Franklin says:

> The denial of death along with the perceived inconvenience of the body is prevalent in Western society. Not only have we forgotten how to participate in the dying process, we have also become strangled by our latent anxiety around the subject of death. The result is manifested in a cruelty toward those who are trying to live with various disease, particularly those that slowly decay the body. We are all susceptible to the limitations of our body and AIDS reminds us of this reality.

In the wake of AIDS, artists are formulating cultural images of the disease that go beyond stigma and stereotype to reveal the essential truth of the human encounter with dying and death. The creation of visual images and other artistic responses to the crisis is helping to transform harmful attitudes into more healing ones.

Indeed, the artistic response to AIDS has pointed up the value of employing creative expression as a means of coping with loss. In the nineteenth century, Americans conjoined classical and Christian symbols of death to simultaneously assuage their grief and memorialize public figures and family members.[59] Such symbols appeared on a variety of objects, jewelry, and pottery, as well as textiles and prints. Common motifs included urns, trees, and gardens. Embroidered mourning memorials were hung in the most important room of the house, the parlor. Mourners also made quilts to both memorialize the dead and express their grief. Such mourning art provided not only a means of perpetuating memories of a loved one, but also a focus for physically working through grief. The same sort of motives exist in individuals who have come together from every state in the nation to participate in constructing a massive quilt commemorating those who have died from AIDS: The Names Project AIDS Memorial Quilt.[60]

The AIDS Quilt is an impressive example of contemporary mourning art, as is the Vietnam Veterans Memorial located in Washington, D.C. Designed by architect Maya Lin, the impetus for the Memorial's construction came from a broad community of bereaved individuals who had the desire to create a memorial to loved ones whose deaths resulted from the war. Both the AIDS Quilt and the Vietnam Memorial exemplify how the social taboo against open mourning can be resisted by defying the suppression of grief and creating new modes for its articulation.[61]

The Present Milieu: Death Attitudes and Awareness

David Stannard tells us that in societies in which each individual is unique, important, and irreplaceable, death is not ignored but is marked by a "community-wide outpouring of grief for what is a genuine social loss."[62] But in societies in which one individual is not considered to be very different from any other, it is felt that "little damage is done to the social fabric by the loss of an individual" and therefore outside one's immediate circle the death receives little or no acknowledgment.

The ambivalent attitudes toward death in American society are reflected when one educator can applaud the study of death as the "last of the old taboos to fall" while another contends that death is "not a fit subject for the curriculum." This ambivalence is also reflected in the occasional spurts of media interest in death education, sometimes in response to campaigns initiated by special-interest groups determined to expose the "evils" of death education. In one instance, students who had agreed to be interviewed by a network film crew felt violated when they saw their positive comments twisted and misrepresented by the way resulting "film bites" were pieced together, apparently in an effort to create a more sensational story for the evening news.[63]

Patrick Dean observes that, if death education has been seen as the "bastard child of the curriculum hidden in the closet," then those who value death education may owe a debt of gratitude to the few but vocal critics whose protests provide opportunities to highlight the importance of death education as preparation for living.[64] Death education, says Dean, could appropriately be renamed "life and loss education," because "only through awareness of our lifelong losses and appreciation of our mortality are we free to be in the present, to live fully."

The first step in gaining new choices among behaviors and attitudes regarding death is to become aware of how denial or avoidance of death estranges us from an integral aspect of human life. The term *thanatology* is usually defined as the "study of death"; but, as Robert Kastenbaum suggests, it might be better defined as "the study of life, with death left in."[65] In the final analysis, sufficient motive for studying death and encountering the reality behind the image is eloquently stated by Octavio Paz: "A civilization that denies death ends by denying life."[66]

Pioneers in Death Studies

A convenient watershed from which to date the modern impulse to systematically study death and dying is Herman Feifel's book, *The Meaning of Death,* which was published in 1959. Based on a symposium held in 1956, this compilation brought together authorities from different disciplines whose essays encompassed theoretical approaches, developmental and attitudinal studies, cultural and religious concepts, and clinical insights. Death was shown to be an important topic for public as well as scholarly consideration. At the time, however, there was resistance to open discussions about death. Feifel says:

> The realization soon began to sink in that what I was up against were not idiosyncratic personal quirks, the usual administrative vicissitudes, pique, or nonacceptance of an inadequate research design. Rather, it was personal position, bolstered by cultural structuring, that death is a dark symbol not to be stirred—not even touched—an obscenity to be avoided.[67]

Feifel recalls that he was emphatically told that "the one thing you never do is to discuss death with a patient."

Essentially the same message was communicated to Elisabeth Kübler-Ross, whose publication of *On Death and Dying* in 1969 captured public attention and helped create demand for a fundamental reappraisal of how dying patients were treated. The notion that patients could offer important lessons for health care professionals was viewed as radical. Cicely Saunders also addressed the needs of dying patients in her pioneering work, *Care of the Dying* (1959), which helped to stimulate interest in hospice care for the dying. The impact of bereavement was brought to increased public attention through literary works such as C. S. Lewis's *A Grief Observed* (1961), and John Hinton's *Dying* (1967) provided a timely review of contemporary attitudes toward death.

During the same period, Jacques Choron examined the broader questions of death from a philosophical vantage point in his *Death and Western Thought* (1963) and *Death and Modern Man* (1964). Robert Fulton's *Death and Identity* (1965) addressed both theoretical and practical issues, with articles by noted scholars and practitioners. Also during the 1960s, Barney G. Glaser and Anselm L. Strauss applied the tools of sociology in studying how the awareness of dying affected patients, hospital staff, and family members. Glaser and Strauss found that medical personnel were reluctant to discuss death and tried to avoid telling a patient that he or she was dying. Glaser and Strauss's *Awareness of Dying* (1965) and *Time for Dying* (1968) are classics of the early literature about death and dying, as is Jeanne Quint Benoliel's pioneering study, *The Nurse and the Dying Patient* (1967), which called for systematic death education for nurses.

Meanwhile, attention was being focused on social customs surrounding death. Geoffrey Gorer's essay, "The Pornography of Death" (1955), marked the beginning of what would become an enthusiastic and often critical appraisal of how death was dealt with in modern societies. Funeral practices were critiqued in Jessica Mitford's *The American Way of Death* and Ruth Harmer's *The High Cost of Dying*, both published in 1963. In *The Loved One* (1948), Evelyn Waugh used satire to shed light on hypocritical and death-avoiding attitudes. These publications sparked efforts by consumer advocates to examine American funeral practices and led to governmental regulation of the funeral industry.

The present milieu is quite different from that encountered by the pioneers who began exploring the field of death studies in the 1950s and 1960s. A revitalized awareness of the place of death in our lives is reflected in the recent success of such titles as *Embraced by the Light* by Betty Eadie and *How We Die: Reflections on Life's Final Chapter* by Sherwin Nuland, which won the National Book Award for nonfiction in 1994. Many books dealing with death are published in the self-help category, offering advice to the bereaved and the dying, and to those who care for them. Indeed, the authors of a recent survey report that such self-help books have become "a ubiquitous part of American health care and culture."[68] Kübler-Ross's *On Death and Dying* was found to be the self-help book most read, as well as most prescribed, by psychologists who responded to the survey. Most bookstores now devote a special section to death-related books for children as well as adults.

There is a burgeoning professional literature dealing with issues related to dying, death, and bereavement. Two scholarly journals are devoted exclusively to thanatology: *Omega: Journal of Death and Dying* and *Death Studies*. Care of the dying is the precinct of *The Journal of Palliative Care* and *Hospice Journal*. Ethical issues are addressed in such journals as *The Hastings Center Report* and *Second Opinion*. Indeed, the literature on death and dying is expanding so fast that it is difficult for even seasoned practitioners to keep up with it. Publications dealing with AIDS have grown from just a trickle to a veritable flood within a short time, as a harrowing epidemic is addressed from every conceivable angle and discipline. To judge by the volume of published material now available, it appears that interest in death and dying is alive and well.

The Rise of Death Education

There is growing acknowledgment of the fact that death and failure are not necessarily synonymous, that the meaning of death lies beyond such categories. Still, there are frequent reminders that death remains a taboo and fearful topic for some. Take a death-and-dying course or read a book like this and quite likely someone will ask, "Why would you want to take a class about

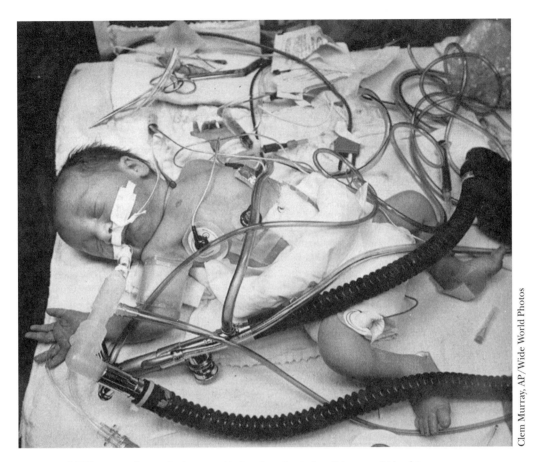

Clem Murray, AP/Wide World Photos

Lifelines—tubes and wires monitoring heartbeat, breathing, and blood pressure— increase this premature baby's chances of survival in the intensive care unit of Philadelphia's Children's Hospital. The special-care nursery often becomes an arena for many of the most difficult ethical decisions in medicine.

death?" or "Why in heaven's name would you be reading about death?" Clearly, we are in a period of transition.

Our understanding of death and dying has been blurred by euphemistic language, by isolation of the terminally ill in hospitals and nursing homes, by medical technology that alters the conventional understanding of life and death, and by social institutions that assume the tasks of dealing with the dying and dead. Our contact with death and dying tends to be limited to vicarious experiences presented in the mass media.

Yet, death unavoidably impinges on our lives. War, violence, and terrorism have been joined more recently by the specter of new diseases like AIDS and warnings about global environmental catastrophe. People of the present era have been described as *hibakusha*, a Japanese word meaning "explosion-affected." Initially applied to the survivors of the atomic bombing of Hiroshima, it connotes a pervasive anxiety about the threat of possible annihilation.

The emergence of the so-called death awareness movement and the rise of formal death education is due to a number of historical and social factors, including (1) the destruction of Hiroshima and Nagasaki by the atomic bomb at the end of World War II, ushering in the nuclear age and its attendant anxieties; (2) the increasing numbers of aged persons in society; (3) the "psychology of entitlement," which asserts the rights of various groups, including the dying; (4) the extension of the "dying interval" due to medical technology and modern health care; (5) a reaction against dehumanizing technology and advocacy of natural approaches to biological phenomena like birth and death; and (6) the desire to find meaning in death despite the waning influence of religious belief in modern secularized societies.[69] AIDS, too, has been a wake-up call for many people, dramatically altering perceptions and expectations about death and dying.

Considered broadly, death education embraces formal instruction as well as informal discussion of dying, grief, and related topics. Informal death education occurs in the context of "teachable moments" that arise out of events in daily life. The precipitating event may be the death of a gerbil in an elementary school classroom, or it may be an event experienced widely, as when an explosion killed the *Challenger* astronauts. Broadcast live to millions of school children as it happened, this disaster stimulated discussion of death-related issues in schools everywhere. Teachers had little choice but to help students deal with their concerns, questions, and anxieties.

More formally, death education is a regular part of the academic curriculum. Systematic death education is offered in some elementary and secondary schools, although courses at the college and university level are more common. The first regular program in death education at an American university was initiated by Robert Fulton at the University of Minnesota in the spring of 1963.[70] The first formal conference on death education was held at Hamline University in Minnesota in 1970.

The interdisciplinary nature of death education is attested to by the fact that courses are taught in a variety of departments, including sociology, social work, psychology, religious studies, philosophy, health science, nursing, gerontology, English, law, and education.[71] Death education benefits from this broad base of academic support as well as from the contributions of physicians, nurses, counselors, ethicists, hospice workers, and other professionals. Death education also conjoins cognitive and affective content.[72] That is, comprehensive death education addresses both objective facts and subjective concerns.

The larger picture of death education includes training for physicians, nurses, allied health workers, and other professionals whose duties involve contact with dying and bereaved individuals.[73] This last group includes police officers, fire fighters, and emergency medical technicians (EMTs). As witnesses to human tragedy in the line of duty, they are called upon to comfort victims and survivors. The stoic image of the police officer, EMT, or fire fighter who "keeps it all in" and never shows emotion is challenged by the recognition that such a strategy is physically and psychologically harmful. Death education, in advance of experiencing the deaths of others, can help individuals identify the range of emotional responses that may be encountered and experienced.

As death education has matured, both local and national organizations have been formed to serve as focal points for interaction and communication around issues of death and dying. Groups like the Association for Death Education and Counseling (ADEC) possess an international scope; others, like the Minnesota Coalition for Terminal Care, conduct similar programs at the regional and local level.[74] The International Work Group on Death, Dying, and Bereavement (IWG) includes many of the leading voices in the field and provides a forum for developing and disseminating policy statements concerning key issues relating to death, dying, and bereavement. Its publications include a helpful set of statements describing the assumptions and principles underlying death education, as well as specific guidelines for education directed to health care and human service professionals and to volunteers and other nonprofessionals who engage in mutual aid activities through self-help groups and other social support programs.[75]

Surveying the status of death education in settings that range from elementary schools to universities, as well as among health professionals and the general public, Hannelore Wass observes that, despite noteworthy beginnings, the vision of high-quality death education is yet to be fully realized. In the end, death education can help us "leap from a parochial to a global view," transcending self-interest in favor of concern for others.[76] "Death education," Wass says, "is about love, care, and compassion; it is about helping and healing."

Where death is concerned, the adage, "What you don't know won't hurt you," is a fallacy. Avoiding the thought of death doesn't remove us from its power. Such ostrichlike behavior only limits the choices for coping effectively. When we bring death out of the closet, we give ourselves the opportunity to clear away the accumulated rubbish and preserve what we find valuable. "The unexamined death," wrote Robert Kavanaugh, "is not worth dying."[77]

The Response to AIDS

Since the early 1980s, AIDS (acquired immunodeficiency syndrome) has been a major force in heightening our awareness of death. What images and feelings do you become aware of as you think about AIDS? For many people, AIDS is synonymous with death: a dread disease, contagious and epidemic, a twentieth-century plague. The pace of medical discovery relative to AIDS has been more than matched by its rapid spread. Robert Kastenbaum points out that the symbolism of AIDS embodies the stigma of many earlier forms of catastrophic dying, including disfiguration, dementia, and skeletonization. It conveys multiple meanings about human vanity and pride, divine punishment, attack by an enemy from within, the terror of life in death and the despair of death in life, and the romantic exit of brilliant and beautiful doomed youth.[78]

From the first reported cases in 1981, through 1993, more than 441,000 Americans have been diagnosed with AIDS and more than 250,000 have died.[79] In 1993, infection with the AIDS virus, HIV (human immunodeficiency virus), became the leading cause of death among Americans twenty-five to forty-four years old. Between 800,000 and 1 million Americans are infected with HIV.[80] Medical scientists emphasize that the "take-home message" behind the statistics is the increasing importance of the heterosexual AIDS epidemic. Although AIDS is a significant health problem in many smaller cities and towns, its greatest impact is in large cities, with African Americans and Hispanics bearing the brunt of new AIDS cases. In 1993, the AIDS rate was more than five times higher among African Americans and three times higher among Hispanics than among white Americans.[81]

The United States and sub-Saharan Africa have been the main "epicenters" of the AIDS pandemic, with more than 10 million people in sub-Saharan Africa believed to have the AIDS virus. Within the past few years, however, the virus has been making rapid inroads in Asia. AIDS is now spreading faster in Asia than anywhere else—mainly in India, Burma, and Thailand, although it is also appearing in Vietnam and Cambodia. Globally, more than 17 million people are HIV-infected, including about 1 million children, with over 6000 people becoming infected with HIV every day.[82] The rate at which the disease is spreading makes it difficult to stay current with statistics; each updated report evokes astonishment.

From the first inklings that AIDS was a new disease that would challenge our economic and emotional resources, the public response has involved questions about allocating economic, medical, and social resources. The community response to AIDS has been mixed.[83] Although some communities responded with a variety of health and public service programs, others reacted by preventing efforts to reach out to victims. When Elisabeth Kübler-Ross proposed a hospice for infants with AIDS in rural Virginia, some members of the community acted swiftly to deny the necessary permits. Fear of contagion won out over the desire to help sick and dying infants.

Society still seems uncertain about how to respond to AIDS. In California, the Department of Motor Vehicles (DMV) refused to provide a customized license plate requested by a registered nurse who specializes in AIDS care.[84] The plate, reading "AIDS RN," was requested by Steve Lee, who said he wanted the new plate on his 1994 Thunderbird to show pride in his work and AIDS awareness. After the DMV turned down the request and deemed the plate offensive, Lee said, "What [DMV] is kind of saying is the way the general society wants to deal with AIDS—they don't want to deal with it." After the

Smithsonian Institution

© Albert Lee Strickland

The making of a memorial quilt was among the elaborate personal and social mecha-nisms for dealing with grief widely practiced during the nineteenth century, as in the top example memorializing a granddaughter who died in infancy. This traditional mourning custom was revived recently to commemorate and remember persons who died from AIDS; in the example at bottom, words and symbols express beloved qualities of Joe's life. For survivors, the creation of such memorials provides not only a focus for physically working through grief but also a means of perpetu-ating the memory of the loved one.

DMV eventually reversed itself, a manager at the agency reported that some AIDS groups had told the DMV they didn't want plates to be issued bearing the words "AIDS" or "HIV" because they would be reminders for people with the virus. On the other hand, the clinical supervisor of an AIDS project said the DMV's rejection of Lee's plate was the "ultimate in political incorrectness." As a commentary on attitudes toward AIDS, this saga of a license plate exemplifies the powerful, and often confusing, images associated with AIDS.

AIDS reminds us that infectious diseases remain a threat and that human beings remain uncertain about how to respond to epidemic disease. AIDS presents a challenge to the health care system and to society as a whole. By putting pressure on medical resources, the epidemic has stimulated interest in hospice and home care. It presents a personal challenge to those directly affected by the disease, and to their caregivers and loved ones. Viewed in a larger context, it challenges all of us. Placing AIDS in historical perspective, Charles Rosenberg says:

> Mortality is built into our bodies, into our modes of behavior, and into our place in the planet's ecology. Like other epidemics, AIDS has served well to remind us, finally, of these ultimate realities.[85]

As AIDS confronts us in different social and individual contexts, it is altering our attitudes and practices as they relate to dying and death.

Is Death Out of the Closet?

In assessing the phenomenon of death avoidance that has characterized much of American life in the twentieth century, attention should be directed to what researchers term *institutional denial.*[86] A student remarked, "Sometimes I feel there's too little space in our society for a person to scream, to cry, to shout, to sing, to touch, to be human." Death evokes all these aspects of human behavior. Yet a grieving person may find it difficult to express his or her natural emotions. Elisabeth Kübler-Ross has said that hospitals should make available a "grief" room, a place set aside for expressing the intense emotions of loss and bereavement.

Death has been brought some distance out of the closet into the light of public attention. The student of death and dying is likely to become uncommonly aware of the social and political issues that relate to death. Death education can promote a deeper appreciation of the reality underlying media reports that speak of death only in statistical or melodramatic terms. Hazards to public safety—often discussed in tedious analyses of risks versus benefits—are perceived more humanely by people who have learned about the very real impact of death on human beings.

The study of death and dying embraces a wide range of issues and topics, from the nuts-and-bolts subject matter of knowing the options in selecting mortuary services or the elements of a will and procedures involved in probating an estate, to more ethereal matters such as speculation about what happens after death and whether the soul enjoys a blissful afterlife. It embraces, too, such here-and-now but elusive issues as the "right to die" and physician-assisted suicide. Such issues have captured public interest through the activities of Dr. Jack Kevorkian, a Michigan pathologist who has assisted in the deaths of more than twenty individuals since 1990. As Kevorkian's challenge to Michigan's ban on assisted suicide made its way to the U.S. Supreme Court, similar cases in other states were also working their way through the court system, including a measure passed by Oregon voters in 1994 that would legally permit physician-assisted suicide for the terminally ill.

As populations grow worldwide, so do deaths. In the aggregate, the terminally ill, along with their families and friends, represent a significant constituency that is challenging, publicly and privately, worrisome or unacceptable aspects of the contemporary health system and the modes of dying embedded within it.[87] Scholars point out that we now live in a *postmodern* era, "surrounded by images and artifacts from all periods and of all geographical and cultural locations."[88] This means that "we are aware of the entire experience of the human race in ways that were not available to previous generations." This is reflected in the eclecticism found in art, philosophy, ethics, social and political matters, and life style. Thus, the postmodern perspective opens up possibilities that allow us to select ideas from all historical periods and cultures, thereby creating a synthesis that is new and personally satisfying.

Examining Assumptions

The changes in American attitudes toward death since the beginning of the twentieth century are evident in the lives of two age groups whose encounters with death have been quite different. The first group was born prior to the advent of the atomic bomb; the second group was born after. Individuals in the first group knew death as visible, immediate, and real. Robert Fulton and Greg Owen remark that their families "lived in terms of the simple round of life that humankind had known and accepted since the beginning: birth, copulation, and death."[89] Dying took place in the home, witnessed by child and adult alike. The second group, in contrast, has mostly experienced death at a distance.

Technological innovation has played a major role in affecting how we die and how we care for our dead. However, the social response to change does not always keep pace with such innovation. *Cultural lag* is a term used by social scientists to describe the phenomenon of societies falling behind in dealing with new social problems caused by such technological innovation.[90]

As we approach the twenty-first century, people are beginning to examine their assumptions about death. The quest for a personally meaningful relationship to death can lead different individuals to different outcomes. For example, questions about the conventional funeral have caused many people to consider their preferences for last rites. Some turn away from traditional

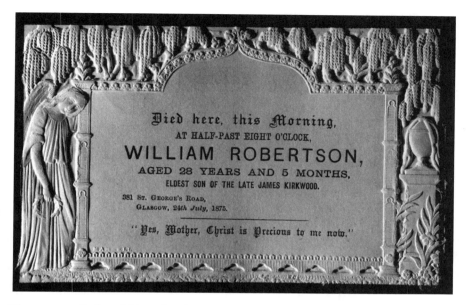

Figure *1-4 Embossed Linen Death Notification Card, 1875*
This card exemplifies the formality of nineteenth-century mourning customs. The etiquette books of the period often devoted considerable space to the procedural details associated with the wearing of mourning clothes, the issuance of funeral invitations, and other behaviors appropriate to the survivors of a death.

funerals in favor of alternatives that offer swift and inexpensive disposition of the body. Others find this trend disturbing. Since time immemorial, rituals and ceremonies marking death have provided a framework for meeting the social and psychological needs of survivors, and for acknowledging the place and meaning of death in human social life (see Figure 1-4). Is something of importance lost when survivors are not given an opportunity to participate in social ritual commemorating the death of a significant other? Underlying these contrasting attitudes, a common intention can be discerned—namely, the desire to find a personally meaningful response to the fact of death.

The hospice movement, with its focus on emotional support for the dying person and his or her family, is an example of how the reality of death is being acknowledged by restoring, in ways appropriate to the present milieu, certain aspects of attitudes and practices that were more prevalent in the past. In societies that preserve traditional beliefs and practices, such as the Amish, death is part of the natural rhythm of life. Death initiates a time of social reinforcement and support, for the bereaved family and for the wider society.

The social patterns that the Amish find helpful in coping with death include open communication about the process of dying and its impact; maintaining, to the extent possible, a normal life style during the course of illness; commitment to the independence of the dying person; and support of the bereaved.[91] Hospice care adapts the core elements of such traditional attitudes and practices to the modern social setting. As Andrew Ziner says:

> Like nearly every other aspect of our lives, our understandings and feelings about dying and death are derived from our involvement in the myriad of groups, organizations, and institutions that represent our communities and, ultimately, constitute our society. As these religious, economic, legal, and familiar structures change over time, we also undergo change. This is because, as social beings, all of the meanings we attach to personal and cultural concerns—including dying and death—are inexorably tied to our social worlds. Independent of the freedoms and constraints attached to our membership in these groups, the idea, impact, and reality of humanity simply could not exist. For example, how do you feel when you hear the word *death*? If you were born a century earlier, would you feel the same way? Is the difference due to individual or social factors?[92]

Death is intrinsic to human experience. Yet many people try to cram it into a dark closet and shut the door. There it stays until, bursting the hinges, the door flies open and death is again forced upon our awareness. Death is like a mysterious stranger at a costume ball, whose mask conceals the face beneath. Perhaps the disguise is more terrifying than the reality, yet how can we know unless we risk uncovering the face hidden behind the mask? Learning about death and dying can help us identify the attitudes and behaviors that keep us from lifting the mask so that we may each confront our mortality in a way that is meaningful for our own lives.

Further Readings

Martha Cooper and Joseph Sciorra. *R.I.P.: Memorial Wall Art*. New York: Henry Holt, 1994.

James K. Crissman. *Death and Dying in Central Appalachia: Changing Attitudes and Practices*. Urbana: University of Illinois Press, 1994.

Roger Y. Dufour-Gompers. "Watching the Violence of Warfare in the 'Theatre' of Operations," *International Social Work Journal* 44, no. 2 (May 1992): 247–265.

Lynne Ann DeSpelder and Albert Lee Strickland, eds. *The Path Ahead: Readings in Death and Dying*. Mountain View, Calif.: Mayfield, 1995.

James Kinsella. *Covering the Plague: AIDS and the American Media*. New Brunswick, N.J.: Rutgers University Press, 1990.

Lawrence L. Langer, ed. *Art from the Ashes: A Holocaust Anthology*. New York: Oxford University Press, 1995.

Dan Nimmo and James E. Combs. *Nightly Horrors: Crisis Coverage by Television Network News*. Knoxville: University of Tennessee Press, 1985.

Jay Ruby. *Secure the Shadow: Death and Photography in America.* Boston: MIT Press, 1995.

William Simon, C. Allen Haney, and Russell Buenteo. "The Postmodernization of Death and Dying," *Symbolic Interaction* 16, no. 4 (1993): 411–426.

Tony Walter. "Modern Death: Taboo or Not Taboo?" *Sociology* 25 (May 1991): 293–310.

Robert F. Weir, ed. *Death in Literature.* New York: Columbia University Press, 1980.

A SIOUX WARRIOR'S GRAVE 1879

In January 1879, frontier photographer L. A. Huffman recorded this scene showing the burial platform of a Sioux warrior who had died and been placed on the scaffold only a few days before. Surrounding the gravesite is a vast plain, crisscrossed with the trails of wild herds of buffalo.

Perspectives on Death: Cross-Cultural and Historical

*D*eath is a universal human experience, yet the response it elicits is shaped by the attitudes that are prevalent in a given culture. Attitudes, which include components of belief, emotion, and behavior, develop out of the interplay between individuals and their cultural environment. The shared consciousness among its members makes a culture distinct; it gives a particular cast to experiences and the meanings ascribed to them. In the previous chapter, we traced the influence of social changes on the characteristic American mode of dealing with death and dying. To gain broader perspective, we now turn our attention to cultures that in many respects differ from our own. Yet, customs that first appear exotic nevertheless share common ground with familiar practices. Understanding how other people perceive and behave toward death sheds light on our own beliefs and behaviors.

The term *culture* provides a shorthand way of referring to the way of life of a given group of people. Cultures can be ranged on a continuum from "death-welcoming" to "death-denying." In reading about the cultures discussed in this chapter, note where each might be placed on the welcoming–denying continuum. As you reflect on your study, consider where your own "cultures"—the national, ethnic, and family groups of which you are a part—might fit on such a continuum. Whatever the particulars of a culture's beliefs about death, they represent efforts to rationalize—that is, make sense of—the world as it is known at a particular time and in a particular place.

Figure 2-1   *Neanderthal Burial*

Death in Early and Traditional Cultures

Archaeological evidence demonstrates that human concern for the dead predates the advent of written history. In Neanderthal burials more than 50,000 years ago, food, ornamental shells, and stone implements were buried with the dead, implying a belief that the dead would find such items useful during their passage from the land of the living to the land of the dead. In many ancient burials, the corpse is stained with red ochre and placed in a fetal posture, suggesting beliefs about the revitalization of the body after death and subsequent rebirth (see Figure 2-1).[1] Evidence from these early burials shows characteristic human concern with the meaning of death and with rituals that formalize the relationship between the living and the dead. In considering the different rituals surrounding death in the cultural settings discussed in this chapter, you may find it useful to keep in mind the definition provided by William LaFleur. Ritual, he says, "is poetry that human beings have taken up with their bodies and turned into a special kind of social practice . . . [it]

When the first man, the father of the human race, was being buried, a god passed by the grave and inquired what it meant, for he had never seen a grave before. Upon receiving the information from those about the place of interment that they had just buried their father, he said: "Do not bury him, dig up the body again." "No," they replied, "we cannot do that. He has been dead for four days and smells." "Not so," entreated the god, "dig him up and I promise you that he will live again." But they refused to carry out the divine injunction. Then the god declared, "By disobeying me, you have sealed your own fate. Had you dug up your ancestor, you would have found him alive, and you yourselves when you passed from this world should have been buried as bananas are for four days, after which you shall have been dug up, not rotten, but ripe. But now, as a punishment for your disobedience, you shall die and rot." And whenever they hear this sad tale the Fijians say: "Oh, that those children had dug up that body!"

Figure 2-2 *Fijian Story (Traditional): The Origin of Death*

provides activities that fuse a wide variety of things that seem otherwise unrelated."[2]

In most cultures, mythological themes about life and death provide a foundation for human attitudes, values, and behavior. Death is viewed not as an end but as a change of status, a transition from the land of the living to the world of the dead. Thus, the living are careful to aid the dead as they journey to the spirit world. In some cases, these precautions also offset fear about the potential malevolence of the dead if they are not shown proper respect by the living. Cultural myths serve four main functions—namely, they (1) reconcile human consciousness with the conditions of its existence; (2) render an image of the cosmos that is consistent with the science of the time; (3) validate and maintain the social order; and (4) shape individuals to the aims and ideals of their social groups.[3]

It is clear from evidence such as the Neanderthal burials that speculation about death and orderly practices for coping with it date from the earliest human societies. The essential concern for living well—and dying well—seems to be present in all human experience. Traditional cultures embody indigenous knowledge—that is, the shared knowledge of a local community as it evolves over time in a particular environment. The idea of "passing down" through successive generations the beliefs, customs, and values of a given culture is inherent in the word *tradition,* which comes from the Latin *tradere,* meaning "to hand down." A culture's understanding of death and its place in people's lives can be found in its rituals and stories.

Origin of Death

How did death first become part of human experience? The answers from traditional cultures to this enigma are couched in myth.[4] In some myths, death

When Hare heard of Death, he started for his lodge & arrived there crying, shriek-ing, *My uncles & my aunts must not die!* And then the thought assailed him: *To all things will come!* He cast his thoughts upon the precipices & they began to fall & crumble. Upon the rocks he cast his thoughts & they became shattered. Under the earth he cast his thoughts & all the things living there stopped moving & their limbs stiffened in death. Up above, toward the skies, he cast his thoughts & the birds flying there suddenly fell to the earth & were dead.

After he entered his lodge he took his blanket and, wrapping it around him, lay down crying. *Not the whole earth will suffice for all those who will die. Oh, there will not be enough earth for them in many places!* There he lay in his corner wrapped up in his blanket, silent.

Figure 2-3   *Winnebago Myth: When Hare Heard of Death*

is portrayed as originating because ancestral parents or an archetypal figure transgressed divine or natural law, either through poor judgment or disobedi-ence (see Figure 2-2). Sometimes the origin of death involves a test of some person or group. When the test is failed, death becomes a reality. A Luba myth from Africa describes how god created a paradise for the first human beings and endowed it with everything needed for their sustenance; however, they were forbidden to eat of the bananas in the middle of the field. When the humans ate the bananas, it was decreed that humankind would die after a lifetime of toil. This motif is akin to the biblical story of Adam and Eve's transgression in the Garden of Eden, an account of death's origin that contin-ues to be relevant in the religious traditions of Judaism, Christianity, and Islam.

In other myths, a crucial act that would have ensured immortality was not properly carried out; an *omission* rather than an *action* introduces death to humankind. Sometimes there is a messenger who was supposed to deliver the message of eternal life but the message was garbled due to malice or forget-fulness, or it did not arrive on time to save the day. The Winnebago story from North America involving the trickster figure, Hare, is an example of this motif (see Figure 2-3). Momentarily forgetting his purpose, Hare failed to deliver the life-saving message. A variant of this motif tells how two messengers were sent—one bringing immortality, the other bringing death—and the messen-ger bringing death arrived first.

In the "death in a bundle" motif, death is introduced into human expe-rience when a bundle containing the mortal fate of all humankind is opened, either inadvertently or because of poor choice. A story told by Aesop from Greek mythology gives a variation on this theme (see Figure 2-4). Another motif, involving sleep and death, describes how a message of immortality was addressed to human beings but people were not awake to receive it.

Although most myths portray death as unwelcome, in some it is wel-comed, even actively pursued, because of weariness with life or disgust with its

It was a hot, sultry summer afternoon, and Eros, tired with play and faint from the heat, took shelter in a cool, dark cave. It happened to be the cave of Death himself.

Eros, wanting only to rest, threw himself down carelesslessly—so carelessly that all his arrows fell out of his quiver.

When he woke he found they had mingled with the arrows of Death, which lay scattered about the floor of the cave. They were so alike Eros could not tell the difference. He knew, however, how many had been in his quiver, and eventually he gathered up the right number.

Of course, Eros took some that belonged to Death and left some of his own behind.

And so it is today that we often see the hearts of the old and the dying struck by bolts of Love; and sometimes we see the hearts of the young captured by Death.

Figure 2-4   *Aesop: Eros and Death*

misery. In some myths, death is sought as a remedy for overpopulation. In others, human beings barter for or purchase death from the gods so that life does not continue interminably.

Despite their variety, these myths echo a theme that is surprisingly familiar: Death comes from outside; it cuts short what otherwise would be an immortal existence. This notion continues to influence our attitudes. Death seems somehow foreign, not really part of ourselves. Even when we understand the biological processes of disease and aging, we may harbor feelings that, if only this defect could be repaired or the deterioration reversed, we could remain alive. Death still seems an anomaly.

Yet the recognition of our own mortality cannot be avoided. The epic of Gilgamesh describes this awakening as the epic relates the odyssey of Gilgamesh, a king whose journey is precipitated by the death of his friend, Enkidu. After undergoing great peril in his search for the power to renew one's youth, Gilgamesh returns from his quest empty-handed. There, grieving the death of his beloved friend Enkidu, Gilgamesh realizes that he too will die. Like Gilgamesh, our acknowledgment of death's reality may be experienced most profoundly as we grieve a loved one's death.

Causes of Death

Having examined the question of how death became part of human experience generally, we turn now to the particular causes that bring about the deaths of *individual* human beings. Death sometimes results from wounds sustained in battle or from accidental injuries that occur unexpectedly in the course of daily life. The proximate cause of death is clear, but the ultimate cause can be questioned: Why did this situation come to this person at this particular time? Could the death have resulted from some malign influence, possibly induced by magical means? Among many traditional peoples, there are no "natural" causes of death. Thus, the explanation for a person's death must be sought by looking to supernatural and other less obvious causes. Although a magical explanation does not lend itself to either proof or disproof, it can provide comfort by making sense of what otherwise seems inexplicable.

Among the Senufo of Africa's Ivory Coast, for example, the death of a child is considered unnatural; it therefore entails an obligation for the survivors to discover the cause of such misfortune. After all, the misfortune of a child's death affects the entire community. In much the same way, cases of sudden death—whether due to violence or accidental injury—also threaten the community's welfare. Actions must be taken that go beyond the obvious cause to uncover what lies behind it. Elaborate precautions may be set into motion, and sacrifices and medicines may be called upon to purify the land and protect the community from further calamity.[5]

Traditional societies like the Senufo typically embrace an ecological orientation with respect to their search for causes of disease and death.[6] They look to the supernatural realm, and also investigate the possible role of phenomena such as the wind or moon, heredity, and behavioral excesses such as not getting enough sleep. They may examine a range of socioeconomic and psychosocial factors. Perhaps the cause of death is somehow related to the person's social interactions. Could anger, anxiety, fright, or envy be involved? Did the person offend the ancestors or neglect proper rites for the dead?

Traditional societies view illness and death as public, not private, events. Death and disease signal the fact that something is "out of balance." Medicine and religion are not put into separate compartments of life, but are viewed as parts of a whole. The health of individuals as well as the entire community depends upon maintaining a correct relationship with the environment, including its unseen aspects. The search for answers to why individuals die occurs within a communal environment that includes both the living and the dead, as the ancestors continue to hold an important place in the ongoing life of the people.

Power of the Dead

In cultures that maintain a strong bond between the living and the dead, "the land echoes with the voices of the ancestors."[7] It is the living and dead who, together, comprise the clan, the tribe, the people. This relationship is celebrated as a sign that the community endures beyond the limits imposed by death. A semblance of this communal sense is displayed when people refer to the "founding fathers" of a nation or college. Such notables are spoken of metaphorically as "being with us in spirit" on occasions when members of the living group—be it nation or college convocation—meet to celebrate their common purpose with those who preceded them in the life of the community.

For traditional societies, the relationship between living and dead can be perilous. The dead may harm the living, especially during the transitional period after death. Grief may be expressed with loud wails or with silent tears,

Death Knells

During many centuries one item of expense for survivors was the fee that must be paid for the ringing of the soul bell. Every cathedral and church of medieval Christendom had such a bell, almost always the largest one in the bell tower.

By the time John Donne wrote the immortal line "for whom the bell tolls," ringing of the soul bell—in a distinctive pattern, or knell—was popularly taken to be merely a public notice that a death had occurred. This use of the soul bell came into importance relatively late, however.

Not simply in Christian Europe but also among primitive tribes and highly developed non-Christian cultures of the Orient, bells have been linked with death. Notes from bells (rung in special fashion) served to help convince a spirit that there was no need to remain close to a useless dead body. At the same time, noise made by bells was considered to be especially effective in driving away the evil spirits who prowled about hoping to seize a newly released soul or to put obstacles in its path.

Ringing of the soul (or passing) bell was long considered so vital that bell ringers demanded, and got, big fees for using it. Still in general use by the British as late as the era of King Charles II in the seventeenth century, bell ringers then regulated the number of strokes of the passing bell so that the general public could determine the age, sex, and social status of the deceased.

Webb Garrison,
Strange Facts About Death

but almost always there is deep respect for the still-powerful soul of the deceased. If the soul or spirit of the deceased is not treated properly, harm may result. Funeral rituals help ensure the successful journey of the soul into the realm of the dead, a journey that also benefits the living. Of special concern in many traditional societies are the malevolent, or evil-intentioned, spirits that wander about aimlessly, seeking to disrupt the well-being of the living. Such spirits are typically associated with catastrophic deaths and deaths in child-birth.

Experiences that include an element of mystery commonly provoke awe and uncertainty. Consider the eerie feelings associated with "haunted houses" and the strange foreboding experienced when passing through a cemetery at night. The context is different in traditional societies, but the basic impulse is strikingly similar: One does not wish to disturb the dead.

Yet, generally speaking, traditional peoples do not shun their dead. Most of them hold ceremonies periodically to celebrate and honor the dead. In the rhythm and flow of communal life, the person—in death as in life—is part of the whole. As unseen members of an ongoing social order, the dead may be allies who perform services for the living—as interpreters, intermediaries, and ambassadors in the realm beyond the reach of sensory perceptions. Often, this communication with the dead is facilitated by the *shaman,* a visionary member of the community who projects his or her consciousness to other realms as an intermediary between the worlds of living and dead.[8]

For Hawaiians living within the intimate relationships of the *'ohana,* or family clan, a close bond existed between living family members and their ancestors.[9] In addition to serving as role models upholding standards of conduct, the ancestors were a crucial spiritual link between human beings and powerful—but distant and impersonal—gods. Keeping alive the memory of one's ancestors and calling upon them to intercede with the gods sustained family loyalties beyond death.

Names of the Dead

If calling a person's name is a way of summoning the person, then refraining from using a name will presumably leave its bearer undisturbed. Hence, one of the most prevalent of all practices related to the dead is name avoidance: The deceased is never again mentioned, or else is referred to only obliquely, never by name.

Among some aboriginal tribes of Australia, for example, the deceased is referred to as "that one" rather than by his or her name. Elsewhere, allusions are made to particular traits or special qualities a person was known for during his or her lifetime. Thus, "Uncle Joe," who gained renown as an expert fisherman, might be referred to after his death as "that relative who caught many fish." Or a woman who had demonstrated extraordinary bravery might be called "that one who showed courage." In other cases, the person is referred to by his or her relationship to the speaker—but again, never by name. Name avoidance can be so thoroughgoing that living individuals who bear the same name as the deceased are forced to adopt new names, and even words describing ordinary objects are removed from the society's vocabulary when they are the same as the dead person's name.

In other instances, rather than being avoided, the name of the deceased person is given special emphasis. It may be conferred on a newborn child in the deceased's family, for example. According to the particular beliefs that motivate the practice, this naming may represent a wish to honor the memory of a loved one or it may be done as a way to ensure that the soul of the dead person is reincarnated. In the traditional Lapp culture, when a woman is near the time of giving birth, a deceased ancestor appears to her in a dream and tells her which of her ancestors is to be reborn in her infant; the dream determines the name her new baby receives.[10] Among indigenous Hawaiians, children were sometimes named for ancestors or even named by the gods. Names bestowed by the gods, which were communicated through dreams, were considered most important, followed by names linking a child with his or her forebears. Sometimes the name of a child who died earlier would be given to a child born later. Naming a child for a deceased relative made the name live again.[11]

We see examples of these traditional naming practices in modern societies. Avoiding the use of the deceased's name may stem from a desire to minimize grief. Whereas people living in traditional cultures may avoid mentioning the deceased's name because of anxiety about provoking its spirit, people in modern societies may avoid the deceased's name to prevent conjuring up mental images that add to the pain of loss. Whereas one society manages grief by postulating the existence of spirits that should not be disturbed, another relies on custom and etiquette to accomplish a similar goal. Similarly, when a child is named after a beloved grandparent or respected friend who has died, aren't the parents hoping that some of the qualities valued in the namesake will be "reborn" in the child? In this, as in the explanations offered for how death came into the world and how it affects particular individuals, there is a common thread that runs through all of human experience, even though cultural forms differ.

Death and Dying in Western Culture

With the beginning of the medieval period in the fifth century of the present era, and continuing for roughly a thousand years, most people living in the milieu of Western European culture accepted death as part of human existence. This attitude was consistent with a view of the universe as bound together by natural and divine law. In Christianized Europe, the teachings of the Church were a source of hope for the afterlife; they affected the manner in which people died as well as the disposition of their earthly remains. This religious outlook, and the general acceptance of death it engendered, lasted until the great cultural Renaissance of the fifteenth and sixteenth centuries, a period that Philippe Ariès has characterized as one of "tamed death" (see Figure 2-5).[12]

Of course, during the course of this lengthy historical period, attitudes and practices concerning death evolved and changed with the times. From about the fifth century to the twelfth century, a sense of collective destiny was the norm. In the religious world view of the time, death was seen as the common fate of all people. Those who had passed on were "asleep in Christ," entrusted to the Church's keeping until their bodily resurrection at the apocalyptic return of Jesus Christ. Cultural values and practices emphasized the fact that "Everyone dies."

By roughly the twelfth century, death was being viewed with a more particular awareness about the fate of each individual person. "Everyone dies" had been transformed into "I will die my own death." This change coincided with an overall enrichment in culture and more complex social structures. There was a general opening to new intellectual pursuits as people achieved a larger sense of individual identity and self-awareness. Whereas residing in the bosom of the Church had been sufficient to ensure resurrection on the Last Day and entry into Heaven, people now began to feel more personally anxious about Judgment Day, the cosmic event that would separate the just from the damned. The *liber vitae,* or Book of Life, which had been pictured as a sort of vast cosmic census, was now being imagined as containing the biographies of individual lives, a kind of balance sheet by which each person's soul would be weighed. Thus, the act of dying became an event of supreme importance, a

Ritual of dying: the recumbent figure of the dying person, presiding amidst protocol and custom, over an essentially public ceremony. Everything done with simplicity, no great show of emotion. Custom and social observances dictate the style of dying and the deathbed scene. Death is familiar; there is an awareness of dying: "I see and I know that my death is near."

As the initiative passes from the dying person to the family and then to the medical arena, there arises a desire to spare the dying person, often by means of pretence, from the "ugliness," of death. Death becomes taboo.

Place of burial is the charnel house, the outer part or courtyard of the church. With the rise of the cult of martyrs, there is a desire to be buried near the great saints of the church; burials take place near or in churches, instead of outside cities, as during pagan times.

Gradually, a greater sense of individuality is reflected in death customs. A new self-awareness becomes evident first in the use of inscriptions and plaques to mark a person's biography and death; later, effigies and death masks herald the individuality of the dead. Eventually, the tombs of the notable dead are embellished with sculptures portraying both the appearance of the body when alive and its ultimate putrefaction after death, a stark reminder of mortality and individual responsibility.

The "cult of memory" demonstrated by ornate memorials to the dead was often accompanied by hysterical mourning on the part of the bereaved survivors. More recently, however, these once-customary signs of mourning have been largely replaced by the avoidance of emotional display and by discreet and brief funeral ceremonies. Uncertainty and anxiety become the characteristic emotions elicited by "invisible death" in the twentieth century.

500 600 700 800 900 1000 1100 1200 1300 1400 1500 1600 1700 1800 1900 2000

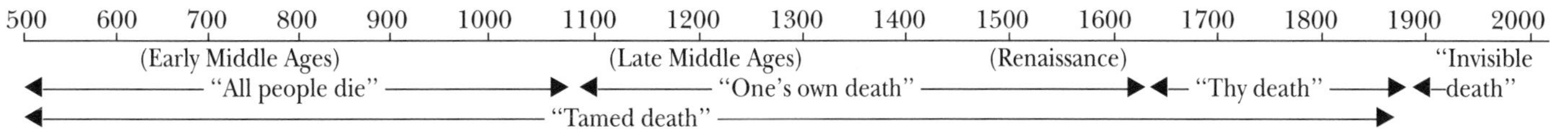

500　600　700　800　900　1000　1100　1200　1300　1400　1500　1600　1700　1800　1900　2000

(Early Middle Ages)　　　(Late Middle Ages)　　(Renaissance)　　　　　　　　"Invisible

—— "All people die" ——　—— "One's own death" ——　—— "Thy death" ——　▼—death"

"Tamed death"

Universe bound together by natural and divine law. Death a familiar and accepted part of this order. Individuals experienced themselves as participants in a collective destiny of humankind, presided over by the Church.

General enrichment throughout culture; intellectual advances, influenced by Greek thought and Roman law.

Age of exploration and conquest; old geographic and intellectual boundaries giving way.

Increasing secularization of social and intellectual life.

Belief in the Apocalypse (Christ's return at the end of time). Resurrection of the dead on the Last Day. The dead "asleep in Christ," to awake in Paradise. Salvation based on participation in the communal Body of Christ, not on individual moral actions.

Concept of the Resurrection incorporates belief in the Last Judgment, when the soul will be judged on its record in the "Book of Life," an individual account that is closed on the Last Day.

Emphasis on Judgment predominates; the "Second Coming" fades into background. The time of Judgment shifts to the deathbed scene, which becomes the final test in the cosmic struggle. Between death and "the Last Day" there is an extension of being into purgatory.

Challenges to religious belief lead to a reexamination and reinterpretation of scripture and sacred traditions. The interplay between reason and faith creates a diverse and pluralistic religious and social environment.

Figure 2-5 *Death and Dying from the Middle Ages to the Present*

Death is a subject to me which you can see and think of but cannot talk of. Indeed however ill he be I could never think of the death of one I love. It may be reconed [*sic*] as a want of faith! I know it is not. I do not mean by that, that I shall not be prepared to die when the time comes.

From the *Diary* (1858) of Annie de Rothschild, age thirteen

phenomenon that is examined more closely in a subsequent section of this chapter.

The next great transformation with respect to attitudes and behaviors relative to death in Western European culture came toward the end of the seventeenth century, as the death of the other, "thy death," took center stage. This change in beliefs and customs gave rise to impassioned expressions of grief and desires to memorialize the dead. The ideal of the "beautiful death" was part of a general fascination with the imaginative and emotional appeal of the heroic, the mysterious. The sad beauty of death elicited feelings of melancholy, though still tinged with optimism that there would be an eventual reunion with the beloved in a Heavenly home. To a greater extent than before, the bereaved began to visit the graves of their loved ones, and expressions of mourning became highly visible as the arts were pressed into service to memorialize the dead. By around the nineteenth century, the deaths of others had largely overshadowed the earlier concern with one's own mortality.

In summary, through more than a thousand years of Western European history, we can trace the progression of attitudes toward death from the communal mentality that "everyone dies," to the more emphatically personal awareness that "I will die," to the preoccupation with the deaths of others, "thy death." Notwithstanding these changes, the entire period surveyed thus far can be represented by the overarching image of "tamed death." Death was not hidden from view. On the contrary, it held a prominent place in the culture as a whole and in the lives of individuals.

Then, with great rapidity, the era of "tamed death" came to an end. Death, once a public and corporate experience, became increasingly private. The deathbed was displaced from the home to the hospital, funerals became shorter and more discreet, grief was suppressed, and the customary signs of mourning disappeared. In the modern period, particularly since the beginning of the twentieth century, our attitudes and behaviors toward death have been characterized by the image of "invisible death." Charles O. Jackson says:

Because the dead world is largely understood as irrelevant to our lives, death tends to become without significance and absurd. . . . [B]ecause we have this perspective on the end of life, it becomes difficult to avoid the same view on all of life.[13]

Hans Holbein the Younger, authors' collection

MIGUEL Y LA CRIADA.

Antonio Guadalupe Posada, Swann Collection, Library of Congress

The somber mood of Hans Holbein's depiction of Die Totentanz, *or Dance of Death, contrasts with the treatment of the same theme by Mexican artist Antonio Guadalupe Posada. In Holbein's medieval woodblock print,* The Child, *we see the anxiety of family members as the skeletal figure of Death ominously takes a child; in Posada's print, there is a sense of gaiety and festivity. Although expressed differently, the two works convey a common message: Death comes to people in all walks of life; no one is exempt.*

Although a chronology is evident in tracking the changes that occurred over the long period of "tamed death," which ended with the significant break characterized as "invisible death," these transitions can also be considered from the point of view of different "mentalities" that exist within a society or even within an individual at different times.[14] To understand more clearly how such mentalities evolve through the interplay between social forces and individuals, we need to examine more closely the evolution of attitudes and behaviors toward death as manifested in the Dance of Death, the death-bed scene, and customs surrounding burial and memorialization of the dead.

The Dance of Death

The *danse macabre,* or Dance of Death, has been expressed through a number of forms, including drama, poetry, music, and the visual arts. With origins in ecstatic mass dances, the Dance of Death achieved its most notable expression in the late thirteenth and early fourteenth centuries with the conjoining of ideas regarding the *inevitability* of death and its *impartiality*. It was sometimes performed as a masque, a short entertainment in which actors costumed as skeletons danced gaily with figures representing people at all levels of society. In art, the Dance of Death is illustrated in paintings that depict individuals being escorted to graveyards by skeletons and corpses, a grim reminder of the universality and imminence of death.[15] In whatever form, the Dance of Death conveyed the notion that death comes to *all* people and to *each* person, regardless of rank or status.

As a reaction to war, famine, and poverty, the Dance of Death was influenced most significantly by the mass deaths caused by the plague of the mid-fourteenth century. Called the Black Death, the plague arrived in Europe via a Black Sea port in 1347. By the time the first wave of pestilence ended in 1351, at least a quarter of the population in Europe had died.[16]

In the oldest versions of the Dance of Death, death seems scarcely to touch the living as it warns or singles them out. Death has assumed a personal meaning, but it is clearly still part of the natural order of things. Toward the end of the medieval period, however, the Dance of Death reflected a shift in attitudes: The individual is now portrayed as being forcibly taken by death. Death is a rupture, a radical and complete break, between the living and the dead. With this changed perspective, the Dance of Death took on erotic connotations. The radical break with ordinary modes of consciousness brought about by death was likened to the "small deaths" that occur during sexual intercourse when there is a momentary break with ordinary consciousness.[17]

Blatantly erotic ideas about death were sublimated into an obsession with beauty and the "beautiful death." Previously, ideas about the relationship between love and death had been confined to religious martyrdom; now they were extended to include romantic love. Romances like those of Tristan and Isolde or Romeo and Juliet dramatized the idea that where there is love, death can be beautiful, even desirable. During the eighteenth and nineteenth centuries, such notions would flower in the popular imagination, and historical antecedents were found in the code of chivalry and ideal of courtly love. Exalted and dramatized, death became important not because it embodied religious ideas about the destiny of one's own soul, but because it affected the other, the loved one whose memory could be perpetuated through elaborate mourning rituals and in ornate cemeteries.

Dying and the Deathbed Scene

"I see and know that my death is near": Thus did the dying person in the medieval period acknowledge impending death. On pious deathbeds, the dying offered up their suffering to God, expecting nothing more than to meet death in the customary manner. Sudden death was rare; even wounds received in battle seldom brought instantaneous death. (The possibility of sudden, unexpected death was feared because it caught the victim unaware and unable

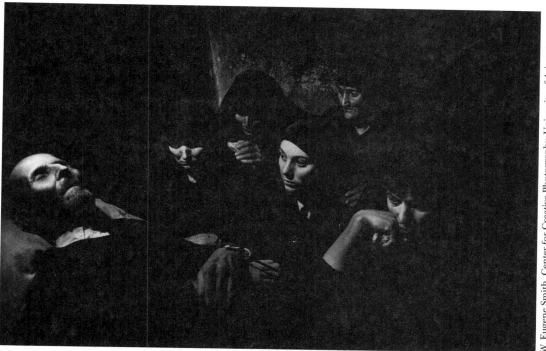

This deathbed vigil in a Spanish village is characteristic of the way in which human beings have responded to death for thousands of years. Only recently have such scenes been superseded in modern societies by the specter of dying alone, perhaps unconscious, amid the impersonal gadgetry of an unfamiliar institutional environment.

to properly close earthly accounts and turn toward the divine.) Those who stood near the deathbed could say with confidence that the dying person "feels her time has come" or "knows he will soon be dead." Death was generally anticipated by natural signs or by a conscious inner certainty. Death seemed manageable.

The dying person enacted customary ritual gestures to make sure that dying was done properly. Ariès describes the main features of a dignified death during the early Middle Ages: Lying down, with the head facing east toward Jerusalem, perhaps with arms crossed over the chest, the dying person expressed sadness at his or her impending end and began "a discreet recollection of beloved beings and things." Family and friends gathered around the deathbed to receive the dying person's pardon for any wrongs they might have done, and all were commended to God. Next, the dying person turned his or her attention away from the earthly and toward the divine. A confession of sins to a priest was followed by a prayer requesting divine grace. The priest then granted absolution. With customary rites completed, nothing more need be said: The dying person was ready for death. If death came more slowly than expected, the dying person simply waited in silence.

The recumbent figure in the deathbed, surrounded by parents, friends, family, children, and even mere passersby, remained the predominant deathbed scene until modern times. Dying was more or less a public ceremony, with the person who was dying clearly in charge. Emotion was neither suppressed nor given vivid expression. Everything was directed toward simplicity and ceremony.

As greater individualism emerged, the deathbed scene began to change subtly. *How* you died became profoundly important. Now, hovering over the entourage of public participants was an invisible army of celestial figures, angels and demons, battling for possession of the dying person's soul. Thus, death became the *speculum mortis,* the mirror in which each person could discover his or her nature and destiny. Because free will implies moral responsibility for one's acts, the dying person tallied the moral balance sheet of his or her life. As a unique opportunity to review one's actions and make a final decision for good or ill, the moment of death became the supreme challenge and ultimate test of an entire lifetime.

Then, as the understanding of death came under the influence of a secular, scientific outlook that emphasized natural reason rather than divine revelation, religion was forced to share the stage with the materialistic orientation of rationalism. The world view of the Middle Ages, embodied in the iconography of the Church with its attendant comforts and fears, gave way to a mentality that viewed death as untamed yet beautiful, like wild nature.

Even with the new secularism, however, the deathbed scene was little changed outwardly; family and friends still gathered as participants in the public ritual of a person's dying. But religion no longer dominated the thoughts of the dying person or the grief of survivors. The images of Heaven and Hell in the iconography of the Church were being replaced by a secular hope for the soul's immortality and eventual reunion with loved ones. Whereas their forebears had contemplated the terrors of death and the torment of a fiery Hell as prods to good behavior, people now likened death to the emergence of a butterfly from its cocoon.

Burial Customs

Burial customs during the early medieval period in Europe remained much the same as they had been during the Roman Empire. Because these customs reflected the belief that the dead might come back to haunt the living, graveyards were usually located away from towns and cities. Although they had different beliefs about the dead, early Christians generally followed customary practices, at first being buried in the pagan cemeteries and then later in their own cemeteries, but still outside populated areas.

Within the first two or three centuries of Christian practice, however, a cult of martyrs arose that introduced a new element into Christian burial practices.[18] Believers came to adopt the notion that the saintliness of the martyrs was powerful even in death. Thus, the saints could help others avoid the pitfalls of sin and the horrors of hell. It became desirable to be buried near the grave of a martyr in hope of gaining merit by such proximity. (A modern analogy might be a movie fan wishing to be buried near a film star at Forest Lawn or a veteran requesting burial near a Medal of Honor winner, although people of the medieval period were concerned with the soul's eternal welfare rather than with earthly prestige or vanity.)

As pilgrims began journeying to graves to venerate the martyrs, a need was created to establish a focal point for worship. Thus, altars, chapels, and eventually churches were built on or near the martyrs' graves. Later, the great urban cathedrals began to allow burials to take place within their precincts. Although such burials were limited at first to the notables and saints of the Church, eventually common folk also were buried in the churchyards and surrounds of urban cathedrals as well as rural churches. Over time, the state of the dead became intimately linked with the Church.

Charnel Houses

The custom of burial within churchyards eventually led to the development of *charnel houses,* arcades and galleries where the bones of the dead were entrusted to the Church. Limbs and skulls were arranged artistically along various parts of the churchyard, as well as within and near the church. (In Paris, one can still visit catacombs where, as one wide-eyed visitor exclaimed, "piles of femurs and skulls" are "stacked eight feet high and ten yards deep, as neatly as lumber in an Oregon mill yard."[19]) The bones in these charnels came from common graves of the poor, which were periodically opened so that the bones could be turned over to the Church for safekeeping until the Resurrection. "As yet unborn," Ariès says, "was the modern idea that the dead person should be installed in a sort of house unto himself, a house of which he was the perpetual owner or at least the long-term tenant, a house in which he would be at home and from which he could not be evicted." Most burials were anonymous. Except for burials involving notables of the Church or royalty, graves had nothing to identify who was buried in them.

Reflecting the familiarity with death and with the dead during the medieval period, the charnel house was a public place. As the Romans had congregated in the Forum, so their medieval counterparts met in the charnel house. There they would find shops and merchants, conduct business, dance, gamble, or simply enjoy being together. Such familiarity is also evident in public anatomy demonstrations, which were attended by surgeons and medical students as well as by curious townspeople. During the sixteenth century, the University of Leiden used the apse of a church as a setting for public dissections of the human body. In this "Anatomical Theater," as it was called, human

Library of Congress

This ossuary located at a European monastery is a survival of the medieval charnel house, a gallery of skeletons and skulls and bones.

remains were displayed artistically or posed in dramatic gestures. Frank Gonzalez-Crussi cites, as an example, a child's arm "clad in an infant's lace sleeve," and, held in the hand, "between thumb and index finger—as gracefully as an artist's model might hold a flower by the stem—a human eye by the optical nerve."[20] In remarking on how shocking such a display would be today,

Gonzalez-Crussi observes that, in the modern period, we have "banished the dead from our midst."

Memorializing the Dead

The growing individualism that became evident in the twelfth and thirteenth centuries was accompanied by moves toward preserving the identity of the person buried in a particular place, although this was a gradual process initially limited to notables. Simple grave markers of the "Here lies John Doe" variety began to appear, as did, to a lesser extent, effigies of the dead. As time passed, these effigies became increasingly realistic and macabre themes developed.

By the seventeenth century, the striving for realism had become so great that the deceased person was sometimes portrayed twice; first as he or she looked while alive and a second time as a severely decomposed corpse. Of course, effigies portrayed only the most notable personages, but they nonetheless provide insight into how the dead were perceived by the living. Survivors discovered that bonds with the dead could be maintained by perpetuating the *memory* of the deceased. As the center of attention shifted to the bereaved, mourning became correspondingly more important.

Such memorialization of the dead came into broader use as cultural changes produced a fascination with the deaths of loved ones and a desire to perpetuate their memory. By the 1830s, the rural cemetery movement had begun in America, and resplendent monuments were erected to honor the dead in perpetuity. The untended graveyards of the Puritans, who disdained the body whether living or dead, were replaced by lush, well-kept cemeteries like Mount Auburn in Cambridge, Massachusetts, and Woodlawn in New York City. In these parklike settings, the bereaved could commune in memory with the deceased.[21]

The hallmarks of such memorialization of the dead were elaborate mourning rituals, ornate tombstones, and various kinds of mourning paraphernalia.[22] Death's finality was made to seem less severe by imagining the deceased's existence in heaven, where survivors hoped to be eventually reunited with loved ones (see Figure 2-6). Paradoxically, the emphasis on mourning the dead began to undercut the acceptance of death that had prevailed for a thousand years. Individuals and societies in the Western European orbit began to exhibit desires to mute the harsh reality of death.

Invisible Death

By the early twentieth century, the era of "tamed death" had been superseded by "invisible death." Care of the dying and dead was relegated to professionals; death was no longer a familiar element of people's lives. Deathbed scenes came to be dominated by efforts to delay death by any means available. The customary role of family and friends as witnesses to a loved one's dying was deemphasized and virtually lost. Mourning customs were abbreviated as funeral services became shorter and more private.

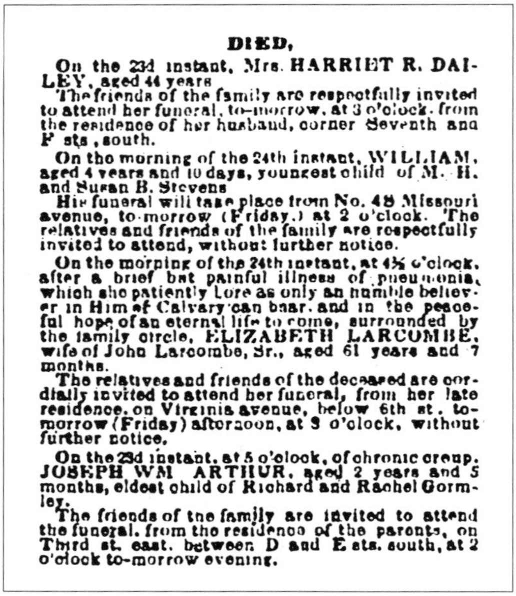

DIED,

On the 23d instant, Mrs. HARRIET R. DAILEY, aged 44 years

The friends of the family are respectfully invited to attend her funeral, to-morrow, at 3 o'clock, from the residence of her husband, corner Seventh and F sts., south.

On the morning of the 24th instant, WILLIAM, aged 4 years and 10 days, youngest child of M. H. and Susan B. Stevens

His funeral will take place from No. 48 Missouri avenue, to-morrow (Friday,) at 2 o'clock. The relatives and friends of the family are respectfully invited to attend, without further notice.

On the morning of the 24th instant, at 4½ o'clock, after a brief but painful illness of pneumonia, which she patiently bore as only an humble believer in Him of Calvary can bear, and in the peaceful hope of an eternal life to come, surrounded by the family circle, ELIZABETH LARCOMBE, wife of John Larcombe, Sr., aged 61 years and 7 months.

The relatives and friends of the deceased are cordially invited to attend her funeral, from her late residence, on Virginia avenue, below 6th st, to-morrow (Friday) afternoon, at 3 o'clock, without further notice.

On the 23d instant, at 5 o'clock, of chronic croup, JOSEPH WM ARTHUR, aged 2 years and 5 months, eldest child of Richard and Rachel Gormley.

The friends of the family are invited to attend the funeral, from the residence of the parents, on Third st. east, between D and E sts. south, at 2 o'clock to-morrow evening.

Figure 2-6   *Newspaper Death Notice from the 1860s*

Despite the welcome advances in medical care as well as in other areas of life in the twentieth century, the dying and bereaved may previously have had greater access to a source of comfort that is now often lacking—namely, the presence of other people. Fulfillment for human beings is associated with what Norbert Elias describes as "the meaning one has attained in the course of one's life for other people."[23] Even when a person has reached significant goals in life and enjoys a sense of completion, dying may be painfully hard if it is felt to be meaningless. Today, the *meaning* of death is hardly considered, while death is generally thought to be synonymous with extinction. Herman Feifel writes,

> In the Middle Ages man had his eschatology and the sacred time of eternity. More recently, temporal man lived with the prospect of personal immortality transformed into concern for historical immortality and for the welfare of posterity. Today we are vouchsafed neither.[24]

In every age, dying and death have been encountered with the aid of cultural support systems. However, the ritual dimensions of dying that guided our ancestors have been replaced for the most part by a technological process. The result is that death occurs, as Ariès says, "by a series of little steps," making it difficult to discern the moment of "real death." He goes on to note that "All these little silent deaths have replaced and erased the great dramatic act of death, and no one any longer has the strength or patience to wait over a period of weeks for a moment which has lost a part of its meaning."

Four Cultural Case Studies

In the following case studies, we highlight four cultures that exhibit ways of coping with death that are distinctly their own. Cross-cultural comparisons provide us with perspective that allows both appreciation and criticism of our own beliefs and customs.[25] To begin, we review some of the attitudes and behaviors that have traditionally been a part of Native American societies. Although the indigenous peoples of North America share many cultural features in common, the individual tribal groups also display diversity in their attitudes and practices related to death. Next we turn to an exploration of attitudes toward the dead in the African tradition, with particular attention to the funeral rites of the LoDagaa. Returning to the Western hemisphere, we investigate the customs surrounding the Mexican fiesta *el Día de los Muertos,* or Day of the Dead. In the final case study in this chapter, we journey to modern Japan, where we find that an emphasis on the role of ancestors continues to be important even in an advanced technological setting.

Although some death customs are shared widely among different cultures, they are manifested in distinct ways by each particular society. For example, although ancestors occupy an important place in all of the cultures discussed here, each cultural tradition embodies distinctive attitudes and behaviors toward them. At first glance, the mourning rituals of the LoDagaa seem very unlike the death ceremonies encountered by most Americans. And the boisterous flaunting of death that occurs during the Mexican fiesta *el Día de los Muertos* contrasts with the reverential attitude most Americans associate with death. Upon closer consideration, however, significant correspondences are found to exist between the "foreign" and the "familiar," correspondences that can evoke insights about behaviors and attitudes that, because they are familiar and our own, we have not really observed. Thus, the study of death in other cultures leads the way toward opportunities for enlivening practices and beliefs that have become a matter of rote rather than a consciously chosen response in our own encounter with death.

Native American Traditions

Within Native American traditions, death is generally viewed as part of a natural process. Broadly speaking, the attitude toward death of the indigenous peoples of North America can be summarized as follows: Death is not to be ignored, but neither should it be feared. It is good to make room for death. The traditional understanding of death in Native American societies emphasizes "the significance of living one day at a time, with purpose, grateful for life's blessings, in the knowledge that it could all end abruptly."[26] This way of relating to death is typified in the Lakota battle cry: "It's a good day to die!"

For most Native Americans, time is not considered a linear phenomenon, proceeding in only one direction, but a recurring cycle. Åke Hultkrantz says that Native Americans are "mainly interested in how this cycle affects people in

© Lawrence Migdale

Among members of the Northwest Coast culture, which extends more than 2000 miles from the northern limits of California to the panhandle of Alaska, the potlatch, or "giveaway" ceremony, reinforces tribal identity and helps determine an individual's rank and prestige in the community. This potlatch was given by David Baxley, a totem-pole carver of the Tsimshian on the island of Metlakatla in southeastern Alaska, to honor his grandfather who would have been 100 years old. The old man had died two years earlier. Marked by the host's lavish distribution of gifts,which may take months or years to accumulate, the potlatch is a celebration of life, a way of honoring the deceased as well as others in the community, and saying "thank you."

this life and have only a vague notion of another existence after death."[27] Dogmatic beliefs about the state of the dead or the afterlife are of little or no importance. Instead, says Hultkrantz, "One individual might hold several ideas about the dead at the same time [because] different situations call for different interpretations of the fate of humans after death." The Wind River Shoshoni, for example, embrace a number of beliefs about death: The dead may travel to another world or may remain on earth as ghosts; they may be born again as people or may transmigrate into "insects, birds, or even inanimate objects like wood and rocks." Hultkrantz remarks that "most Shoshoni express only a slight interest in the next life and often declare that they know nothing about it."

Numerous accounts have been related about Native Americans who faced death stoically, even indifferently. Sometimes they composed "death songs" as

Two Death Songs

In the great night my heart will go out
Toward me the darkness comes rattling
In the great night my heart will go out

   Papago song by Juana Manwell
   (Owl Woman)

The odor of death,
I smell the odor of death
In front of my body.

   A song of the Dakota tribe

expressions of their confrontation with death. In some cases, a death song would be "composed spontaneously at the very moment of death" and "chanted with the last breath of the dying person."[28] These death songs express a resolve to meet death fully, to accept it with one's whole being, not in defeat and desperation, but with equanimity and composure. The death song is a summary of a person's life and an acknowledgment of death as the completion of being, the final act in the drama of earthly existence.

Although this attitude toward death is pervasive, we also need to recognize that there is extraordinary diversity among the indigenous peoples of North America.[29] Moreover, long-standing practices were often altered dramatically by the cultural upheaval caused by the "westward expansionism" of white society.[30] Thus, even within a particular tribal group or culture area, traditional beliefs and practices are unlikely to have persisted unchanged down to the present time. Among many groups, however, the dead are considered to be guardian spirits or special envoys of the shamans. Burial places are usually considered sacred. This attitude of reverence toward the dead was stated eloquently by Chief Seattle: "To us the ashes of our ancestors are sacred and their resting place is hallowed ground. . . . Be just and deal kindly with my people, for the dead are not powerless. Dead, did I say? There is no death, only a change of worlds."[31]

Among some tribal groups, the soul or spirit of the deceased is thought to linger for several days near the site of death before passing on to the afterworld. This is a time that typically requires great care, both to ensure the progress of the deceased toward the supernatural realm and to safeguard the living. The Ohlone of the California coast adorned the corpse with feathers, flowers, and beads, and then wrapped it in blankets and skins. Dance regalia, weapons, the medicine bundle, and other items owned by the deceased were gathered together and, along with the corpse, placed on the funeral pyre. Mourners sometimes threw some of their own valued possessions onto the pyre as gifts for the deceased. Destroying the deceased's possessions helped to facilitate the soul's journey to the "Island of the Dead" and also removed reminders of the deceased that might cause the ghost to remain near the living. This belief is echoed in a Yokut funeral chant which says: "You are going where you are going; don't look back for your family." For the Ohlone, the dangerous period lasted from six months to a year.

Warrior Song

I shall vanish and be no more
But the land over which I now roam
Shall remain
And change not.

Hethúshka Society, Omaha tribe

Still, it was considered disrespectful to utter the deceased's name. In *The Ohlone Way,* Malcolm Margolin writes: "While the mere thought of a dead person brought sorrow, the mention of a dead person's name brought absolute dread."[32] By destroying the deceased's belongings and avoiding his or her name, the survivors confirmed the separation of the dead from the living.

For many tribes of the plains, it was customary to expose the corpse on a platform above ground or to place it in the limbs of a tree. This form of burial not only hastened the decomposition of the body, it also helped speed the soul's journey to the spirit world. Later the sun-bleached skeleton would be retrieved for burial in sacred grounds. As Old Chief Joseph of the Nez Percé lay dying, he told his son, "Never forget my dying words. This country holds your father's body. Never sell the bones of your father and mother." These words were remembered by Younger Chief Joseph as he led warriors into battle to preserve the sanctity of the lands that held the bones of the ancestral dead. (There have been disputes in recent years concerning artifacts and bones retrieved from sacred burial places by archaeologists; also, public display in museums violates the sanctity of ancestral remains.[33])

Even in societies where the dead are feared and the corpse disposed of quickly, the dead can become objects of ritual attention. By drawing upon David Mandelbaum's comparison of death customs among the Hopi and the Cocopa, we find that Native Americans were variable in the extent to which they exhibited fear of the dead.[34] Mandelbaum found that, when a Cocopa dies, surviving family members wail in an "ecstasy of violent grief behavior" that lasts twenty-four hours or more and continues until the body is cremated. Clothes, food, and other articles are burned with the body. The deceased will use these items in the afterlife, but the Cocopa also hope they will help persuade the spirit of the dead person to pass on from the earth. Later, a ceremony is held to mourn and commemorate the deceased.

Although the name of the dead cannot be spoken at other times, at this special mourning ceremony, deceased relatives who have passed into the spirit world are publicly summoned, and their presence may be impersonated by living members of the tribe. A house constructed especially for the spirits may be burned as a gift. The mourning ceremony is conducted to both honor the dead and persuade lurking spirits to come out in the open and leave the

Burial Oration

You are dead.
You will go above there to the trail.
That is the spirit trail.
Go there to the beautiful trail.
May it please you not to walk about where I am.
You are dead.
Go there to the beautiful trail above.
That is your way.
Look at the place where you used to wander.
The north trail, the mountains where you used to wander, you
    are leaving.
Listen to me: go there!

            Wintu tribe

earthly realm. Whereas the initial cremation ritual is focused on the grief of the bereaved family, the subsequent mourning ceremony is focused on affirming the integrity of the family and the community.

Unlike the Cocopa, the Hopi keep death at a distance. Death threatens the "middle way" of order, control, and measured deliberation that the Hopi cherish. This attitude toward death is reflected in Hopi funeral rituals, which are attended by very few and held privately. Death is mourned, but without public ceremony. Mourners are reticent in expressing their grief. For the Hopi, the goal is that the whole matter be "quickly over and best forgotten." In contrast to the Cocopa mourning ceremony, the Hopi have no desire to invite departed ancestors to a communal gathering. Once a person's spirit leaves the body, it is a different class of being, no longer Hopi. Thus, it is important to make sure that the "dichotomy of quick and dead is sharp and clear."

Mandelbaum's descriptions of the Cocopa and the Hopi illustrate how, even within a more or less similar cultural setting, different social groups can create distinctive responses to death. Although, in a general sense, both the Hopi and the Cocopa fear the dead, their ways of coping with this fear are quite different: The Hopi wish to avoid the dead completely while the Cocopa invite the spirits of the dead to join them in celebration, even if only temporarily and under controlled circumstances.

Reflecting on the distinct emphases within the Hopi and Cocopa societies can help us evaluate our own attitudes and values relative to death. What do you find valuable about each of these ways of coming to terms with death? Although the rites of passage surrounding death share common elements—themes of separation, transition, and reincorporation—the way in which these elements are realized through ceremony and other mourning behaviors reflects a society's unique path toward resolution when death comes to a member of the community.

African Traditions

The term *ancestor worship* is sometimes used to label African traditions that may be more accurately described as reverence for the deceased members of a community. This communion with the "living dead" in African societies can be compared with our own relationships to deceased loved ones. When some event or stimulus evokes the memory of a person who was dear to us, we may pause a moment, reflecting on the qualities that made that person beloved, experiencing again our feelings of affection. Such momentary reverie often involves a sense of communion with the deceased. We may feel that this reverie results in some insight that is helpful in our lives. Even though American society lacks formal rituals for acknowledging this kind of experience, its essential qualities are much the same as those known in the context of African culture.

In the African context, this reverence for the dead involves the deceased members of a community who are still remembered by name. As generations come and go, and memory fades, the long-dead ancestral members of the community are replaced by the more recently deceased.[35] Thus, the ongoing community of the "living dead" consists of ancestors who are recalled in the minds of the living. This relationship with the ancestors is illustrated by the system of age grouping practiced by the Nandi in Kenya. Once past childhood, a male member of the tribe moves through the junior and senior warrior levels and eventually enters the age group of senior elders; he next becomes an old man and ultimately, at death, an ancestor, one of the living dead, whose personality is remembered by survivors. When he is no longer remembered by people now alive, he merges with the anonymous dead. By this time, the Nandi believe, the dead man's "soul stuff" may have already reappeared in a new-born child of the tribe, thus continuing the recurrent pattern of a person's passage through the levels of the age-group system.[36]

Kofi Asare Opoku says that the traditional African attitude toward death is essentially positive because "it is comprehensively integrated into the totality of life."[37] In the modern Western world, life and death are generally conceived of as opposites; in the African tradition, "the opposite of death is birth, and birth is the one event that links every human being, on the one hand, with all those who have gone before and, on the other, with all those who will come after."

The death of a person elicits a response from the entire community. The rituals surrounding death function as "symbolic preparations for the deceased to enter the abode of the ancestors." Messages may be given to the deceased to take to the other side, just as one might give a message to a person going on a trip to convey to those he meets at his destination. There is, in fact, a "this-world orientation" to the traditional African conception of the afterlife.

Delmar Lipp. Eliot Elisofon Archives, National Museum of African Art

A woman and child in mourning are depicted in this Yombe memorial figure from Zaire. Installed in a shed constructed on the grave, such adornments are thought to provide the deceased with companionship or protection in the afterlife.

Kwasi Wiredu says, "The land of the dead is geographically similar to our own [and] its population is rather like us."[38]

This reverence toward the dead persists into modern times among individuals who follow the way of traditional African religions. When the body of a Nigerian villager of the Ibo people was recently shipped by air from the United States to her home village, the coffin arrived in a damaged condition and, somewhere along the line, her body had been wrapped in burlap and turned upside down—violating strict tribal taboos concerning abuse of a corpse. Despite the family's offerings of yams, money, and wine to appease the insult, members of the tribe reported seeing the woman's spirit roaming about, and relatives began to experience various reversals of fortune, which they characterized as a "curse" brought about because of the mistreatment of their dead relative. According to the woman's son: "My mother was treated as if she were nothing." As a result, her spirit was angry and not at peace. In bringing suit against the airline to which the body had been entrusted, the son said, "If this had been done to us by an individual, my whole tribe would have gone to war. If I win the case, it would be like bringing back someone's head. It would prove I'm a warrior . . . it will show the gods I have done something against someone who shamed my mother."[39]

Jack Goody's study of the LoDagaa of Northern Ghana offers us an excellent description of the mourning customs practiced within an African society.[40] Among the LoDagaa, funeral ceremonies span at least a six-month period and sometimes continue over several years. They occur in four distinct, successive phases, each focusing on specific aspects of death and bereavement.

The first stage begins at the moment of death and lasts six or seven days. Initially, during the first several days, the body is prepared for burial, the deceased is mourned by bereaved relatives and others in the community, rites are performed to acknowledge the separation of the deceased from the living, kinship ties are affirmed, and some of the social and family roles occupied by the deceased are redistributed. These public ceremonies, which last about three days, conclude with the burial of the corpse. The remaining three or four days of this first stage are devoted to private ceremonies in which preparations are made for redistributing the dead person's property.

About three weeks later, in a second ceremony, the cause of death is established. Whereas most Americans would consider, say, a snakebite to be the cause of death, the LoDagaa would view the snakebite as an intermediate agent but not the final cause of death. The real cause of death is seen as a function of the network of spiritual and human relationships. Thus, inquiries are made to uncover any tension that may have existed between the deceased and others.

At the beginning of the rainy season, a third stage of funeral ritual is held. These rites, although resembling those of the first stage, mark a transitional period in the deceased's passage from the role of the living to that of an ancestor. At this time, a provisional ancestral shrine is placed on the dead person's grave.

The final stage of LoDagaa ceremonies follows the harvest. At this time, the final ancestral shrine is constructed and placed on the grave, and the close relatives of the deceased are formally released from mourning. The care of offspring is formally transferred to the deceased's tribal "brothers," and final rites conclude redistribution of the deceased's property.

Throughout the long period of mourning, the ceremonies serve two purposes: First, they *separate* the dead person from the bereaved family and from the larger community of the living; certain social roles formerly occupied

> If we knew the home of Death, we would set it on fire.
>
> Acholi funeral song

by the deceased are assigned to living persons. Second, they gather together, or *aggregate;* that is, the dead person is joined with the ancestors and the bereaved are reincorporated into the community in a way that reflects their changed status. This rhythm of separation and gathering together is common to all funeral ceremonies. The rites of the LoDagaa are noteworthy because of the formality with which these basic functions of funeral ritual are accomplished. They provide a model of explicitness in mourning against which our own customs can be compared and contrasted.

The explicitness of LoDagaa mourning is evident in the use of "mourning restraints," made of leather, fabric, and string. These restraints, which are generally tied around a person's wrist, indicate the degree of relationship of the bereaved to the dead person. At a man's funeral, for example, his father, mother, and widow wear restraints made of hide; his brothers and sisters wear fiber restraints; and his children wear restraints made of string, tied around the ankle. Thus, the strongest restraints are provided to the mourners who had the closest relationship with the deceased, usually through kinship and marriage but sometimes through strong friendship bonds. Weaker mourning restraints are worn by persons with correspondingly less intimate relationships to the deceased. In all cases, one end of the mourning restraint is attached to the bereaved person while the other end is held by a "mourning companion" who assumes responsibility for the bereaved's behavior during the period of intense grief.

The LoDagaa mourning restraints thus serve two related purposes: Being something that can be seen and felt, they validate that the bereaved's expression of grief at the loss of someone close is commensurate with the intensity of relationship with the deceased. Second, they discourage expressions of grief that would exceed the norms of the community. Immediately following a death, expressions of grief are likely to be fervent. During the three-day period of the initial funeral ritual, the expression of grief gradually becomes more routine and systematized as mourners begin adjusting to the loss.

The LoDagaa way of mourning invites participation by members of the community, but the grave is dug and made ready for the burial by men specially designated and trained for this function. They learn not only how to prepare a grave properly but also how to protect themselves against the mystical dangers that surround care of the dead. The LoDagaa pay for these funeral services by giving offerings of food and other goods to the gravediggers at the conclusion of the ceremonies. Even though gravedigging is performed by specialists, the LoDagaa occasionally make therapeutic use of this task to counteract excessive fear of the dead. If a LoDagaa boy displays debilitating fear at the sight of a dead person or during a funeral, for example, he may be forced to join in digging the grave. The LoDagaa believe that a repulsive act performed under controlled circumstances can have curative as well as preventive effects. Direct confrontation with the reality of death is a way of working through fears. Among the LoDagaa, people come to terms with death by confronting it directly. The elaborate and lengthy funeral rites, the use of mourning restraints, and the therapy of gravedigging all demonstrate the LoDagaa choice to deal explicitly with death.

Funeral traditions such as those associated with the LoDagaa are increasingly threatened by the encroachment of modernity, which exerts intense pressure to give up the old ways. Conversely, traditional death customs have sometimes helped African peoples maintain cultures that are threatened by change. The Sakalava of Madagascar, for example, continue to organize their lives around the royal ancestors who once governed them, while participating only minimally in the national political economy.[41] They have resisted the destruction of their indigenous institutions by "hiding" their values in the now-illicit realm of the dead. Despite changes brought by colonization and subsequent political independence, ancestral tradition remains the ideal guide to action.

Similarly, the use of obituary publication among the Yoruba of southwestern Nigeria provides a modern form for ancient customs. The status and prestige of the deceased is denoted in various ways, most obviously in the size of the obituary publication, which sometimes occupies a full page. Olatunde Bayo Lawuyi says that it is common to "mark the return of the dead every ten years," although this decreases over time.[42] This use of obituary publication, says Lawuyi, "demonstrates the possibility of continuity in ancestral beliefs" and "is a symbolic manifestation of a tradition that has taken a new cultural form."

Mexican Traditions

From ancient times, Mexico has echoed themes of death, sacrifice, and destiny. In the religion of the Aztecs, the very creation of the world was made possible by sacrificial rites enacted by the gods, and human beings were obliged to return the favor. The sacrificial victims in Aztec rites were named *teomicqueh,* the "divine dead," and, according to the divine-human covenant, they participated in a destiny that had been determined at the origin of the world. Through sacrifice, humans did their part to maintain life on earth as well as in the heavens and the underworld.[43] When the Spanish conquerors arrived in Mexico, they brought with them a cult of immortality that in some ways resembled indigenous beliefs. A willingness to die for ideals is exemplified in Spanish history by the mass suicide at Sagunto in 219 B.C., when the city's leading citizens showed that death was preferable to capture by the Carthaginians. Such acceptance of fate was familiar to the ancient Mexicans.

An ironic attitude toward death characterizes the Day of the Dead fiesta in Mexico. Death is satirized while memories of deceased loved ones are cherished by the living. Family members often place the names of deceased relatives on ornaments such as this candy skull and these candy coffins. This practice assures the spirits of the dead that they have not been forgotten by the living and provides solace to the living in the form of tangible symbols of the presence of deceased loved ones.

Commenting on these themes as they manifest themselves in modern-day Mexico, Octavio Paz says, "Death defines life. . . . Each of us dies the death he has made for himself. . . . Death, like life, is not transferable."[44] Folk sayings confirm this connection between death and identity: "Tell me how you die and I will tell you who you are." In the Mexican consciousness, death mirrors a person's life. Surrounded by references to death, the Mexican, says Paz, "jokes about it, caresses it, sleeps with it, celebrates it [and makes it] one of his favorite toys and his steadfast love."

Mexican artists and writers confront death with an attitude of humorous sarcasm. Death is portrayed as an equalizer that not even the wealthiest can escape; the emotional response it generates is often one of apparent impatience, disdain, or irony. The engravings of Antonio Guadalupe Posada superficially resemble the woodcuts of the medieval *danse macabre,* in which people from all walks of life danced with their own skeletons; Posada's skeletons, however, do not exhibit an anxious premonition of death.[45] In Mexican culture, symbols of death abound. The suffering Savior is portrayed with bloody vividness; glass-topped coffins display the remains of martyrs, saints, and other notables of the Church. Awareness of death is manifested in graffiti and in ornaments that decorate cars and buses. Newspapers seem to revel in accounts of violent deaths, and obituaries are framed with conspicuous black borders that attract attention to death. Mexican poetry contains similes comparing life's fragility to a dream, a flower, a river, or a passing breeze.[46] Death, in contrast, is described as awakening from a dreamlike existence.[47]

Once a year, Mexicans celebrate death in a national fiesta known as *el Día de los Muertos,* the Day of the Dead. Occurring in November, it coincides with All Souls' Day, the Church's feast of commemoration for the dead. Blending both indigenous ritual and the imposed dogma of the Church, the fiesta is a unique occasion for communion between the living and the dead. Bread in the shape of human bones is eaten; sugar-candy skulls and tissue-paper skeletons poke fun at death and flaunt it. Although the fiesta is celebrated throughout Mexico, the most traditional observances are found on the Island of Janitzio in Michoacán and in the Zapotec villages in the Valley of Oaxaca.[48] The following description of the celebration of *el Día de los Muertos* in the village of Mixquic is representative of observances throughout the country.[49]

The fiesta begins at midday on October 31, as bells toll to mark the return of dead children. In each house, the family "sets a table adorned with white flowers, glasses of water, plates with salt (for good luck), and a candle for each dead child." The next day, following a special breakfast of chocolate, bread, fruit, and atole (a thick, sweet drink made of corn starch) in honor of the children, families gather at San Andres Church, where bells are rung at noon to signify the departure of the "small defunct ones" and the return of the "big defunct ones." Then, before nightfall, several thousand graves near the Church are cleaned and decorated with ribbons, foil, and marigold-like cempasuchil flowers.

> The celebration kicks into high gear on the evening of November 1 and into the next morning, when thousands file into the small candle-illuminated graveyard carrying tamales, pumpkin marmalade, chicken with "mole"—a spicy sauce of some 50 ingredients including chili peppers, peanuts, and chocolate—and "pan de muerto," or bread of the dead—sweet rolls decorated with "bones" made of sugar. People sit on the graves and eat the food along with the dead ones. They bring guitars and violins and sing songs. There are stands for selling food for the visitors. It goes on all night. It's a happy occasion—a fiesta, not a time of mourning.[50]

Commenting on the meaning of *el Día de los Muertos,* Octavio Paz says it is a time for revolting against ordinary modes of thought and action; it reunites "contradictory elements and principles in order to bring about a renascence of life."[51] Celebrants break the ordinary bonds that separate the dead from the living. Failure to pay respect to the dead can bring scorn to the family that neglects its responsibilities. But mourners are cautioned against shedding too many tears; excessive grief may make the pathway traveled by the dead slippery, burdening them with a tortuous journey as they return to the world of the living at this special time of celebration.

The Mexican commemoration of the dead bears witness to the continuing importance of Mexico's ancient past. As with the joining of the Aztec goddess and the Christian Virgin in the national cult of the virgin of Guadalupe, *el Día de los Muertos* represents a blending of both indigenous and adopted beliefs, a syncretic joining that reflects spiritual as well as historical roots.[52] The result is a heightened awareness of death in Mexican culture. This consciousness of death is part of everyday life in Mexico, though it receives special emphasis as people throughout the country gather in their communities each year to mark the enduring ties between the living and the dead.

Japanese Traditions

Respect for the ancestors is also a hallmark of Japanese traditions relating to death.[53] During the annual festival known as *bon* or *o-bon*, usually observed in August, people in Japan celebrate the return of ancestral spirits to their families. Known in English as the Festival of the Dead, the Feast of Lanterns (because lamps are lit to guide the spirits in their journeys home), the Feast of All Souls, or simply as the midsummer festival, *o-bon* is a contemporary expression of ancient Japanese beliefs and customs relating to the souls of the dead and the reverence due them by the living.

The first reference in the Japanese chronicles to the *bon* festival occurs in the *Nihon-shoki,* which reports that, in the year 606, Empress Suiko ordered its observance in all the temples of the country. *Bon* represents a fusion of indigenous beliefs and Buddhist concepts. Based on a Buddhist sutra known in Japanese as the *urabon-kyo,* the festival weaves strands of tradition from Indian Buddhism, Chinese Taoism and Confucianism, and Japanese practices that eventually became associated with Shinto, Japan's indigenous religion. Despite this assimilation of elements from other cultures, the Japanese manage to keep their own traditional values and outlook. The strands of different traditions are woven almost seamlessly into "the Japanese way."

Ancestor worship occupies a central place in the lives of the Japanese. In European and American usage, ancestors are thought of as "all the dead people from whom one is descended." Ancestors are part of a person's

Death-Song

If they ask for me
  Say: He had some
  Business
In another world.

  Sokan

biological and social past, but they tend to be of little importance for living one's life. In Japan, however, ancestors are "the members of the household who are dead and who are cared for by the living." One becomes an ancestor not through his or her own achievements or virtue, but through rites performed by family members and priests. In this way, funeral and memorial rituals transform the ancestors into sources of blessing for their descendants. As Dennis Klass points out, "The dead still care for the living, not by granting favors like Western saints, but in the sense that the dead share the joys of any positive achievement of a family member, and indeed may be given credit for the success."[54]

Although the practice of ancestor worship in Japan draws upon the historical traditions of both Shinto and Buddhism, the Japanese generally do not distinguish between the two religions so much as adopt elements from each to fulfill certain purposes in their individual and community life.

> The phrase "born Shinto, die Buddhist" reflects the general social and religious reality for many Japanese. It is customary to take newborn babies to Shinto shrines to receive the blessing and protection of the *kami* [spirits or divinities]; at death it is the Buddhist temple to which one turns.[55]

As the phrase "born Shinto, die Buddhist" suggests, for the Japanese, practicing one religious tradition does not mean rejecting all others. A person might feel allegiance to a number of different traditions insofar as they become an integral part of his or her way of life. We will discuss, in turn, the main contributions of each of these religious traditions to ancestor worship in Japan.

Shinto, the indigenous religion of Japan, is called "the way of the gods." It is perhaps best described as "an amalgam of attitudes, ideas, and ways of doing things that through two millenniums and more have become an integral part of the *way* of the Japanese people."[56] This "way" has been faithfully preserved among the Japanese. The chief feature of Shinto involves reverence for or worship of nature, ancestors, and the ancient national heroes. It places special emphasis on the sacredness of *kami,* or sacred spirits. Among the most important of these is *Amaterasu-omikami,* the Sun Goddess and legendary ancestor of the Japanese imperial family who is enshrined in the Inner Shrine of the Grand Shrine of Ise.

Traditionally, anything that inspires awe or expresses a special quality or sense of vitality can be viewed as a *kami* or as the abode of a *kami.* This broad category of things and beings includes deities of heaven and earth, as well as the spirits of the shrines where such deities are worshipped; it includes human beings as well as birds, beasts, trees, plants, seas, and mountains. The Japanese feel that we, as human beings, owe our lives to the *kami* and to the ancestors who, through countless generations, have made our lives possible. It is appropriate to express gratitude for such all-encompassing love.

Besides the indigenous Shinto religious heritage, the great tradition of Buddhism plays a major role in Japanese life. In modern Japan, as the phrase

Ink stone cold
joy and grief
one brush

Mitsu Suzuki

"born Shinto, die Buddhist" implies, funerals are usually conducted within the purview of Buddhist priests and ceremonies. This was not always the case in Japan, however. In ancient times, because Shinto priests did not concern themselves with the dead or with death rites, funerals were conducted by the people themselves. Nor did the early monks who brought Buddhism to Japan concern themselves with funeral rites (at least for secular devotees). On the contrary, the original scriptures of Buddhism inform us that the Buddha himself forbade monks from participating in funerals.[57] Yet, today, it seems that the main concerns of Japanese Buddhism involve funeral services and memorial rites for ancestors. How did this state of affairs come about? To explain requires a brief diversion about the history of Buddhism in Japan.

After Buddhism's entry into Japan, the general public began to view its metaphysical concerns as having a bearing on death and the repose of souls. Over time, the Buddhist clergy began to take responsibility for conducting funeral services, and this function grew to become more and more central to Japanese Buddhism. It became virtually universal in Japan during the Tokugawa Shogunate (1603–1868), when every household was forced to affiliate with a Buddhist temple to prove that none of its members was practicing Christianity, which was at that time a forbidden religion and considered an undesirable foreign influence. (A trace of this prohibition is evident today in the practice of Buddhist priests coming to the home of the deceased and looking under his or her pillow to see if there is a rosary that would suggest that the person was a Christian.[58]) As a result of this historical progression, nearly every person in Japan has a connection with a Buddhist temple, and that connection chiefly has to do with funeral services. "It may be a bitter irony," Hajime Nakamura says, that "Buddhist circles in Japan count as their most essential social function what the monks of original Buddhism jeered at as nonsense."[59]

Let us now turn our attention to some of the ways that the Japanese venerate their ancestors (see Table 2-1 for a glossary of terms). The main thrust of Japanese funeral ritual involves transformation. Ian Reader says, "Death calls into action a series of rites and actions that simultaneously remove the dead soul from this world and install it as an ancestral spirit enshrined in the home of its living kin."[60] Although in recent years some of these rituals have been abbreviated, traditionally there are seven weekly ceremonies, culminating, on the forty-ninth day after death, in the dead person's transformation

T A B L E 2-1   *Japanese Death Customs: Glossary of Terms*

kegare: uncleanness; impurity; pollution; defilement; contamination. The most serious impurity is connected with death, especially with the death of human beings. Words that relate to death may be considered impure; for example, if a person were to say "grave" in the presence of another, the person speaking, the one hearing, and the place in which it was uttered would be polluted.

ancestors: the spirits of the dead members of a household who have been transformed by funeral and memorial rituals into benevolent sources of blessing for descendants. One becomes an ancestor not through one's own achievements or virtue, but through the rituals that other family members perform and have priests perform.

kami: spirits or divinities that inspire a sense of awe. As ancestral spirits lose their individual identity, they merge with the ancestral *kami* of the family. It is felt that the ancestral family *kami* is responsible for birth, and an ancestral spirit may be reborn in the form of a baby born to the family. The term *kami* is an honorific for noble, sacred spirits, which implies a sense of adoration for their virtues and authority.

kaimyo: a posthumous Buddhist name. On the seventh day after death, the dead person is given a *kaimyo,* which confers a new Buddhist identity on the dead person. The *kaimyo* is eventually inscribed on an *ihai* or memorial tablet that is placed in the *butsudan.*

koden: money given by relatives to the primary mourner to help defray funeral expenses; the amount increases as kinship ties become closer (for example, a widow would receive a larger amount from an elder son than from a cousin).

ihai: ancestral tablet; Buddhist mortuary (memorial) tablet with the deceased's posthumous name *(kaimyo)* inscribed on it. The permanent *ihai* is generally made of black lacquer, with the posthumous name embossed in gold. The *ihai* is placed in the *butsudan.*

butsudan: household (family) Buddhist altar; a lacquered or finished cabinet in the main room of the home in which Buddhist divinities and family ancestors are enshrined. Generally contains various Buddhist accoutrements, including candles, an incense burner, a bell, and perhaps a small Buddhist statue or scroll. The altar found in most houses today is a standing cabinet whose doors are usually opened only when some activity is being directed toward the memorial tablets of the family's ancestors. The largest altars are almost ceiling high; the smallest can be set on an ordinary bookshelf.

haka: grave, tomb, or sepulcher. Most Japanese visit the graves of deceased family members to make offerings, pray to the dead (who are regarded as ancestors and protectors of the living), and to clean the graves. Such visits are made especially at *o-bon.*

bon; o-bon: midsummer festival commemorating the return of ancestral spirits to their families. Families pray in front of the home altar *(butsudan)* and family grave *(haka),* offering flowers, incense, and small sweets. Lanterns are lit to guide the spirits in their journeys home, and so the *bon* festival is also called the Feast of Lanterns. After the *bon* season is over, the spirits are said to return to heaven.

into a benevolent ancestor. These rituals are distinctive not only because of their duration, but also because there is a strong association of the ancestor's spirit with the benefit of the ongoing family.

In the traditional view, the spirit of the dead is thought to linger around the family home for the first forty-nine days after death. During this period, rites are held to remove the pollution of death and prepare the soul for enshrinement in the *butsudan,* or household altar, where the ancestors are honored. The family invites Buddhist priests to the home and prayers are said to help emancipate the deceased's spirit. The body is cremated, and the ashes and some pieces of bone are placed in an urn, which is interred at the family grave following a funeral service where incense is offered and Buddhist scriptures are read by priests (the number participating depends on the amount of money the family wishes to spend on the funeral). At this time, the deceased also receives a special posthumous or "Buddhist name," indicating that the material aspect of the person is extinguished. This name *(kaimyo)* is eventually inscribed on an *ihai,* or memorial tablet, that is placed in the family's *butsudan.*

Memorial services continue to be held for the deceased at periodic intervals—typically, on the hundredth day after death, on the first anniversary, the third anniversary, and at fixed intervals thereafter (the seventh, thirteenth, and twenty-third), until the thirty-third, or sometimes the fiftieth, anniversary. The memorial tablets *(ihai)* placed in the Buddhist altar in the home are regularly honored by the family with simple offerings and scripture readings. In addition, the priest of the family's parish temple may, upon request, perform memorial masses in the home, especially on anniversaries of the person's death.

The contemporary Japanese film, *The Funeral* (1987), directed by Juzo Itami, provides a glimpse into modern Japanese death ritual by portraying the experiences of a family in rural Japan. Staged with elements of comic relief, this film gives the viewer a realistic look at Japanese customs. American viewers have noted particularly how young children are incorporated into ritual observances and taught the proper way to behave. For example, after the coffin is closed but before it is taken from the family home, each member of the family uses a stone to strike a blow on the lid of the coffin, symbolically sealing it. In the film, a child of perhaps three or four, apparently fond of the sound the stone makes as it hits the wood, starts banging the stone on the coffin lid repeatedly, whereupon he is admonished kindly by an older relative, and the stone is passed along to the next family member.

Besides the family *butsudan* in the home, the other main focus of ancestral rites is the *haka,* the family grave, where ashes of family members are interred. The grave must be maintained properly, which includes cleaning it and making offerings to the dead. As an important aspect of the ongoing relationships between the living and the dead, such maintenance allows the living to express their feelings for the dead while allowing the ancestors to look after the living.

This butsudan, *prominently situated in the home of a Japanese-American family in California, is representative of altars found in Japanese homes where deceased relatives and ancestors are honored through prayers, gifts of food, and other ways of showing respect. As a focal point for ongoing relationships between the living and dead members of a household, the* butsudan *is a place where such relationships are demonstrated through concrete actions.*

> Empty-handed I entered the world
> Barefoot I leave it.
> My coming, my going—
> Two simple happenings
> That got entangled
>
>   Kozan Ichikyo

Just as with the family *butsudan,* the grave is a place of ritual. Incense and flowers are offered to the ancestors, and water is poured over the gravestone, a gesture of purification that probably dates to Japanese antiquity and which people may now perform without fully recognizing its ancient meaning and symbolism.

And so, with the *butsudan* and the *haka,* we come, in a sense, full circle in our discussion of the rituals surrounding death in Japanese life. In the annual festivals commemorating *o-bon* and the New Year, there are themes that relate to the central role of ancestors in the lives of modern Japanese. During *bon,* folk dances are held in the evening to entertain the ancestors (and the living participants!). At both the midsummer *bon* festival and at the New Year's festival, tradition says, the ancestors pay special visits to the family home. In these annual celebrations, as in other rites honoring the ancestors, there are elements of both Shinto and Buddhism.

Yet many Japanese hardly consider *o-bon* or the New Year's festival religious at all, despite the fact that they travel to religious centers (shrines and temples) and participate in activities that ordinarily would be called religious. Such activities are perceived as social and cultural events that center on family obligations and traditions. The centrality of ancestor worship in Japan reminds us that the social forms in which grief is expressed always relate to larger cultural meanings. Japanese attitudes and practices with respect to the dead support the idea (increasingly acknowledged by Western grief theorists) that survivors seldom sever their bonds with deceased loved ones; rather, "inner representations" of the dead continue to have an active role in the bereaved's ongoing life.[61] Reverence for one's ancestors has been a hallmark of family and social life in Japan since ancient times, and it remains so at the end of the twentieth century.

Rediscovering the Commemoration of Death

Traditionally, as exemplified in the cultures surveyed in this chapter, shared experience and a sense of community have shaped the beliefs and customs that relate to death in a particular society and among its members. This is true even in modern technological societies like the United States, where mourning behaviors and other practices for coping with dying and death tend to be less explicit. The way we deal with death is a product of the interactions between society and individuals. Attitudes and behaviors are not static; they are subject to change; indeed, change is unavoidable.

What seems clear, however, is that some cultures provide a more extensive network of social support for dealing with death than do others. In most of the cultures surveyed in this chapter, the ancestors retain important roles in the lives of the living. Ceremonies and rituals define the nature of this relationship and provide opportunities for celebrating it. In the United States, there are comparatively few socially sanctioned opportunities to commemorate death or honor our forebears.

Religious faith offers an avenue for expressing the profound thoughts and emotions associated with death. But in an avowedly secular and pluralistic society, religion has a problematic role in communal life, even though it can be significant in the lives of individuals. If ceremony is important to human life, perhaps we need to devise rituals that serve present needs without discarding traditional insights. An examination of the practices followed in the cultures included here can provide food for thought. One should not imagine that rituals or traditions can be lifted from one society and placed intact into another. It is possible, however, to learn from others and adapt those things that are felt to have value in one's own life. As implied in the root meaning of *tradition,* "to hand down," our ways of coping with death are not created out of thin air. Each generation receives them from the one preceding, alters them a bit, and passes them on.

In the context of contemporary funeral rites, probably the most frequently heard question is: "Should the children be allowed to attend?" Many people seem to be more likely to exclude children from ceremonies commemorating a person's death than to make a special place for them. Yet, children are not only members of the community, they also represent its future. It is through the processes of socialization that individuals learn the concepts and conventions that have currency in a particular society. The customs related to dying and death embody the attitudes, beliefs, and values of a given community in its relationship to death. We look more closely at the processes of socialization in the next chapter.

Further Readings

Philippe Ariès. *Images of Man and Death.* Cambridge, Mass.: Harvard University Press, 1985.

Richard A. Etlin. *The Architecture of Death: The Transformation of the Cemetery in Eighteenth-Century Paris.* Cambridge, Mass.: MIT Press, 1984.

Patrick J. Geary. *Living with the Dead in the Middle Ages.* Ithaca, N.Y.: Cornell University Press, 1994.

John Greenleigh and Rosalind Rosoff Beimler. *The Days of the Dead: Mexico's Festival of Communion with the Departed.* San Francisco: HarperCollins, 1991.

Åke Hultkrantz. *Shamanic Healing and Ritual Drama: Health and Medicine in Native North American Religious Tradition.* New York: Crossroad, 1992.

Dennis Klass. "Ancestor Worship in Japan: Dependence and the Resolution of Grief," *Omega: Journal of Death and Dying* (in press).

Thomas A. Kselman. *Death and the Afterlife in Modern France.* Princeton, N.J.: Princeton University Press, 1993.

John S. Mbiti. *Introduction to African Religion,* 2d ed. Oxford: Heinemann, 1991.

Philip A. Mellor and Chris Schilling. "Modernity, Self-Identity, and the Sequestration of Death," *Sociology* 27, no. 3 (August 1993): 411–431.

A father and son make an offering at the grave of their Chinese ancestors during village cremation ceremonies held in 1994 in Peliatan, Bali. In this way, religious and cultural traditions are passed along to successive generations through socializing processes that are important to the ongoing life of the community.

Learning About Death: The Influence of Sociocultural Forces

*I*magine yourself as a child. Someone says, "Everybody's going to ziss one of these days. It happens to all of us. You, too, will ziss." Or, one day as you're playing, you are told, "Don't touch that, it's zissed!" Being an observant child, you might notice that when a person zisses, other people cry and appear to be sad. Over time, as you put together all your experiences of "zissing," you begin to develop some personal feelings and thoughts about what it means to ziss.

The understanding of death evolves in much this way. As a child grows older, incorporating a variety of experiences related to death, his or her concepts and emotional responses to death begin to resemble those of the adults in the child's culture. Just as a child's understanding of "money" changes over time—at first it is a matter of little or no concern; later it seems to come into the child's experience almost magically; and finally, it engages the child's attention and participation in many different ways—so, too, does the child develop new understandings about the meaning of death. Like other aspects of human development, the understanding of death evolves during the years of childhood and, although less dramatically, on into the adult years, as experiences provoke a reevaluation of previously held knowledge, beliefs, and attitudes.

A Mature Concept of Death

Whatever our beliefs about death or what it is like to die or what happens afterward, the known facts can be easily summarized: Death is inevitable; it happens to one and all. It is final; biological death marks the end of our known existence. The conscious recognition of these facts is said to reflect a mature understanding of death.

In their observations and interactions with children at different ages and developmental stages, psychologists have attempted to outline the gradual evolution toward a "mature" concept of death and define the specific components of that concept. In reviewing more than 100 such studies, Mark Speece and Sandor Brent conclude that "It is now generally accepted that the concept of death is not a single, unidimensional concept but is, rather, made up of several relatively distinct subconcepts."[1] Drawing on the work of Speece and Brent, we can make a formal statement of the empirical, or observable, facts about death. The statement has four components:

1. *Universality.* All living things eventually die. Death is all-inclusive, inevitable (unavoidable), and unpredictable with respect to its exact timing.
2. *Irreversibility.* Organisms that die cannot be made alive again.
3. *Nonfunctionality.* Death involves the cessation of all physiological functioning, or signs of life.
4. *Causality.* There are biological reasons for the occurrence of death.

It is important to add, however, that nonempirical ideas about death—that is, ideas that are not subject to scientific proof—are also held by individuals who possess an understanding of the observable facts. Such nonempirical ideas about death deal mainly with the notion that human beings survive in some form after the death of the physical body. Questions and concerns about the possibility of an "afterlife" are important for adults as well as children. What happens to an individual's "personality" after he or she dies? Does the self or soul continue to exist in some form after the death of the physical body? What is the meaning of death? Finding personally satisfying answers to such questions is part of the process of acquiring a mature understanding of death. Naturally, different individuals will arrive at different answers, because questions involving "noncorporeal continuity"—the term used by Speece and Brent in categorizing such concerns as the fifth component of a mature understanding of death—are matters of belief rather than proof.

In addition, what a person "knows" about death may differ from time to time, according to circumstances. For example, we may possess conflicting notions about death, especially our own. Under certain conditions, a hard-nosed acceptance of the facts can give way to a more childlike attitude that presumes an ability to bargain where death is concerned. For example, a patient told by a doctor that he or she has only six months to live may imagine that by some kind of "magical" act, some bargain with God or the universe, the death sentence can be postponed. Thus, although the main development toward understand-

Children who experience the death of someone close may look to adults for models of appropriate behavior. Amidst the regalia of high military and political office that characterized the funeral of President John F. Kennedy, young John F. Kennedy, Jr., salutes the flag-draped casket containing his father's body as it is transported from St. Matthew's Cathedral to Arlington National Cemetery. The day also marked John-John's third birthday.

T A B L E *3-1*   *Nonmaterial Aspects of Culture*

Knowledge: Conclusions based on empirical evidence.
Beliefs: Conclusions for which there is not sufficient empirical evidence for them to be
   seen as necessarily true.
Values: Abstract ideas about what is good and desirable.
Norms: Social rules and guidelines that prescribe appropriate behavior in particular
   situations.
Signs and symbols: Representations that stand for something else; this category in-
   cludes language and gestures.

Source: Adapted from Norman Goodman, *Introduction to Sociology* (New York: HarperCollins, 1992), pp. 31–34.

ing death occurs during childhood, how a person understands death through
his or her lifetime fluctuates among different ways of "knowing."

Sociocultural Influences on Our Understanding of Death

The acquisition of a mature understanding of death is part of the developmental process known as *socialization,* which involves learning and internal-
izing the norms, rules, and values of one's society. It is the means by which the
members of one generation in a society acquire knowledge, behavior, and
ideals from older generations in that society. Although the primary agents of
socialization are family, school, and peers, the process of socialization does not
stop with childhood's end, but continues throughout life. Nor is socialization
a one-way process whereby individuals simply learn to fit into their society and
culture. As people redefine their social roles and obligations, the norms and
values of society are also modified.

Society can be defined as "a group of people who share a common culture
(which they transmit to succeeding generations), a common territory, and a
common identity, and who feel themselves to constitute a unified and distinct
entity which involves interacting in socially structured relationships."[2] A society is characterized by the social systems and institutions that give it a distinctive flavor or set it apart in some way from other societies. This sense of
distinctiveness is captured in the term *culture,* which refers to all the ways of
thinking, feeling, and acting that people learn from others as members of a
given society. People often speak or write about societies in ways that highlight
this distinctiveness—for example, Japanese culture, Western European culture, and the like. What do we mean when we say that the members of a society
share a common culture?

Culture may be divided into two main components: material and nonmaterial. Material culture consists of "things"—the manufactured objects (buildings, consumer goods, and the like) or physical manifestations of the life of a
people. The nonmaterial aspects of culture relate to the realm of ideas, beliefs,
values, and customs (see Table 3-1). In this sense, culture can be defined as "all
that in human society which is socially rather than biologically transmitted."[3]

It is important to recognize that these elements of culture are dynamic; that is, they are subject to change as the members of a society reevaluate their inherited beliefs, values, customs, and so on in light of changing circumstances and experiences. Recall, for example, the discussion in Chapter 2 concerning the ways in which burial and memorialization practices in Western European culture changed over the period from the early Middle Ages to the present.

Theoretical Perspectives

Sociology provides useful tools for increasing our understanding about how social and cultural factors affect people's attitudes and behaviors relative to death.[4] To help with our investigation, we review here three theoretical approaches to how societies work. The first takes a broad (macro-level) view of social institutions and social structures. It highlights the interrelationships among such major elements of society as the family, the economy, and the political system. The second theoretical perspective takes a narrower (micro-level) view of the social relations and interactions that occur among members of a society. This approach calls attention to the active manner in which people shape and are shaped by the society in which they live, and the ways in which social meaning is created and shared. Finally, the third theoretical perspective draws on both psychological and sociological insights to present a model of how people become integrated as members of their society through the complex interplay of personality, behavior, and environment.

The Structural-Functionalist Approach

Much as in studying the human body, where we look at the structure and function of various organs and their interrelationships, we can also view society as an organic whole, with constituent parts working together to maintain each other and the society as a whole. Recurring patterns of ordered interaction among the members of a society are part of that society's *social structure*. Such structures include kinship and religion, as well as values and roles. Essentially, social structures are aspects of social life that can "structure," or influence, other aspects of social life. They make social life orderly and predictable. In this sense, a social institution can be thought of as a set of social norms, values, beliefs, groups, and organizations that attend to the basic needs of society and that have received society's approval.

Sociologists usually delineate five major social institutions: (1) the economy, (2) the educational system, (3) the family, (4) the political system, and (5) religion. These institutions relate to one another in such a way that a change in one leads to changes in others (see Figure 3-1).[5] For example, the meaning of death in Western culture has evolved from a position of being defined almost exclusively by religion to a position of openness to alternative meanings and explanations from other social sources. A change in the social institution of religion has brought about changes in other institutions, including the family. In commenting on this change, Talcott Parsons says, "There is

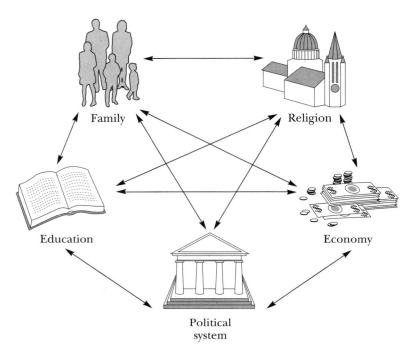

Figure 3-1   *Structural-Functionalist Approach*

a new freedom, for individuals and sociocultural movements, to try their hand at innovative definitions and conceptions."[6]

Similarly, economic constraints exert an influence on how people relate to death. For example, in northeastern Brazil, a region where many people live in extreme poverty, the municipal authorities pay little attention to keeping accurate statistics about infant mortality among the poor.[7] In this example, attitudes toward death are affected by the impact of the economy on the political system; the function of one social institution influences another, with consequences that are evident in the social reality of the Brazilian poor.

As these examples suggest, taking the broad view of society provided by a functional or structural approach helps us gain an appreciation of the institutionalized cultural foundations of attitudes and behaviors concerning death. This approach does not focus on the way individuals perceive or experience their own dying or the death of another, but rather, on the relationship of dying or death to society as a whole. In North America, for example, the predominant attitudes and expectations about "appropriate" death reflect a social reality consistent with a technology-oriented and bureaucratic society that places a premium on ensuring smooth functioning among social institutions. An appropriate death, therefore, is one that occurs naturally and is correctly timed (that is, occurs in old age).[8] Robert Blauner points out that the

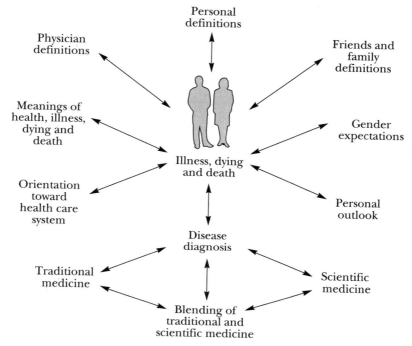

Figure 3-2   *Symbolic Interactionism*

bureaucratic aspect of death in modern societies is designed to prevent disruptions and preserve the equilibrium of social life.[9] Thus, in this structural framework, death is removed from the center of social life to its periphery.[10]

Symbolic Interactionism

The theoretical approach to understanding society known as symbolic interactionism emphasizes "the freedom of individuals to construct their own reality as well as to potentially reconstruct that which has been inherited."[11] People are seen not as passive elements in society but as responsive to the social structures and processes in their lives. This theory highlights the fact that socialization is a two-way process; it is not simply "putting in" information at one end and "getting out" a finished product at the other (see Figure 3-2).

Myra Bluebond-Langner, commenting on the findings from her study of terminally ill children in a leukemia ward, points out that our perspective is too limited when children are defined in terms of "what they will become," while adults are viewed as the active "agents" of their socialization.[12] Bluebond-Langner's remarks apply not only to the socialization of children, but also to social interactions between adults. This is illustrated in Joseph Kaufert and John O'Neil's study of the cultural mediation of dying and grieving among

TABLE 3-2   *The Social Construction of Reality*

1. People create culture (both material artifacts and nonmaterial elements).
2. These cultural creations become reality. That is, they become a natural part of the social landscape.
3. People absorb this reality. That is, individuals adopt their culture's perception of reality.

Source: Adapted from Norman Goodman, *Introduction to Sociology* (New York: HarperCollins, 1992), p. 94.

Native Canadian patients and their families in urban hospital settings.[13] Euro-Canadian caregivers and Native Canadian patients bring to their encounter differing interpretations of what constitutes appropriate care for dying and grieving individuals. By engaging in interactions designed to resolve the conflict between different views, attitudes and behaviors are altered on both sides. New "meanings" emerge through such human interactions and, as a result, the hospital "culture" is changed.

As social beings who are connected to one another in myriad ways, we live in an interactive and dynamic social world (see Table 3-2). This process is referred to by social scientists as the *social construction of reality:*

> Each society constructs its own version of the world, its "truths." In some societies the guiding forces of the world are seen as supernatural; in others they are the impersonal forces of nature. Some individuals structure their lives around their belief in a personal deity. . . . For others no such supreme being exists. Different versions of reality are not limited to weighty issues like religion. They also come into play in everyday events in people's lives.[14]

Applying this process to the study of dying and death, it follows that our concepts of death are socially constructed, or, as expressed by Robert Fulton and Robert Bendiksen, "the 'meaning' that death has for anyone is a result of the socially inherited ideas and assumptions that have been formed over the lifetime of the society in which one lives."[15]

The social construction of reality is also illustrated in a comparison of medical systems associated with different cultural settings. Because illness and its consequences are disruptive to the social order, all human societies devise medical systems that, regardless of their form or style, represent adaptive responses to the threat of illness.[16] In Western medicine, the physician, when presented with a range of symptoms in a patient, seeks to determine the particular disease that is being "expressed" in the individual; the focus is on treating (and curing) the illness, not the patient.

In contrast, the patient occupies a more central role in Chinese medicine, which views health and illness as encompassing a variety of influences that must be considered before making a diagnosis or proposing treatment. When seeking causes and cures, social as well as individual factors are considered.[17] The idioms that characterize traditional Chinese medicine involve the balance between "hot" and "cold" elements in the body as well as the relation between

Two great fears of the traditional Aboriginals are to be hospitalized away from their homelands and to die in the hospital and/or meet the "mamu" spirits of people who have died in the hospital. Aboriginals believe that good health results from harmonious relationships among physical, human, and supernatural environments; sickness results from disruption in these relationships and is directly attributable to the intervention of supernatural forces. These forces are known by various names, one of the most common is "mamu."

Generally, there are two types of forces, and both are potentially dangerous. The first is a kind of "devil," an indeterminate being capable of moving around the same space as ordinary people. . . . The second mamu is more fearful, from the adult Aboriginal's point of view. It is the spirit of the dead, particularly the recent dead. Although not hostile to people, these spirits are dangerous because they seek to rejoin the living. . . . This belief impels people to avoid using the dead person's name and to move camp as soon as a relative dies in camp, as the spirit will look for relatives in the last place they were seen in life.

Death at the time of hospitalization, in a hospital miles from home . . . means that the spirit of the Aboriginal child who dies cannot find its way to the tribal territory to await rebirth. It also means that the life force of adults who die, particularly those who have been repositories of tribal law and knowledge, are separated from their country; the strength of dreaming is weakened, to the eternal loss of all survivors. And a hospital in which many have died becomes a terrifying threat to Aboriginal patients because of the concentration of the mamu spirits of those who died and were unable to find their way back to their individual homelands.

Ruth Walter and Brenda Garneau, "Australia: Its Land, Its People,
Its Health Care System, and Unique Health Issues"

yang and *yin*, both within the individual and within his or her social world. By calling upon a vast library of medical experience that goes back at least two thousand years, the physician designs the optimal treatment for a particular patient.[18]

Chinese and Western physicians both rely on experience as a guide to diagnosis and treatment, but the manner in which such experience is accessed and applied corresponds to the way in which each culture constructs its social reality. It is important to note that a constructed social reality is not static, but is rather an ongoing, dynamic process. In the modern era, Chinese practitioners adopt aspects of the Western medical system, while Western practitioners adopt aspects of the Chinese system, particularly its emphasis on a holistic view of illness and health. (Blue Cross and other health insurers now pay for acupuncture and certain other "alternative" treatments.) In today's increasingly global context, the social construction of reality takes place in an environment that transcends conventional cultural boundaries.

Although death is a biological fact, its meaning is created by socially shaped ideas and assumptions. Consider, for example, the experience of

Hmong refugees recently arrived in North America. As immigrants in an unfamiliar environment, they encounter a kind of culture shock between the ideas and assumptions associated with the culture of their homeland and the ideas and assumptions that predominate in American culture. This clash is exemplified in the efforts of the Hmong to practice their traditional death customs.

The traditional Hmong funeral involves extensive public ceremony. Oxen and buffalo are slaughtered to provide food for the mourners, and there is a funeral procession from the place of death to the burial site. The traditional elements of Hmong funeral ritual cannot readily be accomplished in urban settings in North America. As accommodations are made in response to the American social setting, Hmong traditions are being altered significantly as individuals adapt to new social norms and values.

As with the Hmong experience with funeral practices, the experience and expression of grief is determined by cultural norms prescribing certain emotions as appropriate for a given social situation.[19] In summarizing a study of bereavement patterns in the midwestern United States, social scientists concluded that the response to loss is culturally learned, not genetically determined. They said, "Humankind does not 'naturally' grieve any more than it 'naturally' laughs or cries."[20] Wolfgang and Margaret Stroebe point out that

> Grief is channeled in all cultures along specified lines [and] there are substantial differences in the rules laid down by cultures as to how long the deceased should be grieved over and how long mourning should last. . . . What is sanctioned or prohibited in one culture may differ dramatically from what is or is not permitted in another.[21]

In summary, then, we find that our understanding of death is a product of the interactive relationship between ourselves and our culture.

The Social Learning Approach

In the social learning view, behavior, personality, and environmental factors operate as interlocking determinants of each other. Albert Bandura says, "From a social learning perspective, human nature is characterized as a vast potentiality that can be fashioned by direct and vicarious experience into a variety of forms within biological limits."[22] According to social learning theory, we learn through conditioning how to behave as members of a society. Behavior is shaped "by the stimuli that follow or are consequences of the behavior, and by imitation or modeling of others' behavior."[23] When we conform to social norms, our behavior is rewarded; when we fail to conform, our behavior is punished or goes unrewarded. This mechanism is evident when parents discipline their children for some behaviors and reward them for others, according to the norms and standards that the parents wish the child to emulate and learn.

The learning process need not be overt and is not mechanical. Much of our learning about how to function according to social norms occurs subtly

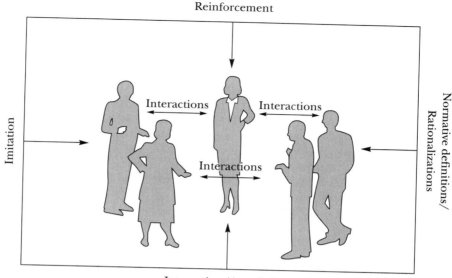

Figure 3-3   *Social Learning Approach: Four Main Dimensions*

through direct and vicarious reinforcement, imitation, interaction, rationalization, and other behavioral and cognitive processes (see Figure 3-3).[24] Often, we are not even aware that we are conforming to some social norms because they are embedded in our way of life; we accept them as natural, "the way things work." In modern American society, people are unlikely to consider the possibility of disposing of a relative's corpse by placing it on a scaffold outdoors where it will gradually decompose; yet, to Native Americans living on the Great Plains in the last century, platform burial was a normal and natural part of that society's social norms.

Thus, it is worth remembering that the norms we accept uncritically may be perceived as deviant by a person whose cultural orientation is otherwise. Ronald Akers says:

> Every society and group has a set of social norms, some applying to everyone in the system, some to almost everyone, and others only to persons in particular age, sex, class, ethnic, or religious categories. Some norms apply to a wide range of situations; others govern specific situations. In a heterogeneous society, different systems of normative standards exist side by side, and one may automatically violate the expectations of one group simply by conforming to those of another.[25]

In a modern, heterogeneous society like the United States, we have ample opportunity to apply the insights provided by social learning theory to expand our understanding of customs and behaviors associated with dying, death, and bereavement. A young Hispanic-American woman who recently attended her first "Anglo" funeral remarked that she was "genuinely puzzled" at the absence of storytelling and gentle humor about the deceased's life. "Everyone was very respectful of the family," she said, "but I was surprised that it was all so serious; I'm used to people talking and laughing at funerals." Recognizing that social norms function in a manner similar to the rules of a game or the script of a drama, we can detect their presence and influence in the ways people grieve and in the ceremonies they create to mark a loved one's death.

Agents of Socialization

Individuals do not come of age in society as a whole, but rather in a particular community, school, and family. Thus, cultural influences are expressed within particular social settings.[26] It is difficult, if not impossible, to pinpoint the genesis of ideas about death that a person may acquire in the natural course of socialization. Consider the following incident, involving two siblings, ages eight and ten. When asked to draw a picture of a funeral (see Figure 3-4), they got out their colored pencils and immersed themselves in the task. After a while, Heather (ten) said to Matt (eight), "Hey, you've got smiles on those faces! This is supposed to be a funeral. What are they doing with smiles on their faces?" In her model of appropriate death-related behavior, people don't smile at funerals; to her younger brother, smiles were perfectly acceptable. One can only surmise the influences that lead to such strong statements about what kind of behavior is appropriate at funerals, but in interactions like this, attitudes about death are incorporated into a child's understanding of death.

In modern societies, socialization involves a variety of influences, beginning with the family and extending to the mass media and other social forces. Although the main phases of socialization occur during the years of childhood and adolescence, the process is lifelong. *Resocialization*, a term that refers to the "uprooting and restructuring of basic attitudes, values, or identities," occurs when adults take on new statuses or roles that require replacing existing values and modes of behavior.[27] This may happen, for example, in the context of a religious conversion or upon starting a new job, getting married, having children, or surviving the death of a mate. Indeed, for both men and women, widowhood involves dramatic changes in many areas of life, as new roles and activities are taken on.[28] Rapid social change also brings about resocialization, as, for example, in the case of social changes related to women's roles over the past few decades. Finally, resocialization occurs when many of the general and abstract norms and values we learn in childhood are modified as we put them into practice later in life.

Family

Comparative studies of family life reveal considerable differences with respect to such issues as individualism and collective welfare. For example, Chinese families are often described as being situation-oriented, valuing family and tradition, harmony, emotional restraint, proper conduct, and accep-

Kid Love

A week or so after the funeral
my niece Kate called and I told her,
'Kate, you know, I can't eat anything but
white food. Mashed potatoes, noodles,
Cream of Wheat, Bimbo bread.' 'Yeah,'
she said, 'I do know. Me too. Me,
the live-right health food maven.'

Then she told me that the other day, Budi,
he's eleven, said, 'Kate,'—he calls her Kate
like my kids call me Maudie—'Kate,' he says,
'I can't believe you're eating that junk stuff.'
And she answered, 'Kid food, Budi. Right now
I need this kid food—you know, comfort stuff.'

Next day he came home from school,
walked past Kate, real cool,
mumbled, 'swapped my lunch,'
and dropped a Hostess Twinkie on the table.

Maude Meehan

tance of social obligations. They traditionally place greater significance on social and moral values than on personal values and competence in achieving individualistic goals or self-fulfillment.[29] Conversely, white, middle-class American families are characterized as prizing individualism, autonomy, and creativity. Unlike Chinese families, these American families tend to encourage children to become self-reliant and independent. An examination of families in other cultures would reveal similar kinds of distinctions based on social and cultural orientations.

As with other broad cultural orientations, attitudes and behaviors related to dying and death are also communicated in the context of family interactions. Think back to your childhood. What messages did you receive about death that remain to this day in the back of your mind? Possibly some messages were conveyed directly: "This is what death is," or, "This is how we behave in relation to death." Perhaps some messages were indirect: "Let's not talk about it. . . ." How would the rest of that sentence go? Let's not talk about it . . . because it's not something that people talk about? When, as a child, she encountered a dead animal on the highway, one woman was told, "You shouldn't look at it." Her mother admonished, "Put your head down; children shouldn't see that." That is a message about what constitutes appropriate behavior toward death.

Other parental messages about death may be communicated unconsciously. Consider the notion of replaceability. A child's pet dies, and the

A

B

Figure *3-4* *Children's Drawings of a Funeral*

Instructed to draw a picture of a funeral, a sister (age ten) and brother (eight) did so. The ten-year-old, whose drawing is A, emphasizes the emotional responses of the survivors. We see the picture as if we are looking in (and down) upon their grief. The figures in the first two pews have tears streaming down their faces and one woman shouts "No!" At ten, this child reflects on the sorrowful and unwelcome nature of death. When questioned about the empty pews, she said they were for anyone who came late.

The eight-year-old's drawing (B) is viewed from a similar perspective (looking in and down at the scene). Here we see the survivors grouped around a flag-draped and flower-bedecked coffin. The figures are portrayed with smiles on their faces. The focus in this drawing is on the symbols of death (e.g., the casket) and the ceremony rather than emotions. During the drawing session, the older sister commented that her brother's picture was "too happy" for a funeral scene.

parent says, "It's okay, dear, we'll get another one." Although children differ in their emotional response to the death of a family pet, some do experience significant grief when a beloved pet dies. The quick replacement of a deceased pet may not allow sufficient time for acknowledging the loss. What lesson about death is taught when a parent moves too hastily toward replacing a pet that has died? Imagine a situation in which a mother's grief over her mate's death is interrupted by her child's remark, "Don't worry, Mommy, we'll get you another one." The lessons about death that are learned in the family are conveyed by actions as well as words.

A woman now in her thirties tells the following story: "I can remember a time when my mother ran over a cat. I wasn't with her in the car, but I recall my mother coming home and just totally falling apart. She ran into the bedroom and cried for hours. Since that time, I've been extremely conscientious about not killing anything. If there's an insect on me or in my house, I'll pick it up and carry it outside." Parental attitudes, and the attitudes of other family members, shape the behavior not only of the child but also of the adult that the child will become, and how that adult conveys attitudes toward death to his or her own children.

School and Peers

As a child progresses through the school years, the social interactions that occur combine with the family's influence to shape attitudes, values, and behavior. Schools teach children much more than "reading, 'riting, and 'rithmetic." Even the style of teaching is a culturally conditioned phenomenon: In some societies, teachers are viewed as professionals and addressed with honorifics; in other societies, teachers are viewed as "friends" or "coaches." Either way, messages about the society's values and norms are conveyed through the medium of schooling.

A child's social world broadens dramatically during the school years. This broadening is due partly to expanded opportunities for interactions with peers. Even before they enter school, however, children enter the world of their peer group—that is, children of the same age and general social status.

The influence of school and peers is seen in children's and adolescents' views of roles and distinctions associated with gender socialization. To illustrate, a study of junior high students found that attitudes toward death differed between males and females, and these differences tended to reflect expectations based on traditional sex roles.[30] In comparison with males, females generally placed higher value on funerals and expressed greater concern about what happens to bodies after death. When asked about the issue of capital punishment, boys were about equally divided, pro and con, whereas girls tended to express uncertainty or opposition. Asked about their beliefs about life after death, males were "more decisive" and females "more variable" in their beliefs. Although such gender-related differences result from a child's social encounters in a variety of contexts, they are significantly influenced by attitudes that are prevalent among peers.

Childhood activities such as "playing dead" can be a means of experimenting with various concepts, trying them on for size, and thus arriving at a more comprehensive and manageable sense of reality.

Mass Media

Television, motion pictures, radio, newspapers, magazines, and books, as well as videos, records, cassettes, and compact discs—all are forms of mass media. These media convey information about ideas, values, and norms to large numbers of people—and they frequently include references to, and depictions of, death-related attitudes and behaviors. These references and depictions have a pervasive socializing influence on both children and adults. Sometimes this influence occurs as an unintentional by-product of the primary message or story being communicated; at other times, the communication of socially accepted norms is a primary and acknowledged aim. For example, the children's television program, "Mister Rogers' Neighborhood," has produced and aired a number of segments that focus creatively on the topic of death, with the explicit intention of helping children deal with it.[31] In other instances, media messages that embody death-related attitudes are not intentionally directed to children, yet they nonetheless reflect society's understanding of death. Consider, for example, the message about attitudes toward death that is communicated by "content warnings" that preface television programs which include graphic depictions of violence. What impact do such messages have on children and adults with respect to cultural attitudes toward violent death?

Recently my seven-year-old son hopped in my lap and we watched the evening news together. The concluding line of a report on environmental pollution was a quote from U.N. scientists predicting that in twenty years the world would be uninhabitable. As the TV switched to a Madison Avenue jingle designed to encourage us to purchase a non-greasy hair tonic, my son turned to me with a terribly small voice and asked: "Dad, how old will I be when we all die?"

Robert D. Barr, *The Social Studies Professional*

Intended as a caution to viewers who might wish to avoid such scenes, these messages reflect a social consensus about death-related programming.

News reports of disasters or death—and the reactions of individuals to such reports—convey information about a society's attitudes toward dying and death. How children relate to such messages depends on their level of cognitive development as well as their individual life experiences. As Martha Wolfenstein and her colleagues discovered when they conducted a study of children's reactions to the death of President John F. Kennedy, from the mass of details about the president's assassination, children selected particular aspects relevant to their own developmental concerns.[32] Young children expressed concern about the appearance of the president's body and the effect of the death on members of his immediate family; older children were more concerned with the impact of the president's death on society and the political system.

Similar developmentally related concerns appeared in children's reactions to the deaths of the *Challenger* astronauts. When a group of first graders was asked to draw pictures of the shuttle accident, many depicted the astronauts as returning safely to earth where they could be saved by rescue teams.[33] One child's picture showed the astronauts coming down in parachutes while debris from the rocket falls around them. Another picture showed all seven astronauts in the water, apparently waiting to be rescued. In some of the drawings, the astronauts' bodies were shown intact; in others, the bodies were in pieces but the child-artists said they could be made whole again by rescue crews or hospital workers. One boy drew a picture of an astronaut in the grass and told his teacher that rescue crews would find the astronaut and take him to a hospital, where he would be made well again. This kind of interest in the condition of the astronauts' bodies and in possibilities of rescue is appropriate and usual for children of this age group. Developmental issues during childhood and adolescence are discussed in greater detail in Chapter 10.

Children's literature is also a source of messages about life and death. Many of the classic children's stories depict death, near deaths, or the threat of death. Here, too, the presentations convey cultural attitudes and values. Consider, for example, the contrasts found in the European and Chinese versions of the tale of Little Red Riding-Hood.

Little Red Riding-Hood

... "Dear me, Grandmamma, what great arms you have!"
 The wolf replied:
 "They are so much better to hug you with, my child."
 "Why, Grandmamma, what great legs you have got!"
 "That is to run the better, my child!"
 "But, Grandmamma, what great ears you've got!"
 "That is to hear the better, my child."
 "But, Grandmamma, what great eyes you've got!"
 "They are so much better to see you with, my child."
 Then the little girl, who was now very much frightened, said:
 "Oh, Grandmamma, what great teeth you have got!"
 "THEY ARE THE BETTER TO EAT YOU UP!"
 With these words the wicked wolf fell upon Little Red Riding-Hood and ate her up in a moment.

Journeys Through Bookland, Volume One

In the Western version, Little Red Riding-Hood goes by herself to visit her grandmother, encounters the wolf, and is tricked into believing the wolf is her grandmother. In the traditional version of the story, the wolf eats Little Red Riding-Hood, but she is saved by a woodsman who kills the wolf and slits its stomach, allowing Little Red Riding-Hood to emerge unharmed. In recent versions, Little Red Riding-Hood's screams alert the woodsman, who chases the wolf and then returns to announce that she will be bothered no more (the killing of the wolf occurs off-stage and is not mentioned).[34]

The Chinese tale of *Lon Po Po* (Granny Wolf) derives from an oral tradition thought to be over a thousand years old. In this version of the story, three young children are left by themselves while their mother goes away to visit their grandmother. The wolf, disguised as Po Po (Grandmother), persuades the children to open the locked door of their house. When they do so, he quickly blows out the light. By making perceptive inquiries, the oldest child cleverly discovers the wolf's true identity and, with her younger siblings, escapes to the top of a gingko tree. Through trickery, the children convince the wolf to step into a basket so they can haul him up to enjoy the gingko nuts. Joining together, the children begin hauling the basket up. But, just as it nearly reaches the top of the tree, they let the basket drop to the ground. The story says, "Not only did the wolf bump his head, but he broke his heart to pieces."[35] Climbing down to the branches just above the wolf, the children discover that he is "truly dead." Unlike the European version, which has an individual child facing the threat of the wolf by herself and ultimately being saved by someone else, the Chinese version of this folk tale illustrates the value of being part of a group effort to do away with the wolf.

The Three Little Pigs

. . . This made the wolf so angry that he vowed he would eat the pig, and that nothing should stop him. So he climbed up on the roof and jumped down the chimney.

But the wise little pig was ready for him, for he had built a big fire and hung a great kettle of water over it, right under the chimney. When the pig heard the wolf coming he took the cover off the kettle, and down fell the wolf right into it. Before he could crawl out, the little pig popped the lid back on again, and in a trice he had the wolf boiling.

That night the little pig had boiled wolf for supper. So he lived in his brick and mortar house till he grew too big for it, and never was he troubled by a wolf again.

Journeys Through Bookland, Volume One

Themes of death and violence are also found in lullabies.[36] Consider the message about death communicated in this well-known lullaby:

Rockabye baby, in the treetops.
When the wind blows, the cradle will rock.
When the bough breaks, the cradle will fall.
Down will come baby, cradle and all.

Some lullabies can be classified as "mourning songs," which describe the death or funeral of a child; others are "threat" songs that warn of violence if a child does not go to sleep or perform some other action in the expected manner. In studying such lullabies, researchers note that the subject matter and presentation of lullabies change as higher standards of living, better nutrition, and a more secure sense of the future evolve.

A considerable amount of death imagery is found in nursery rhymes as well. Of two hundred nursery rhymes examined in one study, about half described the wonder and beauty of life while the other half dealt with the ways in which humans and animals die or are mistreated.[37] Death-related themes in these rhymes included accounts of murder, choking to death, torment and cruelty, maiming, misery and sorrow, stories of lost or abandoned children, and themes depicting poverty and want.

Some stories are written especially to help children find answers to questions about dying and death. In many such books, particularly those written for very young children, death is presented as an event that occurs as part of the natural cycle. These stories often include the suggestion that, like the transition from one season to the next, after each ending in life there is renewal. One writer says, "It is consistent that a society which produced children's books explaining the mysteries of molecules and atoms, of evolution and birth, should also produce works of facts and fiction which attempt to define and explain death."[38] A selected list of children's books about death is included in Chapter 10.

TABLE 3-3   *Four Functions of Religion in Societies*

1. Religion provides a shared set of beliefs, values, and norms around which people can form a common identity. Thus, religion is a unifier, "the social glue that binds a group together by giving it a common set of values."
2. Religion provides answers to the "big questions" about human existence and purpose. It addresses issues of life and death, outlines the kind of life people are expected to lead, and explains what happens to them after they die.
3. Religion often provides a foundation for the norms and laws of a society. Laws acquire a moral as well as legal force when they are embedded in religious values.
4. Religion is a source of emotional and psychological support to people, especially at times of crisis.

Source: Adapted from Norman Goodman, *Introduction to Sociology* (New York: HarperCollins, 1992), pp. 205–206.

Religion

Even in modern "secular" societies, religion plays a surprisingly large role (see Table 3-3). As defined by David Balk and Nancy Hogan, "Religion is the attempt to give organized, cultural form to experiences of the sacred."[39] For the bereaved, religion provides solace to the extent that it suggests some meaning in dying, and it provides mourning rituals that can ease the pangs of grief. In considering the social functions of religion and its impact on individuals, it is useful to distinguish between two related concepts: *religious affiliation* and *religiosity*. Consider, for example, two members of the same religious group. They share the same religious affiliation. Yet, their religiosity—that is, the relative importance of religion in their lives—may differ significantly. Thus, the individual who attends religious services as an avenue for social interaction may have a very different experience of the consolations of religion when death intrudes on his or her life than the person who participates in religious activities because he or she finds deep personal meaning in the religion's creeds and beliefs.

The concept of religiosity embraces several dimensions that are likely to be emphasized differently by different individuals and cultural groups. These include:[40]

1. Emotional ties to a religion (*experiential* religiosity)
2. Extent of participation in the religion (*ritualistic* religiosity)
3. Strength of religious commitment (*ideological* religiosity)
4. Degree to which religion is integrated into the person's daily life (*consequential* religiosity)
5. Range and depth of the person's knowledge about the religion's traditions, beliefs, and practices (*intellectual* religiosity)

Any or all of these dimensions can have a significant impact on an individual's characteristic way of facing death and coping with loss. For example, a young man from a Filipino-American family mentioned the comfort he felt in

After Her Husband Died, Doña Carlota Was So Alone

After her husband died, Doña Carlota was so alone
she wanted nothing more than to die
One day she decided how she would end her life:
leave the gas on
After fixing some tortillas, frijoles for her son
to eat when he arrived home from work
But as she turned a tortilla over she beheld
the image of her husband scorched on it
A sign from God she should live,
spend the rest of her days in peace
The tortilla I am told is in her living room
next to a photo of her dearly-departed Esteban
so unbelievingly striking in resemblance,
preserved forever in Saran Wrap

Leroy Quintana

connection with a funeral Mass held for his father in the Church where his family worshipped. Commenting on the use of Latin during the service, he said, "You know, I've never known exactly what those prayers are all about, but the soothing rhythms of the chants and the pungent smell of the incense make me feel that my dad is taken care of, that he's really okay." This young man's experience includes elements of experiential, ritualistic, and consequential religiosity.

Other Agents

In addition to the possible agencies of socialization we have already mentioned, there are others. We might single out the influence of neighbors as well as social organizations such as the Boy Scouts, Campfire Girls, fraternities and sororities, recreational clubs, and the like. Sports, organizations, and hobbies integrate adolescents into a social world, connecting them to a community and a particular set of social norms.[41] Socialization about death occurs in such groups when, for example, a participant dies or a coach or leader is commemorated following his or her death. With the broadening of an individual's social network, there are corresponding increases in the number of possible encounters related to the deaths of those with whom he or she has formed significant relationships.

Agents of socialization influence our understanding of death and dying in myriad ways. What we understand of death is usually less a result of systematic instruction than of happenstance. However, cultural attitudes toward dying and death are sometimes communicated through programs designed espe-

I saw death. At the age of five: it was watching me; in the evenings, it prowled on the balcony: it pressed its nose to the window; I used to see it but I did not dare to say anything. Once, on the Quai Voltaire, we met it: it was a tall, mad old woman, dressed in black, who mumbled as she went by: "I shall put that child in my pocket." Another time, it took the form of a hole: this was at Arcachon; [we] were visiting Madame Dupont and her son Gabriel, the composer. I was playing in the garden of the villa, scared because I had been told that Gabriel was ill and was going to die. I was playing at horses, half-heartedly, and galloping round the house. Suddenly, I noticed a gloomy hole: the cellar, which had been opened; an indescribable impression of loneliness and horror blinded me: I turned round and, singing at the top of my voice, I fled. At that time, I had an assignation with it every night in my bed. It was a ritual: I had to sleep on my left side, my face to the wall; I would wait, trembling all over, and it would appear, a very conventional skeleton, with a scythe; I then had permission to turn on my right side, it would go away and I could sleep in peace.

Jean-Paul Sartre, *Words*

cially to provide children and other interested persons with opportunities to confront and discuss these topics. An innovative example of this kind of educational presentation occurred when the Boston Children's Museum put together a participatory show entitled "Endings: An Exhibit About Death and Loss." A combination of songs, stories, games, videotapes, and other exhibits was designed to stimulate the sharing of thoughts and feelings about death between parents and children. Although the exhibit was criticized by some as an impingement upon children's "innocence" and "sense of joy" by forcing them to think about dying and death, most parents, educators, and child-development professionals praised the exhibit.

Early Experiences with Death

As we have seen, an array of interrelated sociocultural sources serve as socializing agencies with respect to the norms, beliefs, and behaviors of a given society. In addition to the influence of the sociocultural environment, personal experiences are crucial in shaping an individual's attitudes and behaviors. Thus, it is important to recognize the effect of each person's unique experiences with dying and death.

Ernest Becker points out in his landmark study, *The Denial of Death*, that there are two main schools of thought concerning the "fear of death" in human beings.[42] On the one hand, the "healthy-minded" argument maintains that individuals are not *born* with a fear of death; rather, this fear is engendered by experiences of parental deprivation or "hostile denial" of a child's life impulses by his or her parents (or by society more generally). The "morbidly minded" argument, on the other hand, maintains that the fear of

Cpl. Edward Belfer, U.S. Army Photo

Children experience the impact of war on their lives in a variety of ways. For the German child seen here, war brought a stark encounter with death. This child was one of many German citizens who, at the end of World War II, were ordered by the provisional military government of the U.S. Third Army to view the exhumed bodies of Russians, Poles, and Czechs killed while imprisoned in the concentration camp at Flossenberg. For Amanda Wille (facing page), the impact of war was felt in terms of the anticipated loss of her father, a Navy computer technician, as he prepared to board the USS John F. Kennedy for service during the Persian Gulf War. Understanding only that her father was going away, the three-year-old seemed anxious and bewildered until she found a piece of string on the Norfolk, Virginia, dock. After her father broke the string and tied one piece around his wrist and the other around hers, Amanda cried and hugged him goodbye.

I recall with utter clarity the first great shock of my life. A scream came from the cottage next door. I rushed into the room, as familiar as my own home. The Larkin kids, Conor, Liam and Brigid, all hovered about the alcove in which a mattress of bog fir bedded old Kilty. They stood in gape-mouthed awe.

I stole up next to Conor. "Grandfar is dead," he said.

Their ma, Finola, who was eight months pregnant, knelt with her head pressed against the old man's heart. It was my very first sight of a dead person. He was a waxy, bony specimen lying there with his open mouth showing no teeth at all and his glazed eyes staring up at me and me staring back until I felt my own ready to pop out of their sockets.

Oh, it was a terrible moment of revelation for me. All of us kids thought old Kilty had the magic of the fairies and would live forever, a tale fortified by the fact that he was the oldest survivor of the great famine, to say nothing of being a hero of the Fenian Rising of '67 who had been jailed and fearfully tortured for his efforts.

I was eleven years old at that moment. Kilty had been daft as long as I could recall, always huddled near the fire mumbling incoherently. He was an ancient old dear, ancient beyond age, but nobody ever gave serious consideration to the fact he might die.

Leon Uris, *Trinity*

death is natural and affects everyone. Indeed, in this view, fear of death is the "basic fear that influences all others." Although evidence can be gathered to support either of these views, as a practical matter it can be said that most people do exhibit, if not fear, at least anxiety toward death; and these feelings surface initially during childhood.[43]

Self-concept influences a child's ability to cope with death. A child with a good self-concept is generally less fearful about death, and the same correlation applies to adults. People who are comfortable with themselves, who see themselves as active, vital, and interesting, and who have caring relationships with others tend to be less fearful about dying and death. Consider the responses to death that you have observed. Whereas one person is curious to know all the details about a death, someone else prefers to know as little as possible. The ten-year-old's phrase, "It's sickening, don't talk about it!" can survive into adulthood.

Children who participate in the activities surrounding the death of a close family member or a friend can arrive at an understanding of death that is usually associated with children who are at a later stage of development. One six-year-old who witnessed the accidental death of her sibling expressed what was apparently a clear understanding that death is final, that people die, and that she herself could die. She was concerned about how she could protect herself and her friends from the dangerous circumstances that led to her brother's death. Her attitude was reflected in admonitions to schoolmates that they should be aware of preventing accidents. Along with this understanding of the reality of death, her attitude toward death reflected the particulars of her experience.

Encounters with violent death and warfare powerfully alter a child's understanding of death. In drawings made by Cambodian children living in refugee camps, the predominant theme is death.[44] Having experienced the deaths of parents and others from starvation, these children reflected that experience in their drawings. One such picture shows a woman in the midst of about six smaller bodies; it was captioned by the child, "Mother's Dead Children." James Garbarino says, "Few issues challenge our moral, intellectual, and political resources as does the topic of children and community violence—war, violent crime on the streets, and other forms of armed conflict."[45]

In 1994, a diary written by a young girl in war-torn Sarajevo brought renewed attention to issues involving the effects of violence on children. Zlata Filipovic's diary displayed an evolution from the ordinary concerns of teenage life to a shattering preoccupation with destruction and death as warfare disrupted normal life. In one entry, Zlata writes: "War has crossed out the day and replaced it with horror, and now horrors are unfolding instead of days."[46] Many children and teenagers growing up in America's cities experience warlike disruptions due to the prevalence of drug-related violence and gang warfare, a situation that writer and musician Ice T characterizes as "the killing fields" of America.[47]

Catastrophic experiences of violent death alter a child's understanding of death. In addition to having a more mature conceptual orientation toward death, children who experience firsthand the reality of death because of war or pervasive violence, or in connection with other forms of catastrophic death, often exhibit a fatalistic attitude toward death that contrasts with children whose experiences of death occur in more benign circumstances.[48] When questioned about the "ways people die," children living in violent or death-saturated environments tend to answer quite differently from those whose lives are comparatively sheltered from such experiences (see Figures 3-5 and 3-6).

Socialization is influenced not only by experiencing death-related events, but also by the environment in which such life experiences occur. Take a moment to consider your own circumstances. Do you live in a rural, urban, or small town environment? What region of the country do you live in? The North, East, South, or West? Was your school environment ethnically and religiously diverse? Your response to death is likely to be influenced by such factors. When children in a lower-middle class, urban school in Germany were asked about the ways people die, their responses corresponded to their environment. Violent deaths were described as being caused by "weapons" and "sharp knives." Conspicuously absent was any use of the word *gun*.[49] In Germany, handguns, being illegal, are not available to the general populace; they are carried only by police. Environmental factors play an important role in determining how people think about and respond to death.

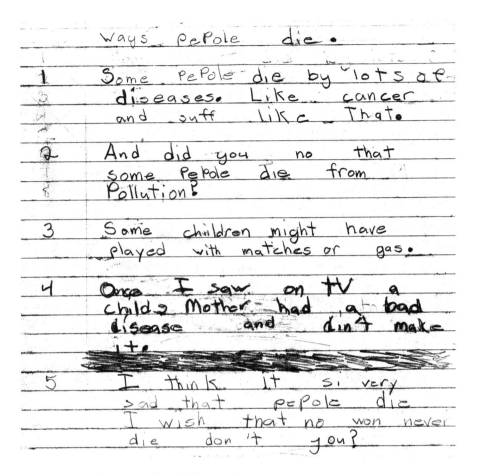

Ways PePole die.

1   Some PePole die by lots of
    diseases. Like cancer
    and suff like That.

2   And did you no that
    some PePole die from
    Pollution?

3   Some children might have
    played with matches or gas.

4   Once I saw on TV a
    childs Mother had a bad
    disease and dint make
    it.

5   I think It si very
    sad that pePole die
    I wish that no won never
    die don't you?

Figure 3-5   *Ways People Die: Children's Explanations*
Environment, including both time and place, influences a child's understanding of death. The impact of environment on children's views of death
can be evoked by asking them to make a list or draw a picture in response
to the question: "What are the ways people die?" The list shown above was
written in 1978 by a seven-year-old Caucasian girl living in a small coastal
California town. It stands in sharp contrast to the 13-item response (*facing
page*) written in 1995 by a seven-year-old African-American boy living in a
major Midwestern city. Although both lists were created by children of the
same age, the second list reflects both the passage of time (17 years) and
the circumstances of life in an inner-city metropolitan environment.
Whereas the first child's list focuses on diseases and accidents, the second
child's explanation shows familiarity with a broad range of causes of death,
few of which relate to "natural" events. His illustration of item number
11, "cut your head off," is shown in Figure 3-6.

1. Heart Attack
2. Smoke / Cancer
3. Drugs
4. Choke on food
5. Shot to death
6. Car AAccident
7. Stabbed
8. Stroke
9. Killeb by a bomb
10. Fire in house
11. Cut your head off
12. Drinking too much
13. Drown

In summary, life experiences—particularly those that involve an encounter with significant loss or death—can be powerful in shaping a person's attitudes and beliefs about death. In some cases, especially when such experiences occur in early childhood, it is only as an adult that a person becomes fully aware of the impact.

Teachable Moments in Socialization About Death

Through the normal course of life, opportunities abound for children to learn about dying and death. Consider, for example, a mother who discovers her eleven-year-old son sitting at her new computer writing his will. Taken aback, she pauses for a moment as thoughts race through her head: Why is he writing a will? How did an eleven-year-old become interested in giving away his

Figure 3-6 *Ways People Die: Children's Images*
Above: A seven-year-old African-American boy in a large Midwestern city draws a picture of murder by decapitation. (In separate incidents, two young girls in his city had been recently killed in this manner.)
Below: In contrast, the drawing created by a seven-year-old Caucasian boy attending Catholic school in a small California town portrays the child's concept that people die when "God calls you home." Notice the child's depiction of the voice of God and heavenly "pearly gates."

favorite treasures? Does he believe he is going to die soon? What should I do? What can I say? Gathering her courage, she cautiously adjusts her tone to suggest a neutral inquisitiveness and asks, "What has made you think about writing a will?"

Turning to her, the joy of accomplishment lighting up his face, the boy says, "I was looking at the menu on your computer and found *Willmaker 5*. The program came up and all I have to do is fill in the blanks. It's easy, see? Then I can print out my very own will."

Thus we encounter the concept of a "teachable moment," a phrase used by educators to describe opportunities for learning that arise out of ordinary experiences.[50] Because of their immediacy, such naturally occurring events are ideal vehicles for learning. The learner's own questions, enthusiasm, and motivation guide the educational process. Teachable moments have been defined as "unanticipated events in life that offer potential for developing useful educational insights and lessons, as well as for personal growth."[51] Although this is a useful definition, it can be expanded.

First off, who is the teacher? If we assume that learning about death always flows in a single direction, from adult to child, we overlook the quintessential quality of education as an interactive process. In the foregoing example of the young boy filling in the blanks of a computerized will-making program, the mother appears to occupy most clearly the role of the learner. She learns something about her son's exploration of the new computer and, more important, she learns the crucial lesson of gathering information before reacting.

Suppose this mother, acting out of initial shock at her son's apparent interest in death, had hastily responded, "Stop that! Children shouldn't be thinking about wills or about dying!" A lesson about death would surely be taught, but it would not promote a healthy understanding of death. So, in thinking about how to apply the concept of teachable moments to guide children in their understanding of death, it is useful to ask: *What* is being taught? Does the "teaching" result from a conscious design? Or is it unintentionally conveying unhealthy messages about death?

Let's return to our story of the mother and son. Having elicited information from her child and refrained from acting on her initial fears, the mother is able to use this interchange with her son as a teachable moment, an opportunity to discuss death in a nonthreatening and unemotional context. She might broach the subject by calling her son's attention to the entry for "Designated Guardian for Minor Children," thereby taking advantage of the opportunity to inform him about the steps she has taken to ensure his well-being ("Did I tell you that Aunt Martha and Uncle John are listed in my will as your guardians?") as well as to respond to his concerns ("No, I do not intend to die for a long time"). They might spend a few minutes discussing other aspects of death and how people prepare for it. In a brief conversation, considerable learning can take place. An atmosphere of openness in talking about death is promoted as information is exchanged between adult and child.

Although teachable moments are often defined in the context of un-planned or unexpected occurrences, it is useful to recognize that parents, educators, and other adults can consciously create situations that encourage such learning opportunities.[52] There is no rule specifying that we must wait until such events happen spontaneously. Indeed, in the foregoing example, the mother used her son's experience with the computer program as a way of introducing their subsequent discussion about death. The key to capitalizing on such occurrences is adequate preparation by trusted adults in the child's environment.

Although it is natural to emphasize the impact of socialization on chil-dren, it is important to be aware also of the opportunities that present them-selves in the form of "teachable moments" for adult learning. Such learning can take place not only between adults and children, but also in adult-to-adult encounters. Asking questions, observing behavior, and listening to language cues can lead to possibilities for increasing understanding.

On an airplane trip, an executive for a large corporation engaged one of this book's authors in light conversation. Upon hearing about this textbook and its subject, however, his tone changed slightly and he said: "Could I ask your opinion on a personal matter?" Naturally, the question concerned death. It involved a family dispute about whether the man's five-year-old son should attend his grandfather's burial ceremony at Arlington National Cemetery. He was sure that the military ceremony—with uniforms, marching soldiers, and a twenty-one gun salute—would scare his son unnecessarily. After he shared additional information about his family and child, suggestions were offered concerning some ways that parental support could be provided to the child during the funeral rites. Hearing these suggestions made it possible for the man to reconsider his earlier decision to exclude the child. With specific recommendations in hand, he decided to include the child as a participant in his grandfather's funeral. Of course, individuals do not have to be textbook authors to offer information that may be useful to people who are coping with death-related issues. As you read this book, you will gain information that can be appropriately offered.

Death in Contemporary Multicultural Societies

Culture differs among societies as well as within societies that include social groups with distinctive customs and life styles. The United States, for example, is often characterized as a "nation of immigrants," a term that reflects its cultural diversity. Thus, sociologists speak of *subcultures*, groups within a given society that share a distinctive identity and life style that set them apart from the overall society. Some subcultures represent a particular ethnic heritage or economic circumstance; others are unique because of their history or place of origin. Subcultures often share a distinctive language or, if they share the same language as the wider culture, a distinctive jargon or slang. Although subcultural differences can be a source of tension and discord within societies, Norman Goodman says, "The cultural mosaic created by subcultures can be seen as enriching a society."[53]

Distinctive Traditions: Ethnicity and Pluralism

David Clark observes that "in the last analysis, human societies are merely men and women banded together in the face of death."[54] Certainly, death presents the ultimate challenge to human pretensions. How individuals cope with this challenge is revealed in their social life and cultural accomplishments. The charge has frequently been made that, in modern societies, death is hidden, if not forbidden. The popularity of memorial services without the body of the deceased present, as well as the sequestration of the dying in hospitals and the professionalization of funeral services, are cited as indicators that death is pushed aside and avoided in modern societies. Upon closer examination, however, we find that the manner of dealing with death in modern societies is not uniform. Although a certain set of attitudes and behaviors may be characterized as "The American Way of Death," for example, the fact is that this phrase encompasses many different "ways of death,"

The Shroud

A mother once had a little seven-year-old boy with such a sweet, beautiful face that no one could look at him without loving him, and she loved him more than anything in the world. Suddenly, the child fell sick, and God took him. The mother was inconsolable and wept day and night. Soon after he was buried, the child began to appear in places where he had sat playing in his lifetime. When his mother wept, he too wept, and when morning came he vanished. Then when the mother could not stop crying, he appeared one night wrapped in the little white shroud he had been buried in and wearing a wreath of flowers on his head. He sat down at her feet and said: "Oh, mother, if you don't stop crying I won't be able to sleep in my coffin, for my shroud is wet with all the tears that fall on it." When she heard that, the mother was horrified, and from then on she shed no tears. The next night the child came again. He held a candle in his hand and said: "You see, my shroud is almost dry. Now I can rest in my grave." After that, the mother gave her grief into God's keeping and bore it silently and patiently. The child never came again, but slept in his little bed under the ground.

Grimm's Tales for Young and Old

reflecting the social life and customs of diverse immigrant groups as well as the lifeways of the continent's original inhabitants. Addressing this issue, David Olson and John DeFrain point out, "It is important to remember that tremendous diversity exists among the people who are commonly grouped together."[55]

Of course, the extent to which traditional cultural patterns are maintained by the different groups that comprise American society varies widely, both between the different ethnic groups and among individuals who share a particular ethnic heritage. Nevertheless, in studies of behaviors related to dying, death, and bereavement, ethnic and other subcultural differences can be identified relative to such matters as methods of coping with life-threatening illness, the perception of pain, social support for the dying, behavioral manifestations of grief, mourning styles, and funeral customs.

A comparative analysis of the bereavement practices of ethnic and cultural groups in the United States suggests that "while adapting partly to Western patterns, at the same time these groups adhere to the bereavement procedures of their own cultures."[56] Ronald Barrett's descriptions of contemporary African-American funeral and mourning customs illustrate the persistence of traditional customs despite time and circumstance.[57] Strands of traditional African practices relative to dying and death remain important to many African Americans, and they are exemplified in such practices as gathering at the gravesite to bid godspeed to the deceased and in the perception of funeral ritual as a "home-going" ceremony honoring the spirit of the dead. In much the same fashion, although altered by their contact with American culture, Hmong funeral traditions are being preserved and perpetuated insofar as it is possible to do so in a very different cultural setting.[58]

In societies that value pluralism, different groups are able to retain distinctive identities while enjoying equal social standing within the culture as a whole. Encouraging diversity in death attitudes and customs allows the entire society to benefit from a wealth of cultural resources that can assist in coping with death.

Yet, it must be recognized that the diversity of customs and beliefs in pluralistic societies also presents challenges. One of any society's functions is to help keep the "dread" felt by human beings toward death "bracketed"—that is, contained within a social framework that lessens anxiety about it. When all the members of a society share common beliefs and customs, it is relatively easy for individuals to enact socially sanctioned ways of dealing with death-related issues and emotions. This comforting situation may be jeopardized by cultural diversity because it becomes less clear which practices are acceptable to a community for managing death and minimizing existential dread.[59] Uncertainty about social norms for dealing with death are evident in the modern phenomenon of people in attendance at a funeral feeling anxious about how to act or what to say. This was the situation faced by the man who was unsure about whether or not to permit his young son to attend his grandfather's burial service.

In contemporary societies, socially sanctioned rites for dealing with death are in flux. The dynamic of the "melting pot" metaphor in American society is being modified as individuals and groups strive to honor and reinterpret, rather than discard, the distinctive attitudes and customs of their forebears. This challenges the assumptions of caregivers, who must carry out their professional missions in an environment that requires attention to individual and group differences.

Mixed Plate: Ethnic Identity in Hawaii

Hawaii is a unique example of cultural diversity and accommodation. Eleanor Nordyke points out that Hawaii "is the only region where all racial groups are minorities and where the majority of the population has its roots in the Pacific Islands or Asia instead of Europe or Africa."[60] The colonization of Hawaii took place from about the third to the sixth centuries of the current era, when Polynesians sailed their canoes to the Hawaiian archipelago.[61] The first contact with Europeans came in 1778 with the exploration of the Pacific by Captain James Cook. Later, successive waves of immigrants came—including Chinese, Japanese, Portuguese, Okinawans, Koreans, and Filipinos—many arriving as temporary laborers in sugar cane fields and then remaining to make Hawaii their home.[62] Today, Hawaii's residents include Caucasians from both North America and Europe, Samoans, Vietnamese, Laotians, and Cambodians, as well as African Americans, Latin Americans, Pakistanis, Tongans,

The Dead Mouse

We had been out of town and the neighbors had been caring for our various pets. When we returned, we found that our cat had, as cats will, caught and killed a mouse and had laid it out ceremoniously in front of his bowl in the garage. I discovered that that had happened when I heard loud screams from the garage. "Pudley's killed a mouse. There's a dead mouse in the garage!" Loud screams, for the whole neighborhood to hear. I went downstairs. It was the first time that I had a chance to observe how my children dealt with death. I said, "Oh, there is?" "Right here," they said, "Look!" They began to tell me how they had determined it was dead. It was not moving. They had poked at it several times and it didn't move. Matthew, who was five years old, added that it didn't look like it was ever going to move again. That was his judgment that the mouse was dead.

I said to him, "Well, what are we going to do?" I could feel myself being slightly repulsed; my fingers went to my nose. It was obvious to me that the mouse was dead—it had started to decay. Matt said very matter-of-factly, "Well, we'll have to bury it." Heather, seven, climbed on a chair and announced, "Not me. I'm not going to touch it. Don't bring it around here. Aughhh, dead mouse!" At that time, she was intent on being what she thought was feminine, and part of the stereotype involved not getting herself dirty.

So Matt volunteered for the job. "I'm going to need a shovel," he said. I stood back and watched, interested to see what would happen. I noticed that he didn't touch the mouse. From somewhere he already had gotten the idea that it wasn't appropriate to touch dead things. He carefully lifted it with the shovel and took it into the backyard to dig a hole. Heather peered around and watched at a safe distance.

After the mouse was buried, Matt came back and said, "I'm going to need some wood, a hammer, and a nail." I thought, "Oh great! He's going to perform some kind of little ceremony and place a symbol of some kind on the grave." Matt went to the woodpile and carefully selected a piece of wood maybe two inches long and another piece a bit wider, perhaps three inches wide and about four or five inches long. I thought, "Tombstone?" He got the nail and put the pieces of wood together in the shape of a cross.

Fijians, Micronesians, people from other parts of Oceania, and others. In just two hundred years, Hawaii has experienced a dramatic transition from an ancient Polynesian agrarian society to an urban industrialized community of mixed ethnic derivation.

The population of modern-day Hawaii represents a rich ethnic and cultural blend. Each group has its own story, with a unique history and corresponding traditions. Although scholars have addressed issues related to the dynamics of Hawaii's mixed population, relatively little work has been done in comparing the customs and behaviors of the different groups with

I thought, "Oh. A cross, religious symbol, burial, funeral—all the things I knew about what happens with a dead body." Matt picked up a marking pen and wrote on the front of the cross: "DEAD MOUSE. KEEP OUT!" And he pounded it into the ground in front of where the mouse was buried. I thought, "What's going on in this kid's mind?"

I asked him, "Does that mean that when I die there should be a sign saying, "Dead Mommie. Keep out"? He put his hand on his hip and looked at me with that disgust that five-year-olds can muster for somebody who is *so* dumb, and said, "Of course not. You're going to be buried in one of those places where they have bodies. This is a backyard. Kids could ride their bikes over it. Who would know that there is a mouse buried back here?" I was flabbergasted.

A few weeks later there was a long discussion about what the mouse would look like at that time. My first thoughts were, "Don't do that! You can't dig it up. It's not nice. It's not good. The mouse has to rest his spirit." Then I realized that all those things were coming from that place in me that didn't want to see what a month-old dead mouse looked like.

So I kept quiet. They dug and dug, and I could feel the sweat dripping off me. They dug a huge hole, but could find no remnants of the mouse. I was a bit relieved. But that brought up all kinds of questions about what happened to the mouse. I made this elaborate picture of a compost pile, really a lengthy explanation. Finally I realized that they didn't understand at all and that what I was saying was of no interest to them.

I said, "Well, it's like if you buried an orange." Something safe, I thought, something I can deal with that can be dug up day by day to see how it goes back into the earth.

They buried an orange and dug it up and dug it up and dug it up. And it wasn't an orange anymore.

I came away from that experience thinking, "Where did they learn all that? Matt's behavior, particularly . . . Where did he get that from?"

respect to death and dying. Yet, because of its ethnic diversity and the close intermingling of different cultural traditions, Hawaii can be viewed as a model for other societies that wish to preserve the cultural richness of distinctive traditions by accommodating and, indeed, welcoming their expression.

Characteristics of Hawaii's Peoples

For native Hawaiians, the extended family group, or *'ohana*, is at the center of traditional values.[63] This emphasis on family is displayed in a variety of ways: Children occupy an important place in all family gatherings, including funeral rituals. Ancestral remains are considered to be sacred, especially those of the *ali'i*, members of the royal family. Indeed, the Hawaiians' love of family is the basis for their renowned love of the land. George Kanahele says,

> In a religious society in which ancestors were deified as *'aumakua* and genealogy elevated to prominent status, a place, a home, was much more valued because of its ties with the ancestors. A Hawaiian's birthplace was celebrated not simply because he happened to be born there, but because it was also the place where so many generations of his ancestors were born before him. It was a constant reminder of the vitality of the bloodline and of the preciousness of life past, present, and future.[64]

Hawaiians exhibit a profound capacity for experiencing the sacred and expressing—through myth, symbolism, and ritual—the transcendent realities of life. In the spring of 1994, the Hawaiian community was shocked into mourning when two *ka'ai*, or woven caskets, containing bones believed to be those of deified Hawaiian chiefs were taken from the Bishop Museum in Honolulu.[65] A grief-filled ceremony was held at the Royal Mausoleum to inform the ancestors of the missing bones and express the desire that the bones be returned safely. Chants and wailing laments asking the ancestors' forgiveness formed part of a ritual that was said to have been last held a hundred years ago.

The Chinese were among the earliest immigrants to Hawaii.[66] Like the native Hawaiians, the Chinese embody cultural values emphasizing family and relationships. In traditional Chinese society, the family is, in effect, a religious institution. A key concept in Chinese philosophy is *harmony*, a quality manifested in an emphasis on proper conduct in interpersonal relationships. This emphasis on proper conduct stems from the central importance of the ancestral cult in Chinese culture. The descendants of a common ancestor share a lineage that often dates back centuries. In traditional Chinese funeral rites, the wearing of specific mourning garments highlights the degree of kinship between the bereaved and the deceased (much as the LoDagaa in Africa use mourning restraints to indicate the closeness of family ties; LoDagaa customs are discussed in Chapter 2).[67] The motivation for such practices can be found in the Chinese ideal of *hsiao* (filiality or filial piety). The assumption is that "the living and dead are dependent on each other, the latter for sacrifices and the former for blessings."[68]

Although historical funeral and mourning practices have been modified to fit the demands of modern societies, the Chinese in Hawaii retain core elements of traditional practices.[69] For example, in accordance with the belief that the needs of the dead resemble those of the living, Chinese funerals in Hawaii typically include offerings of food, money, and other items that will be needed by the deceased in the afterlife. Papier-mâché "servant dolls," placed in front of the casket, are given chanted instructions by a Taoist priest about how to take care of the deceased in Heaven. The boy servant might be told, "Take care of your master; fetch him water and firewood." To the girl servant,

© Anna Ordenstein, Williams Mortuary, Honolulu

Constructed by the Taoist priest who officiates during the funeral and placed directly in front of the casket, these "servant dolls" exemplify the elaborate customs relative to traditional Chinese beliefs about the afterlife. During the funeral rites, family members place servings of rice, also prepared by the priest, into a ceremonial bowl that will be buried in a special niche within the grave where, symbolically, it provides nourishment for the deceased for 10,000 years.

© Albert Lee Strickland

Located in a setting of great natural beauty on the Hawaiian island of Oahu, this Chinese cemetery is situated on a hillside that gently slopes down toward the city of Honolulu and the ocean beyond. Following Chinese custom, care is taken to ensure proper siting of the grave so that the deceased's spirit can easily depart this world. As in the case of this cemetery located above a bustling, metropolitan city, certain aspects of traditional practices retain their importance even in modern social settings.

the priest might say, "Keep the house clean and, when you go shopping, don't waste your master's money." In the typical Taoist funeral, which can continue throughout most of a day, the priest chants and musicians play instruments while family members perform rituals at the priest's direction. Symbolic money (sometimes called "Hell Notes"), which the dead person will use in the next world, is contributed by mourners and burned in a container as the service proceeds. The notion is that, the more money that is burned, the more the deceased has in the next life. All of this goes on while people visit and express their condolences.

Following Taoist traditions that are thousands of years old, the contemporary Chinese funeral in Hawaii uses the ancient principles of *fêng-shui* (often termed "geomancy" in Western writings). Briefly stated, *fêng-shui* is "a system of divination for determining the auspicious siting of human dwellings—for the living or for the dead."[70] During the funeral, the foot of the casket is positioned facing the door so that the spirit or soul of the deceased will have an unobstructed pathway into the next world. It is a duty of the living to make sure that the spirit of the dead goes on to Heaven; that's part of a survivor's responsibility to the deceased relative. The Chinese cemeteries in Hawaii are situated amid great natural beauty and on sloping ground, in accordance with the principles of *fêng-shui*. As with the placement of the casket during the funeral service, burial on sloping ground facilitates the journey of the spirit to the afterlife. Conscientious attention to such traditions allows the bereaved family to be certain that everything is done in the proper way and that the ancestors are honored.

The Japanese comprise yet another important segment of Hawaii's population. Like the Hawaiians and the Chinese, they value highly the family and its extended household. In many respects, the Japanese in Hawaii have lived out the "American dream" since their forebears immigrated to Hawaii as field workers, although they maintain an identity that reflects a distinctive Japanese heritage.[71] Whereas Chinese customs typically involve ground burial of the corpse, the Japanese generally prefer cremation followed by interment of the ashes in a *haka*, or family memorial. In Hawaii, *haka* usually provide space for a dozen crematory urns, although the larger ones can accommodate several times this number.

At Japanese funerals, the primary mourner is often given *koden*—that is, contributions of money to help defray the expenses, with the amount donated increasing as kinship ties become closer. An elder son, for example, would make a larger contribution than, say, a cousin. As is true of Japanese elsewhere, *butsudan*, or family altars where ancestors are honored, are given an important place in many households. The midsummer *o-bon* festival (discussed in Chapter 2) is celebrated widely in Hawaii, and not just by Japanese families. Celebrations like *o-bon*, as well as the similar Chinese festival *ch'ing ming*, are community affairs in Hawaii, with people of varying ethnic backgrounds and traditions participating.

Indeed, all of the groups now living in Hawaii have brought their own distinctive traits and customs and added them to the unique cultural mix that is modern-day Hawaii. Generally speaking, they all share an emphasis on the value of family ties and, in most cases, reverence for their ancestors. As John F. McDermott says,

> In all groups, except perhaps the Caucasian, the extended family plays a central role. There is an emphasis on the family as a key social unit, and on family cohesion, family interdependence, and loyalty to the family as central guiding values. The individual is seen as part of a larger network, and duties and obligations, as well as much of the sense of personal security, derive from that context. . . . Caucasians, too, value the family, but they face the world as individuals.[72]

This distinction, which makes Caucasians stand out from other groups in Hawaii, may be explained by David Plath's remarks concerning how the life

© Patrick Dean

In this celebration of el Día de los Muertos, *or Day of the Dead, held in a California community, a child enters into the festivities by drawing a skull, an activity that reinforces her identity as a participant in age-old traditions that mark her culture's particular attitudes and behaviors relative to death. In pluralistic societies, such celebrations both perpetuate cultural traditions and allow them to be shared with people from the wider community, who may choose to adopt elements of those traditions in their own lives, thereby creating a distinctive sense of local identity with respect to death-related customs and practices.*

course is conceived of among people of European background or ancestry compared to those in Asia, specifically Japan. Plath says, "In the Western view, individuality is already God-given; in Japan [and, by extension, elsewhere in Asia], it has to be evoked in relationships."[73]

Euro-American culture plays a central role in modern Hawaii, although it is appropriate to think of Caucasians not as the dominant force in contemporary Hawaiian society but as one of the several groups that constitute the "ethnic mosaic" of the islands. Nevertheless, most Caucasians who arrive in Hawaii from the mainland tend not to think of themselves as migrants; rather, they view themselves as representing mainstream culture and expect others to adapt, not themselves.[74]

Assimilation and Accommodation in Death Rites

In Hawaii, each "subcultural" group maintains much of its distinctive identity and culture while sharing elements of this identity and culture with the wider community. With the arrival of various ethnic groups in the islands, a common language, known as "pidgin," developed and became a symbol of local identity. Pidgin, a unique mix of words and grammar borrowed from the native tongues of its speakers, is not only an expressive means of communication among people of disparate backgrounds, but also a way for these people to identify with their adopted homeland. Today, pidgin provides a means of transcending cultural boundaries and establishing rapport on the basis of "local" identity. For example, a Caucasian nurse described how she employed pidgin in talking with a Filipino man who was dying. As the man's body wasted away from the disease, he became frightened of dying. Offering comfort, the nurse told him, "Spirit good, body *pau* [finished]." In using a pidgin word drawn from the Hawaiian language, she affirmed that the man's spirit was strong while acknowledging that the life in his body was ending, consumed by a terminal disease.

Local identity is demonstrated by familiarity with the customs of other groups and flexibility in adopting elements of those customs in one's own life. For example, the native Hawaiian tradition of feasting at important ceremonial events, such as those commemorating the life-course markers of birth and death, is widespread among Hawaii's residents. At funerals in Hawaii, mourners often gather after the ritual to share food and conversation. In fact, mortuaries accommodate this custom by having kitchen and dining facilities where food can be prepared, brought by mourners (pot luck), or catered and served to the gathered family and friends. Most funeral announcements in Hawaii include the notice, "Aloha attire requested," and mourners respond by wearing colorful shirts and *mu'u mu'u* (long "missionary" dresses), along with fragrant and beautiful flower leis. In traditional Hawaiian culture, the lei is very special, and various flowers and leis carry symbolic meanings. For example, a *hala* lei is associated with the breath *(ha)* and connotes passing away or dying. The popular ginger, or *'awapuhi,* lei is used as a symbol of things that pass too soon, as indicated in the Hawaiian folk saying, "*'Awapuhi lau pala wale*," which translates as "Ginger leaves yellow too quickly."[75] In the "feasting" that follows a funeral and the wearing of flower leis, customs associated with the indigenous people of Hawaii have become widely adopted as an expression of local identity and community feeling.

Because of the variety of religious traditions practiced in Hawaii— Christianity, Buddhism, and Taoism, among others—mortuaries are generally prepared to offer the appropriate ritual accoutrements and symbols for all these traditions. In one mortuary chapel, for instance, the central portion of the altar is designed as a revolving display so that the images and symbols of the appropriate religious tradition can be easily provided—whether it be Catholic, Protestant, or Buddhist.

In surveying death customs in contemporary Hawaii, we see how the creation of an "ethnic mosaic" involves both assimilation and accommodation. *Assimilation*, in this context, "refers to the incorporation of the values of a new group by the dominant existing group so that it fits into the existing social network, while *accommodation* suggests movement in the other direction, that is, a new individual or group adapting to the existing or dominant group values by changing in order to continue to live with them."[76] The boundaries between different ethnic groups have become loosened through social interaction among the groups. The boundaries are "soft instead of hard, often overlapping rather than sharply defined," resulting in a unique situation wherein "no group has totally surrendered the core of its traditional cultural identity."[77]

It seems that the people of Hawaii have not tried to minimize differences between groups so much as to appreciate and make room for their expression. As individuals marry outside their heritage group, and families from different cultural traditions are joined as kin, customs, beliefs, and practices blend together. Spouses from different traditions adopt elements of each other's culture, and their children become acquainted with the beliefs and customs of both cultures. In Hawaii today, mixed race, or *hapa,* is the fastest growing ethnic group in the Islands. Despite this blending, however, observers note that ethnicity remains very powerful, an important part of every interaction.[78]

The Mature Concept of Death Revisited

As the examples given in this chapter illustrate, the process of socialization is both complex and ongoing. Our understanding of death evolves throughout the life course. As we experience loss in our lives, we are likely to modify previously held beliefs, exchanging them for new ones that provide a better fit with our current understanding of death and its meaning in our lives. In studying the conceptualization of death among adults, Sandor Brent and Mark Speece have found that the "mature" concept of death, which is acquired by children at about age ten, forms the basis for further development as

© Patrick Dean

In contemporary societies where a variety of cultural traditions are practiced by differ-ent ethnic and subcultural groups, people may find themselves "trying on" customs and practices that differ from those of their own heritage group. The opportunity to participate in the rites and ceremonies of other cultures, to assume a "local iden-tity," even if only temporarily, can broaden our understanding and expand our range of choices for revitalizing even those customs with which we are most familiar.

the child grows into adulthood.[79] In a sense, this basic understanding of death serves as "the stable nucleus, or core, of a connotational sphere that the child continues to enrich and elaborate throughout the remainder of life by the addition of all kinds of exceptions, conditions, questions, doubts, and so forth."

Instead of the "neat, clean, sharply delineated concepts of formal sci-entific theories of reality," the result of this process may be a kind of "fuzzy" concept that acknowledges the reality of death while leaving room for a variety of elaborations about its meaning. A recent study comparing the concept of death among Chinese and U.S. children and adolescents found such "fuzzy" concepts about death to be present, especially among older children.[80] In this sense, the binary "either/or" logic used by young children who grasp the core components of a mature concept of death may be viewed as a precursor to the greater sophistication in understanding death that develops later in life. As this process unfolds into adulthood and old age, the agencies of socialization discussed in this chapter exert a powerful influence on beliefs and behaviors. Broadening our perspective to include cultural approaches to dying and death that differ from our own increases the range of choices that can prove useful in our encounters with death. In making this journey of understanding, we can benefit from taking a broad view in defining "community." As David Plath says,

> We are born alone and we die alone, each an organism genetically unique. But we mature or decline together: In the company of others we mutually domesticate the wild genetic pulse as we go about shaping ourselves into persons after the vision of our group's heritage. Perhaps the growth and aging of an organism can be described well enough in terms of stages and transitions within the individual as a monad entity. But in a social animal the life courses have to be described in terms of a collective fabricating of selves, a mutual building of biographies.[81]

The antidote to ethnocentrism—that is, the fallacy of making judgments about others solely in terms of one's own cultural assumptions and biases—is easy to acquire once we broaden our perspective in a way that engages the ideas and customs of people in other cultural contexts. Most studies in death and dying have focused on phenomena associated with the Euro-American experience; one frequently cited survey of ethnic practices in the United States was completed two decades ago.[82] However, this situation is beginning to change as scholars and practitioners recognize the need for adequate information about the diverse populations that make up a pluralistic society. Such information is important for individuals who care for the dying, help grieving families, or otherwise do "death work" where broadened vision and sensitivity to a variety of cultural practices is required. Coping with cultural diversity can be both challenging and rewarding. Seeing others as they see themselves, sharing in some way their perceptions and customs, enriches individual as well as social life, and, indeed, may be the very essence of true education.

Further Readings

Zygmunt Bauman. *Mortality, Immortality, and Other Life Strategies.* Stanford, Calif.: Stanford University Press, 1992.

David Clark, ed. *The Sociology of Death: Theory, Culture, Practice.* Cambridge, Mass.: Blackwell, 1993.

David R. Counts and Dorothy A. Counts, eds. *Coping with the Final Tragedy: Cultural Variation in Dying and Grieving.* Amityville, N.Y.: Baywood, 1991.

Robert Fulton and Robert Bendiksen, eds. *Death and Identity*, 3d ed. Philadelphia: The Charles Press, 1994.

Donald P. Irish, Kathleen F. Lundquist, and Vivian Jenkins Nelsen, eds. *Ethnic Variation in Dying, Death, and Grief.* Washington, D.C.: Taylor and Francis, 1993.

Nancy Scheper-Hughes. *Death Without Weeping: The Violence of Everyday Life in Brazil.* Berkeley: University of California Press, 1992.

Debra Umberson and Kristin Henderson. "The Social Construction of Death in the Gulf War," *Omega: Journal of Death and Dying* 25, no. 1 (1992): 1–15.

James L. Watson and Evelyn S. Rawski, eds. *Death Ritual in Late Imperial and Modern China.* Berkeley: University of California Press, 1988.

Unni Wikan. "Bereavement and Loss in Two Muslim Communities: Egypt and Bali Compared," *Social Science and Medicine* 17, no. 5 (1988): 451–460.

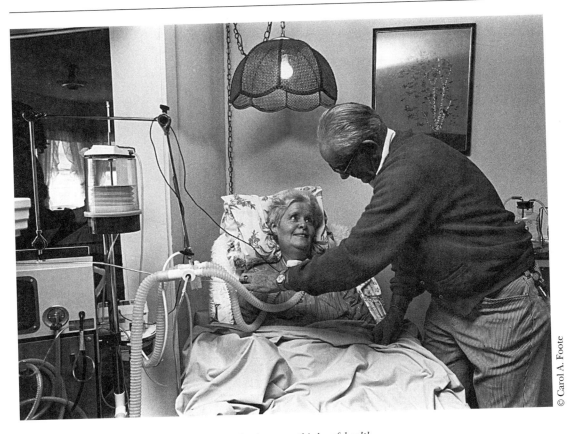

Home care may not come immediately to mind when one thinks of health care systems, yet this centuries-old tradition of care for the ill and the dying is once again emerging as an option for many. Innovations in sophisticated medical life-support equipment often make it possible for the seriously ill to be cared for at a high level of medical technology within the home.

Health Care Systems: Patients, Staff, and Institutions

*T*he struggle to come to grips with the finiteness of physical existence is a constant of human experience. The way we die is not. The act of dying has been significantly altered by medical technology and the advent of the modern hospital. Medical institutions are designed to soothe and heal; yet their salve is not always comforting for the dying.

Think about the end of your own life. What do you fear about dying? Many people say that they fear dying in pain and loneliness amid complicated machines that hum softly in an impersonal setting. Oriented toward the goal of preserving life, the medical system has sometimes been remiss in meeting the needs of dying patients and their families. Death may be treated as an anomaly.

In this chapter, we examine the components of the modern health care system, with particular attention to practices related to terminal care. Patients with life-threatening illness usually receive a combination of both acute and supportive care. As conditions change, a patient may need the acute care skills and resources of a hospital at some times and, at other times, the services of a hospice or nursing home. Institutional care may alternate with home care when outpatient services suffice to meet the patient's needs. Each of the three major categories of institutional medical care—hospitals, nursing homes, and hospices—is designed to optimally serve a specific purpose within the overall health care delivery system.

The first hospitals were established centuries ago to aid the homeless and the hopelessly ill. (The word *hospital* derives from the Latin *hospitium,* meaning a place that receives guests.) A distant relative of modern hotels and hostels, early hospitals aided sick travelers and victims of disaster. Members of religious orders provided nursing care, while physicians generally functioned independently. The close association between physicians and hospitals is a comparatively recent development.

Modern hospitals are devoted mainly to acute intensive care. They are designed to provide highly specialized care to patients. Aggressive techniques are employed to diagnose symptoms, provide treatment, and sustain life. The typical patient expects to regain well-being after a short period of treatment and then return to normal life. Recent data indicate that the average length of a hospital stay has been steadily decreasing and is now about six days.[1] Among the factors contributing to this decline are advances in treatment as well as increased use of home care and outpatient care.

Nursing homes (a category that includes convalescent care and extended-care nursing facilities) provide a less sophisticated level of care than do hospitals. They are chiefly designed to provide care for the chronically ill. About three-quarters of nursing home patients eventually return to the community; the remaining one-quarter includes both patients who require ongoing nursing care and those who die while in a nursing home. Nursing homes designated as skilled nursing facilities have a registered nurse on duty around the clock and a skilled paramedical staff. Those designated as intermediate-care facilities offer less intensive care and have either a registered nurse or licensed vocational nurse on duty during day shifts.

Although about 80 percent of terminal care in the United States is provided by hospitals and nursing homes, hospice care is increasingly important. Hospice care is distinguished by its orientation toward the needs of dying patients and their families. Such care may be provided in a free-standing facility devoted to the care of terminally ill patients; in a palliative care department within a general medical center; or in the patient's home, with care provided by family members, friends, visiting nurses, and other allied health workers. Palliative care is treatment that is intended to provide comfort to the patient, rather than to cure a disease.

Modern Health Care

A person entering a health care facility does so to receive medical and nursing care appropriate to a particular malady. The kind and quality of care provided depends on the relationships among the patient, the institution, and the medical and nursing staff. Each side of this health care triangle—patient, staff, and institution—contributes to the overall shape of health care. Consider the patient's relationship to the administrative and organizational patterns of the institution. Because providing health care for large numbers of

"I think in the next 10–20 years we'll have 'warehouses' with patients on life support systems, if the American public and physicians don't come to grips with and resolve the inherent conflicts involved in the present 'common' method for handling the terminally ill patient." *General practitioner*

"I do not think anybody should have the right to be God and decide death. In view of age and circumstances life may be prolonged to the benefit of patient and family." *Orthopedic surgeon*

"I am a doctor and I feel I should do all in my power to diagnose disease and sustain life." *Internist*

"We should not prolong misery when it's not indicated for other reasons. Everyone has a time to die and should be allowed to die with some dignity." *Urologist*

"The Physician Speaks,"
The Newsletter of Physician Attitudes

people requires efficient use of staff and facilities, procedures are standardized and made routine. Thus, the capacity to meet the needs of each individual patient is limited. When the elderly aunt did her dying at home, she could be spoon-fed her favorite homemade soup by a member of her family. Today, in the hospital or nursing home, she is more likely to receive a standard diet, perhaps served impersonally by an overworked and harried aide. The patient's experience is influenced by rules, regulations, and conventions—written and unwritten. The trade-off for more sophisticated health care may be less personal comfort.

The family of a terminally ill patient may be relegated to maintaining a deathwatch in the corridor or the waiting room down the hall, with one family member at a time squeezing into the patient's room to keep a bedside vigil. There may be little or no private space where relatives can gather to discuss their concerns with staff. Hallway meetings symbolize for many the impersonality of the hospital. To counteract this sense of impersonality, it has been suggested that hospitals set aside a "grief room," insulated from other activities, where family members can feel safe in expressing volatile emotions—anger, pain, sadness—without fear of upsetting institutional routine. Such a room could also be used for meetings between the family and medical personnel when disturbing news about the patient's condition is discussed. In the public setting of a waiting room or hospital chapel, grieving relatives may feel obliged to contain or repress their emotions. The institution of a "grief room" within the hospital setting validates the powerful emotions evoked by loss and acknowledges the grieving person's experience. You might find it interesting to survey the hospitals in your area to determine whether this kind of facility is available.

Unwritten rules, no less faithfully executed than written ones, can contribute to a sense of alienation in institutional settings. Hospitals may follow the convention that only physicians can respond to a patient's or family's questions about treatment or prognosis; nurses are expected to reply to such queries with the statement: "Ask your doctor." When convention prevails, it can result in needless fears and unfounded suspicions, increasing the anxiety of patients and their families.

Depersonalization and abstraction are part of the scientific method that makes possible many of the medical innovations we applaud. Yet these mechanisms also tend to make medical care less humane. Depersonalization is most likely to occur when a disease is not well understood; medical practitioners may display greater interest in the disease than in the patient. In addition, the power structure of a medical institution may create a work environment that promotes a defensive reaction among staff members and, thus, an impersonal experience for patients.[2] Objectivity and detachment may become avoidance when a patient is dying. Nurses may take longer to answer the bedside calls of terminally ill patients than the calls of patients who are less severely ill.[3] This is not the case with all institutional health care, of course, but avoidance of dying patients is unfortunate whenever it occurs. Charles Rosenberg observes that "we expect a great deal of our hospitals: alleviation of pain, extension of life, [and] management of death and the awkward and painful circumstances surrounding its approach."[4]

The rapid acceptance of the hospice philosophy as an option in terminal care is the result not only of concerns about the *care* of dying patients, but also of concerns about the *costs* of health care. Health care expenditures have been growing rapidly; in 1991, they totaled over $750 billion, about 13 percent of the gross domestic product (see Figure 4-1).[5] Hospital care accounts for about 38 percent of the health care dollar—more than for any other category of care (see Figure 4-2). Over the course of recent decades, the way Americans finance their health care has undergone several major changes.[6] In 1965, the federal government created the Medicare and Medicaid programs to extend health care to more people. The 1980s saw changes in methods of reimbursement to hospitals, physicians, and other health care providers. The most important of these changes involved the institution of DRGs (diagnosis-related groups) and prospective payment to health care providers. With reimbursements paid not on the basis of costs incurred, but on the basis of a set fee per case as determined by diagnosis, medical procedure, and other such factors, patient care increasingly came to be viewed in terms of standardized "products." Many insurers began requiring patients to obtain a "preadmission utilization review," confirming the need for a particular medical service, before being admitted to a hospital. In the wake of these developments, the patient may seem to be forgotten.[7] "Dollars saved" appears, in some instances, to be the primary measure of outcome.[8]

Related to health care financing is the trend toward adopting ever more costly medical technologies.[9] For example, physicians rely increasingly on

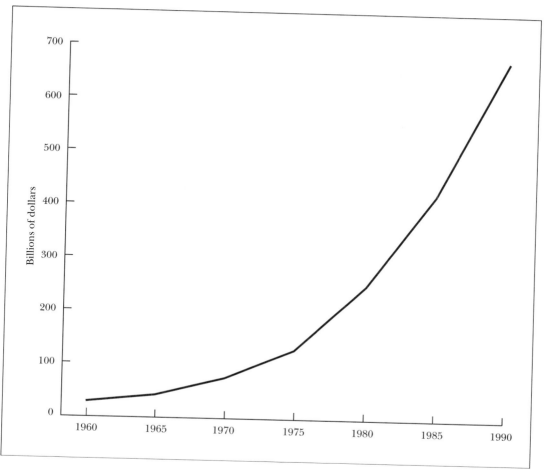

Figure *4-1*   *National Health Expenditures, 1960–1990*
Source: Bureau of the Census, *Statistical Abstract of the United States 1994,* p. 109.

expensive medical tests, some of which may be less accurate than one would wish.[10] There is a growing consensus that society is not obligated to provide every life-sustaining intervention that a patient or health provider believes might be beneficial. Technology generates demand.

To alleviate pressures on the system, experts suggest that health care resources be rationed. In fact, rationing is already occurring, particularly in the area of critical care. Rationing involves the allocation of scarce resources among competing individuals, and it occurs "when not all care expected to be beneficial is provided to all patients."[11] The scarcity of health care resources is also being driven by an aging society and by a growing population of "potentially salvageable" patients. If rationing is necessary or is already occurring,

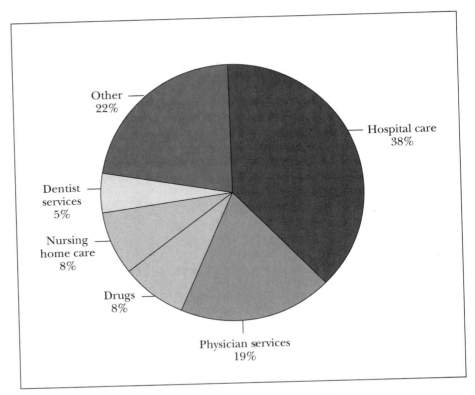

Figure 4-2   *Allocation of National Health Expenditures, 1991*
Source: Health, United States, 1993 (Hyattsville, Md.: Public Health Service, 1994), p. 44.

many people believe, a yardstick of some kind is needed to measure the outcomes of health care choices in relation to available resources. One such measure involves the use of "quality-adjusted life years" (or QALYs) to find an appropriate balance between length of life and quality of life.[12] The idea is that individuals might be willing to accept a trade-off. For example, a person might equate the prospect of living *fewer* years in *perfect* health to the prospect of living *more* years in *less than perfect* health.

To avoid rationing would necessitate altering either the supply or the demand side of the health resources equation. The demand for critical services, for example, might be reduced through education about the limits and consequences of certain medical procedures and technologies. Daniel Callahan argues that a "principle of symmetry" could be usefully applied in acknowledging the inherent limits of medical progress.[13] Callahan says, "A technology should be judged by its likelihood of enhancing a good balance between the extension and saving of life and the quality of life." Conversely, "a health care system that develops and institutionalizes a life-saving technology

T A B L E *4-1*   *What Is Driving Up Health Costs?*

1. The increase in morbidity [incidence of disease] rates due to good medicine. Good medicine keeps *sick* people alive.
2. The expanding concept of health. Our assumptions about health and illness are altered as medicine "discovers" new disorders; even normal aspects of aging have been reclassified as diseases for which treatment can be provided.
3. The seduction of technology and the deception of marketplace models. Decision making becomes distorted whenever extreme risks are involved, and our perceptions of probability vary significantly depending on the setting. People will pay anything to defend against the possibility of death, all the more so when the money involved doesn't come directly out of their own pockets.
4. The American character and appetite. Americans want things solved completely and they want them solved now. Americans refuse to believe there are limits—even to life itself.

Source: Adapted from Willard Gaylin, "Faulty Diagnosis: Why Clinton's Health-Care Plan Won't Cure What Ails Us," *Harper's Magazine* (October 1993), pp. 59–62.

which has the common result of leaving people chronically ill or with poor quality of life ignores the principle of symmetry." This principle is especially important with respect to the application of medical technology at the end of life.

Decisions about allocating medical resources are not just the concern of experts and legislators. The choices that individuals make in pursuit of their own well-being affect the health care system and ultimately determine its character (see Table 4-1). For example, rather than undergoing expensive and futile treatments at the end of life, many people are choosing to complete living wills and other directives that make their wishes known regarding the use of life-sustaining medical technologies. "Medicine overreaches itself," says Daniel Callahan, "when it sets as its implicit goal that of curing all diseases and infinitely forestalling death."

Care of the Dying

When Elisabeth Kübler-Ross set out years ago to educate the interns in an urban hospital about the special needs of the dying, she wanted to let terminally ill patients speak their own case. When she informed staff members about her intentions, however, she was told that no one was dying on their wards; there were only some patients who were "very critically ill."[14] As this story illustrates, even when dying and death are commonplace in one's environment, the operative response still may be to deny reality. In shedding light on the circumstances surrounding terminally ill patients, Kübler-Ross' work became a springboard for the movement toward sensitive care of the dying.

Dedicated to saving lives, medical and nursing personnel may suppress their feelings of helplessness when they are unable to prevent death. The physician who relates to a dying patient in a cold, detached manner could be

Dr. Elisabeth Kübler-Ross, seen here with a patient who has been diagnosed with a life-threatening illness, is widely recognized for her pioneering efforts toward increased awareness on the part of the patient, family, and medical staff relative to the issues that arise in caring for the dying.

compensating for feelings of inadequacy that are too painful to acknowledge. The nurse who recognizes that death will soon sever a relationship with a patient may worry about becoming too personally involved. Robert Kastenbaum identifies five strategies that may be employed in responding to a patient's desire to discuss death: (1) reassurance ("You're doing so well");

(2) denial ("Oh, you'll live to be a hundred"); (3) changing the subject ("Let's talk about something more cheerful"); (4) fatalism ("Well, we all have to die sometime"); (5) discussion ("What happened to make you feel that way?").[15] Jeanne Quint Benoliel says that, in their relationships with dying patients, caregivers need to be aware that "open communication does not necessarily mean open talk about death, but it does mean openness to the patient's verbalized concerns."[16]

Death may seem taboo in some medical institutions. The patient who is near death may be given medications to prevent disrupting the schedule or upsetting staff members or other patients. The patient's family may also be urged to accept tranquilizers to subdue their emotional reactions. Instead of encouraging the expression of natural responses, hospital personnel may emphasize subduing, controlling, and restricting reactions that could jeopardize institutional decorum. Citing the practice of urging drugs on family members to keep emotional disruption to a minimum, Robert Blauner observes that some hospitals exhibit features of a "mass-reduction system," which undermines the subjecthood of dying patients and their families.[17]

When death occurs, it may be treated so secretly that one would hardly be aware that sometimes patients die. Aside from a few individuals charged with the task of preparing the body and trundling it off to be picked up by the mortician, even hospital workers are sheltered from death. The false-bottom gurney, which transports the corpse to a nondescript exit, camouflages its odious human cargo. Death is compartmentalized, shut away from public view.

In some places, this bureaucratization carries over to public announcements of death. Newspaper obituaries and death notices often do not mention the hospital or nursing home where death occurs; instead, they refer to a nameless "local hospital." This evasiveness is apparently intended to convey the message that hospitals are in business to effect cures and save lives; acknowledging that patients die might be deleterious to a hospital's image in the community.

Despite this bleak description of medical institutions as places where death is taboo and the dying patient an anomaly, there are positive signs of change. Many physicians and nurses are aware of the fact that meeting the emotional needs of patients and their families can be as important as caring for bodily needs (see Figure 4-3). Contact that spans the professional distance reduces the sense of alienation between patients and staff. A nurse who steps into the room, sits down by the patient's bed, and demonstrates a willingness to listen is likely to be more successful in providing comfort than the nurse who breezes in, remains standing, and quips, "How're we today? Did we sleep well?" Skillful communication is crucial to the goal of providing health care for the whole person.

A century ago, physicians did perhaps as much to console as to cure patients. Indeed, consolation and palliative (comfort) measures were often all the medical practitioner could offer. Today, our expectations are such that if a

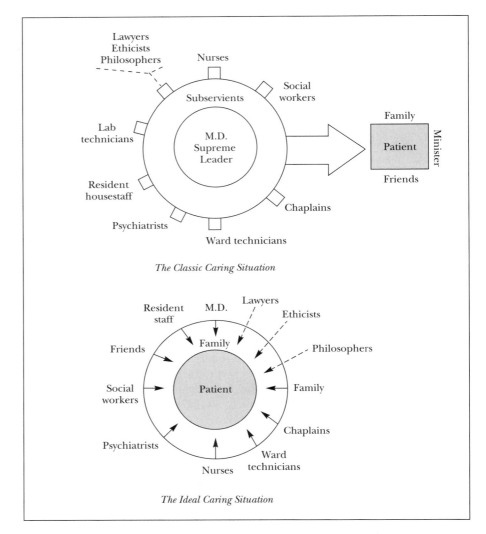

Figure *4-3*   *Classic and Ideal Caring Situations*
Source: David Barton, ed., *Dying and Death: A Clinical Guide for Caregivers* (Baltimore: Williams & Wilkins, 1977), p. 181.

cure is not forthcoming, we feel cheated. Doctors may become scapegoats when a course of treatment does not bring the desired outcome.

We cannot expect institutional care to be as personally focused as care provided by the patient's family. But the question remains: Are there alternatives that can bring about more compassionate care of the dying? One possible option is proposed by William Buchholz, an oncologist and hospice consultant. Referring to the Greek word *eschaton,* meaning "last things," Buchholz suggests that medical practitioners implement a "medical eschatology," in which the roles of caregiver and scientist are combined in the pursuit of knowledge about a phenomenon that "begins not with death, but when the end first draws into sight."[18]

Medical eschatology becomes possible when the illusion of immortality is broken by the recognition that all our biographies have an end. This can pave the way for asking questions that result in a better understanding of the human experience of dying and, in turn, better care of dying patients. These questions include: Which coping mechanisms are most effective, and under what circumstances? What role do psychosocial and transpersonal factors play with respect to life-threatening illness? What is the validity of our expectations regarding stages of dying? Prerequisite to answering such questions is the awareness that *caring* is not always synonymous with *doing.* Although knowledge is important, we must also be open to *not* knowing. "Learning," Buchholz reminds us, "can occur only when something is as yet not understood."

There is an ongoing search for answers to the question of how best to provide care—physical, emotional, and spiritual—for the whole person. Some counsel disidentification with the body; others emphasize beliefs about the afterlife. But the main issue is whether caregivers can put aside their own beliefs and find out what's appropriate for the patient. Those who care for dying patients must attend to clues that lead to discovery of what is appropriate for a particular person in a given situation. Dying, like birthing, is a natural event, often better witnessed than managed. In tracing the thinking that gave rise to the modern hospice movement and techniques of palliative care, Balfour Mount observes that care of the dying involves both heart and mind: "The dying need the friendship of the heart with its caring, acceptance, vulnerability and reciprocity. They also need the skills of the mind embodied in competent medical care. Neither alone is sufficient."[19]

Emergency Care

The roots of present techniques in trauma care can be traced at least as far back as the Civil War, when Army Major John Letterman developed the "triage" system for evacuating casualties. Designed to reduce the time between injury and care, triage involves assigning priorities to patients based on the seriousness of their injuries. Highest priority is given to patients whose injuries are serious, but survivable. Lower priorities are assigned to patients with only a remote chance of survival and to those with comparatively minor injuries. Many procedures that are now commonplace in emergency medicine represent adaptations of techniques used by the military in combat situations. These include the use of helicopter air ambulances, advances in team surgery and orthopedics, and treatment for burns and shock.

In 1992, about 86,000 Americans died from injuries sustained in accidents.[20] Roughly half of these deaths involved motor vehicles. Falls, drownings, fires, and poisonings accounted for most of the remainder. When injury

© Albert Lee Strickland

*Emergency personnel, including search-and-rescue workers and police officers, engage
in the grim task of recovering and identifying the bodies of two people who died in
the crash of a helicopter about a thousand yards offshore. Such work is stressful and
involves an extensive network of helping professionals who typically receive little or
no formal training in methods of coping with the impact of multiple encounters with
death, which occurs in the performance of their duties.*

occurs, time is the enemy. Experts in emergency medicine refer to the critical
"golden hour" following injury. Victims usually require immediate surgery,
often to stop internal bleeding. Although about half of all deaths from traumatic injury occur within the first hour (the first fifteen minutes are particularly crucial), the survival rate for those who receive appropriate care during
this period is 90 percent.[21] Timely treatment is critical.

In 1969, Dr. R. Adams Crowley brought together the Maryland State
Police and the Maryland Institute for Emergency Medical Services to form
the first civilian helicopter medevac program. In 1972, St. Anthony's Hospital
in Denver established the first hospital-based helicopter program. There are
now about 150 trauma centers in the United States. Although these centers
reduce the number of deaths from serious injuries, results could be much
better if sophisticated emergency care were more widely available. The National Research Council calls injury "the principal public health problem in
America today," yet it receives scant funding in comparison with other public
health programs. "The lack of a system," John Grossman says, "is killing
people."[22]

"The hospice movement is a great movement, not because it was legislated by Congress, or mandated by the Federal Government, but because it evolved out of the hearts of people who care."

> Senator Edward M. Kennedy (Massachusetts),
> from his keynote speech at the first annual
> meeting of the National Hospice Organization,
> Washington, D.C., October 1978

Hospice

The philosophy of hospice care emphasizes keeping patients as pain free and comfortable as possible, while refraining from dramatic medical interventions when death approaches. Many advances in pain control, particularly in cases of advanced cancer, have come about through hospice and related forms of palliative care. A salient feature of hospice care is its response to the conventional message to terminal patients that "nothing more can be done."[23] Hospice care reflects the belief that, even when no further treatment of the disease is available or appropriate, something more *can* be done by focusing on the relief of pain and other discomforting symptoms and by creating an environment in which dying can take place amid familiar faces and surroundings. Hospice exemplifies a team approach to care that involves the expertise of physicians, nurses, social workers, home health aides, and trained volunteers. It also draws upon the care and support provided to patients by family members and friends.

The hospice movement can be viewed as a response to what many people—patients and medical practitioners alike—perceived to be inadequate care for the dying. It reflects changing social expectations about health care, "from cure to care, extension of life to quality of life."[24] The roots of modern hospice care, with its emphasis on comfort rather than cure, can be traced to religious traditions of care for the sick and dying. The Judeo-Christian tradition includes the concepts of *diakonia* (serving and caring for others), *metanoia* (turning within to a deeper self or divine power), and *kairos* (a unique moment of fulfillment).[25] Hospice-style care goes back to medieval religious orders, which kept "places of welcome" for pilgrims and travelers. Sandol Stoddard says that people who were dying "received special care and honour, for they too were seen as pilgrims, closer than others to God."[26] Historically, these early hospices formed a contrast to early hospitals, which were built by the Romans on what Stoddard describes as a "military model of efficiency" to provide quick repair of gladiators and slaves.

In the modern era, the most notable and influential model of hospice care is St. Christopher's Hospice in Sydenham, England, which was inaugurated in 1967, after twenty years of planning, by Dr. Cicely Saunders.[27] Named for the patron saint of travelers, St. Christopher's draws most of its patients

I Know (I'm Losing You)

Have you ever touched your father's back? No, my fingers tell me,
as they try to pull up a similar memory.
    There are none. This is a place we have never traveled to, as
I try to lift his weary body onto the bedpan.
    I recall a photo of him standing in front of our house. He is
large, healthy, a stocky body in a dark blue suit.
    And now his bowels panic, feed his mind phony information,
and as I try to position him, my hands shift and the news
shocks me more than the sight of his balls.
    O, bag of bones, this is all I'll know of his body, the sharp
ridge of spine, the bedsores, the ribs rising up in place like new
islands.
    I feel him strain as he pushes, for nothing, feel his fingers
grip my shoulders. *He is slipping to dust,* my hands inform me,
you'd better remember this.

            Cornelius Eady

from within a six-mile radius of the hospice, an area with about 1.5 million inhabitants. Most of St. Christopher's patients have been diagnosed with terminal cancer, although some are elderly patients who can no longer function independently.

Filled with flowers, photographs, and personal items, the rooms at St. Christopher's are cheerful and familiar. To the extent they are able, patients are encouraged to pursue familiar interests and pleasures. Extensive visiting hours allow for considerable interaction between patients and their families, including children and even family pets. Parties are frequently held for patients, staff members, and families, accentuating St. Christopher's personal approach to patient care. St. Christopher's promotes an aura of tranquillity and an acceptance of the process of dying. Its highest priority is making the patient comfortable by controlling pain and other symptoms. Devices for prolonging life are absent. The largest portion of operating costs at St. Christopher's is for staff salaries, reflecting what Dr. Saunders calls a "high person, low technology and hardware" system of health care.[28]

When a patient dies, family, friends, and members of the hospice staff gather around the bed for their farewells. If they wish, relatives can take time to sit with the body. Later, the body is bathed and prepared for viewing in a small chapel. A clergyperson may be invited in to offer words of comfort. The participation of family and friends is encouraged throughout. Death is treated familiarly at St. Christopher's.

Home care is an important adjunct to residential care at St. Christopher's, and it is a feature of hospice care that has been widely emulated. Home care makes it possible to extend the benefits of hospice care to nonresidential patients and their families. St. Christopher's home care program serves individuals who have never been residential patients, as well as former residential patients who have been discharged to their homes. About 10 percent of the residential patients do return home when symptoms are controlled or for brief visits during holidays.

The home care program is essentially an outpatient program. Medication schedules are planned by the hospice staff, and hospice nurses regularly visit patients at home to monitor their conditions. A nurse is on call around the clock to provide help or answer questions from patients and family members. Knowing that backup is available is a source of confidence for patients and families in the outpatient program. Patients who are receiving home care may be admitted to the residential program when the family is worn out, emotionally drained, or otherwise unable to provide the necessary level of support. Augmenting its residential program with home care greatly increases the number of persons who can be served by St. Christopher's.

The first full-service hospice in the United States was established in New Haven, Connecticut. The Hospice of New Haven began serving patients in 1974 through a home care program funded by the National Cancer Institute.[29] Later, it added an inpatient facility. The spread of hospice care in America was stimulated by interest in the program at St. Christopher's and by Dr. Cicely Saunders' visit to Yale University in the 1960s. Indeed, the Hospice of New Haven's first medical director, Dr. Sylvia Lack, had served at St. Christopher's. In discussing another pioneering hospice of the early 1970s, Hospice of Marin in California, William Lamers recalls that it was created out of a desire to improve the quality of life for patients with incurable illness, patients who were being "slighted in a health care system that stressed aggressive therapies aimed at cure or rehabilitation, but that seemed to offer disincentives for care aimed at relief of illness."[30]

From these beginnings, hospice has experienced rapid growth. More than a thousand hospice programs of various kinds now exist in the United States. In many communities across the nation, hospice care is available by picking up the phone and calling a local hospice organization. Hospice care is now reimbursable under Medicare/Medicaid programs as well as by some private health insurers. As the hospice concept has grown, specialized programs have been instituted to serve particular patient populations, including terminally ill children.[31] Hospice care is provided in both home and inpatient settings, although most care is provided by *community-based* groups that do not have free-standing patient facilities. Typically, hospices provide a range of medical, nursing, and psychosocial services to patients and their families, with the aim of supplementing care received from other health care institutions. In carrying out this mission, hospices rely on a cadre of trained volunteers.[32]

Despite the enthusiastic welcome given to hospice care as an alternative to conventional treatment programs for terminally ill patients, such care is still available only to a fraction of the patients who desire it. Hospices are limited in their resources and depend upon contributions of both time and money. As

TABLE 4-2   *Questions for Contemporary Hospices*

1. *The question of access.* Is hospice care available to everyone who desires it? How can access to hospice care be improved for underserved populations such as minorities and people with AIDS?
2. *The question of spiritual care.* Is care related to the spiritual dimensions of life—that which "connects an individual to a sphere beyond himself or herself"—being adequately addressed by hospice?
3. *The question of finances.* What is the effect of the increasing imposition of bureaucratic regulation and budgetary controls on hospice care?
4. *The question of innovation.* How should present hospice services be expanded and new services created?
5. *The question of choice.* What is the role of hospice care in the growing debate about quality of life, euthanasia, and physician-assisted suicide?

Source: Adapted from Inge Baer Corless, "A New Decade for Hospice," in *A Challenge for Living: Dying, Death, and Bereavement,* ed. Inge B. Corless, Barbara B. Germino, and Mary A. Pittman (Boston: Jones and Bartlett, 1995), pp. 77–94.

mainstream health care agencies and institutions adopt the principles of hospice care, we can expect to see increases in the number of hospice programs operated as commercial rather than non-profit ventures. In addition, as hospice care is adopted ever more widely, becoming another item in a menu of medical options for terminal care, it is being challenged by questions that potentially threaten the traditional philosophy of hospice care (see Table 4-2).

In a sociopolitical environment that makes hospice care subject to governmental policies and bureaucratic schedules of reimbursement, what effect does acceptance of hospice care have on the grassroots enthusiasm and rugged independence that distinguished pioneering efforts? Early hospice programs were willing to experiment with different approaches to the delivery of services; now, as Inge Corless observes, the "politicization of reimbursement for hospice care" is resulting in regulations that require all programs wishing to obtain certification "to comply with a set of standards based on one model of care."[33] The impact of AIDS is also putting severe strains on the resources hospices need to carry out their mission. Hospice has proved its worth as a humane way to provide care to terminally ill patients and their families. Many hospice personnel, both staff and volunteers, are selfless in their commitment to hospice care. Whether such commitment can be sustained in the face of regulatory red tape and increased demand for services remains to be seen.

Palliative Care in Hospitals

As palliative care resembling the hospice model becomes increasingly available in conventional medical settings, it represents yet another challenge faced by hospices. Recent statistics indicate that nearly half of all hospice care programs in the United States are based in hospitals.[34] The conventional definition of hospitals as places devoted to acute care is being expanded to include various dimensions of outpatient and extended care, as well as home

There are some people who really can't deal with being told the truth about their illness. If you tell them at the wrong time or in the wrong way, it's too devastating for them.

First of all, get to know the patient. Sit down and talk with him, not about his illness particularly, but general topics. Very soon you get a feeling as to whether or not the patient wants to know. There are two groups: those who want to know and don't mind knowing, and those who very plainly don't want to know. There are some patients who have been told they have cancer, hear doctors discussing it, see their charts, and will still turn around and deny that they have cancer. And, of course, that's a gray area. You're not sure if they want to know. If they want to know, tell them. Don't hide the fact.

Quoted from *Death and Dying: The Physician's Perspective,*
a videotape by Elizabeth Bradbury

and hospice care.[35] Hospitals are developing programs to address issues related to death and dying, including specific initiatives concerning perinatal loss, support groups for terminally ill patients and their families, AIDS task forces, and hospice-style programs.[36] In hospitals where nurses are given time to get to know dying patients, where caregivers are assigned responsibility for individual patients rather than tasks, where supportive relationships exist between staff members, and where a policy of open disclosure of diagnosis and prognosis prevails, care for the dying approaches the ideals of hospice care.[37]

Broadly speaking, we can distinguish two programs of hospice-type palliative care within hospitals. In the first, a separate ward is set up to provide care for terminally ill patients; in the second, terminal care is integrated within the overall treatment program. Instituting a separate ward for terminal patients makes it possible to relax hospital regulations and procedures, thereby creating an environment more conducive to meeting the needs of patients and their families. Rules governing the length of visits and visiting hours can be made less stringent than elsewhere in the hospital. Age requirements can be relaxed to allow children visits with their dying relative. A separate palliative care ward may also help in placing the focus of staff on controlling pain and making the patient comfortable rather than on life-sustaining (or death-postponing) interventions.

However, instituting a separate ward may involve costly reorganization of facilities and resources. In addition, isolating the terminally ill away from the general patient population may stigmatize dying patients. When a patient is admitted to the "terminal ward," the message is clear that the prognosis is death. Patients and families may not want to face death so openly. Also, some health care practitioners prefer to work with patients with favorable odds for recovery; thus, the hospital may find it difficult to recruit staff whose duties involve ministering to the dying instead of working with a range of patients and conditions.

Because of these possible drawbacks, some caregivers advocate integrated care of terminally ill patients; such care places patients within the overall patient population but with special programs designed to supplement standard practices and procedures. Integrated care occupies a broad spectrum of possibilities, from offering counseling support as an addendum to otherwise conventional services to providing terminal patients with a comprehensive program managed by specially trained staff.

In both forms of hospital-based palliative care, hospice volunteers and clergy provide additional support, visiting patients to discuss their concerns and generally assisting in whatever ways are appropriate. The presence of someone familiar with hospital organization and routine—who can therefore act as an informal liaison between staff and patients—is comforting. Palliative care is usually most successful when it evolves from the vision of someone who is an advocate for the dying. That person may be a pastoral care worker or minister, a nurse or physician, a social services worker or a hospice volunteer. The hallmark of palliative care is open-hearted concern with a focus on alleviating the mental as well as physical pain of dying patients and their families.

Home Care

In many cases, home care offers a number of advantages as a setting for terminal care, including the obvious fact that the patient is *at home,* which, for most people, is a "center of meaningful activity and connectedness to family, friends, and community."[38] Amid familiar surroundings, home care provides a greater sense of normalcy than is found in hospitals or other institutional settings. There are also more opportunities for sustaining relationships and exercising self-determination. Home care minimizes the need to "live to a timetable," as is the case in hospitals with their scheduled routines. Home care also allows for reciprocity, a mutuality of care and concern, that families often find gratifying in caring for an ailing family member.

To realize these attractive features, home care requires that adequate support be available, not just from family and friends, but also from medical and nursing personnel who can supervise home care services and provide guidance or relief as needed. Home care is a 24-hour-a-day job. Whether family member, friend, or outside volunteer, someone must always be available to attend to the various tasks that constitute appropriate care of the patient. Home care is increasingly being recognized as an integral element in the overall health care system, partly due to the impact of AIDS and the provision of at-home care to AIDS patients.[39] Many of the costs associated with home care are hidden, but they are nonetheless real. It has been observed that "Home care may sound domestic and low key, but it is quietly bearing massive burdens in the health care system."[40]

Despite the recognition that the presence of a willing and able family member is the main ingredient in successful home care, the importance of family caregivers is sometimes overlooked. The workload of patient care can be

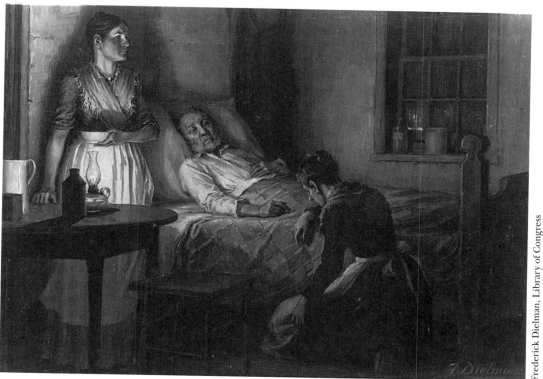

This 1895 illustration captures, in posture and expression, the weariness that accompanies round-the-clock care for the seriously ill and dying. Today's caregivers may feel this burden as much as ever while expecting themselves to put such feelings aside to conform to an image of professionalism.

alleviated by outside support services provided by visiting nurses and ancillary caregivers. Adequate guidance must be provided with respect to the management of pain and other symptoms. Finally, the physical environment of the home itself must be suitable for meeting the patient's needs. Regardless of how genuine and heartfelt the commitment of family caregivers to home care, it is clear that "You can't always make a home into a hospital."[41]

Periods of home care typically alternate with stays in the hospital. Weakness or loss of mobility may require more assistance than can be provided in the patient's home. Problems with control of bowels or bladder, or other difficulties in managing elimination needs, may call for hospitalization, as may inadequately controlled pain. Finally, even when home care is successfully carried out, the patient may need to be admitted to a hospital or skilled nursing facility at times when his or her family feels "out of control," temporarily unable to provide the necessary level of care. Although home care is not an option for everyone, people who have cared for a terminally ill relative at home usually report that the experience is overwhelmingly positive.

Support Groups

Care of the terminally ill is often supplemented by social support groups that focus on specific interests and needs. Usually composed mainly of volunteers, such groups conduct programs for patients and their families, as well as for health professionals and laypersons. Social support is a key component in coping effectively with the trauma of life-threatening illness.

At the national level, one can find support groups like "I Can Cope," a program originated in 1977 by two oncology nurses at the North Memorial Medical Center of Minneapolis and sponsored by the American Cancer Society.[42] Designed for cancer patients and their families, "I Can Cope" helps participants develop a better understanding of cancer and its treatment, learn to manage side effects, deal with fears and feelings, and improve their sense of physical and emotional well-being. Education is provided through lectures, reading materials, and audiovisual media, as well as through the direct sharing of concerns by participants. The program aims to decrease feelings of helplessness and passivity while increasing self-satisfaction, self-esteem, and confidence.

The Shanti Project is another example of social support programs that exist to aid the terminally ill.[43] Organized by Charles Garfield in 1974, Shanti established a central telephone number that people could call to be put in touch with volunteers willing to aid the dying. From the beginning, the Shanti Project followed a policy of accepting only firsthand referrals, which allowed the organization to focus its efforts on people who request help or information for themselves. Assistance is provided to families as well as patients, and educational outreach is done with community groups and medical staff.

After a referral is made, a Shanti volunteer becomes an advocate for the patient, a role that includes such tasks as emptying ashtrays and cleaning the patient's room, as well as consulting on the patient's behalf with medical personnel and health care agencies. Shanti encourages the use of peer counseling, whereby one patient helps another, and someone who has experienced grief helps an actively grieving person. In recent years, Shanti has focused its attention on helping those with AIDS.

Another example of a community group that provides volunteer-oriented emotional support services is Kara, in Palo Alto, California. Taking its name from the Gothic root of the word *care*—meaning to reach out, to care, and to grieve with—Kara works closely with the nearby Veterans Administration Hospital and with other hospitals and hospices in neighboring communities. Besides counseling dying and bereaved clients, Kara provides training and consulting services to professionals and laypersons and, with the VA Hospice, sponsors an annual conference.

Support groups like the Shanti Project and Kara can be found in most areas of the country. Although the various groups do exhibit distinctive traits

I know that, during my own illness in 1964, my fellow patients at the hospital would talk about matters they would never discuss with their doctors. The psychology of the seriously ill put barriers between us and those who had the skill and the grace to minister to us.

There was first of all the feeling of helplessness—a serious disease in itself.

There was the subconscious fear of never being able to function normally again—and it produced a wall of separation between us and the world of open movement, open sounds, open expectations.

There was the reluctance to be thought a complainer.

There was the desire not to add to the already great burden of apprehension felt by one's family; this added to the isolation.

There was the conflict between the terror of loneliness and the desire to be left alone.

There was the lack of self-esteem, the subconscious feeling perhaps that our illness was a manifestation of our inadequacy.

There was the fear that decisions were being made behind our backs, that not everything was made known that we wanted to know, yet dreaded knowing.

There was the morbid fear of intrusive technology, fear of being metabolized by a data base, never to regain our faces again. There was resentment of strangers who came at us with needles and vials—some of which put supposedly magic substances in our veins, and others which took more of our blood than we thought we could afford to lose. There was the distress of being wheeled through white corridors to laboratories for all sorts of strange encounters with compact machines and blinking lights and whirling discs.

And there was the utter void created by the longing—ineradicable, unremitting, pervasive—for warmth of human contact. A warm smile and an outstretched hand were valued even above the offerings of modern science, but the latter were far more accessible than the former.

Norman Cousins, *Anatomy of an Illness*

and methods, their central mission is substantially similar: They serve an important function in the community by supplementing the services provided through hospice or hospital-based programs of terminal care. This can be illustrated by a closer look at the activities of the Zen Hospice Project, a program of social support established in 1987 under the auspices of the San Francisco Zen Center.[44]

At Zen Hospice Project, volunteers receive extensive training in the fundamentals of hospice work, equipping them to provide practical, emotional, and spiritual support to individuals who are in the final weeks of their lives. About 30 percent of the people served have been diagnosed with cancer; the other 70 percent have AIDS. Each year, some 75 volunteers collectively provide 20,000 hours of care for 250 patients at the Project's Guest House (a homelike residence providing 24-hour care that serves about 30 individuals annually) and at Laguna Honda Hospital (a large public care facility with a 28-bed hospice and AIDS unit). Since its inception, the Project has served about 1400 clients and has trained over 300 volunteers. Supported mainly by charitable donations, Zen Center Hospice has an annual budget of about $300,000. Although the predominant spiritual practice of volunteers is Buddhist, other spiritual traditions are also represented; services are provided without regard for religious or sexual preference, gender, ethnicity, age, national origin, or ability to pay. Inspired by a 2500-year-old tradition, Zen Hospice Project aims to foster awareness and compassion in the lives of caregivers and to provide sensitive care for people approaching death. To this end, each caregiver cultivates the "listening mind" through regular meditation or spiritual practice. Frank Ostaseski, Director of Zen Hospice Project, says: "As hospice workers, one of our central tasks is to be available when stories are ready to be told."[45]

The Patient-Caregiver Relationship

Physicians and other health care providers occupy a place of honor in society. Aesculapius, the first physician according to Greek legend, was elevated to the pantheon of gods and, along with Hygeia and Panacea, ruled over health and illness in Greek mythology.[46] As a realm of activity closely associated with the elemental experiences of birth, life, and death, medicine carries high symbolic importance. But the "Aesculapian authority" of medical practitioners is increasingly being challenged. Criticism often centers on the issue of *paternalism,* the assumption of parentlike authority by medical practitioners who make decisions at the expense of the patient's autonomy or freedom to choose. Along with concerns about patients' rights, there is an evolving emphasis on the "patient as person." Much of the recent concern stems from the "perception that medicine's science is at odds with medicine's art and with its sense of humanism."[47]

The social contract between physicians and patients includes qualities of a *covenantal* relationship, which implies a mutuality of interests between health care providers and patients, and between medical professionals and society. Stanley Joel Reiser suggests that patients' experiences in coping with illness can be usefully employed in shaping the missions of health care.[48] The recognition that we are all engaged in a "web of interhuman reciprocity" provides an access point for enacting true covenantal relationships in medicine.[49] Another avenue for resolving the perceived imbalance between the science and art of medicine is available in George Engel's suggestion that the conventional "biomedical" model of disease be replaced with a "biopsychosocial" model.[50] Such a model would focus not merely on an identifiable disease, but also on "the patient in the life system." To implement Engel's suggestion, the training of physicians must be expanded beyond teaching them "to think of human beings as machines."[51] The biopsychosocial model of illness reflects the ancient view of healing as "restoring wholeness" or, to phrase it in modern systems terms, "restoring equilibrium." This model has application not only to

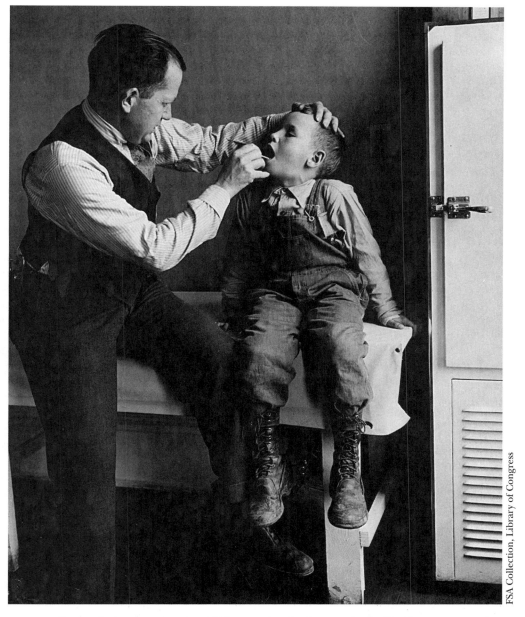

From today's perspective, this 1935 scene of medical care in Reedsville, West Virginia, seems less formal than that found in modern clinics and hospitals. Although the practice of medicine has been enhanced by new methods of diagnosis and treatment, most people still believe that the relationship between physician and patient is central to the outcome of an illness.

patients who expect to recover from their illness, but also to those who face the prospect of dying.

Disclosing a Life-Threatening Diagnosis

If you were diagnosed as having a life-threatening illness, would you want to know about it? Some people answer, "Of course, I want to know about everything that's going on with me!" Others say, "If I could be spared the truth, I'd rather not know that I'm about to die; ignorance is bliss." Consider your own attitudes and preferences with respect to other difficult matters in your life. The person who has spent a lifetime as a perennial fighter against the odds is likely to have a very different response from the person whose typical pattern of coping involves strong efforts to shun stress.

Most people say that they would want to be informed if diagnosed with a life-threatening illness, but the questions of *when* and *how* such information should be delivered may be more difficult to answer. Physicians have an obligation to present the news of a life-threatening diagnosis in a manner that will serve the best interests of the patient. With few guidelines available, doctors must rely on experience. The patient's personality, emotional constitution, and capacity for continued function under stress must all be considered anew in each instance.

Doctors worry that frank knowledge about such a condition might adversely affect a patient's ability to cope. Thus, it could be in the patient's best interest to minimize the threat of the illness. Most physicians subscribe to the belief that it is crucial to offer reassurance and support to the patient, to help the patient maintain hopefulness. The full extent of an illness and its likely consequences may be withheld until the patient or a family member displays a readiness to be told. Although the general facts of an illness are likely to be disclosed voluntarily by physicians, some of the depressing details may be withheld unless the patient takes the initiative by asking questions. A diagnosis of life-threatening illness affects not only the patient but also members of the patient's family. Indeed, sometimes it is a member of the family who learns the truth first. Those who know assume a burden of responsibility, for they must decide what to tell the patient.

Achieving Clear Communication

Once a patient is diagnosed with a life-threatening condition, how should this information be conveyed? Communicating the diagnosis is a critical event in patient care; it can influence a patient's response to treatment, attitude toward the illness, and ability to cope with it constructively. In the initial meeting between physician and patient, what is said depends on a number of factors, including the doctor's preferences for breaking the news about a life-threatening illness to a patient, the patient's receptivity to the facts as presented, and the expected prognosis. During this meeting, the patient should be given a truthful report of the diagnosis and the proposed course of treatment. Information about the disease should be provided, with the

I clearly made Dr. Mueh nervous. He was clearly up to his ears in patients and spread very thin.

He took 90 minutes to talk to me and my wife about my disease. He started out with terminal care and told me I'd get all the narcotics I would need to eliminate pain and that tubes could be used to provide nourishment.

I was amazed that he talked that way, as if I were dying.

Pierre Bowman, *Honolulu Star-Bulletin*

physician giving as much detail as the patient desires. Because this initial meeting between the patient and his or her physician can have an important influence on their subsequent interaction and the type of relationship they maintain during the course of treatment, sufficient time should be made available to fully explore the patient's questions and concerns.[52]

Achieving clear communication in the physician-patient relationship is not automatic. Candace West, a sociologist who conducted a five-year study of how doctors and patients relate to each other, found what she calls a "communications chasm" that hinders the healing process.[53] In particular, she observed a lack of "social cement"—the introductions, greetings, laughter, and use of patient's names—that are part of ordinary social interactions and that help to bring people closer together. West also found that physicians tend to "advance questions which restrict patients' options for answers," while patients tend to be hesitant about asking questions of their doctors. Physicians must "listen" with their eyes as well as their ears, paying attention to the nonverbal communication of gestures and body language that reveal a patient's unease or anxiety about the content of a medical conversation. In the context of modern medicine, highly technical diagnostic and therapeutic interventions can also become obstacles to effective communication.[54]

We expect a great deal of physicians and other caregivers. Although encounters with death and dying may seem routine for health professionals, the human drama of life or death can nevertheless be emotionally affecting. An encounter with death may be fraught with difficulty for the provider as well as the patient. Richard Sandor observes that the knowledge required to master modern medicine, designed to be a haven from confusion, can itself become an instrument of bewilderment. Relatively few caregivers really know anything about death. Sandor says: "We detect subtle disturbances of heart rhythm, manipulate faltering blood pressure to within a few millimeters of mercury, and regulate minute changes in blood chemistry, but what about the person who is dying?"[55]

Communication is an interactive and transactional process: One cannot *not* communicate. Consider the role that nonverbal communication plays in

Generally, the doctor's announcement of the death was made within the first or first two sentences, usually in the course of one long sentence. An interesting feature of his presentation, more common in the DOA situation than in announcements of the deaths of hospital patients, was that in announcing the death he provided, in some way, that the death be presented as having followed a course of "dying." In nearly every scene I witnessed, the doctor's opening remarks contained an historical reference. . . . This was true in accident as well as "natural" deaths, and true whether or not the physician had any basis for assuming a likely cause of death. . . . Physicians seem to feel in such situations that historicizing their delivery of news, no matter how much their limited knowledge of the case may restrict the range of possibilities, helps not only reduce some of the shock value of "sudden deaths" but aids in the very grasp of the news. The correctness of the physician's supposed cause of death is of secondary significance relative to the sheer fact that he provides some sequential formulation of its generation, some means whereby the occurrence can be placed in a sequence of natural or accidental events. This is felt particularly to be necessary in the DOA circumstance, where many deaths occur with no apparent "reason," particularly the so-called "sudden unexpected deaths," not uncommon among young adults.

David Sudnow,
Passing On: The Social Organization of Dying

the health care setting. Such communication includes not only facial expressions, gestures, and body postures, but also *iconics*—that is, objects that convey meaningful information. Labels such as M.D. and R.N., as well as titles such as doctor, nurse, and patient, are examples of symbolic identifiers that can influence the process of communication.[56]

The effect of doctor-patient communication on the patient's well-being was a special concern of Norman Cousins, who wrote about his own experiences with life-threatening ailments, including ankylosing spondylitis and a massive coronary. A serious or life-threatening diagnosis, Cousins said, can be communicated as a "challenge rather than a verdict."[57] Psychoneuroimmunology, an emerging branch of medicine that deals with the interaction of the brain and the immune and endocrine systems, lends credence to Cousins' view that the style of medical communication can exert either a positive attitude, one that promotes faith in the ultimate outcome, or a negative attitude, with corresponding feelings of despondency and despair.[58] If the patient leaves the physician's office in a state of despair, the conditions for effective treatment are impaired. Clear and effective communication between caregiver and patient can play an important role in motivating the patient's own "healing system," thereby creating the potential for a positive outcome regardless of the ultimate prognosis.

The Patient's Story

In learning to think like a medical scientist, I was forgetting the whole patient. To help the patient in times of suffering, the physician must know the patient: not only as a case but as a person. Each patient has a history, a unique story to tell, which goes beyond the information in the medical history. Different patients have different senses of what makes life important to them, what they want out of life, and how far they are willing to go to preserve it. The patient's full story, like any person's story, includes his or her cultural background, childhood circumstances, career, family, religious life, and so on. It includes the patient's self-understanding, appearance, manner of expression, temperament, and character. In short, it includes those attributes that make the patient a person—and not only a person, but this particular person.

Richard B. Gunderman,
"Medicine and the Question of Suffering"

Providing Total Care

The care of seriously ill and dying patients is not limited to merely attending to a patient's physical needs; the patient's personality—a unique combination of mental, emotional, and spiritual needs—must also be considered. Such care requires continuity of contact between at least one caregiver and the patient, opportunity for the patient to remain informed of his or her condition and treatment, participation by the patient in decisions that affect him or her, and behavior by staff members that elicits the patient's trust and confidence.[59] When caregivers follow these guidelines, they provide patient care that is both *personal* and *comprehensive*.

Accommodations can sometimes be made to help patients cope with the inconvenient and bothersome aspects of an illness. For example, treatment schedules may be adjusted in ways that allow patients to continue working or going to school or caring for their families. It is important to recognize that the entire family unit is affected when one of its members requires supportive care. A family is likely to experience a transition of "fading away" as the death of one of its member becomes imminent.[60] The perception of the patient's "fading away" involves a task of redefinition, which requires individuals and families to deal with the burden of letting go of the old before picking up the new. A period of chaos, confusion, fear, and uncertainty may ensue. This may result in feelings of emptiness: "Nothing feels solid anymore." During this period of transition, the family copes with the paradox of caring for a dying loved one while having to carry on with the normal business of living. The model of total care includes attending to the needs of the patient's family (see Table 4-3).

T A B L E *4-3*   *Ways to Meet the Needs of Families*

1. Facilitate discussion and the therapeutic flow of feelings by being aware of nonverbal as well as verbal modes of communication. Caring communication is an important accompaniment to physical care.
2. Alleviate concerns about pain and discomfort. Share information as well as hope.
3. When death is imminent, make a special effort to provide care for the family as well as the patient. Even when a patient is comatose, he or she can be treated as a person worthy of care and attention. Encourage family members to talk to the patient even though he or she is unconscious or otherwise unresponsive. Inform family members about procedures and prepare them for what to expect.
4. After death, as the focus of caregiving turns to meeting the needs of the survivors, keep the lines of communication open. Simple actions—bringing a cup of coffee, making a phone call, just spending time—can be a meaningful demonstration of support and loving affection.

Source: Adapted from Eileen Renear, "Confronting Expected Death," in *Dealing with Death and Dying* (Nursing Skillbook), 2d ed. (Horsham, Pa.: Intermed Communications, 1980), pp. 63–72.

Stress in the Helping Professions

Physicians, nurses, and other health care professionals work in environments where death is more commonplace than it is in most walks of life. This includes "first-responders" such as emergency medical technicians (EMTs), paramedics, and search-and-rescue personnel, as well as firefighters and police officers who provide aid to victims at scenes of an accident or disaster. The impact of working in a death-saturated environment was evident on the faces of rescue personnel in the aftermath of the Oklahoma City disaster in 1995. Caring for seriously ill and dying individuals may make death more familiar, but it may still be stressful.

Besides the stress related to the normal emotional response to the death of another person, caregivers are exposed to stress related specifically to the helping role. The inability to produce a cure may be perceived as an inability to provide adequate care to patients. The most stressful situations are usually those in which caregivers feel helpless, unable to do anything that would make the situation better. Attending to patients who are suffering intractable pain or who are manifestly afraid to die can increase the stress associated with terminal care.[61] Physicians, nurses, and other health care professionals may also experience the "what ifs" when losses occur. If stress is not dealt with appropriately, the result can be harmful.

Trauma Care

Think about the compelling images associated with the emergency room drama of immediate response to life-or-death situations. The pressure to perform is intense. As an ER staffer at one hospital put it, "You can be sitting there almost lulled to sleep during a quiet period, then suddenly everything is

Members of the Newburgh, New York, Volunteer Ambulance Corps are overcome with tears at the end of a memorial held for seven children killed at a local elementary school by a tornado. Emergency personnel who work in closely knit communities often have personal relationships with those they serve, and thus may experience the tragedies that befall their neighbors with special intensity.

© Susan Ragan, AP/Wide World Photos

happening at once because there's just been a five-car crackup.'' Medical interventions must be rapidly and efficiently mobilized if life is to be sustained. For some, the pressure is overwhelming; the rhythms of patient care in other wards may be less stressful. Others gain professional satisfaction from participating in situations in which their skills must be quickly brought to bear to save lives.

Trauma situations may allow no opportunity to establish a relationship with the patient. Emergency room patients are frequently comatose or incoherent due to shock. The ER staff frequently must take action that can make the difference between life and death while receiving little or no feedback from the patient. The patient who survives and is transferred to the intensive care unit may not be seen again by those who labored to sustain his or her life.

When a patient dies, staff members are faced with the task of delivering bad news to relatives and handling their reactions. This task is an underemphasized part of trauma care. Emergency room staff may receive little training in how best to deliver bad news, yet the manner in which such news is conveyed will remain with the survivors and, if handled badly, may leave emotional scars.[62] Usually, news of a patient's death is provided by a doctor, perhaps with other staff members on hand to assist distressed relatives. The communication of such information must be tailored to the situation and the relationship of the person who is told.

Despite the comparative impersonality of the patient-caregiver relationship in trauma care, frequent exposure to death is itself stressful. The notion that everyone can be saved may be a worthy objective, but it is not conducive to coping with the realities of the emergency room. When the circumstances surrounding a death provoke the caregiver's own anxieties about death, or when a death is exceptionally tragic—the death of a child, for example, or the death of a family in an automobile accident on Christmas Eve—caregivers are likely to be affected more profoundly.

Coping with Dying and Death

What constitutes the proper degree of a caregiver's involvement with a patient? How much should a doctor or nurse personally care about a dying patient? Conflicts between emotions and professional responsibilities can contribute to guilt, confusion, and avoidance behavior—all factors that can increase stress. If caring is defined as curing, medical personnel are vulnerable to feelings of failure when a patient dies.[63] To avoid these feelings, caregivers may take refuge in hospital routine and standardized policies. Their desire to avoid being exposed to a patient's pain can create delays in administering medications, adding to confusion and guilt. All of these are symptoms of conflicting emotions caused by uncertainty about what constitutes "proper and correct" involvement with patients. Caregivers may also be uncertain and anxious about feelings of grief experienced in connection with a patient's death.[64]

Once a patient's condition is diagnosed as "terminal," nurses are likely to have more contact with the patient than the patient's physician. Yet the physician's instructions about life-sustaining interventions and related treatment issues significantly influence the type of treatment the patient receives. It is not always possible to "follow doctor's orders." For instance, if a doctor has indicated that medical heroics are to be avoided, who decides whether a particular procedure is "heroic" or "ordinary" in a given set of circumstances? Caregiv-

ers may resent being thrust into what one nursing educator calls "the instrument of death by delegation."[65] Thus, the relationships among members of
the health care team may also contribute to stressful situations.

A study of stress experienced by nurses at a cancer center found a number
of concerns among the caregivers, including feelings of inadequacy, a sense of
isolation from colleagues, questions about the effectiveness of active treatment
for dying patients, reluctance to express these concerns openly because of fear
of criticism and mistrust, and frustration stemming from the failure of physicians to resolve these problems omnipotently. The nurses said that their training had led them to believe there should be answers where often there are
none.[66]

How can caregivers deal with these difficulties? The first step involves
establishing a supportive environment in which death is discussed openly
among those involved in the patients' care. Second, policies should be implemented to mitigate the stresses associated with care of the dying. For example,
opportunities can be provided for caregivers to come together to discuss their
feelings and the issues that arise in connection with terminal care. In one
nursing home, staff members' schedules are rotated so that, when a patient's
death is imminent, someone is with the patient almost constantly. The patient's
family is notified and, if desired, a member of the clergy is called. If no relatives
live nearby, the staff assists in making arrangements for the funeral or disposition of the body. Caregivers who had developed a close relationship with the
patient are given time off to attend funeral services if they wish. Other patients
who express an interest are informed of the death. A short time later, staff
members who cared for the patient in any way—the nursing staff, housekeeping personnel, dietitians, recreational and special service personnel—gather
to discuss their responses to the patient's illness and death. Although there is
no way to completely eliminate stress from the work environment of those who
care for seriously ill and dying patients, it is possible to recognize the presence
of stressful situations and to institute constructive methods for coping with the
stress they experience.

Being with Someone Who Is Dying

People often feel uncomfortable in the presence of a person who has been
diagnosed with a life-threatening illness. What can we say? How ought we to
act? It may seem that anything we might think of to express our feelings is really
little more than a stale platitude. As a result, we may shy away from real
communication. Questions about the illness may be directed to a member of
the patient's family rather than directly to the person who is ill. Discomfort and
uncertainty may be exhibited through either excessive sympathy or obsessive
avoidance.

Life review, a counseling tool used widely with older people, often opens
up possibilities for discussing issues that are of concern to someone facing

> A person's in the room with me and they're very close to dying and afraid. I can feel the fear of death in myself. I'm working through my fear. I give them an opportunity, silent though it may be, to work through theirs. If I come into a room saying, "Oh, there's nothing to be afraid of. We go through death and then into another rebirth," that's not very useful. That's a way of not dealing with the power of the moment— the suffering in that room in the fellow on the bed, and the suffering in the mind of the fellow next to the bed.
>
> Stephen Levine, *A Gradual Awakening*

death. Reviewing the course of one's life can help empower individuals to make choices they value in completing the last chapter of their lives.[67] By reviewing past relationships and events, the person is given an opportunity to finish up unfinished business. The informal use of supportive techniques such as life review provides a means for friends and family members to offer encouragement and support to someone who is facing death.[68]

Being with someone who is seriously ill or dying, we confront our own mortality. We appreciate how precious life is and how uncertain. Such a context offers us a special opportunity to share the deepest part of ourselves. What is shared may well be anger, frustration, pain, guilt, blame, or denial. But few opportunities in life present us with the chance to be as vulnerable, to touch and express aspects of ourselves that are usually kept hidden. In an account of her mother's illness and death, Janmarie Silvera describes how the blossoming of a "huge, luminous full moon" through a hospital window becomes an occasion of "wonderment," a moment of intimacy that acknowledges both life and death.[69]

Further Readings

Daniel Callahan. *What Kind of Life: The Limits of Medical Progress.* New York: Simon & Schuster, 1990.

Arthur L. Caplan. *If I Were a Rich Man Could I Buy a Pancreas? And Other Essays on the Ethics of Health Care.* Bloomington: Indiana University Press, 1992.

Deborah Chase. *Dying at Home with Hospice.* St. Louis: C. V. Mosby, 1986.

Norman Cousins. *The Physician in Literature.* Philadelphia: Saunders, 1982.

Harold L. Klawans. *Life, Death, and in Between: Tales of Clinical Neurology.* New York: Paragon House, 1992.

Melvin Konner. *Medicine at the Crossroads: The Crisis in Health Care.* New York: Pantheon, 1993.

Vincent Mor, David S. Greer, and Robert Kastenbaum, eds. *The Hospice Experiment.* Baltimore: Johns Hopkins University Press, 1988.

Balfour Mount. "Whole Person Care: Beyond Psychosocial and Physical Needs," *American Journal of Hospice and Palliative Care* 10, no. 1 (1993): 28–37.

Carol Pogash. *As Real As It Gets: The Life of a Hospital at the Center of the AIDS Epidemic.* New York: Birch Lane Press, 1992.

Anselm Strauss, Shizuko Fagerhaugh, Barbara Suczek, and Carolyn Wiener. *Social Organization of Medical Work.* Chicago: University of Chicago Press, 1985.

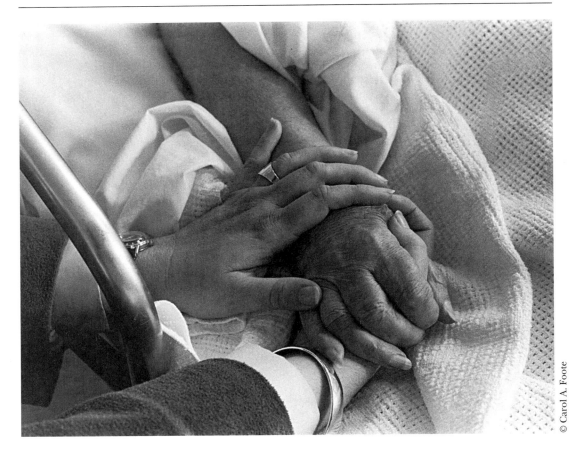

Total care for the patient with a life-threatening illness includes warm, intimate contact with caring persons who are able to listen and share the patient's concerns.

Facing Death: Living with Life-Threatening Illness

*C*ancer. Heart disease. AIDS. For most of us these words send frightening repercussions echoing through the corridors of our minds. The famous, as well as our friends and relatives, die from these illnesses. To many people, cancer seems virtually synonymous with death and dying, though in fact the prognosis for a cancer patient is not always death. Similarly, heart disease—the leading cause of death for Americans—encompasses a number of specific ailments, many of which can be treated with sophisticated medical technologies ranging from drug therapies to heart transplantation.

In this chapter, we examine the experience of facing life-threatening illness and discuss various ways of responding to it, both medically and personally. Although cancer is preeminent in many people's minds as "the" long-term, life-threatening illness, the circumstances faced by individuals with other life-threatening diseases are much the same. Patients diagnosed with heart disease, cerebrovascular disease, acquired immune deficiency syndrome (AIDS), and other serious illnesses encounter similar kinds of medical and nursing care, methods of coping, and support systems. Thus, although the discussion in this chapter focuses primarily on cancer and heart disease, what is said here applies generally to other life-threatening illnesses as well.

We begin by investigating the taboo of life-threatening illness, which causes many people to avoid discussing it. How does this taboo affect the patient's ability to cope?

Next we investigate the personal and social costs of life-threatening illness. The heart of the chapter is then devoted to an exploration of the meaning of life-threatening illness for persons who receive such a diagnosis and the methods they use to cope with it. Following a discussion of the dying trajectory, the chapter concludes by examining the social role of the dying patient.

The Taboo of Life-Threatening Illness

A patient with acute leukemia compared her experience to that of someone with the Black Death during the fourteenth century in Europe. The origin of the disease in one's body is somewhat mysterious, the result of factors not easily discernible or completely understood. Nature seems somehow to have gotten out of control, and, though not fully comprehending the chain of events that led to such bleak fortunes, the patient feels a responsibility to put things right.

Magical thinking—assuming oneself responsible though it's unclear just how—places a great burden on the patient with a life-threatening illness: "What did I do to bring this condition upon myself? If I had done this, or not done that, maybe I wouldn't be in this predicament." Throughout this self-questioning, the patient may feel a pervasive sense of helplessness, a sense of trying to combat unknown natural forces that have gone awry, forces that seem bent on destroying one's body.

Besides self-deprecation, the patient is likely to feel the effects of the social stigma associated with the disease. Many people tend to avoid the person who has a life-threatening illness, almost as if they feared it might be catching, even when they know it is not. More likely, we might catch a sense of the confrontation with death. This confrontation with death exposes our fear of loss and separation from all that we love, our fear of pain, and the imagined horror of dying. It shatters our image of ourselves and our plans for the future.

Heart disease is often thought of as a disease of superachievers, people who are goal-oriented and whose lives are active and filled with accomplishments. Cancer, on the other hand, is often portrayed as the uncontrollable madness of the body's cells gone wild—the body devouring itself from within. The cancer patient is seen as passive and powerless. In fact, however, both heart disease and cancer affect all manner of people. Both illnesses are found at all strata of income and in all occupations, among people of widely divergent life styles. AIDS, too, is a disease that affects people in all walks of life, even though it first came to public attention in this country mainly in populations of homosexual men and intravenous drug users.

Personal and Social Costs of Life-Threatening Illness

Although the mortality rate from heart disease has been declining, it remains the leading cause of death in the United States, accounting for 915,000 deaths in 1992, or about 40 percent of all deaths (see Figure 5-1).[1]

When I first realized that I might have cancer, I felt immediately that I had entered a special place, a place I came to call "The Land of the Sick People." The most disconcerting thing, however, was not that I found that place terrifying and unfamiliar, but that I found it so ordinary, so banal. I didn't feel different, didn't feel that my life had radically changed at the moment the word *cancer* became attached to it. The same rules still held. What had changed, however, was other people's perceptions of me. Unconsciously, even with a certain amount of kindness, everyone—with the single rather extraordinary exception of my husband—regarded me as someone who had been altered irrevocably. I don't want to exaggerate my feeling of alienation or to give the impression that it was in any way dramatic. I have no horror stories of the kind I read a few years ago in the *New York Times;* people didn't move their desks away from me at the office or refuse to let their children play with my children at school because they thought that cancer was catching. My friends are all too sophisticated and too sensitive for that kind of behavior. Their distance from me was marked most of all by their inability to understand the ordinariness, the banality of what was happening to me. They marveled at how well I was "coping with cancer." I had become special, no longer like them.

Alice Stewart Trillin,
"Of Dragons and Garden Peas:
A Cancer Patient Talks to Doctors"

Cancer, the second leading cause of death in the United States, caused about 521,000 deaths in 1992. In 1900, about one of every twenty-seven deaths was attributable to cancer; it now accounts for roughly one in five. Whereas the death rate from heart disease is declining, it appears that some individuals saved from that disease are now dying from cancer.[2]

In addition to costly medical care, patients with life-threatening diseases such as heart disease and cancer face loss of earnings as well as repeated and sometimes lengthy hospitalization. Emotional havoc accompanies the discovery that one has a life-threatening illness: mental and emotional anguish, pain and discomfort, fear, a sense of hopelessness, depression and anxiety, feelings of loneliness. The patient's family shares this burden. Indeed, looking at the family as a "system," we see that, as the illness affects the family life of the patient, the changed family circumstances have a reciprocal impact on the physically ill patient.[3]

Society also pays a high price. Public as well as private funds are allocated to programs of research, education, prevention, and care. There are indirect costs as well. When a seriously ill patient can no longer work or fulfill social responsibilities, there are resulting social costs related to decreased productivity and the retraining of workers.

For the patient, fears excited by the prospect of undergoing treatment may compound the anxieties related to the disease itself. Patients with a life-threatening illness may fear the loss of their sexual functioning or

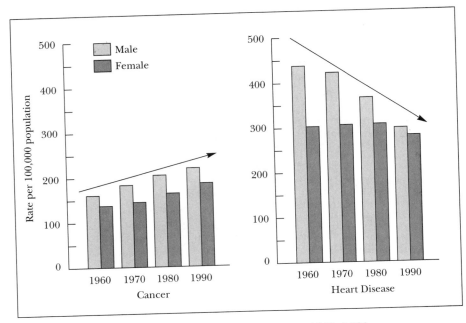

Figure 5-1   *Death Rates from Cancer and Heart Disease, 1960–1990*
Source: Bureau of the Census, *Statistical Abstract of the United States 1994,* pp. 98–99.

attractiveness, either as a direct result of the disease or as a side effect of the treatment. Self-concept is intimately related to sexual identity. Consider, for example, the importance of the face in interpersonal relationships. Facial cancer patients confront anxieties related not only to the disease but also to their interactions with others, including their intimate, sexual relationships. In learning to live with a clearly visible mutilation, such patients need social support in adapting to a new self-image.[4] The possibility of disfigurement or a reduction in physical abilities raises concerns about the integrity of the body that must be considered within the context of a person's whole psychosocial sexual role.

For instance, a man who derives his sense of virility and masculinity from his work role may become sexually dysfunctional if illness makes it impossible for him to keep his job. A feeling that he is "less of a man" in one area of his life may become generalized to other parts of his life, including his sexual identity. Or a woman whose breast is removed because of cancer may worry that she is less of a woman—less able to fulfill her role as a wife or mother, or, indeed, to function in business or social settings. Conversely, a patient who has been diagnosed as having a terminal condition may become compulsively preoccupied with sex, feeling that within the limited time remaining it is all the more important to produce offspring or to maximize sexual experiences. Whether problems with sexual identity are manifest in avoidance or in compulsive activity, they can have a tremendous effect on the patient's self-concept and his or her relationships with others.

Self-concept encompasses our attitudes, beliefs, thoughts, feelings, goals, fears, fantasies, personal history, sense of self-worth, body image, and psychosexual roles. Although self-concept is learned, and thus changeable, the least flexible aspects of self-concept are those relating to body image, sexuality, and work. The presence of serious illness dramatically affects each of these aspects of a person's self-concept.

Few patients are ever completely free of the fear that the disease may someday return, even when a cure is apparently successful.[5] The conflict and stress, and indeed panic, arising from the confrontation with death that a life-threatening illness presents, the adjustments in life style and psychosocial role necessitated by such an illness and its treatment—such experiences are common to most seriously ill patients. Nevertheless, much can be done to alleviate the stress, anxiety, and uncertainty that typically accompany life-threatening illness.

Therapeutic tools—including education, counseling, support groups, and communication skills—can be brought to bear on the experience of life-threatening illness. Gaining information about the disease and its treatment, sharing experiences with others in an atmosphere of mutual support, using counseling services to clarify personal and emotional issues, and developing ways of communicating more effectively with caregivers as well as family members and friends—all these are examples of positive approaches that can be taken in dealing with life-threatening illness.[6] These techniques can promote an understanding that places the crisis in a more affirmative context, making one's experience less confusing and melodramatic, and restoring a sense of personal control over the situation.

The Experience of Life-Threatening Illness

Imagine one day you wake up and notice symptoms in your body that you associate with cancer. What goes through your mind? Perhaps you just barely admit to yourself the possibility that you're sick. Then you quickly push away such thoughts and go about your day's activities. "After all," you say, "there's no reason to suspect it's anything serious; it's probably just some minor infection."

You forget about it for a while. But, more and more persistently, the symptoms you noticed become demanding of your attention. "This better not be anything serious," you tell yourself, "I've got too much to do." Yet, part of you recognizes that it really might be serious. You admit your concern, starting to feel a bit anxious about what the symptoms might mean.

So you make an appointment with your doctor, describe your symptoms, submit to an examination, and wait for the results. Perhaps right away, or maybe only after additional tests are ordered, you learn the diagnosis. Your doctor informs you that you have a tumor, a malignancy. Cancer.

I'm forty. So, obviously things happened to me before I came in here. . . . I was married—I had a wife, and I had a son. But my wife divorced me. I was served with the papers the day I went to the hospital for the operation. My son will be twelve this October, I guess. I've never seen him since.

In the beginning, I was bewildered-like. I didn't know what the hell was happening to me. I didn't know what was wrong. And I kept going from doctor to doctor—and getting worse all the time. Slipping and slipping. I was like up in a cloud—and I was cross then. And bitter. I couldn't see why God had made such a big decision on me. I saw my brothers and sisters walking around so healthy-like—and I couldn't understand why it had happened to me and not to them. Things like that. . . . But, after a while, I decided you've got to take what the Lord decides, and make the best of it. . . .

Quoted in Renee Fox,
Experiment Perilous

Now your thoughts and emotions really become agitated. "What will the doctors do for me? How are they going to treat this illness? What kind of changes will I have to make in my life? Should I postpone the trip I've been planning? What about the pain? What course of treatment should be followed? Are there side effects? Can they even cure this kind of cancer? Will I die?"

As the drama unfolds, you begin to find ways of coping with this new crisis. Your earlier fears about the symptoms are transformed into concerns about the diagnosis, treatment, and outcome of the illness. You wonder how your life will be affected and what kind of adjustments you will have to make.

As time passes, perhaps you experience a remission: The tumor seems to have stopped growing. The doctors give you optimistic reports. Still, you wonder whether the cancer is really gone for good or just temporarily. You feel like someone in limbo. You're happy that things seem to be going well, but your optimism is mixed with uncertainty and fear. Perhaps after a while you begin to relax and feel less anxious about the cancer's returning. It seems "your" cancer was curable.

On the other hand, you may sooner or later again notice the onset of symptoms. If the cancer is declared incurable, you may fear metastasis, the spreading of the cancer to other areas of your body. Now you wrestle with the questions, "Is it going to be painful? What organs will eventually be affected? How long do I have to live?"

This scenario, though in many ways typical, is experienced differently by different patients. Some cancers can be cured by relatively minor forms of treatment. Other cancers persist for a time and then, with treatment, diminish or become stabilized. The prognosis in other cases offers little hope for survival. To whatever degree cancer is perceived as a threat to one's well-being, this scenario is likely to resemble the cancer patient's actual experience and, by extension, the experience of anyone with a life-threatening illness.

Once the disease is judged incurable, the patient's fears may focus on the uncertainty surrounding dying and death. These fears probably have been present from the first, underlying the changing concerns about symptoms, diagnosis, and treatment. Yet when cancer was nothing more than a possibility represented by a particular set of symptoms, attention was directed to what the symptoms might mean. After the diagnosis is learned and as treatment progresses, the fear of death becomes more present, though it is still mitigated by the need to carry out all the various activities that accompany the role of being a patient with a life-threatening illness. Fear is balanced by hope.

As death confronts us squarely, we may yet hope for some last-minute remission, some change for the better that the doctors haven't foreseen. We may fight to the end, thinking, "I've always outwitted the percentages. Why not now?" Or we may cope with the end of life in a very different way, taking charge as much as possible of the remaining time, surrounding ourselves with those closest to us, and accepting our dying. The way each of us copes with dying will likely reflect the ways we've coped with living, the ways we've coped with other losses and changes in our lives.

Coping with Life-Threatening Illness

Undoubtedly the best-known description of the emotional and psychological responses to life-threatening illness is the one recorded by Elisabeth Kübler-Ross on the basis of her work with dying patients.[7] These responses may include denial, anger, bargaining, depression, and acceptance. In an idealized model, an early period of shock, disbelief, and denial eventually gives way to some degree of acceptance. However, a variety of coping mechanisms may be employed to prevent full recognition and acknowledgment of the truth. When confronted by death or loss, a person may respond with avoidance or denial of the truth, or by suppressing or excluding it from consciousness. Setting oneself apart from thoughts or actions that might bring a recognition of the truth— that is, dissociating oneself from it—is another coping mechanism that may come into play when a person faces an unwelcome reality.

Even after the predicament has been acknowledged, however, there is often considerable anger, vulnerability, and dependency. The anger is often manifest as displaced hostility: "Okay, maybe I could've done something to keep this from happening to me, but, damn it, if it isn't safe, why doesn't the government put a stop to it!" Caregivers often become the object of such displaced hostility. The patient's anger at being ill might be displayed in complaints about food or other aspects of care: "Why can't you fix me a good cup of tea? You know I can't do it for myself!" Such coping mechanisms, difficult and possibly painful for patient and caregiver alike, serve to mask the underlying problem: the confrontation with the illness itself and what it portends.

Bargaining, or attempting to strike a deal with fate or with God, is yet another common response. The patient tries to discover some way to enter an

"Bloom County," drawing by Berke Breathed, © 1985 by Washington Post Writers Group

agreement that may postpone the inevitable. Perhaps "good behavior" may be exchanged for an extension of life. Whatever the particulars of the attempt to bargain, such efforts represent a quest to alleviate suffering and to postpone the dreaded outcome.

As the symptoms of illness become stronger and the body weakens, the effort to remain stoic in the face of reality may be replaced by a sense of loss and depression. The sense of loss engendered by the prospect of death may be made heavier by the burdens of treatment and hospitalization, as well as by the financial costs resulting from the illness and by the many disruptions that occur in one's personal life, including the areas of job and family. Kübler-Ross differentiated two kinds of depression: the first, a *reactive* depression to the kinds of issues just described; and the second, a *preparatory* depression that "the terminally ill patient has to undergo in order to prepare himself for his final separation from this world."

After the initial responses—"Oh, no, it can't be me! I don't want to hear about it! Those test results must be for someone else; they got mixed up!"—comes acknowledgment of one's situation: "Yes, I am seriously ill, and I've got to deal with that fact in the best way I can." After a time, many patients come to some acceptance of their situation. They are able to explore more dispassionately its inherent issues and possibilities, and they begin to establish productive ways of dealing with the changed circumstances of their lives. When ready to discuss these concerns, the patient needs a good listener, someone who can be present without judging or trying to persuade the patient to think or feel otherwise.

If the patient is able to confront the fact of illness and find ways of coping with the eventuality it represents, then chances are he or she will experience some resolution of the crisis. Acceptance does not mean giving up or losing hope; rather, it implies coming to an essentially positive, personally satisfying adjustment. Consider the words of Harold Brodkey as he faces the prospect of dying from AIDS:

66—Real Estate Wanted

FORMER President — Major Manufacturing Company. age 56, with possible terminal disease interested in lease purchase of old home. Reasonably large. Farm house with property, condos, land with run down cabin or home in total disrepair. Probably in foothills between Santa Cruz and Castroville. Option period 18 months or final diagnosis — whichever is first. Any remodeling by permission of owner in his name. Will arrive from Seattle on Tuesday evening. Please leave number at Box 9, c/o this newspaper.

Figure 5-2 *Life Change with Life-Threatening Illness: Real Estate Want Ad*
The confrontation with a life-threatening illness may activate desires to accomplish in the present plans that previously had been visualized as occurring in the future.

Source: Register-Pajaronian (Watsonville, Calif.), March 11, 1981.

I have liked my life. I like my life at present, being ill. I like the people I deal with. I don't feel I am being whisked off the stage or murdered and stuffed in a laundry hamper while my life is incomplete. It's my turn to die—I can see that that is interesting to some people but not that it is tragic. Yes, I was left out of some things and was cheated over a lifetime in a bad way but who isn't and so what? I had a lot of privileges as well. Sometimes I'm sad about its being over but I'm that way about books and sunsets and conversations.[8]

Each person's adjustment is unique, determined by such factors as the patient's personality, the kind of helping resources available in his or her environment, and the specific nature of the illness (see Figure 5-2).

These stages of coping with illness should not be thought of as strict categories that occur in a fixed sequence. A variety of emotions—anger, resentment, sadness, acceptance—may be experienced at any time during the process of dealing with illness and the prospect of death. Although there may be movement from initial shock and anger toward eventual acceptance of the situation, a patient who has exhibited great acceptance of his or her death may die raging against the inevitable. Conversely, the angry fighter may find quiet resignation in the final moments of life, dying a peaceful death.

In addition, the adaptive response to loss can vary as circumstances change. Herman Feifel says, "Coping with a life-threatening illness or death threat varies in significant fashion not only among differing groups but among situations."[9] Throughout the experience of coping with the changes caused by life-threatening illness—from the moment one notices the symptoms and wonders what they mean to the final moments awaiting death—hope and honesty exist in a delicate balance unique to each person: honesty to face

Dear Friends,

In company with our dear Mother Earth, I have arrived at the time of autumn in my worldly life, that time of transition between life and death. Before long, just as the leaves drop from the trees to continue Life's cycle of generation and regeneration, so will my body be shed and become part of the muttering earth. Like the tree gathering in energy to prepare itself for winter, I feel a need to gather energy for the process of dying. Also, I want to share a last celebration with you dear friends. To do this, I have planned a ritual of transition to take place on Sunday, November 3, at 2:30 p.m. here at my home.

I would love it if you can participate with your presence; and if you cannot, I would appreciate your joining us in spirit with loving energy via the ethers that afternoon.

If you can come, please bring a pillow to sit on and a symbolic gift of your energy and blessing for me in this process I am going through--something from nature (rock, shell, feather, etc.); a poem, picture or song; something written or drawn; or whatever you are inspired to bring. Please also bring a casserole, salad or dessert or beverage to contribute to our potluck supper following the ritual.

There is a new joy that is beginning to be realized in me as I acknowledge the prospect of having my spirit float free of my tired body. I look forward to sharing this with you too.

Love and blessings,

Joan Conn

Figure 5-3 *Invitation to a Going-Away Party*

Ritual and companionship can assist in dealing with impending death. This celebration was attended by close friends and family, who said the occasion was an extremely moving experience. Knowing that she would soon die from cancer, Joan created a ritual that involved drawing a line on the floor and, in her weakened condition, she was helped across it by her ex-husband and her children while members of the gathering played music and sang. Although such an event would not be appropriate for everyone, Joan's farewell party aptly reflected her life style and values. She died seven months later.

TABLE 5-1   *Four Primary Dimensions in Coping with Dying*

1. *Physical.* Involves satisfying bodily needs and minimizing physical distress in ways consistent with other values.
2. *Psychological.* Involves maximizing psychological security, autonomy, and richness in living.
3. *Social.* Involves sustaining and enhancing significant interpersonal relationships; and addressing the social implications of dying.
4. *Spiritual.* Involves identifying, developing, or reaffirming sources of spiritual energy or meaning and, in so doing, fostering hope.

Source: Adapted from Charles A. Corr, "A Task-Based Approach to Coping with Dying," *Omega: Journal of Death and Dying* 24 (1991–1992): 81–94.

reality as it is, hope that the outcome is positive. It is interesting to note how the object of hope changes. The initial hope that nothing is really wrong gives way to hope that there will be a cure. If the disease seems incurable, then one hopes for more time. When time runs out, one hopes for a pain-free and comfortable death, a good death (see Figure 5-3).

The stage-based model of coping with dying devised by Kübler-Ross has been an important stimulus to increasing our understanding of dying and death; it has directed caregivers and lay people alike to thoughtful consideration of issues related to dying patients, as well as to the universal human confrontation with death. However, since its introduction almost three decades ago, scholars and practitioners have issued warnings against using the model indiscriminately. Charles Corr points out, for example, that using the model in a rote manner can "erect obstacles to individualization," thereby "risking stereotyping vulnerable individuals who are coping with dying."[10] As an alternative, or amplification, of what has become the conventional model, Corr offers a task-based approach that distinguishes four primary dimensions in coping with dying (see Table 5-1). Corr says, "There is no single right way to cope with dying, although there may be better, worse, and even unacceptable models from the standpoint of those involved."

Awareness of Dying

In observing family interactions in response to life-threatening illness, sociologists Barney Glaser and Anselm Strauss noted four distinctive ways in which a context of awareness is established and maintained with respect to a dying patient.[11] These contexts of awareness include both the content and the style of communication.

In the *closed awareness* context, the dying person does not recognize that death is impending, although other people may know. In general, closed awareness does not allow for communication about the illness or the probability of death.

In the *suspected awareness* context, the patient suspects that the prognosis is death, but this is not verified by those who know. The dying person may try to confirm or deny his or her suspicions by testing family members, friends,

I remember her as she lay in her hospital bed in July. Unable finally to deny the pain. And for the first time in our relationship of 21 years forced to allow someone else to take care of her. My father could not stand the sight and so he stayed outside, pacing up and down in the hallways. I could not help staring at her. Disbelief that this person with tubes running in and out like entrances and exits on a freeway was the same woman who just six months before had laughed gaily and danced at my wedding.

Ruth Kramer Ziony,
"Scream of Consciousness"

and medical personnel in an effort to elicit information known by others but not openly shared. Despite the secrecy, however, the patient is aware that the illness is severely disrupting the family's usual style of relating, and may sense others' fearfulness or anxiety about his or her condition, thus tending to confirm the suspicions in the patient's mind.

The *mutual pretense* context can be likened to a dance in which participants sidestep a direct confrontation about the patient's condition. Typically, this involves complicated, though usually unspoken, rules of behavior designed to sustain the illusion that the patient is getting well. With mutual pretense, everyone—including the patient—recognizes the fact that death will be the outcome, but all act as if the patient will recover. Mutual pretense may be practiced right to the end, despite any violation of unspoken rules that might have prompted disclosure of the patient's true condition.

Underlying mutual pretense is the notion that everyone should strive to avoid "dangerous" or "threatening" topics. Such topics include facts about the disease and prognosis, medical procedures, other patients' deaths, and future plans and events. Obviously, this eliminates from discussion a considerable portion of the family's current experience. The pattern of mutual pretense usually begins early; subtle signals are communicated among participants that the method being used to cope with the crisis is to pretend that things are normal.

When something threatens to break the fiction and disclose the reality of the situation, the parties to mutual pretense act as if the threatening event did not occur. Distancing strategies may be called upon to preserve the illusion that the person is not seriously ill—typically by avoiding interactions that threaten disclosure of the truth. Children may respond to the risk of disclosure by becoming angry or withdrawn; adults may excuse themselves by saying they need to go out for a walk or make a phone call. In the short term, the strategies used in mutual pretense can be useful in coping with a difficult and painful situation.

Glaser and Strauss's fourth designation, the context of *open awareness*, describes situations in which the likelihood of death is acknowledged and discussed. Such openness does not necessarily make death easier to accept, but it offers the possibility of sharing support in ways that would not otherwise be available.

The awareness context is a crucial element in determining the interaction among medical and nursing staff, family members, and the patient. As new information is presented to the patient or family members, the awareness context may change. For example, a context of closed awareness or mutual pretense may prevail throughout a succession of medical procedures. Then, with news of yet another series of tests or a new treatment program, the illness may be acknowledged as life threatening. At that point, the awareness context may shift from closed or suspected to open.

Creating a context of open awareness does not necessarily mean the situation will be easier or that one will cope more successfully. At times, it may make coping more difficult, because the option to distance oneself from the experience by avoidance or denial is less available. Open awareness is not a static or unchanging condition; the awareness context may be variable, with transitions from comparative openness to greater closure or mutual pretense, depending upon the intensity of the immediate experience and the capacity or desire of the persons involved to cope with that reality.

Congruency of—that is, agreement between—beliefs and actions is an important determinant of how a crisis is experienced. When your beliefs and actions are congruent, you are more likely to cope successfully with a crisis. If, in your value system, a style of mutual pretense is viewed as useful in coping with threatening or discomforting situations, and if such a style of communication is customary in your family's interactions, then pretense may be an effective means of coping with crises. Suppose, conversely, that you value openness and honesty, and your family has always been scrupulously honest with one another. If a family member is dying, yet everyone is pretending that the crisis really doesn't exist—that the person is getting well—then anxiety is likely to be made even more unbearable by the conflict between beliefs and actions.

Maintaining Coping Potency

It has long been a truism in medicine that hope plays a key part in a patient's ability to cope with illness. When a patient is seen as a passive participant, merely following the program outlined by the physician, options that rightfully belong to the patient may be unwittingly taken away. How a patient is perceived by his or her caregivers is important. It influences the patient's access to resources that he or she may need to cope with the realities of serious illness. When a patient is treated as a whole person, his or her sense of self-worth and dignity is enhanced. As the patient's preferences are respected, he or she is further empowered to make choices that embody a sense of purpose.[12]

The capacity to maintain a sense of self-worth, to set goals and strive to meet them, to exercise choice out of an awareness of one's power to meet

We've got this 17-month-old rascal in the other room that right now is getting recharged. His battery pack is nuclear. I want to grow up with him, I want to be able to play with him, I want to throw the ball and do the things that my father was unable to do with me because of his time schedule. I would love to teach him how to ski and do all the things that I would really like to do. I think that's one of the things that keeps me fighting against my disease. I probably want to do it more for my benefit than for his at this particular time.

Don

challenges, to engage in active interactions with one's environment—all of these reflect a "coping potency" that sustains the will to live in the face of death. It is said, for example, that both John Adams and Thomas Jefferson managed to live until July 4, 1826, the fiftieth anniversary of the signing of the Declaration of Independence; and, according to Jefferson's physician, his last words were, "Is it the Fourth?"

Essential to maintaining a positive attitude under the stress of life-threatening illness is the patient's self-image. Those who interact with the patient can be critical in this regard. Their fears and misconceptions about serious illness can significantly affect the patient's perception of his or her physical condition and self-worth. The late Orville Kelly, founder of Make Today Count, described his own response and the reactions of others after he was diagnosed with cancer.[13] Given a prognosis of six months to six years to live, Kelly was depressed and contemplated suicide, fearing that he might become a burden to his family. Relatives and friends began to show signs of being uncomfortable in his presence. One woman asked his wife, "How is he?"—despite the fact that Kelly was just a few feet away. Though alive, he was being subjected to a kind of social death, his full humanity already being written off by uneasy friends and relatives.

Despite the frightening prognosis, Kelly soon realized that in fact he was still alive. He could still love and be loved. No matter how short a time he might have to live, he could make the best of each day. Each person—whether or not he or she is diagnosed with a terminal illness—faces the challenge of making each day count. Recognizing that the mortality of every generation is ultimately 100 percent, Kelly began talking openly about his feelings and expressing the concerns of someone with a terminal illness. An article he wrote for his local newspaper elicited such a response that it led to the formation of Make Today Count, a nationwide support group for the terminally ill. Support groups like Make Today Count offer terminal patients and their families a comfortable and supportive environment where they are free to express themselves about the impact of life-threatening illness in their lives.

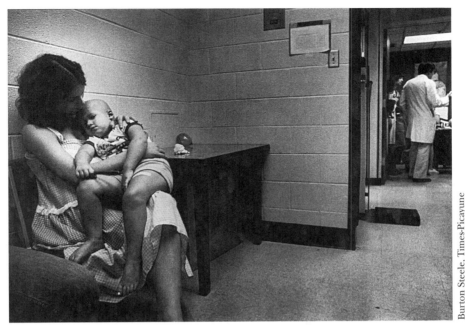

Burton Steele, Times-Picayune

With her seriously ill daughter, this mother waits for the test results that will help determine the next step in care and treatment.

Treatment Options and Issues

The treatment options for life-threatening illness depend on the nature of the disease and the patient's particular situation. As new medical technologies become available, treatment options may change drastically. Typically, however, medical advances occur gradually, steadily increasing the choices available to patients. For example, among the new technologies for diagnosing heart problems is an advance in computer tomography that allows stop-action photos to be taken of the beating heart. The device allows cardiologists to measure and analyze data about the heart's functioning that otherwise could be obtained only through invasive and expensive procedures such as catheterization.

The options available for treatment depend not only on the nature of the disease and the medical technologies available to treat it, but also on decisions made by society at large. The treatment for sudden cardiac death, a subset of coronary heart disease, is a case in point.[14] Of the 1.5 million heart attacks suffered by Americans each year, about three-quarters of the victims are admitted to hospitals, where they receive advanced care; of these patients, more than 80 percent survive and are discharged. Often, however, a heart attack is the first indication of any coronary problem. The key to life-saving intervention in cases of sudden heart attack and similar emergencies is a rapid and coordinated medical response. In communities that have placed a high priority on providing this kind of response and where emergency personnel are equipped with cardiac care units, fatalities have declined. Such care can be costly, however. Thus, a community's ability or willingness to pay for this kind of care can affect a patient's options for treatment.

Ethical issues must sometimes be resolved before a new therapy can be applied widely. The artificial heart is an example. Although artificial hearts and heart-assist devices have been implanted in more than 200 patients worldwide, many of them as "bridges" to a heart transplant provided by a donor, serious questions remain concerning the fairness of the selection process and whether such patients can understand sufficiently what is in store for them before they give their informed consent to the procedure.[15] Although proponents say the artificial heart could extend the lives of many people, critics respond that it does not really save patients' lives—it only changes the way they die. Economic questions also must be considered in making decisions about a proposed therapy. Again using the artificial heart as an example, with perhaps 35,000 potential candidates for the device each year in the United States, at a cost of $150,000 per implant, the procedure could add $5 billion to the nation's health bill. Critics argue that this money could be better spent on health education aimed at preventing heart disease; proponents point out, however, that this cost is not any greater than the amount Americans spend each year on video games. Thus, innovative therapies often bring with them questions that are not amenable to easy or quick resolution.

Current research in cancer treatment suggests promising roles for recombinant DNA technology and for "monoclonal antibodies" that can be tailored to attack selected targets on cancer cells. With greater understanding of disease processes and improved diagnostic procedures, there is increasingly better "staging" of the disease to determine its precise characteristics and when to apply appropriate therapies. In the management of serious illnesses, emphasis is being placed on individualized treatment. Although different illnesses require forms of treatment specific to each, the options available to patients can be illustrated by focusing on the treatment modalities associated with cancer.

As a general term, *cancer* encompasses many different types of malignant, or potentially lethal, growths that occur in many parts of the body. Because cancerous cells reproduce in a manner unregulated by the body's normal controls on cell growth, over time there is the possibility of unlimited expansion. First affecting tissues in one part of the body, cancer may spread either by invading adjacent tissues or by *metastasis,* a process whereby diseased cells travel in the blood or lymph system or through body tracts, to more distant parts of the body.[16] Successful treatment of cancer requires the destruction or removal of all cancerous tissue; otherwise, the disease recurs.

A number of therapies—primarily surgery, radiation therapy, and chemotherapy—have been applied to the management of cancer. But none is

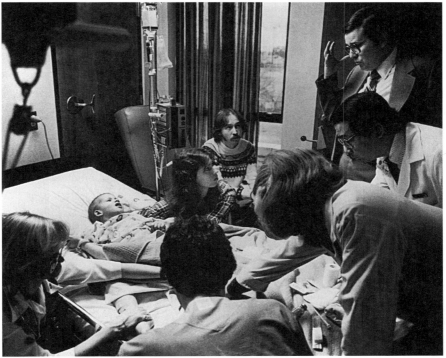

Burton Steele, Times-Picayune

Family members and consulting physicians gathered around the bedside of a seriously ill child discuss the impending brain surgery that everyone hopes will bring a favorable prognosis.

effective for all of the forms in which cancer may appear in the body. A treatment with a high rate of success with one type of cancer may be ineffective with another. Frequently, a combination of therapies is recommended, each designed to accomplish a particular aim within a comprehensive treatment program. Some treatments of life-threatening illness create the need for adjunctive therapies to counteract the side effects of the primary mode of treatment. As we discuss the various methods of treating cancer, the benefits and disadvantages of each type of therapy will be emphasized, along with its effects on the patient's experience. (Key terms used in conjunction with the treatment of cancer and other diseases are defined in Table 5-2.)

Surgery

The greatest percentage of cancer cures has been due to the use of surgery. Indeed, most of the progress in cancer survival has come about because of improvements in surgical techniques and in preoperative and postoperative care, especially in control of infection. At present, surgery has

T A B L E 5-2   *Medical Treatment Word List*

Alkylating agents: A family of chemotherapeutic drugs that combine with DNA (genetic substance) to prevent normal cell division.

Analgesic: A drug used for reducing pain.

Antimetabolites: A family of chemotherapeutic drugs that interfere with the processes of DNA production, and thus prevent normal cell division.

Benign: Not malignant.

Biopsy: The surgical removal of a small portion of tissue for diagnosis.

Blood count: A laboratory study to evaluate the amount of white cells, red cells, and platelets.

Bone marrow: A soft substance found within bone cavities, ordinarily composed of fat and developing red cells, white cells, and platelets.

Cancer: A condition in which there is the proliferation of malignant cells that are capable of invading normal tissues.

Chemotherapy: The treatment of disease by chemicals (drugs) introduced into the bloodstream by injection or taken by mouth as tablets.

Cobalt treatment: Radiotherapy using gamma rays generated from the breakdown of radioactive cobalt-60.

Colostomy: Surgical formation of an artificial anus in the abdominal wall, so the colon can drain feces into a bag.

Coma: A condition of decreased mental function in which the individual is incapable of responding to any stimulus, including painful stimuli.

Cyanotic: A blue appearance of the skin, lips, or fingernails as the result of low oxygen content of the circulating blood.

Diagnosis: The process by which a disease is identified.

DNA: Abbreviation for deoxyribonucleic acid, the building block of the genes, responsible for the passing of hereditary characteristics from cell to cell.

Hodgkin's disease: A form of tumor that arises in a single lymph node and may spread to local and then distant lymph nodes and finally to other tissues, commonly including the spleen, liver, and bone marrow.

Immunotherapy: A method of cancer therapy that stimulates the body defenses (the immune system) to attack cancer cells or modify a specific disease state.

Intravenous (IV): Describing the administration of a drug or of fluid directly into a vein.

Leukemia: A malignant proliferation of white blood cells in the bone marrow; cancer of the blood cells.

Lymph nodes: Organized clusters of lymphocytes through which the tissue fluids drain upon returning to the blood circulation; they act as the first line of defense, filtering out and destroying infective organisms or cancer cells and initiating the generalized immune response.

Malignant: Having the potentiality of being lethal if not successfully treated. All cancers are malignant by definition.

Melanoma: A cancer of the pigment cells of the skin, usually arising in a preexisting pigmented area (mole).

Metastasis: The establishment of a secondary site or multiple sites of cancer separate from the primary or original site.

Multimodality therapy: The use of more than one modality for cure or palliation (abatement) of cancer.

Myelogram: The introduction of radiopaque dye into the sac surrounding the spinal cord, a process that makes it possible to see tumor involvement of the spinal cord or nerve roots on X-ray.

TABLE 5-2   *(continued)*

Oncologist: An internist (specialist in internal medicine dealing with nonsurgical treatment of disease) who has subspecialized in cancer therapy and has expertise in both chemotherapy and the handling of problems arising during the course of the disease.

Parkinson's disease: Degenerative disease of the brain resulting in tremor and rigid muscles.

Prognosis: An estimate of the outcome of a disease based on the status of the patient and accumulated information about the disease and its treatment.

Prosthesis: An artificial structure designed to replace or approximate a normal one.

Regression: The diminution of cancerous involvement, usually as the result of therapy; it is manifested by decreased size of the tumor (or tumors) or its clinical evidence in fewer locations.

Relapse: The reappearance of cancer following a period of remission.

Remission: The temporary disappearance of evident active cancer, occurring either spontaneously or as the result of therapy.

Sarcoma: A cancer of connective tissue, bone, cartilage, fat, muscle, nerve sheath, blood vessels, or lymphoid system.

Subcutaneous cyst: A cyst located beneath the skin; usually benign.

Symptom: A manifestation or complaint of disease as described by the patient, as opposed to one found by the doctor's examination; the latter is referred to as a sign.

Terminal: Describing a condition of decline toward death, from which not even a brief reversal can be expected.

Therapeutic procedure: A procedure intended to offer palliation (abatement) or cure of a condition or disease.

Toxicity: The property of producing unpleasant or dangerous side effects.

Tumor: A mass or swelling. A tumor can be either benign or malignant.

Source: Excerpted and adapted from Ernest H. Rosenbaum, M.D., *Living with Cancer: A Guide for the Patient, the Family and Friends* (St. Louis: C. V. Mosby, 1982).

no peer in the cure of cancer, although with some forms of cancer it is not successful.

Surgery is a routine modern medical practice, and surgery to remove diseased tissues or organs was one of the earliest types. Nevertheless, many people fear surgery as a violation of the body and the loss of some part of it; often they fear possible disfigurement, disability, or loss of bodily function. In cancer surgery, not only is the organ or tissue with the malignancy removed, but a wide margin of the adjacent tissue, possibly including adjacent organs, may also be removed to prevent the spread of the cancer. In the case of breast cancer, for example, radical mastectomy (breast removal) has been a common method of treatment. In radical surgical procedures, even if nearby lymphatic nodes appear normal, they are removed to prevent the persistence of any malignant cells that might cause a recurrence of the disease. Such radical techniques have achieved a high percentage of cures in such diseases as breast cancer, although many practitioners are now seeking less disfiguring methods of successfully removing the cancerous tissue.

Reconstructive techniques are also important to the overall success of surgery. For example, patients who undergo surgery for cancer of the colon or rectum can now be supplied with relatively simple devices for waste elimination. Improvements in such reconstructive and rehabilitative techniques have lessened the impact of radical surgery on the patient's life style and have shortened recovery time.

Despite the progress achieved by surgery, however, fewer than 50 percent of cancer patients can be cured by this procedure alone. Therefore, great effort has gone into discovering auxiliary therapies that can be given following surgery.

Radiation Therapy

One of the most widely employed of these auxiliary therapies is *radiation,* which is used to treat more than half the cancer patients in the United States. The potentialities of radiation for treating cancer were recognized soon after the discovery of radium in 1898. Radiation therapy uses ionizing radiation to destroy cells, thus preventing further cellular division and growth. Radiation affects both normal and cancerous tissues, but because cancer cells usually grow more rapidly than normal cells, they are more seriously damaged. Not all forms of cancer respond to radiation therapy, however. Some growths and tissues are quite sensitive to radiation; others are relatively resistant.

Radiation does seem to be effective in at least slowing the growth of many types of malignancy. Remissions, though sometimes lasting for a year or less, frequently occur after radiation therapy. Even when a cure is not achieved or the growth arrested, however, a palliative effect often occurs, lessening the severity of the symptoms.

Conversely, radiation therapy can cause uncomfortable side effects. Most patients who receive radiation therapy are scheduled for frequent, intense treatments, commonly as often as three or four times a week over a period of several months. The radiation dose is prescribed on the basis of the stage of the disease and the patient's ability to withstand the side effects. Nausea, vomiting, tiredness, and general weakness often accompany treatment, and patients undergoing radiation therapy often express dread of additional treatments. Because the side effects are so frequently debilitating, many patients must curtail their activities in order to get necessary bed rest.

Although the successes with radiation therapy tend to be less dramatic than those possible with surgery, its continued achievement of at least moderate successes with many patients makes radiation therapy one of the most commonly practiced methods of treating cancer, either alone or in concert with other modes of therapy. As with surgery, however, radiation by itself is not a cure for most cancers—the dosage required to eradicate all the cancer cells would also kill the patient.

Chemotherapy

Chemotherapy is the use of toxic drugs to kill cancer cells. It originated from the observation that the toxic effects of mustard gases during World War I

THE BODY SCAN, BONE SCAN, HEAD SCAN AND INTERNAL ORGAN SCAN WERE ALL NEGATIVE. THE BAD NEWS IS THAT YOU'RE RADIOACTIVE."

Drawing by Harley Schwadron, © 1994 Wall Street Journal, Cartoon Feature Syndicate

included damage to the bone marrow. Following World War II, clinical trials with chemotherapy began and the early results were encouraging. Today, many different chemotherapeutic agents are employed, in various combinations, for treating cancer. Chemotherapy has been called the leading weapon for increasing the number of patients who can be cured of cancer. To be effective therapeutically, the dose must be strong enough to kill the malignancy or slow its growth but not so potent that it might seriously harm the patient. Ideally, a chemical agent of this kind would attack only the cancerous cells in the body without affecting normal, healthy tissue.

All the diverse chemotherapeutic agents basically work by blocking the metabolic processes involved in cellular division. Because cancer cells divide more rapidly than do most normal cells, the agents used in chemotherapy are designed to preferentially affect the cancerous cells.

Like radiation therapy, chemotherapy brings discomforting side effects to many, though not to all, patients: loss of hair, sleeplessness, nausea, difficulty in eating and digestion, bleeding sores around the mouth, ulceration and bleeding in the gastrointestinal tract, and various other toxic effects. Sometimes the visible side effects can be quite alarming to the patient's family and friends.

Whether the particular drug used in chemotherapy prevents cells from making genetic material (DNA), blocks nucleic acid synthesis, or stops cell division and induces other cellular changes, chemotherapeutic agents owe their effectiveness to the fact that they are poison. As a result, they damage normal as well as diseased tissue. In addition, some cancer cells eventually become resistant to the drugs. To overcome these limitations, and because chemotherapeutic agents generally destroy only the portion of the cell population that is currently undergoing division, several drugs that act on cells in different ways are usually administered in combination.

Although chemotherapy does not usually result in a cure, it has been used successfully with some forms of cancer. It has produced long-term, disease-free remissions in many children with acute leukemia, for example, and in many patients with advanced stages of Hodgkin's disease. Some of these patients have been in remission for five years or more and may, in fact, be cured. In certain forms of malignant diseases, the palliative effects achieved by chemotherapy have allowed patients to lead comparatively normal, even prolonged, lives. Some skin cancers have also responded favorably to applications of certain chemotherapeutic ointments.

Interestingly, chemotherapy appears to be most effective with the less common forms of cancer and least effective with the more prevalent forms—cancers of the breast, colon, and lung. Nevertheless, with many cancers, chemotherapy does bring about a partial or temporary remission or some palliation of symptoms. Often, a more comfortable life, if not a cure, is achieved for the patient.

Organ Transplantation

Of all the recent innovative medical techniques for saving patients formerly considered hopeless, probably the best known is the transplantation of human organs. Acceptance of organ transplantation, as well as the number of such procedures, has been growing at a steady pace since the first kidney transplant, from one identical twin to another, in 1954 at the Peter Bent Brigham Hospital in Boston. Early transplant efforts were not always successful and, as Leonard Bailey observes, "cadaveric organs were virtually unavailable in the 1950s and most of the 1960s because we did not know how to define death appropriately."[17] The establishment of new criteria for defining so-called brain death in 1968 and the discovery of the immunosuppressive drug cyclosporine in 1976 advanced transplantation science, transforming the 1980s into what Bailey calls "a halcyon decade of organ transplantation." During 1992, the most recent year for which statistics are available, 10,210 kidneys, 3059 livers, and 2172 hearts were transplanted, and over 42,000 cornea grafts, 350,000 bone grafts, and 5500 skin grafts were done.[18]

In some cases, the organ donor is a living person; sometimes donor and recipient are members of the same family. The transaction involved in the gift of an organ from one's own body for transplanting into the body of another can generate feelings of altruism and a sense of pride. In a very real way, such a gift allows another person to live.

Yet the donor's decision may also involve feelings of masochism or guilt. Perhaps a donor feels "backed against the wall" by other family members who want the transplant operation to take place. At the same time, the potential recipient of an organ may experience conflict concerning the transaction. The recipient may feel guilty that another person has to give up an organ to the possible jeopardy of the donor's health; there may be anxiety about the outcome: "What if we all put ourselves through this procedure and my body rejects the donated organ? I'll feel responsible for ruining someone else's life, and we'll all be losers." Thus, both donor and recipient may have mixed feelings. Generally, the medical team responsible for the transplant operation tries to make sure that the psychological issues are resolved just as successfully as those related to the physiological concerns.[19]

Because fewer organs are donated than are needed, physicians must choose among prospective recipients. Thus, the physician or the medical team becomes a "gatekeeper."[20] Once a prospective recipient has been certified as physically suitable for a transplant, other factors are considered. Emotional stability, age, and ability to withstand stress all influence the chances of achieving a successful outcome. The ideal candidate for a transplant is a patient whose condition is deteriorating despite the best conventional medical treatment available and for whom a transplant offers a reasonable likelihood of recovery—in other words, someone who is likely to die in the absence of radical intervention. Thus, the alternative—death—makes the risks associated with a transplant procedure acceptable.

Organ transplantation has become an important part of current medical interventions, and there is a constant need for replacement body parts: liver, kidney, heart, and so on. When a living donor is unavailable, or when the needed organ—a heart, for example—cannot be removed from a living human being, an alternative must be found. The practice of medicine now routinely includes the transplantation of organs from the body of a person who has been declared dead into the body of a living person who can continue to receive the life-giving benefits of the transplanted organ. The donated organ may come from someone who agreed before his or her death to allow organs to be taken for transplantation, or the deceased's next of kin may give permission. Bereaved families usually experience intense feelings about the decision to give a gift of such importance to another human being.

Organ transplantation has caused quite dramatic changes in the way we think about death—in particular, the moment of death. Current medical technologies allow doctors to maintain the viability of body organs by sustaining certain physiological functions in the body of a person who has been declared dead. When artificial life-support systems are used to maintain breathing and heart action, the definition of death is blurred. The determination of death in such cases proceeds from methods of defining death that were only recently formulated.

Other Therapies

In the discussion that follows, we make a distinction between adjunctive therapies, which may be pursued alongside conventional treatment approaches of the sort already mentioned, and unorthodox therapies, which are often disparaged by the medical establishment. We begin by discussing one of the most common techniques for healing that is used in conjunction with conventional treatments.

Adjunctive Treatment

Among the techniques used for treating the emotional and physical aspects of illness, probably the best known is *visualization*. Here, the patient creates a mental state in which he or she attempts to take control of bodily processes by imagining the diseased parts of the body becoming well again. Affirmations that one already exists in a state of wellness and creative fantasies directed toward wholeness are used to generate a sense of well-being (see Figure 5-4). These methods originated with the discovery that cases of spontaneous remission shared a common factor: The patient viewed himself or herself as being well again.

Imaginative techniques such as visualization are frequently used in conjunction with conventional therapies. With chemotherapy, for instance, the patient visualizes the chemical agent inside the body, working to diminish the cancer and to restore well-being. The belief systems of the patient, the patient's family, and the physician must be considered in a holistic way in applying such adjunctive therapies to aid healing.

At Shibata Hospital in Japan, conventional treatments for cancer are accompanied by a psychotherapeutic technique called *ikigai ryoho,* or meaningful-life therapy.[21] David K. Reynolds explains that "the theory of meaningful-life therapy is that it is in our control over our behavior that hope lies." Despite fears or the quirks of our own personality, it is possible to "take responsibility for what to do in the time remaining to us." The cancer patients at Shibata Hospital begin with acknowledgment of their own private suffering and gradually proceed, first, to the recognition that others are also suffering, then to an acceptance of the reality of the illness and the fight that must be carried on, and, finally, to "an ability to live fully and deeply within the realistic limits posed by the illness." A four-part outline summarizes the approach taken in meaningful-life therapy:

1. We must accept the inevitability of dying.
2. It is impossible to eliminate our basic dread of death; we must live alongside it.
3. Behind our fear of death is the strong desire to live fully, realistically.
4. Our fear need not pressure us unconditionally; we can live each day doing well what needs to be done.

Unorthodox Treatment

Because the orthodox, or conventional, forms of treatment for cancer—surgery, radiation, and chemotherapy—are not always sufficient to bring about a cure, patients sometimes pursue experimental or unconventional therapies that seem to offer hope. Within the medical establishment, a peren-

Figure 5-4   *Good Cells and Bad Cells: A Child's Drawing*
In this drawing by a child with cancer, the health-giving good cells are depicted as being victorious over the diseased bad cells. Such imaginative
techniques can be ways of enlisting the patient's internal resources as an
adjunct to conventional therapies.
Source: Center for Attitudinal Healing, *There Is a Rainbow Behind Every Dark Cloud* (Millbrae,
Calif.: Celestial Arts, 1978), p. 71.

nial search is under way for more effective methods of treating disease; and, as
new discoveries are made, the response from patients is often dramatic. When
the National Cancer Institute announced the possibility of using Interleukin-2,
a protein produced by the immune system, to boost the body's own natural
defenses in attacking some forms of cancer, within a week's time the Institute
logged over a thousand calls from people wanting to know how to avail themselves or a family member of the new therapy. Although researchers emphasized that the discovery was a "first step" and "not a cure for cancer," many of
the callers were desperate and felt they had "nothing to lose" from trying an
experimental treatment.

Unconventional or unorthodox therapies encompass methods of treatment that the medical establishment considers unproved or potentially

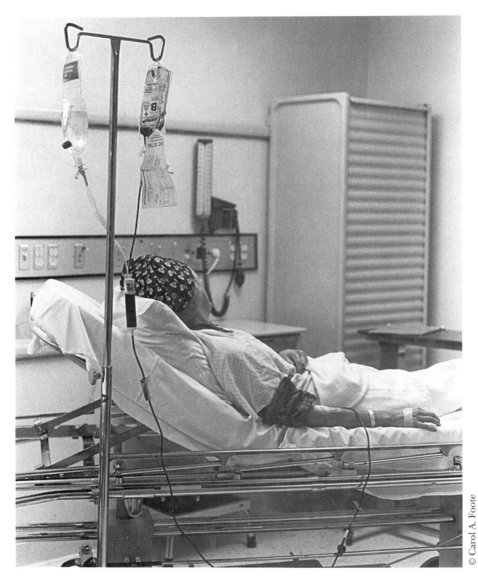

© Carol A. Foote

As part of her medical treatment, this chemotherapy patient is receiving a blood transfusion. Some treatments of life-threatening illness create the need for adjunctive therapies to counteract the side effects of the primary mode of treatment.

harmful. Those who advocate such remedies may be branded as quacks and their methods characterized as contemporary editions of Dr. Feelgood's Medicine Show, a form of snake oil medicine that, even if intrinsically harmless, diverts patients from conventional medical programs where they might receive help.

What comes to mind when you hear the word unorthodox? Not accepted? Outside of the establishment? Ineffective? That a supposed cancer cure derives from the pits of apricots or almonds may push the limits of credibility; and, indeed, such "cures" may actually be harmful. Yet many of our most common medications are derived from such seemingly unlikely sources. Such medications, whether in natural or synthetic form, comprise a significant portion of the armamentaria of conventional medicine. Penicillin is naturally produced from molds. Digitalis, prescribed for some heart ailments, derives from the plant foxglove. The active ingredient of common aspirin is close kin to a substance found in the bark and leaves of the white willow. Clearly, the source of a proposed medicinal substance ought to concern us less than the question, Does it work?

Some of the methods banned from use in conventional medicine are unproved simply because of insufficient research to determine their possible validity. Interferons, for example, are considered by many to be among the most promising of the unproved therapies. Simply put, interferons are a family of proteins produced by the body's cells in the presence of viral infection. At present, interferon therapy is experimental. Preliminary results tend to cast doubt on whether interferons represent a dramatic breakthrough in cancer therapy, but there are indications that they can beneficially affect some cancers. It is not yet clear how interferons might eventually fit into the total scheme of cancer therapies.

Most patients prefer orthodox therapies, but others distrust or lose faith in the conventional approach and choose unsanctioned alternatives as their course of therapy. Some patients try to find a comfortable balance between medically approved therapies and innovative but unproved approaches. For example, they may follow their doctor's prescription for radiation therapy or chemotherapy while at the same time pursuing techniques such as biofeedback, meditation, or visualization that are designed to mobilize the body's own resources. Some alternative approaches to treatment can be combined with an orthodox medical approach; others cannot and require a radical departure from conventional medical practices.

Anson Shupe and Jeffrey Hadden have proposed the term *symbolic healing* to identify the varied therapies known under such names as "faith healing," "supernatural healing," and "folk healing."[22] Accepting the validity of symbolic healing means acknowledging the reality that "human beings do not live in the physical world alone but also in a world mediated for them by symbolic meanings provided by their culture" and that "symbols cue and prompt responses, not just in brains but in glands as well." In short, what we take to be meaningful—what we believe—about the way of the world potentially affects the functioning of our bodies. The concept of symbolic healing places the human organism within a series of overlapping environments: biological, social, and cultural.

When we look at concepts of illness and health cross-culturally, say Shupe and Hadden, we find that "human understandings of illness, or disease, usually posit an imbalance among different realms of a patient's life." At

its most basic, therefore, healing "consists of restoring balance." This traditional understanding is in essential agreement with the integrated mind/body
model now being advocated by a growing number of physicians and medical
scientists. The brain has been called "the major organ of adaptation," and
Shupe and Hadden remark that "the function of the brain is to seek a stable
health homeostasis through the integration of emotions, cognitions, and
socio-symbolic relationships with the chemistries of immune, cardiovascular,
and endorphin systems, among others."[23] In other words, the brain naturally
seeks to bring about a healthy state of functioning.

Now, what meaning does all this talk of symbolic healing have for patients
and caregivers? Perhaps most significantly, it reinforces the importance of
attending to the dynamics of the healer-patient relationship. Shupe and Hadden cite several elements that are critical in this regard: First, the patient must
have confidence in "the legitimacy and credibility of the medical system, even
if the details of its technology are not understood." Second, the patient must
trust "in the wisdom and expertise of the healer." Third, the healer must have
"confidence in the validity of his or her medical intervention." Fourth, the
context of healing must employ "culturally consistent myths and symbols" that
actively involve the patient.

These insights from cross-cultural studies of the physician-patient relationship can be usefully applied to situations involving persons diagnosed with
a terminal illness. As Norman Cousins said shortly before his death, "The great
tragedy of life is not death but what dies inside us while we live."[24] The shock
of a terminal diagnosis and the reality of living with serious illness can "kill" or
wreak damage on the human spirit, that part of the person which is the
reservoir of zest for life and positive accomplishment. Despite the statistical
probabilities of an illness or the incapacitation it brings into a person's life,
healers and patients can join together in encouraging (giving heart to) the
inner human spirit while acknowledging the grim reality.

Doctors are beginning to accept the notion that orthodox treatments
may not be sufficient for all cases and that confronting patients with an
"either/or" situation—forcing them to choose between orthodox or alternative treatments—may at times do more harm than good. With the increase
over the last few decades of people with cancer being cured or surviving
longer, greater public attention has been brought to the possibility of
"beating" cancer by assuming an attitude of "heroic self-healing" through the
use of positive thinking, healing imagery, and personal growth techniques.[25]
Even though the empirical, or scientific, support for such a psychospiritual
influence on illness is considered by most researchers to be tenuous, the psychological implications of belief in such influences may be important in their
own right. For some patients, identifying with the notion of "heroic self-
healing" offers a method for coping with illness that enhances their quality of
life, if not its duration. To be sure, some alternative or unorthodox treatments
are harmful to patients. Yet it is also true that other alternative or unorthodox
therapies may not only empower patients and give them renewed hope but in
some cases also serve as useful adjuncts to conventional methods of treatment.

Infection

Because life-threatening illnesses typically lower the body's resistance to microorganisms, patients with such diseases tend to be extremely susceptible to infection. Some believe infection to be the most significant cause of mortality and manifest ill health, or wasting away, in cancer patients. Similarly, the diminished immune response associated with AIDS renders people with this disease vulnerable to opportunistic infections and tumorous growths. Pneumocystic carinii pneumonia is frequently the first infection to occur with AIDS and is the most common cause of death. In addition, many AIDS patients develop cancers, the most common of which include Kaposi's sarcoma, non-Hodgkin's lymphoma, and Hodgkin's disease.

Infection can result from both endogenous, or resident, organisms and exogenous, or external, organisms. All three of the primary modes of treating cancer—surgery, radiation therapy, and chemotherapy—carry risks of infection. And although surgery always involves some risk of infection, the risk to cancer patients is increased significantly because their resistance tends to be lower and because malignancies tend to be conducive to the growth of microorganisms. Radiation therapy and chemotherapy increase the risk of infection because they work by suppressing the body's natural immune system. That hospitals are poor environments for avoiding infection is an additional argument against unnecessary hospitalization.

Treating infection is often difficult because the use of antibiotics to combat the infection may disturb the balance of normal microbial flora. Those who care for patients with cancer and other such diseases need to be aware of the various preventive and therapeutic measures that are available for reducing the threat of infections.

Pain Management

In discussions about the experience of life-threatening illness, one of the frequently mentioned phenomena is that of pain. Indeed, pain is the most common symptom of terminally ill patients.[26] The effective management of pain is a chief goal of palliative care and a hallmark of the comfort-oriented focus associated with hospice care. Although we often speak of pain as if it were a well-defined entity, the fact is that the experience of pain is "subjective in nature and ultimately unshareable." Linda Garro points out that "pain cannot be directly measured or observed; it is a perceptual experience that can only be communicated through verbal means and/or by behavior interpreted as indicating pain."[27]

In an article on culture and pain, Garro goes on to discuss the way that languages differ in their "lexicon" for talking about pain. For example, English speakers use several basic terms when describing pain: pain, hurt, sore, and ache. To these basic terms, qualifiers are added to make the description of pain more specific to the actual experience. We talk about having a "burning" or "stabbing" pain, or about having an "unbearable ache" or "soreness in the shoulder." In this way, a particular experience of pain is further defined in terms of temporal, spatial, thermal, pressure, and other qualities. Notice that

But You Look So Good

It's with me each day.
I wake, thinking
Today it will go away.
But the pain seems to stay . . .
Persistent, resistant, consistent.
People say,
But you look so good.
If only I could
Feel like I look.
Or, should
I look bad?
So they'll know
How I feel
is real.
Do they doubt?
I wish the pain
Was on the outside—
something you see.
Not only the pain
Do I need to survive,
But also my
Paranoid imaginings
Of others' disbelief.

Judy Ellsworth

the tendency is to treat pain as an object: "I have a pain." For a Thai speaker, on the other hand, "the basic pain terms are verbs and refer to the active perception of sensations." Pain is perceived not as an object, but as process. As these differences in language usage illustrate, the response to pain is to some extent culturally shaped.

Although home care for dying patients is considered by many to be a highly desirable method for providing terminal care, effective pain and symptom control is not always a reality in the home setting.[28] Families and friends may encounter relatively few difficulties with respect to supplying adequate nursing care, but pain management typically requires attention by skilled professionals. Yet physicians with experience in home care and a willingness to exercise the needed flexibility for a workable program are in short supply.

Michael Levy notes that pain can be technically defined as an "unpleasant sensory and emotional experience associated with actual or potential tissue damage or described in terms of such damage."[29] More practically, however, he asserts that "pain is what the patient says it is and occurs when he or she says it does." Levy points out that the two main goals of caring for the terminally ill are "to optimize the quality of their remaining life and to alleviate the distress of their survivors." Pain control is crucial to achieving both of these aims.

The three basic approaches to reducing pain—modifying the source of the pain, interfering with its transmission, and altering perception of the pain—can be implemented by a number of methodologies. These include palliative surgery, radiation therapy, and hormonal therapy, as well as a wide variety of drug therapies.

The "politics of pain management" is cited as an important factor relating to the delivery of pain-reducing techniques to terminally ill patients. In some instances, for example, highly addictive but nonetheless effective drugs are withheld or given only sparingly despite the fact that a patient's limited prognosis makes concerns about possible addiction irrelevant. The consensus within the medical community appears to be that, despite considerable advances in recent years, pain control remains inadequate for a large number of patients.

Hospice and palliative care programs have taken a leading role in advocating greater attention to pain management, especially as applied in cases of terminal illness. Interdisciplinary approaches, combining both conventional and innovative techniques, are endorsed by many in the field as offering a way to address the "total pain"—physical, psychological, social, and spiritual—experienced by the terminally ill person. These approaches often make use of techniques that enhance a patient's ability to maintain a positive attitude and a feeling of greater control over his or her situation. When effectively managed, this combination of conventional medical wisdom and innovative techniques intended to elicit the body's own powers of healing can result in an easing of physical, as well as mental and emotional, discomforts arising out of the experience of life-threatening illness.

The Dying Trajectory

Our expectations about dying may be quite different from what most people actually experience. In a recent study, Robert Kastenbaum and Claude Normand compared deathbed scenes as *imagined* by the young and *experienced* by the old.[30] The young people (students of college age) imagined themselves living into old age and then dying at home, with the companionship of loved ones, quickly, and without pain or other symptoms, while remaining alert and lucid until the end. The researchers found that the respondents tended to substitute "desired" for "most likely to happen" in imagining the end of their lives. The presence of pain, nausea, constipation, pressure sores, and insomnia—all too often part of the dying experience—were virtually absent from the imagined deathbed scenes.

The expectation of a "quick" death is not borne out by the reality experienced by most people, who typically live with a debilitating condition for weeks or months. Although the researchers caution that this study is exploratory and tentative, its findings suggest that our picture of dying and death may

There Are Days Now

There are days now
when I can see
the souls of elephants
being towed to heaven;
and the whales, the whales,
those hulls full of sadness!
Soon the trees will be loosed from their moorings
and sail off
like a chorus of Greek Women
rigid with grief.

I am resigned to this,
and yet
with each of their passings
there is a crumbling
along the banks of my bloodstream.
So if I touched you now,
my friend,
how could it be with my whole hand,
the fat resting firm beneath the palm,
and not with a clutch of fingers,
as though I had grabbed you in passing
and were holding on?

Morton Marcus

be influenced more by images portrayed in the media than by what is likely to actually take place.

Most deaths today occur in institutional settings, and dying occurs over a period of time.[31] This time-course, or trajectory, followed by a dying patient can be regarded as fitting into one of the following categories:

1. Certain death at a known time
2. Certain death at an unknown time
3. Uncertain death, but a known time when the certainty will be established
4. Uncertain death and an unknown time when the question will be resolved

With respect to dying trajectories, two types are of particular importance: (1) the lingering trajectory, in which "a patient's life is fading slowly, gradually, and inevitably," and (2) the expected quick trajectory, such as occurs in "the acute or emergency situation in which life or death hang in the immediate balance."[32] The expectations of medical professionals, family members, and other interested parties concerning a patient's course toward death are likely to play an important part in determining the nature and kind of care received by the dying person. From the perspective of the dying person, the psychological process of dying can be organized in terms of the three stages categorized by Avery Weisman: (1) from the time symptoms are noticed until the diagnosis is confirmed, (2) between diagnosis and the final decline, and (3) the stage of final decline.[33]

When death is made to seem less a natural event than a medical failure, biological death, the cessation of physical functions, may be preceded by *social death*. Eric Cassell writes: "There are two distinct things happening to the terminally ill: the death of the body and the passing of the person."[34] The death of the body is a physical phenomenon whereas the passing of the person is a nonphysical (social, emotional, psychological, spiritual) one; yet, these aspects tend to become confused.

If the deathbed scene imagined by the young respondents is to become a reality, society will need to ensure that management of pain and other symptoms, and the participation of family and friends, become important elements in a comprehensive program of terminal care.

The Social Role of the Dying Patient

As sociologist Talcott Parsons discovered in the 1950s, a particular social role accompanies illness.[35] Like all social roles—parent, child, student, employee, spouse—the role of the "person who is sick" includes certain rights as well as responsibilities. For example, when we are ill, others exempt us from our usual tasks. We may stay home from work. Someone else may take on our share of housecleaning or child care. Commitments may be neglected. We are granted the right to be sick. We assume a particular social role that causes others to make allowances for our behavior that otherwise might result in social penalties. Whereas taking off from work just to enjoy a day in the sun is likely to be frowned upon, an absence due to illness elicits sympathy rather than reprimands.

The sick person not only enjoys exemptions from many of the usual social obligations but also receives special consideration and care. Others make an effort to ensure that the patient is comfortable, is receiving adequate treatment, and so on. Personal and financial resources may be devoted to the patient's care and treatment. Such care is part of the social role of being sick, of being a patient.

But these rights are balanced by responsibilities. The sick person must want to get well. Malingerers, those who pretend to be sicker than they really are, receive little or no respect from those whose job it is to provide care or help carry the additional burden imposed by their supposed illness. It's okay to receive special treatment when you're really ill or when you've suffered an injury, but the role of the patient demands that you demonstrate that you'd really rather be well. You've got to take your medicine. You're expected to cooperate with those who are prescribing and administering treatment.

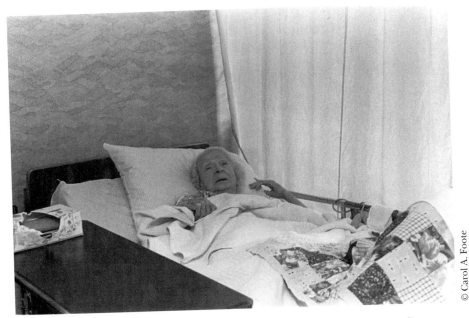

© Carol A. Foote

Being with a loved one who is dying confronts us with the fact of our own mortality as well as with the losses associated with that person's death. Even when communication is hampered by physical disability, such times can be precious opportunities for sharing our deepest feelings with someone we love whose presence will be missed in our lives.

At one time or another most people have experienced the role of patient as well as the role of caregiver. The role of the dying patient is quite different. Although sharing some aspects of the curable patient's social role, the dying person's illness does not fit the pattern of a temporary condition leading to an eventual return to wellness. Yet, in our society, a social role for the dying is not well defined. The same expectations may be placed on the dying person as on patients whose prognosis is rehabilitation and return to normal modes of living. Even when circumstances are clearly contrary, the dying person may be urged to maintain a hope of recovery, to deny the reality of what he or she is experiencing. If the dying person does not exhibit this cheerful will to live, friends and family may feel angry or rejected.

The person who is dying assumes a different role in relation to the medical community. When cure is no longer perceived as a medical possibility, palliative (comfort-oriented) care takes the place of active intervention and treatment. Typically, the physician begins to devote less time to mapping out hopeful strategies and takes on a more supervisory role, while the patient is expected to assume more responsibility for his or her own care.

The lack of a clear consensus on care of the dying and the role of the dying patient can lead to actions that seem quite incongruous. Consider, for example, the hopelessly ill patient in the final stage of a terminal condition who is rushed into the intensive care unit and subjected to heroic medical attempts to sustain life. Meanwhile, the patient's family may be waiting outside, experiencing a lingering uncertainty or false hopes for the patient's survival. In such circumstances, death may be far from peaceful or dignified. It may be difficult for the patient to deal with the prospect of death in a personally appropriate and comforting way.

Until about the middle of the twentieth century, a social role for the dying person was more or less fixed by custom and circumstance. The rapid and pervasive social and technological changes of recent times have largely eliminated the traditional role of the dying, while offering few guidelines in its stead. What would a newly rediscovered and updated role for the dying look like? It would undoubtedly draw upon historical precedent, while also reflecting the social and technological changes in our present modes of caring for dying patients.

Let us imagine some of the attributes of such a newly evolving role for the dying: No longer would the patient need to maintain an appearance of expecting to live forever, of getting well again, of sustaining false hope. At the same time, the patient would assume a more independent role, able to exercise more self-determination, and entitled to a greater degree of cooperation from others involved in caregiving. Caregivers, family members, and the patient would work together to nurture a sense of "empowerment" that emphasized the possibility of the patient's "owning" his or her own life.[36]

The patient whose resources had been mobilized in the effort to effect a cure would now turn his or her attention to the prospect of death. Relatives and friends, understanding this change of perspective as natural, would allow the patient to disengage from the activities and relationships that prevailed before the onset of illness. Such disengagement would not necessarily mean the terminal patient wanted to "separate" from others.[37] Indeed, in a study of "farewells by the dying," researchers found that most (80 percent) of the terminally ill persons in the sample expressed a desire to communicate their farewells—primarily through giving gifts, writing letters, and having informal conversations—and wanted these farewells to take place late in the course of their dying.[38] Although some degree of social disengagement is likely to occur as a person nears his or her death, maintaining valued relationships is important for most people right to the end of life.

As the desire of dying patients to communicate their "farewells" suggests, the evolving social role of dying patients must encompass spiritual as well as physical and emotional needs. These include:[39]

1. *The need for meaning and purpose.* This involves reviewing one's life (including relationships, work, other achievements, and religious concerns) and

Your Caring Presence: Ways of Effectively Providing Support to Others

1. Be honest about your own thoughts, concerns, and feelings.
2. When in doubt, ask questions:
      How is that for you?
      How do you feel right now?
      Can you tell me more about that?
      Am I intruding?
      What do you need?
      What are the ways you can take care of yourself?
3. When you are responding to a person facing a crisis situation, be sure to use statements such as:
      I feel _____
      I believe _____
      I would want _____
   Rather than:
      You should
      That's wrong
      Everything will be ok.
   which are statements that may not give the person the opportunity to express his/her own unique needs and feelings.
4. Stay in the present as much as possible: How do you feel RIGHT NOW? What do you need RIGHT NOW?
5. Listening is profoundly healing. You don't have to make it better. You don't have to have the answers. You don't have to take away the pain. It's his pain. He needs to experience it in his own time and in his own way.
6. People in crisis need to know they have decision-making power. It may be appropriate to point out alternatives.
7. Offer any practical assistance that you feel comfortable giving.
8. If the situation warrants it, feel free to refer individual to appropriate agency.

The Centre for Living with Dying

attempting to make sense of it, to place it within a larger perspective that has meaning.

2. *The need for hope and creativity.* Whereas the first item on this list involves looking back over one's life to discover meaning and purpose, this spiritual need is oriented toward the future. It may involve the aspiration for improved well-being, to be free of pain; the desire to accomplish a personal goal or to achieve reconciliation with others; or it may involve the hope of an afterlife. This need may also center on the hope, as Roderick Cosh puts it, "that that which has been of meaning and purpose to the individual may be affirmed by those who are important to him or her."

3. *The need to give and receive love.* As Cosh says, "We all need to be reassured that we are loved and that others need our love." Reconciliation is a key element in satisfying this human spiritual need.

A "good" death—that is, one appropriate to the person who is dying—is as much anticipated as was the earlier hope of recovery. The dying person is recognized as the protagonist in an important and potentially valuable experience of life.

Further Readings

Judith Ahronheim and Doron Weber. *Final Passages: Positive Choices for the Dying and Their Loved Ones.* New York: Simon & Schuster, 1992.

Geoffrey M. Cooper. *The Cancer Book: A Guide to Understanding the Causes, Prevention, and Treatment of Cancer.* Boston: Jones and Bartlett, 1993.

Kenneth J. Doka. *Living with Life-Threatening Illness: A Guide for Patients, Their Families, and Caregivers.* New York: Lexington, 1993.

Norbert Elias. *The Loneliness of the Dying.* New York: Basil Blackwell, 1985.

Renee C. Fox and Judith P. Swazey. *Spare Parts: Organ Replacement in American Society.* New York: Oxford University Press, 1992.

Arthur W. Frank. *At the Will of the Body: Reflections on Illness.* Boston: Houghton Mifflin, 1991.

David B. Morris. *The Culture of Pain.* Berkeley: University of California Press, 1991.

Sherwin B. Nuland. *How We Die: Reflections on Life's Final Chapter.* New York: Alfred A. Knopf, 1994.

Barry D. Schoub. *AIDS & HIV in Perspective: A Guide to Understanding the Virus and Its Consequences.* New York: Cambridge University Press, 1994.

Arthur Selzer. *Understanding Heart Disease.* Berkeley: University of California Press, 1992.

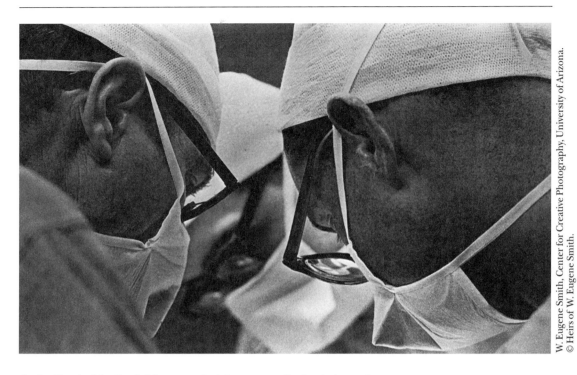

At the Hospital for Special Surgery, physicians use medical techniques that call for teamwork and expertise. Life-sustaining interventions made possible by advances in medical technologies require physicians and society as a whole to consider difficult issues of medical ethics.

Medical Ethics:
Dying in a
Technological Age

*G*reat-grandpa was born before Henry Ford put his first automobile on the road, and he died shortly after Neil Armstrong set his foot on the moon. From Michigan to outer space, he experienced an unprecedented advance in the technological capacities of our society. At the time of his death, he was surrounded by technological innovations. The canvas-topped, hand-cranked two-seater car he hand-built in 1922 had been replaced by a factory-built vinyl-topped, four-door automatic, with power steering and power brakes. A retired auto worker, he had begun to question the consequences of the automobile on the quality of his life. If he had been conscious as he lay dying, he might have talked about the consequences that the machines sustaining his life brought to the quality of his death.

Advances in biomedical technology present us with new and sometimes confusing choices. Surgery repairs physical dysfunctions that once were fatal. When repair is not feasible, it may be possible to replace the defective organ. Medical centers across the country regularly perform major organ transplants. In 1981, heart transplants were being performed by only 8 medical centers in the United States; by 1992, they were being performed by 163 centers.[1]

It is commonly said that the great advances in medicine have come about because physicians take seriously the Hippocratic obligation to keep people alive.[2] But the practice of this worthy maxim can lead to confusing consequences. Techniques for

The Oath of Hippocrates

I swear by Apollo the physician, and by Aesculapius [god of medicine], Hygeia [goddess of health], and Panacea [goddess of healing], and all the gods and goddesses, that, to the best of my ability and judgment, I will keep this oath and agreement: to regard my teacher in this art as equal to my own parents; to share my living with him and provide for him in need; to treat his children as my own and teach them this art if they wish to learn it, without payment or obligation; to give guidance, explanations, and every other kind of instruction to my own children and those of my teacher, and to students who subscribe to the Physician's Oath, but to nobody else.

I will prescribe treatment to the best of my ability and judgment for the benefit of my patients and will abstain from whatever is harmful or pernicious. I will give no poisonous or deadly medicine, even if asked to, nor make any such suggestion; neither will I give any woman a pessary to produce an abortion. I will both live and work in purity and holiness. I will not operate, not even on patients suffering from the stone, but will leave this to specialists who are skilled in this work. Into whatever houses I enter, I will make the patient's good my principal aim and will avoid all deliberate harm or corruption, especially from sexual relations with women or men, bond or free. Whatever I see or hear about people, whether in the course of my practice or outside it, if it should not be made public, I will keep it to myself and treat it as an inviolable secret.

While I abide by this oath and never violate it, may all people hold me in esteem for all time on account of my life and work; but if I break this oath, let the reverse be my fate.

cardiopulmonary resuscitation (CPR) and respiratory assistance have progressed to the point where physicians can interrupt the "normal" dying process; unfortunately, some of the patients saved by the use of such techniques "have their cardiac and respiratory functions restored, but remain with irreversible damage to the brain."[3] The average person might question the obligation to keep people alive in certain instances, such as when a person is maintained in a hopelessly comatose condition, or when heroic medical procedures are undertaken to keep a seriously deformed baby alive. The sophisticated and innovative technologies, which now have an unprecedented impact on the way we die, present a great challenge to us as we confront the prospect of our own or another's death.

Most deaths in modern societies are anticipated, the result of a malady that may linger months or even years. Yet even irreversible, debilitating ailments that are ordinarily expected to result in death are being actively combated. Now that infectious diseases of the past have been largely controlled, the medical community is waging war against the diseases that threaten us today.

The human organism can often be kept going despite the cessation of normal heart, brain, respiratory, or kidney function. When medical technologies spare patients' lives and enable them to resume more or less normal functioning, the results are gratifying. But, paradoxically, the very technologies designed to prolong our lives may prolong our dying as well. When life is sustained artificially, while the person shows no signs of personality or consciousness and there is no likely chance of recovery, ethical questions arise.

When death mercifully does come in such instances, who or what finally "dies"? Put another way, what in fact is death? When does it occur? Until quite recently, cessation of breathing and heartbeat defined death. In our time, the definition of death is less clear.

The social and technological advances that have brought about improved health care and greater choices in medical services have also resulted in questions about how best to use these choices and improvements. When these questions impinge on the ethical realm of decision making, the choices are difficult for individuals and for social institutions alike. Ethical decision making becomes even more complicated in a climate of medical economics in which traditional "virtue-centered" ethics are being eroded by growing self-interest and the "businessification" of medical care.[4] Although judicial intervention by the courts in an attempt to sort out what is ethically proper in bioethics cases has become relatively commonplace, the burden of such decision making ideally rests with individuals, families, and caregivers who, acting together, form a community of interest, with firsthand knowledge about a particular case and the will to make moral decisions.[5]

Fundamental Ethical Principles

To provide a framework for discussing such issues as informed consent, euthanasia, and withdrawing or withholding medical treatment, it is worth examining what is meant when people talk about behaving ethically or morally. Although the definitions of such terms are often taken for granted, understanding how they are applied in the context of medical care provides a foundation for the ensuing discussion.

To begin with, *ethics* refers to the investigation of what is good and bad, especially as these concepts relate to moral duties and obligations. Ideally, the outcome of this investigation will be a set of moral principles or values that can serve to guide proper behavior. When we think of *morals,* or moral principles, we are dealing essentially with notions of right and wrong. Although the two terms—morals and ethics—are closely related, we can distinguish them, in one way, by noting that morals generally means conforming to established codes or accepted notions of right and wrong, whereas ethics suggests grappling with more subtle or challenging questions of rightness, fairness, or equity. Briefly stated, then, ethics is concerned with what are usually difficult issues relating to value and obligation. The ethical pursuit is characterized by attempts to answer the question, "What is the good?," along with its corollary, "What is to be done?"

In applying ethical principles to the realm of medicine, there are several concepts with which one should be familiar. The first of these, *autonomy,* refers to an individual's right to be self-governing—that is, to exercise self-directing freedom and moral independence.[6] Personal autonomy may be limited by the corresponding rights of others to exercise their autonomy, and it may be limited by society, which may exercise countervailing rights in the name of the community at large. A common example is the requirement that a traveler must obtain inoculations before being granted a visa to enter certain countries; the traveler's autonomy or personal choice is subjected to restrictions relating to public health that are imposed by the larger community.

In discussing the principle of autonomy in health care ethics, we are really talking about respect or regard for the autonomy of others.[7] Personal autonomy is complex and often ambiguous. Although it is wrong to subject a person's actions or choices to coercion, autonomy does not imply that an individual cannot willingly yield to decisions proposed by others. For example, a patient may not wish a detailed presentation of the pros and cons of a particular treatment, preferring to trust in the relationship established with his or her physician. Of course, it is not always a simple matter to determine a person's choices or preferences, which may be ambivalent or even contradictory, and which can change over time.

Furthermore, respect for autonomy does not mean forcing individuals to arrive at decisions independent of their social support networks. Among the elderly, for example, there appears to be a relationship between a sense of control over one's decisions and positive outcomes as one ages. Yet, as Marshall Kapp points out, this "empowerment" of the elderly should not be used to impose a burden of self-determination on individuals who prefer guidance from others or even want physicians, family members, or close friends to take on primary responsibility for medical decisions.[8] In other words, an individual has the right to choose the degree to which his or her capacity for autonomy will be exercised. Respect for autonomy does not mean that we abandon people in their decision making.

Family members and others close to the patient may have a legitimate voice in determining the kinds of choices a patient makes. John Hardwig refers to human connectedness, particularly the interconnectedness of the family, as a basis for balancing respect for individual autonomy and respect for the values of others with whom one has significant relationships.[9] While acknowledging that the ill deserve special consideration, Hardwig rejects the notion that they deserve exclusive consideration. That is, the effect that an individual's decision is likely to have on others must also be considered. In advocating a role for "intimate others" in medical decision making, Nancy Jecker argues that, if decisions are made without considering their effect on the "family commons," those choices may rightfully be overridden to prevent harm to the commons.[10] Despite the limits inherent in the principle of autonomy, it is an important constraint on actions by others. The concept of autonomy supports the "respect for persons" needed in the patient–provider relationship.

Another term important to medical ethics is *beneficence,* which can be understood as doing good or as conferring benefits that support personal or social well-being. This principle of beneficence as applied to medical care is sometimes expressed by its counterpart, *nonmaleficence,* or the injunction to "do no harm."

Finally, medical ethics is concerned with the principle of *justice,* a term that, like "the good," is difficult to define simply. Justice embraces the qualities of impartiality and fairness, as well as right and proper action. In the aspect of fairness, justice implies going beyond one's own feelings, prejudices, and desires in the effort to reach a balance between conflicting interests. You will find it helpful to keep these three fundamental principles of medical ethics— autonomy, beneficence, and justice—in mind while exploring the specific issues discussed in the remainder of this chapter.

Informed Consent to Treatment

The relationship between patient and physician implies the existence of a contract whereby each party agrees to perform certain acts designed to achieve the desired results. Fundamental to the contract are self-determination and informed consent. It is generally acknowledged that patients have the right to self-determination regarding a proposed plan of treatment. In practice, we usually rely on the physician's judgment, accepting the diagnosis of an illness and acceding to the proposed course of treatment; we follow the doctor's advice and expect a more or less speedy recovery. We see our doctor to obtain medication to cure the flu or to mend a broken arm, and we give little consideration to possible alternative treatments. The etiology, or cause, of the disease or injury generally concerns us less than obtaining relief from its symptoms.

More complex, however, is the question of the patient's consent to treatment when the illness is serious or life threatening. Not only has life-threatening illness vastly greater consequences for the patient, but the physician's role is fraught with greater ambiguity. Frequently, several different treatment plans are available, each with its own set of potential risks and benefits. Medical practitioners may be uncertain about what might be the most promising treatment. Too, with diseases like cancer, the side effects of surgery, radiation, and chemotherapy may be nearly as frightening or as discomforting as the disease itself.

Clearly, then, the patient's *informed consent* to a plan of treatment is crucial. Informed consent is based on three principles: First, the patient must be competent to give consent. Second, consent must be given freely and voluntarily. Third, consent must be based on an adequate understanding of what is involved in the treatment program. In an ideal model, the physician informs the patient about the risks of the proposed therapy, about alternative methods of treatment, and about the likely outcome of undertaking no treatment.

Burton Steele, Times-Picayune

Informed consent is a fundamental ethical principle in medicine. Even fairly routine procedures, such as mending a small fracture, may become complicated when the patient is leukemic, as is this child: Alternatives must be weighed more carefully before a course of treatment is chosen.

The antecedents of informed consent go back hundreds of years in English common law. Although the phrase "informed consent" did not achieve legal definition until 1957, the doctrine of informed consent has been recognized in case law or statute in nearly all American jurisdictions. The President's Commission for the Study of Ethical Problems in Medicine noted that "the legal doctrine of informed consent imposes on physicians two general duties: to disclose information about treatment to patients and to obtain their consent before proceeding with treatment."[11]

Decisions about medical care involve values and goals as well as methods and behavior. The values underlying informed consent include serving the patient's well-being and respecting his or her right to self-determination. To make these values a reality, attention must be paid not only to the patient's capacity to make decisions about his or her care, but also to the communication process between patient and practitioner.

Although it has foundations in law, the doctrine of informed consent is essentially an ethical imperative. It cannot be equated with a formal recitation of the risks of a particular treatment but involves instead a process of shared decision making based on mutual respect and participation. Because people differ in their attitudes toward autonomy and choice relative to medical care, the process of informed consent must be flexible.

A survey conducted for the Commission found "a universal desire for information, choice, and respectful communication about decisions," yet many people have only a vague notion of informed consent. When asked, "What does the term informed consent mean to you?" 21 percent of those surveyed said they did not know. About half said that informed consent meant "agreeing to treatment" or "letting the doctor do whatever is necessary or best." Only 10 percent mentioned having information about risks, and less than 1 percent mentioned being told about alternatives. Among physicians, about half described informed consent as "generally informing patient about condition and treatment," while somewhat fewer added that it included "disclosing treatment risks to patient." Only 14 percent mentioned telling patients about treatment alternatives.

Physicians generally believe they have a responsibility to inform patients about the facts of a life-threatening condition, but this attitude has not always prevailed. A study in 1961 found that doctors at that time demonstrated a strong and general tendency to *withhold* information.[12] None of the doctors surveyed reported having a policy of telling every patient. Only about 12 percent said they would usually tell patients of a diagnosis of incurable cancer. When they did inform patients, descriptions of the disease were often couched in euphemisms. They might tell a cancer patient that he or she had a "lesion" or a "mass." Some used a more precise description such as "growth," "tumor," or "hyperplastic tissue." Often the description was phrased to suggest that the cancer was benign. Adjectives were used to temper the impact of the cancer diagnosis. The tumor was "suspicious" or "degenerated." Such descriptions allowed physicians to explain the medical situation in general terms while eliciting the patient's cooperation in the proposed course of treatment.

The climate of truth telling has changed significantly in recent decades. A 1977 study found an almost complete reversal of attitudes compared with the earlier study: About 97 percent of the doctors said they would usually tell cancer patients the diagnosis.[13] As was true of the 1961 study, however, the doctors pointed out that the determining factor in revealing a diagnosis was their own clinical experience and personal conviction. In a second follow-up study, physicians said they were willing to engage in some deception when confronted with situations involving difficult ethical problems.[14] Researchers concluded that physicians "appear to justify their decisions in terms of the consequences and to place a higher value on their patients' welfare and keeping patients' confidences than truth telling for its own sake."

Informed consent requires that patients *and* caregivers be prepared for shared decision making. It becomes increasingly important when medical care is provided by teams of highly specialized professionals whose responsibilities may be defined less by the overall needs of the patient than by particular diseases or organ systems. No single individual may be charged with responsibility for the entire care of the patient—no familiar person to whom the patient can turn for information, advice, and comfort. The threat such a situation poses to the patient's autonomy cannot be remedied by formal disclosure of remote risks on informed consent forms.

Although some have argued that patients cannot fully understand medical information relevant to their health care, the majority of physicians surveyed by the Commission reported that virtually all of their patients could understand most aspects of their condition and treatment, if sufficient time and effort were given to explanation. The Commission noted that "questions of patient capacity in decision making typically arise only when a patient chooses a course—often a refusal of treatment—other than the one the health professional finds most reasonable."

Although forced, coercive treatment is rare, caregivers can—unwittingly or not—exert undue influence on patients by means of subtle or overt manipulation. Once the patient is in a health care institution, cooperation with caregivers is generally expected. The tacit communication may be that the patient has no choice. Thus, the communication process itself may be the key factor in determining whether informed consent is present. When medical information is presented, the facts and possible outcomes must be tailored so as to facilitate a discussion attuned to the needs, capabilities, and emotional state of a particular patient.

When the physicians in the survey were asked about how they treated the issue of informed consent, slightly more than half (56 percent) said they always discussed their diagnosis and prognosis with patients, and another 42 percent said it was their usual practice. When asked what they would tell a patient who had a fully confirmed diagnosis of advanced lung cancer, however, only 13 percent said they would give a straight statistical prognosis. A third said they

Nurse: Did they mention anything about a tube through your nose?

Patient: Yes, I'm gonna have a tube in my nose.

Nurse: You're going to have the tube down for a couple of days or longer. It depends. So you're going to be NPO, nothing by mouth, and also you're going to have IV fluid.

Patient: I know. For three or four days, they told me that already. I don't like it, though.

Nurse: You don't have any choice.

Patient: Yes, I don't have any choice, I know.

Nurse: Like it or not, you don't have any choice. (laughter) After you come back, we'll ask you to do a lot of coughing and deep breathing to exercise your lungs.

Patient: Oh, we'll see how I feel.

Nurse: (emphasis) No matter how you feel, you have to do that!

President's Commission for the Study of Ethical Problems in Medicine and Biomedical and Behavioral Research, *Making Health Care Decisions: A Report on the Ethical and Legal Implications of the Patient-Practitioner Relationship*

would tell the patient they didn't know how long he or she might live, "but would stress that it could be for a substantial period of time"; 28 percent would say they "couldn't tell how long, but would stress that in most cases people live no longer than a year"; and 22 percent would "refuse to speculate on how long the patient might live."

To the degree that a proposed course of treatment is elective, the outcome uncertain, and the procedure experimental, the patient's informed consent becomes correspondingly more important. For example, the drawing of a blood sample is a widely known and common procedure that entails little risk to the patient. Consequently, we do not expect to receive a detailed explanation of risks when we roll up our sleeve for the insertion of the needle. However, a complicated surgical procedure, one that involves a nearly equal proportion of risks and benefits, makes the matter of the patient's informed consent crucial.

A gray area involving informed consent relates to the use of *placebos* in medical practice. A placebo is an "inert substance made to appear indistinguishable from an authentic drug," with an inactive component such as sugar substituted for the active drug.[15] Placebos are commonly used in testing new drugs to provide an evaluation by comparison, and such use is not ethically questionable. However, the prescribing of placebos by doctors in routine medical practice raises questions related to deceiving patients, even though it can be argued that the aim is worthy. Typically, placebos are prescribed when no organic cause for an ailment is found, and it is believed that the placebo will have a beneficial psychological effect. Some authorities estimate that 35 to 45 percent of all prescriptions are essentially placebos. David Towle says that

The doctor who fears being subjected to a malpractice suit if he doesn't tell the worst, and who tells the worst, may actually help to bring on the worst. . . . A serious diagnosis can be communicated as a challenge rather than as a verdict. The physician who volunteers a terminal date, for example, or allows himself to be pressured into offering a terminal date may actually be putting a hex on the patient.

Norman Cousins, "Tapping Human Potential"

"those physicians who use placebos argue that the end, curing the patient, takes precedence over the means: in this case, the deception of the patient."[16]

The ideal of informed consent is not always easy to attain. It may be difficult to clearly determine what constitutes sufficient information on which the patient can base a decision. Some patients take an active role in their treatment, even suggesting alternative methods of treatment to their physician; they are eager to receive a full disclosure of the medical facts and insist on understanding the various options. Other patients prefer simply to follow the program outlined by their doctor; they do not want to know about potential risks or the percentage of failures.

Patients devise different strategies for coping with their illnesses; full disclosure may be a help to some patients, a hindrance to others. This difference can present a dilemma to the medical practitioner. Required to obtain the patient's informed consent before proceeding with treatment, the physician must be sensitive to the patient's preferences for the amount and kind of information given.

In addition, the patient's family may have an agenda regarding truth telling that complicates issues of informed consent. Margot White and John Fletcher describe a case in which the spouse of a dying patient told doctors: "You can't tell my husband he's dying; it will kill him."[17] She insisted that the truth of her husband's illness be withheld from him, refusing the doctors' requests to speak with him about his condition and preferences for treatment. From "Mrs. Doe's" point of view, she knew her husband better than anyone— certainly better than the doctors—and she knew what was best for him. For the medical staff, however, this "interference" raised serious questions about whether their patient's autonomy was being unreasonably compromised. In such circumstances, it is difficult to find solutions to the problem of informed consent that satisfactorily meet the needs of all the concerned parties.

Informed consent also has a bearing on the need for physicians to safeguard themselves against the threat of malpractice suits, which may arise when patients do not adequately understand the possible consequences of a course of treatment. Unfortunately, some physicians may view the concept of informed consent as a nonmedical legalistic and bureaucratic intrusion that interrupts the practice of medicine. Such a viewpoint is not likely to result in physicians providing information in a way that truly meets the needs and desires of patients. Informed consent should not be interpreted as merely reciting "an exhaustive list of risks of any particular medical procedure."[18] On the contrary, if informed consent is to become an integral part of patient care, doctors must make their reasoning about a proposed course of treatment "transparent" to the patient. To this end, the physician must disclose the basis for choosing a proposed treatment and provide opportunities for the patient to ask questions and have them answered to his or her satisfaction. In this way, informed consent becomes more than simply a laundry list of risks recited to avoid potential complaints or legal problems; it facilitates true patient–physician cooperation in working toward a common goal of optimal health care.

Choosing Death: Euthanasia and Allowing to Die

Throughout most of the history of medicine, the Hippocratic obligation of physicians to care for patients has been interpreted to mean, "Thou shalt not kill, but needst not strive officiously to keep alive." This traditional understanding of the Hippocratic obligation acknowledges that in some circumstances medical treatment is futile, offering no further benefit to the patient. With the advent of modern medical technologies, however, the slogan of the medical practitioner has often seemed to be: "Keep the patient alive at all costs." This fundamental change in the aims of medical care not only affects the dying and their relatives, it also presents a burdensome paradox to physicians. What is the proper balance between preserving life and preventing suffering when further treatment is likely to be futile? Although today's medical technologies offer tremendous possibilities for sustaining life, what effect do these life-sustaining technologies have on the *quality* of patient's lives?

Ethical questions about the "right to die" have become prominent since the landmark case involving Karen Ann Quinlan. On April 15, 1975, at age twenty-one, Karen was admitted to the intensive care unit of a New Jersey hospital in a comatose state. Soon her vital processes were being artificially sustained via a mechanical MA-1 respirator. When she remained unresponsive, in a so-called "persistent vegetative state" with no known hope of recovery, Karen's parents asked to have the respirator disconnected so that nature might take its course. This request was opposed by the medical staff responsible for Karen's care, and their refusal resulted in a suit before the New Jersey Superior Court to determine who should have the right to act on Karen's behalf: her parents or the medical staff. Although the Superior Court ruled in favor of the medical staff, thereby keeping Karen on the respirator, this decision was overturned by the Supreme Court of New Jersey in March of 1976.[19] Artificial respiration was discontinued and Karen was eventually transferred to a nursing care facility where she died in June 1985 at age thirty-one, having become a focal point for issues pertaining to "death with dignity," which continue to be debated intensely.

When suffering outweighs the benefits of continued existence, some would argue that individuals have a "right to die," whether or not that right is exercised. Patients themselves often make last-ditch attempts to end their lives. Joseph Fletcher reports that patients may "swallow Kleenex to suffocate themselves, or jerk tubes out of their noses or veins, in a cat-and-mouse game of life and death which is neither merciful nor meaningful."[20] Surrounded by an array of machinery and tubes, the patient may seem less a whole human person than an objectified extension of medical technology.

Even when a patient is deemed to be irreversibly comatose or in a persistent vegetative state—that is, profoundly unconscious, lacking any sign of normal reflexes controlled by the brain stem or spinal cord, unresponsive to all external stimuli, and with no reasonable hope of change for the better—medical personnel are duty bound to render beneficial treatment.[21] But what constitutes beneficial treatment in such cases? Is preserving life the only ethical choice, regardless of the circumstances? Should useless treatment be withheld or withdrawn even though such a decision is virtually certain to result in the patient's death? When confronted with the case of an irreversibly comatose patient or an end-stage terminal patient in great suffering, should a physician consider actively *hastening* or assisting in a patient's death?

Such questions are central to the debate concerning *euthanasia,* which is defined as the act of bringing about a gentle, painless death. In practice, the term is usually understood as "intentionally taking the life of a terminal patient who requests it in order to end a painful dying."[22] In discussions of euthanasia, a distinction is often made between *active* euthanasia (that is, actively bringing about death by, for example, administering a lethal injection) and *passive* euthanasia (allowing death to occur as a result of withdrawing or withholding some treatment that might otherwise sustain life). This distinction is sometimes characterized as the difference between "killing" and "letting die," and it is central to the current debate over physician-assisted death (see Figure 6-1).

When a patient is hopelessly ill or irreversibly comatose, medical ethicists delineate three "treatment" options that can be considered: (1) active treatment to forestall death; (2) active intervention to terminate life; and (3) passive management, a middle course involving neither extraordinary life-saving measures nor active hastening of death. In practice, active intervention to intentionally terminate a patient's life occurs infrequently. It is much more likely that the choice will be made to pursue either active intervention (using extraordinary measures to sustain life) or a course of passive management (using only "ordinary" or "essential" means of treatment).

In the United States, taking active measures to end someone's life is a capital crime. In contrast, it is widely considered to be good medical practice not to artificially prolong the life and suffering of a person who is dying from a fatal disease.[23] Forgoing life-sustaining treatment (that is, doing without a medical intervention that would be expected to extend life) encompasses both

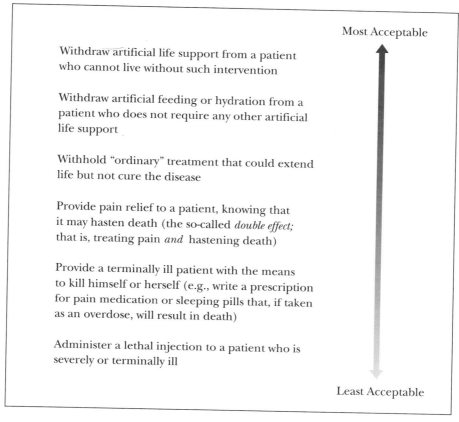

Most Acceptable

Withdraw artificial life support from a patient who cannot live without such intervention

Withdraw artificial feeding or hydration from a patient who does not require any other artificial life support

Withhold "ordinary" treatment that could extend life but not cure the disease

Provide pain relief to a patient, knowing that it may hasten death (the so-called *double effect;* that is, treating pain *and* hastening death)

Provide a terminally ill patient with the means to kill himself or herself (e.g., write a prescription for pain medication or sleeping pills that, if taken as an overdose, will result in death)

Administer a lethal injection to a patient who is severely or terminally ill

Least Acceptable

Figure *6-1*   *Public Acceptance of Voluntary Euthanasia*
Note: Involuntary euthanasia occurs when someone acts arbitrarily, without the patient's consent, to end the patient's life.

withholding (not initiating) treatment and *withdrawing* (discontinuing) an ongoing treatment.

Antibiotics and artificial nutrition, as well as respirators, kidney machines, and other technologies of modern medicine are examples of therapies that sustain life. Reviewing the range of today's medical technologies, the President's Commission for the Study of Ethical Problems in Medicine reported: "For almost any life-threatening condition, some intervention is capable of delaying the moment of death. . . . Matters that were once the province of fate have now become a matter of human choice."[24]

There is a general feeling that when a person is without hope of regaining consciousness or the semblance of normal human activity, he or she should be allowed to die as peacefully as possible. A patient whose case is utterly without

When I was a junior physician in a hospital, we were once called urgently to the bedside of a lady of ninety. The nurse had used the term "cardiac arrest"—the old lady's heart had stopped (as hearts are apt to do, around ninety!). But because the cardiac arrest alarm was raised, I and the other houseman launched into a full-scale resuscitation. With violent drugs injected directly into the heart, blasts of electric current through her chest, noise and chaos, she had anything but a peaceful death. On reflection we realized that all this had been inappropriate, but nothing in our medical student training gave us any guide. Indeed once the emergency is in the air, there is not time to weight up the pros and cons. The decision is rarely a doctor's anyway, because usually the only person on the scene when an emergency occurs is a nurse—probably a relatively junior one if it is night time—and she decides whether or not to resuscitate. Needless to say, it is a very courageous nurse who decides not to. Once things have started, it is very difficult for the doctor when he arrives to stop everything, particularly if the patient is showing signs of reviving.

Richard Lamerton, *Care of the Dying*

hope may be designated "Code 90," or "DNR" (Do Not Resuscitate), or "CMO" (Comfort Measures Only), each a message to the medical and nursing staff that, when death appears to be imminent, extraordinary life-saving measures are not to be applied. Efforts are directed toward easing pain and making the patient as comfortable as possible until death comes. In the absence of a physician's written DNR order, most hospitals require the active initiation of cardiopulmonary resuscitation (CPR) in the event of cardiac or respiratory arrest. Yet, when such resuscitation is clearly futile, some observers believe that it should be withheld, as would other forms of treatment that offer no benefit to the patient.[25]

Ordinary care includes the use of conventional, proven therapies that are maximally effective with minimal danger. *Extraordinary measures,* however, usually entail significant risks and unpredictable results. Typically, such treatment is intended as a temporary measure to sustain life artificially until the patient's own restorative powers can take over. Of course, given the particulars of a situation, a treatment considered by some as ordinary or essential may be considered by others as extraordinary or even intrusive. The use of antibiotics to combat pneumonia in an end-stage cancer patient is an example of how a normally ordinary and essential treatment may be viewed as extraordinary because of the circumstances in which it is administered. Although there now appears to be general agreement among medical practitioners as well as among the public that extraordinary measures need not be used when a patient is hopelessly ill, it is nonetheless true that many areas of uncertainty remain.

Many ethicists and medical practitioners express concern about blurring the distinction between "allowing to die" by withholding or withdrawing treatment and actively "helping to die." In an article published in the *Journal of the American Medical Association,* Charles Sprung says that, even though active euthanasia is considered by many people as "unconscionable" and unlikely to be accepted, "the seeds of active euthanasia have already been planted in our country."[26] Prominent physicians have voiced the belief that "it is not immoral for a physician to assist in the rational suicide of a terminally ill patient." An example of acting on such a belief was the controversial case of "Debbie," a twenty-year-old woman with terminal ovarian cancer who was killed by her physician because he "wanted to help put her out of her misery."[27] Even if the medical profession or society as a whole disavows such actions, individual physicians may act without ethical sanction. Public awareness of the ethical issues concerning euthanasia has been heightened in recent years by the activities of Michigan pathologist Dr. Jack Kevorkian, who has provided aid-in-dying to more than twenty individuals since 1990. (The legal issues in physician-assisted death are discussed in Chapter 9.)

David Roy, director of the Center for Bioethics in Montreal and editor of the *Journal of Palliative Care,* believes that the distinction between euthanasia and allowing to die must be maintained: "This distinction is a recognition of the limits of modern medicine's power, and of the limits of the medical profession's mandate; a recognition also that horrible and intolerable abuse is as much a possibility for us today as it has already proved to be a reality in the past."[28] The challenge of civilization to our societies, he says, is not to legalize euthanasia, but rather to transform our care of the suffering and dying. Most people who endorse the philosophy of hospice or palliative care would agree that the provision of adequate treatment for pain and depression essentially does away with any reason for considering active measures to prematurely end a terminal patient's life.

In the Netherlands, physicians are permitted to take *active* steps, under certain circumstances, to end the lives of patients who request a "dignified death."[29] Although Dutch law states that anyone who takes another person's life—even at their explicit request—can be punished, it also states that such an act is not punishable if "driven by an overwhelming power, a sudden conflict of duties or interests in a situation in which a choice must be made." Decisions during the 1970s and 1980s by the Dutch courts formed a consensus that euthanasia would not be prosecuted as long as certain conditions were met. In 1993, the Dutch legislature affirmed this consensus when it passed a bill regarding voluntary active euthanasia and physician-assisted suicide. Although both acts remain illegal in the Netherlands, the 1993 bill specifies that physicians will not be prosecuted if they act in accordance with specific requirements to ensure responsible practice.

Consonant with prevailing medical ethics in the Netherlands, the criteria established by Dutch courts and affirmed by the parliament include the presence of a confirmed terminal diagnosis; the patient's unwavering desire, confirmed in writing, of his or her wish to die; the presence of unbearable and incurable physical suffering; and a second medical opinion. Out of 129,000 deaths each year in the Netherlands, about 2300 (1.8 percent of all deaths)

Dying of a prolonged disease is less an event than a difficult process, which, like birth, requires understanding help.

Medicine should prolong life, not the process of dying. There comes a point in a degenerative disease when further "aggressive" treatment would intensify the patient's suffering without substantial benefit. Then concern for the patient should become concern for a dignified death, for palliative care for symptoms and needs. This point is difficult to determine, because much is unknown about the behavior of advanced malignant disease. But the point must be determined.

Hospices . . . are an answer to demands for euthanasia (meaning not the patient's legal right to demand withdrawal of life-support treatment, but the right to demand a killing act). Support for euthanasia legislation derives, in part, from the mistaken fear that doctors are obligated to prolong life with all available technologies, however severe the ordeal and cost, and the mistaken fear that unremitting pain in terminal diseases, especially cancer, is unavoidable. With hospice care as an alternative, there would be little demand for euthanasia.

George F. Will, *The Pursuit of Virtue & Other Tory Notions*

result from voluntary euthanasia at the patient's explicit request, with death typically being hastened by lethal doses administered by sympathetic physicians. An additional 400 cases (0.3 percent of all deaths) fit into the category of assisted suicide. This results in about 2700 cases of euthanasia and assisted suicide annually. Thus, in the Netherlands, acts of voluntary active euthanasia and assisted suicide, although illegal, are nevertheless "tolerated" within a socially sanctioned set of guidelines and practices.

Some argue that euthanasia is morally permissible when it prevents an even greater cruelty—namely, preventing someone who is in pain and wishes to die from obtaining the release offered by death. According to this view, both the patient and the physician ought to be free to pursue the course indicated as in the patient's best interests, given his or her terminal condition.

Critics of this argument respond by emphasizing the dangers of allowing euthanasia to become an acceptable and routine policy. Objections to euthanasia include the difficulty of obtaining a patient's clear consent, the risk of incorrect diagnosis, and the uncertainty of whether an innovative treatment might become available in time to offer a cure. Another objection has been characterized as the "wedge" or "slippery slope" argument: One should not permit acts that, although possibly moral in themselves, might eventually pave the way for acts that would be immoral. If we were to permit euthanasia in cases of irreversible terminal illness today, tomorrow the practice might well be expanded to situations that are far less justifiable, leading to acts of killing motivated by caprice or whim, or perhaps darker motives.

(Another argument that can be made against euthanasia relates to the notion held by some Buddhists, for example, that the period surrounding dying offers an extraordinary opportunity for awakening or enlightenment. That there may also be a biochemical basis for this belief is suggested by recent research on endorphins, which are natural products of the body that seem to relieve pain while enhancing clarity of thought during the dying process.)

Pioneers in care of the dying, such as Elisabeth Kübler-Ross and Cicely Saunders, have argued strongly against voluntary euthanasia among the terminally ill. Such a practice, they say, is unlikely to remain voluntary; soon, the irreversibly sick will be made to feel guilty for not agreeing to end it quickly. Others involved in palliative care concur with the notion that permitting euthanasia to become an accepted policy is not only morally dangerous, but also unnecessary because the suffering of dying patients can be treated. In summary, their argument states:[30]

1. There is an inherent risk that a legally sanctioned "right" to euthanasia might come to be experienced by the patient as an obligation, with a subtle pressure to "end it all" so as to lessen the burden on loved ones.
2. Where would one draw the line once the slippery slope of euthanasia has been embarked on?
3. When the pain and depression are treated and the sources of anxiety addressed, the infrequent request for euthanasia may disappear.

In surveying the arguments for and against euthanasia, Charles Dougherty calls attention to a consideration of what constitutes the "common good" for society as a whole with respect to questions involving euthanasia and physician-assisted death.[31] Perhaps an overemphasis on individualism has caused us to lose sight of the fact that no aspect of human experience is wholly personal and private. On the contrary, says Dougherty, "The way we die—when, under what circumstances, and from what cause or reason—is shaped in profound ways by relationships with others and by large social and institutional forces." If dying in the modern medical environment sometimes involves excessive pain and suffering, and costs too much, then society's common good would be best served "by measures that add simplicity and dignity to the process of dying and contain unnecessary spending." Practical steps toward enhancing the common good in caring for the terminally ill include: (1) increasing the use of home hospice care; (2) developing strategies for more aggressive pain management; (3) refining protocols for timely diagnosis of terminal illness; (4) making the right to refuse extraordinary care universally available to patients; (5) expanding the use of DNR orders to avoid prolonged, expensive, and unnecessary care at the end of life; (6) providing universal access to an appropriate combination of care options (home, hospice, and so on); and (7) instituting a health insurance system that ensures adequate and appropriate care for everyone. In suggesting these measures, Dougherty says, "Respect for the common good demands creation and protection of social realities that serve all persons."

Nutrition and Hydration

In several states, families of irreversibly comatose patients have sought and obtained court rulings allowing removal of artificial feeding tubes. In Florida, for example, a District Court of Appeals said that artificial feeding is similar to

Assistance in providing nutrition to chronically ill and dying patients ranges from help with eating, as seen here with these nursing home residents, to total reliance on artificial feeding. The issue of artificially providing nutrition to comatose, hopelessly ill patients is one of the newest ethical issues in medicine.

other extraordinary means of sustaining life, such as the respirator. It ruled that the right of privacy includes the right to remove nasogastric tubes from persons who are in persistent vegetative states with no prospect of regaining cognitive brain function. In a unanimous decision, the court said that when the use of medical technologies results in a situation where all that remains is the forced function of bodily processes, including artificial sustenance of the body itself, "we recognize the right to allow the natural consequences of the removal of those artificial life-sustaining measures."[32] Concurrence in such decisions is reflected in a policy announced by an ethics panel of the American Medical Association stating that artificial feeding and the infusion of water can be stopped in cases of irreversible coma.

Some commentators have condemned judicial decisions authorizing the withdrawal of nutrition from a "preservable unconscious patient," even going so far as to characterize such actions as the intentional killing of a human being. Others, holding to the distinction between active euthanasia and forgoing a medical intervention, contend that the withdrawal of artificial nutrition is consistent with traditional medical and legal doctrines.[33] Among those who believe that removal of artificial nutrition is tantamount to intentional killing, some argue that the symbolic significance of nourishment justifies the continuation of artificial nutrition and hydration even when all other medical treatments have been stopped. Feelings about the provision of food and drink and about the specter of "starving" a patient to death are deeply rooted in the human psyche. On the other hand, those who believe it is indeed moral to withdraw artificial nourishment argue that these everyday sentiments about the symbolic meaning of food and water "cannot be transferred without distortion to the hospital world," and that, indeed, "authentic sentiment may demand discontinuance of artificial feeding."[34]

This "conceptual ambiguity" about the artificial delivery of food and fluids, say James McCartney and Jane Trau, "derives from the traditional consideration of nourishment as simple care."[35] When such nourishment is withheld, it brings up images of burdening the patient with "the pain of death by starvation." But the invasive nature of delivering such nourishment and the skills required to administer it, as well as the pain and discomfort experienced by many patients, argue against the perception that such artificial delivery of sustenance is merely providing care. Instead of viewing the artificial provision of nourishment as simple care, McCartney and Trau find that, in actuality, these procedures more closely resemble palliative or even therapeutic treatment. As Dena Davis remarks in the context of a case involving whether or not to implant a permanent feeding tube into the body of an eighty-year-old woman, the issues relating to providing nourishment are highly charged emotionally, and "we need to be very careful to sort out the physiological aspects of providing nutrition from the social phenomenon of 'feeding.'"[36]

In 1987, the New Jersey Supreme Court ruled on cases involving the removal of feeding tubes from two patients in that state. Nancy Ellen Jobes, thirty-one years old, was four months pregnant in April 1980 when she was in a car accident, and she had fallen into a coma when doctors removed the fetus (which died). The other patient, Hilda Peter, sixty-five years old, had suffered a stroke in 1984 and had been in a coma since that time, a condition that her physicians said could continue indefinitely. In deciding the cases, the court stated that it recognized that "the state has an interest in preserving life," but that those interests "weaken—and the individual's right to privacy becomes stronger—as the degree of bodily invasion (affected by the medical treatment at issue) increases and the prognosis dims."[37]

The opinions of the Florida and New Jersey courts relative to the removal of artificial feeding devices are not universally shared, however. This fact was clearly illustrated by the June 1990 decision of the United States Supreme Court regarding the case of Nancy Beth Cruzan. As a result of injuries sustained in an automobile accident when she was twenty-five, Cruzan had been in a persistent vegetative state since January of 1983. Although paramedics restored her breathing after the accident, her brain was deprived of oxygen for so long that she never regained consciousness. In February 1983, doctors implanted a feeding tube in Cruzan's stomach, the only form of life support she was receiving. Prior to the Supreme Court's deliberations, the Missouri Supreme Court had denied her parents' petition to end artificial feeding, a treatment that Nancy's physicians said could prolong her life for as long as thirty years. As Nancy's guardians, her parents claimed legal standing to assert her right to be free from "unwarranted bodily intrusions." However, absent Nancy's express consent to remove life-sustaining artificial nutrition and hydration, the state court held that her guardians could not exercise her right to refuse treatment and that the state's "unqualified" interest in preserving life should therefore prevail.[38]

As the case went before the U.S. Supreme Court, the American Medical Association and other groups, including Concern for Dying, filed *amicus curiae* briefs in support of the Cruzans' position. Other groups, including the Association of American Physicians and Surgeons, filed opposing briefs, arguing that a physician's obligation to patients who are comatose or in a persistent vegetative state "does not depend upon the prospect of recovery."

In its 5–4 decision, the Supreme Court ruled that Missouri could enforce the standards expressed in its statute by reason of the state's interest in protecting life. Although the Court affirmed a patient's right to refuse medical treatment, including artificial nutrition and hydration, it said that states are justified in requiring that only the patient—in a clear and competent expression of his or her wishes—can decide to withdraw treatment. Here is a synopsis of the Court's decision:

> The scope of the Court's considerations was quite narrow. It sought to determine whether Nancy Cruzan had a right under the United States Constitution that would require the hospital to withdraw life-sustaining treatment. The Court answered in the negative. While acknowledging that a competent person has a constitutional right to refuse life-sustaining medical treatment on the basis of "liberty interests" (not privacy) protected by the 14th Amendment, the Court held that there is nothing in the United States Constitution that forbids Missouri from establishing the procedural requirements it did (that is, clear and convincing evidence) for decision making by surrogates for incompetent patients.[39]

Thus, despite the Cruzans' insistence that they were in a position to voice their daughter's wishes (as her court-appointed guardians), the Court's decision hinged on the fact that Nancy had not formally made her wishes known by executing a living will or similar advance directive stating her preferences. (Advance directives such as living wills and durable powers of attorney are discussed in Chapter 9.) Although the motives of the Cruzans were not questioned by the Court, which found them to be "loving and caring parents," its ruling reflected the opinion that the motives of family members in other cases could be "not entirely disinterested." Thus, in the majority opinion of the Court, "A state is entitled to guard against potential abuses in such situations." The Cruzan case highlights the importance of leaving written instructions for relatives and doctors to follow in the event of incapacitating and terminal illness. Notice, if you will, how the principles of autonomy, beneficence, and justice were applied in this case.

The Supreme Court's decision effectively returned further consideration of the case back to the Missouri courts. In December 1990, a Missouri judge

A number of years ago, before all the discussion about defining brain death and maintaining life on a respirator and so on, a patient of mine, a young pregnant woman at term, suddenly developed extremely high blood pressure. Then she had a stroke and the baby's heartbeat stopped, so we supported her by artificially maintaining blood pressure and other vital functions, including breathing. But she had had a complete brain death immediately. And she had lost the baby. We got an EEG [electroencephalogram], and it was completely flat. We repeated it twenty-four hours later, and again it was completely flat.

It was the worst tragedy I've ever seen, because in just a few minutes she was gone and the baby was gone—just within moments. I talked with her husband, her mother, and her father. (Now, this was long before the issues surrounding definition of death had become so contentious that the lawyers got involved.) I told them that the thing to do was turn off the machine. Just as I had not read about all this, they as a family had not read about it. It seemed quite logical to me.

So we picked a time when we were going to do it, and they all came and waited outside the door. I told them again what I was going to do, and they said to go ahead and do it. I went in and turned off the machine. The nurse and I watched her, and in five minutes her pulse rate had stopped. I think this is the proper way to handle this sort of situation when brain death is involved. I think it has a negative effect to continue life support systems for weeks and months. It was a tragedy, and given the tragedy, what options do you have? Continue the life support system or don't continue it. To me, there's no argument whatsoever to continue the life support system.

Quoted from *Death and Dying:
The Physician's Perspective,* a
videotape by Elizabeth Bradbury

reconsidered the case in light of the Supreme Court's decision and new testimony from three of Nancy's friends, who claimed to have had conversations with her to the effect that she would not want to live "like a vegetable." The attorney general of Missouri had, in the meantime, asked the court to drop the state as a colitigant, saying that the state no longer had a "recognizable legal interest" in the case and would not contest the Cruzans' attempts to end their daughter's life. In addition, Nancy Cruzan's court-appointed guardian recommended that the feeding tube be removed. A doctor who had previously testified against removing the feeding tube now reversed himself and testified that he believed it would be in Cruzan's best interest to end her "living hell." At this point, the state court ruled that the "clear and convincing evidence" standard had been met and granted permission for removal of the tube supplying food and water. Thirteen days later, while anti-euthanasia protesters congregated outside the hospital, Nancy Cruzan died. "She remained peaceful throughout and showed no sign of discomfort or distress in any way," the Cruzan family said in a statement. "Knowing Nancy as only a family can, there remains no question that we made the choice she would want."

Following Nancy's death, columnist Ellen Goodman wrote: "The Cruzan case, like that of Karen Ann Quinlan, became a story that made America talk publicly and at length about death in the technological age."[40] As the first case of its kind to come before the Supreme Court, the Cruzan case focused national attention on "right to die" issues and helped prompt legislation requiring that patients be informed of their right to refuse treatment.[41]

Whereas the Cruzan case caused many people to think about formally expressing their wishes while still able to do so, the recent case of Carrie Coons, an 86-year-old New York stroke victim may give some of them pause.[42] For more than four months following her stroke, Mrs. Coons showed no signs of alertness. Doctors, lawyers, and family members believed her to be in a persistent and irreversible vegetative coma, and so petitioned the court for the right to disconnect her life support—an action previously approved of by Mrs. Coons. This permission was granted. Two days later, Mrs. Coons began to stir, eventually eating small portions of food and saying a few words. When her physician asked what should now be done about her case, Mrs. Coons replied, "These are difficult decisions," and fell asleep. The court withdrew permission to disconnect her feeding tube.

Ethical issues involving forced feeding of *noncomatose* patients became prominent in the California judiciary when the decision of Elizabeth Bouvia, a quadriplegic, to refuse such treatment was upheld by that state's Supreme Court. The ruling said that mentally competent, informed patients have the right to refuse any medical treatment, including life support provided by mechanical or artificial means. This historic ruling allowing Elizabeth Bouvia to refuse forced feeding was hailed by some as a victory for individual liberties; others called it "legal suicide."[43]

Given the degree of uncertainty currently surrounding many ethical issues in medicine, who should make decisions about forgoing life-sustaining treatment? In the final report of its studies, the President's Commission emphasized the importance of: (1) respecting the choices of individuals who are competent to decide to forgo even life-sustaining treatment; (2) providing guidelines and procedures for making decisions on behalf of patients who are unable to do so on their own; (3) maintaining a presumption in favor of sustaining life; (4) improving the medical options available to dying patients; (5) providing respectful, responsive, and supportive care to patients for whom no further medical therapies are available or elected; and (6) encouraging health care institutions to take responsibility for ensuring that adequate procedures for decision making are available for all patients.[44] Probably no other topic of death and dying generates as much debate as does the ethical issues related to the hopelessly ill.

Seriously Ill Newborns

The ethical issues that arise from the dilemma of whether to sustain life or to allow death are perhaps most sensitively realized in the case of infants. Throughout this century, and especially within the past few decades, the

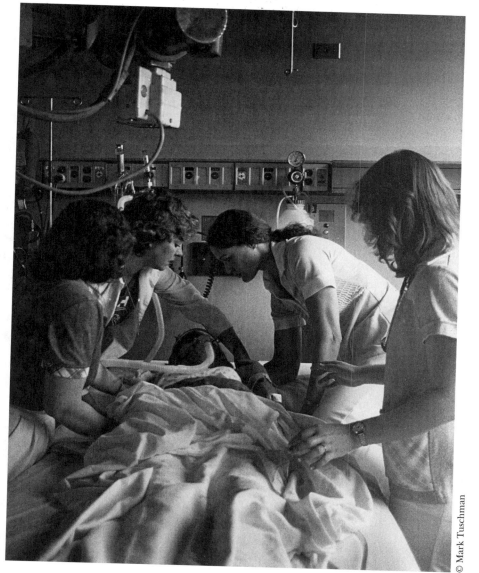

In the intensive care unit, both human and technical considerations combine to make necessary the evaluation of ethical questions regarding the meaning of life and death.

© Mark Tuschman

mortality rate among infants and children has been reduced, largely through advances in both the knowledge and techniques of neonatal care. In hospitals with specialized infant intensive care units, for instance, the neonatal mortality rate is roughly half that of hospitals not having such special care nurseries. Neonatal treatment now includes "the use of respirators, sensitive monitoring of blood pressure, oxygenation, blood flow and biochemical parameters, and other evolving nursing and medical technologies," and "new techniques have been developed in heart, intestine, liver, kidney, and brain surgery to correct congenital anomalies."[45]

The special care nursery, which can make a crucial difference in an infant's chances of survival, is an innovation in medical practice that virtually everyone would applaud. As Marie McCormick reports, "Neonatal intensive care continues to be effective in saving lives" and "the majority of survivors do not suffer from severe to moderate handicap."[46] Unfortunately, some of the infants whose lives are spared will never be capable of living what is considered a normal human life. They may suffer from cardiopulmonary ailments or brain damage, or they may be severely handicapped by some congenital malformation. Formerly, such dysfunctional conditions in infancy would almost surely have resulted in death. Now that many of these infants survive because of the specialized care they receive, we are confronted by ethical questions concerning the quality of their lives and the guidelines that should be operable in determining whether or not medical intervention is the best course of action.

Should the life of an infant with intestinal blockage be spared by surgical intervention? Is the answer always "Yes, life should be saved," or does the answer change according to circumstances? What if the infant is brain-damaged or severely retarded?

Consider the following case: An infant was born with his entire left side malformed, with no left eye, and practically without a left ear; his left hand was deformed, and some of his vertebrae were not fused. Being also afflicted with a tracheo-esophageal fistula (an abnormality of the windpipe and the canal that leads to the stomach), he could not be fed by mouth. Air leaked into his stomach instead of going to the lungs, and fluid from the stomach pushed up into the lungs. One doctor commented, "It takes little imagination to think there were further internal difficulties as well." In the ensuing days, the infant's condition steadily worsened. Pneumonia set in; his reflexes became impaired; and, because of poor circulation, severe brain damage was suspected. But despite the seriousness of all these factors taken together, the immediate threat to his survival, the tracheo-esophageal fistula, could be corrected by a fairly easy surgical procedure.

The debate began when the parents refused to give their consent to surgery. Some of the doctors treating the child believed that surgery was warranted and took the case to court. The judge ordered surgery, ruling that "at the moment of live birth, there does exist a human being entitled to the fullest protection of the law. . . . The most basic right enjoyed by every human being is the right to life itself."[47]

In another case, which provides some contrasts to the one just cited, the mother of a premature baby overheard the doctor describing her infant as having Down's syndrome with the added complication that the intestines were blocked. Ordinary surgery can correct this kind of blockage; without correction, the child cannot be fed and will die. The mother felt that "it would be unfair" to her other children if a retarded child were brought into the home. Her husband supported this decision, and they refused their consent for surgery.

One of the physicians argued that the degree of mental retardation in children with Down's syndrome cannot be predicted; and, in the physician's words: "They're almost always trainable. They can hold simple jobs, and they're famous for being happy children. They're perennially happy and usually a great joy. When further complications do not appear, a long life can be anticipated." However, in this case, the hospital staff did not seek a court order to override the parents' decision against surgical intervention. As a result, the child was placed in a side room and, over the following eleven days, it starved to death.

The differences between these two cases are instructive. The severely malformed infant in the first case seemed to have less chance of survival or of living a normal life than the afflicted infant in the second example. Yet the hospital staff in the first case chose to seek a court order granting treatment, whereas the staff at the second hospital chose to abide by the parents' wishes even though the child could probably have been saved.

In commenting on the second case, James Gustafson argues that the child's right to life was not adequately explored, either by the physicians or by the parents.[48] From the doctors' point of view, once the decision was made not to proceed with the operation, the child became terminal, and thus further means of sustaining life were unwarranted. Gustafson, however, argues that the subsequent withholding of ordinary means of treatment was in actuality an *extraordinary* nonintervention.

Whatever our feelings may be about the decisions just described, a distinction between cases involving infants and those involving terminal patients with a prolonged illness is worth noting. Generally, in the latter case, all procedures that might prolong life have been tried or at least presented to the patient as options. But, in cases involving infants, Gustafson says, the withholding of treatment results from a "decision not to act at all."

The difficulty inherent in making decisions about the treatment of seriously ill newborns was highlighted in the study by the President's Commission. While affirming that parents should have the power of decision in most instances, the Commission also stated that medical institutions should pursue the best interests of an infant "when those interests are clear."[49] Using as an example the situation of an otherwise healthy Down's syndrome child whose life is threatened by a surgically correctable condition, the Commission said that such an infant should receive surgery because he or she would benefit. While stating that therapies expected to be futile need not be provided, the Commission added that, even in cases when no beneficial therapy is available, action should be taken to ensure the infant's comfort. Based on a review of current neonatal care technologies and present standards for determining treatment, medical ethicist Arthur Caplan concludes that decisions regarding disabled newborns ought to be based on a standard that combines "the best interest of the child," an infant-centered approach, with considerations about the "relationship potential" of such a child, an approach that "allows the interests of others—for example, the family or society—to weigh in the decision about whether to treat."[50]

Defining Death

On the face of it, the definition of death might seem quite obvious: A person dies, is dead, and the corpse is disposed of. But as soon as someone asks, "What do you mean by 'a person dies'?" the whole matter begins to unravel. What at first may seem simple turns out to be amazingly complex. Indeed, there are many historical accounts of people being thought dead who in fact were in a state that only mimicked biological death.

Not too many years ago, one could hear horror stories about bodies lying in a morgue coming back to life, as it were, and startling the bereaved family, not to mention the mortician. A state of unconsciousness, perhaps, or an extreme slowing of body functioning resulted in the appearance of death. To provide a safeguard against the threat of being buried alive, some people gave instructions that their bodies be placed in coffins with bells or some other attention-getting device that the "corpse" could activate even after burial should consciousness return after a mistaken determination of death (see Figure 6-2).

Think for a moment. When would you consider yourself to be dead? How would you know that death had occurred in someone else? The answers to these questions range from the definite ("when decay and putrefaction have set in") to the more difficult ("when I can no longer take care of myself"). A person using the first method for making a determination of death would hardly be pleased to be judged dead by the standards of the second.

The present concern with defining death is, of course, more sophisticated, taking into account complex scientific data. Although we still must make determinations of death from observable indications that life has ceased, these observable signs can be interpreted differently, depending on how death is defined. In other words, how we define death establishes the empirical procedures to be used in determining that a person has died. To better understand the issues relating to defining and making a determination of death, some writers distinguish five levels at which decisions are made with respect to the death of a human being: First, a conceptual understanding of what constitutes death must be established; second, general criteria and procedures for determining that a person has died must be selected; third, these criteria must be applied in a particular case to determine if the patient meets the criteria; fourth, if the criteria are met, the person is pronounced dead; and fifth, the death is attested on a certificate of record.[51]

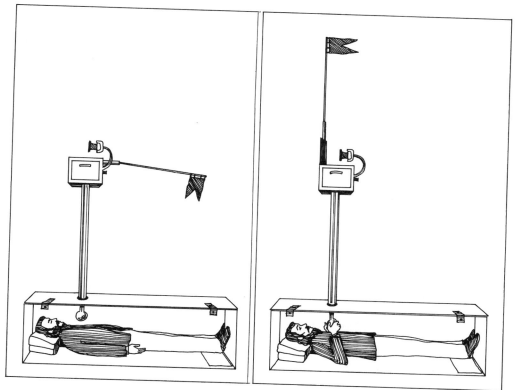

Figure *6-2*   *Coffin Bell-Pull Device*
To prevent premature burial in cases of doubtful death, devices such as this
French "life-preserving" coffin were invented and patented. If activated,
the box above the ground opened to let in air and light, the flag raised,
a bell rang, and a light came on to signal that the buried person was still
alive. The person who had been mistaken for dead could also call out, and
his or her voice would be amplified by the device. The fear of being buried alive stemmed from the period of great plagues and epidemics when, in
the hasty disposition of the dead, a mistaken determination of death might
result from a state of illness that only mimicked death.

The Traditional Signs of Death and the New Technology

Historically, the death of the human organism has been ascertained by the
absence of heartbeat and respiration. With the cessation of these vital signs,
and as the cells and tissues of the body die, certain advanced signs of death
become evident: the lack of certain reflexes in the eyes, the fall of body
temperature (algor mortis), the purple-red discoloration of parts of the body
as blood settles (livor mortis), and the rigidity of muscles (rigor mortis). Even
today, most deaths are determined by the absence of these vital signs.

However, respirators and other sophisticated devices, which sustain vital processes artificially, render the traditional means of determining death inadequate. Using traditional criteria, a patient in an irreversible coma with no brain wave activity could be termed alive on the basis of *artificially* maintained breathing and heartbeat. Efforts to expand the criteria for determining death have focused on "brain" death or, in some instances, cerebral death (that is, cessation of activity in the upper part of the brain, the cerebrum, which is regarded as the locus of conscious mental processes). As a result, medical practitioners have adopted a definition of death that equates it with irreversible coma, as determined by a flat electroencephalogram (EEG) reading. Confirmatory signs of irreversible or "terminal" coma include unresponsiveness to all external stimuli and lack of any sign of normal reflexes controlled by the brain stem or spinal cord.[52]

As pointed out in an editorial in the British medical journal *Lancet*, the problem of defining brain death arises only when a patient is put on a respirator and is thus sustained artificially; indeed, the editorial stated bluntly, the resulting dilemma about brain death is of the doctor's own making.[53] In fact, the dilemma is one that relates to a host of medical, legal, ethical, moral, and religious concerns. The debate about new definitions of death and how they should be applied has become a public policy issue of interest to both professionals and laypersons, much like the debate over nuclear armaments. Just as the history of the nuclear debate can be traced to a particular event—the development of the atomic bomb—so the debate concerning how death should be defined and determined can be traced to the development of the respirator. Thus, the current situation is the result of a technological innovation. Clyde Nabe says:

> Technology seldom presents itself in a value-free way. There are usually trade-offs involved; the respirator saves lives and allows many human beings to continue productive lives that would otherwise be lost. But it also presents us with situations wherein we are uncertain we are dealing any longer with a human life; the morality of continuing to respirate a body that may or may not be a human being is unclear.[54]

Rather than replacing the traditional clinical means of diagnosis—pulse, heartbeat, and respiration—the new criteria for determining death supplement them, being applicable to instances that arise from the new technology. The widespread use of organ transplantation procedures has been an important impetus to recent efforts to arrive at a new definition of death. In many cases, transplanted organs are taken from donors who have suffered brain death but whose heartbeat and breath are maintained artificially. With regard to organ transplantation, two issues are central: (1) determining when death can be said to have occurred, and (2) deciding when it is permissible to remove the deceased's organs. Even when the second of these issues is not relevant to a particular patient's situation, however, the determination of death can still present a dilemma. As the *Lancet* editorial emphasized, once a patient is placed on devices that artificially sustain vital functions, a variety of complex medical, legal, and ethical questions may impinge on how death is defined.

If alternative definitions of death are to be assessed, the distinction between clinical death and cellular death must be understood. As we have seen, *clinical death* is determined by a set of criteria imposed on a particular array of vital signs (such as blood flow and breathing). Thus, when a patient's breathing or heartbeat stops—even if temporarily, as during certain surgical procedures—it can be said that the patient was clinically dead during the time these vital functions had ceased. However, it can be argued that when the state of cessation of vital functions is reversible, it would be imprecise or unwarranted to term such a cessation clinical death.

Cellular death refers to a process that is gradual and that involves complex variables, including such vital signs as blood flow and breathing, but that also encompasses physiological processes within the body's cells. Death is defined biologically as "the cessation of life resulting from irreversible changes in cell metabolism."[55] Because the living cell is an unstable system, it requires a continuous input of energy; otherwise, "it will degrade into a nonliving collection of molecules." Without oxygen, body cells vary in their survival potential. The cells of skin and connective tissues may survive for several hours; the neurons of the brain can last only five to eight minutes. When there is a loss of neurons in the midbrain and medulla, the brain center that controls breathing is destroyed; the death of neurons in the cerebral cortex destroys intellectual capacity.

As cellular death proceeds, the body's major systems and organs undergo an irreversible process of deterioration. The breakdown of these metabolic processes, the sum of which we call life, results in a loss of organic functions— that is, death. We have already seen how, as death progresses at the cellular level, such phenomena as algor mortis, livor mortis, and rigor mortis occur in the body.

Cellular death may affect some organs of the body, causing irreversible breakdown, while other organs of the body are sustained by artificial means. Medical science now allows for the manipulation of the dying process so that some parts of the body cease to function while other parts can be maintained indefinitely. This ability of modern medicine to alter the natural sequence and process of cellular death has brought about a need to redefine the physiological meaning of death and to institute new procedures for making a clinical determination of death.

Conceptual and Empirical Criteria

What is death? How can it be determined that a person has died? These questions, though closely related, involve separate issues that must be distinguished. As Clyde Nabe points out, to untangle the complexity of these issues, we must "make plain the distinctions between the *clinical criteria* for determining when death has occurred, and the *decision* as to what *constitutes* death, and what we mean by 'death.'"[56] Definitions of death involve conceptual issues;

methods of making a determination that death has occurred involve empirical and procedural issues.

Robert Veatch has outlined four levels that must be addressed in the inquiry concerning the definition and determination of death.[57] The first level involves formally defining *death*, an essentially conceptual or philosophical endeavor. Veatch supplies a formal definition: "Death means a complete change in the status of a living entity characterized by the irreversible loss of those characteristics that are essentially significant to it." This definition encompasses the deaths not only of human beings but also of nonhuman animals, plants, cells, and indeed can even be understood metaphorically as applying to a social phenomenon such as an organization of a society or culture. Whatever the instance, however, it is clear that death is a dramatic change in the status of the entity.

To give content to this formal definition, we must address Veatch's second level of inquiry, again a conceptual or philosophical question: What is so essentially significant about life that its loss is termed *death*? Some answers have included the flow of vital bodily fluids (breath and blood, for example), the soul, and in more recent definitions, consciousness. We will examine each of these in greater detail shortly.

The third level distinguished by Veatch concerns the question of the *locus* of death: Where in the organism should one look to determine whether death has occurred? With this question, we move from conceptual issues to an empirical inquiry, although the answer to this question depends on the conceptual basis used to define death.

At Veatch's fourth level of inquiry the criteria of death must be formulated: In other words, what technical tests must be applied at the locus to determine if an individual is living or dead?

To summarize these four levels: We must first establish a general definition of death; then give that definition content by stating what is essentially significant about the change of status from life to death; then locate where in the organism one can observe the signs of this change; and finally describe the tests that should be applied to determine whether a person is alive or dead. Veatch believes that it is the confusion of these four levels that has confounded much of the current debate and efforts to establish new standards for determining death.

Four Approaches to the Definition and Determination of Death

Veatch then identifies four "plausible approaches" to defining and determining death. Whereas the formal definition of death applies to all of these approaches, the subsequent levels of inquiry—that is, those involving a particular concept of death, the locus of death, and the criteria for determining death—are distinctive for each approach. Each approach relates death to a loss: the first, of the flow of vital fluids; the second, of the soul by the body; the third, of the capacity for bodily integration; the fourth, of the capacity for social interaction. As you read about each approach, you can see how death is determined according to the way it is defined.

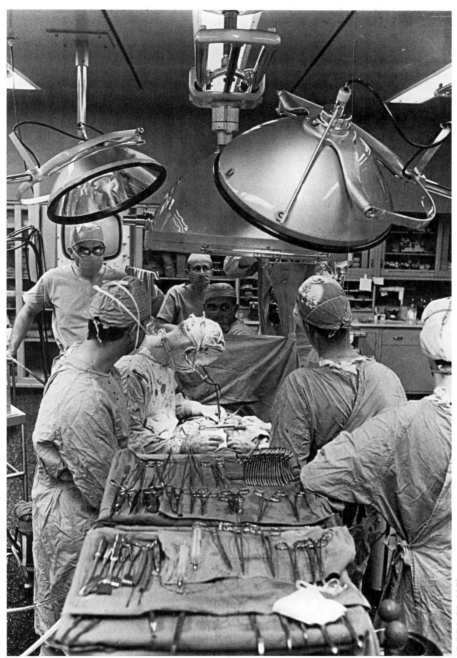

At the Stanford University Medical Center, Dr. Norman Shumway and his colleagues perform open-heart surgery. Advances in transplantation procedures and related medical therapies make such operations more feasible, yet they also raise questions that are difficult, at times quite painful, to resolve.

Irreversible Loss of Flow of Vital Fluids

The first approach pertains to the cessation of the flow of vital bodily fluids. With this conceptual understanding of death, one looks to the heart, blood vessels, lungs, and respiratory tract as the locus of death. To determine whether an individual is alive or dead, one would observe the breathing, feel the pulse, and listen to the heartbeat. The more sophisticated modern methods of electrocardiogram and direct measurement of oxygen and carbon dioxide levels in the blood can be added to these traditional tests because they focus on the same loci and criteria for determining death.

This approach to defining death is adequate for making a determination of death in most cases, even today. When vital functions are artificially sustained by machines, however, no unambiguous determination of death can be made by this definition. For instance, a patient is connected to a heart-lung machine that keeps the vital fluids of blood and breath flowing through the body. According to this definition, the patient is alive. If the patient is disconnected from the machine, these vital functions cease and, by this definition, the patient is dead. Yet during open-heart surgery, these circulatory systems are interrupted—making it possible to consider the patient clinically dead under this definition. But we know the patient is not dead, because such temporary cessation is simply part of the surgical procedures.

The ambiguity of this first approach to defining death results from defining death on the basis of physiological criteria that, although intimately related to life processes, do not seem to constitute the most significant criteria for identifying human life.

Irreversible Loss of the Soul from the Body

In the second approach to defining death—one used in many cultures worldwide and from time immemorial—the criterion is the presence or absence of the soul in the body. Within this framework, as long as the soul is present, the person is alive; when the soul leaves, the body dies. Indeed, some traditions define death in precisely this way. The *Tibetan Book of the Dead*, for example, presents the view that life is terminated in a series of gradual steps, from a state of life to the state we call death. Christian theologians and other religious ethicists also grapple with this question.

This second conceptual definition of death, then, involves the irreversible loss of the soul from the body. The locus of the soul has not been scientifically established (nor has its existence), although some believe the soul is related to the breath or the heart, or perhaps, as seventeenth-century philosopher René Descartes believed, to the pineal body, a small protrusion from the center of the brain. For those who hold this concept, the criteria for determining death would presumably involve some means of ascertaining death at the particular locus where the soul is thought to reside. For example, if the soul is thought to be coincident with the breath, then absence of breath would indicate the loss of the soul and, hence, death. In a study conducted in 1907, dying people were placed on a very sensitive scale to determine whether any weight loss occurs at

Knowing What a Human Being Is

Rolling Thunder often repeated, "We do so many unnatural things, we don't know what's natural anymore." One day he and I were sitting on the ground out in the desert. He was describing a young Indian apprentice from another tribe and making designs in the sand with a stick. Suddenly he said, "You people don't even know what a human being is!" I did not see the connection between the subject at hand and that sudden exclamation, but I had learned to understand what he meant by "you people." It was not a judgmental finger-pointing to be taken personally, but a sort of generalized identification to be applied wherever it fit. "You can look right at someone's empty body and think that you're lookin' at the person when they're not even there. Time and time again, you people speed to the scene of an accident, pick up an empty body and take it down the highway at eighty miles an hour, leaving the person miles behind, not knowing what the heck is going on!"

As an example, he then described to me an episode in which he went into the hospital to assist a young lady—a friend of friends—who had been in a head-on collision and was a long time in a coma.

"But the moment I took a good look at the body, I could see she wasn't even there. I had to find her—go get her—and she was way out in the field where the car'd flipped over the cliff, and she was sittin' on a rock. Her friend who was driving was killed. And this one sittin' on the rock, she didn't even know where she was. But, boy, she was determined to stay there. She was totally disoriented. I had to pull her, nearly force her back. Only time we can do that is when we know their own will isn't working—otherwise we always leave it up to their own choice.

"Well, in the early days, most everyone could tell when a person wasn't in their body. That was just natural to see that. That's been lost now, mostly. Only thing I can say is, until you learn to understand these things, you should never, never move an unconscious body. Unconscious means the person is not in there. So treat the body on the scene and never, never move it. Not until you learn how. People can't find their own way back to the body—not when they've been pulled loose that way by some accident or something. Time and time again, traumatized people get abandoned that way. Time and time again, people die in a coma because of that."

Quoted in Doug Boyd, *Mystics, Magicians, and
Medicine People: Tales of a Wanderer*

the moment of death. Researchers noted a loss, averaging from 1 to 2 ounces, leading to speculations about whether the loss indicated the departure of the soul from the body at death.[58]

To most people living in modern, urban-technological societies, in which secular beliefs are prominent, this approach to defining death is simply not relevant. Our first difficulty would be to adequately define the soul. And even if this difficulty could be surmounted, we would need some way to ascertain whether the soul was present or absent at a given time. Moreover, this definition of death forces an examination of whether death occurs because the soul departs from the body, or, conversely, whether the soul departs from the body because death has occurred. In other words, does the soul "animate" the body, giving it life, or do the physiological processes of vitality in the body provide a vessel wherein the soul resides? Such questions may elicit fascinating speculations, but they bear little relevance to the dilemmas posed by modern medical practice in a scientific age.

Irreversible Loss of the Capacity for Bodily Integration

In the third approach, death can be defined as the irreversible loss of the capacity for bodily integration. This approach is more sophisticated than the first because it refers not simply to the traditional physiological signs of vitality in the body (the flow of breath and blood), but to the more generalized capability of the body to regulate its own functioning. The approach recognizes the fact that a human being is an integrated organism with capacities for internal regulation through complex homeostatic feedback mechanisms.

This definition at least partly resolves the ambiguity of the first definition, for a determination of death would not be made merely because a person's physiological functioning was being maintained by a machine. Rather, a determination of death could be made when the organism itself was no longer capable of bodily integration. In other words, artificial life support would not constitute the determining factor; rather, only with the irreversible loss of the capacity for bodily integration could there be a determination of death. The locus for such a determination is currently considered by clinicians to be the central nervous system—more specifically, the brain. The determination of death that results from this definition is often characterized as "brain death" (although this term is somewhat misleading because it focuses attention on the death of a part of the organism, not the whole organism).

In 1968, the Harvard Medical School Ad Hoc Committee to Examine the Definition of Brain Death proposed criteria for determining death by this new definition. The Harvard committee identified four essential criteria for brain death: (1) lack of receptivity and response to external stimuli; (2) absence of spontaneous muscular movement and spontaneous breathing; (3) absence of observable reflexes, including brain and spinal reflexes; and (4) absence of brain activity, signified by a flat electroencephalogram (EEG). [The Harvard criteria call for a second set of tests to be performed on the patient after twenty-four hours have elapsed. They also specifically exclude cases of hypothermia (body temperature below 90 degrees Fahrenheit) as well as situations involving the presence of central nervous system depressants such as barbiturates.] Notice that these criteria incorporate the traditional means of determining death—heartbeat and blood flow. Procedures for applying these criteria have been widely adopted, particularly when the traditional means of determining death are inconclusive.

Irreversible Loss of the Capacity for Consciousness or Social Interaction

Although the Harvard criteria have gained wide acceptance in clinical settings, some argue that they fail to specify what is *significant* about human

Modern medicine raises a thicket of difficult social and ethical issues. We have grown used to seeing members of the medical community try to resolve them in the courtroom. Sometimes they're there as expert witnesses, sometimes as defendants in malpractice suits. At other times they come seeking the protection of a judicial ruling, for example, on the circumstances in which a gravely ill patient has "the right to die" and "heroic" life support can be withdrawn. Once in a while it's a criminal matter. . . .

Moral uncertainties will continue to abound in medicine. No hospital rule book can do justice to the ambiguous circumstances in which lower-level line staff must translate institutional policy to humane practice. This is true, incidentally, not only for a licensed practical nurse at the bottom of a hospital pecking order, but for a policeman or social worker or a member of a dozen other occupations whose members deal daily with humanity's most painful contradictions. This is often underrespected, underpaid, emotionally draining work with impossibly complex multiple objectives: How simultaneously to follow a rulebook, get the job done and be humane?

Excerpts from an
editorial in the *Boston Sunday Globe,*
November 8, 1981

life. Veatch, for example, says that it is the higher functions of the brain—not merely reflex networks that regulate such physiological processes as blood pressure and respiration—that define the essential characteristics of a human being. Thus, the fourth approach to defining death emphasizes the capacity for consciousness and social interaction. The implicit premise of this approach is that for a person to be fully human, not only must certain biological processes operate, but the social dimension of life—consciousness or personhood—must be present. Being alive implies the capacity for conscious interaction with one's environment and with other human beings. According to this definition, when the capacity for social interaction is irreversibly lost, a determination of death would follow.

Using this approach, where should one look to determine whether an individual is alive or dead? Current scientific evidence points to the neocortex, the outer surface of the brain, where processes essential to consciousness and social interaction are located. If this supposition is correct, the EEG alone would provide an adequate measure for determining death.

In the theoretical debate regarding how death should be defined, this fourth approach is known as a "higher-brain" theory, in contrast to the "whole-brain" theory advocated by those who define death as the irreversible loss of function of the organism as a whole. As Karen Gervais points out, however, "By emphasizing the brain's integrating role in the human organism the whole-brain theory of death reduces to a lower-brain theory of death."[59] Observing that human beings are "ontologically unique and complex organisms," Gervais says that "it is loss of consciousness and not loss of biological functioning that should determine when human life is over." According to this view, the death of a *person* is synonymous with the death of a human being. In commenting on the search for a more precise definition of human death, Gervais concludes that we are left with a basic choice about the definition of human life—namely, whether we consider a human being as an organism or as a person.

Considering Ethical Issues in Medicine

In reviewing the rapidity with which issues of medical ethics have come to the forefront of discussion during the past three decades, Leon Kass observes that "today the ethics business is booming," with medical schools offering courses in medical ethics, hospitals establishing ethics committees, courts adjudicating ethical conflicts, and blue-ribbon commissions analyzing and pronouncing on ethical issues.[60] Yet, Kass argues, much of this "action" is really just talk—philosophical theorizing and rational analysis—with comparatively little time devoted to "what genuinely moves people to act—their motives and passions." This is not to say that rational analysis and abstract problem solving are not relevant, but that the "morality of ordinary practice" must also receive attention. As Kass says, "Every human encounter is an ethical encounter, an occasion for the practice (and cultivation) of virtue and respect, and, between doctors and patients, for the exercise of responsibility and trust, on both sides."

The discussion in this chapter can form a basis for intelligent consideration of ethical issues in medicine. Applying fundamental ethical principles to issues of informed consent, euthanasia, and the definition of death provides a framework for understanding such issues in a clearer light. As medical technologies evolve and assume greater importance in health care, an increasing number of people will be faced by the prospect of grappling with such issues at a personal level. One sign of this is the space increasingly being devoted to coverage of euthanasia and other issues of medical ethics in the popular media. Public concern about issues involving euthanasia, for example, is evident in a widespread political movement that seeks to change existing laws regarding physician aid-in-dying. Indeed, the euthanasia issue has been characterized as "the abortion debate of the next century."[61] However, as we have seen in the examples given in this chapter, concerns about ethical decision making in medicine apply not just to the realm of public policy, but also bear directly, and sometimes painfully, on the lives of individuals and families.

Further Readings

Lisa Belkin. *First, Do No Harm.* New York: Simon & Schuster, 1993.
Rasa Gustaitis and Ernle W.D. Young. *A Time to Be Born, A Time to Die: Conflicts and Ethics in an Intensive Care Nursery.* Reading, Mass.: Addison-Wesley, 1986.

Frank Harron, John Burnside, and Tom Beauchamp. *Health and Human Values: A Guide to Making Your Own Decisions.* New Haven: Yale University Press, 1983.

Albert R. Jonsen, Mark Siegler, and William J. Winslade. *Clinical Ethics: A Practical Approach to Ethical Decisions in Clinical Medicine.* New York: Macmillan, 1982.

Stanley Joel Reiser, Arthur J. Dyck, and William J. Curran, eds. *Ethics in Medicine: Historical Perspectives and Contemporary Concerns.* Cambridge, Mass.: MIT Press, 1977.

Earl E. Shelp. *Born to Die? Deciding the Fate of Critically Ill Newborns.* New York: Free Press, 1986.

Robert M. Veatch. *Cross Cultural Perspectives in Medical Ethics.* Boston: Jones and Bartlett, 1989.

William J. Winslade and Judith Wilson Ross. *Choosing Life or Death: A Guide for Patients, Families, and Professionals.* New York: Free Press, 1986.

UPI/Bettmann Newsphotos

*Grief encompasses a range of emotions in survivors. Bereavement is often a
time of turning inward, of clutching to reminders of the deceased and to
the memories they evoke.*

Survivors: Understanding the Experience of Loss

We are all survivors. Not everyone has experienced the loss that occurs with death, but everyone has experienced losses of some kind. Reflect for a moment on something—material or nonmaterial—that you have lost. You may recall the loss of a job, a friend's moving away, misplacing an important letter, any number of things. Whether such losses seem big or small, they are a fact of life for everyone.

Endings are another way to think about loss: The end of summer vacation, graduating from school, leaving a familiar neighborhood, confronting the prospect of retirement—all these endings typify changes that arise in the course of living, changes that often occasion feelings of grief. Some writers call such experiences "little deaths." As you recall some of the "little deaths" in your own life, think about how you responded. Shock, disbelief, resentment, sadness, and relief are natural reactions. Generally, the more valuable or emotionally charged an experience or relationship, the greater a person's reaction to its loss.

As you read these words, you are alive. You are a *survivor* of the many changes that have taken place in your life up to the present moment. Keeping this fact in mind as you learn about bereavement, grief, and mourning will increase your awareness of the issues related to surviving the death of someone close to you.

249

For many people, grief has negative connotations. They say, "Oh, don't talk about that subject, it's too depressing," or "I'd rather just think positive thoughts, not dwell on all that negativity." Expanding our knowledge of survivorship allows us a more encompassing and accurate picture of what grief and mourning represent in human experience. Among the most impressive facts is the continuity and essential unity in the human experience of bereavement, grief, and mourning.

Bereavement, Grief, and Mourning

The word most often associated with loss by death is grief. We hear that someone is bereaved, is grieving, or has "grief work" to do. We say that the person is mourning. Understanding the definitions of bereavement, grief, and mourning broadens our understanding of what it means to be a survivor. Although these terms are often used somewhat interchangeably, each refers to a distinct aspect of the encounter with loss.

Bereavement comes from a root word meaning "shorn off or torn up"—as if something had been suddenly yanked away. The word thus conveys a sense of a person's being deprived, of having something stripped away against one's will, of being robbed. Bereavement signifies a force that comes from outside as a violent, destructive action taken against us. Obviously, if we think about bereavement only as a violent event, our understanding will be different from that of the person who defines bereavement as a change that is natural, a normal event in human experience. Thus considered, bereavement can be defined simply as the objective event of loss.

Grief refers to a person's response to the event of loss. It includes emotions, mental perceptions, and physical reactions. Like bereavement, grief is often thought of in negative terms: heartbreak, anguish, distress, suffering—a burdensome emotional state. Yet, among the range of emotions that may be present in a survivor's grief are not only sorrow and sadness, but also relief, anger, disgust, and self-pity. Limiting our definition of grief reduces the chances of accepting all of the responses that may be present.

Mourning is closely related to grief and, indeed, is frequently used as a synonym for it. Still, it is useful to distinguish somewhat between the two terms. If we define grief as an individual's response, or reaction, to loss, then mourning refers to those behaviors whereby the bereaved individual incorporates the experience of loss into his or her ongoing life. In this sense, mourning is a *process* actively engaged in by the bereaved rather than a *reaction* to the event of loss itself. The behaviors associated with mourning are determined to a significant degree by social and cultural norms that prescribe appropriate ways of coping with loss within a given society. Thus, mourning denotes both the coping behaviors that an individual utilizes in coming to terms with loss and the social customs by which that loss is acknowledged in the community.

In every society, certain behaviors are socially or culturally defined as appropriate for making known the fact that a person is mourning. These

Working through our endings allows us to redefine
our relationships, to surrender what is dead
and to accept what is alive,
and to be in the world more fully to face the
new situation.

Stanley Keleman,
Living Your Dying

"rules" are manifested in such customs as temporary seclusion of the bereaved in the period after a death. Seclusion enforces on the survivors a period of abstinence from social relationships. Perhaps you have heard someone say, "That family just experienced a death in the family and is in mourning; they aren't going out socially." Philippe Ariès traced the practice of seclusion back to the Middle Ages and noted that it served two purposes: First, it allows the unhappy survivors to shelter their grief from the world, and, second, it prevents survivors from forgetting the deceased too quickly.[1]

Conventional forms of mourning behavior include wearing black armbands or clothes of subdued colors and, if the deceased was a public figure, flying the national flag at half-mast. Following the death of George Washington, for instance, Congress led the nation in a thirty-day period of mourning, during which some citizens wore black bands on which were stamped in white letters the inscription that appeared on the President's coffin plate: "General George Washington—Departed this life on the 14th of December, 1799."[2] In some societies, widows commonly dress in black for many years following the death of a spouse, outwardly acknowledging their loss and their mourning. The veiled woman dressed in black, a *mater dolorosa*, arrived on the scene in the nineteenth century, emphasizing how nearly impossible it was for the living to forget the departed. The practice of altering one's appearance in some way as a sign of mourning is a common custom that occurs in different ways in different societies. Among Native American people, for instance, great significance is attached to hair; long hair is often considered a sign of status and wealth. Terry Tafoya says, "To cut the hair short is a symbolic and actual sacrifice in memory and respect of the one lost. It is also an immediate sign to visitors that such a loss has taken place. It is a strong visual symbol of grief."[3]

In modern societies, mourning behavior is generally less formal than it is among traditional cultures or than it was historically. Because we lack rigorous definitions of what constitutes appropriate mourning behavior, there is sometimes conflict between conventional notions of mourning and the ideas of the deceased or the survivors, as illustrated by the following anecdote: A young girl wrote to an advice columnist about a "sweet sixteen" party that her dying father had asked the family to celebrate for her, even if the party should occur on the day of his funeral. The girl said that she had not felt like having a party, but the family decided to honor the promise to her father. So the party was held two days after her father's death, and it turned out to be a good experience for all who attended. The problem arose when several relatives became horrified because, in their view, enjoying a party was inappropriate behavior during a time of mourning. What advice would you give to this girl? In a pluralistic social environment, the customs and coping behaviors for dealing with loss are not rigorously defined. Consider, for example, the situation confronted by the Hmong (discussed in Chapter 3). It is useful to suspend our judgments about what constitutes appropriate mourning behavior and to recognize that a broad spectrum of behaviors is appropriate in today's pluralistic and multicultural society.

Tasks of Mourning

In a landmark study published in 1944, "The Symptomatology and Management of Acute Grief," Erich Lindemann identified three primary tasks necessary for satisfactorily mourning a loss: first, *accepting* the fact of the loss; second, *adjusting* to a life without the deceased; third, *forming new relationships*.[4] This basic model of "grief work" has subsequently been modified by theorists and practitioners in ways that expand our understanding of bereavement, grief, and mourning. In presenting an overall view of the process of coping with loss, we make use of a model described by William Worden.[5]

The first task of grieving involves *accepting the reality* of the loss. Even when a death is anticipated, the reality may be difficult to accept fully. "Denying the facts of the loss," says Worden, "can vary in degree from a slight distortion to a full-blown delusion." One signpost at this point in the journey toward coming to terms with loss is the survivor's choice of words when talking about the deceased person. Most significant is the transition from present to past tense, from *is* to *was*, as, for example, from "Randy is a wonderful carpenter" to "Randy was a wonderful carpenter."

The second task involves *working through the pain* of grief. This includes both the physical pain as well as the emotional and behavioral pain of loss. As Worden says, "Not everyone experiences the same intensity of pain or feels it in the same way, but it is impossible to lose someone you have been deeply attached to without experiencing some level of pain." A significant danger for survivors at this point involves the misuse of "pain killers" such as alcohol and drugs (prescription or not). Experiencing the pain does not mean "deadening" it. Social support, including support groups focusing on the specific needs of survivors, can be beneficial at this point in the journey of grief. Humor, too, can lighten the weight of grief, providing a respite for survivors as they come to terms with the loss.

The third task involves *adjusting to a changed environment* in which the deceased is missing. It may take considerable time to make this adjustment, especially when a relationship was of long duration and exceptional closeness. Often, the many roles fulfilled by the deceased in the bereaved's life are not

Grief may indeed range the gamut. It may be shrill and maniacal; it may be subdued and reflective; it may be philosophical. The recording of grief and of the response to it, of the sadness that is virtually physiological and is certainly deeply mysterious in its fullest psychological character, serves, as Aristotle and the later students of tragic catharsis have suggested, as a kind of purgation, as a means of releasing the terrible suppressed tensions, fears, anxieties, deeply fearsome in their potential for still greater unknown effect. Identifying the full range and depth of the symptoms must always come first, must be the basis on which understanding, management, and assimilation of grief into the totality of living rests.

Morris Freedman, "Notes on Grief in Literature"

fully realized until after the loss occurs. The term "changed environment" encompasses the physical, emotional, and spiritual dimensions of life. The adjustments made by survivors often include physical changes, such as rearranging the furniture or changing the place settings at the dining table. It is important to understand that the changes undertaken may intensify grief. For instance, one family decided to travel to a foreign country during the first holiday season following the death of their daughter. Although they were not sitting around the fire at home crying, their sorrow was nonetheless felt while on the tour. Later, they acknowledged that the urge to radically alter their usual holiday rituals arose from a desire to adjust to the changed environment in which one of the family members was no longer present. Yet their grief traveled with them. As it happened, because the surviving family members were aware of their feelings and open with each other, the trip proved to be healing.

Finally, the fourth task of grieving has to do with *emotionally relocating the deceased and moving on with life.* This task can seem problematic, either because it apparently involves a dishonoring of the deceased's memory or because of anxiety about investing emotional energy into another relationship that could also end in loss. Working through this task entails "letting go" of past attachments and forming new ones. The accomplishment of this task is founded on the recognition that, although one does not love the deceased person any less, there are also other people to be loved.

Although some scholars and practitioners have been rather emphatic about "breaking bonds" between the bereaved person and the deceased, recent thought about the nature of grief suggests that this view should be modified. First, it has become increasingly clear that the manifestations of grief and mourning are highly variable, depending on both individual and cultural differences. Second, contemporary studies of grief provide convincing evidence that the resolution of grief is more complex than simply severing the affectional bonds with the deceased and going on with one's life.

Edward V. Gillion

© Albert Lee Strickland

The nineteenth-century Romantic view of death is reflected in the Lawson memorial, which characterizes both the devotion of the bereaved to the deceased and the belief that loving relationships continue beyond the mortal framework of the human lifespan.

Contemporary memorial stones often reflect a similar emphasis on the unending love felt by survivors for the deceased and on the faith that bonds forged during a person's lifetime can remain strong despite death.

Mourning is a process of transformation whereby the bereaved incorporates the loss into his or her ongoing life. In some cultural settings, this occurs in the context of rituals that locate the deceased in the realm of beloved ancestors. In others, it means keeping a special place for the deceased in one's heart and mind. This kind of continuing bond with the deceased is not an aberration in grieving that needs to be rectified; rather, it is testimony to the enduring strength of love. Dennis Klass notes that bereaved parents participating in the support organization, The Compassionate Friends, often gain solace by maintaining continuing bonds with their children who died untimely deaths due to terminal illness.[6] "Memory," he says, "binds family and communities together." Through religious beliefs and objects linking the parents' thoughts with memories of the deceased child, a kind of immortality is granted to the child in the lives of surviving family members. Work done by Phyllis Silverman, Steven Nickman, and William Worden in the Child Bereavement Study lends similar support to the notion that children, too, maintain a connection with their deceased parents through memories and linking objects.[7] Futhermore, as David Balk and Nancy Hogan point out, "A remarkable bit of evidence for on-going attachment is the millions and millions who visit the Vietnam War Memorial each year to remember and leave literally tons of connections for their deceased loved ones."[8] Balk and Hogan add that a similar link with memories of the dead can be seen in the example of pilgrimages to the Wailing Wall in Jerusalem.

Thus, the view that resolving grief necessarily means breaking affectional ties with the deceased is giving way to a paradigm that is both more encompassing and more accurate in describing the range of behaviors and emotions that may be elicited by loss. Recognizing the variability in grief, however, we should be wary of generalization. As Margaret Stroebe and her colleagues suggest, it seems appropriate to "search for an appreciative understanding of grief in all its varieties."[9] With respect to grief therapy, "this would mean curtailing the search for ideal therapeutic practices and focusing instead on tailor-made treatments." As these writers note, the awareness of cultural context and the multiplicity of mourning behaviors is just beginning to penetrate the field of bereavement research.

In casting a more expansive light on the fourth and "final" task of mourning, it may be helpful to adopt the perspective suggested by John Kelly, in which our lives are seen as "stories."[10] When someone we love dies, we encounter the prospect of re-forming our life story. In this view, coping with loss is seen as involving a re-forming of our story so that we achieve a new integration of the deceased into our lives and adjust all of our relationships in ways that restore wholeness.

The Experience of Grief and Mourning

Keeping in mind the four tasks of mourning described by Worden, let us look more closely now at the parameters of grief and mourning. Bereaved persons are often alarmed by the confusing flood of emotional and physical reactions that can occur following a significant loss. People often ask, What constitutes normal or appropriate grief and mourning? Are the feelings, bodily reactions, and other symptoms that may be part of the bereaved person's experience of grief normal—and how long do they last? After the initial shock subsides, how long should one expect to actively mourn or grieve before reaching a sense of resolution? Indeed, what is the normal course of mourning? How does the experience of grief evolve in the weeks and months after bereavement? If the bereaved is not "over" the loss in some specified period of time, does that mean he or she is experiencing pathological grief or mourning inappropriately?

Such questions reflect natural human concerns. Any attempt to define normal grief and mourning must include a consideration of the circumstances of a death, along with a number of other factors that affect a particular survivor's experience. Before examining the variables that influence the nature of grief and bereavement, we need to acquire an appreciation for the wide range of physical, mental, and emotional reactions associated with grief, as well as an overview of the typical progression and duration of mourning.

Comparing the extent and form of emotional responses to announcements of death in various circumstances, I found a considerable amount of variability. On some occasions there was no crying whatever; the doctor's mention of the death was responded to with downward looking silence. On other occasions, his utterance "passed away" or "died" spontaneously produced hysterical crying, screaming, moaning, trembling, etc. . . . In numerous instances I have seen men and women tear at themselves, pulling their hair, tugging at their garments, biting their lips.

David Sudnow,
Passing On: The Social Organization of Dying

Symptoms of Grief

Bereavement studies provide a fairly detailed picture of the range of somatic symptoms, or body reactions, that may be present with normal grief. Somatic disturbances can include tightness of the throat, choking, shortness of breath, the need for frequent sighing, an empty feeling in the abdomen, muscle weakness, chills, and tremors. These bodily sensations may be accompanied by intense mental distress: tension, loneliness, and anguish.

The survivor's perceptions may be disorganized. Events may seem unreal, sensory responses undependable and erratic. Survivors describe periods of hallucination or even euphoria. During such times, the survivor experiences a heightened perceptual and emotional sensitivity to people and events in the immediate environment. It is common for survivors to be preoccupied with images of the deceased. Often, survivors are highly irritable or even hostile. They may talk incessantly about the deceased. Or they may talk about everything but their confrontation with loss and the circumstances of the death. Survivors often manifest a general restlessness.

In addition to feelings of sadness, longing, loneliness, and sorrow, there may be feelings of guilt or anger. The survivor may feel anger and outrage at the apparent injustice of the loss and tremendous frustration and a sense of impotence at the inability to control events. As survivors, we may feel that if we could arrange the world more to our liking, we would not have included loss as part of the human experience.

The symptoms and behaviors appropriate to normal grief clearly make up a broad range of responses. But no particular survivor will necessarily experience all of them, nor must all be present if grief is to be considered normal. If a person has mental images of the deceased and says, "Oh no, I shouldn't be thinking like this," the denial can create additional conflicts and greater difficulties in coming to terms with the loss. In contrast, if a survivor is aware that many kinds of feelings are acceptable, the experience of grief is likely to be much more easily managed.

When loss occurs, the usual patterns of living are disrupted. People stop doing the things they ordinarily do. Their actions may be so unlike their usual

An Elegy on the Death of John Keats

Ah, woe is me! Winter is come and gone,
But grief returns with the revolving year;
The airs and streams renew their joyous tone:
The ants, the bees, the swallows reappear;
Fresh leaves and flowers deck the dead Seasons' bier;
The amorous birds now pair in every brake,
And build their mossy homes in field and brere;
And the green lizard, and the golden snake,
Like unimprisoned flames, out of their trance awake.

Alas! that all we loved of him should be
But for our grief, as if it had not been,
And grief itself be mortal! Woe is me!
Whence are we, and why are we? of what scene
The actors or spectators? Great and mean
Meet massed in death, who lends what life must borrow.
As long as skies are blue, and fields are green,
Evening must usher night, night urge the morrow,
Month follow month with woe, and year wake year to sorrow.

Percy Bysshe Shelley, "Adonais"
(excerpt)

behavior that an outsider, or even an acquaintance, might judge it bizarre or aberrant. In an early study of grief, "Mourning and Melancholia," Sigmund Freud addressed this concern from the psychoanalytic perspective.[11] According to this view, although grieving behavior may be quite different from a person's usual behavior, normal grief is not a pathological condition nor is its presence a cause for medical treatment. Grief is the normal reaction to loss. In its application to grief, the *attachment theory* postulated by Freud, John Bowlby, and others can be briefly summarized:[12] When the bereaved perceives that the love object no longer exists, grief arises, along with a defensive demand to withdraw libido (energy) from the object to which it had been attached. This demand may meet with opposition, causing the survivor to temporarily turn away from reality in an attempt to cling to the lost object. According to this model, the libido eventually becomes detached from the love object, and the ego (personality) becomes free of its clinging attachment to the deceased.[13]

This model has been criticized because of its apparent assumption that attachment objects can be replaced. As Colin Murray Parkes points out, "Each love relationship is unique, and theoretical models which assume that libido can be withdrawn from one object in order to become invested in another similar object, fail to recognize this uniqueness."[14] Bereavement, says Parkes, is revealed as one category of "psychosocial transition," a concept that is highly relevant to the study of loss and change. This transition was described by

Theorist	GRIEF						
	Onset ⟵————————————————⟶ Resolution						
GORER	Shock		Intense grief work		Reestablishing physical and mental balance		
KAVANAUGH	Shock	Disorganization	Volatile emotions	Guilt	Loss and loneliness	Relief	Reestablishment
RAPHAEL	Shock, numbness, disbelief		Separation pain		Psychological mourning process		Reintegration
WEIZMAN and KAMM	Shock, disbelief, denial		Undoing	Anger		Sadness	Integration

Figure 7-1   *Grief Models by Theorist*

the father of a dead child who said, "Living without my son has meant adding another room onto the house in my mind; not so I can shut the door on his death, but so I can move in and out of the experience of my loss." As this father recognized, the psychosocial transition resulting from loss requires space and attention.

Studies have led to the conclusion that acute grief possesses the qualities of a definite syndrome, with both psychological and somatic symptomatology. However, the signs of grief may either appear immediately or be delayed; they may even be absent. Symptoms may be distorted, exaggerated, or highly variable—differing among individuals and according to circumstances. In short, grief is seen to be a complex, evolving process with multiple dimensions.[15] As Dennis Klass wisely observes, "Bereavement is complex, for it reaches to the heart of what it means to be human and what it means to have a relationship."[16]

Phases of Grief

In an attempt to understand and delineate the various processes associated with grief, researchers have devised a number of models that present these processes within a framework involving a theory of stages (see Figure 7-1).[17] Some models postulate three stages, others seven or ten. To outline the stages of grief work in this manner seems to suggest a linear progression from the first stage, through the second, and so on, until the process has been completed. Although this notion might provide comfort to those who wish to evaluate a survivor's journey toward reintegration after loss, it is important to place these theories in their intended context.

The theories concerning stages of grief represent an effort to specify various aspects of a process that occurs in highly individualistic ways. Thus,

The upper middles would probably drink themselves silly at the funeral. Although a few years ago this would have been frowned on. When my husband in the sixties announced that he intended to leave £200 in his will for a booze-up for his friends, his lawyer talked him out of it, saying it was in bad taste and would upset people. The same year his grandmother died, and after the funeral, recovering from the innate vulgarity of the cremation service when the gramophone record stuck on 'Abi-abi-abi-abi-de with me,' the whole family trooped home and discovered some crates of Australian burgundy under the stairs. A rip-roaring party ensued and soon a lower middle busybody who lived next door came bustling over to see if anything was wrong. Whereupon my father-in-law, holding a glass and seeing her coming up the path, uttered the immortal line: 'Who is this intruding on our grief?'

Jilly Cooper, *Class*

although models of grief can be very helpful in increasing our understanding, we should not superimpose a particular structure on the actual grief experience of a particular survivor. Furthermore, although each of the phases of grief may be considered as distinct emotional states, they are not necessarily separate; they will invariably intertwine and overlap.

The earliest phase of grief is typically characterized by *shock* and *numbness,* usually lasting from the time the survivor learns of the death until the final disposition of the deceased's body. *Disbelief* and *denial* are components of the grief experienced at this time. Confused and bewildered by the impact, the bereaved may feel vulnerable and seek protection by isolation and withdrawal. During this period the survivor is occupied with activities surrounding the disposition of the deceased's body, such as arranging for burial or cremation, and sorting out the deceased's personal and family affairs. This is the time when sympathy cards arrive and the survivor accepts the condolences of friends and relatives. There may be feelings of *disorganization,* which Robert Kavanaugh has likened to the bereaved person, motionless and helpless, being stranded in the middle of a fast-flowing stream while water and debris rush about him or her. Mourning rites during the period of shock help reintegrate the family following the disruption caused by the death of one of its members. The initial phase of grief fades as the bereaved moves through the funeral rites and the reality of the death is gradually acknowledged.

Social institutions and customs may perform a valuable service to the survivor during the initial phase of grief. The presence of family and other social groups and the need to actively attend to the various details of the funeral and disposition of the body may help to define the role and behaviors expected of survivors at a time of crisis. The regimen provided by such activities is in marked contrast to what often occurs afterward. Typically, after the final disposition of the deceased's body, friends and family disperse, leaving the bereaved largely on his or her own to find adequate ways of coping with the loss. Much of the intense grief work takes place just when support systems are most lacking.

The middle phase of grief is a period of *intense grief work* and *separation pain*. During this time, the bereaved experiences intense yearning for the person who has died. Then, as the finality of the loss is increasingly accepted, the bereaved begins to review and sort through all the bonds and "bits" of interaction that built the relationship. There is an intense reexperiencing of the whole history of the relationship, and the bonds of attachment are slowly relinquished. This is also a time of *undoing:* The bereaved wishes to undo the calamity, to make everything as it was before. Fantasies of alternatives that would have prevented the death are characteristic of this phase. Varying considerably among survivors, this phase generally lasts from several weeks to several months. During this period the bereaved's attention is withdrawn from external events, and many of the physiological symptoms associated with intense grief may be present. For example, the survivor may experience restlessness and disturbed sleep, perhaps with dreams in which the deceased figures prominently. Lack of appetite and weight loss are also common. Paradoxically, at a time when grief is often most intense, the survivor usually receives relatively little support from family, friends, or the community or by way of formal rituals, because the funeral, memorial service, or the like have already passed. This stage is often a time when the bereaved is left alone with his or her grief. As survivors, and as caring persons, we should remember that a lack of support at this crucial time can limit opportunities for the bereaved to express feelings of grief, with the possible result that these feelings will be suppressed and normal readjustment delayed or thwarted.

The middle phase of grief is characterized by *volatile emotions*, which suggests the image of boiling water, intermittently giving off steam, like a volcano, while at other times appearing relatively dormant. *Anger* is commonly experienced, with the object of the anger being the deceased loved one ("How could you abandon me?"), God ("How could you let this happen?"), or the situation itself ("How could this happen to me?"). Anger is sometimes displaced toward persons in the bereaved's environment, such as family members or friends. *Guilt,* too, may be experienced, as well as a sense of *longing and loneliness* as needs and dependencies that previously were satisfied by the deceased become painfully apparent to the survivor. This is a time of "if onlys" and "what ifs," as the bereaved comes to terms with issues of responsibility and power relating to changing the reality that is: The person is dead. As the reality of the death begins to be absorbed, the predominant feeling becomes one of *sadness.* During this *psychological mourning process*, the world at first seems disorganized and chaotic; eventually, as the bonds of the relationship are undone, the emotions are freed for reinvestment in life once more.

The last phase of "active" grief is a period of *reintegration,* of *reestablishing physical and mental balance.* The survivor no longer constantly experiences acute physical or emotional turmoil at being bereft. Although sadness doesn't disappear completely and may be stimulated when a reminder or memory is especially poignant, it recedes into the background. Sleep and appetite return to normal, and the survivor is again an interested participant in the outside world. *Relief* may be felt as the pain subsides and the attachment diminishes, bringing a new freedom to the bereaved's life (which may be difficult to admit to others). The bereaved person begins to move ahead with his or her life, and the present concerns of life become the foreground on which to focus.

Keep in mind that models of mourning as a process distinguished by specific phases are intended to help us comprehend the functioning of grief and its effect on survivors. But we should not mistake the map for the territory. Although "stage-theories," descriptions of phases of grief, are useful in defining certain aspects of grief that may be encountered by a survivor, the actual experience resembles a series of dance steps more than it does a cross-country walk.

When you recall a loss in your life, you may remember the elements of shock, intense emotions, and becoming reestablished, but not in a neat and clearly delineated sequence of mutually exclusive states. Sometimes it may have felt as if all the feelings were present at once. Part of you may have been feeling shock while another part was calm. We are capable of experiencing many emotions, even conflicting ones, at the same time.

Duration of Grief

Research suggests that the more acute and intense experience of grief, immediately following a loss by death, usually lasts about four to six weeks. During the first year following bereavement, however, the survivor is likely to experience anniversaries, birthdays, holidays, and other special occasions that previously had been shared with the deceased in ways that involve coming to grips with the deceased's absence. Although the most acute phase occupies a comparatively brief time, the death of a close relation typically results in a response that is measured in years rather than in weeks. During this period, the survivor gradually comes to accept the loss and reorient his or her life without the deceased.

Prolonged grief or unresolved grief is described not so much in terms of duration but in terms of its effect on the survivor. Determinations of behaviors that are truly "abnormal" are best made by professionals who have been exposed to a broad range of grief responses. Severe, persistent problems with sleeplessness or loss of appetite may be symptomatic of difficulties, as may such medical complaints as ulcerative colitis, rheumatoid arthritis, or asthma. Depression—especially when accompanied by serious emotional problems, alcohol or drug abuse, or suicidal behavior—may be a correlate of unresolved grief, signaling the need for professional intervention to help deal with the underlying reasons for difficulty in coming to terms with the loss.[18]

The attempt to make a sharp distinction between normal and *pathological grief* has been largely replaced, however, by a greater awareness of individual and cultural differences in the expression of grief. In short, the "gradual erosion of categorical thinking" about grief has resulted in a more cautious

Tears stream down the face of accordion player Graham Jackson as the body of President Franklin Delano Roosevelt is carried to the train at Warm Springs, Georgia, the day after his death—a poignant example of how bereaved people express their loss in public as well as private.

attitude about labeling particular manifestations of grief as pathological or abnormal.[19] For example, the onset of intense pain years after a loss may in fact be the response to a "new" death or loss and, thus, a time-appropriate rather than delayed response.[20] To illustrate, a young woman whose husband had died nearly four years earlier reported a bout of intense grief. Bewildered by the experience, she said, "I don't understand myself; it feels almost like the day he died." In conversation with her counselor, she discovered the event triggering her pain: Within a few days, the couple's seven-year-old daughter would be celebrating her first communion. Although happily remarried, successfully back to work, and obviously healing from her loss, this devoutly religious woman grieved the absence of her child's father from a celebration that had been discussed and anticipated since the child's birth. Even in cases where the issue seems to be prolonged or pathological grief, normal grief reactions can be restored, even years after a death, through appropriate therapeutic means.

With a major loss such as death, the survivor's overwhelming experience is the sense of finality. For this reason, and because the loss is so important, the survivor may experience a recurrence of grief for that loss at various times throughout his or her life, although with decreasing frequency. Certain incidents that arise naturally in daily life will again bring to mind that what once was is no more. For example, it is now recognized that, although most widows and widowers do not actively mourn after the turmoil of the first one to three years, the loss nevertheless remains a part of them, and feelings of grief never cease entirely. A longitudinal study of widows and widowers, none of whom was older than forty-five years, found that the forces of bereavement and adjustment usually operate over a period that is more appropriately termed a period of "life transition" than a "life crisis," with bereaved spouses continuing the psychological work of mourning for the rest of their lives.[21] Similarly, an individual who was bereaved as a child by a parent's death may mourn that death anew many years later when his or her own child is born. The experience of loss has an ongoing developmental quality; it corresponds to the situation in which a person finds himself or herself at different stages of life.

In our own lives we can recognize the recurrence of mourning for earlier losses. We may mourn the loss of childhood and its experiences. A woman told about visiting her parents after some years of living on her own. One day, while poking around in the attic, her mother opened a trunk and pulled out a collection of dolls that had belonged to the daughter when she was a child. Seeing the dolls elicited feelings of grief for the childhood that was now lost to the past. She said, "I looked at those dolls and their tiny clothes, and I got in touch with the loss of that time in my life when my mother had taken care of me and had made clothes for my dolls. There I was, sitting in the attic, just bawling." Each of us has undoubtedly experienced similar situations in our own lives. Some event, picture, place, melody, or other stimulus has provoked feelings of grief related to something or someone no longer present in our lives.

The Mortality of Bereavement

To be a survivor is to experience not only symptoms of physical disease but dis-ease of a psychological and social nature as well. We have already enumerated some of the observable symptoms that may arise in the body with the onset of grief: tightness of the throat, loss of appetite, difficulty in breathing, and a host of others. These body responses constitute one aspect of the biology of grief.

However, another aspect of the biological response to grief can have more serious consequences for the survivor. W. D. Rees and S. G. Lutkins examined the mortality of bereavement and found that the death rate among survivors during the first year of bereavement was nearly seven times that of the general population.[22] And research by Arthur C. Carr and Bernard Schoenberg has shown that some chronic diseases have a higher incidence among the recently bereaved.[23] These diseases include cancer, tuberculosis, ulcerative colitis,

All that day I walked alone. In the afternoon I looked for a church, went into a cafe, and finally left on the bus, carrying with me more grief and sorrow than I had ever borne before, my body in tatters and my whole life a moan.

Oscar Lewis,
A Death in the Sanchez Family

asthma, obesity, rheumatoid arthritis, congestive heart failure, leukemia, and diabetes. In another study, conducted by Marvin Stein at Mount Sinai School of Medicine, diminished immune response was found among a group of widowers during the first few months following bereavement.[24] Other studies have produced similar results, showing a significant depression of lymphocyte (T-cell) function during the early period following bereavement.[25] Although no direct cause-and-effect link has yet been established between bereavement and the onset of disease, the evidence does suggest that reaction to loss can contribute to the epidemiology of certain diseases, especially those related to stress.

Hans Selye's studies point to the existence of an acute alarm reaction, or mobilization of the body's resources, in situations of high emotional stress.[26] According to Selye, the alarm reaction is a "generalized call to arms" of the body's defenses, and it manifests itself in various physiological changes that prepare the organism to cope with the agent or situation that elicited the reaction. If this reaction is not followed by some form of adaptation or resistance to the agent eliciting it, severe damage or even death can ensue. In addition, the stress associated with bereavement appears at times to aggravate a physical condition that may have been latent, causing symptoms to become manifest or to develop more rapidly. Stress is a component of the grief process that plays a crucial role in the survivor's ability to cope with loss.

One researcher, George Engel, compiled a number of case reports indicating a relationship between stress and sudden death.[27] He then classified the various stressful situations into eight categories, four of which can be considered as either a direct or an indirect component of grief and mourning: (1) the impact of the death of a close person, (2) the stress of acute grief, (3) the stress that occurs with mourning, and (4) the loss of status or self-esteem following bereavement.

On first thought, loss of self-esteem may not seem to be a corollary of experiencing bereavement. Guilt, however, tends to lower self-esteem, and guilt is a common component of grief. Consider the bereaved person who says, "If only I had tried harder, if I had done something differently, my friend might not have died." In addition, situations in daily life may work to lower a survivor's self-esteem following the death of a spouse, close friend, or family member. For instance, a widower who used to attend social functions with his spouse may find that he is now left off the guest list. A widow may decline invitations or avoid situations that she considers activities for couples. The financial status of the bereaved person often changes. If self-worth has been dependent on a certain income level, then less money and tighter finances may lower self-esteem. The loss of status enjoyed because of a deceased mate's professional or community standing can have a similar effect.

During the fifteenth century, grief was one of the legal causes of death that could be listed on death certificates. Can a bereaved person indeed die of a "broken heart"? Although the idea that severe grief can somehow damage the heart has persisted since ancient times, Colin Murray Parkes notes that "the fact that bereavement may be followed by death from heart disease does not prove that grief itself is a cause of death."[28] When stress is not dealt with adequately, however, disease can result. The determinant is not so much the presence of stress as the ability to cope with it. How a person copes with catastrophic losses—such as the death of a mate, close friend, or family member—tends to be consistent in many respects with how that person copes with the everyday stresses and small losses of daily living. It is important, therefore, to be aware of stress and its potentially harmful effects, and to take constructive steps to manage the level of stress in one's life. Social support may be the key to helping the bereaved mitigate the potentially harmful effects of grief with respect to heightened mortality or morbidity following loss.[29]

Intellectual Versus Emotional Responses

When there is a marked difference between the survivor's emotional and intellectual responses to death, and the survivor believes that only one response can be right, the result is conflict. To expect the head and the heart to react the same to loss is unrealistic; disparity between feelings and thoughts is likely. During the process of working through grief, many different emotions will be felt, and many different thoughts will arise. By allowing them all and withholding judgment as to the rightness and wrongness of particular emotions or thoughts, the survivor is much more likely to experience grief as healing.

One must give oneself permission to experience feelings of loss. Survivors often have rigid rules about what kind of feelings can be expressed in grief, and when—such as where and when it is acceptable to be angry, or to open to the pain and release an intense outburst of sadness.

Permission to have and express feelings is of immense importance in dealing with the issues of survivorship. Intellectually, we may think, "How can I be mad at someone for dying?" Yet anger may indeed be a component of grief; consider the example of someone who died because of driving while intoxicated, or of the suicide. Of course, anger may be present even if death was seemingly unavoidable and beyond the victim's control. One young mother told of walking past a photograph of her recently deceased child and noticing, amid the grief and pain, a small voice within her blurting out, "Brat! How could you die and leave me as you did!" In a purely intellectual sense, we might be tempted to think this mother's behavior quite out of place. How

A Letter from the Canadian Prairie

Heather Brae, Alberta
January 12, 1906

Miss Jennie Magee
Dear Sister:

You will be surprised to hear from me after so many years. Well I have bad news for you. My Dear little wife is Dead and I am the lonelyist Man in all the world. She gave Birth to little Daughter on the 27th of December three Days after she went out of her mind and on the 7th of January she took Pnumonia and Died about half past three in the afternoon. We buried her tuesday afternoon in a little cemetery on the Prarry about 15 miles from here. I am writing to you to see if you will come and keep house for me and raise my little Baby. I would not like to influence you in any way as I am afraid you would be lonely when I have to go from home as I will now and again. You are used to so much stir in the city. I have 400 acres of Land and I have 9 or ten cows and some hens. If you come you can make all you can out of the Butter and eggs and I might be able to Pay you a small wage. . . . Write and let me know as soon as Possible what you think about the Proposition. I am writing to the rest tonight to let them know the bad news. I think this is all at Present from your affectionate Brother.

William Magee

Linda Rasmussen, Lorna Rasmussen,
Candace Savage, and Anne Wheeler,
A Harvest Yet to Reap: A History of Prairie Women

could she be angry at her child for dying? Yet that sense of rage, that frustrated anger, is typical in the experience of survivors.

Survivors must allow themselves to experience those feelings, to feel anger at the person for having died and anger at themselves for not having been able to prevent the death—indeed, they must give themselves permission to experience all the feelings that arise. Thus, they need not judge themselves as uncaring or bad.

Practical Management of Life's Affairs

Survivors are sometimes urged to take a hand in the practical management of their everyday affairs as soon as possible following bereavement. During the early period of bereavement, especially, there is a need to find a balance between the *bridging* activities that will lead the survivor to a future without the deceased and the *linking* activities that give the survivor familiar ties to the past.

The survivor must deal with the impact of change, which may affect virtually every detail of life: The family unit is different; the social realities have changed; legal and financial matters require attention. The survivor must face these issues and answer the question, "How can I make the necessary adjustment in each of these areas?" Because the loss of someone close brings tremendous change, it is usually helpful if, in the management of life's affairs, the survivor limits the number of other changes that occur at the same time.

Variables Influencing Grief

Just as no two persons are alike, no two experiences of grief are alike. The circumstances of a death, the personality and social roles of the bereaved, his or her relationship with the deceased—these are among the factors that influence the nature of grief. An understanding of these factors can provide not only knowledge about the processes of grief but also clues about why some deaths seem especially devastating to survivors.

Survivor's Model of the World

A survivor's experience of loss and grief is conditioned to a large extent by his or her model of the world—that is, by his or her perception of reality and judgment about how the world works. In considering how a person's model of the world applies to the experience of bereavement, four factors identified by Edgar Jackson are particularly important in conditioning a person's emotional reaction to bereavement.[30]

Personality

The first factor is the individual's personality. Personality, of course, influences how we relate to life experiences generally: Some people seem to ride easily over large bumps, but may receive quite a jolt from a small shock; for others, the situation is reversed. In this respect, self-concept is an important determinant of how a person responds when death occurs. An immature, dependent personality will be more vulnerable to the loss of a person in whom a large amount of emotional capital has been invested. Such an investment may represent an attempt to compensate for feelings of personal inadequacy by projecting part of one's self-identity onto another person. When bereavement occurs, more of this projected self is involved in the loss. In contrast, the person with greater self-esteem and a stronger self-concept is not so prone to such overcompensation, with the result that grief is likely to be less devastating. Similarly, it has been found that, when bereavement occurs, people who report a high degree of purpose in life tend to cope more effectively than do people who report a low purpose in life.[31]

Social Roles

The second conditioning factor identified by Jackson relates to social roles, which provide the framework wherein the survivor copes with grief. Again, it is the way in which a person incorporates social roles into his or her model of the world that influences the response to death. This response is determined in part by answering the question, What does society say should be

This portrait of the Saltonstall family, painted in 1611 by David Des Granges, pro-
vides a record of living family members and their relational links with the deceased,
whose influence is still felt. The husband and father, Sir Richard, is portrayed as
if standing at the bedside of his dead wife, whose arm reaches toward their two chil-
dren. Seated in the chair and holding her baby, the newest member of the family, is
Sir Richard's second wife, whom he married three years after the death of his first
wife.

a particular survivor's response to death in general or to a particular death? A
soldier in combat is expected to perform his duties despite any personal
feelings of grief or loss when comrades die. Among some primitive societies a
widow knows in advance what kind of behavior is expected, and the members
of her society gather to ensure that grief is expressed in quite specific ways. In
most modern societies, people generally have greater freedom to determine
for themselves what kind of behavior is appropriate. Even so, the social and
cultural environment is important in shaping a person's grief and mourning.
For example, in a study of the effect of ethnicity on death attitudes, over half
of the Japanese Americans and Mexican Americans in the population studied
felt that at least one year (and preferably two or more years) should pass before
a widowed spouse remarries; among African Americans and Anglo Americans,
only one-fourth of the sample held such a position.[32]

David Des Granges, Tate Gallery, London

Perception of the Deceased's Importance

The third factor that conditions a grief reaction is the survivor's perception of the relative importance of the deceased. Was the deceased an important person in my life? Will my life be changed greatly by this death? Importance may also be considered in terms of the survivor's *perceived similarity* to the deceased. The hypothesis here is that the more similar to the deceased a survivor believes he or she is, the greater is the grief.[33]

The deaths of family members and close friends usually cause the deepest grief, but the deaths of others who have been significant in our lives can also cause strong grief reactions. Americans grieved over the deaths of President John F. Kennedy, Robert Kennedy, Martin Luther King, and the *Challenger* astronauts, even though the vast majority had never met any of them personally. In the case of President Kennedy's death, researchers found a tendency for individuals to react to the assassination in terms of personal grief and loss rather than in terms of a more generalized concern for the future or of political or ideological concern.[34] A similar outpouring of grief on a nationwide scale occurred when Abraham Lincoln was killed by an assassin's bullet.

Values

The fourth conditioning factor identified by Jackson is the person's value structure—that is, the relative worth assigned to different experiences and possible outcomes. For example, we sometimes hear people say something like, "Of course, his wife misses him terribly, but she is also relieved that he is no longer enduring such pain and suffering." In other words, the knowledge that her husband's suffering is over helps mitigate her grief at his death. Jackson cites an example of a husband who, knowing that he will soon die from a terminal illness, prepares his wife for the time when he will not be present to manage their financial affairs. Again, the value that this couple placed on being prepared was a conditioning factor in their experience of facing the husband's dying and the wife's subsequent grief.

More generally, value structures that allow death an appropriate place in a person's philosophy of life can be a significant determinant of how he or she experiences loss and grief. For example, religious beliefs can influence the way individuals relate to the meaning of death and, thus, can shape to a significant extent the experience of loss and grief. Even when such belief offers the bereaved hope of an eventual reunion with the deceased loved one, however, the individual's present response to grief is nonetheless a reality that must be recognized. As Richard Leliaert says: "To suggest that faith itself can drive out the pain of bereavement is to counsel badly."[35] Although religious faith can indeed offer consolation and comfort during a time of mourning, the path of grief must nevertheless be trod. Leliaert notes that "good spiritual caregiving for bereaved persons needs a fine balance between the human need to grieve adequately and the spiritual grounds for hope provided by formal religions or spiritual belief systems." The spiritual or philosophical underpinnings that can give death an appropriate place in our view of human existence need also to embrace the processes of grief and mourning.

Mode of Death

How a person dies affects a survivor's grief. The type of death—be it natural, accidental, homicide, or suicide—influences the grief experience, as does the survivor's previous experience with that type of death.[36] Consider the various ways in which people die. We think of the aged grandmother, dying quietly in her sleep; the young child pronounced DOA after a bicycle accident; the innocent bystander caught in the crossfire of violence or terrorism; the chronically ill person whose dying is prolonged, a "lingering death"; the despondent executive who commits suicide. Our minds (not to mention the evening news) can provide us with many such examples—powerful, heart-wrenching images. Each mode of death, each set of circumstances by which death occurs can uniquely affect the survivor's ability to integrate the loss.

Sudden Death

In a recent address before a group of death educators and counselors, Yvonne Ameche described her experience on the night two policemen came to her door with news of her son's unexpected death. Despite having experienced the deaths of her grandparents during her childhood and, later, the deaths of both her parents, Ameche said, "I don't know if anything prepared me for the knock on the door the night Paul died. . . . I remember reeling back [and feeling] like I had been physically assaulted."[37] The sense of overwhelming shock caused by the unexpected nature of her son's death was accompanied by feelings that her own familiar sense of self had been "lost" as well. The journey of survivorship from head to heart, as Ameche describes it, "where I started to internalize what I had so carefully intellectualized," took a long time and, she adds, "it was a long time before I felt like myself." Sudden deaths that occur in the context of specific kinds of events—war, for example—result in a particular set of circumstances surrounding death, and this constellation of circumstances affects how survivors deal with the loss.[38]

Anticipated Death

The phenomenon of *anticipatory grief* can be understood as a response to prior knowledge of an impending death, with the result that the survivor has time to contemplate its effect before it actually occurs. Some researchers believe that, when death is anticipated, as in the case of chronic illness, it may be easier to cope with than when death occurs suddenly, without warning.[39] Others, however, say that anticipatory grief does not significantly diminish the grief experienced when the loss becomes an objective fact. This is not a question to be resolved easily, but there is general agreement that the element of shock is more intense and overwhelming when death is unexpected.

A phenomenon associated with anticipatory grief is *secondary morbidity,* which refers to "difficulties in the physical, cognitive, emotional, or social

The other day I heard the father of a boy who had committed suicide say, "Everyone has a skeleton in their closet. But the person who kills themselves leaves their skeleton in another's closet." The grief and guilt that arise in the wake of suicide often leave a legacy of guilt and confusion. Each loved one wracks the mind and tears the heart questioning, "What could I have done to prevent this?"

Stephen Levine, *Who Dies? An Investigation of Conscious Living and Conscious Dying*

spheres of functioning that may be experienced by those closely involved with the terminally ill person."[40] For example, the burden of caring for a dying relative may cause a caregiver to pay inadequate attention to his or her own health care needs, with the result that the caregiver becomes sick or feels "run down." Such manifestations of secondary morbidity can extend to professional or volunteer caregivers as well as to family members and friends of the dying person.

Suicide

Consider some of the qualities that are unique to survivors whose bereavement occurs in connection with suicide. Such survivors are often left with a numbing feeling of, "Oh, my God, he did it to himself!" If someone close to us was in such pain that he or she chose suicide, we may be burdened with guilty questions: "Why didn't I see the predicament and do more to help? What could have been done to respond to the cry for help?" The impact of suicide can intensify survivors' feelings of blame and guilt. That someone we know has willingly chosen to end his or her life adds an element of personal confrontation. Besides guilt and self-questioning, the survivor may direct strong feelings of anger and blame toward the person who committed suicide. Suicide is seen as the ultimate affront, the final insult—one that, because it cannot be answered, compounds the survivor's frustration and anger.

Moreover, feelings of guilt and blame may be made more difficult to cope with because of societal attitudes toward suicide and related perceptions of the bereaved family members. Survivors are, to some degree, more likely to be "held responsible" for a death by suicide than for a death by illness. This negative reaction to suicide survivors may be especially directed toward the parents of a child who died by suicide.[41] As Gordon Thornton and his colleagues point out, one result of such societal attitudes may be a comparative lack of social support for individuals who are bereaved by suicide.[42] Counselors and others who are aware of this unfortunate result must therefore make corresponding allowances in providing the necessary support.

Furthermore, as with other types of sudden death, a suicide is typically unexpected. The shock magnifies the survivor's sense that death was wrong or inappropriate. Like the death of a child, a death by suicide goes against the grain of our intrinsic belief that people should live on into old age. Thus, the survivor may be left with an additional, burdensome feeling that the death was premature.

Some researchers and clinicians believe that individuals who have been bereaved as a result of suicide tend to be especially vulnerable to unusually severe grief or other adverse effects. However, the survivors of such deaths do not necessarily exhibit more pathological reactions or a more complicated and prolonged grief process than do other survivors.[43]

Homicide

If the deceased was a victim of homicide, the survivor's predominant emotions may be anger and fear. The world may be experienced as dangerous and cruel, unsafe and unfair. The suddenness and apparent injustice of the circumstances of death affect the experience of grief. Furthermore, as Lula Redmond points out, "the raw wound of the grieving homicide survivor is overtly and covertly affected by the performance of law enforcement officials, criminal justice practitioners, media personnel, and others after a murder."[44] Dealing with the criminal justice system extends the normal grieving period as the case drags on, with no assurance that the result will give the survivor a sense of justice being done. Among the "trigger events" that Redmond cites as restimulating grief in cases of homicidal death are:

1. Identification of the assailant
2. Sensing (hearing, smelling, and so on) something that elicits recollection of an experience acutely associated with the traumatic event
3. Anniversaries of the event
4. Holidays and other significant events in the life of the family (such as birthdays)
5. Hearings, trials, appeals, and other criminal justice proceedings
6. Media reports about the event or about similar events

Disaster

People who have survived a disaster in which others died also have special concerns in grieving.[45] They have become survivors twice over—survivors of a catastrophic event that could have ended their own lives, and survivors of the deaths of others, perhaps friends or relatives. In studies of survivors of the Holocaust, researchers often found a deep sense of guilt about having survived the camps and the torture while others were not as fortunate.[46] Although there is evidence that such feelings tend to be intensified by disasters or events such as the Holocaust, this sense of guilt at still being alive can affect any survivor.

High-Grief Versus Low-Grief Deaths

A major influence on the experience of grief is whether the circumstances of a death classify it as a *high-grief* or *low-grief* death.[47] A high-grief death is

© James Van Der Zee

Many people believe the death of a young child to be the most heartrending of all bereavement experiences—what researchers term a high-grief death because it tends to elicit a tremendous sense of loss.

characterized by the intense emotional and physical reactions to loss usually associated with normal grief; a low-grief death, although emotionally affecting, is less devastating, and thus the reaction is less severe and the bereaved is able to cope more readily. The death of a child is often cited as the classic example of a high-grief death, whereas the death of a person in old age, someone we think of as having lived a long and varied life, is likely to be a low-grief death. It is the circumstances of a particular death and its effect on a particular survivor, however, that determines whether the emotional response is of high or low grief. The survivor's age may also be a factor. For example, the death of a parent may be more catastrophic to a young child or an adolescent than to a grown child who has lived apart from his or her parents for many years.

Bereaved persons in most cultures may dream that a beloved person has come back. In the early stages of bereavement, this, as well as hallucinating the dead, is a normal manifestation of grieving. However, Hawaiians usually see the dead in dreams more often, for more reasons, and for longer periods after a death than do, for example, Western Caucasians. In modern Western culture, when dreams (or hallucinations) of the dead continue too long, they are usually symptoms of pathological grief: the process or "work" of grieving has not progressed through the normal stages.

For the Hawaiian who is emotionally close to his ethnic roots, such prolonged dreaming or envisioning of the dead may or may not be a sign of blocked grief work. In the Hawaiian tradition, the dead do return: in dreams and visions, in sensations of skin, in hearing the voice or smelling the perfume or body odor of the one who has died.

The difference between what is culturally normal and what may be pathological is only partly spelled out by the dream content. We must also know what is going on in the life and family life of the dreamer; we must know how much and what kind of emotion the dream aroused. Especially, we must know what were the relationships in life between the one who died and the survivor who dreams.

Mary Kawena Pukui, E. W. Haertig, and
Catherine A. Lee, *Nana I Ke Kumu (Look to the Source)*

Intense grief also can be elicited when a survivor's circumstances involve *multiple losses.* Often, the event that precipitates such loss involves war or natural disaster. For example, Terry Tafoya points out that Native Americans "hold in common a heritage of death following initial contact with Europeans."[48] Within two generations of white contact, it is estimated that 80 percent of the Native people in the Pacific Northwest had died in the encounter with newly introduced diseases to which they had no immunity. A similar pattern was experienced by Native peoples throughout the Americas. Genocide, the systematic destruction of a racial or cultural group, is often an accompaniment to war, as in the Nazi Holocaust, which resulted in the deaths of 6 million Jews, and, more recently, in the mass killing of Cambodians at the hands of the Khmer Rouge. Catastrophe, whether natural or human-caused, can result in multiple losses that are difficult to grieve. Overwhelmed by loss, survivors may be so devastated that the predominant feeling is numbness, a sense of total disorientation that prevents the expression of normal emotions. In the wake of multiple losses experienced by many people in the current AIDS crisis, survivors may feel that they have "run out of tears," that they are bereft of emotional resources to express further feelings of grief. Thus, in situations involving multiple losses, a "high-grief" death may not necessarily result in a correspondingly intense outpouring of emotions. It's as if the normal expression of grief is somehow short-circuited by the ongoing experience of loss.

Relationship to the Deceased

The experience of bereavement is profoundly influenced by the relationship between the deceased and the survivor. Think for a moment about the various kinds of relationships in your life. As you name them, you will notice that a variety of labels come to mind—parents, children, pets, neighbors, coworkers, teachers, friends, and lovers. The *form* of a given relationship is one determinant of a survivor's experience of grief. Generally speaking, the death of a family member or other close relative requires a greater adjustment by the survivor than does the death of a coworker or neighbor. But the outward form of relationship is not the sole determinant of a survivor's experience of grief. The grief resulting from the death of a close friend may parallel the bereavement patterns associated with surviving a death within the family.[49]

Whatever the outward form—kin, friend, neighbor, or mate—relationships vary according to the degree of intimacy involved, the perception of each other's roles, the expectations of the other person, and the feelings about the quality of the relationship itself. In Bali, for example, family members and other kin are rarely referred to by their *personal* names, but rather by the *degree of relationship,* thus placing emphasis on the social roles. In our culture, most people do refer to siblings and other relatives by their personal names, yet how many refer to a parent by his or her given name?

A person's relationship with his or her parents may reflect the socially defined roles of "parent" and "child" more than feelings of friendship or personal intimacy. For some, however, a parent may occupy additional roles of business associate, neighbor, and close friend. These differing roles and expectations are likely to result in a very different experience of grief when the parent dies.

As we see, then, a number of factors influence whether a particular relationship is *central* or *peripheral* to a person's life. A death involving someone central to the survivor's life generally will be much more affecting than the death of someone felt to be on the periphery. The degree of relationship, level of intimacy, and the roles and expectations associated with the relationship all influence whether we categorize a particular relationship as central or peripheral to our lives.

The severity of the grief response may be predicted to some extent by relating a survivor's relationship to the deceased (categorized as central or peripheral) with the survivor's *belief* about the circumstances of the death (whether preventable or unpreventable).[50] In other words, a survivor's attachment to the deceased and his or her sense of the appropriateness of the death will generally determine the response. For example, given a *central* relationship between the survivor and the deceased and the belief that the death was *preventable,* one would expect the grieving process to be both intense and prolonged. However, if the survivor had a *peripheral* relationship with the deceased and believed that the death was *not preventable,* one might expect the grieving process to be mild as well as relatively brief.

Ambivalence is another factor influencing relationships and subsequent grief. Such feeling about the quality of a relationship, reflecting a push-pull struggle between love and hate, may be subtle or dramatic. Perhaps no relationship is entirely free of ambivalence or questions about its quality. But when feelings of ambivalence are intense and prolonged, grieving can be complicated by unresolved emotions.

Available Social Support

The experience of grief also varies according to the amount of social support available. For instance, after the death of an unborn child, whether through miscarriage or induced abortion, a survivor is likely to receive little support from the social conventions that comfort other survivors in their grief. Often, no funeral or other ceremony is observed, and the loss may not be acknowledged at all by the larger community. Thus, the usual processes that allow a survivor to confront a loss and to take leave of the deceased are greatly hampered. These kinds of losses may be accompanied by *disenfranchised grief*—that is, grief experienced in connection with a loss that is not socially supported or acknowledged through the usual rituals.[51]

Grief may also be less than fully recognized not because of the circumstances of the loss, but because of certain qualities that others may wittingly or unwittingly associate with the bereaved himself or herself. For example, as Darlene Kloeppel and Sheila Hollins point out, significant complications may occur when a death in the family is combined with a family member having a mental handicap.[52] These complications may affect both the family's functioning and the retarded person's grieving process. It is important to recognize, write Kloeppel and Hollins, that "death and mental retardation are both taboo subjects in our society," and that "taboos elicit fear and avoidance." Specific interventions designed to alleviate the potential difficulties inherent in such situations may be needed to assist both the family and its mentally handicapped member on their journey through grief.

When grief is disenfranchised, either because the significance of the loss to the survivor is not recognized or because the relationship between the deceased and the bereaved is not socially sanctioned, the person suffering the loss has little or no opportunity to mourn publicly. The surviving same-sex mates of persons who die with AIDS face this situation. Although AIDS affects people in all walks of life, the homosexual partners of persons with AIDS may find comparatively little support from the wider community as they cope with their loss. How many community resources, such as spousal support groups, are welcoming of persons with a differing sexual orientation? The answer to this question undoubtedly varies depending on the community and the mindset of a particular support group. For example, in one medium-sized community, a support group composed of parents who experienced neonatal loss successfully integrated a lesbian couple whose baby died, thus providing a measure of community support. When a high-grief death is treated by society

The Reassurance

About ten days or so
After we saw you dead
You came back in a dream.
I'm all right now you said.

And it *was* you, although
You were fleshed out again:
You hugged us all round then,
And gave your welcoming beam.

How like you to be kind,
Seeking to reassure.
And, yes, how like my mind
To make itself secure.

Thom Gunn

as if it were not a significant loss, the process of adjustment is unnecessarily made more difficult for survivors.

Unfinished Business

Unfinished business can be aptly termed "business that goes on after death." Something remains incomplete at the time of death. The content of unfinished business, how it is handled, and how the survivor is affected by it all have an impact on the experience of grief. Unfinished business can be thought of in one or both of two ways relative to its effect on survivors: first is the fact of death itself; second is the relationship between deceased and survivor. As to the first, perhaps an earlier death of a parent, child, sibling, or someone else close continues to be a vivid reminder of the survivor's uncertainty and fears about death. Regardless of an individual's particular beliefs or values, the more "finished" the business of death is—that is, the more a survivor feels resolved within himself or herself toward it—the easier it will be to accept death and to cope with grief and mourning. If a person rails against death, denying it and refusing to accept it, the experience of grief is more likely to be difficult and perhaps prolonged. Accepting death, giving it a place in our lives, allows us to be finished with otherwise unresolved issues about death itself.

Second, and probably more crucial in alleviating the stress and pain of grief, is the unfinished business between the deceased and the survivor. Something in the relationship was left incomplete—perhaps some long-standing conflict was never resolved during the deceased's lifetime, and now the survivor feels it is too late. Such unfinished business can include things that were and were not said, things done or not done. The work of Elisabeth Kübler-Ross and others points up the importance of finishing business between the person who is dying and his or her survivors. Open and uninhibited discussion at the time of an impending death can yield significant benefits both for the person who is dying and for the survivor.

People who have experienced the death of someone close often say that the things left unsaid or undone seem to come back to pain them, to give them bad times in the night. The sense of never being able to resolve the conflicts left by unfinished business is what amplifies the suffering. Consider the image of a son standing over his father's grave saying, "If only we had been closer, Dad. We ought to have taken more time to visit each other."

It may be possible to resolve some unfinished business even after the person's death by working through the unresolved experiences with the help of various techniques of counseling and therapeutic intervention. But it is easier and clearer to work toward resolving unfinished business daily, in all our relationships and especially our intimate ones.

Another category of unfinished business relates to the plans and dreams that a survivor had shared with the deceased person. Perhaps there were places they talked about going together at some time in the future; now, these travel plans will never be fulfilled. Perhaps the survivor and the deceased shared dreams and plans related to personal or family matters—plans about their children or "retirement years," for example. Perhaps they shared plans relating to starting or building a business together. Such plans and dreams can involve a variety of areas in the survivor's life. Death brings an end to all the things the survivor had imagined doing with the deceased.

Deathbed promises constitute a particular kind of unfinished business, and they affect more people than we might at first imagine. Picture the classic scene in which the person who is dying elicits some promise from the survivor to perform a particular action after the person dies. Most survivors agree to enact the promise, whether or not they really want to comply with the deathbed request. Thus, a deathbed promise can later cause considerable conflict for the survivor, who may be torn between fulfilling the promise and taking a contradictory course of action. Some people carry through a deathbed promise and find it to be a gratifying choice; others find that a deathbed promise needs to be reevaluated in the light of their own wishes and circumstances.

Coping Mechanisms for Survivors

From the dawn of human consciousness, survivors have used a variety of activities, rituals, and social institutions to help them cope with the fact of loss. Funerals and other rites surrounding disposition of the body serve this purpose by providing an orderly and acceptable framework for dealing with the initial shock of loss. However, because the process of coming to terms with a loss continues beyond the brief period taken up with such rituals, many survivors seek additional sources of support.

Pam Price, UPI/Bettmann Newsphotos

Family members leave the church after attending the funeral of a son and brother. As a focus of familial and community support for the bereaved, the funeral ceremony performs a unique function among the social rituals devised to mark significant events in the lives of members of a community.

Much of this support is provided within the family and the close-knit community of friends and relatives. With changes in the patterns of social life, such as smaller families and greater geographic mobility, some of these traditional sources of support may be unavailable or insufficient to meet the particular needs of survivors. Thus, many bereaved people seek support by sharing their concerns with others who have had similar bereavement experiences. Such survivor support groups extend communal support beyond the initial period of the funeral rites and provide supportive resources that may be otherwise lacking in the survivor's milieu. We will look briefly at how each of these coping mechanisms—funerals, other leave-taking rituals, and support groups—can help survivors in the process of mourning.

Funerals and Other Leave-Taking Rituals

Funerals and other leave-taking rituals provide a sense of closure on the deceased's life and thereby help survivors integrate the loss into their ongoing lives. Such rituals typically represent an opportunity for a "controlled expression of anger and hostility, and also for a lessening of guilt and anxiety."[53] The role of the wake among traditional Hawaiians illustrates these remarks. Everyone in the *ohana,* or extended family, came to the wake, including children. With each new arrival, a relative would say—as if telling the dead person—"Here comes Keone, your old fishing companion," or "Tutu is coming in now; remember how she used to massage you when you were sick." The mourners then addressed the dead, recalling their memories and perhaps describing their feelings of abandonment, even scolding the deceased for dying. A fishing companion might exclaim, "What do you mean, going off when we had planned to go fishing! Now who will I fish with?" Or a wife might say, "You had no business to go. You should be ashamed of yourself. We need you."[54]

Although these customs were not consciously planned to vent grief, they nevertheless facilitated it. The practice of scolding the corpse, for instance, provided an opportunity for survivors to vent hostility toward the dead who had abandoned them. What a contrast to the Western cultural notion that one should "not speak ill of the dead," which may deny feelings of anger at the deceased.

In one culture funerals are occasions for weeping and wailing, even literally "tearing one's hair out," magnifying the emotional response to provide catharsis; another culture emphasizes keeping emotions subdued, not demonstrating grief, not "breaking down." There may be discrepancies between expressed norms and observed grief behaviors.[55] Even within a particular social group, some survivors express their grief with intense fervor, others adopt a nearly stoic expression of grief. Still, as a culturally condoned vehicle for expressing grief behavior, funerals and other death rituals can facilitate mourning by providing survivors with a social framework for coping with the fact of death.

Indeed, the role of funeral rituals in gathering social support may be especially important in societies like the United States, which is typified by loose social networks. Whereas dense social networks—the small or medium-sized Israeli kibbutz, for example—have social structures that allow mourning to take place within an intimate circle of family, friends, neighbors, and

Advice for the Bereaved

Realize and recognize the loss.

Take time for nature's slow, sure, stuttering process of healing.

Give yourself massive doses of restful relaxation and routine busy-ness.

Know that powerful, overwhelming feelings will lessen with time.

Be vulnerable, share your pain, and be humble enough to accept support.

Surround yourself with life: plants, animals, and friends.

Use mementos to help your mourning, not to live in the dead past.

Avoid rebound relationships, big decisions, and anything addictive.

Keep a diary and record successes, memories, and struggles.

Prepare for change, new interests, new friends, solitude, creativity, growth.

Recognize that forgiveness (of ourselves and others) is a vital part of the healing process.

Know that holidays and anniversaries can bring up the painful feelings you thought you had successfully worked through.

Realize that any new death-related crisis will bring up feelings about past losses.

The Centre for Living with Dying

coworkers, looser social networks may capitalize on explicit forms of funeral ritual to generate an adequate sense of social support for the bereaved.[56]

Traditional mourning rituals have inspired other forms of leave-taking ritual, such as various forms of "directive mourning therapy," that allow the grieving survivor to take symbolic leave of the deceased.[57] This kind of ritual is also used to help individuals who wish to move from a maladaptive to an adaptive style of grieving.[58] Such leave-taking typically uses *linking objects* that are symbolic in some way of the survivor's relationship to the deceased.[59] An example would be the writing of a farewell letter to the deceased, and its subsequent burial or burning. Such an activity can be followed by a "reunion" ritual, perhaps in the form of a ceremonial dinner with family and friends. In this way, the movement of separation and joining found in traditional rituals can be adapted to the circumstances of a particular survivor.

Survivor Support Groups

By offering opportunities for bereaved persons to share their concerns and empathy with one another, support groups provide important help to survivors in coping with grief and mourning. Such groups are usually based on the concept of *perceived similarity*. Having experienced similar losses, members of support groups come together to support one another as they work toward integrating those losses into their lives. A well-known example of such mutual support would be organizations of widows (often known as widow-to-widow groups) that provide opportunities for widows to share experiences of being a woman alone and encourage one another in the task of coping with the death of a spouse.

Other mutual-help groups providing social support for the bereaved include organizations like Bereaved Families of Ontario (BFO), which was established in 1978 to assist families coping with the death of a child. It later expanded its mandate to include children, adolescents, and young adults who had suffered the death of a parent or sibling. In describing the aims of BFO, Stephen Fleming and Leslie Balmer note that it is "designed to facilitate the grieving process, emancipate the bereaved from crippling attachments to the deceased, assuage fears that one is 'going crazy,' educate the survivors about the nature and dynamics of grief to normalize their experience, and promote the usual curative qualities found in groups (the installation of hope, altruism, group cohesiveness, catharsis, and insight)."[60]

The meetings of some support groups resemble encounter sessions, the rule being to accept and express feelings. Others function more as social groups, providing a place for the survivor to come and be with others who have had similar experiences. Some groups are composed entirely of peers; others are facilitated by a trained professional or lay counselor.

Many hospice and palliative care programs provide specially trained volunteers to help families cope with their grief.[61] The coming of a greater openness about death has been accompanied by growing attention to bereavement care in many countries.[62] In Britain, for example, the organization Cruse has a national network of trained volunteer bereavement counselors who are supported by social workers, psychiatrists, and other professionals. Israel provides support services to war widows. And, in the United States, groups such as the Widow-to-Widow program have spurred the development of widespread mutual help groups and other forms of bereavement support.

Bereavement as an Opportunity for Growth

Survivors are better able to cope if they are aware that death and bereavement can be an opportunity for growth. This perspective allows movement toward resolving the loss. One can begin to reformulate the loss, thus freeing up energy that had been bound to the past. As John Schneider says, "There is a change in perceptual set from focusing on limits to focusing on potential; from coping to growth; and from problems to challenges."[63] The tragic event of the loved one's death is reformulated in a way that offers new opportunities. This reframing of the experience can carry over into other areas of the person's life, so that beliefs and assumptions that were once limiting may be reassessed with greater self-confidence and self-awareness. The process of resolving loss and working through grief provides incentives that make possible significant life changes.

In this way, the loss is transformed. The intensive focus on self-awareness gives way to a new sense of identity whereby the loss is placed within a context of growth and life cycles. Grief becomes a unifying rather than alienating human experience, and the lost relationship is viewed as changed, but not ended. Transforming the loss involves integrating what was lost into one's own life energies. Being a survivor may allow changes in beliefs and values—understanding about death and about life—that might not otherwise have been possible. Recollecting their grief, bereaved individuals have described themselves as stronger, more competent, more mature, more independent, and better able to face other crises; for many, bereavement led to positive experiences with their social support systems of family and friends.[64]

As we have seen, the process by which a survivor integrates a loss into his or her life varies. In many cases, turning to inner sources of creativity gives form to the experience of grief. Creatively responding to loss can bring forth remarkable results. Those who work with the bereaved can spark a grieving person's creative response, as in the case of a young woman who had experienced the sudden, unexpected death of her son at birth. Overwhelmed by feelings of sadness, depression, and inability to do anything other than grieve, she was despairing of words to communicate her feelings. In a counseling session six months after her son's death, she remarked, "I haven't touched a lump of clay since Justin died." The obvious question was, What had she done with clay before his death? She said that her sculptures of whales and seals had sold at a local seaside crafts shop. The counselor pointed out that the reason for her inability to return to her art might lie in the source of her creative energies. Although whales and seals might one day reemerge from the lumps of clay, her creativity at present might take a different form. The client agreed to find a quiet moment when she would put her hands to the lump of clay as an experiment to see what might emerge.

Both the bereaved mother and the counselor were amazed at the results (see Figures 7-2a,b,c). Over the course of twelve months, a series of some twenty-two figures emerged. The earliest were naked, later works were draped with blankets, and, with the final pieces, the fabric of the blankets had been turned into clothing. The mother's creativity not only gave form to her loss, but also manifested an unconscious understanding of the process of recovery and the integration of her loss. Subsequently, the sculptures were photographed and published, along with her prose, giving comfort to other survivors.[65]

Death is a community event. Death does not end the survivor's membership in family, community, or nation. Attitudes toward the dead are largely a continuation of the natural affections and styles of relationship that hold for the living in any given culture. People maintain connections with deceased loved ones through memories as well as through personal or social rituals that periodically provide a "space" in their ongoing lives for acknowledging affection and love for the deceased. Bereavement, grief, and mourning are complementary threads in the fabric of life, part of the warp and weft of human experience.

A survivor's response to death is complex, encompassing a multitude of personal, family, and social factors. It is influenced also by the circumstances

Figure 7-2(a)   *Anguish of loss*

Figure 7-2(b)   *Sharing the grief*

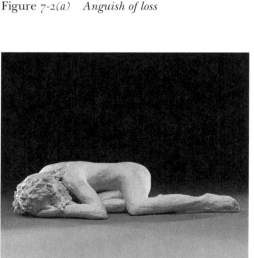

Figure 7-2(c)   *Collapsing*

"The anguish of loss is overpowering and vast," begins the prose accompanying the sculpture by Julie Fritsch pictured here, part of the series created following the death of her son. "Sharing the grief" states the theme of the second sculpture, acknowledging that "together we must comfort and be comforted." The third sculpture portrays the bereaved artist "collapsing from the weight of emotions I cannot control." The prose accompanying this sculpture continues: "Drained of any ability to cope or carry on, I must collapse now. And feel myself overcome by absolute grief."

surrounding the death. By becoming aware of the vast range of responses that can be present in the experience of loss and grief, we increase our choices for dealing with loss. By understanding the issues involved in survivorship, we offer ourselves greater opportunity to cope successfully with loss and to use the experience of loss as a means of becoming more fully human.

Further Readings

Kenneth J. Doka, ed. *Disenfranchised Grief: Recognizing Hidden Sorrow.* Lexington, Mass.: Lexington Books, 1989.

Marian Osterweis, Fredric Solomon, and Morris Green, eds. *Bereavement: Reactions, Consequences, and Care.* Washington, D.C.: National Academy Press, 1984.

Colin Murray Parkes. *Bereavement: Studies of Grief in Adult Life,* 2d ed. Madison, Conn.: International Universities Press, 1987.

Catherine M. Sanders. *Grief, The Mourning After: Dealing with Adult Bereavement.* New York: John Wiley and Sons, 1989.

Margaret S. Stroebe, Wolfgang Stroebe, and Robert O. Hansson, eds. *Handbook of Bereavement: Theory, Research, and Intervention.* New York: Cambridge University Press, 1993.

Judy Tatelbaum. *The Courage to Grieve: Creative Living, Recovery and Growth Through Grief.* New York: Harper & Row, 1982.

Vamik D. Volkan and Elizabeth Zintl. *Life After Loss: The Lessons of Grief.* New York: Collier, 1994.

Familiarity with the choices available in funeral services can help us appreciate our many options, perhaps alleviating some of the stress of making such choices in the midst of crisis. The roles of the funeral director and others who can provide assistance in coping with the practical matters of death may also be better understood.

Last Rites:
Funerals and Body
Disposition

*O*ur choices regarding last rites tell something about our attitudes and beliefs about death. The ceremonies that a community enacts to mark the passing of one of its members express, through symbol and metaphor, how death is perceived within that particular social group. A society's attitude toward death, as well as toward the meaning and purpose of life, is revealed in its funeral customs.

A young musician describes the ceremony he would choose to mark his death: "My body would be cremated and the ashes put into an Egyptian urn. My friends would place the urn on stage at a rock concert and, as the band plays on, everyone will dance and celebrate the changes that we all must pass through eventually."

Some people find the musician's choice lacking in solemnity. "That's not a funeral," they might say. "It's a party." The friends of the musician, however, might respond that his death style is consistent with his life style. His funeral bespeaks an emphasis on celebrating the joys of life. His preference for cremation may reflect a belief that existence is transitory. It's as if he were saying, "Life is a passing show. When the movie's over for me, why should my body be preserved?" The urn in which the ashes are placed may symbolize the musician's view that he is somehow part of a historical continuity that transcends even death. In short, each component of the musician's death ceremony tells us something about his concept of death.

The Metropolitan Museum of Art, Rogers/Harkness Funds, 1920

The presence of mortuary goods helped ensure a pleasant afterlife for the ancient Egyptians. Dating from the Eleventh Dynasty, about two thousand years before the present era, this funerary model of a paddling yacht comes from the tomb of Meket-Re.

Examining the death customs of the ancient Egyptians, we see a culture preoccupied with acquiring mortuary goods and preparing for the afterlife.[1] A dominant theme in Egyptian religion was belief in life after death. If adequate preparations were made, there was no reason to fear death. The body was mortal. Yet within it were immortal elements: the *Ba,* a soul or psychic force, and the *Ka,* a spiritual double representing the creative and preserving power of life. At death, the *Ka* flew to the afterlife while the *Ba* lived on in the body.

As the permanent dwelling place of the *Ba,* the body was preserved by mummification and protected by wooden coffins, sometimes placed within stone sarcophagi; and the tomb was built to resemble one's earthly home. By providing a home for the *Ba* (often depicted in the form of a bird hovering above the mummy of the deceased), continued enjoyment of the afterlife was ensured. However, if the *Ba* were destroyed, one would suffer "the second death, the death that really did come as the end." It would be as if the person had been annihilated, as if he or she had never come into existence. Preservation of the physical form, either as mummy or as statue, was necessary for survival. This relationship between the identity of the person and the body lying in the tomb, which may in some sense be universal, is found in the feeling of connection with the deceased that one has at graveside.

Likewise, the customary American funeral contains a wealth of information concerning how we relate to death in our society. Consider, for example, the practice of cosmetically restoring the corpse to a more or less "lifelike" appearance. Some believe that this effort at disguise bespeaks a tendency to deny death. Lavish displays for the dead have aroused criticism at least since the time of the Greek philosopher Herodotus in the fourth century before the present era. But, as some writers have observed, ours is the first society that apparently wishes to do away with all traces of death by masking its reality and quickly disposing of the corpse.

In considering whether contemporary funeral practices encourage the denial of death, we must consider these questions: Who does the funeral serve—the living or the dead? What is the purpose—socially and psychologically—of last rites? What are the essential elements of ceremonies that mark the passing of a member of the community?

In contrast to cultures in which the funeral is seen as a vehicle for preparing the dead to successfully migrate to the afterworld, the American funeral is focused on the welfare of the survivors. Socially, the funeral provides a setting wherein the bereaved family makes a public statement that one of its members has died. The wider community uses the occasion to respond with sympathy and support for the bereaved. Psychologically, the funeral provides a framework within which survivors confront the fact of their loss. By enacting the funeral ritual, survivors move toward resolving the crisis and accepting the loss.

Psychosocial Aspects of Last Rites

Funeral ceremonies and memorial services are rites of passage that reflect a community's acknowledgment that one of its members has died. Often termed *last rites,* they mark the final transition or passage of an individual in his or her status as a member of the larger social group (see Table 8-1). Just as a community convenes to commemorate the other major social transitions in a person's life, the funeral facilitates a gathering together of the survivors to commemorate the deceased's participation as a former member of the community and his or her passage from the group by death. This communal acknowledgment of death serves both social and psychological purposes.

Death Notification

A death occurs. First to learn about it, besides the attending medical team, are usually members of the immediate family. Then, in a gradually widening network, other relatives and friends of the deceased are notified. David Sudnow observed that notification generally occurs in a consistent pattern from the immediate family to the wider community (see Figure 8-1).[2] Those with closest relationships to the deceased are notified first, followed by those with less intimate relationships. Sudnow also found that such notification generally takes place between people in a peer relationship. For example, a bereaved

TABLE *8-1*   *Elements of Funeral Ritual*

1. *Death watch* (also known as the death vigil or "sitting up"). As death nears, relatives and friends gather to say farewells and show respect for the dying person, as well as give support and care to his or her family. Historically, a death watch might continue for hours, days, or even weeks or months.
2. *Preparation of the deceased.* Involves various tasks associated with preparing the corpse for ultimate disposition, usually burial or cremation.
3. *Wake* (also known as "visitation" or "calling hours"). Traditionally held on the night after death occurs, this funeral practice involves laying out the corpse and keeping a watch or "wake" over it. Wakes have historically been observed as a safeguard against premature burial, as an opportunity for paying respects to the deceased, and, in some cultures, as an occasion for lively festivities focused on allaying fears by "rousing the ghost."

   With changes in the social patterns of mourning, the traditional wake has been largely transformed into the practice of setting aside time for viewing of the body prior to the funeral service. Such viewing confirms that the death has occurred and is a psychological impetus enabling the bereaved to begin the journey toward resolving grief. As with the traditional observances, the modern "visitation" provides opportunities for social interactions that can be healing in the aftermath of loss.
4. *Funeral.* As the "centerpiece" of ceremonies and rituals surrounding death, the funeral is a rite of passage for both the deceased and his or her survivors. Services are usually held in a mortuary chapel or church, although they may be held in the home or at the gravesite. The body may or may not be present; if it is present, the casket may be open or closed. Funeral services typically include music, prayers, readings from scripture or other poetry or prose, a eulogy honoring the life of the deceased, and, less frequently, a funeral sermon focusing on the role of death in human life generally. In modern times, funerals are usually held within a few days after death, and they are increasingly being scheduled in the evening or on weekends so that mourners who work can attend the service.
5. *Procession.* Traditionally, funeral rites include a procession conveying the corpse from the site of the funeral to the place of burial. It is considered an honor to be among the friends and relatives chosen to carry the deceased's body to its final resting place. Funerals for national leaders and other notables may include a lengthy procession, or cortege, with the corpse attended by honorary pallbearers.
6. *Committal.* A ceremony held at the grave or crematorium, the committal service is held after, or sometimes in lieu of, the funeral service. When it follows a funeral service, it usually consists of a brief ceremony focusing on disposition of the deceased's remains.
7. *Disposal of the corpse.* In modern societies, disposition usually means burial or cremation.

---

mother might first call the child who had been closest to the deceased, and that person then calls the other brothers and sisters. They, in turn, notify more distant kin.

A similar pattern of notification occurs among those who are not directly related to the deceased. For instance, a coworker or neighbor informed about the death notifies others who had a similar relationship with the deceased. This process of notification—taking in a gradually widening circle of relatives,

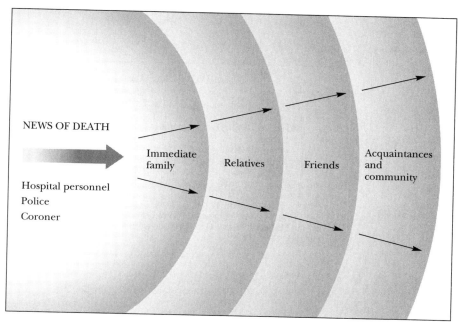

Figure *8-1*   *Widening Circles of Death Notification*

friends, and acquaintances—continues until virtually everyone affected by the death is notified.

Death notification also takes place by means of notices that appear in the newspaper (see Figure 8-2). We expect these announcements to appear in a timely fashion. When they do not, the results can be upsetting. The following complaint is typical: "The obituary did not appear in the newspaper until the morning of the funeral. . . . We had a number of calls and letters from people who didn't know about the funeral until it was too late to attend."

When the deceased is well known, news of the death is broadcast more widely, because it affects more people. Thus, notification about the deaths of public figures is carried out on a grand scale. The death of President John F. Kennedy, for example, was known by about 90 percent of the American people within an hour of its official pronouncement at Parkland Hospital in Dallas.[3]

Human beings feel the need to respond to the death of a significant other. The person who learns the news of a death only after the final disposition of the body may regret not having been able to participate in the final ceremonies marking that person's death. Because the mutual support of the community of bereaved persons is not likely to be as available after the initial period of mourning has passed, the belatedly notified person may feel alone in dealing with grief. The value placed on timely notification is emphasized in an article by Ronald Barrett focusing on funeral traditions within the African-American

---

Obituaries

Spirit Bird Benton

HAYWARD – Spirit Bird Benton, 17, Rt. 5, Hayward, died Friday, April 19, 1991, in Albuquerque, N.M. in an automobile accident.

Spirit Bird was born August 22, 1973 in St. Paul, Minn., the son of Edward J. and Delma (Arrow) Benton. He was a student at Lac Courte Oreilles High School.

He is survived by his father, Edward, Hayward; his mother, Delma, Tama, Iowa; three brothers, John Wedward and Ramon, both of Hayward and Eddie, Green Bay; four sisters, Marilyn, Nancy and Sherrole, all of Hayward and Natalie, Oneida; and a grandmother, Elizabeth Arrow, White River, S.D.

Tribal rites were held on Tuesday, April 23 at the Eagle Lodge, Hayward. Burial was in the Hayward Indian Cemetery in Historyland.

Anderson-Nathan Funeral Home of Hayward was in charge of arrangements.

Figure 8-2   *Newspaper Obituary*
Source: The County Journal (Bayfield County, Cable, Wis.), April 25, 1991.

community. Barrett says: "The immediacy of notification is equated with importance and respect. To not be informed of the death in a timely manner is considered insensitive, lacking respect, and an insult."[4]

The process of death notification also helps to set apart the bereaved during the period of mourning. In some societies, the black armband, mourning colors and garb, as well as various other signs and symbols, distinguish the bereaved person from those not in mourning. Those traditional signs of mourning have almost vanished from American life. Yet most people still feel that the bereaved deserve special consideration during their distress.

A woman who became involved in an automobile accident several days after the death of her child said later that she wished she could have had a banner proclaiming her status as a "mother whose child has just died." With no outward symbol of her bereavement, she was subjected, as any of us would be, to the strain of waiting around and filling in seemingly endless accident report forms. Had she lived in a small town, the process of notification itself might have set her apart in such a way that the task of completing the paperwork would have been made easier and more convenient.

Though often taken for granted, the process of death notification is important. It can elicit support that is helpful to survivors in dealing with their loss, and it provides an impetus for coming to terms with the fact that a significant loss has taken place.

Mutual Support

When people learn about the death of someone significant to them, they tend to gather together, closing ranks to provide support and comfort in their

In an earlier time, when society was more agrarian, the whole community could pause from the daily round and rally to the support of the family at the funeral. In this urban age, however, when families live anonymously and work miles from their bedroom communities, and when approximately 60 percent of the women are in the work force, it is increasingly difficult for people to attend daytime funerals unless the deceased is a close relative. The policy of many companies is to give released time to employees only for the funeral of an immediate family member. Consequently, the tendency is for acquaintances to call at the parlor during evening visitation hours and for only the closest friends and relatives to attend the funeral itself. Many clergy feel this deprives the family of a powerful support system and renders impossible a corporate celebration of the life of the deceased.

Frank Minton, "Clergy Views of Funeral Practice"

mutual bereavement. Generally, this emotional and social support is directed primarily toward the bereaved family. When a small child asked her mother why they were going to visit a bereaved family, the mother replied, "It's important for people to know that you care." What we think we can or cannot do for the bereaved family matters little. What counts is that somehow we demonstrate our care and concern. J. Z. Young says, "Probably the very act of coming together symbolizes communication. A symbol is a sign that points to some state that is of emotional importance. The very fact of assembly gives reassurance that we are part of a larger whole and the individual life is strengthened thereby."[5]

Those who gather at the home of the bereaved participate in a unique social occasion. Unlike other social interactions, this one is not by "invitation only"; generally speaking, anyone who wishes may come. Some persons stay only a short while, expressing their condolences and then leaving. Others, usually relatives or close friends, stay for a longer time, perhaps assisting with the preparation of food, caring for children, helping with funeral arrangements, greeting visitors, or doing whatever else needs doing during the crisis.

Gathering together to support and comfort the bereaved continues throughout the events of the funeral. This pattern of social interaction has important psychological implications for the bereaved as well. It serves to corroborate the fact that a loved one has died. It expresses the notion, "Our community of family and friends has undergone a significant change of status; one of our members is dead." The coming together of the community members to support one another confirms the significance of that loss.

Death is a change of status for the person who dies, and it brings a change of status for the survivors. Funeral rituals embody the rhythms of separation and integration. The survivors come together as a community to let go of the dead person, and to acknowledge that their situation is no longer the same. This change of status is sometimes reflected in language, as when we refer to someone as a widow or widower. The use of a special term to designate a

Thousands of American citizens joined in the funeral observance honoring the Unknown Serviceman of the Vietnam era. Here the procession is crossing Memorial Bridge between two rows of a Marine honor cordon, on its way to Arlington National Cemetery. Replete with full military honors, the funeral was an occasion for expressing national gratitude and grief in response to the ultimate sacrifice of those who died in the wartime service of their country.

William E. Rosemund, U.S. Army Photo

surviving husband or wife calls attention to the social and psychological impact that is associated with a spouse's death.

Impetus for Coping with Loss

Death must be confronted not only within the social setting in which it occurs, but within the psyche of the bereaved person. The processes of death notification and visitations are forms of social interaction, but they also provide a potent psychological means for coming to terms with a death.

When death occurs, the most immediate need of the survivors is the disposition of the corpse, which involves both a mental process (deciding what is to be done) and a physical activity (carrying out the course of action decided upon). Making arrangements for disposition of the body engages the survivor in a process that helps to reinforce the recognition that the deceased is really dead. This gradual realization of the loss occurs whether the survivor simply talks with someone about funeral arrangements or actively constructs the coffin and digs the grave.

As with people of other times and other cultures, survivors today frequently choose to bury funerary artifacts or "grave goods" with their dead.[6] Jewelry, photographs, rosaries, Bibles, favorite hats, military medals, stuffed animals, and organizational emblems are among the items most commonly placed in the casket or buried with the deceased. Tobacco, alcohol, and articles related to a favorite activity such as golf or fishing are also frequently mentioned by morticians as examples of grave goods placed with the deceased. The personal sentiment expressed by such placement bespeaks yet another way that funeral rituals help survivors deal with the crisis of loss. Surrounding the final disposition of the body is a complex of social, cultural, religious, psychological, and interpersonal factors that determine the ritual form in which this basic task of body disposition is accomplished. These ceremonies give significance to the events that lead to the final disposition of the deceased's body.

The American Funeral

Most Americans give the funeral service trade positive marks. Nevertheless, because the activities and costs of funeral services are unfamiliar to most people, some critics point out that funeral directors are in a position to take advantage of their customers. The funeral industry is viewed as a "mystery business," about which the average person knows little. Thus, despite general satisfaction with funeral service, there are questions about whether a consumer would know if he or she were being ripped off.

Criticisms

The American funeral has been criticized on several grounds, from general objections to what a funeral represents to criticisms of particular funeral practices. Bertram Puckle's *Funeral Customs: Their Origin and Development*, published in 1926, was a general attack against lavish concern for the dead. To

If you have an uncomfortable feeling about funerals, which are the accepted social pattern for confronting death in our culture, if you try to avoid or eliminate them, that might be a sign that you're dealing with major residual death anxiety. That's one of the things that shows up in our culture: the way people delude themselves and retreat from the major therapeutic resources that are provided culturally. There's a notion that if we have a mini-funeral, we'll have mini-grief. But we know that the exact opposite is true.

The more you reduce your emotional acting out at the time of the event, the more you prolong the pain of grief and postpone the therapeutic work of mourning.

That's why in a culture such as ours, where you have an unwise management of grief, you have a very large proportion of illness responses after the death experience. People act it out physically, rather than doing it psychologically or socially. That's a very heavy weight.

But in primitive cultures, such as the aboriginals in Australia, where you have almost a two-week funeral process, where there are all kinds of acting out of deep feelings, you come to the end of that two weeks and a major portion of the grief work has been done, and the survivor is ready to move into the period of resolution through the mourning process, which takes quite a bit longer usually.

Edgar N. Jackson,
from an interview with the authors

Puckle, the funeral was a vestige of the superstitious fear of the dead characteristic of the pagan and the primitive.

In 1959 LeRoy Bowman, in *The American Funeral: A Study in Guilt, Extravagance, and Sublimity,* documented the commercialism and conspicuous display connected with funerals while investigating their social and psychological value. Bowman concluded that funeral practices were overlaid with such ostentation that the fundamental meaning and dignity of the funeral rite had all but disappeared. The American funeral, he said, "appears to be an anachronism, an elaboration of early customs rather than the adaptation to modern needs that it should be."[7] Bowman urged Americans to become more aware of the essential social, psychological, and spiritual functions of funeral rituals. In this way, Bowman believed, people could avoid the potential for exploitation associated with the materialistic features of contemporary practices.

To Bowman, the funeral director was a tradesman, often selling wares that were unnecessary and unwanted. The function of the funeral director, Bowman said, should be to help the family fulfill its own wishes. In this, he urged greater flexibility in carrying out last rites. "The uniformity of present usage should give way to individually adapted procedures, whatever they may be." These insights continue to have value to anyone wishing more participation in the design of funeral rituals.

In 1963 two books appeared that brought criticisms about the American funeral to public attention: Jessica Mitford's *The American Way of Death* and

"You've got to admit—he looks good."

Drawing by Jack Ziegler, © 1994 The New Yorker Magazine, Inc.

Ruth M. Harmer's *The High Cost of Dying*. Both books criticized the materialism of the contemporary funeral and called for reform.

Mitford said that conventional funeral practices were bizarre and morbid. In her view, the attempt to disguise and prettify death makes it more grotesque. She took issue with the euphemisms employed to soften the reality of death: the metamorphosis of coffins into "caskets," hearses into "coaches," flowers into "floral tributes," and cremated ashes into "cremains." The language of the funeral service industry came under especially heavy assault by Mitford's penetrating wit. The corpse, she pointed out, lies in state in the "slumber room." The undertaker, now a "mortician" or "funeral director," displays a solid-copper "Colonial Classic Beauty," replete with a "Perfect-Posture" adjustable innerspring mattress, in a choice of "60 color-matched shades." Within this handsome arrangement, the deceased wears "handmade original fashions" from a "gravewear couturiere" and "Nature-Glo, the ultimate in cosmetic grooming."[8] Mitford's satiric criticisms sparked concern among those in the funeral trade and promoted the rise of alternatives, such as non-profit funeral and memorial societies. Many funeral directors responded to criticisms by offering a wider range of choices in funeral service, thereby encouraging the trend toward more individualized services.[9]

Traditionally, the clergy has played a significant role in dealing with the bereaved family and in making preparations for the disposition of the corpse. Today, however, funeral services are seldom held in churches, having been moved to the chapels that are part of the modern funeral establishment. Some clergy would like to reverse this practice, particularly in the case of funerals for their parishioners.[10]

Although a study conducted as part of a Federal Trade Commission (FTC) investigation found substantial public approval of funeral practices, lingering concerns prompted the Commission to implement the "Trade Regulation Rule on Funeral Industry Practices" in 1984.[11] The Funeral Rule, as it is called, stipulates that funeral providers give detailed information about prices and legal requirements to people who are arranging funerals. It requires disclosure of itemized prices, both over the telephone and in writing. Misrepresentations about the disposition of human remains are prohibited, as are certain practices such as embalming for a fee without prior permission, requiring customers to purchase caskets for a direct cremation, or making the purchase of any funeral good or service conditional on the purchase of any other funeral good or service.[12]

History

The detailed regulations promulgated by the FTC can be viewed as the natural outcome of a historical process that removed death from the purview of family and friends and placed it in the hands of professional morticians. When families themselves took care of the disposition of their dead, any criticism of their manner of performance would have been irrelevant. And, of course, it was not designed to produce a profit. Disposition was simply a human task to be carried out in a spirit of compassion, kindness, and respect. Even though we are now accustomed to giving over the care of our dead to the mortician, we may yet carry residual feelings that realizing a profit from performing these services is somehow macabre.

Another source of our discomfort about the commercialization of funeral services arises from anxiety about death and an aversion to touching or being in the presence of a corpse. (Such aversion can perhaps be attributed to our unfamiliarity with personal care of the dead—an effect, rather than a cause, of current practices.) Yet when the corpse is of someone we loved, our aversion may be mixed with guilt; we are pulled in opposing directions, and feel uncomfortable about the dead. We may unconsciously resent the funeral director who handles the body of our loved one. Thus, we feel a confusing range of emotions regarding the dead: aversion, guilt, resentment, affection, and anxiety.

Formerly, the family's ceremonial occasions were held within the home. The undertaker was a merchant who supplied the materials and funeral paraphernalia—such items as the casket and carriage, door badges and scarves, special clothing, memorial cards and announcements, chairs, robes, pillows, gauze, candles, ornaments, and so on, which were used to equip the home for the mourning ritual (see Figure 8-3).

By the end of the nineteenth century, however, the undertaker had assumed a much larger role. No longer merely a tradesman who furnished goods

Figure *8-3*　*City Directory Listing for a Cabinet Maker and Supplier of Funeral Furnishings, circa 1850*

to the bereaved family, the undertaker had become a provider of services. He was being asked to take more control and to assume a larger role, actually taking part in the disposition of the dead: laying out the body for the wake, transporting it to the church for the funeral, and, finally, taking it to the cemetery for burial.

Embalming the dead came into use around the time of the Civil War. President Lincoln's funeral procession, which traveled from Washington, D.C., to Springfield, Illinois, was a public event that increased awareness of the new practice of embalming.[13] Still, other means of temporarily retarding decomposition of the corpse continued in use (see Figure 8-4).

(There is evidence that embalming was performed on some of the soldiers killed during the Civil War, which allowed their bodies to be returned home. Through World Wars I and II and down to the Korean conflict, however, battlefield dead were typically buried in the particular theater of operations in which they had been killed, with a possibility of final disposition to the United States after the end of hostilities. The Vietnam conflict was the first in which battlefield dead were returned from a foreign battle zone for stateside burial as a matter of course. The military services have their own mortuary officers, who may be given specialized training to help them carry out their duties.[14])

With the coming of smaller houses and increased urbanization, the place where the dead were prepared for burial changed: The viewing of the body moved from the parlor of the family home into a room reserved for such use by the tradesman-undertaker. The funeral "parlor" in town gradually substituted for the ceremonial room that people no longer had in their own homes. This one-room funeral parlor was the forerunner of the present-day funeral home or mortuary.

By the late nineteenth century, undertakers had become "morticians" and were starting to think of themselves as "funeral *directors.*" The Funeral Directors' National Association, established in the 1880s—now the National Funeral Directors Association (NFDA)—was among the first of the new trade organizations designed both to promote business and to establish minimum

J. C. TAYLOR & SON'S
PATENT IMPROVED ICE CASKETS,
FOR PRESERVING THE DEAD BY COLD AIR.

The Pioneer Corpse Preserver, Over 3,500 in Use.

PRICES AND SIZES:

6 Feet 4 Inches Long, 20 Inches Wide, $60 00. | 4 Feet 10 Inches Long, 17 Inches Wide, $48 00.
5 " 10 " " 20 " " 58 00. | 3 " 10 " " 15 " " 42 00.

Send for Illustrated and Descriptive Price-List, Containing full Particulars.

FOR SALE AT MANUFACTURERS' PRICES, BY

Paxson, Comfort & Co., 523 Market St., Philadelphia.

Figure *8-4*   *Refrigerated Casket Advertisement, 1881*
Undertakers of the 1880s could keep a body for viewing over a longer period of time by using an ice casket, such as the one shown in this advertisement. When embalming became widespread, these cold-air preservation
devices became obsolete.

standards for service. Trade publications, such as *The Casket* and *Sunnyside*,
facilitated communication among funeral directors. In 1917 the National
Selected Morticians was formed as a limited-membership group dedicated to
the ideal of service. The National Foundation of Funeral Service was formed in
1945 to conduct research, establish a library of funeral service information,
and sponsor an institute providing professional education for funeral directors. Today, most states require that funeral directors be certified by state
licensing, and all states require that embalmers be licensed.

Selecting Funeral Services

The purchase of funeral services is a transaction unique in commerce.
Most people give it little or no thought until they find themselves in the midst
of an emotional crisis. As with other purchases, however, the customer who
winds up with the least regrets is likely to be the one who takes time beforehand
to fully explore his or her options. When arrangements for funeral services are
made during a time of crisis and confusion, the customer is confronted with

> The funeral director is caught between ambivalent demands: On the one hand, he is encouraged to disguise the reality of death for the survivors who do not possess the emotional support once provided by theology to deal with it; on the other hand, he is impelled to call attention to the special services he is rendering. Thus, he both blunts and sharpens the reality of death.
>
> Robert Fulton and Gilbert Geis,
> "Death and Social Values"

the need to make an on-the-spot decision about a purchase that cannot be returned. Caskets do not bear a notice saying, "Return in thirty days if not completely satisfied." Once made, the decision is final. Lack of information, coupled with lack of forethought about funerals or body disposition, may lead to decisions that will be regretted later.

The choices involved in selecting funeral services tend to be quite different from those involved in most other purchases. When purchasing a new car, for example, you can shop around and test-drive various makes and models. If you encounter a salesperson who uses high-pressure techniques, you can either submit to such tactics or walk away: You have a clear choice. Yet, rarely do the emotional conditions in which funeral services are purchased allow for such coolheadedness or presence of mind that the bereaved can simply walk away and go elsewhere to compare prices. In some localities, there may be only one mortician to serve the entire community. When a death has already occurred, it can be too late to start investigating the options.

Unfortunately, the funeral may become an occasion for an expensive or lavish display, as survivors attempt to assuage guilt or compensate for some unresolved conflict with the deceased. Spending a huge sum of money on a funeral, under such circumstances, may thwart the real purpose of last rites—namely, to acknowledge publicly that a member of the community has died and to effect closure on that person's life for the bereaved.

The funeral is a setting for private sorrow and public loss in which the burden of grief is reduced by sharing with others. It effects the disposition of the corpse while acknowledging that indeed a life has been lived. The funeral is a statement from the family to the community: "We have lost someone, and we are grieving." Ideally, it is a personal statement based on felt needs and values. It is worth remembering that the purpose of the funeral can be realized whether it is garnished with diamonds and rubies, or with poetry and a song.

Funeral Service Charges

The National Funeral Directors Association has distinguished four categories of charges that together make up the cost of a conventional American funeral. The first category includes the services provided by the funeral director and mortuary staff, the use of mortuary facilities and equipment, and the casket and related funeral merchandise selected by the customer.

The second category pertains to the actual disposition of the body. Depending on the method of disposition chosen, this can include the purchase of a gravesite and costs for opening and closing the grave; or, if above-ground entombment is chosen, the cost of a mausoleum crypt; or, if the body is cremated, the cost of cremation and the subsequent interment, entombment, or scattering of the cremated remains, as well as the cost of an urn to hold the ashes, if desired.

The third category is made up of costs related to memorialization. For burials, this can include a monument or marker for the grave; for cremated remains, it can include an inscription or plaque for the niche (recessed compartment) in a *columbarium,* an above-ground structure with a series of niches for urns.

The fourth category involves miscellaneous expenses either paid directly by the family or reimbursed to the undertaker. These may include a clergy member's honorarium, the use of limousines and additional vehicles (if not included in the funeral services category), flowers, notices of the death that appear in newspapers, and transportation outside the local area.

In summary, then, the total cost for the final disposition of the deceased includes funeral service charges, body disposition costs, memorialization expenses, and miscellaneous or supplemental expenses.

Until recently, the funeral director's portion of these expenses might be quoted to customers in a variety of ways. The most widespread form of pricing, and the simplest, was the single-unit method: A single price was quoted for a standard funeral; the specifics of the service and the total price depended on the type of casket selected. A more expensive casket thus became the centerpiece of a correspondingly more ornate and elaborate ceremony.

With the advent of the Federal Trade Commission's "Funeral Rule" in 1984, itemized price information became a requirement for all funeral providers. The rule requires, at minimum, that prices be itemized for seventeen specified goods and services, if those items are offered by the funeral provider (see Table 8-2). These goods and services must be specified on the provider's General Price List, which has been called "the keystone of the Funeral Rule," so that customers can compare prices or choose only those elements of a funeral they want. It is important to note that FTC requirements do not prohibit funeral directors from also offering package funerals, as discussed earlier.

The average cost of a funeral, excluding cemetery costs, is now about $4000. Funeral costs vary among regions of the country, as well as between rural and metropolitan areas. A mid-1980s survey of nearly 700 firms revealed that charges for individual funerals ranged from a low of $100 to a high of $23,560.[15] With about 2.2 million Americans dying each year, expenditures for funeral services total about $8 billion.[16] Although many of the 15,000 funeral

T A B L E *8-2* *Funeral Rule Itemization Requirements*

Forwarding of remains to another funeral home[1]
Receiving remains from another funeral home[1]
Direct cremation[1,2]
Immediate burial[1]
Transfer of remains to funeral home
Embalming[3]
Other preparation of the body
Use of facilities for viewing
Use of facilities for funeral ceremony
Other use of facilities[4]
Hearse
Limousine
Other automotive equipment
Acknowledgment cards
Casket prices[5]
Outer burial container prices[6]
Charge for professional services of the funeral director[7]

1. Any fee for professional services must be included in the price quoted for this item.
2. If a provider offers direct cremations, consumers must be allowed to provide their own container if they desire, as long as it meets state or crematory requirements. Also, if direct cremations are offered, the provider must make available either an unfinished wood box or alternative container for consumers who request it. A disclosure to this effect must be included in conjunction with the price for direct cremations.
3. In addition to the quoted price for embalming, there must be an affirmative disclosure stating, in part, that "except in certain special cases, embalming is not required by law."
4. Other facilities might include, for example, a tent and chairs for a graveside service.
5. Casket prices must be disclosed either on the General Price List or on a separate Casket Price List.
6. Prices for Outer Burial Containers may be listed on the General Price List or on a separate price list. Also, a disclosure must be made to the effect that "in most areas of the country, no state or local law requires you to buy an outer burial container; however, many cemeteries ask that you have such a container so that the grave will not sink in. Either a burial vault or a grave liner will satisfy these requirements."
7. As noted above, charges for services entailed in forwarding and receiving remains, direct cremations, and immediate burials are not involved here, since the FTC rule requires that service costs be included in the prices for those items. The fee for professional services may be listed separately from other items, or it may be included in the price of caskets. Whichever method is chosen by a funeral provider, a disclosure to that effect must appear on the General Price List.

service firms in the United States are operated as small businesses, taken in the aggregate, disposition of the dead is clearly big business.

Typically, the funeral business resides in a rather large, possibly colonial style building, the floor plan of which may be adapted or designed especially for its function as a funeral home. Funerals have been compared to theatrical presentations, with certain activities taking place, as it were, off stage.[17] The backstage area, hidden away from the public's gaze, is where the body is prepared by embalming and application of cosmetics for its eventual role in the funeral drama. There is generally no hint of these backstage regions to those who enter by the front door. The funeral chapel itself has been described as "a model of theatrical perfection" that might well "make a Broadway star envious." Usually arranged in such a way that there are several entrances and exits, it "may be served by back doors, halls, tunnels, and passageways that lead from the preparation room without ever trespassing frontstage areas."

Funeral directors regard themselves as professionals who provide critical services to people who are in crisis. Although funeral directors, as a group, have been criticized by some for taking on the role of "grief therapists" and perhaps using this role as a marketing ploy, some funeral directors consider this function essential to meeting the needs of bereaved families. Grief counseling requires skills that are obtained only through comprehensive training and certification; although some funeral directors do indeed pursue advanced training in this field, others may attend, at best, a weekend workshop or "aftercare" seminar providing only the briefest overview of grief therapy. As in any business or industry, funeral service establishments differ with respect to their integrity and overall philosophy of how to best satisfy customers' needs.

Comparing the Costs

Comparing the costs of competing funeral establishments may be difficult, even when costs are itemized. Different funeral providers do not always offer the same goods and services, and they may choose different methods of presenting prices. Thus, the comparison shopper may be trying to compare what seems like apples and oranges, with confusing results. Nevertheless, it is useful to distinguish among the charges that may be assessed. (As you read the following discussion of funeral goods and services, you may find it useful to refer to Table 8-3, which shows the relative costs of various items that are typically part of mortuary services; actual prices will vary from region to region and generally increase on a par with rises in the Consumer Price Index.)

Charge for Professional Services

Funeral costs include a basic charge for the services provided by the funeral director and his or her staff. It is payment for arranging the funeral, consulting with family members and clergy, directing the visitation and funeral ceremony, and preparing and filing necessary notices and authorizations related to body disposition. This latter service may include filing the death certificate and certain claims for death benefits.

The fee for professional services covers a pro rata share of the overhead expenses required to maintain facilities and staff around the clock. The method of arriving at this charge is, of course, left to the discretion of each funeral provider, and it varies according to a number of factors, including the clientele served and the prices charged by competitors.

Cemetery or crematory services, flowers, and placement of newspaper notices are generally not covered in the basic service charge. Those items are usually billed separately, and there may be a charge for the funeral director's services in purchasing such items on the customer's behalf.

According to the Funeral Rule, if direct cremation or immediate burial is chosen, any fee charged for professional services must be included in the price quoted for those methods of disposition. Similarly, the fee for professional services must be included in prices quoted for forwarding remains to another funeral home or receiving remains from another funeral home.

TABLE *8-3*   *Sample Funeral Service Prices*

Transfer of remains to mortuary	
Direct cremation	$75
with container provided by purchaser	$575
including alternative container	$625
including cloth-covered wood casket	$925
Immediate burial	
with container provided by purchaser	$530
including cloth-covered wood casket	$900
including oak-finished pine casket	$1500
Embalming	$150
Other body preparation	
Cosmetology and hairstyling	$60
Dressing and placing remains in casket	$60
Use of facilities for viewing (per day)	$65
Use of facilities for funeral ceremony	
Chapel	$260
Smaller stateroom	$160
Use of automotive equipment	
Hearse	$85
Limousine	$60
Acknowledgment cards (box of 25)	$30
Memorial folders or prayer cards (first 100)	$40
Register book	$25
Cremation urn	$75–$400
Casket	$400–8000
Outer burial container	$100–2000
Charge for professional services	$450
Miscellaneous services	
Staff conducting graveside service	$65
Scattering cremated remains	$75–250

As an alternative method of pricing, the FTC rule allows funeral providers to incorporate a fee for professional services into the prices of caskets. When casket prices include a fee for professional services, however, a description of those services must be placed on the casket price list.

Intake Charge

The intake charge is the fee for transporting the remains from the place of death to the mortuary. There may be a surcharge for a nighttime pickup to cover additional costs of staff.

Embalming

In *Death to Dust,* Kenneth Iserson says, "An unembalmed body buried six-feet deep in ordinary soil without a coffin normally takes ten to twelve years to decompose down to the bony skeleton; a child's body takes about half that time."[18] Environmental conditions can delay or hasten decomposition; for

"Now, Mr. Barlow, what had you in mind? Embalmment of course, and after that incineration or not, according to taste. Our crematory is on scientific principles, the heat is so intense that all inessentials are volatilized. Some people did not like the thought that ashes of the casket and clothing were mixed with the Loved One's. Normal disposal is by inhumement, entombment, inurnment or immurement, but many people just lately prefer insarcophagusment. That is *very* individual. The casket is placed inside a sealed sarcophagus, marble or bronze, and rests permanently above ground in a niche in the mausoleum, with or without a personal stained-glass window above. That, of course, is for those with whom price is not a primary consideration."

Evelyn Waugh, *The Loved One*

example, corpses buried in coffins or caskets take longer to decompose than those buried without such containers, and bodies exposed to the environment will generally be reduced to skeletons rather quickly. "Originally," Iserson says, "embalming meant placing balm, essentially natural sap and aromatic substances, on a corpse."[19] Over the course of history, methods of embalming have differed widely among cultures, with correspondingly varied results with respect to preservation of the corpse. In modern usage, embalming involves removing the blood and other fluids in the body and replacing them with chemicals to disinfect and temporarily retard deterioration of the corpse.

Nowhere in the United States is embalming required by law, except in certain circumstances. Yet embalming is such an accepted mortuary practice in America that hardly anyone questions it. Embalming is usually considered a practical necessity by most mortuary establishments when a body will be viewed. With few exceptions, however, the FTC rule requires that mortuaries obtain express permission to embalm from the family in order to charge a fee for the procedure.[20] Furthermore, the price list must include the following disclosure next to the price for embalming:

> Except in certain special cases, embalming is not required by law. Embalming may be necessary, however, if you select certain funeral arrangements, such as a funeral with viewing. If you do not want embalming, you usually have the right to choose an arrangement which does not require you to pay for it, such as direct cremation or immediate burial.

Embalming laws vary from state to state. In Connecticut, for instance, embalming is required only when a body is to be transported across state lines by common carrier (bus, train, plane, or commercial vehicle). In Kentucky, embalming is not mandatory under any circumstances. The District of

Columbia requires that a body be embalmed only when death results from communicable disease. In Louisiana, a body must be embalmed if it is held longer than thirty hours before final disposition. California requires embalming only when the body is to be transported by common carrier. In summary, depending on the specific requirements of each state, special circumstances may make embalming mandatory.

If refrigeration is available, a mortuary may offer the alternative of storing a body for a short time without embalming. A refrigerated, unembalmed body will remain relatively preserved for about three days, although some mortuaries stipulate that they will not hold an unembalmed body for longer than forty-eight hours. The cost of refrigeration is likely to be somewhat less than for embalming.

Some mortuaries have a combined charge for embalming and body preparation; others itemize each of the procedures involved in readying a body for viewing and for the funeral. Thus, in addition to embalming charges (or, if embalming is not done, in lieu of such charges), separate fees may be charged for each of the procedures performed in the preparation room.

Other Body Preparation Charges

Body preparation includes minimal antiseptic hygiene procedures, such as washing the body. Some funeral establishments list separate charges for embalming; for cosmetology, hair styling, and manicuring; and for dressing the body, placing it in the casket, and composing it for viewing.

Casket Prices

Of all funeral costs, people usually feel the most important is that of the casket because of its symbolic and emotional value in honoring the deceased. The customer is faced with a wide range of options, and, whereas many other items of the funeral service are based on a standard fee, the price of a casket is highly variable. The latitude in choice ranges from inexpensive cardboard containers all the way to solid mahogany, copper, or bronze caskets costing thousands of dollars. Depending on the socioeconomic status of their clientele, most funeral homes can provide caskets in a wide range of prices. Because funeral homes are free to determine their own methods of pricing caskets, the customer may discover that a casket selling for $1000 in one funeral home costs twice as much in another. This price difference may be due to a higher markup designed to increase the profit margin; or, as mentioned earlier, it may result from the fact that the funeral provider has chosen to include the fee for professional services in the casket price rather than charging for it separately. Because of this variability, prices of caskets can be discussed here only in general terms, with the aim being to describe the types of caskets available.

At the lower end of the price range, a conventional casket may cost from several hundred to a thousand dollars. These caskets are typically made of

Library of Congress

The funeral has traditionally been a time when family and friends come together to pay respects and to say farewells. It is a time of mutual support for the bereaved and of tribute to the deceased. The display of flowers surrounding this casket bespeaks the affection felt for the deceased while she was alive and the sense of loss at her absence from the community.

plywood and covered with cloth, and contain a mattress that is likely to be made of straw covered with an acetate sheet.

At the next pricing level, refinements appear. Although these are also made of wood, they may be covered with copper or bronze sheathing. Gasketed steel caskets are available at prices ranging from about $1000 to several thousand dollars. The mattress, too, exhibits refinements, being constructed with springs, over which is a layer of foam rubber and a covering of acetate material. In this range, some caskets are available with devices designed to ensure an airtight environment within the casket. (Although a solace to some people, any added protection is debatable; critics contend that such devices actually hasten decomposition.)

The price tag on a top-of-the-line casket ranges upwards to $10,000 or more. For this sum, one obtains a casket constructed of mahogany, copper, or bronze and fitted out with all the accoutrements of the casket manufacturer's art. Deluxe models feature an adjustable boxspring mattress that can be tilted to enhance the display of the corpse.

Marketing analysis indicates that the gasketed steel casket is most popular with Americans. Based on recent statistics indicating the number of caskets shipped to funeral directors, the gasketed steel casket holds a 44 percent share of the market, trailed by nongasketed steel (19.1 percent), cloth-covered (17.5 percent), hardwood (13.4 percent), copper or bronze (2.3 percent), and stainless steel caskets (0.8 percent).[21]

Our choices for displaying and disposing of the dead are regulated less by the force of law than by custom and by ignorance of alternatives. For example, many people are surprised to learn that there is no law requiring a body destined for cremation to be placed in a casket. Most crematoria require only that the body be delivered in a rigid container. Most mortuaries can provide a cardboard box, which suffices for this purpose, at a small charge. The FTC rule prohibits funeral providers from telling consumers that state or local law requires them to purchase a casket when they wish to arrange a direct cremation (that is, a cremation that occurs without formal viewing of the remains or any visitation or ceremony with the body present). For firms that do arrange for direct cremations, the rule stipulates that the following disclosure be made to customers:

> If you want to arrange a direct cremation, you can use an unfinished wood box or an alternative container. Alternative containers can be made of materials like heavy cardboard or composition materials (with or without an outside covering), or pouches of canvas.

Finally, as regards caskets, the FTC rule requires funeral providers to supply customers with a list of the prices and descriptions of available caskets. This may be handled in one of two ways, either on the General Price List or on a separate Casket Price List.

Facilities Charges

The use of a visitation or viewing room is a common component of most funerals. In the itemized listing of prices, the funeral director may use whatever method of pricing is preferred or follow common practice for that particular area. For example, various settings in the funeral home might be listed, along with the charges for each by day, half day, or hour. Similarly, if a funeral ceremony is held at the mortuary chapel, a charge for the use of that facility will be specified by the funeral provider. When other facilities are made available to customers (for example, a tent and chairs for graveside services), the charges for their use must be stated on the funeral provider's price list.

Epitaph

The Body of
B. Franklin,
Printer;
Like the Cover of an old book,
Its Contents torn out
And Stript of its Lettering and Gilding,
Lies Here, Food for Worms.
But the Work shall not be wholly lost;
For it will, as he believ'd, appear once more,
In a New & more perfect Edition
Corrected and amended
By the Author.

Vehicles

As with other aspects of funeral service, mortuaries follow different pricing policies for the use of vehicles. According to the FTC rule, charges for the use of a hearse, limousine, or other automotive equipment must be itemized separately on the General Price List. Sometimes additional vehicles are requested for the use of pallbearers, family members, or other participants such as clergy. A "flower car" may be used to transport floral arrangements to the cemetery. If a motorcycle escort is desired, there is a charge for each escort.

Outer Burial Container Prices

If outer burial containers are offered by the funeral home, their prices must be listed, either separately or on the General Price List. In addition, the following disclosure must be made:

In most areas of the country, no state or local law makes you buy a container to surround the casket in the grave. However, many cemeteries require that you have such a container so that the grave will not sink in. Either a burial vault or a grave liner will satisfy these requirements.

Because many funeral homes do not sell burial vaults or grave liners, this item may not appear on the price lists of the mortuaries in your area. Further information about the types of outer burial containers is given in the discussion of burial and entombment costs later in this chapter.

Miscellaneous Charges

Under the miscellaneous category are charges for goods or services provided directly by the funeral home, as well as charges by outside sources

Albert Lee Strickland

For individuals whose deaths occurred away from their ancestral villages, traditional Chinese custom involved disinterring the bones after perhaps ten years of burial and eventually returning them to the village where the person was born. In the interim, the bones were kept in a structure like this one at the Ket-On Society cemetery in Hawaii.

incurred on behalf of the customer. This latter category includes such "cash-advance" items as floral arrangements and newspaper notices. The customer may be billed for the actual amounts of the items, or the funeral provider may add a surcharge for arranging these cash-advance items. If an additional charge is made, a notice to that effect must be shown on the General Price List.

The FTC rule specifically mentions that acknowledgment cards must be itemized if the funeral provider sells those items or performs the service of filling out and sending them for customers.

Other items that come under the heading of miscellaneous costs are any fees or honoraria for pallbearers, an honorarium for the clergyperson who conducts the funeral service, and the cost of any burial garments purchased from the mortuary.

Direct Cremations and Immediate Burials

Not all funeral homes offer direct cremations and immediate burials to consumers, although the number of those that do is increasing. These methods of body disposition usually occur without formal viewing of the remains or any visitation or ceremony with the body present. (Some mortuaries are responding to consumer requests for viewing and for informal ceremonies by placing the body on a cloth-covered gurney.)

If direct cremation or immediate burial is offered by a funeral home, the charge—including the fee for professional services—is shown on the General Price List. When direct cremation is selected, the customer must be given the option of providing the container or of purchasing an unfinished pine box or alternative container (such as canvas pouch, or a box made of cardboard, plywood, or composition material). Similarly, for immediate burials, the customer has the option to provide a container or purchase a simple casket, such as one made of wood and covered with cloth. (If a funeral home offers immediate burials but does not offer direct cremations, the FTC rule does not require the firm to make available an alternative container or unfinished wood box, although a funeral director might choose to do so.)

Funeral and Memorial Societies

Funeral and memorial societies aim to provide body disposal services to members at a lower cost by arranging with a mortuary or crematorium to provide services based on volume purchasing. As with other areas of funeral service, customers are usually able to select exactly the services they want with respect to burial or cremation. Many such societies operate as non-profit organizations, advocating dignity, simplicity, and economy in after-death arrangements. Currently there are over 175 funeral and memorial societies in the United States and Canada. On the whole, although additional options may be available, such organizations follow a minimalist plan with respect to disposition of the corpse.

Judging by their rapid growth, funeral and memorial societies meet a need felt by many people for low-cost and simple methods of body disposition. It is perhaps easier now than at any time since funerals were moved from the family parlor to the mortuary to compare the costs of funerals and body disposition options among competing establishments. In most cases, a telephone call is all that is necessary to obtain relevant pricing information for your own locality.

Body Disposition

Think for a moment about the manner you would choose for the disposition of your body after you die. When Americans are asked their preferences, responses usually fall into one of three categories: burial, cremation, or donation to science. Corpses must be disposed of because of

Assume that we are confronted with the dead body of a man. What disposition shall we make of it? Shall we lay it in a boat that is set adrift? Shall we take the heart from it and bury it in one place and the rest of the body in another? Shall we expose it to wild animals? Burn it on a pyre? Push it into a pit to rot with other bodies? Boil it until the flesh falls off the bones, and throw the flesh away and treasure the bones? Such questions provoke others which may not be consciously articulated, such as: "What do men generally think this body is?" And, "What do they think is a proper way of dealing with it?"

Robert W. Habenstein and William M. Lamers,
The History of American Funeral Directing

sanitary considerations, though it is unlikely that a person's choice of method is influenced by that fact. It is more likely that preferences result from social, cultural, and philosophical reasons.

Religious beliefs often influence the method of body disposition. For example, Jews and Christians have traditionally practiced ground burial, whereas Hindus and Buddhists prefer cremation. Each method of disposing of the corpse carries symbolic meanings that can be important to followers of the respective religious tradition. Among Hindus, cremation is seen as a gesture of purification and symbol of the transitory nature of human life. Orthodox Judaism, in contrast, views cremation as a form of idolatry; burial represents a return of the body to the "dust" from whence it was created by God. In the modern era, other branches of Judaism take a less strict view of this ban on cremation. Similarly, the historical Christian prohibition against cremation has undergone change, with some churches supporting or at least tolerating cremation while others maintain a requirement, or at least a strong preference, for burial.

The decomposition of the body is hastened in some societies by washing the flesh from the bones when the corpse is partially decomposed; parts of the body are then retained as a memorial. In other societies, the body is left to the elements and generally decomposes quite rapidly (except in very dry, desert climates, where the heat removes the moisture from the body, acting thereby to preserve it). Some Indian tribes of the American plains constructed platforms on which the corpse was exposed to the effects of the sun, wind, and rain. In some societies, the remains of the dead are consumed by birds of prey or other animals. In India, for example, one can visit the Towers of Silence on Bombay's fashionable Marabar Hill, where the Parsi community disposes of its dead by leaving corpses to be devoured by vultures. As followers of Zoroaster, they regard earth, fire, and water as sacred, not to be defiled by the dead. Their beliefs are not shared, however, by the residents of high-rise luxury apartments

U.S. Navy Photo

Burial at sea is a naval tradition the world over, particularly during times of war.
Here the body of a seaman is committed to the deep during burial services aboard the
USS Ranger *in 1963.*

whose windows look out upon what they consider a grotesque method of body disposition.

A method of body disposal practiced by mariners since ancient times is water burial, or burial at sea. Depending on circumstances and cultural practices, this form of body disposition might involve either ceremonially sliding the corpse off the side of a ship or placing the corpse inside a boat that is set aflame and then set adrift.

Another method of body disposition, although decidedly less popular than burial or cremation, is donation to science. The person who chooses this method may gain satisfaction from the notion that he or she is making a contribution to the advancement of knowledge: "My body will serve a useful function even after I'm gone." This option tends to be limited, however, because most medical schools and similar institutions can readily obtain an adequate supply of cadavers. Thus, donation to medical science is an option that may be difficult to exercise.

Burial vaults, such as those seen here in Oaxaca, Mexico, represent an alternative to underground burial that is found in many parts of the world. When space is at a premium, bodies may be removed from the vaults after a certain period of time and given underground burial.

An unorthodox method of body disposition, cryonics, is attractive to some people. Cryonics is not a method of body disposal in the sense used so far. Rather, it is a method of subjecting a corpse to extremely low temperatures—in effect, keeping the body frozen—until some future time when it is envisioned that medical science will have advanced to a point where the body can be resuscitated and the cause of death reversed. Most people view cryonics as a curiosity more than as a realistic alternative to conventional methods of body disposition, but it does have a small number of adherents.

From the burials of prehistory to space-age cryonics, human beings have chosen from a variety of alternatives for disposing of the dead. Although few people give much thought to the subject of body disposition, it is nonetheless fraught with emotional and psychological importance, as the following story illustrates: When Major Edward Strombeck was killed in a plane crash while on duty in Vietnam, the military cremated his body and forwarded the ashes, by mail, to his home in Hawaii. Shocked at the lack of proper ceremony, his

Elmer Ruiz: Gravedigger

Not anybody can be a gravedigger. You can dig a hole any way they come. A gravedigger, you have to make a neat job. I had a fella once, he wanted to see a grave. He was a fella that digged sewers. He was impressed when he seen me diggin' this grave—how square and how perfect it was. A human body is goin' into this grave. That's why you need skill when you're gonna dig a grave.

The gravedigger today, they have to be somebody to operate a machine. You just use a shovel to push the dirt loose. Otherwise you don't use 'em. We're tryin' a new machine, a ground hog. This machine is supposed to go through heavy frost. It do very good job so far. When the weather is mild, like fifteen degrees above zero, you can do it very easy.

But when the weather is below zero, believe me, you just really workin' hard. I have to use a mask. Your skin hurts so much when it's cold—like you put a hot flame near your face. I'm talkin' about two, three hours standin' outside. You have to wear a mask, otherwise you can't stand it at all. . . .

The most graves I dig is about six, seven a day. This is in the summer. In the winter it's a little difficult. In the winter you have four funerals, that's a pretty busy day. . . .

The grave will be covered in less than two minutes, complete. We just open the hoppers with the right amount of earth. We just press it and then we lay out a layer of black earth. Then we put the sod that belongs there. After a couple of weeks you wouldn't know it's a grave there. It's complete flat. Very rarely you see a grave that is sunk. . . .

I usually tell 'em I'm a caretaker. I don't think the name sound as bad. I have to look at the park, so after the day's over that everything's closed, that nobody do damage to the park. Some occasions some people just come and steal and loot and do bad things in the park, destroy some things. I believe it would be some young fellas. A man with responsibility, he wouldn't do things like that. Finally we had to put up some gates and close 'em at sundown. Before, we didn't, no. We have a fence of roses. Always in cars you can come after sundown. . . .

A gravedigger is a very important person. You must have hear about the strike we had in New York about two years ago. There were twenty thousand bodies layin'

mother and other family members expressed their dismay and gained the attention of U.S. Senator Daniel Inouye. The result was a change in policy, which ordered that the ashes of military personnel be escorted home with dignity and honor.[22] Proper disposition of human remains is a matter of considerable significance not only to the immediate survivors but also to the larger community. What do your own preferences regarding body disposition tell you about your attitudes and beliefs toward death?

Burial

Historically, in most societies associated with the Western European tradition, the preferred method for disposing of the corpse has been burial. In and nobody could bury 'em. The cost of funerals they raised and they didn't want to raise the price of the workers. The way they're livin', everything wanna go up, and I don't know what's gonna happen.

Can you imagine if I wouldn't show up tomorrow morning and this other fella—he usually comes late—and sometimes he don't show. We have a funeral for eleven o'clock. Imagine what happens? The funeral arrive and where you gonna bury it? . . . .

There are some funerals, they really affect you. Some young kid. We buried lots of young. You have emotions, you turn in, believe me, you turn. I had a burial about two years ago of teen-agers, a young boy and a young girl. This was a real sad funeral because there was nobody but young teen-agers. I'm so used to going to funerals every day—of course, it bothers me—but I don't feel as bad as when I bury a young child. You really turn. . . .

This grief that I see every day, I'm really used to somebody's crying every day. But there is some that are real bad, when you just have to take it. Some people just don't want to give up. You have to understand that when somebody pass away, there's nothing you can do and you have to take it. If you don't want to take it, you're just gonna make your life worse, become sick. People seems to take it more easier these days. They miss the person, but not as much.

There's some funerals that people, they show they're not sad. This is different kinds of people. I believe they are happy to see this person—not in a way of singing—because this person is out of his sufferin' in this world. This person is gone and at rest for the rest of his life. I have this question lots of times: "How can I take it?" They ask if I'm calm when I bury people. If you stop and think, a funeral is one of the natural things in the world. . . .

I believe I'm gonna have to stay here probably until I die. It's not gonna be too bad for me because I been livin' twelve years already in the cemetery. I'm still gonna be livin' in the cemetery. (Laughs.) So that's gonna be all right with me whenever I go. I think I may be buried here, it look like.

Quoted in Studs Terkel, *Working*

speaking of burial, however, we should note that the term encompasses a variety of related practices. Burial may be accomplished by digging a single grave in the soil or by entombment in a multitiered mausoleum. It may refer not only to burial of the whole body, but also to burial of the bones or even cremated remains. Despite its continued popularity as a means of body disposal, burial is becoming a more limited option in some areas. For example, in response to soaring real estate prices and lack of burial space at Buddhist temples, where the Japanese have traditionally interred the cremated remains of loved ones, a "high-rise condominium cemetery" was recently erected in Tokyo as a concession to modern living.[23] With land near urban areas at a premium, and as older cemeteries fill up, space for burials is being developed farther from cities. (Similar problems have beset "pet cemeteries," where the side effects of urban sprawl have caused animal cemeteries to suspend operations or even close facilities that were intended to be the final resting place for beloved animals.[24])

In addition to the cost of a cemetery plot, which can range from less than $100 to more than $5000, cemeteries usually require a grave liner or vault to support the earth around and above the casket. This adds about $250–$500 to the cost of ground burial, although some types of vaults designed (but not guaranteed) to seal out moisture cost substantially more.

The cost of entombment in a mausoleum or outdoor crypt averages about $2000, although prices vary considerably. Historically, the term *crypt* denotes a subterranean burial vault or chamber, often situated beneath the floor of a church. In modern usage, the term also refers to space in a *mausoleum,* an above-ground structure of concrete, marble, or other stone in which one or more bodies are entombed. The most expensive crypt spaces are usually those at eye level, with the least expensive spaces at the top and bottom. With both burial and entombment, additional charges are normally levied for opening and closing the grave or crypt. These range from about $75 to $350, depending on the area of the country and the particular facility.

A simple bronze or stone grave marker is likely to be available at a cost upwards of about $200. The average cost for a simple, flat-on-the-ground grave marker is about $300, the name plate for a mausoleum crypt somewhat less. Other, more elaborate, memorials cost from a few hundred to many thousands of dollars.

Finally, most cemeteries also assess an endowment or "perpetual care cost" to subsidize upkeep of the cemetery. Endowment costs range upwards of $100 and are sometimes included in the basic cost for burial or entombment.

Cremation

In the United States, the practice of cremation extends back to the nineteenth century (cremation had long been practiced by the original inhabitants, of course). In Europe, the practice is considerably older, going back at least to the Bronze Age. It is the most common method of body disposal in many countries, including India and Japan.

The process of cremation involves subjecting the corpse to extreme heat, approximately 2000 to 2500 degrees Fahrenheit. It has been carried out by means ranging from a simple wood fire to sophisticated electric or gas retorts. In the United States, natural gas is the most commonly used fuel. An average-size body takes about one and one-half hours to be reduced to ashes weighing from five to seven pounds. (The term *ashes* leads some people to believe that the cremated remains will look and feel like wood or paper ashes. In reality, the ashes are composed of pieces of bone, which look and feel like

A papier-mâché bull symbolizing the deceased's caste is a focal point of this cremation ceremony in a Balinese village. According to local custom, corpses are buried until families accumulate the necessary funds to pay for the cremation ritual; at that time, the body is disinterred, wrapped in cloth, and placed, along with various offerings, in ritual objects such as the bull, shown here at the cremation site.

coarse coral sands whose shell-like components are worn by the wind and waves.)

Although relatively few Americans choose to be cremated, it is quite clearly a method of body disposition that is growing in acceptance. In the late 1980s, cremation was the disposition of choice in about 14 percent of all deaths in the United States, almost double the rate of ten years previously. It is projected that by the year 2000 cremation will become the preferred method of body disposition in nearly one-quarter of all deaths in the United States, a proportion that Canada reached in 1985.[25]

Cremated remains can be buried in a cemetery plot, placed in a columbarium niche, interred in an urn garden, kept by the family, or scattered at sea or on land, in accordance with state and local laws. The Cremation Association of North America encourages memorialization of the deceased in conjunction with cremation, just as with traditional burials. Urns to hold cremated remains can be purchased at prices from about $50 to $400, though more expensive urns are available. If the ashes are to be entombed, columbarium niches (a small vault in which the urn is placed) are available, with the cost depending on the size and location of the niche. Among some families and ethnic groups, a family tomb is the resting place for the ashes of several generations of deceased ancestors.

Laws Regulating Body Disposition

As a general rule, the deceased's next of kin is responsible for arranging for the final disposition of the body. The options for doing so, however, may be circumscribed by local ordinances and state laws governing the manner in which disposition can be effected. For example, some communities have enacted ordinances that prohibit burial within city limits. Similarly, laws regulating the disposition of cremated remains vary among states and localities. For example, a California law (now removed from the books) prohibited the scattering of ashes by private citizens. If this law was violated, the person scattering the ashes could be charged with a misdemeanor, punishable by a fine or imprisonment; if two or more persons participated, it could be considered a conspiracy, and a felony could be charged against them. Thus, although there is some degree of uniformity throughout the United States, laws governing body disposition are subject to variation among states and local jurisdictions.

When the deceased has provided for donation of his or her body or body parts, the final disposition of the remains may be left to the discretion of the hospital, medical school, or other institution that has possession of the body. Even in these instances, however, the next of kin is usually given a say in determining the final disposition once the medical or scientific purposes of the donation have been achieved. When the next of kin does not request return of the remains for private disposition, most medical schools and other such institutions have policies ensuring that cadavers are treated ethically and that human remains are disposed of properly. In some cases, a memorial service is held to acknowledge the human gift that is represented by the donation of the body to science.[26]

When the deceased has left no money to cover the cost of body disposition, and his or her relatives are unwilling or unable to pay, the state may be forced to intervene. County jurisdictions generally have an "indigent burial fund" that is made available in such cases. Depending on the circumstances, the public administrator's office may be called upon to make a determination that distinguishes between "inconvenient to pay" and "unable to pay." When funds are, in fact, not available from private sources, the local jurisdiction picks up the cost. Payment is made to a contracting mortuary that provides direct cremation, with burial of the cremated remains. If the next of kin opposes cremation, the corpse may be placed in a casket and buried in a plot donated by the cemetery for indigent burials (or, again, paid for out of community funds).

Making Meaningful Choices

The funeral has been defined as "an organized, purposeful, time-limited, flexible, group-centered response to death."[27] If this definition can be applied to our modern approaches to caring for the dead, then, in view of the varied styles of funeral service now available, can we identify any single set of values to guide our actions in memorializing the dead and providing for the needs of the survivors? Probably not. Increasingly, the choices that are made relative to funerals and body disposition reflect individual rather than community judgments. Nevertheless, resources are available to help individuals and families create or adapt funeral ceremonies from both religious and humanist traditions.[28]

In a pluralistic society, there are many ways of dealing meaningfully and appropriately with death. Some choose a minimal role in caring for their dead loved ones; others seek more active participation. Becoming aware of the alternatives enables us to make more meaningful choices. The experience of a couple following the death of their young son is illustrative. Initially, they had planned no formal funeral ceremony. They intended that the body would simply be cremated and the ashes scattered. On the day before the body was released from the coroner for cremation, however, they found themselves experiencing the acute grief that comes with a sudden and intimate loss.

As they struggled to come to terms with their emotions and the loss of their son, someone in their circle of friends suggested that they direct their energy into building a coffin. Soon, friends and members of the family, including the five-year-old brother of the child who was killed, were busily engaged in the task of constructing a coffin. Later they said they were relieved to have had the opportunity to "do something" (see Figure 8-5). For the participants, building the coffin became a meaningful way to honor the dead child as well as a means of working through their own feelings, allowing them to get a better handle on their experience. This, then, is the real value of learning about and investigating the options: finding the response that is meaningful to us personally.

Figure 8-5   *Three Views of a Child's Coffin*

Top View: When the wooden coffin constructed by the family and friends had been completed, the surviving child ran his hand over the surface and voiced his approval but said that it "needs something more." He gathered his marking pens and began to ornament the coffin with drawings. The inscriptions on the outer surface of the lid show the child's interest in identifying by name and by picture the fact that this coffin was built for his brother. His own participation in the making of the coffin is also connoted by the inclusion of his name and by the demonstration of his newly developed skills with the use of numerals and letters.

Detail of Lid Interior: In this closeup of a portion of the interior lid, viewed from left to right, one can see a chrysalis—indicating a transition from caterpillar to butterfly—along with some of the younger brother's favorite television characters: Big Bird, Oscar the Grouch, and the Cookie Monster.

Interior of Lid: In contrast to the matter-of-fact inscriptions placed on the outer surface, the inside of the coffin lid is filled with representations of experiences, events, and objects that brought joy into the life of the child's younger brother. Many of the dead child's favorite activities, such as listening to the stereo with headphones and sitting on a horse at grandma's house, are depicted. The surviving child depicts himself as sad because of his brother's death, yet also as happy because of the shared experiences he enjoyed with his brother. It is interesting to notice the degree of detail and the variety of images placed on the interior of the coffin lid.

If funeral rituals provide closure on the deceased's life for survivors and allow the community to affirm the timeless rhythms of separation and integration, then what should our feelings be when the social elements of the funeral are lacking or absent, as with "take-out-and-cremate" practices? Can the emotional and psychological issues that accompany bereavement be resolved satisfactorily? Many would say no, yet there is a paucity of hard data to establish the conventional funeral as the most effective vehicle of psychological resolution.

Commenting on the changing attitudes toward funerals and traditional methods of body disposition, Robert Fulton and Greg Owen observe that the obligations—religious, emotional, and economic—that a funeral imposes on a family have come to be seen by many people as both burdensome and inappropriate.[29] In surveying the contemporary situation, they note that:

> Advocacy of a memorial service, with the body absent, and medical donation of the body or its parts are attempts within the context of contemporary values to resolve the different problems associated with the disposition of the dead. Other

attempts to contain or limit the social impact of a death upon the family or community can be seen in the decline of public obituaries, the dramatic rise in immediate disposition and/or cremation of the body, the increasing formalization of rules governing an employee's time off for bereavement, and the direct implementation of Federal Trade Commission guidelines on the business practices and procedures of American funeral directors.

Yet, as Edgar Jackson points out, despite the changes that have occurred in American funeral practices over the past decades, funeral directors receive more expressions of gratitude from the people they serve than do the members of any other helping profession. Jackson notes that the funeral director is there at a time when the family is experiencing an acute crisis. The immediate response and help in sorting out the events of the days following the death of a loved one provide stability and reassurance for the bereaved family.[30] Robert Fulton corroborates this view, adding that funeral directors are in a unique position to assist the bereaved and are potentially a valuable part of a community's mental health resource and helping network.[31]

The social support that accompanies meaningful ritual need not be limited to the period immediately following a death. In traditional Hawaiian culture, for example, the bereaved community holds a memorial feast on the first-year anniversary of the day of death for any person—man, woman, child, even a newborn baby.[32] For the extended family, this is considered as "one of the three greatest occasions, the others being the feasts of rejoicing for the first-born and the marriage festival." Although this occasion is called the *'aha'aina waimaka* or "feast of tears," because it embraces everyone who had shed tears out of respect and love for the deceased, it is in fact "a happy occasion, a joyful reunion of all who had previously shed tears together." In the words of one participant: "There was drinking, eating, singing and dancing. We had a *lu'au* when all the grief was done."

Further Readings

Robert W. Habenstein and William M. Lamers. *The History of American Funeral Directing.* Milwaukee: Bulfin Printers, 1962.

Robert W. Habenstein and William M. Lamers. *Funeral Customs the World Over.* Rev. ed. Milwaukee: Bulfin Printers, 1974.

Kenneth V. Iserson. *Death to Dust: What Happens to Dead Bodies?* Tucson: Galen Press, 1994.

R. Moroni Leash. *Death Notification: A Practical Guide to the Process.* Hinesburg, Vt.: Upper Access, 1994.

Ernest Morgan. *Dealing Creatively with Death: A Manual of Death Education and Simple Burial,* 11th ed. Burnsville, N.C.: Celo Press, 1988.

Elaine Nichols, ed. *The Last Miles of the Way: African-American Homegoing Traditions, 1890–Present.* Columbia, S.C.: South Carolina State Museum, 1989.

Gay Petrillo. "The Distant Mourner: An Examination of the American Gravedigger." *Omega: Journal of Death and Dying* 20 (1989–1990): 139–148.

Vanderlyn R. Pine. *Caretaker of the Dead: The American Funeral Director.* New York: Irvington Publishers, 1985.

Seen here testifying in a Michigan courtroom, Dr. Jack Kevorkian has become a symbol of the debate over the ethical and legal issues that pertain to physician-assisted death. The legal system touches on many aspects of dying and death, from organ donation and death certification to the making of wills and settling of estates.

The Law and Death

*F*rom the relative simplicity of filing a death certificate to the settling of a complicated estate, the law impinges upon our experiences of death and dying. In some cases, laws serve to increase our options; in other cases, they restrict them. In the case of organ donation as formalized by the Uniform Anatomical Gift Act, for example, our options for dealing with death have been broadened. In other areas, such as physician-assisted death, the law constrains our behavior and choices.

In this chapter, we examine a variety of legal issues related to dying and death. We begin with a discussion of several important issues that have become prominent in the public arena, including legislation defining death, the use of advance directives regarding medical treatment, and physician-assisted death, or aid-in-dying. These issues are at the forefront of the contemporary debate over ethical and legal issues involving death and dying.

Following this discussion, the next section provides a comprehensive overview of the legal and administrative aspects of organ donation, death certification, the role of the coroner and the medical examiner, and autopsies. This section deals with the question: How are societal interests in the circumstances of death reflected in governmental and institutional policies and procedures?

We then look closely at the procedures involved in making a will, probating an estate, paying estate and inheritance taxes, and claiming insurance and other death benefits.

As with the other topics discussed in this chapter, these activities, which occur following a death, also reflect the interests of society. In the context of the laws relating to it, death is a public matter, not a private one.

Legal Issues in the Public Arena

In the recent past, public concern about the legal aspects of dying and death has been focused primarily in three areas: defining death in a way that meets the demands of modern life-support technology; allowing individuals to express their wishes concerning medical treatment at the end-stage of life through the use of advance directives; and sanctioning physician assistance in terminating one's life when hopes for recovery fail. All three of these issues have generated considerable debate, reflecting a range of public attitudes and opinions. Whereas the legalities involving wills, probate, autopsies, and the function of the coroner have had a long history in Western societies, the legal issues discussed in this section are of recent vintage, growing largely out of the contemporary encounter with sophisticated medical technologies.

Legislation Defining Death

The definition of death touches upon many aspects of social life. Criminal prosecution, inheritance, taxation, treatment of the corpse, and mourning are all affected by the way society "draws the dividing line between life and death."[1] Many states have recognized that the conventional definition of death—that is, the cessation of the flow of vital bodily fluids—is inadequate at times in the present technological setting.

In 1970, Kansas became the first state to adopt brain-based criteria for determining death. A number of other states subsequently adopted similar statutes. Because the Kansas-inspired statute contained dual definitions of death (one based on cessation of vital functions and the other on brain functions), it did not provide a unitary description of death and therefore was criticized as potentially confusing.

In 1972, Alexander Capron and Leon Kass proposed an improvement on the Kansas statute that related the two standards for determining death.[2] This proposal was governed by the following five principles:

1. The statute should concern the death of a human being, not the death of cells, tissues, or organs, and not the "death or cessation of his role as a fully functioning member of his family or community."
2. It should move incrementally, supplementing rather than replacing the older cardiopulmonary standards.
3. It should avoid serving as a special definition for a special function such as transplantation.
4. It should apply uniformly to all persons.
5. It should be flexible, leaving specific criteria to the judgment of physicians.

Uniform Determination of Death Act

1. [*Determination of Death.*] An individual who has sustained either (1) irreversible cessation of circulatory and respiratory functions, or (2) irreversible cessation of all functions of the entire brain, including the brain stem, is dead. A determination of death must be made in accordance with accepted medical standards.
2. [*Uniformity of Construction and Application.*] This act shall be applied and construed to effectuate its general purpose to make uniform the law with respect to the subject of this Act among states enacting it.

Figure *9-1*　*Uniform Determination of Death Act*

Source: President's Commission for the Study of Ethical Problems in Medicine and Biomedical and Behavioral Research, *Defining Death: A Report on the Medical, Legal and Ethical Issues in the Determination of Death* (Washington: Government Printing Office, 1981), p. 73.

Although this proposal was adopted with various modifications by several states, it was also criticized because it did not address the issues raised by organ transplantation procedures; that is, it did not require at least two physicians to participate jointly in determining death, nor did it stipulate that the physician who pronounces death not be a member of the medical team seeking organs for transplantation. In response to the criticism, Capron and Kass asserted that transplant considerations ought to be dealt with in separate legislation, such as the Uniform Anatomical Gift Act.

Another model statute was proposed in 1975 by the American Bar Association. It was designed to provide a definition of death "for all legal purposes." This proposal virtually ignored traditional cardiopulmonary criteria for determining death, focusing instead on the "irreversible cessation of total brain function." As with the earlier statutes, the ABA proposal, verbatim or with modification, was adopted by a number of states. These proposals were followed in 1978 by the Uniform Brain Death Act and, in 1979, by a model proposed by the American Medical Association.

Finally, the President's Commission for the Study of Ethical Problems in Medicine proposed a model statute: the Uniform Determination of Death Act (see Figure 9-1). It was endorsed by the American Bar Association and the American Medical Association, both of which approved it as a substitute for their own models. The first states to adopt it were Colorado and Idaho; and, by 1988, twenty-five states had adopted the statute. This proposal was designed to be broadly acceptable, thus easing the enactment of uniform law for defining and determining death throughout the United States.

According to the report of the President's Commission, the Act "addresses the matter of 'defining' death at the level of general physiological standards rather than at the level of more abstract concepts or the level of more precise criteria and tests," because these change over time as knowledge and techniques are refined.[3] Because irreversible circulatory and respiratory cessation will be the obvious and sufficient basis for diagnosing death in most cases, the statute acknowledges that fact. In such cases, death is determined on the basis that breathing and blood flow have ceased and cannot be restored or replaced. When a patient is not supported on a respirator, the need to evaluate brain functions does not arise.

The Commission also said that a statutory definition of death should be kept separate and distinct from any provisions concerning organ donation and the termination of life-sustaining treatment. In contrast to most of the earlier proposals, which stated that a person would be "considered dead" when the criteria were met, the language of the Uniform Determination of Death Act is clearer and more direct. It states simply that a person who meets the standards set forth in the law "is dead."

Confusion about the definition of death had arisen, the Commission said, "because the same technology not only keeps heart and lungs functioning in some who have irretrievably lost all brain functions but also sustains other, less severely injured patients." The result is a "blurring of the important distinction between patients who are *dead* and those who are or may be *dying*." The Commission concluded that "proof of an irreversible absence of functions in the entire brain, including the brain stem, provides a highly reliable means of declaring death for respirator-maintained bodies."

It also noted that the 1968 "Harvard criteria" for making a determination of death have been reliable, adding that "no case has yet been found that met these criteria and regained any brain functions despite continuation of respirator support." It pointed out, however, that although the criteria are intended to define a state of "irreversible coma," or death, the phrase is misleading because the word *coma* refers to a condition of a living person, whereas "a body without any brain functions is dead and thus *beyond* any coma." Irreversible loss of functions of the whole brain is generally the result of: (1) direct trauma to the head, such as from a motor vehicle accident or gunshot wound, (2) massive hemorrhage into the brain from a ruptured aneurysm or from complications of high blood pressure, or (3) anoxic damage from cardiac or respiratory arrest or severely reduced blood pressure.

The Commission argued that it would radically change the meaning of death to expand our definition to include persons who have lost all cognitive functions but still are able to breath spontaneously. Death is an absolute and single phenomenon, the Commission said. Thus, even terms such as "brain dead" are misleading. When brain stem functions remain—for example, when respiration occurs naturally but there is no cognitive awareness—the condition of such a patient can be described as "persistent vegetative or noncognitive state." Although one may observe involuntary movements and unassisted breathing in a person's body, the lack of higher brain functions indicates an absence of awareness of self and the environment. Sustained by medical and nursing care, including artificial feeding through intravenous or nasogastric tubes and antibiotics to fight recurrent infections, such patients may survive for years without a respirator. (The longest such survival, according to the Commission's report, was over thirty-seven years.)

The Commission emphasized a "whole-brain" formulation in preference to a definition based on functions of the so-called higher brain. In doing so, it cited the nearly universal acceptance of the "whole-brain" concept by both the medical community and the general public. A higher brain formulation, however, would require agreement on the meaning of personhood, a concept that does not enjoy such consensus. If "personhood" is made to depend on a certain state of awareness or consciousness, then the severely senile or retarded individual could be excluded. Likewise, according to some proposed definitions, a person whose higher brain functions have been permanently damaged but whose lower brain continues to function might lack the qualities of "personhood." At the present level of understanding and technique, said the Commission, "the 'higher brain' may well exist only as a metaphorical concept, not in reality."

Modern medical technologies create a need to define more specifically the locus of death when the traditional criteria prove insufficient to make a determination of death. Yet perhaps the precise moments of both our entry into and exit from life will prove to be elusive. The search for scientific criteria that allow a definite determination of death may provide ever more precise, but still not absolute, definitions. This is not to suggest that the search is futile. But ultimately there is no alternative to the human responsibility for making ethical decisions on matters of life and death in circumstances of fundamental ambiguity.

Advance Directives

Living wills, natural death directives, and durable powers of attorney for health care—known collectively as advance directives—are acknowledged to be increasingly important in medical decision making.[4] The concept of a "living will" was initially developed in support of the argument that persons should not be kept alive by artificial means against their will. Advance directives express the desire that medical heroics be avoided when death is imminent, that life-sustaining devices and extraordinary medical procedures not be used when there is no chance of recovery. By providing written evidence that an individual does not want to be artifically kept alive when terminally ill, advance directives also serve to protect doctors and hospitals from accusations of malpractice and from civil liability or criminal prosecution when following a patient's directive to forgo medical heroics.

Originally, living wills had no force in law. They were merely an expression of a person's wishes. During the late 1970s, however, state legislatures began to consider the question of laws that would require physicians to honor patients' desires at the end of life. By 1989, most states had enacted some type of legislation regarding advance directives.[5] As the letters in Figure 9-2 indicate, however, advance directives have been controversial. Whereas opponents

Editor: If the governor signs the bill currently before him, this will become the first state to legalize suicide.

I believe this measure is immoral, bizarre, and tainted with Mephistophelian connotations.

Legislators, at all levels, should legislate laws pertaining only to life, as we know it. Death, in any manner, is nature's absolute domain, and no one should attempt to trespass on that domain.

I trust the governor is wise enough and sane enough to veto the bill presently lying heavily and cadaverously on his desk.

Editor: We have explored this bill and its implications in death and fully support the right of an individual, who wishes to do so, to be allowed to make a legally recognized written directive requesting withdrawal of life-support systems when these procedures would serve no purpose except to artificially delay the moment of death.

We reiterate our belief in the basic human right of an individual to control his destiny. We have communicated our support of this bill to the legislature and to the governor.

Editor: This bill, and all other natural-death or death-with-dignity bills, is based on a faulty premise. For when we react to tubes, oxygen and other paraphernalia, our concern is with daintiness, not dignity.

Dignity is the quality of mind having to do with worth, nobility, and forbearance. The dying, with the help of the living, can have dignity—no matter what functions of control are lost.

Instead of unplugging and abandoning our dying patients, we should work to achieve truly compassionate care for them in hospices like those in London, England, and New Haven, Connecticut.

Editor: No physician is required by law to use extraordinary means of preserving life, and none has ever been convicted for failing to do so.

So the real purpose of death-with-dignity or natural-death bills must be to set the stage for letting doctors take positive action: giving lethal injections or denying ordinary means of care to patients who may be handicapped or burdensome to society.

We must be suspicious of any trend which offers death as a solution to problems, no matter how heart-rending those problems may be.

Editor: The bill allowing an adult of sound mind to refuse extraordinary life-preservation measures reaffirms for me the value of life. Life is active choosing toward greater fulfillment and reduced suffering, not the beating of a heart in a pain-wracked and hopeless body. This bill is a public and legal recognition of that principle.

Figure 9-2   *Letters in Response to Proposed Living Will Legislation*

argue that advance directives represent a step toward society's acceptance of active euthanasia, possibly leading to abuses such as arbitrarily withdrawing treatment from patients close to death, proponents argue that living wills safeguard the rights of patients to determine the manner of their own dying.

Differences exist among the states regarding such issues as the assessment of penalties for disobeying a properly executed directive or preventing the transfer of a patient seeking another physician who will respect and follow the patient's wishes.[6] In short, a patient's wishes about the prohibition of life-sustaining treatment may be impeded. Thus, whether the wishes expressed by a patient are followed may depend on the policies of a given health care institution and standard practices within a community or jurisdiction. Uncertainty about the projected course of an illness or a disease may cause doctors to be wary of declaring that a patient is hopelessly terminal. In effect, an advance directive may be less a directive than a request.

Indeed, whether or not an advance directive is followed may in some instances depend largely on the nature of the relationship between patient and physician and, specifically, on the physician's willingness to abide by the patient's wishes. Gender has sometimes been a factor, with the treatment preferences of women being viewed as less reflective, mature, or rational than the treatment preferences of men.[7]

Completing an *advance proxy directive,* or durable power of attorney, provides an additional safeguard that an individual's preferences about life-sustaining treatment will be followed. In 1985, California enacted legislation providing for a Durable Power of Attorney for Health Care. This document allows a person to designate an agent who is empowered to make health care decisions, particularly with respect to the withholding or withdrawal of life-sustaining treatment. The designated person might be a spouse, adult offspring, or friend with whom one has discussed treatment preferences. An agent must act consistently with a patient's wishes, as specifically stated in the document itself or as otherwise made known. In addition, a court may take away the agent's power to make decisions if he or she: (1) authorizes any illegal act; (2) acts contrary to the patient's known desires; or (3) where those desires are not known, does anything clearly contrary to the patient's best interests.

The Durable Power of Attorney for Health Care becomes effective only when the principal (the person executing it) becomes unable to communicate with his or her doctor. For forms executed since 1992, California law provides that, unless revoked by the person making it, the Durable Power of Attorney for Health Care is effective indefinitely. Forms printed prior to January 1, 1992, generally expire at the end of seven years from the date of signing. The Durable Power of Attorney for Health Care does not usually require an attorney's assistance, and forms can be obtained from the state medical association or even from a local stationery store; many hospitals also make such forms available.

Furthermore, as part of the state's Natural Death Act, California law allows an individual to sign a declaration expressing his or her wishes about treatment. This declaration may be incorporated into the Durable Power of Attorney for Health Care, or it may be used independently (see Figure 9-3). The declaration must be witnessed by two individuals who are not responsible for the person's health care, at least one of whom is not a potential heir. The California statute illustrates the evolving nature of legislation

DECLARATION

Natural Death Act
California Health and Safety Code section 7186.5

If I should have an incurable and irreversible condition that has been diagnosed by two physicians and that will result in my death within a relatively short
time without the administration of life-sustaining treatment or has produced an
irreversible coma or persistent vegetative state, and I am no longer able to make
decisions regarding my medical treatment, I direct my attending physician, pursuant to the Natural Death Act of California, to withhold or withdraw treatment,
including artificially administered nutrition and hydration, that only prolongs the
process of dying or the irreversible coma or persistent vegetative state and is not
necessary for my comfort or to alleviate pain.

Signed this _____ day of _____ , 1995.

Figure 9-3   *Statement of Wishes for Optional Use with California's Durable Power
of Attorney for Health Care*

regarding advance directives and of support for the idea that individuals have
the right to make decisions about their own health care even as they approach
death.

Studies indicate that patients are less worried about receiving unwanted
treatment and doctors less worried about the legal consequences of withholding treatment when the patient has executed some type of advance directive
expressing his or her wishes.[8] Although advance directives appear to both
safeguard a patient's autonomy and minimize conflict in a critical care situation, it is important to recognize that they are virtually useless if doctors and
hospitals do not know of their existence. To meet this difficulty, some advocate
the implementation of policies whereby hospitals would routinely ask patients
whether they have completed an advance directive. Such a policy would not
only bring all existing documents to light, it would also give the patient an
opportunity to revise those portions of the directive that no longer accurately
express his or her treatment preferences.[9] The suggestion has also been made
that wallet cards and bracelets (similar to those used for "Medic Alert") be
developed to signify that an individual has completed an advance directive.
Such an innovation might be especially worthwhile in cases when life-
sustaining treatment is routinely initiated (as with paramedics at an accident
scene) or when an individual is unable to express his or her wishes about the
desirability of such treatment.[10]

According to the provisions of the Patient Self-Determination Act
(PSDA), a law passed by Congress in 1990, health care providers who receive

federal Medicare funds—including hospitals, skilled nursing facilities, home health agencies, hospice programs, and health maintenance agencies—are required to: (1) provide adult patients with information about their rights under state law to accept or refuse treatment, and their right to make advance directives for health care decisions; (2) maintain written policies and procedures to ensure that patients receive such information in written form; (3) document in the patient's medical record whether the patient has executed an advance directive; (4) ensure compliance with requirements of state law with respect to advance directives; and (5) provide staff and community education about advance directives.[11] Information about advance directives is to be provided to patients at the time of their admission to the health care facility or when an individual comes under the care of the agency (such as a home care agency or hospice).

The Patient Self-Determination Act has been described as a "medical Miranda warning" (referring to the requirement that police officers advise arrested suspects of their rights) due to its insistence that patients be advised of their rights regarding advance directives and life-sustaining treatment.[12] It has been reported that only about 10 percent of mentally competent adults have signed an advance directive, and that even fewer have designated someone else to make decisions by means of a health care proxy. Although some believe the new requirements will help people decide their own fate, others believe the law will promote the death of patients by devaluing the goal of sustaining life. Another concern is that patients may become unduly alarmed about the state of their health by being questioned as to whether or not they have executed an advance directive. The elderly widow, for example, who enters a nursing home following the death of her husband may be frightened by what she perceives as a warning that she, too, is about to die, thus adding to the anxiety and depression caused by the disruptions in her life.

With respect to how the Patient Self-Determination Act is eventually assessed, there is considerable agreement that much depends on how the law is implemented through state regulations and at the local level, where health care services are delivered to patients. As the case of Nancy Beth Cruzan (discussed in Chapter 6) made abundantly clear to many people, advance directives offer a relatively simple and easy means to provide the requisite "clear and convincing evidence" as to one's wishes concerning life-sustaining medical treatment.

Larry Churchill points out, however, that advance directives emphasize a "procedural ethics" that is concerned with fairness in process but gives little regard to the quality of trust.[13] People write advance directives not so much to express their autonomy or self-directed choice, but because of fear born of mistrust. When the social and communal dimensions of life are lacking, trusting relationships suffer. Advance directives can be an opportunity for conversation that helps rebuild trust. Respect for autonomy is not to be eliminated, but the good that people seek through advance directives is not autonomy

The clock wound by Elizabeth still ticked, storing in its spring the pressure of her hand.

Life cannot be cut off quickly. One cannot be dead until the things he changed are dead. His effect is the only evidence of his life. While there remains even a plaintive memory a person cannot be cut off, dead. A man's life dies as a commotion in a still pool dies, in little waves, spreading and growing back towards stillness.

John Steinbeck, *To a God Unknown*

per se—not an abrogation of the communal dimensions of life—but rather a "good death."

Physician-Assisted Death

Arthur Berger says, "Choosing to die naturally is one thing [but] asking the assistance of others to terminate a life is quite another."[14] Current laws in the United States echo this sentiment: Suicide is not against the law, whereas assisting in the death of another is legally considered homicide or murder. The highly publicized cases of physician-assisted death involving the Michigan pathologist, Dr. Jack Kevorkian, have brought increased public attention to the debate about whether such aid-in-dying should be permitted and, if so, what kinds of laws are needed to regulate such practices.

According to public opinion surveys conducted in the United States, roughly half of the respondents are in favor of legally instituting a "right to die," or, as some prefer to phrase it, legalizing the possibility of choosing *when* to die. Thus, the American public appears to be almost evenly divided about whether aid-in-dying ought to be legally permitted. Organizations such as the Hemlock Society in the United States and the British Voluntary Euthanasia Society (formerly called Exit) actively promote efforts to make aid-in-dying a legal option for terminally ill people. Some argue that this kind of "death control" is most important for elderly people facing severe physical debility, although many younger people with similar physical limitations also appear to welcome such an option.[15] The executive director of the Hemlock Society, John Pridonoff, believes that hospice care and physician aid-in-dying are not necessarily incompatible; on the contrary, they can be complementary aspects of a comprehensive approach to end-of-life decisions.[16]

In several states—including Wasington, Oregon, and California—citizens have sponsored legislative initiatives that would legalize aid-in-dying. In Washington and California, these efforts failed to achieve a majority at the polls. In November 1994, however, Oregonians approved, by a margin of 52 percent to 48 percent, the Oregon Death with Dignity Act, making that state the first place in the world to pass legislation in favor of physician aid-in-dying. At the time of this writing, the Oregon law has been placed on hold for judicial review. If it passes muster and is eventually implemented, the Oregon Death with Dignity Act would allow terminally ill patients with fewer than six months to live to obtain a lethal prescription from a physician after meeting certain requirements (including being mentally competent, giving informed consent, and obtaining a second medical opinion). The Oregon law requires that the patient take the lethal medication without assistance, and it specifically prohibits lethal injections. Physicians opposed to aid-in-dying have the option of refusing to participate, and the provisions of the law are not available to individuals who are not legal residents of Oregon.

The general trend of American law in recent years has been toward greater freedom for individuals to choose when and how they will die, and many observers believe this trend could result fairly soon in the legal recognition of a "right" to physician assistance in bringing death about when certain preconditions are met. As with other legislation involving the freedom to choose, such as in the case of abortion, a right to aid-in-dying might be determined on the basis of a constitutional "right to privacy"[17] or the "due process" clause of the Fourteenth Amendment to the United States Constitution.[18] Whether the issue is ultimately settled due to citizen initiatives, such as those mentioned, or to judicial action independent of the polling booth, questions about physician-assisted death are likely to remain for some time a central issue of public and private debate.

Organ Donation

The Uniform Anatomical Gift Act, approved in 1968 by the National Conference of Commissions on Uniform State Laws and enacted in some form in all fifty states, provides for the donation of the body or specific body parts upon the death of the donor. Because of the chronic shortage of donor organs, the Act was revised in 1987 with the aim of simplifying the donation of organs by removing requirements that the document be witnessed and that next-of-kin give their consent. The major provisions of the Uniform Anatomical Gift Act are presented in Table 9-1.

Many people find it gratifying to know that, by making an organ donation, they can help others even after their own death. Organ donations can be made by completing a form such as the uniform donor card (see Figure 9-4). A donor may specify that *any* needed organs or body parts may be taken or that only certain body parts or organs are to be donated. Besides specifying how one's body may be used after death, the donor may also specify the final disposition of his or her remains once the donation has been effected. Although polls indicate that virtually all Americans are aware of organ transplants and that the overwhelming majority say they would be willing to make an organ or tissue donation, only a small percentage of the adult population carry donor cards. Studies indicate that individuals who are less anxious about death are more likely to sign organ donor cards.[19] In

TABLE 9-1   *Major Provisions of the Uniform Anatomical Gift Act*

1. Any person over eighteen may donate all or part of his or her body for education, research, therapeutic, or transplantation purposes.
2. If the person has not made a donation before death, the next of kin can make it unless there was a known objection by the deceased.
3. If the person has made such a gift, it cannot be revoked by his or her relatives.
4. If there is more than one person of the same degree of kinship, the gift from relatives shall not be accepted if there is a known objection by one of them.
5. The gift can be authorized by a card carried by the individual or by written or recorded verbal communication from a relative.
6. The gift can be amended or revoked at any time before the death of the donor.
7. The time of death must be determined by a physician who is not involved in any transplantation.

any case, many donations are made by relatives at the time of a loved one's death.

Despite the fact that donor cards are legal in all states, a donor's wishes may be thwarted when there are strong objections from relatives. Because most hospitals also obtain consent from the next of kin, a hospital is unlikely to insist on organ donation if close family members adamantly disagree with the deceased's wishes. Thus, as with other provisions that one intends to have carried out after his or her death, plans for organ donation should be discussed with family members to ensure that their feelings are considered in the final decision.

The success achieved with organ transplants has given hope to the seriously ill, and it has also created a waiting list of patients seeking donor organs. The National Organ Transplant Act was enacted by Congress in 1984 "to provide for a comprehensive review of the medical, legal, ethical, economic, and social issues presented by human organ procurement and transplantation, and to strengthen the ability of the nation's health care system to provide organ transplants."[20] The Division of Organ Transplantation was established in the Health Resources and Services Administration of the Public Health Service, and a National Task Force on Organ Transplantation conducted a two-year study of the issues involved in organ procurement and transplantation. The Act also provided for establishment of a central office to help match donated organs with potential recipients. The United Network for Organ Sharing (UNOS), located in Richmond, Virginia, maintains lists of people waiting for transplants and tracks the status of all donated organs in the United States to ensure both the fairness of distribution and the competence of medical centers where organ transplants are performed. Interest in such a network was spurred partly by the potential for abuses resulting from commercialization of donated organs.

Because the demand for donated organs is larger than the supply, most states have enacted "required request" (also known as routine inquiry) laws

DONOR

STATE OF CALIFORNIA
DMV
DEPARTMENT OF MOTOR VEHICLES

Pursuant to the Uniform Anatomical Gift Act.
I hereby give, effective upon my death:

A _____ Any needed organ or parts

B _____ Parts or organs listed _____

_____

_____
Signature of Donor

_____
DL-290 (REV 10/86)   D A T E

DETACH HERE

To pledge a donation, fill out this card. Remove "DONOR" dot and affix it on the front of your license or I.D. card as shown in the diagram. Affix the card on the reverse of your license or I.D. card. If you change your mind, peel off the card and the dot. Whole Body donations require separate arrangements.
If you are unable to sign, instruct two witnesses to sign this card in your presence.

DMV CALIFORNIA
Driver License
DONOR DOT

NOTICE

If you are at least 18, you may designate on your driver license or I.D. card a donation of any needed organs or tissues for medical transplantation. Under the Uniform Anatomical Gift Act (Sec. 7150, Health & Safety Code) donation takes effect upon your death.
NEXT OF KIN (OPTIONAL)

NAME _____

ADDRESS _____

TELEPHONE NO. _____

DETACH HERE

Additional information regarding the Donor program may be obtained by writing or calling The Gift of Life:

National Kidney Foundation of Southern California
6820 La Tijera Blvd., Suite 111
Los Angeles, CA 90045
(213) 641-5245

3430 Fifth Ave., Suite C
San Diego, CA 92103
(619) 297-2470

National Kidney Foundation of Northern California
856 Stanton Road
Burlingame, CA 94010
(415) 697-0110

Figure 9-4   *Donor Card*
Source: California Department of Motor Vehicles.

requiring hospitals to institute policies and procedures for encouraging organ and tissue donations. In 1986, Congress established similar requirements for hospitals participating in the Medicare and Medicaid programs. Such laws require hospitals to develop a protocol for identifying potential organ and tissue donors and to notify and cooperate with organ procurement centers when organs have been donated.

At or near the time of death, hospital personnel must ask whether the individual had agreed to be an organ donor; and, if not, the family must be informed about the option to donate organs and tissues. Hospitals are to exercise reasonable discretion and sensitivity to the family circumstances in discussing organ donation with surviving family members. In many hospitals, a "transplant coordinator," typically a member of the nursing staff, contacts family members and makes the request for organ and tissue donation.[21]

Under the provisions of the Uniform Anatomical Gift Act, organ donation is entirely voluntary. Many ethicists and medical practitioners believe, however, that a voluntary approach is woefully inadequate given the number of

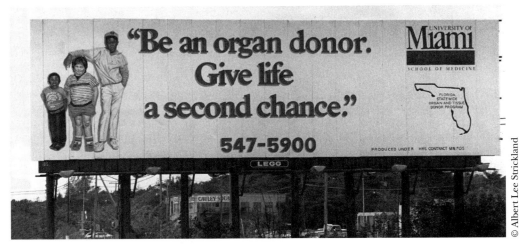

© Albert Lee Strickland

Designed to increase public awareness of organ donation, this billboard on a Florida highway calls particular attention to donations that can save the lives of children.

people waiting to receive donated organs. Although some observers think the answer lies in better public education about organ donation, thereby increasing the pool of voluntary donors, others advocate enactment of a national law that would *require* organ donation unless an individual specifically "opts out" by signing an objection on the back of his or her driver's license or on some other designated document. Such advocacy reflects the view that individuals have an obligation to consent to the removal and transplantation of their organs after death. David Peters, for instance, argues that using terms such as "gift" and "donation" implies that what is taking place is an "act of human kindness beyond the call of duty," but, he says, consenting to transplantation of one's organs after death is a moral duty, "the duty to attempt an easy rescue of an endangered person."[22] David Thomasma, taking a theological approach, bases his support for obligatory organ removal on the premise that "human beings own each other" and that organ donation is not merely a "good deed," but is a profoundly religious, even sacramental activity between human beings.[23] In reviewing the impact of organ transplantation on social attitudes and practices, Robert Fulton and Greg Owen point out that "the harvesting of cadaver kidneys and other organs of the body" has achieved a significance for our society that would have been impossible to anticipate just a few short decades ago, and they note that legislation related to organ donation "has the potential to take from the family survivors the right of decision with respect to the deceased's body, a right that has been integral to family life since before the Christian period."[24]

Another area of recent controversy among medical scientists, ethicists, and other groups concerns the use of fetal tissue transplants to treat such clinical disorders as Parkinson's disease, diabetes, and immunodeficiency and metabolic disorders.[25] Despite the potential good that might result from using fetal tissue for transplantation research, some fear that the procurement of fetal tissue—which is made available as a result of abortion—could lead to serious abuse. Advocates of fetal tissue transplants believe that the Uniform Anatomical Gift Act's stipulations with respect to the use of cadaverous tissue are sufficient to ensure ethical practices.

Closely related to the issue of using fetal tissue for various transplantation procedures is the question of anencephalic infants as potential donor sources. The medical condition of anencephaly is generally defined as "the congenital absence of skull, scalp, and forebrain (cerebral hemispheres)."[26] Infants with this condition are born with all but a small portion of their brain missing. Because this condition is fatal, some medical practitioners and ethicists believe that anencephalics could be an appropriate source of organs and tissues for other infants. However, the laws regarding organ donation require that death be pronounced using brain death criteria or the cessation of heart and respiratory functions. Anencephalic infants do not meet these regulatory requirements because they can exhibit spontaneous breathing and, "if physicians were to wait until all electrical activity from the small portion of the brain present in such infants ceased, there is grave concern that the vital organs and tissues of the infant would be severely damaged."[27] Opponents of using anencephalic infants as organ sources argue that the death of "infant organ donors should be declared with no less certainty than that of adult donors," and, in any event, such transplants may well be unethical.[28]

Death Certification

The death certificate constitutes legal proof of death. The official registration of death is considered the most important legal procedure following a death, and death certificates are required by all jurisdictions in the United States. The causes of death recognized by law include natural causes, accident, suicide, and homicide. Although death certificates vary somewhat from state to state, most follow the format outlined by the United States Standard Certificate of Death.

Death certificates reflect both a private and a public function. On the face of it, the document used to certify the facts of death is quite straightforward, a concise summary of the pertinent data regarding the deceased and the mode and place of death. However, this seemingly simple document has much broader implications than one might at first imagine.[29] In addition to its value and purpose as a legal document that affects disposition of property rights, life insurance benefits, pension payments, and so on, the utility of the death certificate extends to such diverse matters as aiding in crime detection, tracing genealogy, and gaining knowledge about the incidence of disease and other aspects of physical and psychological health.

The typical death certificate now in use (see Figure 9-5) provides for noting only four different *modes* of death: accidental, suicidal, homicidal, and natural. Edwin Shneidman is among those who argue that certification of death ought to be concerned with the facts of death, not only as experienced by the person who died but also as experienced and accounted for by witnesses. As Shneidman points out, the *cause* of death isn't necessarily the same as the *mode* of death. For example, if a death were caused by asphyxiation due to drowning, should such a death be classified as an accident, a suicide, or a homicide? Any of these modes might apply.

Underlying the distinction between mode and cause is the more complex issue of untangling the intentions and subconscious factors, the states of mind and actions, that may have contributed, directly or indirectly, to the death. For instance, if an intoxicated person jumps into a swimming pool with no one else present and drowns, is the death accidental or suicidal? Does it make a difference whether the impetus for alcohol abuse resulted from emotional distress and feelings of despondency? Or what is the mode of death if the cocktails were served by a too-generous host? What if the person serving the excessive alcohol were also an heir of the person who dies?

Obviously, intentions can be far more complex than allowed for by the relatively elementary distinctions concerning mode and cause of death now listed on most death certificates. A study done in Marin County, California, to assess the conventional classifications of mode of death as well as the lethality of the deceased's intention revealed that some deaths classified as natural, accidental, and homicidal were also precipitated by the deceased's own actions; the deceased had lethal intentions against himself or herself. The use of a *psychological autopsy* as an investigative tool for reconstructing the events leading up to a death is discussed in Chapter 12.

The Coroner and the Medical Examiner

Most deaths in the United States result from disease. The physician attending the patient at the time of death completes and signs the death certificate. However, when death occurs in suspicious circumstances or is sudden and there is no physician to sign the death certificate, the cause of death must be determined by a coroner or medical examiner. Besides suspected homicides and suicides, other circumstances of death that require investigation include accidents; deaths that occur on the job, in jails, and in other government institutions; deaths that occur in hospitals or other health care facilities when negligence is suspected or the death was unexpected; and deaths that occur at home when there is no attending physician who is able to sign the death certificate attesting to the cause of death.

The cause of death is determined by use of various scientific procedures, possibly including an autopsy, toxicology and bacteriology tests, chemical analyses, and other studies that are necessary to arrive at adequate findings.

CERTIFICATE OF DEATH
STATE OF CALIFORNIA
USE BLACK INK ONLY/NO ERASURES, WHITEOUTS OR ALTERATIONS
VS-11 (REV. 7/93)

STATE FILE NUMBER | LOCAL REGISTRATION NUMBER

DECEDENT PERSONAL DATA

1. NAME OF DECEDENT—FIRST (GIVEN)
2. MIDDLE
3. LAST (FAMILY)
4. DATE OF BIRTH MM/DD/CCYY
5. AGE YRS. | IF UNDER 1 YEAR MONTHS | DAYS | IF UNDER 24 HOURS HOURS | MINUTES
6. SEX
7. DATE OF DEATH MM/DD/CCYY
8. HOUR
9. STATE OF BIRTH
10. SOCIAL SECURITY NO.
11. MILITARY SERVICE 19___ TO 19___ | NONE
12. MARITAL STATUS
13. EDUCATION ——YEARS COMPLETED
14. RACE
15. HISPANIC—SPECIFY | YES | NO
16. USUAL EMPLOYER
17. OCCUPATION
18. KIND OF BUSINESS
19. YEARS IN OCCUPATION

USUAL RESIDENCE

20. RESIDENCE—STREET AND NUMBER OR LOCATION
21. CITY
22. COUNTY
23. ZIP CODE
24. YRS IN COUNTY
25. STATE OR FOREIGN COUNTRY

INFORMANT

26. NAME, RELATIONSHIP
27. MAILING ADDRESS (STREET AND NUMBER OR RURAL ROUTE NUMBER, CITY OR TOWN, STATE, ZIP)

SPOUSE AND PARENT INFORMATION

28. NAME OF SURVIVING SPOUSE—FIRST
29. MIDDLE
30. LAST (MAIDEN NAME)
31. NAME OF FATHER—FIRST
32. MIDDLE
33. LAST
34. BIRTH STATE
35. NAME OF MOTHER—FIRST
36. MIDDLE
37. LAST (MAIDEN)
38. BIRTH STATE

DISPOSITION(S)

39. DATE MM/DD/CCYY
40. PLACE OF FINAL DISPOSITION

FUNERAL DIRECTOR AND LOCAL REGISTRAR

41. TYPE OF DISPOSITION(S)
42. SIGNATURE OF EMBALMER
43. LICENSE NO.
44. NAME OF FUNERAL DIRECTOR
45. LICENSE NO.
46. SIGNATURE OF LOCAL REGISTRAR
47. DATE MM/DD/CCYY

PLACE OF DEATH

101. PLACE OF DEATH
102. IF HOSPITAL, SPECIFY ONE: | IP | ER/OP | DOA
103. FACILITY OTHER THAN HOSPITAL: | CONV. HOSP. | RES. | OTHER
104. COUNTY
105. STREET ADDRESS—STREET AND NUMBER OR LOCATION
106. CITY

CAUSE OF DEATH

107. DEATH WAS CAUSED BY: (ENTER ONLY ONE CAUSE PER LINE FOR A, B, C, AND D)

TIME INTERVAL BETWEEN ONSET AND DEATH

IMMEDIATE CAUSE (A)

DUE TO (B)

DUE TO (C)

DUE TO (D)

108. DEATH REPORTED TO CORONER | YES | No | REFERRAL NUMBER
109. BIOPSY PERFORMED | YES | No
110. AUTOPSY PERFORMED | YES | No
111. USED IN DETERMINING CAUSE | YES | No

112. OTHER SIGNIFICANT CONDITIONS CONTRIBUTING TO DEATH BUT NOT RELATED TO CAUSE GIVEN IN 107

113. WAS OPERATION PERFORMED FOR ANY CONDITION IN ITEM 107 OR 112? IF YES, LIST TYPE OF OPERATION AND DATE.

PHYSICIAN'S CERTIFICATION

114. I CERTIFY THAT TO THE BEST OF MY KNOWLEDGE DEATH OCCURRED AT THE HOUR, DATE AND PLACE STATED FROM THE CAUSES STATED.
DECEDENT ATTENDED SINCE MM/DD/CCYY | DECEDENT LAST SEEN ALIVE MM/DD/CCYY
115. SIGNATURE AND TITLE OF CERTIFIER
116. LICENSE NO.
117. DATE MM/DD/CCYY
118. TYPE ATTENDING PHYSICIAN'S NAME, MAILING ADDRESS + ZIP

CORONER'S USE ONLY

I CERTIFY THAT IN MY OPINION DEATH OCCURRED AT THE HOUR, DATE AND PLACE STATED FROM THE CAUSES STATED.
119. MANNER OF DEATH
NATURAL | SUICIDE | HOMICIDE
ACCIDENT | PENDING INVESTIGATION | COULD NOT BE DETERMINED
120. INJURY AT WORK | YES | No
121. INJURY DATE MM/DD/CCYY
122. HOUR
123. PLACE OF INJURY
124. DESCRIBE HOW INJURY OCCURRED (EVENTS WHICH RESULTED IN INJURY)
125. LOCATION (STREET AND NUMBER OR LOCATION AND CITY AND ZIP CODE)
126. SIGNATURE OF CORONER OR DEPUTY CORONER
127. DATE MM/DD/CCYY
128. TYPED NAME, TITLE OF CORONER OR DEPUTY CORONER

STATE REGISTRAR

A | B | C | D | E | F | G | H | FAX AUTH. # | CENSUS TRACT

Figure 9-5 *Certificate of Death in Use in California*

When death occurs under suspicious or uncertain circumstances, the coroner or medical examiner usually directs an investigation to determine the cause of death. If foul play is suspected, a police or sheriff's department investigation is undertaken.

Unlike autopsies performed as part of medical training or at a family's request, those done as part of an investigation conducted by a coroner or medical examiner are required by law. The results of such postmortem examination can play a crucial role in court cases and insurance settlements. The outcome of such proceedings are often important not only to law enforcement agencies but also to the families involved: The mode of death—whether it is due to foul play, negligence, suicide, accident, or natural causes—can have a significant emotional effect on survivors. It may also have an economic effect; for example, some life insurance policies cover only accidental death, while others pay twice the face value of the contract in case of accidental death (double indemnity).

Coroners are usually elected officials; medical examiners are usually appointed. The main difference between the two positions, however, has to do with training. Whereas the coroner may not possess any special background or training, the medical examiner is a qualified medical doctor, generally with advanced training and certification in *forensic pathology* (the application of

The office of coroner developed in England approximately 800 to 900 years ago. Coroners were originally referred to as "crowners," the name deriving from the fact that they were officially appointed by the Crown to represent the King's interests in the investigation of violent, unexplained, and suspicious deaths, and more importantly, in the disposition of any personal or real property that became available under the existing laws following a homicide or suicide. The Latin word for crown is *corona,* and hence in later years the name of the office came to be called coroner.

Cyril H. Wecht, "The Coroner and Death"

medical knowledge to questions of law). Besides his or her responsibilities for investigating the cause of death in questionable circumstances, the medical examiner often plays a key role in community health programs such as suicide prevention and drug abuse education.

Autopsies

An autopsy (from the Greek *autopsia,* meaning "seeing with one's own eyes") is a medical examination of a body after death to determine the cause of death or to investigate the extent and nature of changes caused by disease. Autopsies involve detailed examination of both the exterior and interior of the body.[30] Once the abdominal cavity is exposed, organs are removed for examination of their internal structure, and small samples may be taken for later analysis. After the autopsy is completed, organs not needed for further study are replaced in the body cavity and all incisions are closed.

An autopsy may be performed for legal or official reasons (as mentioned in connection with the role of the coroner or medical examiner), or as part of a hospital's teaching or research program. Sometimes, the deceased's family will request an autopsy to determine whether genetic or infectious conditions led to death or to help resolve questions about possible malpractice. Except when required by law, an autopsy can be performed only after the next of kin's consent is obtained or when the deceased has donated his or her body for autopsy under the provisions of the Uniform Anatomical Gift Act.

Within the past decade, forensic science has achieved noteworthy results in investigating human rights violations. In Argentina, for example, a team of forensic scientists helped to identify remains of the *desaparecidos,* the "disappeared," who had been buried in mass graves during a period of military rule and terrorism in that country. The families of the disappeared had often been helpless in their attempts to determine the fate of loved ones. Aided by the techniques of forensic science, including the use of autopsies to determine the cause of death, many families were able to learn the fate of their missing loved ones and to give them a proper burial. Furthermore, during the ensuing trials

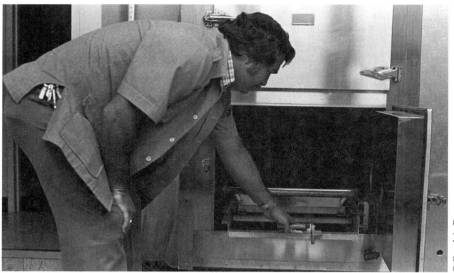

© Carol A. Foote

When a coroner's preliminary investigation reveals the need to scientifically determine the cause of death, the corpse is brought to the morgue, where it is held until an autopsy can be performed.

The autopsy, or medical examination to determine the cause of death, is conducted under the coroner's direction when the circumstances of a death are violent, suspicious, or unexplained, or when a death is medically unattended and a doctor is unable to certify the cause of death. All homicides, accidents, and suicides come under the coroner's or medical examiner's jurisdiction.

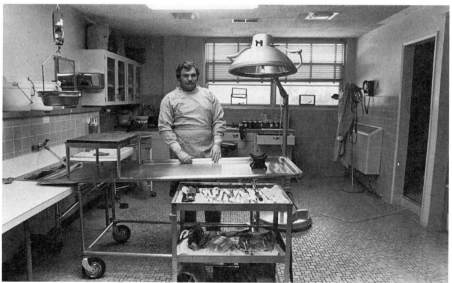

© Carol A. Foote

of several former military leaders, forensic scientists presented expert testimony that helped convict those responsible for the deaths. Members of the
team later expressed hope that "the knowledge that litigation and forensic
documentation can hold governments accountable for their actions may help
deter state-sponsored killings in the future."[31]

Similar techniques for identifying remains are used by the Army Central
Identification Laboratory at Hickam Air Force Base in Hawaii (CILHI). With
nearly 150 staff members, CILHI is the only organization of its kind in the
U.S. military with responsibility for searching for, recovering, and identifying
service members killed or listed as missing.[32] It investigates cases from World
War II, the Korean War, and the Vietnam War, as well as recent military and
civilian cases. As part of a joint task force charged with resolving cases of
Americans missing as a result of the Vietnam War, CILHI has investigated
nearly 700 cases and inspected more than 360 crash or grave sites in Vietnam,
Cambodia, and Laos.

Organized into three sections, CILHI includes teams devoted to search
and recovery, casualty data analysis, and the lab itself. The analysis section
focuses on the medical and dental records of individuals whose remains have
not been recovered. In the lab, recovered remains and other evidence are
examined by physical anthropologists and other experts. Remains arrive at
Hickam in flag-draped caskets with full military honors. Although CILHI does
not expect to be able to recover or identify all of the roughly 2250 individuals
unaccounted for from the Vietnam War, its continuing perseverance in this
task confirms the emotional importance that human beings attach to psychological closure when death occurs.

As a method of conclusively establishing the cause of death, autopsies
serve a number of important purposes in law and medicine. As a tool of
medical investigation, autopsies are used to confirm diagnosis, train doctors,
and conduct research. In this way, autopsies increase the understanding of
disease, thereby leading to improved treatment and life-saving interventions.
Autopsies must be regularly performed by hospitals that aspire to status as
teaching institutions. Because they are *required* in just a few circumstances,
however, the percentage of autopsies performed in the United States is
now only about 14 percent of all deaths. This rate, say medical researchers,
severely limits the number of studies that potentially could result in medical
benefits.

Wills

A legal document expressing a person's intentions and wishes for the
disposition of his or her property after death, the *will* is a valuable tool for
planning one's estate and for conveying property to one's beneficiaries. Conferring a kind of immortality on the *testator* (the person making the will), a will
can be thought of as the deceased's last words. The will can also become a focal
point for powerful emotions, embodying as it does the testator's feelings and

T A B L E 9-2   *Terms Related to Wills and Probate*

Administrator: A person appointed by the court (in the absence of a will, or if no executor is named in one) to carry out the steps necessary to settling an estate. When an administrator is to be appointed, state law requires the drawing up of a preferential list of candidates. Assuming that the necessary qualifications are met, the order of preference typically begins with the spouse of the deceased and continues successively through the deceased's children, grandchildren, parents, siblings, more distant next of kin, and a public administrator.

Attestation Clause: A statement signed by the persons who witness the testator's making of the will.

Codicil: An amendment to a will.

Conditional will: A type of formally executed will that states that certain actions will take place provided that a specified future event occurs. For example, suppose a testator wishes to bequeath money or property to a potential beneficiary who is incapable of self-care, but who has a reasonable chance of recovery. With a conditional will, the money or property could be held in trust for that person until the conditions specified in the will (e.g., recovery) have been satisfied. A problem of conditional wills lies in the difficulty of stipulating with exactitude the nature of events and circumstances that might occur in the future.

Executor: A person named by the testator in his or her will to see that the provisions in the will are carried out properly.

Holographic will: A will written entirely by the hand of the person signing it. Some states do not recognize holographic wills as valid, and those that do generally have stringent conditions for such a document to be deemed valid. Not considered a substitute for a formally executed will.

Intestate: The condition of having made no valid will.

Mutual will: A type of formally executed will that contains reciprocal provisions. May be used by husbands and wives who wish to leave everything to the other spouse with no restrictions, although it limits the range of choices that are available when a will is executed individually.

Nuncupative will: A will made orally. Many states do not recognize a nuncupative will, or do so only under extremely limited circumstances. A few states admit an oral will if the person makes it in fear of imminent death or expectation of receiving mortal injuries, and the peril does result in death. A nuncupative will may also be valid when made by a soldier or sailor engaged in military service or by a mariner at sea; in these instances, the individual need not be in immediate peril. Generally, an oral will must be witnessed by at least two persons who attest that the will is indeed a statement of the testator's wishes.

Probate: The process by which an estate is settled and the property distributed. This process generally occupies an average of nine to twelve months, though it may be longer or shorter depending on circumstances and the complexity of the estate.

---

intentions toward his or her survivors. A glossary of terms relating to wills and probate can be found in Table 9-2.

Many people think of a will as simply a tool for estate planning, perhaps overlooking its important comforting effects for both testator and survivors. Barton Bernstein, a lawyer who has written widely on this point, says that the attorney who helps draw up and execute a will performs a valuable service in helping survivors deal with bereavement and in handling their affairs during the period of mourning.[33]

Many terminally ill patients and their families turn to counselors and other mental health professionals to help them explore their fears, uncertainties, and conflicts as well as devise a plan to meet the prospects that lie ahead. Bernstein believes that lawyers should be included as part of that interdisciplinary team. Otherwise, although the help obtained from such professionals can be a tremendous aid in clarifying concerns, opening communication channels, and enhancing interpersonal relationships, the task of planning for a future that will not include the dying family member may be neglected. The death of a major breadwinner can be especially devastating. Estate planning not only optimizes survivors' financial security but also helps ensure peace of mind to survivors and to the terminally ill person, who can be confident that his or her affairs have been put in order. In addition, the services of a lawyer may be effectively used to ensure that the dying person's wishes regarding organ donation or advance directives for medical care are carried out.

Bernstein outlines three basic legal stages that apply in cases of terminal illness when death follows expected medical probabilities.[34] The *first* stage involves long-range planning, in which the terminally ill person arranges his or her legal and financial affairs for the eventuality of death. During the *second* stage, which occurs shortly before death, the survivors gather pertinent legal papers, obtain sufficient funds to cover immediate expenses, and notify the attorney and insurance representative so they will be ready to make a smooth transition of the deceased's legal and financial affairs. Also at this time, if the dying person intends to make an anatomical gift, the appropriate medical personnel are alerted.

In the *third* stage of legal activity, which follows the death, the will is delivered to an attorney for probate. The effort that went into planning is now rewarded in the survivors' greater sense of security and certainty that affairs have not been left to chance. The survivors can confront their loss without the distraction and worry of complex legal and financial entanglements.

Definitions and Elements of Wills

In many early legal systems, all property belonged to the family, clan, or tribe. The right to make a will is an acknowledgment of the rights of private property rather than communal ownership. The right or privilege of determining how one's property will be distributed following death is not available in all societies, nor is it without limitations. In some countries the government automatically assumes control over the settlement of a person's affairs; in the United States, the individual has considerable liberty in determining how property will be distributed. Still, depending on the laws of a particular state, enforcing and carrying out the provisions of a will may be constrained by circumstances affecting one's heirs. For example, someone may try to avoid willing anything to his or her spouse, but if the will is contested it may be overturned by a court. State statutes usually stipulate that a surviving spouse

© Carol A. Foote

Many of the legal issues surrounding death can be clarified with the help of a competent attorney who is versed in the options available to clients.

cannot be disinherited. Some statutes require that dependent children be provided for in the will. As a rule of thumb, anything that conflicts with ordinary standards of social policy may be abrogated or made invalid if the will is contested.

The person who makes a will must have the mental capacity to understand the nature of the document and the consequences of signing it. He or she must understand the nature and extent of the property being bequeathed by the will and be able to identify the persons who, by convention, ought to be considered when making a will, whether or not they actually become beneficiaries. Given these conditions, and in the absence of any significant delusions, the testator is said to be of sound mind, capable of executing a legal will. State laws generally specify a minimum age at which a person can make a legal will—usually eighteen, though in several states as young as fourteen—and various other requirements, such as the presence of witnesses and execution of the document in a proper form.

In addition to standard information such as the testator's identification and a declaration that the document constitutes the person's last will and testament (along with a statement revoking previous wills, if applicable), a will may include information regarding the property to be distributed, the names of children and other heirs, specific bequests and allocations of property, as well as information concerning the establishment of trusts, the granting of powers to a trustee and/or guardian, other provisions for disposition of property, and payment of taxes, debts, and expenses of administration.

Not all these items are necessarily part of every will, nor is a will limited to the items listed here. For instance, an additional provision may delineate how property is to be distributed when simultaneous accidental deaths occur. Many wills contain a provision spelling out the lines of succession should the primary beneficiary die before the testator.

Most attorneys encourage people making wills to involve spouses in the process to prevent problems that can arise when each spouse makes out a will separately or makes a will without the other's knowledge. When survivors find out after the testator's death that things are not as expected, an added burden of pain and confusion makes coping with the death that much more difficult. There is no requirement, however, that one's mate be involved in the making of a will.

Keeping in mind these general principles regarding wills, we now proceed to an examination of some nuts-and-bolts issues that pertain to making a will.

The Formally Executed Will

The *formally executed will* is the conventional document used for specifying a person's wishes for the distribution of his or her estate after death (see Figure 9-6). If carefully and sensitively prepared, it not only has sufficient clarity of purpose and expression to withstand a court's scrutiny, but can help ease the burden and stress on survivors while demonstrating the testator's affection for those who were close during life.

In making a formally executed will, most people find it beneficial to consult an attorney. A comprehensive review of an estate requires that various records and other information be gathered.[35] Several meetings may be required to carefully plan and consider the ramifications of alternatives concerning the nature of the property and the testator's wishes for its distribution. Once the will's content is determined and its provisions set, the attorney has it typed and an appointment is made for its formal execution. On that occasion, two (in some states, three) disinterested persons are brought in to serve as witnesses, the will is reviewed, and the testator acknowledges that the document accurately reflects his or her wishes and signs it. Although preparation of the will may involve weeks or even months of thoughtful consideration and planning, the actual signing can take less than five minutes. Once the will is signed and witnessed, the testator is assured that the distribution of the estate according to his or her wishes is protected by a valid legal document.

Amending or Revoking a Will

A will is not unchangeable. It can be revoked and replaced by a new will or amended. Amending a will is a means of adding new provisions without having to rewrite it entirely. For instance, a testator who, after the will has been executed, acquires valuable property, such as an art collection, might want to

Will of Tomás Antonio Yorba

In the name of the Holy Trinity, Father, Son, and the Holy Ghost, three distinct persons and one true God, Amen.

1st Clause. Know all [men] who may read this my last will and testament: that I—Tomás Antonio Yorba, native born resident of this department of California, legitimate son of Antonio Yorba and Josefa Grijalva—being sick, but, by divine mercy, in the full enjoyment of my reason, memory and understanding, believing, as I firmly do, in all the mysteries of our holy Catholic faith, which faith is natural to me, since I have lived in it from my infancy and I declare that I want to live in it as a faithful Christian and true Catholic, trusting that, for this reason, his divine Majesty will have mercy on me and will pardon all my sins, through the mysteries of our Lord Jesus Christ and the intercession of his most holy mother, who is my protector and benefactress in these my last moments, so that together with my guardian angel, with St. Joseph, my own name's saint, and all the other saints of my devotion and all the other hosts of heaven, they will assist me before the grand tribunal of God, before which all mortals must render account of their actions—make and decree this my last will and testament as follows, in ordinary paper because of lack of stamped paper.

2nd Clause. Firstly, I commend my soul to God who created it, and my body to the earth, from whence it was fashioned, and it is my wish that I be buried in the church of the Mission of San Gabriel in the shroud of our father St. Francis, the funeral to be according to what my executors and heirs consider that I deserve and is befitting.

3rd Clause. Item: In regard to the expense of the funeral and masses, these should be drawn from the fifth of my estate, according to the disposition of my executors, and I leave the residue of this fifth to my son Juan.

4th Clause. I declare that with respect to my debts, my heirs and executors should collect and pay any legal claims that may turn up or be due according to law. Item: I declare to have been married to Doña Vicenta Sepúlveda, legitimate daughter of Don Francisco Sepúlveda and Doña Ramona Sepúlveda, of this neighborhood, by which marriage I had five children named: (1) Juan; (2) Guadalupe, deceased; (3) José Antonio; (4) Josefa; (5) Ramona. The first being 10 years old, the second died at the age of three, the third six years old, the fourth four years old, and the fifth two years old. Item: I declare to have given my wife jewels of some value as a wedding present, but I do not remember how many nor their value; but they must be in her possession, since I gave them to her. Item: According to my reckoning I have about 2,000 head of cattle, 900 ewes and their respective males, three herds of about 100 mares and their stallions, and three donkeys; about 21 tame horses, 7 tame and 12 unbroken mules; and lastly, whatever cattle, horses or mules may turn up with my brand which may not have been legally sold. Item: I declare to have the right—through inheritance from my father—to part of Middle Santa Ana and Lower Santana, known to be of the Yorbas. I have in Middle Santa Ana an adobe house, its roof being part timber and part thatched, consisting of 18 rooms, including the soap-house. Item: I declare that I have two vineyards with wooden fences which are now planted with bearing vines and some fruit trees; also a section of enclosed land.

5th Clause. I declare that it is my wish to name as executors and guardians of my estate, first, my brother, Don Bernardo Yorba, and second, Don Raimundo Yorba, by joint approval, to whom I give all my vested power, as much as may be necessary, to go in and examine my property for the benefit of my heirs in carrying out this will, and I grant them the power to procure another

continued

continued from previous page

associate [executor] to expedite its due execution, whom I consider appointed as a matter of course, granting him the same authority as those previously named.

6th Clause. I name as my heirs my children and my wife, in the form and manner indicated by the laws, following the necessary inventory.

7th Clause. In this my last will, I annul and void whatever will or wills, codicil or codicils, I may have previously made, so that they may stand nullified with or without judicial process, now and forever, since I definitely desire that the present testamentary disposition be my last will, codicil, and final wish, in the manner and form most legally valid. To this effect I beg Don Vicente Sanchez, Judge of 1st *instancia,* to exercise his authority in probating this will.

To which I, the citizen Vicente Sanchez, 1st constitutional Alcalde and Judge of the 1st *instancia* of the city of Los Angeles, certify; and I affirm that the present testamentary disposition was made in my presence, and that the testator, Don Tomás Antonio Yorba, although ill, finds himself in the full command of his faculties and natural understanding, and, to attest it, I do this before the assistant witnesses—the citizens Ramon Aguilar and Ignacio Coronel—the other instrumental witnesses being the citizens Bautista Mutriel and Mariano Martinez; on the 28th day of the month of January, 1845. The testator did not sign because of physical inability, but Don Juan Bandini signed for him.

Figure *9-6* *Historical Will*
Social custom plays a significant part in the making of a will. The will of Don Tomás Antonio Yorba, dating from the period of Mexican rule in California, presents an illuminating contrast to the modern will with its emphasis on the distrubution of the testator's property. Although Yorba's estate was among the largest of the time—consisting of a Spanish land grant of 62,000 acres known as the Rancho Santiago de Santa Ana in Southern Califonia—only a small fraction of his will relates to matters affecting the distribution of the estate to his heirs.

make a specific provision for the new property without disturbing other parts of his or her estate plan. A codicil, which is executed in the same manner as the original will, would accomplish that objective. Wills should be reviewed periodically to determine if changed circumstances call for revision.

When the addition of codicils makes the will unwieldy or potentially confusing, it is time to review the entire will and make a new one. States vary in their requirements for legally revoking a will. Generally, the testator's *intent* to revoke the will must be demonstrated; the accidental burning of a will, for instance, does not imply revocation. However, if someone turns up with an earlier will, it may be difficult to prove that it was revoked if a subsequent will does not explicitly say so. When in doubt about the validity of a will, seek competent legal advice.

"What would you like for breakfast, Jack?" I asked my son-in-law on Sunday, the day after the funeral.

"A fried egg, over," he replied.

Such a simple thing. Yet, I'd never fried an egg.

Oh, we often had them on weekends; but my husband was the breakfast cook, while I dashed up and down the steps putting clothes in the washer, running the vacuum, and all the other tasks always awaiting a working wife.

I stood there, the frying pan in one hand, the egg in the other.

How many times in the future would I find myself standing the same way? How many things had I never done? How many things had I taken for granted?

Maxine Dowd Jensen,
The Warming of Winter

Probate

During the course of probate the validity of the will is proved; an executor or administrator of the estate is appointed; the necessary matters for settling the estate are carried out; and, with the probate court's approval, the decedent's property is distributed to the beneficiaries. If the deceased left a valid will, property is distributed in accordance with its terms. If there is no will (that is, the person died *intestate,* having left no valid will), the probate court usually names an administrator and the property is then distributed according to the laws of intestate succession in that particular state.

Essentially, the probate period allows time for the deceased's affairs to be resolved, debts and taxes paid, arrangements made to receive moneys due the deceased at the time of death, and finally distribution of the deceased's property. Notices to creditors are generally published in newspapers so that claims outstanding against the estate can be paid prior to distribution of the property to beneficiaries. In addition, the period of probate includes an opportunity for any interested persons to contest the validity of the will.

The Duties of the Executor or Administrator

Someone has to be responsible for carrying out all the steps necessary to settling an estate through probate. Whether an *executor* named in the will or an *administrator* appointed by the court, this person generally must meet certain minimum requirements stipulated by the law of the state in which probate occurs. Once approved by the court, the executor takes an oath to perform all duties faithfully. Some states require the posting of a bond to protect beneficiaries from any potential mismanagement of the estate during the probate period. Once these legalities are in order, then the actual job of settling the estate begins.

NOTICE OF DEATH OF
LEE D. WILLIAMS
AND OF PETITION TO
ADMINISTER ESTATE
Case Number: 11111

To all heirs, beneficiaries, creditors, contingent creditors, and persons who may be otherwise interested in the will or estate of LEE D. WILLIAMS.

A petition has been filed by JANE DOE, in the Superior Court of Santa Cruz County requesting that JANE DOE be appointed as personal representative to administer the estate of the decedent.

A hearing on the petition will be held on March 22, 1982, at 8:30 a.m. in Dept III, located at 701 Ocean Street, Santa Cruz, California 95060.

IF YOU OBJECT to the granting of the petition, you should either appear at the hearing and state your objections or file written objections with the court before the hearing. Your appearance may be in person or by your attorney.

IF YOU ARE A CREDITOR or a contingent creditor of the deceased, you must file your claim with the court or present it to the personal representative appointed by the court within four months from the date of first issuance of letters as provided in section 700 of the California Probate Code. The time for filing claims will not expire prior to four months from the date of the hearing noticed above.

YOU MAY EXAMINE the file kept by the court. If you are a person interested in the estate, you may file a request with the court to receive special notice of the filing of the inventory of estate assets and of the petitions, accounts and reports described in section 1200 of the California Probate Code.

s/ JOHN P. SMITH
Attorney for the Petitioner

JOHN P. SMITH
9999 Pacific Avenue
Santa Cruz, CA 95060
March 7, 9, 14

Figure 9-7   *Newspaper Notice to Creditors*

The prospective executor's or administrator's first duty is to notify interested parties of the testator's death. This is typically accomplished by placing a notification of death in appropriate newspapers (see Figure 9-7). Such a notice serves three purposes: (1) It announces that someone is ready to prove the will of the decedent; (2) it acknowledges that someone is petitioning to be appointed by the court to begin probate; and (3) it gives notice of the death to creditors so that any outstanding claims against the decedent can be submitted for settlement.

The executor makes an inventory of the estate, including all personal and real property owned by the decedent. Bank accounts, stocks, bonds, and other assets are inventoried, as are the contents of the deceased's home and his or her safe deposit box, if any. When a surviving spouse is the estate's primary or sole heir, the inventory of personal and household goods can be less meticulous, though items that have significant worth, such as paintings, jewelry, and antiques, are specified. Important papers are gathered, including insurance policies, Social Security and pension information, military service records, and other documents that require review and possibly action. Several copies of the

When it comes to divide an estate, the politest men quarrel.

Ralph Waldo Emerson,
Journals (1863)

death certificate are obtained to facilitate claims for payment of insurance benefits and the like. Names and addresses of all beneficiaries are compiled.

The executor is responsible for properly managing the estate pending its final disbursement to heirs. Tax returns may need to be filed on behalf of the decedent and the estate. The executor may be charged with paying an allowance to the spouse or to minor children for their support during the period of probate. If the decedent was in business or was a stockholder in a corporation, the executor must skillfully execute a smooth transition that benefits the estate.

An executor or administrator who is not knowledgeable in the law usually enlists the aid of an attorney to make certain that legal requirements are satisfied. Both the executor or administrator and the attorney are entitled to compensation for their services to the estate. These fees are usually a percentage of the value of the estate's assets, the percentage being computed according to fee tables established by state legislatures.

After all the information is compiled about payments due the estate and claims against it, the executor or administrator takes the necessary steps to have the debts paid and to receive moneys due. If an estate's funds are not sufficient to pay all creditors, disbursement is usually made according to guidelines established by state law.

Finally, an accounting and schedule for distributing the estate's property to the beneficiaries is prepared and submitted for the approval of the probate court. Once the court's approval is obtained, the property is distributed and receipts are obtained to certify that the distribution has been made correctly. Assuming that everything has been carried out properly, the court then discharges the executor or administrator. The estate is settled.

Avoiding Probate

Because probate involves delays and can sometimes be expensive, many people take steps to avoid it. Sensible, legal steps can be taken to avoid or at least minimize probate costs. For example, a husband and wife may own their house and other assets in joint tenancy, a form of property ownership that allows a spouse to take full legal possession of the property upon the other's death, without probate.

Some approaches to avoiding probate, however, can have serious pitfalls, particularly the do-it-yourself approach that is taken without obtaining qualified legal counsel. Suppose, for example, that an elderly couple would like their house to go to their grandson after their deaths. Intending to avoid probate, they might visit a local stationery store, purchase the appropriate form to file a change of ownership, add the grandson's name to the property deed, and record this document with the county recorder. So far, so good. But now suppose that several years later they decide to sell the house, or they change their minds about making the grandson their beneficiary and want to remove his name from the deed. To make this desired change, they must obtain the grandson's signature, much as if he were "selling" his right of ownership in the house. Placing a minor's name on a deed may require going into court and requesting that a legal guardian be appointed to act on behalf of the minor should a change of ownership be desired.

Many options are available for setting up one's estate so that probate is minimized or eliminated. Such actions may offer significant savings of legal fees and probate costs. However, all such plans to avoid or minimize probate should be adopted only after careful consideration.

Laws of Intestate Succession

It is estimated that seven out of ten Americans die without leaving a will. Perhaps so many of us fail to make a will because death makes us uncomfortable. Or perhaps, overwhelmed by busyness, we neglect this aspect of financial planning with the questionable excuse that we are not yet at the age when death is statistically probable. Considering the consequence that can result when one dies intestate—that is, without a will—we would do well to give this matter more than passing thought.

Whereas an executor named by the testator is permitted to act more or less independently in the management of the estate provided that he or she acts prudently, the court-appointed administrator may be required to obtain the court's approval before proceeding with sensible and necessary decisions. When an estate is sizable or is otherwise complex, the difference between management of the estate by an executor and management by the court-appointed administrator may be significant.

One of the chief reasons for making a will is to ensure that property will be disbursed according to one's wishes. In the absence of a will, property is distributed according to general guidelines established in state law. The state generally tries to accomplish what it believes the deceased would have done had he or she actually made a will. The laws that dictate the disbursement of property, the care of minor children, and all the matters that pertain to settling the estate reflect society's ideas of fair play and justice. Thus, the values of society, rather than the deceased's personal values, determine the outcome.

If any heirs are minors, their share of the estate will be held in a court-supervised guardianship. Their guardian, even when it is the surviving parent, will have to periodically report to the court on management of the children's

"Aaaaaaaa! . . . It's George! He's taking it with him!"

trust. The complications that arise from dying intestate make a solid argument for making a will.

Although the laws of intestate succession differ among states, some general patterns prevail. In community property states, for example, all community property goes to the surviving spouse. When there is only one child, the estate generally will be divided equally between child and surviving spouse. If there is more than one child, usually one-third of the estate goes to the surviving spouse and the remaining two-thirds is divided equally among the children.

If there is no surviving spouse, property is divided among the children; if no children, disbursement is made to the deceased's parents; if they are not living, property is likely to be divided among the deceased's surviving siblings; if there are none, the estate may be divided among the deceased's siblings' children. In attempting to settle an estate, the court will make a determined

And in a decade or two or more when death taps at the door, your estate may be far larger than you now envisage. It may be so already. One tends to think in terms of a few principal segments of one's estate. For purposes of planning, your "estate" includes everything of monetary value: your home and other real estate; all bank and savings accounts; usables including *objets d'art* and hobbies, such as a stamp collection; your carefully planned investment portfolio; life insurance; rights under a pension plan, if you enjoy that umbrella; as well as growing protection from social security. All must be arranged so as to afford maximum benefit to the beneficiaries.

Paul P. Ashley, *You and Your Will*

effort to locate surviving heirs. If none can be found, however, the proceeds from the estate go to the state.

Because the laws of intestate succession are designed to protect the interests of the surviving spouse and children of the deceased, some people find it convenient to let the state decide how their property is distributed after death. The major flaw in this view, however, is that the decisions made by the state may be quite different from those the person would have made. The distinction between intestate succession and distribution according to the terms of a formally executed will is fundamental: Who would you rather have make the rules and decide the outcome of your estate—the legislature and public officials, or you, the testator?[36]

Estate and Inheritance Taxes

Estate and inheritance taxes have the same rationale as other forms of taxation: the redistribution of wealth. Equality of opportunity is a cornerstone of American society, and taxation is seen as a method of breaking up concentrations of wealth and providing greater economic benefits for a greater number of citizens. Although there may be dissent about *how* wealth is thus redistributed, it is presumed that there is consensus among the American people about the desirability of redistribution. Nevertheless, few people enjoy paying taxes, and many feel that so-called death taxes are among the most abhorrent. Although a case can be made for the philosophical view that inheritance taxes should be 100 percent—"Empty we come into the world, empty we leave"—this notion goes against the grain of human nature.

Estate Taxes

The estate tax imposed by the federal government is a tax paid on the *transfer* of assets from the decedent to his or her beneficiaries. Estate taxes are assessed on the total value of the taxable estate before it is divided. Like individual income tax returns, estate taxes are calculated on the basis of assets

Inheritance

When I was ten years old, my father died. And at that time, of course, I thought my father was the best and finest man there ever was. And some years later when I was eighteen and I began to mingle in the adult community, I introduced myself to strangers and they would ask me if John Estrada was my father. When I said yes, they would say, "Well, let me shake your hand. He was a fine man and a good friend of mine." And then they would tell me wonderful stories about him. Since that time, I have hoped that when I am gone, some people might meet my children and say to them that I was a good man and a good friend. To me that is a finer inheritance than any material possession.

Fred Estrada

less allowable deductions. The estate's assets are those items included on the inventory taken by the executor or administrator, and the value of these assets is generally determined by court-appointed appraisers. Once the gross value of an estate is determined, the next step is to compute allowable deductions. Typical deductions include expenses incurred during a terminal illness; funeral costs; administrative expenses; debts, mortgages, and liens against the estate; net losses that occur during administration of the estate; charitable and public bequests; several categories of tax credits, if applicable to a particular estate; and the marital deduction.

First enacted in 1948, the *marital deduction* was designed to extend to everyone in the United States the same opportunity for tax savings that had been provided to those living in community-property states. Whereas earlier laws placed a limit on the deduction allowed on transfers of property between spouses, current law provides an unlimited marital deduction. This means that no tax need be paid upon the death of the first spouse on whatever portion of the estate is left to the surviving spouse. However, in some cases, particularly those involving large estates, it may not be advantageous to use the unlimited marital deduction because it is designed to allow a postponement of tax (until the death of the surviving spouse), not an avoidance of tax.

Although the marital deduction provides an opportunity to avoid taxation on transfers of estates between spouses, it limits a testator's freedom of choice with respect to the distribution of his or her estate. Thus, some people choose to incur larger taxes as a trade-off for retaining greater control over how an estate will be distributed.

Inheritance Taxes

Whereas estate taxes are levied by the federal government, inheritance taxes are imposed by the states. Taxation rates and regulations vary among the states. Inheritance tax has generally been smaller than the estate tax, although estates exempt from federal estate taxes may be subject to state inheritance taxes. Inheritance taxes may be levied according to the relationship between the decedent and the beneficiary: As the relationship grows more distant, the exempt amount is decreased and the tax rate on the excess is increased.

Some states tax insurance benefits, others do not, and yet others provide exemptions calculated according to the relationship of the named beneficiary to the insured. Information about the specific inheritance tax rates and regulations that apply in your state can be obtained from a local attorney, the state's inheritance tax department, or reference books such as *The World Almanac.*

Trusts

A *trust* can be defined simply as the holding of property by one person for the benefit of another. The many kinds of trusts constitute extremely valuable tools of estate planning. Common forms of trusts include arranging for the financial security of minor children and providing funds for college or similar expenses.

Although we usually think of trusts as a financial planning tool that benefits others, it is possible to set up a trust for oneself. In fact, the person making the trust can serve as both its trustee and beneficiary. A *living trust,* for example, can be established whereby a husband and wife hold their property in trust for themselves. Such a trust differs from a *testamentary trust,* which becomes effective upon the testator's death.

One wise use of the living trust is to provide funds for medical care in the event that the trustor is unable to act in his or her own behalf due to senility or some other incapacity. One instance of the wisdom of planning before need is described by Paul Ashley. An eighty-year-old man established a living trust, designating his attorney to handle his affairs if he should not be able to do so himself. Shortly after setting up this trust, the man suffered a stroke that incapacitated him for nearly three years, making it impossible for him to conduct necessary business and financial transactions. Because he had had the foresight to institute a living trust for just such a contingency, he and his wife were assured of receiving every care and comfort that could be made available during the term of his disability.[37]

Trusts can be designed to serve many different kinds of purposes. They are often an excellent means for avoiding or minimizing the complexity and duration of probate procedures, thus saving time and money.

Life Insurance and Death Benefits

In the United States, the first life insurance company was established in 1759 by the Presbyterian Synod of Philadelphia for Presbyterian ministers. Although life insurance did not become common until the middle of the nineteenth century, it is now a huge industry whose assets grew from $207.3 billion in 1970 to $1665 billion by the early 1990s.[38] Most American households include at least one member who owns some form of life insurance.

T A B L E 9-3   *A Brief Glossary of Life Insurance Terms*

Annuities: Closely related to life insurance, annuities are designed to ensure that a person's accumulated funds will last for the remainder of his or her life by guaranteeing a specified income for as long as he or she lives. The price of an annuity is based on the average life expectancy for persons of a given age; those who die earlier than the average are, in effect, paying to support those who live longer.

Beneficiary: The person (or other entity, such as an institution or a charitable organization) named to receive the proceeds of a life insurance policy that are payable at the death of the insured.

Chartered Life Underwriter (CLU): A designation awarded to agents who complete a college-level course of study in insurance and financial planning.

Endowment: An insurance policy that provides for the payment of the face amount of the policy after a specified number of years, or at a specified age of the insured, or to the beneficiaries of the insured at his or her death. Typically used to accumulate savings, such as for education or retirement, an endowment policy offers less protection in the event of early death than does a whole life policy.

Face amount: The amount of insurance protection under a given policy as stated on the first page, or face, of the agreement; this amount may be increased by dividends or decreased by loans against the policy.

Group life insurance: An insurance agreement covering a group of people, often the employees of a company or, in some cases, the members of a voluntary-membership organization; the premiums may be paid either exclusively by the employer or jointly by the employer and employees.

Insured: The person whose life is insured under the terms of an insurance agreement, often the person who takes out the policy.

Life insurance policy: A written agreement between an insurance company and the insured that provides for payment of a stipulated sum of money to the beneficiary or beneficiaries named in the policy or to the estate of the deceased upon the death of the insured.

Mutual company: An insurance company owned by the policyholders and managed by a board of directors chosen by the policyholders. After administrative expenses are paid, the profits from operating the firm are returned to policyholders in the form of dividends.

Nonparticipating policy: A policy on which no refunds or dividends are paid and which bears a relatively low guaranteed premium.

Paid-up policy: An insurance policy on which no further payments are due and under which there remain outstanding benefits as provided by the terms of the policy.

Participating policy: An insurance policy in which the insured shares in the distribution of dividends resulting from the surplus earnings of the insurance company.

Premium: The amount paid to an insurance company by the insured in exchange for the benefits provided under the terms of the policy.

Stock company: An insurance company owned by its stockholders. Generally, the policies are nonparticipating; that is, no dividends are paid to those who are insured by the company. Instead, profits are shared by the company's stockholders. Although insurance premiums are usually lower with a stock company, when dividends paid over a period of time are taken into account, one may find that costs are ultimately less with a mutual, or participating, company.

Term insurance: The simplest type of policy. Provides protection for a stated period of time (usually from five to twenty years) and expires without value if the insured survives longer than the stated period. Term insurance provides maximum protection for a minimum outlay at a given time.

T A B L E 9-3   *(continued)*

Underwriter: The insurer, or a person acting on behalf of the insurer, who accepts and classifies the life insurance risk; also, the person who solicits insurance as an agent of the insurer and who assumes the obligation on behalf of the insurer by signing the insurance agreement.

Whole life insurance: A policy that continues throughout the insured's lifetime. The premium remains constant since it is based on the expectation that the policy will be held for the person's lifetime. The younger a person's age when the policy is taken out, the lower the premium. In early years, the premium paid is more than the true cost of the insurance; in later years, it is less. Thus, the policy builds up a cash value based on the difference between the premium paid and the true cost of the insurance. This cash value can be "captured" by borrowing on it or by discontinuing the policy and getting a refund. Upon the death of the insured, the policy provides for payment of the stated amount of insurance as increased by any dividends that have been retained and reduced by any loans against the policy. Also called ordinary life and straight life. This type of policy requires a lower cash outlay than other types of policies over a person's lifetime.

Policies and Considerations

Life insurance is a convenient and relatively inexpensive way of providing at least a basic estate for our beneficiaries after we die. It may represent a small portion of a large estate, or the major portion of a smaller estate. Insurance plans can be designed in a number of ways and to suit many purposes. Some policies are part of a total investment portfolio that can be drawn upon during the insured's lifetime. Other policies provide for benefit payments only after the death of the insured. Table 9-3 presents a glossary of insurance terms. Companies licensed to sell insurance must conform to state laws regulating insurance practices.

Those who favor including insurance as part of estate planning argue that life insurance offers some advantages not available from other forms of investment. For example, life insurance benefits payable to a named beneficiary (not the decedent's estate) are not subject to attachment by the decedent's creditors. Too, benefits usually become available immediately following death, unlike assets that must be processed through probate. Thus, insurance benefits can have important psychological and emotional value. Such funds may provide relief and a sense of security to a surviving spouse and other dependents during the period immediately after bereavement. Knowing that money is available to cover anticipated expenses may help to reduce the stress associated with this period of crisis. However, a hasty or ill-informed decision concerning how insurance benefits are spent may ultimately increase the survivor's stress rather than alleviating it. Issues like this, so important for the well-being of one's survivors, should be considered in devising a comprehensive estate plan.

Burial in a national cemetery, such as the Black Hills National Cemetery in South Dakota, is a benefit made available to veterans who have served in American military forces during wartime. Such cemeteries have been established across the United States. Other death benefits for veterans include a lump-sum payment to help defray burial expenses and, under certain circumstances, direct payments to survivors.

© Albert Lee Strickland

Other Death Benefits

Many survivors qualify for various lump-sum and income benefits from government programs and institutions such as Social Security and the Veterans Administration. The dependents of Civil Service employees may be entitled to similar benefits. To obtain current information about any of these death-benefit programs, one can call or write the government bureau administering them. It is important to recognize that a person entitled to benefits under one or more of these programs may not receive them unless a claim is filed. Moreover, delays in filing may result in a loss of benefits. A well-conceived and adequate estate plan includes consideration of benefits that may accrue from government programs such as those mentioned as well as benefits that may be due from employee or union pension programs.

When death results from accident or negligence, various kinds of insurance settlements or other death benefits may become payable to survivors. Such benefits are often related to court cases that involve the attempt to place a "value" on the deceased person's life and what that loss represents to his or her survivors. Although settlements of this kind may indeed be helpful to survivors as they pick up the pieces and try to go on with their lives, the monetary amount of a settlement, no matter how large, is poor compensation for the loss of a loved one (see Figure 9-8).

Death of a Son

"I'm not happy because I no more my son already . . . . I miss him. Even if I get my money, I no more my loved one, my son. I'm not interested in money. Every day, after work, even if I feel tired, I no miss to go visit my boy. Sometimes I cry. Sometimes I give food [for his grave]. Soda. His favorite—Kentucky Fried Chicken. Sometimes fried saimin. Then I give an orange. Ice cream. . . . One day after the crash, my boy, he come my house in spirit. He tell me, 'Daddy, I miss you. I no more hands. I no more eyes.' Ho, I cry."

Figure *9-8   Death of a Son*
Jovencio Ruiz of Molokai, responding to a question about a six-figure insurance settlement in the death of his 14-year-old son, Jovencio Jr., in an air crash.

Further Readings

George J. Annas. *The Rights of Patients: The Basic ACLU Guide to Patient Rights*, 2d ed. Clifton, N.J.: Humana Press, 1991.

Paul P. Ashley. *You and Your Will: The Planning and Management of Your Estate*, Rev. ed. New York: New American Library, 1985.

Joseph M. Belth. *Life Insurance: A Consumer's Handbook*, 2d ed. Bloomington: Indiana University Press, 1985.

Howard Brody. "Assisted Death: A Compassionate Response to Medical Failure." *New England Journal of Medicine* 327, no. 19 (November 5, 1992): 1384–1388.

Ronald Chester. *Inheritance, Wealth, and Society.* Bloomington: Indiana University Press, 1982.

Jack Kevorkian. *Prescription—Medicide: The Goodness of Planned Death.* New York: Prometheus, 1991.

Charlotte Kirsch. *A Survivor's Guide to Contingency Planning.* Garden City, N.Y.: Anchor Press/Doubleday, 1981.

Thane Josef Messinger. "A Gentle and Easy Death: From Ancient Greece to Beyond Cruzan Toward a Reasoned Legal Response to the Societal Dilemma of Euthanasia." *Denver University Law Review* 71, no. 1 (1993): 175–251.

Frank Smith. *Cause of Death: The Story of Forensic Science.* New York: Van Nostrand Reinhold, 1980.

Edward F. Sutkowski. *Estate Planning: A Basic Guide.* Chicago: American Bar Association, 1986.

Cyril Wecht. *Cause of Death.* New York: Dutton, 1993.

A child feels the death of a parent or other close family member or friend as deeply as do adult survivors of a close death. This young girl finds solace and a means of coming to terms with the death of her father by bringing a favorite drawing to the gravesite and spending some time alone with her thoughts and memories of her father and what his loss represents in her life.

Death in the Lives of Children and Adolescents

*C*hange is pervasive in the lives of children and adolescents. Families move. Children leave familiar playmates and friends, their neighborhood, school, and the people and places they have come to know and to which they feel attached. A parent may say, "But, dear, it's only for a year," or, "We'll come back to visit next summer." To a young child, however, a year or next summer is a very long time indeed. Concepts related to time and distance may lie outside the child's frame of reference. Change can bring a very real loss.

Changes in family relationships—divorce or separation, for instance—may be experienced as a kind of death. The child senses that the known relationship has changed, but exactly what the future holds is uncertain and possibly bewildering. Even though such changes may not connote the sense of finality that adults reserve for death, children can experience a lingering uncertainty, a kind of "little death." Separation from one's parents is usually painful whether the separation is due to death, divorce, or some other reason.

Change is experienced as older brothers and sisters grow up and move away from home. As the composition of the family shifts, a child is faced with the need to adjust to new and unfamiliar situations. Perhaps the child delights in the change because it means he or she now enjoys the thrill of having one's own room. However, with the departure of an older sibling, the child may lose an advocate or a confidant who provided support and understanding. Change brings both gains and losses.

Death has a different emotional meaning to young children. In the game of Cowboys and Indians death is not final; the game must continue. The common threat when angered may be, "I'll kill you." One can readily see that the concept of killing is not viewed as final and that there is no association of pain with killing. Perhaps the following example will best prove the point. Upon arriving home from a business trip, a young child's father brought her a gun and holster set. After buckling on her new present she took out the gun, pointed it at her father and said, "Bang, bang, you're dead! I killed you." Her father replied, "Don't hurt me." His daughter's innocent answer was, "Oh, Daddy, I won't hurt you, I just killed you." To many children death is seen only as something in the distant future; "only old people die."

Dan Leviton and Eileen C. Forman,
"Death Education for Children and Youth"

An addition to the family, a new baby brother or sister, can give rise to both excitement and trepidation. The new family member may represent an intrusion upon the child's place in the family, a loss of attention from parents and other family members. Yet the child may also enjoy the adventure and the more mature responsibilities that accompany change. Changes require readjustments.

In addition, children and adolescents may encounter other significant losses: the death of a brother or sister, a parent, or a friend; or confrontation with an illness that threatens his or her own life. As much as we may wish it were otherwise, children are exposed to events of change and loss, experiences of bereavement and grief.

Development of the Understanding of Death

The evolving understanding of death reflects a process of continuous adjustments and refinements as new experiences cause a reexamination of previously held values and responses. This process is often quite rapid; a child's understanding of death can change dramatically in a very brief time. Its progression can be placed in a framework that gives an orderly picture of the relevant processes. By observing and questioning to gather information, and then analyzing the data, researchers identify characteristic patterns of childhood development. (You have probably done this yourself by observing the changes that occur in children with whom you have frequent contact. For example, the kinds of play activities that engross a child change over time; the toys that elicited great excitement at one age become uninteresting at a later time.) By observing children's behavior, developmental psychologists devise models to describe the characteristic concerns and interests of children at various ages. These models are like maps that describe the main features of the

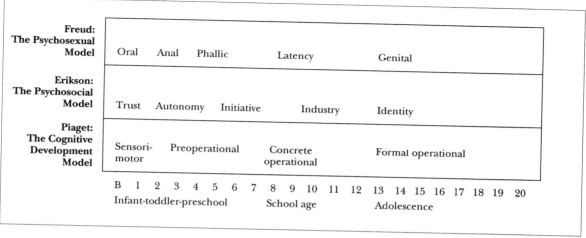

Figure *10-1   Comparison of Major Developmental Models, or Theories, Concerning Childhood Phases of Development*

territory of childhood at different stages of development. The models are useful for describing the characteristics of a typical child at, say, age two or age seven. They give a general picture of each stage of development. But the map should not be mistaken for the territory.

Like maps, models of human development are abstractions, representations, interpretations of the actual territory (see Figure 10-1). Such maps can be helpful in guiding one's way, locating certain landmarks, and sharing knowledge with others. But the particular features of the landscape always possess a uniqueness that cannot be fully described by a map. Children vary in individual rates of development—not only physically but also emotionally and cognitively, or intellectually. Thus, with respect to a child's understanding of death, as with other human traits, developmental levels do not correspond neatly to chronological age.

The child's concerns and behaviors change over time due to the interplay between experiences and the level of maturity brought to understanding them. Or, put another way, the child's understanding of death usually fits with his or her model of the world at each stage of development. Thus, an adult could give a young child a lengthy, detailed explanation of the concept of death as adults understand it, yet the child will grasp its components only as he or she is developmentally ready to understand. However, a child's cognitive and emotional readiness to understand is not simply a matter of age: Experience plays an important role. A child who has had firsthand encounters with death may arrive at an understanding of death beyond what is typical of other children of the same age.

Summaries of Early Studies of Children's Concepts of Death

Paul Schilder and David Wechsler (1934): Schilder and Wechsler listed general statements about children's attitudes toward death:

1. Children deal with death in an utterly matter-of-fact and realistic way.
2. Children exhibit skepticism concerning the unobservables.
3. Children often accept conventional definitions.
4. Children often remain insensitive to contradictions between convention and observation.
5. Children exhibit naivete in solving problems.
6. Children regard death as deprivation.
7. Children believe the devil punishes orally by withdrawing food or by devouring the dead.
8. Children do not believe in their own death.
9. To very young children, death seems reversible.
10. Children believe death may result from disease.
11. Children have a tendency toward undue generalization of limited knowledge.
12. Children believe in death from overeating, violence, and acts of God.
13. Fear of death is rare.
14. Children often fail to understand the meaning of death, but base their attitudes on the actions of adults.
15. Children may exhibit suicidal ideas.
16. Children are always ready to believe in the deaths of others.
17. Children are ready to kill.
18. The tendency to kill may come only in play.
19. The degree of preoccupation of children with violence and death can be seen by the way in which they react to ghost pictures.
20. God appears as a stage magician, controlling ghosts and death, etc.
21. Appearance and reality are not sharply differentiated.
22. Children exhibit the urge to pass moral judgments on every person and picture.
23. Children's professed morality is utilitarian, since children fear punishment.
24. Religious morality enters relatively rarely into children's attitudes toward death.

continued

Until recently, few studies of children's development focused on how children learn about death. Studies done in the 1930s and 1940s generally concluded that children had little or no awareness of death before the age of three or four. Early theoretical models proposed a series of stages with fixed corresponding ages within which particular kinds of behaviors and conceptual developments occurred. As some of the blanks in developmental studies are now being filled in by current research, the picture drawn by earlier research is being refined.[1]

It has become increasingly clear, for example, that emphasizing developmental *sequence* is more reliable than correlating stages of understanding to

continued from previous page

Sylvia Anthony (1940): Before the age of two years, the child has no understanding of death. After age two, most children think often of death. The idea of death seems to take much of its emotional component from its links with birth anxiety and aggressive impulses. Magical thinking pervades much of the child's thoughts about death (i.e., belief that events happen in a certain way because he or she thinks about them happening in a certain way; for example, angry thoughts directed toward someone who subsequently dies makes the child feel himself or herself to be a murderer). As a result, guilt is one of the child's reactions to death.

Maria H. Nagy (1948): Nagy identified three major developmental stages among children three to ten years of age.

Stage 1 (3–5 years): Death is understood as separation, a state of being less alive, a departure or disappearance (i.e., the dead go away and continue to "live" on under changed circumstances). The child does not yet recognize that death involves complete cessation of life; nor is the finality (irreversibility) of death comprehended.

Stage 2 (5–9 years): Death is now understood as final. However, still present is the notion that one might be able to elude death; the inevitability (all die) and personal reference (I die) components are not yet established. Belief that one might be able to outwit or outluck the "Death Man."

Stage 3 (9 or 10 years and older): Death is recognized as final and inevitable.

Irving E. Alexander and Arthur M. Alderstein (1958): Death has a greater emotional significance for children with less stable ego self-concepts than for children with adequate self-concepts. The ages five to eight and the period of adolescence are times of great emotional upheaval and changing demands of growth, which are likely to put existing self-images to a severe test. As a result, the concept of nonbeing (death) may be more threatening during these periods of development.

Sources: Paul Schilder and David Wechsler, "The Attitudes of Children Toward Death," *Journal of Genetic Psychology* 45 (1934): 406–451; Sylvia Anthony, *The Discovery of Death in Childhood and After* (New York: Basic Books); Maria H. Nagy, "The Child's View of Death," *Journal of Genetic Psychology* 73 (1948): 3–27; Irving E. Alexander and Arthur M. Alderstein, "Affective Responses to the Concept of Death in a Population of Children and Early Adolescents," *Journal of Genetic Psychology* 93 (1958): 167–177.

age for describing how children learn about death. Children initially conceive of death as partial, reversible, and avoidable. As their understanding matures, they eventually arrive at the concept of death as final and inevitable. The cognitive resources that permit a conception of death as final and inevitable were long thought to be acquired at around the age of nine. Recent research, however, places this occurrence between the ages of five and seven for most children, although the correlation between age and stage is deemphasized in current studies.[2]

In tracing the development of the death concept in children, it is useful to have a theoretical framework within which to place the distinctive attitudes

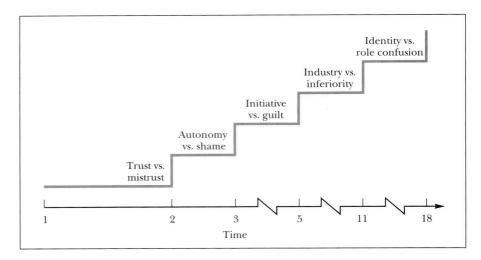

Figure *10-2*   *Five Stages of Preadult Psychosocial Development Proposed by Erikson*
Source: Based on Erik H. Erikson, *Childhood and Society* (New York: Norton, 1964), pp. 247–274.

and behaviors that pertain to various phases of childhood. We use two theories of development—namely, those devised by Erik Erikson and Jean Piaget—in the discussion that follows.

The model of human development devised by psychologist Erik Erikson focuses on the *stages of psychosocial development,* or psychosocial milestones, that occur successively throughout a person's life (see Figure 10-2).[3] In Erikson's model, psychosocial development depends significantly on the environment and is linked to the individual's *relationships* with others. Each stage of development involves a turning point, or crisis, that requires a response from the individual.

Applying Erikson's model, we would expect to find that, depending on an individual's psychosocial stage, certain aspects of death are likely to be more important than others. For instance, to an infant, the sudden loss of a parent may be a major blow to the child's development of *trust* in the environment. The preschooler's fantasies of a parent's death may be accompanied by feelings of *guilt*. The adolescent's experience of a close friend's death may trigger *anxieties* concerning whether death could thwart the realization of his or her own goals and dreams as well. Thus, as we consider the various periods of childhood development, Erikson's model can help to supply insight into the issues children are likely to pay particular attention to at different times in their lives.

Jean Piaget is widely considered to have been the world's foremost child psychologist, a profound theorist as well as an astute observer of children's

TABLE *10-1*   *Piaget's Model of Cognitive Development*

Age (approximate)	Developmental Period	Characteristics
Birth–2 years	Sensorimotor	Focused on senses and motor abilities; learns object exists even when not observable (object permanence) and begins to remember and imagine ideas and experiences (mental representation).
2–7 years	Preoperational	Development of symbolic thinking and language to understand the world. (2–4 years) *Preconceptual subperiod:* sense of magical omnipotence; self as center of world; egocentric thought; all natural objects have feelings and intention (will). (4–6 years) *Prelogical subperiod:* beginning problem solving; seeing is believing; trial and error; understanding of other points of view; more socialized speech; gradual decentering of self and discovery of correct relationships.
7–12 years	Concrete operational	Applies logical abilities to understanding concrete ideas; organizes and classifies information; manipulates ideas and experiences symbolically; able to think backwards and forwards; notion of reversibility; can think logically about things experienced.
12+ years	Formal operational	Reasons logically about abstract ideas and experiences; can think hypothetically about things never experienced; deductive and inductive reasoning; complexity of knowledge; many answers to questions; interest in ethics, politics, social sciences.

behavior. Piaget's focus was on the *cognitive transformations* that occur during childhood (see Table 10-1).[4] In his view, an individual's mode of understanding the world changes, in sequential stages, from infancy to adulthood. Accordingly, four different periods of cognitive, or intellectual, development can be distinguished. These developmental stages are based on the characteristic ways in which individuals organize their experience of the world: *sensorimotor, preoperational, concrete operational,* and *formal operational.*

All children move through these periods in the same order, although the rate of cognitive development for each child is unique. Thus, Piaget's theory emphasizes *sequence,* not a direct age–stage correlation. Although particular cognitive abilities tend to be associated with a specific age range, such abilities develop earlier in some children and later in others. Thus, when statements about age are made in discussing children's development, they should be understood as approximations, not as norms.

Infancy and Toddlerhood

According to the psychosocial model devised by Erikson, infancy is characterized by the individual's development of a sense of *trust* concerning the environment. If the infant's needs are not met, the result may be distrust. Thus, other people in the infant's environment—typically, parents—play an important part in the child's psychosocial development.

During Erikson's second stage, toddlerhood (roughly one to three years of age), the child begins to grapple with the issues of *autonomy* versus shame and doubt. As the toddler explores the environment and develops greater independence, there is usually a clash between what the child wants to do and what others want the child to do. Toilet training typically occurs during this time. In both physical and psychosocial development, this is a period of "letting go" and "holding on."

Turning our attention to Piaget's cognitive model, we find that the first two years of life are characterized as the *sensorimotor* period. During this period, the child develops and strengthens sensory and motor abilities, becoming acquainted with the body and learning about the environment. Because the child has not yet acquired the ability to name objects by use of language, this is not considered to be a period of conceptual development. A parent who leaves the room has simply vanished from the scene; there is no thought "My parent is in the other room." Piaget says, "As long as there is no subject, that is, as long as the child does not recognize itself as the origin of its own actions, it also does not recognize the permanency of objects other than itself."[5]

As the child accumulates experiences of the changing flow of events in the environment, he or she gradually begins to perceive patterns that become generalized into what Piaget terms "schemes." These schemes tie together the common features of actions occurring at different times. About this stage of development, Piaget says, "a Copernican revolution takes place," with the result that "at the end of this sensory-motor evolution, there are permanent objects, constituting a universe within which the child's own body exists also."

Early Childhood

During the years of preschool and kindergarten (roughly three to five years of age), a child's psychosocial development involves issues of *initiative* versus guilt. The child increasingly desires to find his or her own purpose and direction, yet is also concerned about how parents (and other significant adults) perceive these tentative efforts to express initiative and individuality. The egocentric orientation of the infant gives way to the socially integrated self of the older child, which assumes its place as one among many. This transition may involve situations that induce feelings of guilt. For instance, a child who

He lived a long way from here
Lew's mother explained.
You never asked
so I never told you
Grandpa died.

I want him to come back.
I miss him, Lewis said.
I have been waiting for him
and I miss him especially tonight.

I do too
said Lew's mother.
But you made him come back
for me tonight
by telling me what you remember.

Charlotte Zolotow, *My Grandson Lew*

has fantasies of doing away with a parent—expressed perhaps by the frustrated scream, "I wish you were dead!"—may feel guilt about having such thoughts. How others respond to this conflict is important in determining whether the crisis is resolved positively for the child's development. This period marks the beginning of the child's moral sense, the ability to function within socially sanctioned modes of behavior.

Among the fears that may manifest during this period is that of bodily mutilation. Children at this age are racing around on tricycles or big wheels, learning to cut small pieces of paper very precisely, making their muscles work for them, gaining greater control over their bodies. The body is important to the child's self-image. This preoccupation with the body can be illustrated: A five-year-old witnessed the death of his younger brother, who was killed when the wheel of a truck rolled over his head. The parents, who were considering having a wake in their home, asked their surviving son how he might feel if his younger brother's body was brought into the house for a wake. His question was, "Does he look hurt?" This child's concern about bodily disfigurement is characteristic of this stage of psychosocial development (see Figure 10-3).

In Piaget's model, the years of early childhood are characterized as the *preoperational* period. Cognitive development centers on learning to use language and symbols to represent objects. Vocabulary develops at an astounding rate as the child becomes interested in naming everything in sight. During this period, the child's primary task is to explore and appraise his or her situation in the world. Whereas during the sensorimotor period the child perceives the subjective and objective worlds as more or less fused into a single reality, now the child seeks causes and explanations.

How does Piaget's model of cognitive development apply to children's concepts of death? A partial answer is supplied by a study conducted by Gerald Koocher.[6] After being tested to determine which of Piaget's periods he or she fit into, each child was asked four questions about death. You might want to answer each of these questions for yourself.

Figure *10-3*   *Accident Drawing by a Five-Year-Old*
In this drawing by a five-year-old who witnessed his younger brother's accidental death, the surviving child is depicted as riding a "big wheel" on
the left side of the truck that ran over his brother. The four wheels of the
truck are shown, and the younger brother's head is drawn next to the
wheel farthest to the right. This drawing is similar to one drawn by the
child on the night of the fatal accident when he told his parents, "I can't
sleep because I can't get the pictures out of my head." The act of external-
izing these disturbing images by making a drawing had therapeutic value
for this child in coming to terms with the traumatic experience of his
sibling's death.

The first question was, "What makes things die?" Children in the preoperational stage used fantasy reasoning, magical thinking, and realistic causes of
death (sometimes expressed in egocentric terms). Here are sample responses:

- Nancy: "When they eat bad things, like if you went with a stranger and
  they gave you a candy bar with poison on it. [*The researcher asks, "Anything else?"*] Yes, you can die if you swallow a dirty bug."
- Carol: "They eat poison and stuff, pills. You'd better wait until your Mom
  gives them to you. [*Anything else?*] Drinking poison water and stuff like
  going swimming alone."
- David: "A bird might get real sick and die if you catch it. [*Anything else?*]
  They could eat the wrong foods like aluminum foil. That's all I can
  think of."

These findings received corroboration in a study done by Helen Swain.[7]
When the concept of finality was investigated, most of the children in Swain's

I was astonished to hear a highly intelligent boy of ten remark after the sudden death of his father: "I know father's dead, but what I can't understand is why he doesn't come home to supper."

Sigmund Freud, *The Interpretation of Dreams*

study expressed the notion that death was reversible. They attributed the return of life to the good effects of ambulances, hospitals, or doctors whose participation is often summoned magically, as if a dead person could ring up the hospital and say, "Will you send me an ambulance over here? I'm dead and I need you to fix me up."

About two-thirds of Swain's study group said that death is unlikely or avoidable, or is brought on only by unusual events such as an accident or catastrophe. About one-third expressed disbelief that death could happen to them or to their families. Nearly half were uncertain whether they would ever die or else thought they would die only in the remote future.

The Middle Years of Childhood

In Erikson's model, the years from about six to eleven generally correspond to the stage of *industry* versus inferiority. This is typically a time when the child is busy in school, interacting with peers in a variety of ways. As the child's efforts begin to gain recognition and bring satisfaction, there may be anxieties about those areas in which the child senses a failure to measure up. Overcoming these feelings of inadequacy or inferiority becomes the major task of this psychosocial stage. As in all of the psychosocial stages, encouragement from others is crucial to the child's well-being.

In Piaget's framework, this period is denoted by the term *concrete operations*. The child begins to use logic to solve problems and to think logically about things without having to have their relationships demonstrated directly. The ability to do arithmetic, for instance, requires the recognition that numbers are symbols for quantities. Children at this stage are able to manipulate such concepts in a logical fashion, although they are typically unable to engage in abstract thinking. That is, the ability to think logically can be applied to objects, but not yet to hypotheses, which require the ability to carry out operations on operations. Thus, the characteristic mode of thought in this period emphasizes the concreteness and the logic of *things*. Children can think forward and backward in time, and they demonstrate an appreciation of time as "passing," although their comprehension of such measurements as time and space does not yet allow them to manipulate these concepts with the flexibility or abstraction that comes with the ability to engage in formal operations of thought.

During this period of development, children tend to name both intentional and unintentional means by which a person may die. The child is familiar with a wide range of causes of death. Here are some responses from the children in Koocher's study when asked about causes of death:

- Todd: "Knife, arrow, guns, and lots of stuff. You want me to tell you all of them? [*As many as you want.*] Hatchets and animals, and fires and explosions, too."
- Kenny: "Cancer, heart attacks, poison, guns, bullets, or if someone drops a boulder on you."
- Deborah: "Accidents, cars, guns, or a knife. Old age, sickness, taking dope, or drowning."

Adolescence

According to the model of psychosocial development, the years of adolescence are marked by the milestone of establishing an individual *identity*. This period is an important time of personality development. A bridge must be established between the past—the years of childhood and dependency—and the future—the years of adulthood and independence. Thus, it is a period of integration as well as separation.

Remember what it's like being a teenager? Becoming more your own person? Striving to express your own ideas and beliefs? Sorting out the unbelievable tangle of all that's happening to you? Deciding what you want for your life? These years can be confusing and challenging. With the desire for a greater sense of one's own identity—an answer to the question "Who am I?"—there may also come anxieties about framing an adequate answer. Adolescents are just on the edge of beginning to achieve what they want for themselves. The achievement of their goals and dreams seems nearly within their grasp. Death represents a threat to that achievement.

When a major publishing company ran a "young adult" novel competition, the editors were initially surprised to find that the submissions from adolescents predominantly revealed what they called negative themes—illness, death of a loved one, suicide, loss. One editor commented that this result indicated "that kids are writing about what they want to know about."

In Piaget's theory, the years of adolescence are characterized by the term *formal operations*. Marking the fourth and final phase of cognitive development, this period begins at about the age of eleven or twelve and extends into adulthood, although a person's fundamental way of seeing the world is thought to be fairly well established by about the age of fifteen. With the arrival of formal operational thinking, the child is able to "think about thinking"—that is, to formulate or master concepts that are purely abstract or symbolic. As the end point of a complex process of cognitive development, this period is characterized by highly sophisticated operations of thought.

Relations of correspondence or implication between complex sets of statements can be perceived, analogies recognized, and assumptions or deductions made. Such operations make it possible to predict outcomes without having to try them out in the real world. In a chess game, for example, formal operations of thought allow the player to consider a number of complicated strategies, and to predict the likely result of each move, without having to touch a single piece on the board. Likewise, by mentally manipulating related ideas and possibilities, the child can hypothesize the implications of an ethical or political issue. The child is capable of using analysis and reflection to make sense of his or her experience and to formulate a coherent model of the world.

By this point children typically demonstrate possession of a mature concept of death: They understand that death is inevitable and irreversible, that it involves the cessation of physiological functioning, and that it results from biological causes. Although in Koocher's study most of the children who used formal operations of thought were twelve or older, some were as young as nine or ten. The mature understanding of death is reflected in responses to the question "What makes things die?"

- Ed: "You mean death in a physical sense? [*Yes*]. Destruction of a vital organ or life force within us."
- George: "They get old and their body gets all worn out, and their organs don't work as well as they used to."
- Paula: "When the heart stops, blood stops circulating. You stop breathing, and that's it. [*Anything else?*] Well, there's lots of ways it can get started, but that's what really happens."

The Evolution of a Mature Concept of Death

Through successive periods of cognitive development, children's responses to the question "What makes things die?" reflect progress toward a mature understanding of death. Answers to the other questions asked by Koocher also elicited differences corresponding to developmental stages— preoperational, concrete operational, and formal operational. Asked "How do you make dead things come back to life?" children who conceived of death as reversible gave answers like: "You can help them; give them hot food and keep them healthy so it won't happen again." Another child said, "No one ever taught me about that, but maybe you could give them some kind of medicine and take them to the hospital to get better." Children in later developmental stages, however, were able to recognize death as permanent: "If it was a tree, you could water it. If it's a person, you could rush them to the emergency room, but it would do no good if they were dead already." Another child said, "Maybe some day we'll be able to do it, but not now. Scientists are working on that problem."

Asked "When will you die?" children in the preoperational period provided answers ranging from "When I'm seven" (from a six-year-old) to "Three hundred years." In contrast, older children typically expected to live out a

Hasse Persson, UPI/Bettmann Newsphotos

The classmates of a murdered child carry his coffin to the grave. The rituals and ceremonies surrounding death can provide an avenue for children and adolescents to express their grief and to begin the process of coming to terms with loss.

statistically correct lifespan, or a bit more; the usual age at which death was expected was about eighty.

In answer to the researchers' fourth question, "What will happen when you die?" one nine-and-a-half-year-old said, "They'll help me come back alive." The researcher asked, "Who?" "My father, my mother, and my grandfather," the child responded. "They'll keep me in bed and feed me and keep me away from rat poison and stuff." According to some early developmental models of how children learn about death, a child of nine would understand that none of those measures would work. Thus, this example illustrates the point that age-and-stage correlations provide, at best, a rule of thumb concerning how children develop. As with any *model* of human behavior, the age–stage developmental framework is indicative, not rigorously descriptive.

In answer to the same question, an eight-and-a-half-year-old replied, "You go to heaven and all that will be left of you will be a skeleton. My friend has some fossils of people. A fossil is just a skeleton." Notice how the child makes use of comparison to help interpret what happens when death occurs. An eleven-year-old said, "I'll feel dizzy and tired and pass out, and then they'll bury me and I'll rot away. You just disintegrate and only your bones will be left."

A twelve-year-old said, "I'll have a nice funeral and be buried and leave all my money to my son." One ten-year-old said, "If I tell you, you'll laugh." The researcher assured the child, "No, I won't, I want to know what you really think." Thus encouraged, the child continued, "I think I'm going to be reincarnated as a plant or animal, whatever they need at that particular time." The ability to imagine what things might be like in the future is seen in these responses.

Play activities can help children deal with evolving concerns about death. Play can be a means of exorcising fears, trying out roles, making decisions, investigating consequences of actions, experimenting with value judgments, and finding a comfortable self-image.[8] Games like cowboys and Indians and cops and robbers reflect, in part, the child's attempt to reach some understanding about the place of death in his or her world.

Early Childhood Encounters with Death

When does a child first become aware of death? By the time children are four or five, death-related thoughts and experiences are usually evident in their songs, their play, and their questions. Although the awareness of death among younger children is not so readily observed (and, of course, is manifested differently from that of older children), researchers suggest that such experiences begin quite early.[9] The infant's experience of the difference between sleep and wakefulness may involve a perception of the distinction between being and nonbeing. Children begin to experiment with this difference at a very early age. The "peekaboo" game, for instance, may represent the polarities of being and nonbeing. The infant's experience of having a cloth

Small boy. "Where do animals go when they die?"
Small girl. "All good animals go to heaven, but the bad ones go to the Natural History Museum."

Caption to drawing by E. H. Shepard, *Punch,* 1929

thrown over her face, shutting out sensory awareness of the environment, is analogous to death. The "boo," when the cloth is removed, is like being alive again. Thus, death may be experienced in games of this kind as separation, disappearance, and return.

The child's earliest encounter with death usually comes with the ability to distinguish between the animate and the inanimate. The child perceives whether or not something has life. The following story illustrates how this may occur in quite ordinary circumstances. An eighteen-month-old boy was out for a walk with his father when the father inadvertently stepped on a caterpillar. The child kneeled down, looked at the dead caterpillar lying on the sidewalk, and said, "No more!" That is the typical genesis of a child's awareness of death: *No more.*

It should be recognized that similar experiences may produce quite different responses in different children. Encountering a dead caterpillar or dead bird may set off a reaction in one child that lasts for several days, during which time the child is eager to find answers. Another child may pay such an encounter little heed, apparently without a moment's reflection about an event that the first child found provocative and mysterious.

Some theorists believe that much of the behavior shown by infants and very young children is *protothanatic*—that is, preparation for concepts about life and death that will eventually emerge in the child's later interactions with the environment. To what degree such early experiences influence the child's later concepts about death is not clear. However, there is general agreement that children do exhibit some awareness of death quite early.

Psychoanalytic theory suggests that our earliest experiences of separation and loss mark the beginning of death-related anxieties that continue throughout life.[10] According to this view, the infant's lack of physical and psychological resources of self-care leads to anxiety, which is mitigated by the parent's nurture and care.

A central feature of an infant's existence is helplessness. From the infant's perspective, care takes place because of his or her own control over the environment. The infant's cries result in some action on the parent's part to relieve the child's discomfort. Diapers are changed; the child is fed. It's as if imagining or thinking about the breast causes it to appear. The symbiotic union with the parent is so complete that there seems to be no separation between the child's subjective and objective realities.

"Peanuts," drawing by Charles Schulz, © 1995 United Feature Syndicate, Inc.

Inevitably, however, there will be times when the infant's attempt to satisfy needs meets with frustration. Over time, the infant gradually perceives that the parent is a separate entity; the child is a separate self. This perception is the beginning of a kind of love-hate relationship with the parent, who both satisfies and frustrates the striving to have needs met. If mother arrives at the crib for feeding because she has been wished there, then angry thoughts may lead to her disappearance. This kind of magical thinking, which operates on the premise that wishing something can make it a reality, equates separation or disappearance with nonbeing or "death."

The process of individuation, of arriving at a separate self-identity, occurs most notably within the context of the intimate bonding between an infant and parent, and anxiety is likely to be especially acute at the major turning points in a child's development—such as weaning, toilet training, beginning school, or the birth of siblings.

The fears associated with the separation-individuation process during infancy and early childhood may appear in an altered context during adolescence. Just as the infant comes to perceive separation from parents, so too the adolescent strives to come to terms with that separateness on a broader scale. Because the adolescent's developmental tasks with regard to forging an individual identity are conceptually quite different from the younger child's, the anxieties aroused by death also differ.

Death-Experienced Children, Ages One to Three

A study conducted by Mark Speece to investigate the impact of death experiences on children ages one to three suggests that very young children do make efforts to come to terms with death-related experiences.[11] Speece says, "It seems safe to conclude that death experiences occur in the lives of a sizable proportion of children of this age and that those children who do have such experiences attempt to deal with and integrate their specific death experiences into their understanding of the world in general."

Speece found that slightly over half of the children he studied had some experience with death: in some cases, a human death (for example, a grandmother, a cousin, a neighbor); in others, a nonhuman death such as that of a pet (most often birds, dogs, and fish). Speece found that these young children responded to death in observable ways. For example, some actively looked for the deceased pet or person. That these children were trying to come to terms with the experience of death was indicated by their questions about the immobility of the deceased and what happens after death, and by their expression of concerns for the welfare of the living. One child became angry when a pet bird that had died would not come back to life. Thus, the idea that very young children do not experience a meaningful response to the deaths occurring in their environment is falling away as new evidence reveals this notion to be a fallacy.

The Very Young Child and Death: An Example

So, how does one answer the question, "When does the understanding of death begin, and what governs its development?" The dialogue between a twenty-seven-month-old child and his psychologist father provides an illuminating and suggestive case study.[12] (Note how the father's professional skills in listening and his sensitivity to his child's behavior helped him engage in this kind of conversation.)

For two months the child had been waking several times each night and screaming hysterically for a bottle of sugar water. The father describes getting up one night, for the second or third time, and deciding with his wife to use firmness in refusing to meet the child's demand. He went into his son's room and told him that he was too old to have a bottle and would have to go back to sleep without it. The father, his mind made up that enough was enough, started to leave the room.

But then he heard a frightened cry, one of desperation that sounded like the fear of death. Wondering what could be causing the child such alarm, the father turned back into the room, took his son out of the crib, and asked, "What will happen if you don't get your bottle?" The child, no longer hysterical, but very tearful and sniffling, said, "I can't make contact!" The father asked, "What does that mean, 'you can't make contact'?" His son replied, "If I run out of gas, I can't make contact—my engine won't go. You know!"

The father then remembered several family excursions during the previous summer, when vehicles had run out of gas. "What are you afraid will happen if you run out of gas?" Still crying, the child replied, "My motor won't run and then I'll die." At that point, the father recalled another incident his son had witnessed. Some time earlier, when they were selling an old car, the prospective buyer had tried to start the engine, but the battery was dead and the engine wouldn't turn over. The child had heard remarks like, "It's probably *not making contact*," "the *motor died*," and "I guess *the battery's dead*."

With this incident in mind, the father asked, "Are you afraid that your bottle is like gasoline and, just like when the car runs out of gas, the car dies; so, if you run out of food, you'll die?" The child nodded his head, "Yes." The father explained, "Well, that's not the same thing at all. You see, when you eat food, your body stores up energy so that you have enough to last you all night. You eat three times a day; we only fill up the car with gas once a week. When the car runs out of gas, it doesn't have any saved up for an emergency. But with people it isn't anything like that at all. You can go maybe two or three days without eating. And, even if you got hungry, you still wouldn't die. People aren't anything like cars."

This explanation seemed to do little toward alleviating the child's anxiety, so the father tried a different tack. "You're worried that you have a motor, just like a car, right?" The child nodded, "Yes." "So," continued the father, "you're worried that if you run out of gas or run out of food you'll die, just like the motor of a car, right?" Again, the child nodded yes. "Ah, but the car has a key, right? We can turn it on and off anytime we want, right?"

Now the child's body began to relax. "But where is your key?" The father poked around the boy's belly button: "Is this your key?" The child laughed. "Can I turn your motor off and on? See, you're really nothing like a car at all. Nobody can turn you on and off. Once your motor is on, you don't have to worry about it dying. You can sleep through the whole night and your motor will keep running without you ever having to fill it up with gas. Do you know what I mean?" The child said, "Yes."

"Okay. Now you can sleep without worrying. When you wake in the morning, your motor will still be running. Okay?" Never again did the child wake up in the middle of the night asking for a bottle of warm sugar water.

Think of the impressive reasoning that goes on in a child's mind—the way of stringing together concepts. In this case, the father speculates that two experiences contributed to his child's understanding: First, the child had decided that sugar water would give him gas because he had overheard his parents saying that a younger sibling had "gas" from drinking sugar water; second, when the child's parakeet died, his question "What happened to it?" was answered by his father: "Every animal has a motor inside that keeps it going. When a thing dies, it is like when a motor stops running. Its motor just won't run anymore."

A child's understanding of death is composed of a series of concepts, strung together like beads in a strand that is worked with until it eventually becomes a necklace, a coherent understanding of death. The description of this twenty-seven-month-old's complex associations of language and death demonstrates that children are capable of formulating some understanding about death very early in life.

Major Causes of Death in Childhood and Adolescence

Death is often viewed as appropriate only when it comes in old age. Confronting the death of a child uncovers our uneasiness about death in a more dramatic way than when death is seen as the culmination of a long life. A child's death underscores the truth that no one is immune to death.

When I am dead, and laid in grave,
And all my bones are rotten,
By this may I remembered be
When I should be forgotten.

On a girl's sampler, 1736

As the most prominent cause of death during the first half of the human lifespan, accidental injury has been characterized as "the last major plague of the young."[13] Reviewing the main causes of death among children between the ages of five and fourteen, we find that accidents top the list (with a death rate of 9.3 per 100,000), followed by cancer (3.0), homicide (1.6), congenital anomalies (1.2), suicide (0.9), heart disease (0.8), HIV infection (0.3), and pneumonia and influenza (0.3).[14] Of the deaths resulting from accidents in this age group, over half involved motor vehicles.

Injury is devastating to a young person, emotionally as well as physically. Whether or not death results, injury involves significant losses, and when a young person bears responsibility for a peer's injury or death because of an accident, as in alcohol-related and drug-related incidents, the felt loss can be severe. If a person feels that he or she played a role in the events that led to the disability or death of a friend or other loved one, guilt may predominate among the emotions experienced after the loss.

To illustrate, in one situation, involving three brothers playing with a loaded gun, the youngest pushed the oldest, who held the gun, as the bullet was discharged, killing the third sibling. "I have always struggled with myself about whether my brother would have died if I hadn't tried to push my other brother away," said a thirty-year-old man, recalling events that had taken place more than a quarter of a century earlier. "I always thought I did the right thing, but no one ever told me or even talked with me about my feelings. For years, I cried myself to sleep alone in my bed at night." Because accidents occur suddenly and unexpectedly, allowing no time to prepare for the outcome, their aftermath can be especially shocking and devastating to survivors.

Children with Life-Threatening Illnesses

Although more children and adolescents die from injuries received in accidents than from the effects of disease, the situation confronting the child with a life-threatening illness is one of special poignancy. Perhaps we feel, justifiably or not, that an accident is something that just "happens" and is, therefore, not preventable, whereas we expect medicine to provide a cure for disease. In this section, we turn our attention to the ways children perceive an

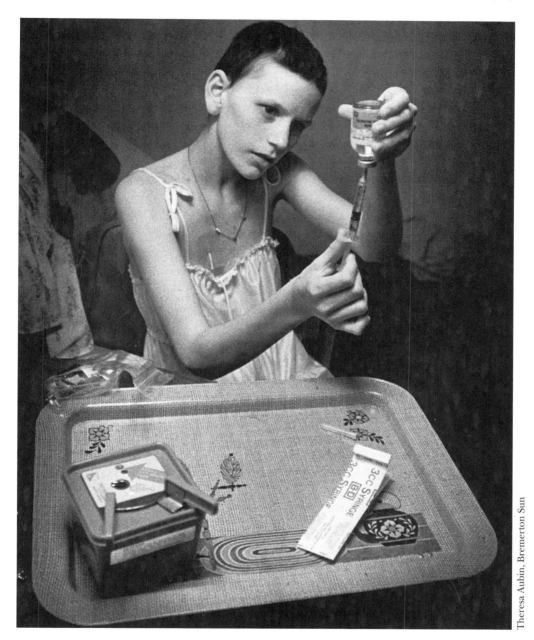

Adolescents and older children with life-threatening illnesses may take on increasing responsibilities for their daily treatment regimes. Here, a young cancer patient flushes her venous access catheter, the route used to administer chemotherapy, which must be cleaned nightly.

experience with life-threatening illness and how they cope with that reality in their lives.

The Child's Perception of Illness

A child's inquisitiveness about his or her illness and its prognosis may be painful for parents and other adults to confront. The child's questions may be met with silence or other forms of avoidance. Is it ethical, or even possible, to withhold information about a serious or life-threatening illness from a child? This question poses a dilemma for those who might wish to keep disturbing news from a child. William Bartholome observes that "The most daunting problem facing parents and caregivers who are caring for a terminally ill child is that the person they are caring for lives in a different reality."[15]

Based on her study of children in a leukemia ward, Myra Bluebond-Langner concluded that children are usually able to guess their condition by interpreting how people behave toward them.[16] For example, children interpret behaviors such as crying or avoidance as indicating the seriousness of their illness and their nearness to dying. Children in the leukemia ward, most of whom were between the ages of three and nine, could assess the seriousness of their illness even though no one had told them that they were very sick or that they were going to die. Although the children sometimes discussed their illnesses with their peers, they refrained from doing so with adults. Apparently perceiving that their conversations made adults uncomfortable, the children talked about the taboo topic among themselves, much as children discuss other forbidden topics, out of range of an adult's hearing.

Bluebond-Langner also observed that the children's interpretations of their conditions changed over time; the illness was first perceived as acute, then chronic, and finally fatal. Similarly, medications were first "healing agents," then "something that prolongs life." As their perception of drugs progressed from something that was "always effective" to "effective sometimes" to "not really effective at all," their behaviors toward taking medication changed likewise. The children generally knew a great deal about the world of the hospital, its staff and procedures, and the experiences of leukemic children. Most were aware of the condition of other children, making comments like "Jeffrey's in his first relapse" and noticing when other children died. Although many children did not know the proper name for their disease, they typically displayed considerable knowledge about its treatment and prognosis.

Fears and Anxieties

Seriously ill children may need "mental first aid" to help them cope with their thoughts and emotions. This may mean simply comforting the child and being supportive through a difficult or painful procedure, or it may require more substantive intervention to successfully deal with anxiety, guilt, anger, or other conflicting or unresolved emotions. Whereas some children seem to cope with traumatic experiences without requiring much outside help, others need support to cope with relatively minor crises. Working with children requires a flexible approach. A child who feels unsupported or unsure about what is happening can experience fantasies that are more frightening than the truth. An atmosphere of support and encouragement in which the child and the parents feel free to express their fears and concerns can alleviate anxiety as well as diminish the child's feelings of separation and loneliness.

Family members can be encouraged to participate in the child's care. Although professional caregivers are equipped to provide for the child's medical needs, a parent's special expertise lies in the nontechnical aspects of child care. Activities such as bathing the child, assisting at meal times, tucking the child in at night, and providing emotional support are all tasks wherein a parent can be involved to the benefit of everyone concerned. However, parents should be wary about performing procedures that might cause the child pain. The parent who helps with a painful procedure may be seen by the child as causing or intensifying pain. Parents should devote their attention to providing comfort and support. Shirley Steele says, "Parents should be helped to participate in the role of a parent rather than trying to play the role of a nurse."[17]

Researchers who have studied seriously ill and dying children report that the primary concern of such children relates to fears of pain and separation. The main sources of stress for hospitalized dying children can be summarized as: (1) separation from the mother (or mother figure), (2) painful or traumatic procedures, and (3) the deaths of other children. Development of the concept of death during childhood is reflected in the sequence of major concerns experienced by sick children. For example, children under five years old tend to be most distressed by separation from the mother. Children in the middle group, roughly ages five to nine, tend to be most concerned about the discomforting and possibly disfiguring effects of the disease and related medical procedures. Older children are likely to experience anxiety caused by awareness of other children's deaths. These findings are consistent with the developmental model: Separation anxiety is typical of the young child; a personification of death, with fears about mutilation and pain, predominates during the middle years of childhood; and older children exhibit anxiety related to the deaths of other children, corresponding to a more mature understanding of death as final and universal. Terminally ill children tend to have a greater awareness of death than do their healthier counterparts.

Children who are dying as a result of perinatally acquired HIV infection represent an especially heartrending case. Typically, their lives are subjected to extraordinary disruption, accompanied by the loss of any sense of security. As Sara Dubik-Unruh says, such children are often members of "dying families."[18] These families may be affected by a multitude of crisis situations, including incarceration, addiction, illness, abandonment or court removal of children, hospitalization, separation from parents and siblings, and homelessness. It is estimated that between one-fourth and one-third of infants with AIDS are not cared for by their biological parents. Dubik-Unruh points out, "The situation of a child who is already ill, who loses one parent, moves from one temporary placement to another, experiences multiple changes in caretakers, and ultimately loses the remaining parent and/or siblings, is staggering to imagine." Negative attitudes expressed by the wider public community can also have a harmful impact on the emotional well-being of these children. Dubik-Unruh concludes that the care of these children "must include their emotional well-being as well as their physical health, to enable those children who do survive to face the future with strength, and to allow those children who do not survive to live the remainder of their lives with their innocence and childhood intact, and their personal integrity respected."

Hospital and Home Care

Illness separates children from the people and the surroundings that are familiar and loved. Besides physical pain, anguish may be felt because of the child's inability to engage in the activities and pursuits of healthy children. The sick child misses school, is restricted from playtime activities, and becomes enmeshed in a more or less alien world of hospitals and medical paraphernalia. Even when a child has grown somewhat accustomed to life in and out of the hospital, new forms of treatment and unfamiliar medical settings or personnel can be upsetting. Change of routine brings added fears and anxieties. This reaction can occur in varying degrees regardless of efforts by hospital staff to create a special environment for sick children.[19] Nursing educator Donna Juenker points out, "Each time a child returns to the hospital he is literally a different person. He is at a wholly new stage of development with correspondingly different fears and expectations."[20]

As with terminally ill adults, various programs exist for providing care to terminally ill children, including hospices specifically designed to meet the needs of children. More common is the practice of home-based palliative care, which many caregivers believe provides significant practical and emotional benefits for terminally ill children, their parents, and their siblings.[21] Whatever the setting—hospital, hospice, or home—families experiencing a child's serious illness and impending death need appropriate professional and community support.[22]

The Child's Coping Mechanisms

The seriously ill child is not simply a passive participant in the medical and social circumstances surrounding the illness. A child experiences psychosocial concerns related to absence from school, changes in family patterns, the threat of increased dependency on others, and the financial or emotional strain on his or her family. Medical concerns relate to the visibility of the illness, physical discomfort, and the symbolic significance attached to the part of the body affected. How a child perceives the illness and the manner in which he or she responds to it depends on age, the nature of the illness and its treatment, family relationships, and past experience.

Sick children use various coping mechanisms to deal with the anxiety and confusion that accompany life-threatening illness. Although a child's developmental stage influences the level of awareness and the kinds of coping mechanisms available, even very young children may exhibit a surprisingly wide range of resources for coping with the prospect of death.

Children with life-threatening illnesses frequently use distancing strategies to limit the number of people with whom they have close relationships. This reduces the risk of a distressing interaction because it allows fewer opportunities for such an occurrence. Using such a strategy, a child selects from the total situation only those aspects or those people that he or she finds least threatening. In this way, the child attempts to construct as safe and secure an environment as possible given the circumstances.

At various times, a child may try to avoid stress by denying the reality of the situation or withdrawing from a potentially stressful situation. The child may cope with a painful procedure by rationalizing that it will help effect a cure. Or the painful treatment may be balanced in the child's mind by making a deal that allows some desire to be fulfilled once the pain is endured. For example, a child asks, "After I get my shot, can I play with my toys?" Some children cope by regressing to a pattern of behavior that reflects a less-demanding, more-comfortable time in their lives. For example, a child may regress to the use of baby talk or "forget" his or her toilet training.

Sublimation or goal substitution is another way that children cope with the infringements of serious illness. For example, a child who is prevented by illness from engaging in a competitive sport may find a substitute for the desired activity by playing board games in a highly competitive way. One might envision scenes of sick children racing through the hospital corridors, IV bottles swinging from their wheelchairs, in a spontaneous competition.

Such coping mechanisms enable children to deal with the uncomfortable and frightening aspects of illness. How a particular child copes with illness depends not only on the circumstances, but also on the child's *perception* of its meaning and consequences.

Children as Survivors of a Close Death

Nearly all parents would wish to spare their children the pain of bereavement. Sometimes rather grand attempts are made to minimize the effects of a loss when it occurs in a child's life. The death of a pet, for example, may be swiftly followed by its replacement with another animal. At best, such a course of action has limited usefulness. Death is a fact of life that eventually cannot be ignored. A more constructive approach when such losses occur is to help the

Suddenly the feeling that this was all just a dream ended. Christopher was angry. It wasn't fair. Why did that dumb man have to hit Bodger?

"I ought to run *him* over with a truck."

"Oh, honey, Bodger ran right in front of him. The man didn't have time to stop."

They took Christopher home to bed where he relived the accident over and over in his mind. He tried to pretend that the truck had missed the dog, or that he hadn't called and Bodger had stayed on the other side. Or he pretended that they hadn't left the dirt road where there were hardly ever any cars. Or that they had stayed home and waited.

But the bad dream always rolled on out of his control until the moment when Bodger was lying in the road.

Carol and Donald Carrick, *The Accident*

child explore his or her feelings about death and develop an appropriate understanding of it.

The Bereaved Child's Experience of Grief

Children are capable of experiencing grief. A bereaved child can experience the same kind of physical and emotional symptoms as adults, including lack of appetite, insomnia, nightmares, and nausea. Although children tend to exhibit considerable resiliency in coping with tragedy, adults can nevertheless help by being willing to listen to the child's expressions of mourning and to communicate and demonstrate support for the child's well-being.

A child's response to loss is similar in many respects to that of adults, but a particular child's experience will reflect the influence of such factors as age, stage of mental and emotional development, patterns of interaction and communication within the family, degree of relationship with the person who has died, and previous experiences with death.[23] Sudden, unexpected death or death as a result of suicide or homicide are added factors that the child must face in coming to terms with loss.[24]

Even among children of the same age, significant differences can be observed with respect to their ability to comprehend death and cope with its effects. For example, one five-year-old might seem devastated by the death of a parent; another child of the same age and similar circumstances might appear to be comparatively unaffected. The first child may put forth intense effort in trying to come to terms with the loss. The second child, in contrast, may seem satisfied with the brief explanation that "Daddy's gone and he won't ever be coming back." Which of these children do you believe exhibits the healthier response to loss?

As you may have guessed, such a question is inappropriate because not enough is known about each child to allow framing an adequate reply.

Suppose, however, that the first child's pattern of coping involves a period of acute grief, followed by acceptance and integration of the loss. Suppose, further, that the second child's apparent indifference is only transitory, a temporary state of mind that is followed by a protracted and painful process of coming to terms with the death, a process that may continue into adolescence or even adulthood before the loss is satisfactorily resolved. As this example suggests, it is not always possible to rely on appearances to assess how a child is coping with loss.

Children may cope with loss by selectively forgetting, or by reconstructing reality in a more desirable and comfortable way. For example, a child may not recall how frightened he was by the sight of a sibling lying in a hospital bed surrounded by awesome medical paraphernalia, or the memory of a protracted illness with long stays in the hospital may be reconstructed so that it seems as if the sibling were only away from home briefly for a few tests. The forgotten details or reconstructed images allow the child to cope with the experience without being overwhelmed by painful memories. At the same time, a child's experience of death can stimulate the development of more mature concepts about death.[25] Although age and cognitive development affect a child's response to loss, many other variables are at work, not least of which are the attitudes exhibited by the significant adults in the child's life.

The Death of a Pet

Often, a child's first experience with death involves a pet, a situation that is not surprising considering that about 63 million cats, 55 million dogs, and 25 million birds are kept as pets in the United States. When a pet dies, parents may wonder how best to help their child cope with the loss. Should one try to minimize the child's loss? Or should the death be seen as a natural opportunity for the child to consider what death means and to explore his or her feelings about the loss?

One mother described the responses of her daughters to the deaths of a new litter of baby rabbits.[26] Upon learning the news, the seven-year-old burst into tears and howled, "I don't want them dead." The five-year-old at first stood silently and then asked to call her father at work. She told him, "If you had been here, Daddy, you could have been the rabbits' doctor," reflecting a belief, appropriate for her age, that it should have been possible somehow to save the baby rabbits or restore them to life. Later, when the children began to dig a grave to bury the dead rabbits, the seven-year-old stopped crying for the first time since learning the news, while the five-year-old kept repeating, "The baby rabbits are dead, the baby rabbits are dead," in a monotone.

In the days following the rabbits' deaths, the girls asked many questions. The seven-year-old was particularly interested in questioning a family friend who was a widow about her dead husband. How often did she think about him and why did people have to be taken away from those who loved them, she wanted to know. The five-year-old, meanwhile, continued to mourn silently until her mother encouraged her to express her feelings. Then she

Children can feel strong attachment to their pets. Involving a child in the experience of a pet's death through ritual or discussion provides a means of coping with the loss.

began to sob. Finally, she said, "I'm glad I'm only five, you only die when you're old."

The younger child's first concern was for herself, the fear that she herself could die. The older child, conversely, worried about the durability of relationships. Although each child had a distinctive response to the loss, both children showed a need to be close to their parents during the days following the deaths of the rabbits, and they told the story of the rabbits' deaths again and again as they dealt with their experience.

Of course, it is not just children who are affected by the death of a pet. A woman described the reaction of her husband to the death of Iggy, a desert iguana.[27] When the iguana died, she reported that her husband "cried throughout the shoebox burial in the backyard." He later said that he was crying "for every pet he had ever loved and lost."

Attachments between humans and pets can be very strong. Yet mourning the loss of a pet sometimes elicits ridicule. Some may say that the bereaved pet owner is overreacting. After all "it was only an animal, a mere pet." Those who counsel individuals who are grieving over the loss of a pet emphasize that feelings should be expressed by adults as well as children. As for replacing a pet, sufficient time should be allowed to mourn the loss before a new animal is acquired. This may take weeks or months, perhaps longer. The bonds of attachment to the pet that has died may jeopardize a healthy transition of affections to another animal if the natural process of grief has been prematurely curtailed or ignored.

A sign of the increasing attention given to mourning the loss of a pet can be seen in the growth of pet cemeteries. The International Pet Cemetery Association reports a total of 400 pet cemeteries in the United States, with the oldest dating back to the 1800s.[28] The appropriateness of grief over the death of a pet has also been acknowledged by veterinarians, some of whom send contributions to pet care research institutions as a memorial to a deceased pet. A major greeting card company recently introduced sympathy cards expressing condolences with respect to the loss of a pet. When the bond between a pet and its owner is broken by death, the significance of that loss is increasingly recognized as a natural occasion for mourning.[29] Indeed, as Avery Weisman observes, "The depth of a human-animal bond often exceeds that between a person and close kith and kin."[30] Thus, mourning for a dead pet is an authentic and normal experience for adults as well as children.

The Death of a Parent

Of all the deaths that may be experienced in childhood, the most affecting is considered to be the death of a parent.[31] A parent's death is perceived as a loss of security, nurture, and affection—a loss of the emotional and psychological support upon which the child could formerly rely. Based on data obtained from the Child Bereavement Study, Phyllis Silverman and her colleagues conclude that children who have lost a parent typically establish a set of memories, feelings, and actions that serve to aid the child in "reconstruct-ing" an image of the dead parent.[32] This reconstruction involves building an inner representation that helps the child remain in relationship with the deceased, and "this relationship changes as the child matures and as the intensity of grief lessens." As with the emerging shift in models of grief (dis-cussed in Chapter 7), the child negotiates and renegotiates the meaning of the loss over time, rather than severing the attachment. The loss is permanent and unchanging; the process of coping with it is not.

Sometimes feelings of guilt result from what the child imagines to be actions that in some way contributed to a parent's death. For example, a child whose parent died of a terminal illness might remember particular instances when she was noisy and her sick parent needed rest. "Perhaps if I had been less noisy," the child thinks, "Mom would have gotten well." As proof of this imagined connection between the child's behavior and the parent's death, the child may cite the fact that "Mom went away and never came back to us." Such feelings are typical of the responsibility that children may assume as they try to understand a close death.

When the death of a parent affects a very young child, the emotional components of grief may focus on mourning the years of relationship that were lost as a result of the parent's premature death. This is a common occurrence, for example, when the parent's death happened in connection with war. There can be a lingering sense of "never having known" the de-ceased parent. Conflicting emotions may lie buried for a considerable time until some stimulus—perhaps the discovery of the parent's military papers or a visit to a memorial for the fallen combatants—brings the unresolved loss to the surface. Sharing the loss with others who are similarly situated can aid healing, even many years later. Some of the children of individuals who died in Vietnam have found solace through joining together in a national support organization, "Sons and Daughters in Touch," where they share a common bond in their efforts to come to terms with the death of their parent.[33] These efforts include talking to other veterans to fill in the picture of a deceased parent the child was never able to fully know.

A child's experience as a survivor may also give rise to feelings of guilt or uncertainty. A drawing made by a four-year-old whose father had died of leukemia illustrates this (see Figure 10-4). Some time after his father's death, as the child was playing with pencils and drawing paper, he asked his mother how to spell various words. Attracted by the child's activity, his mother noticed that he had drawn a picture of his father. In the drawing the father was saying to the child, "I am mad at you!" Surprised at this depiction of her husband's anger toward her son, the mother asked, "Why should your father have been mad at you?" The child explained, "Because you and I can still play together and Dad isn't with us anymore." Amid the confusing feelings resulting from his father's death, the child was attempting to come to terms with the fact of his survivorship.

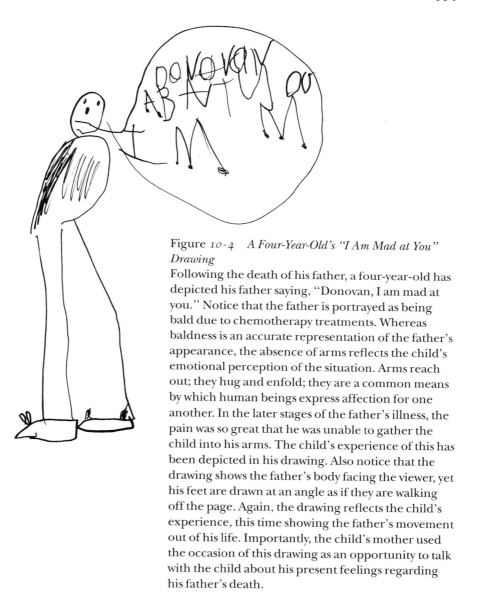

**Figure 10-4 *A Four-Year-Old's "I Am Mad at You"
Drawing***
Following the death of his father, a four-year-old has
depicted his father saying, "Donovan, I am mad at
you." Notice that the father is portrayed as being
bald due to chemotherapy treatments. Whereas
baldness is an accurate representation of the father's
appearance, the absence of arms reflects the child's
emotional perception of the situation. Arms reach
out; they hug and enfold; they are a common means
by which human beings express affection for one
another. In the later stages of the father's illness, the
pain was so great that he was unable to gather the
child into his arms. The child's experience of this has
been depicted in his drawing. Also notice that the
drawing shows the father's body facing the viewer, yet
his feet are drawn at an angle as if they are walking
off the page. Again, the drawing reflects the child's
experience, this time showing the father's movement
out of his life. Importantly, the child's mother used
the occasion of this drawing as an opportunity to talk
with the child about his present feelings regarding
his father's death.

Now, in working with this child as a survivor, his mother did a very wise
thing. She said, "Tell me about this picture." In other words, she asked
open-ended questions to elicit information about the child's feelings. This
allowed her to respond directly to the child's concerns. Spontaneous drawings
and other forms of art therapy are excellent methods for working with young

The Lesson

'Your father's gone,' my bald headmaster said.
His shiny dome and brown tobacco jar
Splintered at once in tears. It wasn't grief.
I cried for knowledge which was bitterer
Than any grief. For there and then I knew
That grief has uses—that a father dead
Could bind the bully's fist a week or two;
And then I cried for shame, then for relief.

I was a month past ten when I learnt this:
I still remember how the noise was stilled
In school-assembly when my grief came in.
Some goldfish in a bowl quietly sculled
Around their shining prison on its shelf.
They were indifferent. All the other eyes
Were turned towards me. Somewhere in myself
Pride, like a goldfish, flashed a sudden fin.

Edward Lucie-Smith

children to help them explore and express feelings that otherwise might remain hidden, yet be disturbing to them.[34] Using art with bereaved children helps them to work through grief by providing a safe, focused environment for expressing their concerns and feelings.[35]

The Death of a Sibling

Unlike a parent's death, a sibling's death rarely represents a loss of security for the surviving child. Still, the effect of such a close death may increase the surviving child's sense of vulnerability to death, especially when siblings are close to one another in age. The surviving child may experience a variety of responses to the death of a sibling. Perhaps the brother or sister was a protector, a caregiver as well as a playmate. The surviving child may be sad that this unique relationship has ended, worried that the protection and care given by the sibling is no longer available, and yet relieved or even pleased that, with the sibling's absence, he or she is now more the center of attention in the family. Such a mixture of emotions can produce guilt and confusion as a child comes to terms with the sibling's death.

For the adolescent survivor of a sibling's death, the struggle to come to terms with the loss may be intertwined with the developmental task of formulating a personal sense of the meaning of life, a task that typically involves intense questioning about the value of religious beliefs and the existence of God. David Balk points out that the death of a sibling shatters "trust in a benign, innocent universe" and "questions about the nature of life and death, about good and evil, and about the meaning of life become personal."[36] The

© Karen Saltzman

Siblings enjoy a special relationship, one conjoining both rivalries and mutual affection and love. The death of a brother or sister thus severs a unique human relationship. The surviving child may feel the loss more intensely because of an identification with the deceased brother or sister. The surviving child recognizes that he or she is also not immune to dying at an early age.

normal developmental struggles over religion become sharper-edged when an adolescent's sibling dies. Coping with a sibling's death can bring about a greater maturity in cognitive development, social reasoning, moral judgment, identity formation, and religious understanding. Indeed, bereaved young people often cite religion as an important resource for coping with loss, a source of meaning that provides solace as they search for significance in the aftermath of tragedy.

Children look to their parents for help in understanding the significance of a sibling's death and in coping with its effects on the family. The parents' methods of coping can play a large part in determining how the surviving child copes. Sometimes the parents' response to a child's death sets into motion dysfunctional family patterns that impair the surviving child's ability to cope. Such dysfunctional responses range from overt resentment of the surviving child to attempts to recreate in that child some of the qualities of the deceased child. The surviving child's feelings of rejection may be further complicated by feelings of guilt concerning a sibling's death. Such parental responses may be present to a lesser extent even among families that appear to be coping successfully. As parents try to come to terms with a child's death, they may unintentionally minimize contact with the surviving child. The living child can be a painful reminder of the child now lost. Conversely, parents may become overprotective of the surviving child.

The bereaved child must be given opportunities to acknowledge and express his or her grief. Feelings of guilt as well as sadness need to be explored and resolved in a loving and supportive atmosphere. When a child expresses guilt, one can ask, "What would it take to forgive yourself?" An open exploration allows the child to find personally satisfying ways of coping with a loved one's death. A surviving child's feelings of guilt are related to normal sibling rivalry. The sister at whom I angrily yell, "I hate you!" in the morning may be lying dead at the morgue in the afternoon, the victim of a bicycle accident. To a young child, the coincidence of anger directed toward a person and that person's subsequent death may be viewed as a cause-and-effect relationship.

This assumption of responsibility is sometimes displayed as a preoccupation with the "should haves." One five-year-old whose younger brother was run over by a truck while they were outside playing told his mother later, "I should have . . . I should have." He saw himself as his younger brother's protector, responsible for his safety. His mother asked him, "You should have what?" He replied, "I just should have!"

His mother then asked, "What do you mean, you 'should have'?" The boy answered, "I should have looked, I should have known, I should have—": a flood of "should haves" about being his brother's guardian and protector. Taking the child into her arms, his mother said, "I understand, honey. Daddy's got the 'should haves.' Mommy's got the 'should haves.' We all have them. It's okay to have them. And it's okay to know that everybody could have done something differently, and that they *would* have if they'd had a choice."

If a child believes that death is something that happens in old age, and then experiences the death of a younger sibling, how does the child reconcile

Figure *10-5* *A Five-Year-Old's "Crooked Day" Drawing*
In this drawing of "The Crooked Day," a five-year-old boy depicts his experience of the events that transpired on the day his brother received fatal injuries in an accident. Contrary to what might be assumed about this drawing, the places on the line where the greatest stress is indicated occurred after the accident itself. The sharp dip in the line at the left-hand side of the drawing represents the accident; the point at which the line crosses back on itself denotes the time when the surviving child was left with a neighbor while his parents were at the hospital with his brother. This was a period of uncertainty and confusion, and the child was angry about not being with the other members of his family. The point at which his parents returned and informed him of his brother's death is indicated by the vertical slash marks, which were literally stabbed onto the paper. The jagged line connoting the remainder of the day represents the emotional upheaval that occurred as the child and his parents together focused their attention on coping with the initial shock of their loss. Importantly, the drawing ends with an upward slanting line that is indicative of an essentially positive attitude—the child's ability to deal constructively with his experience of loss. This drawing demonstrates that even a simple artistic expression, such as a line depicting the chronology of events, can reveal a wealth of detail about a child's experience of a traumatic event such as death.

this clash between concept and experience? The primary means by which a child constructs a bridge between earlier notions about death and present reality is simply to observe how parents and other significant adults respond to the loss and express grief. Allowing a child to participate in the family's experience helps the child cope with crisis, as we see exemplified in a drawing by the five-year-old who saw his younger brother killed. The drawing represented "the day my brother was killed"; the point of greatest stress was shown to be the period of time when he was left at a neighbor's house while his parents were at the hospital (see Figure 10-5). Even more frightening than seeing the wheel of the truck roll over his brother's head was the feeling of being left alone, being separated from the rest of his family, not knowing what was happening with his parents and his younger brother.

This child's parents not only encouraged the child to express his feelings, they also sought out community resources as additional support for coping with the tragedy. Just as the child's work with spontaneous drawings helped bring to light his disturbance at being left out, the parents received support by sharing their experience with others who had survived similar experiences and by calling on therapeutic resources in their community.

When a Family Member Is Seriously Ill or Dying

When a member of a child's family is seriously ill, family routine is disrupted. If the child is kept from learning the truth about a parent's or sibling's illness, or if the family's style of communication is closed, he or she may become confused about the reasons for changes in the family's usual patterns of interaction. The child may feel rejected, left out of family activities, or ignored for no apparent reason: "Why are my parents so nice to my sister, but they ignore me all the time!" or "Geez, I get into trouble about every little thing while my brother gets off scot-free no matter what he does!"

Although openness is an important condition for helping a child cope with the crisis, explanations must be suited to the child's cognitive abilities. For example, a very young child whose parent is seriously ill might be told simply that "Mommy has an ouch in her tummy which the doctors are trying to fix." A school-age child, however, could be given a more complex explanation to the effect that the parent needs medical treatment because something is growing in her stomach that doesn't belong there.

The child who is aware of a parent's or sibling's illness may experience anxiety, which can be manifest in various ways. For example, a child may be angry because "Mommy isn't here," yet feel guilty because of imagined notions about "causing the illness." To help balance these conflicting feelings, the child can be encouraged to participate in comforting the sick family member in appropriate ways. A child might pick a bouquet or make a small drawing as a gift. This activity allows affirmation and expression of love and kindness despite possible feelings of anger or guilt.

Siblings who feel neglected because the family's attention is devoted more and more to a sick brother or sister may resent adjustments that have to be made in their own lives. Conflicting emotions can be balanced by accepting the well child as a fully participating family member who is given information and encouraged to be part of the process of dealing with the sibling's illness.[37] Including the child increases the likelihood that family communication and routines will be maintained. Myra Bluebond-Langer has aptly said: "The well siblings of terminally ill children live in houses of chronic sorrow."[38] Although children cannot be protected from the reality of death, their experiences of it can be made less traumatic when they receive sensitive, caring support from those closest to them.

Helping Children Cope with Change and Loss

How can a parent—or any caring person—help a child come to terms with the experience of loss? In the aftermath of death, what kind of assistance can be offered to a bereaved child? How do family patterns and styles of communication influence a child's ability to cope with change and loss?

Consider what it feels like for an adult to face the terminal illness or death of someone close. Now, how does this person explain these painful circumstances to a child? Because of the nature of the crisis, perhaps coupled with notions about a child's limited ability to understand, the child's feelings and concerns may be dismissed or ignored. Even adults who recognize that children need to know may be uncomfortable about exposing them to painful and disturbing news. Might knowing the truth cause a child more harm than good? In fact, a child's natural curiosity effectively removes the option of withholding information.

Children usually cope more easily with their feelings about a close death or serious illness of a family member when they are allowed to participate in the unfolding experience of grief and mourning. When they are excluded, or when their questions go unanswered, the resulting uncertainty in the child's mind generates additional anxiety, confusion, and pain. Sharing the reality of what is happening allows a child to begin to understand and cope with the experience.

Guidelines for Sharing Information

Although a child's experience of change and crisis is similar in some respects to an adult's, there are also significant differences. These differences in a child's manner of perceiving, experiencing, and coping with change need to be considered by parents and others who wish to be helpful to children in crisis. Responding to a child's natural inquisitiveness and concern about death and dying does not mean that one should overwhelm the child with excessive detail, nor does it mean talking down to the child as if he or she were incapable of comprehending at all. Rather, it implies an openness in responding to the child's concerns within the context of his or her ability to understand. In talking to a child about death, it is important to keep the explanation simple, stick to basics, and verify what the child has understood.

Discussing Death Before a Crisis Occurs

However tempered they may be by the influence of peers and what is learned in the classroom and elsewhere outside the home, parental attitudes significantly influence the child's attitude toward death. Thus, parents have natural concerns regarding what to tell their children about it. What can be told? What should be told? How can I talk about it? What will the child understand? We have seen that children develop their own concepts about death, whether or not they receive parental instruction—even when parents and other adults consider the topic taboo. Children want to learn about death, just as they want to learn about everything that touches their lives. One child wrote, "Dear God, what's it like when you die? Nobody will tell me. I just want to know. I don't want to do it."

© Lawrence Migdale

Exemplifying the age-old oral tradition of elders transmitting culture to the young, this Native American grandmother shares memories and stories as her grandson learns about his deceased grandfather and his place in the family's heritage. Occasions for discussing death with children arise naturally out of our interactions; the most important contribution an adult can make in talking with a child about death is often simply to be a good listener.

Parents explaining death to children should put honesty foremost. Be straightforward. Note, however, that a parent who sets a ground rule that it's okay to be open and honest in talking about death ought to be aware that there may be times when the child wants to initiate a discussion and the parent is tired or would rather avoid the subject.

Second, don't put off introducing the topic of death to a child. When the experience of a close death precedes the discussion, the parent is faced with the need to provide an explanation in the midst of crisis. This unfortunate situation arises when a parent puts off discussing death "because it's not really going to happen," only to find that "I'm confronted with it happening right now in my family and the child has to be told something." When a family member is dying or has died, the explanation to the child is charged with all the emotions that the parent is dealing with, making the aim of clear communication more difficult to attain.

Third, set the level of explanation to the child's capacity to understand. This is determined partly by the child's cognitive stage and partly by his or her unique experience. By using the child's interest and ability to understand as a guide, the parent can provide an explanation that is appropriate to the child's particular circumstances. Such an explanation can help the child cope with his or her general concerns about death as well as with the specific issues that may arise in conjunction with the experience of a close death.

A supportive listener increases the child's openness. Valuing a child's ideas and encouraging candid expression is an excellent way to help a child explore and discuss his or her understanding of death. As their children's mainstay, parents who are open to an interchange on any subject will have a number of skills and resources that can be employed when the discussion turns to death. The most useful approach is to simply talk with the child about what he or she believes, to enter into the child's understanding of what death is all about.

When you talk to children about death, it is important to verify what it is they think you've told them. Have them tell you what they learned or what they heard you saying about death. Children tend to generalize from known concepts to make new experiences fit. This may result in a very literal-minded interpretation of new information, especially among young children, who tend to emphasize the concreteness of things. Recognizing this, try to keep your communication free of associations that might lead to confusion in the child's mind. Metaphorical explanations about death can help provide a child-sized picture that helps understanding, but unless fact is clearly separated from fancy, the child may grasp the literal details instead of the underlying message the analogy was intended to convey.

A story can illustrate how easily confusion can arise when death is explained to children. A girl of age five was told that her grandfather's cancer was like a seed that grew in his body; it grew and grew until he couldn't live in his body anymore and he died. Her parents didn't notice that ever afterward, all through childhood, she never ate another seed. Not one. Not a cucumber seed, watermelon seed, no seeds. Finally, at age twenty-one, she was asked, "Why are you avoiding the seeds? Isn't that a little bizarre? What's wrong with the seeds?" Her automatic response was, "You swallow them and you die." After all those years, she saw the fallacy of her compulsion to avoid eating seeds. It would have been useful if someone had asked her when she was five, "What will happen if you swallow that seed?"

In the Aftermath of Loss

Recognizing that children are individuals and that their methods of coping with loss may differ, it is possible to suggest guidelines that parents and other adults can use to advantage. Foremost among the guidelines for helping children cope with crisis is a *willingness to listen and to accept the reality of the child's experience.* We tend to assume that our experience of the world is shared by others. In fact, each of us perceives the world uniquely. Understanding another person's experience requires the art of listening. The aim is to discover what the other person thinks, feels, and believes: What does he or she think is

George Willard became possessed of a madness to lift the sheet from the body of his mother and look at her face. The thought that had come into his mind gripped him terribly. He became convinced that not his mother but someone else lay in the bed before him. The conviction was so real that it was almost unbearable. The body under the sheets was long and in death looked young and graceful. To the boy, held by some strange fancy, it was unspeakably lovely. The feeling that the body before him was alive, that in another moment a lovely woman would spring out of the bed and confront him, became so overpowering that he could not bear the suspense. Again and again he put out his hand. Once he touched and half lifted the white sheet that covered her, but his courage failed and he, like Doctor Reefy, turned and went out of the room. In the hallway outside the door he stopped and trembled so that he had to put a hand against the wall to support himself. "That's not my mother. That's not my mother in there," he whispered to himself and again his body shook with fright and uncertainty. When Aunt Elizabeth Swift, who had come to watch over the body, came out of an adjoining room he put his hand into hers and began to sob, shaking his head from side to side, half blind with grief. "My mother is dead," he said. . . .

Sherwood Anderson, *Winesburg, Ohio*

important about this situation? What are the person's concerns, fears, hopes, and anxieties? If a need for support or assistance is expressed, then what specific kind of help is being asked for?

Questions of this kind are especially important in relating to children. Sometimes children are asked to be "unseen and unheard," thus thwarting their natural tendency to explore and grapple with the emotions and thoughts generated by change. Particularly when it disrupts familiar patterns of living, change can result in confusion and conflict, creating a tangle of emotions and thoughts that may be difficult to sort out. Paying attention to a child's behavior is useful for gathering information about his or her experience of crisis. Acknowledge and accept the child's feelings. Crying, for instance, is a natural response to the loss of someone significant. Admonishing a fearful child to "Be brave!" or "Be a little man and buck up!" denies the validity of the child's spontaneous emotion.

In helping children cope with loss, adults must strive to *answer the child's questions honestly and directly.* Explanations should be truthful to the facts and should be as concrete as possible. Don't overwhelm the child with information that is beyond his or her developmental level. A child told that her goldfish "went to heaven" may make an elaborate picture of the pearly gates and different sections of heaven. Here is goldfish heaven, this is cat heaven, and over here is people heaven—a very organized concept that makes sense to a child. But we have to be careful that the concepts we convey to a child don't turn out to be dysfunctional.

One woman recalled that when she was three or four a favorite old black dog had to "go away for a long sleep." It wasn't until she was about seven years old that she realized that the dog wasn't away just napping someplace, at the puppy farm having a long sleep. If it was just "off somewhere to sleep," then a casual goodbye was fine. When she discovered that in fact her beloved dog was dead, she felt angry that she hadn't had the opportunity to give it a proper farewell.

Religious beliefs may be important in a family's understanding of death. If so, it is only natural that parents will want to share these beliefs with their children. Children may be comforted by such beliefs, although they deserve to be told that these are *beliefs*. In addition, care should be taken to express such beliefs in a manner that avoids confusing the child. An adult's concept of an afterlife, for example, may be quite different from what a child is able to understand.

This is illustrated in the experience of a woman whose first experience with death occurred when she was three-and-a-half and her mother died. It seemed that her mother had just disappeared; she didn't know what had happened to her. Some time later, she began to realize that her mother had died and she started asking questions. Some people told her that her mother had been buried, and her thought was, "Why don't they dig her up?" Others said that her mother had gone to heaven, so she kept looking at the sky, watching for her. With both of these concepts running through her young mind, she did her best to figure out, "How can my mother be buried in heaven?" That's an example of the concreteness of a young child's concepts about death.

A similar confusion is illustrated in the case of a four-year-old whose brother (nine) told him that daddy had gone to heaven. The four-year-old promptly went and told his mother, "My daddy's on the roof!" She said, "What? Who told you that?" He said, "Andrew did." The older brother then explained, "We were looking out the window and I told him that daddy was in heaven up there." To the four-year-old, the highest "up there" was up on the roof. If you tell a four-year-old that someone who has died is "up there" and you also say that Santa Claus lands on the roof on Christmas Eve, he may decide that Santa Claus and the person who has died are great buddies. He might make up stories about how they work together, making toys, feeding the reindeer, and so on.

A child who is told that "God took Daddy to be with him in heaven" may not feel very kindly toward a being who could be so capricious and inconsiderate of the child's feelings. Religious and philosophical concepts of death may confuse and frighten young children whose emphasis on "concreteness" is not well suited for grasping abstractions. Similarly, fairy tales, metaphors, and the like should be avoided or used with care because children may take such explanations of death literally.

When children are asked about their experiences during crises involving death, many say that the most difficult times were when they did not know what was happening. A child whose diagnosis of life-threatening illness was withheld from her by her family said later, "We'd always done everything with each other knowing what was going on. Suddenly that was different. That scared me more than what was happening to my body. It felt like my family was becoming strangers."[39] A sudden change in family communication patterns can be alarming to a child and actually heighten anxiety about the crisis.

Even in families that encourage openness, a crisis can precipitate breakdowns in communication, as the following story illustrates: A young girl whose mother refused to discuss her illness told a hospital staffer, "I know I'm going to die. I want to talk to Mother, but she won't let me. I know she's hurting, but I'm the one who's dying." When told of this conversation by the staff member, the girl's mother replied angrily, "She wouldn't be thinking of dying if you hadn't made her talk about it."

As the communication between mother and daughter continued to deteriorate, the daughter became increasingly withdrawn. Still refusing to allow her daughter to discuss her feelings about the illness, the mother's communication style finally degenerated into baby talk: "Her doesn't feel goody today . . . her doesn't want to talk." Clearly, the communication style exhibited by this mother and daughter wasn't helping either to cope with the predicament. A lack of openness was hampering satisfaction of normal human needs for affection and reassurance.

Children are apt to point out any inconsistencies in what we tell them about death. When one three-year-old's young playmate was killed, his mother explained to him that Jesus had come and taken his friend to heaven. His concrete response was, "Well, that's an awful thing to do; I want to play with him. Jesus isn't very nice if he comes down here and takes my friend from me." In discussing death with a child, it helps if you understand the child's belief system, the kind of thought processes he or she uses to understand the world; and then, from your very first statement, ask yourself: If I explain death in this way, how will it wind up in the child's understanding?

We can picture communication styles occupying a continuum that ranges from encouraging the child's participation in all facets of the crisis to trying to keep reality hidden from the child. The best gauge of a child's readiness to be informed about a potentially painful situation is the child's own interest, usually expressed through questions. Using the child's own questions as a guide, we can give straightforward answers without burdening the child with facts irrelevant to his or her understanding of the situation. Above all, children in crisis situations need to be reassured that they are loved.

Using Books as Tools for Coping

Bibliotherapy—that is, the use of books as an aid to coping—can facilitate communication between adults and children and create opportunities for discussing feelings and experiences. Most book shops are well-stocked with a variety of children's books about dying, death, and bereavement. Both fiction and nonfiction works can be found dealing with the deaths of parents, grandparents, siblings, other relatives and friends, as well as pets. A four-year-old whose father has died might view a picture book such as *Everett Anderson's Good-Bye,* which depicts a young boy's feelings about his father's death, and be encouraged to talk about his or her own feelings. An adult might ask, "What else do you think someone like Everett might do or say when feeling angry about his father's death?" When a death has recently occurred or is expected, an appropriate book can give adults and children an opportunity to begin talking about each other's experiences (see Figure 10-6).

Bibliographies

Hazel B. Benson. *The Dying Child: An Annotated Bibliography.* Westport, Conn.: Greenwood Press, 1988.

Lyn Miller-Lachmann. *Our Family, Our Friends, Our World: An Annotated Guide to Significant Multicultural Books for Children and Teenagers.* New York: R. R. Bowker, 1992.

Marian S. Pyles. *Death and Dying in Children's and Young People's Literature.* Jefferson, N.C.: McFarland, 1988.

Masha K. Rudman, Kathleen Dunne Gagne, and Joanne E. Bernstein. *Books to Help Children Cope with Separation and Loss: An Annotated Bibliography,* 4th ed. New York: R. R. Bowker, 1993.

Books for Children and Adolescents

Chana Byars Abells. *The Children We Remember.* New York: Greenwillow, 1986. Combines text and photographs from the Yad Vashem Archives to chronicle the story of Jewish children during the Holocaust.

Marion Dane Bauer. *On My Honor.* New York: Clarion, 1986. The story of a boy's feelings of guilt over the role he played in the death of his best friend.

Marinus van den Berg. *The Three Birds: A Story for Children about the Loss of a Loved One.* Illustrations by Sandra Ireland. New York: Magination Press, 1994. A young bird journeys from bewilderment through grief to resolution of his mother's untimely death.

Joeri Breebaart. *When I Die, Will I Get Better?* New York: Peter Bedrick Books, 1993. Written by a six-year-old boy (with the help of his father, Piet), who comes to terms with the sudden illness and death of his younger brother by creating a story about the Robert Rabbit brothers that closely parallels his own experience. A true story with a preface by Harold Kushner.

Eve Bunting. *The Happy Funeral.* New York: Harper and Row, 1982. The funeral of a child's Chinese-American grandfather.

Eve Bunting. *Face at the Edge of the World.* New York: Clarion, 1985. An African-American boy reflects on his friend's last week of life to discover why he committed suicide.

Eve Bunting. *The Wall.* New York: Clarion Books, 1990. Story about a boy and his father who visit the Vietnam Veterans Memorial and find the name of the child's grandfather.

Carol Carrick. *The Accident.* Illustrations by Donald Carrick. New York: Seabury/Clarion, 1976. A young child copes with the death of a pet dog.

continued

Figure *10-6* *Books for Helping Children and Adolescents Cope with Loss*

continued from previous page

Lucile Clifton. *Everett Anderson's Good-Bye.* Illustrated by Ann Grifalconi. New York: Holt, Rinehart and Winston, 1983. A young African-American boy explores his feelings about the death of his father.

Eleanor Coerr. *Sadako and the Thousand Paper Cranes.* Illustrations by Ronald Himler. New York: Putnam, 1977. The story of a Japanese girl's illness and death from leukemia resulting from the Hiroshima bomb, her courage, and the memorial to her by her classmates and community.

Miriam Cohen. *Jim's Dog Muffins.* Illustrations by Lillian Hoban. New York: Greenwillow/William Morrow, 1984. A friend and a teacher help a boy cope with the loss of his dog.

Elizabeth Corley. *Tell Me About Death, Tell Me About Funerals.* Illustrations by Philip Pecorado. Santa Clara, Calif.: Grammatical Sciences, 1973. Information about funerals is presented in a comforting manner to a girl whose grandfather has died.

Tomie DePaola. *Nana Upstairs and Nana Downstairs.* New York: Penguin, 1978. A boy learns to face the eventual deaths of his grandmother and great-grandmother.

Michael Foreman. *War Game.* New York: Arcade, 1994. Patriotism and the atrocities of war are explored in this account of four English boys who heed the call to arms during World War I.

Jason Gaes. *My Book for Kids with Cancer: A Child's Autobiography of Hope.* Aberdeen, S.D.: Melius and Peterson, 1987. A boy's gift to other children with cancer.

Richard García. *My Aunt Otilia's Spirits/Los Espíritus de mi Tía Otilia.* San Francisco: Children's Book Press, 1986. When Aunt Otilia visits from Puerto Rico, her young nephew discovers that she brings her "spirits" with her.

Mordicai Gerstein. *The Mountains of Tibet.* New York: Harper and Row, 1987. Inspired by the Tibetan Book of the Dead, this illustrated tale uses the theme of reincarnation to tell the story of a Tibetan woodcutter who, after dying, is given the choice of going to paradise or living another life anywhere in the universe.

Barbara Girion. *A Tangle of Roots.* New York: Charles Scribner's Sons, 1979. A mother's sudden death and the daughter's readjustment following the loss.

Charlotte Graeber. *Mustard.* Illustrations by Donna Diamond. New York: Macmillan, 1982. A young boy deals with the increasing infirmity and eventual death of a cat that had been part of the family since before he was born.

Eloise Greenfield. *Nathanial Talking.* New York: Black Butterfly Children's Group, 1993. Using rap and rhyme to express his feelings, an African-American nine-year-old boy tells of his experience after his mother dies.

Sharon Greenlee. *When Someone Dies.* Illustrated by Bill Draft. Atlanta: Peachtree, 1992. Using colorful pictures and a writing style directed to children, this book describes how to cope with the confusion and hurt felt by children and adults alike when they are faced with death.

Earl Grollman. *Talking About Death: A Dialogue Between Parent and Child.* 3d ed. Boston: Beacon Press, 1991. A classic nonfiction explanation about death.

Rosmarie Hausherr. *Children and the AIDS Virus: A Book for Children, Parents, and Teachers.* Illustrated with photographs by the author, this book describes how our immune system fights the common cold virus and goes on to explain, in simple terms, the virus that causes AIDS and how it is spread. Includes an account of two children with AIDS who attend school and enjoy other activities.

L. Dwight Holden. *Gran-Gran's Best Trick: A Story for Children Who Have Lost Someone They Love.* Illustrated by Michael Chesworth. New York: Magination Press, 1989. This story about a young girl's experience with her grandfather's illness and death from cancer includes a description of how the lessons she learns about coping can be applied to other losses.

Diane Hoyt-Goldsmith. *Day of the Dead: A Mexican-American Celebration.* Photographs by Lawrence Migdale. New York: Holiday House, 1994. Ten-year-old twins, Ximena and Azucena, celebrate el Día de los Muertos, honoring relatives and friends who have died and marking the spiritual return of the deceased, who share a special feast with the living.

Hadley Irwin. *So Long at the Fair*. New York: McElderry-Macmillan, 1988. Joel Logan, a high school senior, finds that he must remember and work through the past to come to terms with the suicidal death of his girlfriend.

MaryKate Jordan. *Losing Uncle Tim*. Niles, Ill.: Albert Whitman, 1989. When a young boy's uncle dies of AIDS, he strives for reassurance and understanding and finds that his favorite grown-up has left him a legacy of joy and courage.

M. E. Kerr. *Night Kites*. New York: Harper and Row, 1986. A teenage boy grapples with the discovery that his older brother is dying of AIDS.

Jill Krementz. *How It Feels When a Parent Dies*. New York: Alfred A. Knopf, 1981. A photographic essay with children's descriptions of their experiences and feelings.

Jill Krementz. *How It Feels to Fight for Your Life*. New York: Simon & Schuster, 1991. Children from ages seven to sixteen describe their reactions to a variety of life-threatening illnesses; each child's photograph accompanies the text.

Jane Merksy Leder. *Dead Serious: A Book for Teenagers About Teen Suicide*. New York: Avon, 1989. Selected by the American Library Association as one of the best books for young adults on suicide.

Madeleine L'Engle. *A Ring of Endless Light*. New York: Farrar, Straus & Giroux, 1980. A teenage girl copes with the experience of loss, grief, and terminal illness by discovering underlying spiritual and moral dimensions.

Jonathan London. *Liplap's Wish*. Illustrated by Sylvia Long. San Francisco: Chronicle Books, 1994. This beautifully illustrated story about Liplap the bunny offers a metaphorical explanation about coping with the death of a grandparent. Although he keeps expecting to see her step from the house, Liplap eventually realizes that his grandma didn't live to see it snow this year. With his mother, he talks about what happened to grandmother—and it turns out that grandmother is probably a star.

Leonard S. Marcus. *Lifelines: A Poetry Anthology Patterned on the Stages of Life*. New York: Dutton, 1994. This poetry anthology gathers many voices and perspectives on the stages of life from conception to death.

Norma Fox Mazer. *After the Rain*. New York: William Morrow, 1987. The after-school visits of fifteen-year-old Rachel with her dying grandfather begin as a chore and gradually become a central part of her life as she shares his final days.

Jill Westberg McNamara. *My Mom Is Dying: A Child's Diary*. Illustrated by David LaRochelle. Minneapolis: Augsburg Fortress, 1994. When Kristin learns that her mother is dying, she turns to God for help. Through a series of conversations with God, she gradually comes to understand her feelings, recognizing that it is okay to experience fear, anger, and sadness. She finds solace in knowing that God understands her grief. Includes a discussion section to help parents and children talk about death, grieving, and God's love.

Miska Miles. *Annie and the Old One*. Illustrations by Peter Parnall. Boston: Little, Brown, 1971. The story of a Navajo girl's efforts to prevent the inevitable by unraveling each day's weaving on a rug whose completion she fears will bring her grandmother's death.

Joyce C. Mills. *Little Tree: A Story for Children with Serious Medical Problems*. Illustrated by Michael Chesworth. New York: Magination Press, 1993. A tree that grows deep when it cannot grow tall provides a metaphor for children dealing with illness.

Joyce C. Mills. *Gentle Willow: A Story for Children About Dying*. Illustrated by Michael Chesworth. New York: Magination Press, 1993. Bringing back the characters from *Little Tree* (above), this story is written for children who may not survive their illness as well as for healthy children who are facing death and dying in their lives.

continued

continued from previous page

Jane Mobley. *The Star Husband.* Illustrations by Anna Vojtech. New York: Doubleday, 1979. This adaptation of a Native American myth affirms the natural cycle of life, death, and rebirth.

Jeanne Moutoussany-Ashe. *Daddy and Me.* New York: Alfred A. Knopf, 1993. A portrait of tennis pro Arthur Ashe and his six-year-old daughter Camera as they help each other through "good" and "bad" days related to his contracting AIDS from a blood transfusion. An affecting chronicle, told from the child's perspective, of family interactions in coping with AIDS. Mom took the photographs.

Walter Dean Myers. *Fallen Angels.* New York: Scholastic, 1988. The gritty and heartrending story of Richie Perry, just out of high school, who enlists in the Army and spends a devastating year in Vietnam.

Carolyn Nystrom. *What Happens When We Die?* Illustrated by Eira Reeves. Chicago: Moody Press, 1992. Presented from a Christian perspective, this picture book is intended to help children understand why people die and to give them a comforting vision of a Heavenly afterlife.

Carolyn Nystrom. *Emma Says Goodbye: A Child's Guide to Bereavement.* Illustrated by Annabel Large. Elgin, Ill.: Lion Publishing, 1994. Emma's Aunt Sue has always been full of fun, and strong, too—strong enough to climb telephone poles and fix wires. But now Aunt Sue is too ill to work and her body keeps getting thinner and thinner. This change frightens Emma, and she worries that Aunt Sue is not going to get better. Emma becomes angry when God does not answer her prayers. Based on a Christian understanding of illness and death, this story describes family interactions in the context of religious beliefs.

Wendie C. Old. *Stacy Had a Little Sister.* Illustrated by Judith Friedman. Norton Grove, Ill.: Albert Whitman, 1995. Sometimes Stacy loved her new baby sister Ashley, and sometimes she became angry because her parents spent time taking care of Ashley and didn't pay attention to her. When the baby dies suddenly, Stacy questions whether her angry thoughts somehow caused Ashley's death. This book provides good descriptions of death from Sudden Infant Death Syndrome (SIDS), the role of funeral ritual, a child's experience of magical thinking, and positive parent–child interaction.

Barbra Ann Porte. *Harry's Mom.* Illustrations by Yossi Abolafia. New York: Greenwillow/Morrow, 1985. A story for young children about a mother's death.

Patricia Quinlan. *Tiger Flowers.* Illustrations by Janet Wilson. New York: Dial/Penguin, 1994. Joel adores his Uncle Michael; they build a treehouse and root for their favorite baseball teams. Then, when Michael contracts AIDS, he comes to live with Joel's family and they grow even closer. After Michael's death, Joel is heartsick until he learns to find solace in his memories of the beloved uncle.

Eric E. Rofes. *The Kids Book about Death and Dying: By and for Kids.* Boston: Little, Brown, 1985. What is death? What is it like for a child when a friend or relative dies? Is there life after death? These are just a few of the questions a group of students, ranging in age from 11 to 14, answered for themselves while exploring the subject of death and dying under the direction of their teacher, Eric Rofes, at the Fairweather Street School in Cambridge, Mass.

Fred Rogers. *When a Pet Dies.* New York: G. P. Putnam's Sons, 1988. Portrays a family whose dog dies and another family whose cat dies; the grieving children ask questions of their parents and adjust to their losses.

James Shott. *The House Across the Street.* Nashville: Winston-Derek, 1988. A young girl befriends an elderly neighbor whose daughter died twenty years before, and the resulting encounter helps resolve the grief of her newfound friend as well as her own grief at losing her grandmother.

Posy Simmonds. *Fred.* New York: Alfred A. Knopf, 1987. The night Sophie and Nick bury their beloved cat Fred, his cat friends arrive to tell them about his nighttime self and give him a proper funeral and farewell. This picture book for young children validates mourning for the death of a pet.

Norma Simon. *The Saddest Time.* Illustrated by Jacqueline Rogers. Norton Grove, Ill.: Albert Whitman, 1986. This book includes three stories dealing with the deaths of a young uncle from terminal illness, a classmate killed in action, and a grandparent. Promotes the idea that children need to understand death as a natural life event.

Charles H. Slaughter. *The Dirty War.* New York: Walker, 1994. For ages twelve and up, this story focuses on a boy affected by Argentina's military regime in the late 1970s and the thousands of people tortured and killed.

Anne Warren Smith. *Sister in the Shadow.* New York: Atheneum, 1986. During a summer job as a mother's helper, a young girl is confronted by the effects of an earlier experience of crib death on the family's patterns and relationships.

Sara Bonnett Stein. *About Dying: An Open Family Book for Parents and Children Together.* New York: Walker, 1974. A story about death composed of parallel texts providing basic information for children and supplemental information for adults.

Heather Teakle-Barnes. *My Daddy Died: Supporting Young Children in Grief.* San Francisco: Harper-Collins, 1993. Story about how a mother dealt with her young child when the child's father was killed in an automobile accident.

Yukio Tsuchiya. *Faithful Elephants: A True Story of Animals, People, and War.* Boston: Houghton Mifflin, 1988. A poignant story of the horror of war and its effect on animals and people.

Susan Varley. *Badger's Parting Gifts.* New York: Lothrop, Lee and Shepard, 1984. The story of Badger's experience of growing old and dying, as well as his friends' grief and their rituals for relocating him in their lives.

Judith Viorst. *The Tenth Good Thing About Barney.* Illustrations by Erik Blegvad. New York: Atheneum, 1971. A boy thinks of the ten best things about his pet cat, who has died.

Alice Walker. *To Hell with Dying.* Illustrated by Catherine Deeter. New York: Harcourt Brace Jovanovich, 1988. A Pulitzer Prize–winning African-American writer tells the story of old Mr. Sweet. Though often seemingly on the verge of dying, he could be revived by the attention given him by Alice and her brothers. The author tells of discovering Mr. Sweet dead when she was twenty-four and how she coped with her grief and loss.

E. B. White. *Charlotte's Web.* Illustrations by Garth Williams. New York: Harper and Row, 1952. This classic story describes the grief experienced at the death of a close friend—Charlotte, a spider—and the continuing of life through her offspring.

Charlotte Zolotow. *My Grandson Lew.* New York: Harper and Row, 1974. Lew and his mother learn the value of memories of his deceased grandfather.

Support Groups for Children

Community support represents an important adjunct to the family's internal support system. Many organizations dedicated to providing support during the crises of serious illness and bereavement emphasize caring for all members of a family, including the children. Organizations like The Compassionate Friends and Bereaved Families of Ontario, for example, not only provide support to bereaved parents but conduct programs to help children and adolescents cope with loss. Such organizations typically include a peer-support component as well as help and guidance provided by trained volunteers and professional caregivers.

In Maryland, the Hospice of Frederick County (HFC) has experimented with an innovative outreach program in which bereaved children ages six to fourteen were paired with a group of caring adults, many of whom were also recovering from losses. In the context of a weekend camp in an idyllic mountain setting, participants not only enjoyed recreational activities but were given opportunities to explore their losses in a safe environment among peers and "big buddies." Named after a young hospice patient who died before his third birthday, Camp Jamie provided the children with "a haven to learn about coping with grief" and "enabled them to experience the universality of loss through interactions with other children and adults who shared the common bond of bereavement."[40]

Other support groups focus primarily on providing social support to sick or terminally ill children. Help is offered in a variety of ways, ranging from comprehensive support services to specialized activities. An example of the former is HUGS: Help, Understanding, and Group Support for Hawaii's Seriously Ill Children and Their Families, which was founded in 1982. Services are provided free of charge and include 24-hour crisis support, hospital visitation, transportation to and from medical appointments, recreational outings, home visits, and respite care. In addition, children and parents receive counseling to learn how to cope with fear, anger, and heartache. Bereavement support is provided to the family when a child dies. On any given day, HUGS is helping nearly 100 families across the state. Organized around a professional staff and a network of trained volunteers, HUGS provides social services "to help families stay together in the face of overwhelming adversity."[41]

Magic Performers of America Club (Magic PAC) exemplifies organizations that have a more specialized focus. According to its mission statement:"Magic PAC is a place for children to celebrate life in the face of death."[42] Formed in 1992, the program offers an environment where children can laugh, have fun, be supported by their peers, and realize that they are not alone. Besides attending club meetings where they share concerns as well as practice magic tricks and other creative arts, members give presentations to other sick and disabled children in the community. In this way, "both club members and children in the audience experience the exhilaration that is so healing to the body, mind, and spirit." Magic PAC makes its services available to children with cancer or other life-threatening illnesses, and siblings of the ill children, as well as to children of parents with terminal illnesses or whose parents have died.

Telephone support groups represent yet another type of social support that has been effectively used with various populations, including children. The telephone was first used as a method of outreach for suicide prevention by the Samaritans in London in 1953.[43] Recently, the Pediatric Branch of the National Cancer Institute made use of a telephone network to offer social support to HIV-infected children. This type of support was found to be "a creative and therapeutic way to help HIV-infected children and their family members cope with the impact this disease had on their lives." The telephone network provided "a sense of confidentiality not afforded in face-to-face groups," and interactions among participants included considerable self-disclosure and sharing of mutual fears and concerns.

Finally, a number of well-known organizations exist to grant the wishes of children who have been given a limited or uncertain prognosis. The Sunshine Foundation, founded in 1976, and the Starlight Foundation, founded in 1983, are examples of such organizations.[44] Through the efforts of such groups, seriously ill children and their families are given opportunities to take a vacation together or to fulfill some other wish that seemed impossible without the organization's help.

Many adults tend to worry about children, especially so with respect to their encounters with death. Are they doing all right? Will they be okay? Is death going to be too hard for them to handle? Can they survive this particular loss? (Underlying this concern is worry about ourselves too.) In general, children do remarkably well. Erik Erikson said, "Healthy children will not fear life if their parents have integrity not to fear death."

Further Readings

Sol Altschul, ed. *Childhood Bereavement and Its Aftermath.* Madison, Conn.: International Universities Press, 1988.

Robert W. Buckingham. *Care of the Dying Child: A Practical Guide for Those Who Help Others.* New York: Continuum, 1989.

Charles A. Corr and Joan N. McNeil, eds. *Adolescence and Death.* New York: Springer, 1986.

James Garbarino, Nancy Dubrow, Kathleen Kostelny, and Carole Pardo. *Children in Danger: Coping with the Consequences of Community Violence.* San Francisco: Jossey-Bass, 1992.

Shelley Geballe, Janice Gruendel, and Warren Andiman, eds. *Forgotten Children of the AIDS Epidemic.* New Haven, Conn.: Yale University Press, 1995.

Susan Goodwillie, ed. *Voices from the Future: Our Children Tell Us About Violence in America.* New York: Crown, 1993.

Karen Gravelle and Charles Haskins. *Teenagers Face to Face with Bereavement.* Englewood Cliffs, N.J.: Julian Messner, 1989.

Helen Rosen. *Unspoken Grief: Coping with Childhood Sibling Loss.* Lexington, Mass.: Lexington Books, 1985.

Neil J. Salkind. *Theories of Human Development,* 2d ed. New York: John Wiley and Sons, 1985.

Claudine Vegh. *I Didn't Say Goodbye: Interviews with the Children of the Holocaust.* New York: Viking, 1986.

Holding their dead baby, this Harlem couple finds comfort in the sharing of their memories and their grief as they acknowledge the death of their first-born child. Of all the losses that can be experienced during adult life, most people feel that the death of a child is the most painful.

Death in the Lives of Adults

*J*ust as human development does not stop with childhood's end, the patterns of coping with loss continue to evolve throughout a person's lifespan. Even when the circumstances of bereavement are outwardly similar, a person's response to loss depends on many factors, not least of which is age. Although the *event* of a parent's death, for example, may occur during childhood or adulthood, the *experience* will differ at each developmental period. Furthermore, adult life entails losses that happen only during maturity. The death of a spouse occurs in the context of marriage, the death of a child in the context of family and the childbearing and childrearing years.

Studying losses experienced by college students, Louis LaGrand found that events some students considered to be major losses—such as course failure, death of a pet, or suspension of a roommate from school—were viewed by others as less significant.[1] This disparity does not mean that students in the first group were wrong, that their losses weren't so important after all. Neither does it indicate that the other students were insensitive and unfeeling. It does underscore the fact that a person's *interpretation* of loss, its personal meaning in his or her own life, determines its relative significance.

The aspects of death that make us fearful or anxious also differ among individuals. For instance, even though a butcher and a funeral director are both involved in jobs with death-related implications, they may each feel comfortable with their own, but not the other's, work.[2] Similarly, a person's attitude toward the prospect of his or her own death reflects individual differences; in addition, attitudes change over the course of life and depending on circumstances. If death seems a remote possibility, an event not expected to occur for many years, it may cause little alarm or concern. When a medical checkup reveals the presence of a life-threatening illness, however, the response may be otherwise.

The meaning of death is usually interpreted differently as a person ages. One study found that "fear of death/dying was relatively high among the young, peaked during middle age and fell to its lowest point among the elderly."[3] Although the old generally appear to fear death less than do younger people, individual differences remain important throughout the lifespan. Also, although death is perceived as normal and acceptable in old age, *choosing* death is less acceptable for the aged than for younger people.[4] Thus, the relative absence of death anxiety, or fear of death, among older people should not be interpreted as acceptance of actively taking steps to shorten one's life.

In addition to interpreting the significance of losses and the meaning of death in distinctive ways, individuals use various ways of coping. Variability in coping styles—from acceptance to drug intoxication—was noted as one of the most revealing features of student reactions to loss in the study mentioned. Social support, especially talking about the loss with others, was typically important in resolving grief. Successfully handled, the experience of loss can result in meaningful learnings and positive changes of attitude.

The Psychosocial Stages of Adulthood

Just as we can associate distinct developmental tasks and abilities with children of varying ages, so too, we can distinguish distinctive phases and transitions during adult life. In the previous chapter, we discussed the first five stages of psychosocial development proposed by Erik Erikson—namely, those pertaining to the years of childhood and adolescence. The last three stages of psychosocial development, according to this model, occur during adulthood. As in childhood, each stage of adult life requires a particular developmental response, and each stage builds upon previous ones.

Young adulthood is represented by the conflict between intimacy and isolation. This stage involves various forms of commitment and interaction, including sex, friendship, cooperation, partnership, and affiliation. Because mature love takes the risk of commitment, the death of a loved one may be most devastating during this stage and the next.[5] In the study conducted by LaGrand of losses experienced by college students, more than three-fourths involved the loss of a significant other either by death or by separation resulting from the end of a friendship, the dissolution of a love relationship, or divorce.[6]

The next psychosocial stage, according to Erikson, is *adulthood*, which involves the crisis of generativity versus stagnation. This stage is characterized

Among the most poignant losses that can be experienced in adult life are those related
to war. The Vietnam Veterans' Memorial in Washington, D.C., is a focal point for
coping with the grief of individual as well as national losses. For many who fought
the war, as well as for other survivors, the effects are pervasive and felt daily. Here,
visitors reflect on the names of the individuals engraved on the face of the black wall
of the Memorial, following its official dedication in November 1982.

What Personnel Handbooks Never Tell You

They leave a lot out of the personnel handbooks.
Dying, for instance.
You can find funeral leave
but you can't find dying.
You can't find what to do
when a guy you've worked with since you both
      were pups
looks you in the eye
and says something about hope and chemotherapy.
No phrases,
no triplicate forms,
no rating systems.
Seminars won't do it
and it's too late for a new policy on sabbaticals.

They don't tell you about eye contact
and how easily it slips away
when a woman who lost a breast
says, "They didn't get it all."
You can find essays on motivation
but the business schools
don't teach what the good manager says
to keep people taking up the slack
while someone steals a little more time
at the hospital.
There's no help from those tapes
you pop into the player
while you drive or jog.
They'd never get the voice right.

And this poem won't help either.
You just have to figure it out for yourself,
and don't ever expect to do it well.

    James A. Autry

by a widening commitment to take care of the people, things, and ideas one has learned to care for. This emphasis on care helps explain why the death of a child is so painful. Symbolically and actually, a child's death is opposed to the nurturitive psychosocial task of adulthood.

When we reach the stage of *maturity,* the eighth and final stage of the life cycle, the turning point or crisis to be resolved is that of integrity versus despair. Viewing all the developmental phases as connected, each building on the ones

"Bloom County," drawing by Berke Breathed, © 1984 by Washington Post Writers Group

before, the crisis of this stage is especially powerful. It is marked by the end of our "one given course of life." Successfully negotiating this developmental task gives us the strength of wisdom, which Erikson describes as "informed and detached concern with life itself in the face of death itself."[7]

Many illnesses and disabilities are most common among people in the seventh or eighth decade of life or older; nevertheless, the probability of dying steadily increases as we age. Aging doesn't begin at fifty, or sixty-five, or eighty-five. At this moment, we are all aging. The person who festively celebtrates his or her thirtieth or fortieth birthday may find that these milestones of life also bring sobering reflections about the meaning of growing older and the unavoidable losses incurred in taking one particular path in life rather than another.[8]

Besides the experience of coming nearer to our own death, nature dictates that our experiences of others' deaths also increase as we grow older. Children become seriously ill, and some die. Spousal relationships and close friendships come to an end, suddenly or perhaps over a longer period due to chronic illness. Growing older also increases the chances that an individual will experience the death of his or her parents, and, conversely, that a parent may experience the death of an adult child. Eventually, it may become impossible to care adequately for ourselves. Failing health, for example, is among the reasons given by some aged people for preferring death to continued existence (see Table 11-1). Leaving one's own home to live with strangers in a nursing home or other institutional environment can mean losing virtually everything familiar acquired over the course of a lifetime.

You may find it useful to consider the losses that have occurred in your own life, both as a child and as an adult. How have they differed, and in what ways are they similar? Have others responded to your experiences of loss in supportive ways? What coping mechanisms were you able to bring into play to move through the experience successfully? Questions of this kind can form a framework for examining typical losses in adult life.

TABLE 11-1   *Some Reasons Given by Aged People for Accepting Death*

Death is preferable to inactivity.
Death is preferable to the loss of the ability to be useful.
Death is preferable to becoming a burden.
Death is preferable to loss of mental faculties.
Death is preferable to living with progressively deteriorating physical health and concomitant physical discomfort.

Source: Adapted from Victor W. Marshall, *Last Chapters: A Sociology of Aging and Dying* (Monterey, Calif.: Brooks/Cole, 1980), pp. 169–177.

Parental Bereavement

Think about a child being diagnosed as terminally ill, or suddenly dead due to a fatal accident. What makes the loss of a child a high-grief death? To most people, the death of a child connotes the unfinished, the untimely loss of a potential future. Perhaps the parents envisioned the child playing on the local youth soccer team, graduating from school, getting married, raising children—all the various milestones and occasions that comprise a sense of continuity into the future. Death brings an end to the plans and hopes for a child's life. We expect that a child will outlive his or her parents. A child carries something of the parent into the future, even after the parent's death. A child's very existence grants a kind of immortality to the parent; this is taken away when the child dies.

The interdependency between parent and child makes the death of a child a deep experience of loss.[9] Grief may focus on issues of parental responsibility. Parenting is generally defined as protecting and nurturing a child until he or she can act independently in the world. If mourning parents hold such a definition, the death of a child may be experienced as the ultimate lack of protection and nurture, the ultimate breakdown and failure in being a "good parent."

Among the Cree of North America, infants were given "ghost-protective" moccasins to wear. Holes were cut in the bottom of the moccasins to safeguard the baby from death. If the spirit of an ancestor appeared and beckoned, the infant could refuse to go, pointing out that his or her moccasins "needed mending."[10] Such feelings about the parental role of safeguarding a child are universal, and parents expend considerable effort in seeking to guarantee a child's safety and welfare.

Many issues of parental bereavement span the adult life cycle. They are present for forty-year-old parents and for eighty-year-old parents. They are experienced by parents of grown-up children as well as by parents of infants. A parent's fantasies and plans can be just as strong for an unborn infant as for an older child. But to comprehend the nature of parental bereavement and the range of losses involved, both the age of the parent and the age of the child are significant. A sixty-five-year-old divorced or widowed mother may feel considerable loss of security when her thirty-five-year-old child dies suddenly. One such woman said repeatedly: "He was going to take care of me when I got old; now I have no one." Whether or not her son would have indeed taken on the responsibility she envisioned, his death represented the loss of *her* imagined future.

Parental bereavement is a powerful experience that relates to both socio-biological and psychological explanations of human grief. Studies of human bonding and the psychodynamics of family systems contribute to a comprehensive model of parental grief. Research carried out by Dennis Klass, for example, shows that bereaved parents often maintain an inner representation of the dead child that is sustained through memories and religious beliefs.[11] It is in appreciating the uniqueness of the parent–child relationship that we begin to understand the grief evoked by the death of a child. Given the biological, social, and psychological dynamics that form the bond between parent and child, resolving the grief experienced at the loss of a child is truly a family affair.[12]

Coping with Parental Bereavement as a Couple

In counseling bereaved parents, clinicians often note the presence of a kind of "general chaos." Frequently, a directionlessness sets in, part of a pervasive sense that the parents have been robbed of a past and a future. The prevailing attitude may be one of "do it now." Sexual acting out is not uncommon during parental bereavement. The attitudes and behaviors of parents after a child's death reflect the reality of being overwhelmed, which helps explain the incidence of marital disruption and divorce among bereaved parents.

With such a traumatic event, parents are expected to provide support to each other. But the energy expended by each partner in coping with his or her own grief can deplete the emotional resources necessary for mutual support. Some bereaved parents report that, in addition to losing a child, they felt they had lost their spouse for a time. Fathers may feel especially unsupported. Social support outside the marriage is often directed toward the wife, while husbands are expected to be strong. Based on a study of parents who experienced the death of a young child, Kathleen Gilbert says, "Men spoke of the stress of maintaining the family, facing financial worries, going to work, and being expected 'to produce one hundred percent' while at the same time facing the prospect of serving as the only support for their wives."[13] In another study, fathers who experienced a perinatal loss described the period following bereavement as an "intensely active time involving confirmation of the death, managing the physical process of labor and delivery, notifying the extended family and friends of the death and delivery event, and managing the mother's psychological state as well as their own feelings as fathers."[14] Many of the fathers spoke of suppressing or "storing" their own feelings as they helped their spouses cope and attended to other details during the early period following the loss.

Even though they share the same loss, parents typically have different grieving styles, which can leave each of them feeling isolated and unsupported by the only other person in the world who shares the magnitude of the loss. Differences in individual beliefs and expectations can give rise to conflicts in coping styles, thereby reducing the sense of "commonality" in a couple's grief experience.[15] Although husbands and wives do not always or necessarily grieve in an asynchronous or "roller coaster" pattern, it is, nevertheless, not uncommon for bereaved parents to find themselves sometimes grieving "out of synch" with one another.[16]

The sense of commonality in a couple's grief is also affected by their view of themselves as a *couple*. Gilbert found that couples may have difficulty reaching agreement about the best way to regain a sense of stability and meaning in life after the loss of a child, and about how to handle emotions. Despite the desire and expectation of each partner to "go through grief" together, differences in grieving styles may lead to questions about whether one's partner is behaving appropriately.

Conflict can arise out of each partner's *interpretation* of the other's behavior. A father who contains his grief so that he can "be there" for his spouse may be perceived by the spouse as cold and unfeeling. His desire to be caring and protective may be misinterpreted, resulting in conflict rather than comfort. Disagreement or misunderstanding can also center on issues concerning what constitutes "proper" mourning behavior, the public display of grief.

Happily, there are ways to reduce conflict between grieving couples and promote positive interactions. Most important is a willingness to engage in open and honest communication. In her study of bereaved parents, Gilbert found that "exchanging information increased a sense of mutuality and understanding. . . . The ability to convey accurate information was useful in answering immediate questions as well as those that occurred later as the couple attempted to make sense of the death." Furthermore, each partner's emotional expression of loss can help validate the reality of the other's perceptions of loss. Gilbert says, "The ability to cry together and display deep emotions in each other's company" was perceived as helpful toward resolving the loss. In this regard, simply listening to a spouse's expression of deep emotion is meaningful, as is the ability to express support both verbally and through nonverbal cues and signals.

A distinctive characteristic of couples who report little conflict is the positive view that each has of the other and of their relationship. Accepting differences and being flexible about role relationships are also among the factors that contribute to sharing grief. Coming to terms with a grieving spouse's behavior is enhanced by the ability of partners to *reframe* each other's behavior in a positive way. For example, a husband who views his wife's sobbing as "breaking down" can alter his perception so that the crying is seen as emotionally cleansing and valuable. Reframing a spouse's behavior makes it

Käthe Kollwitz, Library of Congress

The overwhelming grief of parental bereavement is expressed in the soft-ground etching Überfahren *(Passing Over), by Käthe Kollwitz, whose art became a means of working through her own sorrow following the death of a child. The dead child is carried by adults bent with the burden of grief; other children look on.*

possible to explain the behavior in positive terms, rather than judging it as inappropriate or dysfunctional. When previously unsettling behavior can be seen as providing emotional release, it allows a mate to support the expression instead of trying to curtail it by urging the spouse to "get it together." As in other areas of relationships, it is often the "little things" spouses do that cause their partners to feel supported and loved.

Childbearing Losses

Pregnancy represents a major life transition for adults. The expected result is the birth of a viable, healthy baby. Miscarriage, stillbirth, or neonatal death is not the anticipated outcome of pregnancy. Yet, such losses do occur. In 1990, nearly 68,000 fetal and infant deaths were recorded in the United States, with about 43 percent of these deaths having been stillbirths, another 36 percent neonatal deaths, and the remaining 21 percent postneonatal deaths.[17]

The grief experienced after a perinatal loss can be as devastating as the loss of an older child.[18]

According to medical definition, *stillbirth* refers to fetal death occurring between the twentieth week of gestation (pregnancy) and the time of birth, resulting in the delivery of a dead child. *Neonatal* deaths are those occurring during the first four weeks following birth. In the statistics given above, *post-neonatal* deaths include those that occur after the first four weeks and up to eleven months following birth.

These statistics do not include deaths from *miscarriage,* which occurs prior to the twentieth week of gestation. Miscarriage, also termed *spontaneous abortion,* is defined as "loss of the products of conception before the fetus is viable."[19] The distinction between miscarriage and stillbirth is based on the logic that most fetuses are viable—that is, able to survive outside the mother's body—after the twentieth week of pregnancy. It is estimated that about 20 percent of all pregnancies end in miscarriage, with about three-fourths of these ending before twelve weeks.[20] In contrast to spontaneous abortion, which occurs naturally, *induced abortion* (sometimes called artificial or therapeutic abortion) is brought about intentionally with the aim of ending a pregnancy by mechanical means or drugs.

Broadly considered, reproductive loss also includes losses resulting from infertility and sterility. Whereas *infertility* refers to "diminished or absent capacity to produce offspring," *sterility* denotes "complete inability to produce offspring," due either to inability to conceive (female) or to induce conception (male).[21] Although most couples are able to produce children without undue difficulty, it is sadly true that "some manage only after years of disappointment and some not at all."[22] Despite advances in medical treatment for infertility, many couples ultimately find themselves facing the fact that they will remain childless, their biological and social urges to reproduce thwarted by forces beyond their control.

Another example of reproductive loss involves giving up a child for *adoption.* Although this might not initially be thought of as a childbearing loss because adoption usually results from choice, grief may accompany such decisions. Often unrecognized, unsupported, and unresolved, the grief following such a loss can have a deep emotional effect on birth parents. Seeing a child at play or walking down the street can spur the reaction of wondering what one's own child might be like at that age. Recognizing adoption as a type of childbearing loss, some communities now offer counseling and other supportive services for birth parents.

A comprehensive view of childbearing losses also includes the losses that ensue when a child is born with severe disabilities, such as congenital deformities or mental retardation. Parents may have difficulty accepting the reality that their child is not as they had wished for and dreamed about; they may grieve the loss of the "perfect" child. Coming to terms with such a loss is not easy. Lost expectations need to be acknowledged and mourned. Coping

Small Son

They have gone.
The last mourner,
the last comfort,
last cliche.

I wrap a pillow
in your blanket.
Lie burying my face
to hold your fading
milk sweet smell.

The silence swells.

    I run

to where the stand
of saplings wait
for clearing.

Chopping, slashing,
small limbs
dragged and pulled
and piled for burning.

I turn away
consumed,
the taste of ashes
in my mouth.

                Maude Meehan

involves finding ways to help themselves and the child lead the most productive lives possible under the circumstances.

All these reproductive or childbearing losses involve the reality of mourning unlived lives. Judith Savage says, "Childbearing losses are mourned not only for what was, but also for what might have been."[23] Grief is felt not only for the physical loss, but also for symbolic losses. Thus, survivors mourn "the child of the imagination, that part of themselves which seems now to have no possibility of embodiment in the world." Writing from the perspective of a Jungian psychologist who by the age of 33 had experienced multiple losses (her adoptive and biological parents, her two brothers, and her infant son), Savage says:

> By unraveling the mystery of the imaginative relationship, that is, the projections of the self onto the unborn child, it becomes clear that primary relationships are not composed merely of interchangeable functional attributes and roles but are uniquely personal bonds that are generated from deep within and are as much a reflection of the individual soul as they are an accurate reflection of the other.[24]

It is important to be aware of two distinct yet related realities: the *actual* relationship and the *symbolic* nature of the parent–child bond. Grieving parents often talk about lost companionship, lost dreams—all the ways in which the child would have enriched their lives. Such discussion is concerned with the actual loss. The symbolic loss relates to the meaning attached to the relationship, as when an individual, by parenting a child, becomes a nurturing, supportive guide. As one bereaved father said, "Not only have I lost a son who might follow in my footsteps, but, without him, I have no feet." It was important for this father to acknowledge and mourn both the loss of his son and the loss of meaning and purpose in his life.

When a person's identity as a nurturing parent has been thwarted, healing the grief requires honoring the archetypal bonds of parent and child. Simply put, an archetype is a basic form that takes shape from our experiences as human beings. Myth, legend, and history shape our understanding of such archetypal forms. In the context of parental bereavement, the archetypal child occupies polar opposites: the divine child (one who is all good) and the terrible child (one who is all bad). Within the experience of childbearing loss, the image of the lost child activates powerful associations.

According to the model suggested by Savage, grief involves merging the "archetypal child" with the actual child. This transforms the search for the "external object" into an inner search whereby the meanings attached to the child are made conscious. In this way, "those attributes which were feared permanently lost are regained and the parent can return to life with hope, imagination, trust, and an openness toward experience."[25] The loss is neither denied nor minimized; instead, it becomes part of a natural process guiding the bereaved parent's journey toward wholeness.

Grief following a childbearing loss may be influenced by the parents' perceptions that the loss is neither understood nor acknowledged by others.[26] Bereaved parents report hearing insensitive comments, such as "It must be easier since you didn't get too attached." Well-intentioned family members and friends may attempt to minimize the death in an effort to console the bereaved parent. They may say, "You're young; you can have another baby," unaware that such a comment, though possibly true, is inappropriate. No other baby will replace the one who has just died. Advice such as this is especially difficult for couples who postponed having children—they may feel the added constraint of time compounding the experience of loss.

Self-esteem suffers when a parent is unable to complete the act of sexual reproduction. Blame can be turned inward as well as directed outward. Questions about the cause of the tragedy abound: Was it that glass of wine, the aspirin, or, as one mother asked in desperation, "Was it the nutmeg I put on my oatmeal?" Even inconsequential actions may be evaluated this way.

Anger may be directed toward the other parent with the accusation, "You never wanted this baby anyway!" Or it may be focused on the baby, resulting in confusing emotions for parents. After all, what kind of person could be angry at an innocent infant? Yet anger is a natural response to loss. As one woman said of her stillborn daughter, "Why did she just drop in and out of my life? Why did she bother coming at all?" Emotional responses may be accompanied by auditory or kinesthetic hallucinations: A baby cries in the night, waking parents from sleep; the baby kicks inside the womb, yet there is no pregnancy, no live child.

Absent a baby, the mother may be confronted by physical reminders of the loss, such as the onset of lactation. One bereaved mother said, "I wanted to go to the cemetery and let my milk flow onto my daughter's grave." Meanwhile, the father may feel culturally constrained to "be brave" so that he can support the mother, who is recuperating physically as well as emotionally. In the process, the father's need to grieve may go unmet, and his emotions may be pushed below the surface until long afterward.

Perinatal bereavement care is important. The program sponsored by the Reuben Center for Women and Children at Toledo Hospital in Ohio is a positive example of support for parents who have suffered a childbearing loss.[27] Established in 1980, the program has a variety of bereavement protocols, including guidelines on how staff and volunteers can offer bereavement support, photographic techniques (photos are taken of all deceased infants and are given to parents either at the time of the death or at whatever time they want them), use of trained support group volunteers, distribution of printed materials on bereavement and grief (including a brochure written expressly to educate relatives and friends of the bereaved about what they can do), use of hospital chaplains, various funeral options, and the availability of other local support groups for families who do not live near the hospital. The hospital hosts regular meetings of a bereavement support group and, if desired, home visits are made. Educational programs and mutual support are also provided for staff members who provide primary care for newly bereaved families. Programs like this demonstrate that comprehensive support for perinatal loss can be provided to families, staff, and the community.

Miscarriage

Many people assume that the loss of a baby during the early stages of pregnancy evokes feelings of disappointment, but not grief. To parents who have dreamed about the baby even before its conception, however, miscarriage evokes pain and confusion. A parent may ask, "Didn't I want this baby enough?" Parents may be told that the loss is simply "Nature's way" of weeding out genetic anomalies. To grieving parents, this remark provides little or no consolation because it was *their* baby that Nature decided to sort. Platitudes that minimize or deny the loss are decidedly unhelpful. When parents experience a series of miscarriages, grief is further compounded.

Parents may have difficulty identifying their loss precisely or making sense of what has happened.[28] One young mother's grief was complicated after a miscarriage because she had no remains to be buried. "I didn't know where my baby was," she said. Even though a miscarriage may have occurred many years ago, grief for an unborn baby can recur with other significant life events—for example, at the birth of a subsequent child or the onset of menopause. A particular marker, such as reaching age forty or age sixty-five, can reawaken feelings of grief.

Induced Abortion

In the United States, about one-fourth of all pregnancies are terminated by induced abortion, resulting in an annual total of about 1.6 million abortions.[29] Although it might be assumed that women who elect to terminate a pregnancy would not experience a grief reaction, this hypothesis is certainly not universally true. The grief reaction to elective abortion can be substantially the same as that following involuntary fetal or infant loss.[30] Such a reaction is influenced by the individual's perception of the pregnancy: Does she perceive herself as simply pregnant, or does she see herself as a potential mother? Similar questions can apply to men who are involved in decisions about elective abortion.

The emotional reaction to abortion varies; some people experience minimal grief while others suffer considerable emotional trauma. In some cases, the repercussions of such decisions are not felt until much later. One woman, who had chosen to abort a pregnancy as a young adult because she and her husband felt their relationship could not withstand the pressures of raising a child at that time, experienced considerable remorse later when she and her husband found themselves unable to have other children. "That may have been our only chance," she lamented. Subsequent pregnancy loss may be experienced as "retribution" for an earlier abortion. In addition, personal and social attitudes toward abortion can affect the resolution of grief. When social support is lacking, people have fewer opportunities to express their feelings about a loss.

In Japan, at places like Hase Temple in Kamakura and Shiun Jizo Temple north of Tokyo, thousands of tiny stone statues called *mizuko* represent children conceived but never born.[31] Some of these "water children" wear bibs and stocking caps. Placed alongside them are toy milk bottles, dolls, and twirling pinwheels, along with memorials written by their sponsors—women who chose to have an abortion rather than give birth. The statues, each one costing several hundred dollars, are erected as repositories for the souls of unborn babies. At Hase Temple, the more than 50,000 *mizuko* are watched over by a thirty-foot-tall wooden statue of the "Goddess of Mercy," who is also the patroness of safe birth. Even though abortion is common in Japan (due to government restrictions on birth control), the popularity of "mizuko worship" bears witness to an intense desire to acknowledge the unborn fetus.

Even when the decision for an abortion results from adverse information about the baby's health, the choice can be a source of conflict that adds to parents' grief. Many genetic diseases are identified by tests during the early phases of pregnancy; and, when the results are unfavorable, terminating the pregnancy may seem the best or only choice. Some tests can be done only well into the pregnancy, after the mother has already felt the baby moving. Parents who decide in favor of a therapeutic abortion often worry that no one will understand their "choice" and that they will be judged harshly. Furthermore, such couples may face not only the death of a particular baby, but also the possibility of a childless future; biological considerations or genetic risk may preclude the choice to conceive again.

Kenneth Doka points out that contemporary views about abortion may place the bereaved in a dilemma: Those who believe a loss occurred may not sanction the act, whereas those who sanction the act may not recognize that grief in response to the perceived loss needs to be expressed and legitimized. Difficulties in grieving may be exacerbated when customary sources of solace and social support are not readily available.[32]

Stillbirth

"Instead of giving birth, I gave death," said a mother whose daughter died in childbirth. Instead of a cradle, there is a grave; instead of receiving blankets, there are burial clothes; instead of a birth certificate, there is a death certificate. After a stillbirth, "a family's wishes and hopes and dreams—the individuals' illusions about what life *ought* to be—are quickly shattered by the reality of what life really *is*."[33] Those who counsel newly bereaved parents of a stillborn baby emphasize the importance of acknowledging the child's birth. Rather than whisking away the stillborn infant as quickly as possible, hospital staff can encourage parents to see and hold their baby. Healthy grief is facilitated by acknowledging the reality of the baby's life and death. A postmortem photograph of the child may assist in the process of grieving.[34] Parents may choose to hold a memorial service for the stillborn baby, a practice that not only acknowledges the reality of what has happened, but that allows an opportunity for finding meaning and solace in a confusing situation.

Support groups dealing with issues of pregnancy loss encourage hospitals to use information packets that include a "Certificate of Stillbirth," which acknowledges the birth as well as the death of the child. Linking objects, such as a lock of hair, a photograph, and the receiving blanket can be comforting to parents, if not at first, then later when they want to hold on to every precious memory. Nearly 90 percent of the parents included in a study by John De Frain named their stillborn baby in recognition that it was indeed part of the family, no matter how briefly: "Naming seemed to help show others that the baby really existed and was important, not just something to be thrown away and forgotten."[35] Most parents of stillborn babies conclude that, even though the hurt may fade as time passes, the memories do not.

Neonatal Death

When a baby is born alive but with life-threatening disabilities due to prematurity, congenital defects, or other causes, the ensuing period can be a nightmare for parents. Frustration and a sense of futility may be overwhelming as surgery or other interventions are attempted and fail. Sometimes a baby born with one or more life-threatening conditions embarks on a life-or-death struggle that lasts weeks.

Parents may be confronted by ethical choices that could result in the baby's death. Meanwhile the costs incurred in keeping the baby alive continue to accrue. After the death of the baby, parents may resent the medical institution and its personnel, feeling as if they survived a painful and futile ordeal only to be billed later for the experience.

In circumstances involving a critically ill newborn, *any* decision may haunt parents as they repeatedly ask themselves if they made the right choice.

© Albert Lee Strickland

The items placed around the grave of this infant in Hawaii—balloons, flowers, and jars of baby food—bespeak the parents' loss and acknowledge the enduring bonds of even a short-lived relationship.

Caregivers who appreciate the heart-wrenching ethical dilemmas that occur in the context of neonatal intensive care are in a position to provide sensitive care and support to parents facing the prospect of making and living with these difficult decisions. When the life of a critically ill infant is being sustained by extraordinary medical means, the decision to terminate the artificial support ought to be handled with as much grace as circumstances allow. The choices made in the context of neonatal care can be troubling for medical practitioners as well as parents. As one young neonatologist remarked, "One of the most difficult and important things for me to learn was to hand over the baby to the parents so it could die in their arms."

Sudden Infant Death Syndrome

Although not, strictly speaking, in the category of reproductive or childbearing loss, Sudden Infant Death Syndrome (SIDS) has many of the same

Last year, a fourteen-year-old boy who suddenly collapsed on the street was rushed to our hospital emergency room. Even though there were no clinical signs of life, at least six physicians frantically attempted resuscitative measures. In the hallway outside the emergency room, I came upon two stunned parents who were standing absolutely alone. None of the physicians wanted to leave the dramatic scene to obtain a history, let alone provide any solace. I did not want to either, the boy was dead (possibly from a cardiac conduction defect—even the autopsy later was unrevealing); but I forced myself to sit down in an adjoining room and listen while they talked of their hopes and their son's aspirations. I am used to talking with parents whose children die of sudden infant death syndrome; this was different and I was overwhelmed. Afterward, I went to my office and cried. I later thought that I should have let my interns and residents witness me cry to learn that professionalism does not preclude expression of human feeling.

Abraham B. Bergman, "Psychological Aspects of Sudden Unexpected Death in Infants and Children"

characteristics and consequences in terms of parental bereavement. SIDS deaths usually affect children under the age of one year; the death is sudden, and often comes at night. Parents are typically left angry, often with a tremendous sense of guilt. The unexpected and sudden nature of the death, age of the child, and uncertainty about the cause of death combine to make SIDS deaths a high-grief loss.

Parents of an infant whose death is attributed to SIDS may be subjected to criminal investigation as concerns about child abuse prompt law enforcement officials to question whether the parents are somehow responsible. With greater understanding about SIDS deaths, most investigations are now handled more sensitively, a result brought about in part because of information disseminated by parent support groups concerned about the effects of misdirected questioning and accusations on grieving parents. Still, parents may question themselves just as sternly, wondering if the death was in any way due to something they did or something left undone; could it have been prevented in some way? The unexplained nature of many SIDS deaths can lead to a quest for answers that ultimately may not be available. Peer support provided by other parents who have dealt with the death of a child from SIDS can be an important source of reliable information as well as emotional comfort through grief.

The Critically Ill or Dying Child

Many of the issues discussed in connection with pregnancy loss, neonatal death, and the death of an infant also pertain to the death of an older child or adolescent. The meaning of such a death is more complex, however, because the relationship between parent and child has been of longer duration, with a correspondingly larger store of memories. A child represents many things to a parent. As Beverly Raphael reminds us, a child is "a part of the self, and of the loved partner; a representation of generations past; the genes of the forebears; the hope of the future; a source of love, pleasure, even narcissistic delight; a tie or a burden; and sometimes a symbol of the worst parts of the self and others."[36] As experiences are shared, the bond between parent and child takes on increasing complexity. During the years of childhood and adolescence, the relationship between parent and child may include feelings of ambivalence, no matter how strong the bonds of affection and love. Thus, the death of a child can be an especially difficult type of bereavement.

When a child's life is threatened by illness, it affects the whole fabric of family life. Parents and siblings, along with other relatives, are all involved in coping with the illness, which gradually becomes integrated into overall family patterns. As the child grows closer to death, there may be—in addition to the physical isolation that accompanies illness—a psychic separation, a distancing from the child by parents, relatives, and even members of the health care team. For the dying child, this psychic distancing can be the most severe pain of all.

If the significant adults in the child's life find it difficult to witness the physical disintegration caused by disease, they may avoid situations that elicit painful feelings. Parents may exhibit an unwillingness to confront the reality of the situation by taking long absences from the child's room or by keeping their interactions with the child as brief as possible. They may create excuses for interruptions when the situation becomes too painful or may avoid altogether any topics related to the child's illness. In these ways, parents signal their limits about what they feel comfortable discussing with the child.

A family's established communication patterns also shape how parents and other family members relate to a child's illness. Few families can sustain complete openness to the reality of a child's terminal illness throughout what may be a lengthy process from diagnosis of the disease to the child's death. The intensity of debilitating or disrupting symptoms also varies. At times, the sick child may function quite normally, and the routine of medical care may become simply another aspect of family life. At other times, the disease will require the family to deal specifically with changes in the child's condition. Families must adjust to fluctuations between hope for recovery and acceptance of terminality, while trying to support the child in the best way possible.

Families that deal openly with a child's illness are typically those in which the parents do not derive their personal identities solely from their role as parents. In other words, although parenting is an important part of their lives, it does not constitute the totality of their self-image, which encompasses other accomplishments and values as well.

Some people who are confronted by the reality of a seriously ill child not only survive, but grow from the experience. Jerome Schulman writes: "Rather than simply coping—in the sense of merely surviving—many parents and children respond to a severe illness by making a more mature reevaluation of their lives and achieving a truer vision of what counts. Their lives become more

We had waited, agonizing through the nights and days without sleep, startled by nearly any sound, unable to eat, simply staring at our meals. Suddenly in a few seconds of radio time it was over. My first son, whose birth had brought me so much joy that I jumped up in a hall outside the room where he was born and touched the ceiling—the child, the scholar, the preacher, the boy singing and smiling, the son—all of it was gone. And Ebenezer was so quiet. All through the church as the staff learned what had happened, the tears flowed, but almost completely in silence.

Martin Luther King, Sr.

significant, more basic, more meaningful. They live one day at a time . . . but they learn to make each new day more enriching."[37]

The Death of an Adult Child

For a young or middle-aged adult to die while his or her parents live on seems unnatural. It is a death "out of sequence," unexpected and difficult to resolve. A study of parents who had lost an adult son during military service found that the parents felt an "existential vacuum," which was expressed through lack of meaning and purpose in life.[38] Even though there is likely to be a degree of separation between an adult child and his or her parent, this does not mean that the parent's grief will be correspondingly less intense.

The older parent who survives the death of a middle-aged child may also be losing a caregiver. The adult child may represent a source of comfort and security that is now gone. Parental bereavement can be complicated by the sense of "competing" with the deceased's spouse or children for the role of "most bereaved." Who has priority in receiving care and comfort? Sometimes the death of an adult child involves circumstances that require parents to assume care of their grandchildren, a result that may be emotionally as well as economically disruptive.

Parents who suffer the death of a child already grown to adulthood may find themselves virtually alone in coping with their grief. In contrast to the situation of parents who lose younger children to terminal illness or individuals who survive the death of a spouse, comparatively few social support resources are available to help parents cope with the death of an adult child. Perhaps because this type of bereavement is an anomaly, it has not been studied extensively. Yet, the death of a child—at whatever age—is clearly a major loss.

Support Groups for Parental Bereavements

Support groups exist to offer information and help to parents who are coping with the serious illness or death of a child. One such group, Compassionate Friends, is directed primarily to the needs of parents who have experienced the death of a child. A group known as the Guild for Infant Survival is composed of parents who have lost children to "crib death," or Sudden Infant Death Syndrome (SIDS). Another group, Candlelighters, is made up of parents of children with cancer. From a child's initial diagnosis with cancer, through his or her treatment and long-term survival or death, there are specific programs for the child, his or her parents, and other family members. These programs range from offering emotional support in coping with the reality of childhood cancer to providing practical information for dealing with problems related to treatment, nutrition, interruption in school attendance, disruption of family patterns, and so on.

Besides providing emotional support for the grief experienced at the loss of a child, some organizations for bereaved parents also engage in political advocacy designed to remedy the situation that precipitated the death. Examples of these peer support groups include Mothers Against Drunk Driving and Parents of Murdered Children. The grief resulting from losses such as those reflected in the names of these two organizations is complicated by the violent circumstances of a child's death, circumstances that may be accompanied by intrusions on the family's grief by media coverage of the event as well as subsequent criminal investigation and judicial proceedings.

There are many ways of offering support to bereaved families: listening, sending cards and letters of condolence or making phone calls, bringing food, doing housework, caring for other children in the family, helping with chores, sharing one's own grief over the loss, letting the parents grieve, giving the parents time to be alone, and touching with one's eyes, arms, and heart.[39] Such support can be offered by relatives, friends, and neighbors who are not afraid to talk about the issues that follow in the wake of a child's death.

Death of a Parent

The death of a parent typically represents the loss of a long-term relationship characterized by nurture and unconditional support. Parents are often described as "always there when the chips are really down, no matter what." The death of a parent is generally followed by a period of upheaval and transition. A parent's death is an important symbolic event for midlife adults. Most people report that the death of a parent changes their outlook on life, often spurring them on to examine their lives more closely, to begin changing what they don't like, and to appreciate more fully their ongoing relationships.[40]

Any death reminds us of our own mortality, but the death of a parent forces a person to realize, perhaps for the first time, that he or she has become an adult. When parents are alive, they usually provide moral support for their children; there is a sense that if real trouble comes a child can call on his or her parents. These feelings can provide a sense of security. When a parent dies, that security is diminished. The bereaved child may feel there is no one left to answer a call for help unconditionally.

You Don't Miss Your Water

At home, my mother wakes up and spends some of her day talking back to my father's empty chair.

In Florida, my sister experiences the occasional dream in which my father returns; they chat.

He's been dead and gone for a little over a year. How it would please me to hear his unrecorded voice again, now alive only in the minds of those who remember him.

If I could, if as in the old spiritual, I could actually get a direct phone link to the other side, I could call him up, tell him about this small prize of a week I've had teaching poetry at a ski resort a few miles from Lake Tahoe, imagination jackpot, brief paradise of letters.

How could I make him believe that I have gotten all of this, this modern apartment, this pond in front of my window, all from the writing of a few good lines of verse, my father, who distrusted anything he couldn't get his hands on?

Most likely, he would listen, then ask me, as he always did, just for safety's sake, if my wife still had her good paying job.

And I can't tell you why, but this afternoon, I wouldn't become hot and stuffy from his concern, think "old fool" and gripe back *Of course I'm still teaching college. It's summer, you know?*

This afternoon, I miss his difficult waters, and when he'd ask, as he always would, *how're they treating you?* I'd love to answer back, *fine, daddy. They're paying me to write about your life.*

Cornelius Eady

There is evidence that the death of one's parents can result in a "developmental push," which may effect a "more mature stance in parentally bereaved adults who no longer think of themselves as children."[41] When both parents have died, there is a role change for the adult child, who no longer has his or her parents to "fall back on," even if only in the imagination. After the deaths of both her parents, one woman said that, although she knew friends and other relatives loved and cared about her, she felt that the love from her parents had been unique, unconditional, and irreplaceable.

The death of a mother is considered by many people a harder loss to sustain than the death of a father. This may be due partly to a mother's traditional status as the primary nurturing caregiver. Another reason, however, may be the fact that, statistically, fathers die before mothers. Thus, when the mother dies, the death represents the loss of having "parents" as the bereaved adult child experiences reactive grief over the death of the other parent as well.

When a family relationship has been dysfunctional, the death of a parent brings to an end the hope of creating a better, more functional relationship.

Upon the death of her alcoholic mother, one middle-aged woman lamented, "With her death, dead also is the dream that she would eventually go into treatment and that we would finally heal the wounds our family has suffered. Although I'm relieved that I can no longer be hurt by her drinking, I wish it could have turned out differently."

For adults, the death of a parent may result in a less intense grief compared with, say, the death of a child. This phenomenon is probably related to the fact that an adult child is involved in his or her own life; feelings of attachment have been largely redirected toward others, such as spouse and children. Nevertheless, a parent's death can have a long-term impact as the bereaved child mourns the loss of the special relationship that had existed with the deceased parent.

Spousal Bereavement

The ties between two persons in a paired relationship are usually so closely interwoven that, as Beverly Raphael says, the death of one partner "cuts across the very meaning of the other's existence."[42] Although we may recognize the likelihood that one spouse will die before the other and that the survivor will be left to carry on alone, such thoughts are generally kept in the background. The pressing activities of daily life occupy our attention until one day the possibility becomes a reality that can't be ignored.

The aftermath of a mate's death has been described as follows: "Everyday occurrences underscore the absence of your mate. Sitting down to breakfast, or dinner, opening mail, hearing a special song, going to bed, all become sources of pain when they were formerly sources of pleasure. Each day is full of challenges and heartbreaks."[43] Although a spouse's death always requires an adjustment from being a couple to being single, the transition may be especially hard for the survivor who is also a parent. With children to care for, there is an added burden of making a transition to single parenthood.

Factors Influencing Spousal Bereavement

Although the loss of a spouse is the most intensively studied of all loss experiences during adulthood, most research has focused on a brief time span immediately after bereavement; there are few studies of the enduring effects of spousal loss.[44] Thus, questions remain: How do factors such as age and gender affect styles of coping with the death of a mate? What role does social support play in coming to terms with such a significant loss?

It is also noteworthy that studies of spousal bereavement tend to focus exclusively on heterosexually paired relationships; homosexual couples who make a lifelong commitment to each other are virtually ignored in the literature. In the wider community, grief in response to the death of a partner in a same-sex relationship is often poorly understood and acknowledged only minimally. Grief may be exacerbated by conflict with a mate's parents who

When a man to whom you have been married for more than thirty years dies, a piece of you that you will never know again goes out the door with him. Sitting dry-eyed in a chair watching the rescue-squad men load him onto the stretcher and strap him in, I was mercifully numb. Yes, I said obediently, I would await a call from the coroner; yes, his doctor could be reached at the hospital; yes, I would be all right alone.

And then they were wheeling him out the door, casting uneasy backward glances at me. Thirty years of being us was suddenly transformed into just me.

Elizabeth C. Mooney, *Alone: Surviving as a Widow*

never made peace with their son's or daughter's unconventional life style. "If I was effectively nonexistent to them before," one surviving mate said, "I really vanished after my partner died. For years, they denied our commitment to each other; now they acted as if they could completely erase me! They claimed everything: the body, our home, and, seemingly, my right to grieve." In reading and thinking about spousal bereavement, notice that the experience of such a loss pertains to the bonds formed by the partners that are broken by death. Even though the automatic reaction is to think of a "marital" bond as signifying a legally sanctioned heterosexual relationship, it is important to recognize that the reality of grief over the loss of a mate is really independent of legal or social sanctions about the nature of relationships.

The patterns of intimacy and interaction between spouses form an important determinant of how the loss of a partner will be perceived by a survivor. One couple derives primary satisfaction from shared activities; another prefers a higher degree of separateness. In some relationships, the focus is on children; in others, the adult partners take precedence. The patterns of any relationship are in flux as circumstances change over time.

Consider the difference in outlook between a young couple, together only a short time, and an older couple, who have shared their lives over many years. When spousal bereavement occurs in old age, it typically follows what has been a lifetime of mutual commitment and shared experiences. In contrast, a young couple just setting out to build a world together is engaged in what Charles Brice characterizes as an "ongoing creative dialogue which, in turn, defines the mature love relationship."[45] When one of the partners dies, the survivor is left alone to reconstitute previously shared aims. During the years from youth to old age, a person's standard of living and overall quality of life are also likely to change, thus affecting the meaning and reality of loss. Furthermore, youth and old age involve differing expectations about mortality.

Age also influences a person's style of coping.[46] Although bereaved spouses of all ages report depressive symptoms during the first year of bereavement, younger people seem to experience more physical distress and tend to

Mr. and Mrs. Andrew Lyman, Polish tobacco farmers living near Windsor Locks, Connecticut, exemplify some of the qualities that contribute to a close relationship. When such a bond is severed by death, the effect is felt in every area of the survivor's life.

rely more on drugs to counter this distress than do older people. However, older people may have health problems that were neglected while caring for an ailing spouse. In the first year following the loss of a mate, there are increases in the morbidity and mortality rates of widows and widowers, with aged people particularly at risk. While caring for a dying spouse, the survivor's ties to the outside world may have lessened, thus increasing feelings of loneliness following bereavement.

Relief following the death of a spouse, although little discussed, is an emotion experienced by many women and men who have cared for an ailing spouse over a long period of time. Death may be viewed as ending further suffering for an ailing loved one. Less socially accepted, or even acknowledged, is relief experienced when a mate's death is welcomed as the end to an unsatisfactory relationship.

Spousal bereavement also elicits distinct behaviors related to culturally sanctioned gender roles. In one culture, a widower might avoid crying publicly because doing so would be viewed as "weak" and shameful. A widower in another culture, conversely, might express his grief through many tears and loud crying because not doing so would suggest a "weakness" in ability to love.

Individuals who have lived out traditional sex roles may find the transition to widowhood especially hard. Learning to manage unfamiliar role responsibilities in the midst of grief can be a formidable task, intensifying feelings of helplessness. The widow who has never written a check or the widower who has never prepared dinner is confronted not only with grief at losing a loved one, but also with major role readjustments. New skills must be learned to manage the needs of daily life. An individual's involvement in multiple roles may be a better predictor of adjustment following bereavement than gender, age, time elapsed from the spouse's death, educational attainment, income level, or degree of religiosity.[47] In other words, widowed individuals whose life styles included multiple roles—such as parent, employee, friend, student, hobbyist, or participant in community, political, and religious organizations—seem to experience a better adjustment to bereavement than do those with fewer role involvements.

Adverse effects of spousal death appear to be more prevalent among widowers, perhaps because men who live out traditional sex roles find it more difficult to manage domestic matters that were left to the now-deceased spouse. Widowers also may be less likely than widows to seek help from others, again a trait of "self-reliance" that may be associated with a traditional sex role. As Judith Stillion points out, men who care for an ailing partner over an extended period of time may be at a disadvantage in coping with the onset of normal physical and psychological problems of bereavement if "their socialization prohibits them from asking for help, showing strain, or even, in some instances, recognizing and discussing their feelings with helping professionals."[48] One study, which followed more than five hundred elderly widows and widowers over a period of six years, found "excess mortality" for males over

> your hair is falling out,   and
> you are not so beautiful:
> your eyes have dark shadows
> your body is bloated;   arms covered with
>   bruises and needlemarks;
> legs swollen and useless . . .
>   your body and spirit
> are weakened with toxic chemicals
> urine smells like antibiotics,
>   even the sweat
> that bathes your whole body
>   in the early hours of morning
> reeks of dicloxacillin   and methotrexate.
>
>   you are nauseous all the time
> i am afraid to move on the bed
> for fear of waking you   to moan
> and lean over the edge
>   vomiting into the bag
>
>   i curl up fetally
>   withdraw into my dreams
> with a frightened back to you . . .
>   and i'm scared
>   and i'm hiding
> but i love you so much;

age seventy-five as compared with males of the same age group in the general population.[49]

Because women statistically live longer than men, it is estimated that three out of every four married women will be widowed at one time or another. Of the 13.7 million widowed people living in the United States, more than 11 million are widows.[50] Widows who want to remarry face not only social pressures but a situation wherein there are few eligible men. However, it has been suggested that widowhood is less difficult for women than retirement is for men. This is because there are many other widows with whom to share leisure time and activities, so that a woman's status actually increases with widowhood, whereas a man's status decreases at retirement.

Social Support for Bereaved Spouses

The availability of a stable social support network is a crucial factor in determining how bereaved spouses adjust to their changed status.[51] The death of a mate results in the loss of a primary source of one's social interactions and alters a person's social role in the community. Maintaining the continuity of

this truth does not change . . .
years ago,
when i met you, as we were falling in love,
your beauty attracted me:
long, golden-brown hair
clear and peaceful green eyes
high cheekbones   and long smooth muscles
but you know—and this is true—
i fell in love with your soul
the real essence of you
and this cannot grow less beautiful . . .

sometimes   these days
even your soul is cloudy
i still recognize you

we may be frightened
be hiding our sorrow
it may take a little longer
to acknowledge the truth,
but i would not want to be   anywhere else
i am here   with you
you can grow less beautiful to the world
you are safe
i will always love you.

A young widow

one's social support network can be important in smoothing the process of adjustment to loss and alleviating disruptions caused by attendant role changes following the death of a spouse.

Maintaining relationships with nonrelatives appears to be especially important, because friendships are based on common interests and life styles. Family relationships, in contrast, may pose a potential psychological threat to the widowed elderly because they contain elements of "role reversal" between the adult child and the aging parent that suggest or demand dependency from the aged widow or widower. Furthermore, an adult child's experience of the loss differs from that of the bereaved spouse, who is likely to value the loss as more significant than does the child and to feel the effects of the loss more intensely with respect to physical and emotional health.[52]

One of the most valuable resources for the recently widowed is contact with peers—that is, other bereaved people who have lost a mate and who can serve as role models during the subsequent period of adjustment. The widowed person acting as role model does not try to minimize the painful or difficult feelings of grief. Rather, exposed to the helper's accepting attitude,

"Widow" is a harsh and hurtful word. It comes from the Sanskrit and it means "empty." I have been empty too long. I do not want to be pigeon-holed as a widow. I am a woman whose husband has died, yes. But not a second-class citizen, not a lonely goose. I am a mother and a working woman and a friend and a sexual woman and a laughing woman and a concerned woman and a vital woman. I am a person. I resent what the term widow has come to mean. I am alive. I am part of the world.

If fate had reversed its whim and taken me instead of Martin, I would expect him to be very much part of the world. I cannot see him with the good gray tag of "widower." He would not stand for it for one moment. And neither will I. Not anymore.

But what of love? The warmth, the tenderness, the passion I had for Martin? Am I rejecting that, too?

Ah, that is the very definition of bereavement. The love object is lost. And love without its object shrivels like a flower betrayed by an early frost. How can we live without it? Without love? Without its total commitment? This explains the passionate grief of widowhood. Grief is as much a lament for the end of love as anything else.

Acceptance finally comes. And with it comes peace. Today I carry the scars of my bitter grief. In a way I look upon them as battle stripes, marks of my fight to attain an identity of my own. I owe the person I am today to Martin's death. If he had not died, I am sure I would have lived happily ever after as a twentieth-century child wife never knowing what I was missing. . . .

But today I am someone else. I am stronger, more independent. I have more understanding, more sympathy. A different perspective. I have a quiet love for Martin. I have passionate, poignant memories of him. He will always be part of me. But—

If I were to meet Martin today . . . ?

Would I love him?

I ask myself. Startled. What brought the question to my mind. I know. I ask it because I am a different woman.

Yes. Of course I would. I love him now. But Martin is dead. And I am a different woman. And the next time I love, if ever I do, it will be a different man, a different love.

Frightening.

But so is life. And wonderful.

Lynn Caine, *Widow*

the newly widowed person learns to live with these feelings and to gain perspective on them. Many "widows" groups now include widowers as well, and separate widower-to-widower support groups also exist.

The Widowed Persons Service (WPS), whose parent organization is the American Association of Retired Persons (AARP), began implementing a concept of mutual help to widowed individuals in 1973, following upon the pioneering work of Phyllis Silverman at Harvard University Medical School.[53] By the late 1980s, more than 200 chapters were functioning across the United

States. As a one-to-one outreach program of peer support, WPS offers help to newly widowed people provided by trained volunteers who themselves have been widowed. Individuals who participate in support groups such as those offered by the Widowed Persons Service report that such help is beneficial in helping them work through grief and achieve a positive resolution of the loss.

Aging and Illness

The expectations most people have about aging or being old differ from the actual experience. Young adults typically expect problems among older people to be more serious than they are for those who experience them. Bernice Neugarten reports that when she first developed a course on Adult Development and Aging "it was generally assumed that you reached a plateau simply called adulthood and you lived on that plateau until you went over the cliff at age sixty-five."[54] The stereotyped image of an aged person is marked by such outward signs as dry and wrinkled skin, graying hair, baldness, failing eyesight, loss of hearing, stiff joints, and general physical debility. Indeed, the physical signs of *senescence*, or the process of becoming old, are rightly associated with the aging of the human organism. (Senescence can be thought of in terms of vulnerability; the risk that an illness or an injury will prove fatal increases with age.)[55]

In developed societies, health promotion activities are devoted to improving the quality of life while "compressing" morbidity and extending "active" life expectancy.[56] In other words, shortening the period of debilitating illness associated with old age enables people to remain relatively active until quite near the end of their lives. Most individuals in modern societies enjoy relatively good health and active life styles until close to the time of death. Recognizing the changing health status of older people, the National Council on Aging uses the terms "young-old" for people ages 60 to 75, "middle-old" for those 75 to 85, and "old-old" for those over the age of 85.

In contrast to the stereotypical image of the aged, old people tend to be more individually distinct than any other segment of the population: They have had more years to create unique life histories. As Neugarten says, "People are 'open systems,' interacting with the people around them. All their experiences leave traces."[57] Mutual respect, faith, communion with others, and concern with existential issues of life are essential to the well-being of the aged.[58]

As a society we provide for the physical care of our aged through such programs as Social Security and Medicare. We appear to be less interested, however, in providing a "place" for the aged in society. The societal wish seems to be only that the old "age gracefully." As Daniel Callahan observes, the impulse to rid ourselves of stereotypes about old age may have the ironic effect of leading us "away from fruitful and valid generalizations about the elderly and fresh efforts to understand the place of old age in the life cycle."[59] While acknowledging individual *differences* among the aged, says Callahan, we should

While There Is Time

I carry the folding chair
for my mother
I carry the shawl
the large straw hat
to shield her from the glare
She leans her small weight
on my arm   Frail legs unsteady
feet now cramped with pain

Each day we sit for hours
at the ocean   The sun is hot
but she is wrapped and swathed
her hands are icy cold
they hide their ache
beneath the blanket

Her eyes follow the
movement that surrounds us
the romp of children
flight of gulls
the strong young surfers
challenging the sea

When the visit is ended
when my mother leaves
I will burst from the house
run empty-handed to the beach
hold out my arms
and swoop like a bird
my hands will tag children
as I pass

I will run and run
until I fall
and weep
for the crushed feet
the gnarled fingers
for her longing
I will run for both of us

Maude Meehan

also appreciate the "*shared* features of old age, the features that make it meaningful to talk about the aged as a group and about old age as an inherent part of individual life." In seeking what Callahan terms a "public meaning" of aging, important questions need to be discussed:

1. Because aging is often accompanied by "private suffering" caused by physical and psychological losses, how can such suffering become a meaningful and significant part of life?
2. What are the moral virtues (e.g., patience, cultivation of wisdom, courage in the face of change) that properly should be associated with preparing for and living old age?
3. What are the characteristic moral and social obligations of the elderly? Is old age a time for devoting one's life to pleasure and well-being, or is it a time for active involvement in the civic life of society?
4. What medical and social entitlements are due to the elderly? If we cannot meet every medical need or pursue every possible line of medical research, how can we arrive at an equitable level of support?

As Callahan suggests, our answers to such questions need to reflect both "what kind of elderly person we want ourselves to be and what ideal character traits we would like to promote and support." In considering one's own future status as an elder, it is worth noting that attempts to meet *all* the "needs" of the elderly must inevitably fail, especially if those needs are defined as the avoidance of disease and frailty. The obvious truth is, says Callahan, "it will *always* be impossible to meet such needs" despite an implicit social ideology that apparently "seeks to neutralize any inevitability about the process of aging and decline."

Despite medical advances that have extended human longevity, there remain haunting questions about the meaning and purpose of life. As Melvin Kimble observes, our culture "appears to lack symbols of transcendence and rituals that would give meaning to the experience of growing old," with the result than "an irrational and anxious dread about aging" begins to manifest itself at much earlier stages of the life cycle than one would normally expect.[60] What used to be called the prime of life is, for many, experienced as decline. The positive images and meanings of growing old are eroded when we regard old age as a pathological state or as an avoidable affliction. Growing old is not essentially a "medical problem." Robert Butler says, "None of us knows whether we have already had the best years of our lives or whether the best are yet to come. But the greatest of human possibilities remain to the very end of life—the possibilities for love and feeling, reconciliation and resolution."[61]

As the culminating phase of human life, the period of old age or maturity is an appropriate time to focus on the tasks specific to that part of the human journey. Such tasks involve an openness to matters associated with death education, including patients' rights, support groups, legal matters, funerals, facing one's own mortality, helping a dying or bereaved family member or friend, and learning to cope with loss and bereavement.[62] Robert Butler says:

> After one has lived a life of meaning, death may lose much of its terror. For what we fear most is not really death but a meaningless and absurd life. I believe most human beings can accept the basic fairness of each generation's taking its turn on the face of the planet if they are not cheated out of the full measure of their turn.[63]

Chronic and Debilitating Conditions

The cumulative effect of the physical and social realities of aging means that, if a person lives long enough, he or she is likely to experience loss on a daily basis. These losses may include diminished physiological functions, changes in self-esteem, inability to continue as a materially productive member of society, and increasing helplessness and vulnerability in all aspects of life.

The most obvious of these losses occur in connection with diseases common to the second half of life, including atherosclerosis, hypertension, and stroke syndrome, which are often found in interrelationship, each condition influencing the onset of the others. *Atherosclerosis,* a buildup of fatty deposits in the arteries that eventually constricts the flow of blood, has been singled out as a nearly universal health problem posing a barrier to any appreciable prolongation of life. *Hypertension,* or high blood pressure, frequently accompanies or

It is hard for me to speak of the regression that I watch. At first, there was a groping to express herself, along with the intense frustration at her every attempt. And then her moments of expression became less frequent, until eventually the struggle stopped. This disease has invaded her brain to such a depth that a state of passivity and helplessness has set in. One scene that is forever impressed on my memory took place in my apartment a little over two years ago. My mother was unable to achieve the simple motion of entering a room to sit in an armchair. She fearfully clung to the door frame, her eyes darting back and forth from chair to door, door to chair. Ultimately, she remained at the door until help came. Today, two years later, I wish I could at least see her standing unassisted.

Princess Yasmin Khan, daughter of Rita Hayworth

contributes to a variety of other illnesses and can lead to death from stroke or heart failure. *Strokes* are caused by a sudden blocking or rupture of the cerebral arteries, thereby interfering with the circulation of the blood in the brain. Even when a stroke is not fatal, it may result in loss of memory, speech defects, emotional problems, paralysis, or loss of control over bodily functions. With such maladies, the threat to well-being is generally cumulative, thus increasing the likelihood of ill effects as one gets older. Other diseases, arthritis and rheumatism, for example, are seldom identified as causes of death, yet they nevertheless result in debilitating losses that limit normal activities.

Degenerative diseases such as Alzheimer's and Parkinson's bring specific losses in their wake, as do hereditary diseases such as Huntington's and amyotrophic lateral sclerosis (ALS). When Alzheimer's disease affects a middle-aged or an old person, for example, there are losses not only for the affected individual but also for family and friends who can no longer relate in the same way to the person they once knew.[64] As the husband of one Alzheimer's patient said, "My wife is standing next to me, but she's not really there; what's standing there is a memory." The symptoms of Alzheimer's include declines in learning, attention, and judgment; disorientation in time and space; difficulty in finding words and communicating; and changes in personality. Conversely, with a disease like ALS, the body is rendered an increasingly useless shell while the mind remains intact and functioning.

The physical signs of aging are often accompanied by *psychological disorders*, including emotional distress (sometimes resulting from stressful and anxiety-provoking conditions) and disorders related to personality, mood, and depression, as well as *psychosomatic symptoms* affecting such physical processes as sleep, appetite, bowel movements, and fatigue. The old may also exhibit a variety of neuroses, psychoses, and brain syndromes. Such conditions, in varying degrees, involve change, transition, and loss.

Besides specific diseases, a variety of dysfunctions can have an impact on the older person's quality of life. Sensory and cognitive impairments can result

The worst fear of people who are at risk for Huntington's disease is that they will eventually get the disease and life will become meaningless for them. For most people, death itself is not nearly as fearful as the possibility of years of meaningless suffering. . . . The meaning of life is not, after all, the same for everybody. It varies from person to person according to a multitude of circumstances. And for each person it varies from day to day, even from hour to hour. The meaning of life constantly changes but *never ceases to exist*. It exists even in suffering. Often it exists especially in suffering. That is fortunate, because suffering is an inevitable part of life.

Dennis H. Phillips, *Living with Huntington's Disease: A Book for Patients and Families*

in loss of hearing or sight, or in a diminished sense of taste and smell. Oral and dental problems can make eating difficult, with the result that nutrition suffers, thus compounding the cycle of poor health. Deficient reaction times and psychomotor responses may increase the chance of accidents. Although any of these disabilities represents a significant loss by itself, in many instances a person experiences a number of these conditions at the same time.

Consider for a moment the effect of even a relatively minor injury on your usual functioning. As you think about the limitations this injury poses, you may gain some insight into what multiple losses may mean in the lives of those who experience them: What was once possible is now lost.

Options in Care of the Aged Adult

Round-the-clock care is sometimes needed to manage the symptoms associated with the debility associated with old age. Such care can have a significant impact on families as well as on the older person. Listen to conversations about care of the chronically ill older adult. Notice how the need for care may be described in language like this: "She couldn't live by herself so her son took her in," or "He was failing and had to be put in a nursing home." A question like, "What will we do with Dad when he is too old to manage by himself?" reflects both loving concern and inadvertent disregard for the aged relative. In light of remarks like these, it is not surprising that many aged people report feelings of being put away, taken in, done to, and otherwise manipulated, their integrity ignored.

Historically, the family has been a haven for ill and aged relatives, and families continue to provide the major portion of care for aged relatives. Some individuals and cultural groups place a very high value on keeping an older person within the family unit as opposed to placing him or her in an institutional care setting. Most aged people live in their own homes or with their families, but some require more assistance than relatives or friends can realistically provide. In the United States, social service programs on behalf of older

Of America's more than 1 million nursing home patients, women outnumber men by about three to one. The majority are white, widowed, and disabled. Few have visitors and only about 20 percent return home; the vast majority will die in the nursing home.

people can be traced to the Depression of the 1930s and passage of the Social Security Act of 1935. It was not until 1950, however, with enactment of the Old Age Assistance Act, that the first federal program designed specifically to relieve problems among the aged was implemented. Following adoption of the Medicare and Medicaid programs in the mid-1960s, federal assistance became an accepted means of providing care for America's elderly. Questions about how to provide adequate, as well as economical, care for the aged continue to be of public concern. Such issues become increasingly important as life expectancy increases; aged people are not only growing in number, but are also constituting a larger proportion of the total population.

When they can no longer continue to live independently and their families are unable to sustain the level of care needed, the aged find themselves

In Europe the availability of domiciliary homes for the elderly goes back to sixteenth-century "alms houses" for the indigent old in England and on the continent. During the Middle Ages, care of the elderly was sporadic, generally perceived of as a moral obligation of the church. In England, the Poor Law of 1601 settled the responsibility of caring for the poor and infirm on the shoulders of each community.

Jon Hendricks and C. Davis Hendricks, *Aging in Mass Society*

facing the prospect of institutional care. The type of institutional care required depends on an individual's physical and mental condition as well as his or her ability to act independently. *Domiciliary care homes,* for example, provide custodial care to residents who need minimal supervision in a sheltered environment and who are otherwise able to care for their own needs. People with more serious disabilities may live in *personal care homes,* which may or may not offer nursing care. Retirement communities and residential hotels or apartments generally fall into these two categories, which comprise about one-fourth of the institutional choices available. At a more comprehensive level of care, *skilled nursing facilities* furnish medical and nursing services as well as dietary supervision.

Alternatives to institutional care also exist for older people who are able to live more or less independently in their own homes. Depending on the resources available in a community, *home health care* may be available to assist in a variety of ways, ranging from medical and nursing visits to preparation of meals, help with exercise and other maintenance needs, and simple (but important) visitation. *Day hospitals* and *elder daycare centers* represent another form of alternative care for the aged. This alternative typically includes health maintenance, financial and general counseling, meals, and other services designed to increase independence, such as housekeeping, shopping, and transportation.

Halfway between institutionalization and independent living is a form of care known as *congregate housing.* This is usually a large residence with individual apartments or a series of structures within a small neighborhood. The distinguishing feature of this form of care is its organizational structure, which, like a series of concentric circles or graduated steps, provides the particular level of care needed by each resident. Within such a community, some individuals are essentially living independently, preparing meals in their own apartments or eating in the dining room when they wish. Other residents receive more help. In this way, older people enjoy a sense of security, knowing that help is available when it's needed, without completely losing their independence.

Despite the image of aged people being "dumped" in nursing homes by uncaring relatives, this is rarely the reality. On the contrary, families often

TABLE 11-2   *Steps in Choosing a Nursing Care Facility*

1. Make a list of local facilities offering the type of services needed.
2. Find out whether the facilities are licensed and certified.
3. Visit the facilities.
4. Prepare a checklist of desirable features and evaluate each facility in light of the needs of the person who would be moving in.
5. Determine the costs.
6. Make your decision.

Source: Adapted from Colette Browne and Roberta Onzuka-Anderson, editors, *Our Aging Parents: A Practical Guide to Eldercare* (Honolulu: University of Hawaii Press, 1985), pp. 204–209.

postpone obtaining adequate care for elders because of reluctance to face the fact that more intensive care is needed than can be provided in the home. Institutionalization is usually viewed as the ultimate personal failure for both the aged person and his or her family. Many elderly people view institutions as the least desirable option, "a sort of confession to final surrender, a halfway stop on the route to death."[65] When supervised, institutional care becomes the only reasonable course open to the family of an aged relative, the best outcome ensues when adequate information is gathered before making a decision about a particular facility (see Table 11-2).[66]

It is unfortunately true that, with rare exceptions, institutional care is depersonalizing. Residents often feel deprived of their self-esteem and integrity as well as their personal property. Rules and regulations dictate a style of life that may be far from what the resident would choose for himself or herself. Even a cherished picture of a loved one may find no place in the resident's room: not the bedstand (that's for bedpans), not the wall (patients are frequently moved)—so where? The answer too frequently is, "Nowhere."

Gerontologists—scholars and practitioners who study the aged and the processes of aging—point out that the "psychological railroading" associated with routinized environments can lead to *institutional neurosis*, the symptoms of which include "a gradual erosion of the uniqueness of one's personality traits so that residents become increasingly dependent on staff direction for even the most mundane needs."[67]

Institutional care is unavoidably oriented toward the efficient provision of necessary services to many residents. This results in a certain degree of routine. Nevertheless, favoring institutional expediency over the unique needs of residents cannot, finally, be justified. Over the coming decades, we will confront changes in the patterns of disease as well as the technology of health care. New forms of care for the aged will be explored and examined. Perhaps most important, however, as individuals and as a society, we need to address the task of envisioning and creating a worthy "place" for the old who live among us.

Further Readings

Colette Browne and Roberta Onzuka-Anderson, eds. *Our Aging Parents: A Practical Guide to Eldercare.* Honolulu: University of Hawaii Press, 1985.

Robert C. DiGiulio. *Beyond Widowhood: From Bereavement to Emergence and Hope.* New York: Free Press, 1989.

Kathleen R. Gilbert and Laura S. Smart. *Coping with Infant or Fetal Loss: The Couple's Healing Process.* New York: Brunner/Mazel, 1992.

Sharon R. Kaufman. *The Ageless Self: Sources of Meaning in Later Life.* Madison: University of Wisconsin Press, 1995.

Dennis Klass. *Parental Grief: Solace and Resolution.* New York: Springer, 1988.

Ronald J. Knapp. *Beyond Endurance: When a Child Dies.* New York: Schocken, 1986.

William R. LaFleur. *Liquid Life: Abortion and Buddhism in Japan.* Princeton, N.J.: Princeton University Press, 1992.

Therese A. Rando, ed. *Parental Loss of a Child.* Champaign, Ill.: Research Press, 1986.

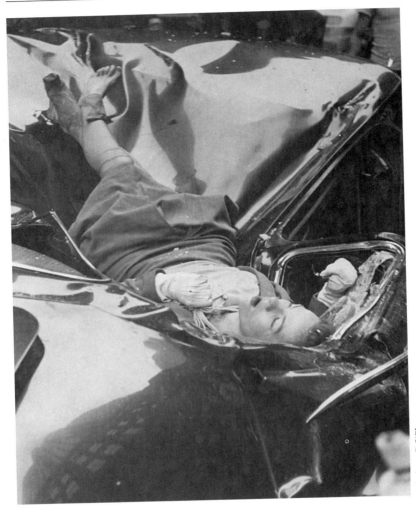

After plummeting eighty-six floors from the observation deck of the Empire State Building—visible in the metallic reflection at lower left—this young woman lies dead, the victim of suicide.

Suicide

*S*uicide, the intentional taking of one's own life, encompasses a variety of motives and behaviors. Although suicide has been characterized by some as a "disease of civilization," suicide is found in virtually all societies. It is influenced by personality and culture as well as by the unique circumstances of an individual's situation. Judith Stillion observes that "suicide is arguably the most complex and the least understood of all human behaviors, although it has been documented throughout recorded history."[1] Altruistic suicide—that is, a person giving up his or her life for others or for a greater good—has likely existed since human beings first banded together in clans.[2] We can imagine situations in which one individual volunteers to draw the attention of a herd of animals to himself, thereby allowing other members of a hunting party to trap the animals more easily. Although the probability of surviving the onrushing herd was low, the reward for the clan was survival. Even in recent times, some nomadic societies accept suicide among the elderly or infirm to maintain the mobility needed for the survival of the group. Indeed, honor may be given to the person who, recognizing that the end of life is near, willingly leaves the community for certain death. In much the same way, suicide has been seen as a way of expressing the ultimate commitment to a moral or philosophical principle. The self-inflicted death of Socrates has stood for twenty-four hundred years as a symbol of dying for one's principles. In feudal Japan,

455

when samurai warriors sacrificed their lives to maintain the honor or reputation of their lords, their suicide was viewed as heroic.

The contemporary context of suicide is quite different. In modern societies, especially those that have developed out of the Western European tradition, suicide is generally not a socially sanctioned action. Only rarely is the act viewed as related to altruism or self-sacrifice on behalf of others. Instead, the basis for understanding suicide involves such factors as depression, low self-esteem, negative life experiences, and chronic physical pain. Thus, when someone commits suicide, the cause is sought primarily in psychological and sociological explanations.

Examining Suicide Statistics

Although the overall suicide rate in the United States has remained fairly constant in the recent past, a significant shift has taken place among certain age groups. Until the late 1960s, suicide rates generally increased directly with age, with the lowest suicide rates among the young and the highest among the aged. More recently, however, a decrease in the rate among older people has been offset by an increase among adolescents and young adults. The rising suicide trend among adolescents is associated with a deteriorating state of well-being for young people, and the generally declining suicide trend among the aged is associated with an improving state of well-being for the elderly.[3] The suicide rate for males is almost four times that of females, and this ratio holds generally for all age groups except the elderly, where the male predominance increases.[4]

The white population in the United States commits the majority of suicides and has rates more than twice as high as those for the nonwhite population as a whole.[5] Within the nonwhite population, however, there is a significantly higher rate of suicide among Native Americans than among other ethnic groups.[6] Taken in the aggregate, the suicide rate among Native Americans is about three times the national average; and, on some reservations, the suicide rate is ten times that of the general population. As these figures suggest, there is considerable variability in suicide rates among Native Americans; therefore, it would be erroneous to attribute one suicide pattern to all Native Americans. To summarize, in broad demographic terms, the groups at relatively higher risk for suicide include males, whites, older adults, adolescents, and Native Americans.[7]

Statistical Problems

There is general agreement that official counts of suicide understate the actual number of suicides, perhaps by as much as half.[8] A death is unlikely to be classified as a suicide unless the coroner or medical examiner suspects such a possibility due to the deceased's history of suicidal tendencies or acts of self-injury, or because the deceased left a suicide note, or because the circumstances of death so clearly point to suicide. Glen Evans and Norman Farberow

Richard Cory

Whenever Richard Cory went down town,
　　We people on the pavement looked at him:
He was a gentleman from sole to crown,
　　Clean favored, and imperially slim.

And he was always quietly arrayed,
　　And he was always human when he talked;
But still he fluttered pulses when he said,
　　"Good-morning," and he glittered when he walked.

And he was rich—yes, richer than a king—
　　And admirably schooled in every grace:
In fine, we thought that he was everything
　　To make us wish that we were in his place.

So on we worked, and waited for the light,
　　And went without the meat, and cursed the bread;
And Richard Cory, one calm summer night,
　　Went home and put a bullet through his head.

　　　　　Edwin Arlington Robinson

observe that "generally, coroners list suicide as a cause of death only when circumstances unequivocally justify such a determination."[9]

Related to the burden-of-proof issue with respect to classifying a death as suicide is the social stigma of suicide. Suicide is commonly viewed as representing failure—on the part of the individual who commits suicide, his or her family and friends, and society as a whole. Open discussion about suicide remains largely taboo. Neighbors and friends who suspect that a terminally ill husband's death was the result of self-inflicted gunshot wounds may refrain from mentioning the circumstances of the death, engaging instead in a form of polite mutual pretense unless and until the barrier to disclosure is somehow lifted.

If the circumstances of a death are equivocal (meaning that the causes are uncertain or unclear) and there is a question about whether the death was a suicide or an accident, it is likely to be classified as accidental. Many automobile accidents, for example, are believed to be suicides in disguise. Indeed, some authorities believe that if these "autocides" were added to known suicides, it would make suicide the number one killer of young people.

Similarly, victim-precipitated homicide may mask an individual's suicidal intentions. The homicide victim who deliberately provokes others by flashing a knife or wielding a gun, or by goading others with threats of violence, may be attempting to gain the unwitting help of others in causing his own death. Such deaths are rarely included in suicide statistics, however, because victim-precipitated deaths tend to be classified as homicides unless further investigation reveals otherwise. Victim-precipitated homicide is thought to occur with greatest frequency among young African-American males.[10] Individuals may create violent situations in which they are likely to be killed, thereby "dying as heroes" and "preserving their definition of masculinity."[11]

In summarizing the problems in compiling suicide statistics, Edwin Shneidman says, "because of religious and bureaucratic prejudices, family sensitivity, differences in the proceedings of coroner's hearings and postmortem examinations, and the shadowy distinctions between suicides and accidents—in short, the unwillingness to recognize the act for what it is— knowledge of the extent to which suicide pervades modern society is diminished and distorted."[12]

The Psychological Autopsy

The investigative methods of the psychological autopsy improve the accuracy of death classification, particularly when the cause of death is uncertain and potentially related to suicidal intent. Initially conceived as a device by which to investigate equivocal cases of suicide on behalf of the Los Angeles County Coroner, the psychological autopsy has been called "one of the most significant research tools to come along since the field of suicidology grew into recognition."[13]

Developed in 1961—primarily by Norman Farberow, Edwin Shneidman, and Robert Litman—the psychological autopsy is an investigative technique used by behavioral scientists in cases of equivocal death.[14] It attempts to recreate the personality and life style of the deceased and the known circumstances of his or her death. Information gathered from interviews, documents, and other materials is used to make a determination concerning the mode of death: natural, accident, suicide, or homicide. With this information in hand, "The historical gestalt that emerges from the data can clarify the most probable mode of death."[15]

Of particular importance is the information pieced together from interviews with the victim's friends and relatives as well as other members of the community. Attention is paid to learning about current and previous stresses, psychiatric and medical histories, and the general life style of the victim as well as any communication about suicidal intent. The deceased's routine in the days and hours before death is carefully considered as investigators attempt to create a picture of the person's character, personality, and state of mind. Based on an assessment of all the data gathered, a judgment is made about the mode of death (see Table 12-1).

In 1989, an explosion aboard the USS *Iowa*, which killed forty-seven sailors, brought increased public attention to the use of psychological autopsies.[16] Based on an "equivocal death analysis" conducted by the FBI, the U.S. Navy attributed the tragedy to alleged suicidal acts by Gunners Mate Clayton Hartwig, a decision viewed in some quarters as a preemptive strike against wrongful death suits filed against the Navy by families of some of the dead

T A B L E *12-1*   *Four Purposes of the Psychological Autopsy*

1. To help clarify the mode of death: natural, accident, suicide, or homicide (a classification system known by the acronym NASH). Note that *mode* of death differs from *cause* of death. The mode of death may be uncertain while the cause is clear.
2. To determine why a death occurred at a particular time; in other words, to examine the possible connection between the individual's psychology or state of mind and the timing of his or her death.
3. To gain data that may prove useful in predicting suicide and assessing the lethality of the suicidal person, thus helping clinicians and others identify trends in suicidal behavior and high-risk groups.
4. To obtain information that can be of therapeutic value to survivors in resolving emotional turmoil and questions that follow upon a loved one's death by suicide.

Source: Adapted from Thomas J. Young, "Procedures and Problems in Conducting a Psychological Autopsy," *International Journal of Offender Therapy and Comparative Criminology* 36, no. 1 (Spring 1992): 43–52.

sailors. Because of questions about the investigation, the House Armed Services Committee convened a panel of distinguished psychologists to conduct a peer review of the FBI's report and the Navy's subsequent conclusion. After weighing the evidence, the Committee rejected the Navy's allegation that Hartwig intentionally caused the explosion and characterized its inquiry as an "investigative failure," particularly with respect to the FBI's analysis. Later tests indicated that the blast may have been due to mechanical error, and the Navy recanted its allegations of Hartwig's responsibility; in 1991, the Chief of Naval Operations issued a formal apology to Hartwig's family.

In commenting about the case, the Committee's psychologists cited several limitations of reconstructive psychological procedures such as the FBI's equivocal death analysis and psychological autopsies (see Table 12-2). They concluded that such psychological reconstruction should not result in an assertion of "categorical conclusions about the precise mental state or actions suspected of the actor at the time of his or her demise;" such conclusions, they said, are at best "informed speculations or theoretical formulations."[17] Legal applications of psychological autopsies were viewed as posing a special concern. Indeed, at present, the judicial system appears to be undecided about the admissibility of psychological autopsies as evidence: Some courts admit them into evidence while others exclude them.

The Hartwig case demonstrates that a lack of scientific precision may lead investigators to erroneous conclusions about the data collected through the use of psychological autopsies. However, as proponents of such investigative techniques point out, even *medical* autopsies are not perfect—yet they are viewed as having the potential to clarify circumstances surrounding death. It is argued that the same can be said about psychological autopsies.

In summary, despite its limitations, the psychological autopsy has proved—over a period of more than three decades—to be a useful tool in assessing risk factors for suicide. It has been especially helpful in increasing the

TABLE *12-2*   *Limitations of the Psychological Autopsy*

1. *Lack of standardized procedures.* Several guidelines for conducting a psychological autopsy have been proposed, but a set of standardized procedures does not exist.
Thus, critics question the reliability and validity of psychological autopsies. Proponents, on the other hand, argue that wide latitude is needed to accommodate
unique situations.
2. *Retrospective nature.* Examiners are required to offer observations or opinions about
a person's past mental state.
3. *Third-party informants may distort representations of the decedent for a variety of reasons.*
Everyone who participates in a psychological autopsy has some stake in its outcome. Information from friends or relatives may be biased; public agencies may
shape the story to fit certain preconceived parameters.
4. *The individual of interest is not available for examination,* a fact that makes this the
greatest limitation of the psychological autopsy.
5. *There are few studies examining the reliability and validity of data obtained by psychological
autopsies.*

Source: Adapted from James R. P. Ogloff and Randy K. Otto, "Psychological Autopsy: Clinical and Legal
Perspectives," *Saint Louis University Law Journal* 37, no. 3 (Spring 1993): 610–614; and Thomas J. Young,
"Procedures and Problems in Conducting a Psychological Autopsy," *International Journal of Offender Therapy
and Comparative Criminology* 36, no. 1 (Spring 1992): 47–48.

understanding of factors that place young people at risk.[18] Indeed, there is
evidence that the investigative methods associated with psychological autopsies may have application as a predictive indicator of people who are at a
heightened risk of suicide because of suicidogenic, or suicide-causing, factors
in their lives.[19] As both an investigative approach and a research tool, the
psychological autopsy deepens our understanding of suicide and suicidal
behavior.

Comprehending Suicide

Most people have at some time in their lives fantasized about the possibility of committing suicide. Such thoughts are not uncommon during childhood and adolescence, and they may crop up from time to time in later life as
well. Thoughts like these occur as a kind of "trying out" or "testing" of the
notion rather than as a serious consideration of suicidal behavior. The subject
of suicide may be dealt with by forced humor, uneasy laughter, or a cerebral
intellectuality that distances us from the real threat of mortality. We mask our
discomfort at the awesome fact that each of us has the power to choose
whether or not we continue to exist. Death is usually conceived of as something
that "happens" to an individual. "Why," it is asked, "would someone willingly
end his or her own life?"

In considering what might influence a person to commit suicide, you may
find yourself thinking, "There's nothing that could cause me to think seriously
about ending my own life." To those who believe they have the resources to

TABLE *12-3*   *Four Definitions of Suicide*

Suicide is . . .

The act or an instance of taking one's own life voluntarily and intentionally, especially by a person of years of discretion and of sound mind. (*Webster's New Collegiate Dictionary*)[a]

Self-killing deriving from one's inability or refusal to accept the terms of the human condition. (Ronald W. Maris)[b]

All behavior that seeks and finds the solution to an existential problem by making an attempt on the life of the subject. (Jean Baechler)[c]

The human act of self-inflicted, self-intentioned cessation. (Edwin Shneidman)[d]

[a]Used by permission. From *Webster's Ninth New Collegiate Dictionary*, © 1986 by Merriam-Webster Inc. Publishers of the Merriam-Webster® Dictionaries.
[b]Ronald W. Maris, *Pathways to Suicide: A Survey of Self-Destructive Behaviors* (Baltimore: Johns Hopkins University Press, 1981), p. 290.
[c]Jean Baechler, *Suicides* (New York: Basic Books, 1979), p. 11.
[d]Edwin S. Shneidman, ed., *Death: Current Perspectives*, 2d ed. (Mountain View, Calif.: Mayfield, 1980), p. 416.

deal effectively with the demands of life, suicide seems a radical solution indeed. Yet suicide is a complex human behavior, one involving diverse motives and intentions. Thus, our first step toward understanding its dynamics must be to develop a working definition of suicide that provides a framework for organizing this complexity into manageable form.

In thinking about the reasons why a person would elect to end his or her own life, it soon becomes apparent that suicide can be studied on the basis of the apparent cause or purpose of the suicidal act, the individual and cultural meanings attached to suicidal behaviors, and the specific populations affected by suicide. The definitions of suicide given in Table 12-3 can help establish a comprehensive working definition that is useful for all of these approaches.

Notice that each definition emphasizes certain aspects of suicidal intention and behavior. The basic dictionary definition is a good starting point for understanding suicide, but it is vague. As you review the definitions, pay particular attention to how each explains the dynamics of suicide. Ask yourself: What kinds of human behavior does the definition include? Is suicide a specific act, or is it a behavioral process? What is the context of suicide?

For example, Ronald Maris's definition focuses on the cause or rationale for suicide. French social scientist Jean Baechler's definition emphasizes suicide as a means of resolving problems. Notice that suicide is defined as a behavior rather than as a specific act. Notice also that suicidal behavior may be immediate or long term. Thus, alcoholism can be considered as suicidal behavior inasmuch as it reflects the attempt to solve an existential problem by making use of something that, over time, can have fatal consequences. Finally, Edwin Shneidman's definition emphasizes intention and action, along with the concept of ending one's conscious existence. From your perusal of these definitions, you can see that suicide involves the mental intention to cause one's own death as well as actions to carry out that intention.

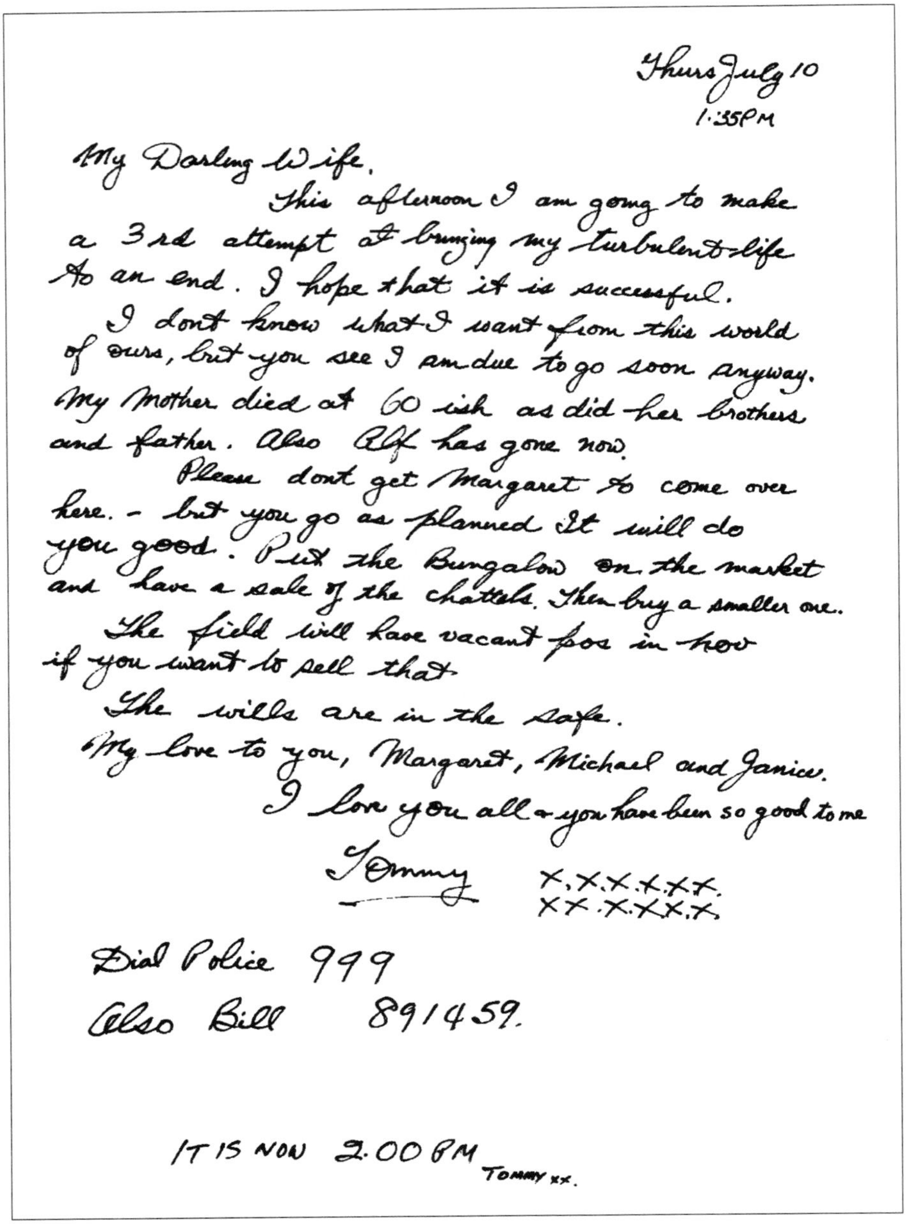

Thurs July 10
1.35PM

My Darling Wife,
This afternoon I am going to make a 3rd attempt at bringing my turbulent life to an end. I hope that it is successful.
I dont know what I want from this world of ours, but you see I am due to go soon anyway. My Mother died at 60 ish as did her brothers and father. Also Alf has gone now.
Please dont get Margaret to come over here. - but you go as planned It will do you good. Put the Bungalow on the market and have a sale of the chattels. Then buy a smaller one.
The field will have vacant pos in now if you want to sell that.
The wills are in the safe.
My love to you, Margaret, Michael and Janice.
I love you all - you have been so good to me

Tommy X.X.X.X.X.X. XX.X.XX.X.

Dial Police 999
Also Bill 891459.

IT IS NOW 2.00 PM
TOMMY xx.

Figure 12-1 *Suicide Note and Report of Death*
Even when a newspaper account is as detailed as this British report (*facing page*), the facts of suicide as described in the newspaper may reveal very little of the intense human factors—the personal and social dynamics—that precipitated the suicidal act.

Retired man's suicide

A HYTHE man aged 64 killed himself because he could not stand old age, an inquest heard yesterday.

Retired maintenance engineer Aubrey Heathfield Aylmore, who lived at Forest Front, Hythe, was found dead in his car by his wife.

The inquest heard that Mrs. Heathfield Aylmore had been to a WI meeting and returned home an hour later than planned.

She found her husband's body in the garage with a length of hose pipe running from the exhaust into the car.

A note was found in which Mr. Heathfield Aylmore said that this was his third suicide attempt and that he wanted to "put an end to my turbulent life."

Dr. Richard Goodbody, consultant pathologist, said cause of death was asphyxia due to carbon monoxide poisoning.

Coroner Mr. Harry Roe said that Mr. Heathfield Aylmore had been depressed at the thought of growing old.

Explanatory Theories of Suicide

The study of suicide has mainly followed two lines of theoretical investigation: (1) the sociological model, which has its foundation in the work of nineteenth-century French sociologist Emile Durkheim; and (2) the psychological model, based on the work of Viennese psychoanalyst Sigmund Freud. Contemporary scholars usually seek an integrated approach to understanding suicide, one that combines sociological and psychological insights (see Figure 12–1).

The Social Context of Suicide

The sociological model, as its name implies, focuses on the relationship between the individual and society. Individual behavior is considered in its social setting and within the context of group dynamics. According to Durkheim, these social forces are manifested in the degree of regulation and integration present in a given society.[20]

Degree of Social Regulation

When a society is loosely regulated, individuals experience a sense of chaos and confusion as well as a loss of traditional values and social mores. Rules, customs, and traditions cannot be relied upon as a definitive guide to behavior. Such circumstances are characterized by a sense of *anomie* (mean-

Suicide Note Written by a Divorced Woman, Age 61

You cops will want to know why I did it, well just let us say that I lived 61 years too many.

People have always put obstacles in my way. One of the great ones is leaving this world when you want to and have nothing to live for.

I am not insane. My mind was never more clear. It has been a long day. The motor got so hot it would not run so I just had to sit here and wait. The breaks were against me to the very last.

The sun is leaving the hill now so hope nothing else happens.

ing "lawlessness"). Because of loose social ties, the individual experiences anxiety, disorientation, isolation, and loneliness. When there is insufficient social regulation, *anomic* suicides result. The classic example of this phenomenon occurs in societies experiencing rapid social change. Set free from traditional moorings, individuals find it difficult to adjust to a changing environment. The sense of identity with the social group may be shaken, leaving the individual feeling upset and confused. Among the Aboriginal people of Australia, for example, the rapid pace of social change relative to their traditional life style is being accompanied by signs of increasing behavioral distress, including suicide.[21]

Sudden trauma or catastrophe can also shatter the relationship between an individual and society. The loss of a job, the amputation of a limb, the death of a close friend or family member—any of these losses might constitute an anomic event. Indeed, any disruptive change—whether it is perceived as positive or negative—can precipitate a state of anomie. Even sudden wealth might stimulate suicidal behavior if the person feels unable to cope with his or her changed status. Calling attention to the disruptions caused by divorce and by economic hardship, Durkheim argued that anomic suicide is a chronic condition in modern societies.

At the other extreme of regulation we find a society characterized by repressive constraints. Lack of freedom and absence of choice may produce what Durkheim termed *fatalistic* suicide. The inability to openly express one's individuality can lead to a sense of fatalism, a feeling that one has nowhere to turn. The high rate of suicides in jails and other detention facilities is due at least partly to the intense regulation that characterizes such facilities.

Degree of Social Integration

Turning to the effect of social integration, at one extreme we find situations in which the individual feels alienated, separate from the significant institutions and traditions in his or her society. In this instance, the person has few ties to the community and is not integrated into the society but is instead dependent on his or her own resources and devices. Durkheim termed the suicides occurring in this type of environment *egoistic*. An individual's mental energies are concentrated on the self to such an extent that social sanctions against suicide are ineffective. People who are disenfranchised or who live at the fringes of society may feel no compulsion to heed life-affirming values because they do not experience themselves as meaningfully related to the wider community. In this sense, anomie (lack of regulation) and egoism (lack of integration) reinforce each other. In Durkheim's view, when a person is detached from social life, the individual personality takes precedence over the collective personality. Thus, egoistic suicide is "the special type of suicide springing from excessive individualism."[22]

Conversely, in the case of *altruistic* or institutional suicide, excessive identification with the values or causes of society produces such a strong sense of integration with the social group that the individual loses his or her own personal identity. The group's values predominate over the individual's. "An integrated social situation," says Ronald Maris, "is one in which individuals are strongly attached to society's governing rules."[23] Norman Farberow observes that an overidentification with the values or causes of a society can produce "a too-ready willingness to sacrifice one's life in a burst of patriotism or martyrdom."[24]

In medieval Japanese society, ritual disembowelment, called *hara-kiri* or *seppuku*, was culturally accepted, even demanded, in certain circumstances, especially among the samurai class. Occasions when suicide might seem the only socially acceptable course included disgrace in battle or the death of a lord, as well as the desire to make a public statement of one's disagreement with a superior. In such cases, *seppuku*, or ritual suicide, became the necessary act for an honorable warrior, and specific customs dictated how the suicidal act was to be performed.[25]

Similarly, until modern times, certain castes in India were expected to practice *suttee*, which called for the wife of a nobleman to throw herself upon his cremation pyre. Such self-immolation was condoned by the prevailing religious and cultural beliefs. A widow's reluctance to perform such ritual suicide was met with social disapproval. Indeed, a reluctant wife might find herself "helped" onto the burning pyre.

To these well-known examples of *seppuku* and *suttee* could be added the deaths of kamikaze pilots in Japan's air attack corps during World War II and the example of the dedicated captain who goes down with the ship. In these examples, suicide is "the self-destruction demanded by a society . . . as a price for being a member of that society."[26] As alluded to in the case of samurai who committed *seppuku* as a means of protesting policies of their superiors, altruistic suicide does not always involve an acceptance of social norms. Suicide as protest came to public attention during the Vietnam war, when Buddhist monks committed suicide by self-immolation to protest governmental policies.

AP/Wide World Photos

Flames engulf the body of a Buddhist monk, Quang Duc, whose self-immolation before thousands of onlookers in downtown Saigon was a protest against alleged persecution of Buddhists by the government of South Vietnam.

A highly publicized instance of institutional suicide occurred on November 20, 1978, in Jonestown, Guyana, when more than 900 persons met their death in what has been called the largest mass suicide in history.[27] At a previously little-noticed jungle clearing, which had been the communal settlement of the followers of the Reverend Jim Jones, many of the victims drank cyanide-laced fruit punch and families died together in one another's arms. In hypnotic tones from his throne above the crowd, Jones urged community members to drink the poison. The customs of the social group influenced the individual's decision to commit suicide.

From the social perspective, then, suicide is seen to be the result of a disturbance in the ties between the individual and society. When there is imbalance or upset with respect to this relationship, the potential for suicide is heightened. Each form of suicide—anomic, fatalistic, egoistic, altruistic—is related to a particular kind of interplay between the society and the individual.

For more than 900 Americans who left their home to join a religious fanatic called the Reverend Jim Jones, death came in the jungles of Guyana with these comforting words from the man who engineered the largest mass suicide the world has witnessed:

> What's going to happen here in a matter of a few minutes is that one of those people in the plane is going to shoot the pilot. . . . So you be kind to the children and be kind to seniors, and take the potion like they used to in Ancient Greece, and step over quietly, because we are not committing suicide—it's a revolutionary act.
>
> Everybody dies. I haven't seen anybody yet didn't die. And I like to choose my own kind of death for a change. I'm tired of being tormented to hell. Tired of it. (Applause)

A few cultists protested. Some women screamed. Children cried. Armed guards took up positions around the camp to keep anyone from escaping:

> Let the little children in and reassure them. . . . They're not crying from pain, it's just a little bitter-tasting. . . . Death is a million times more preferable to spend more days in this life. If you knew what was ahead of you, you'd be glad to be stepping over tonight . . . quickly, quickly, no more pain. . . . This world was not your home. . . .

Here the tape runs out. The sound stops before the report of the pistol that killed Jim Jones, presumably fired by his own hand.

Robert Ramsey and Randall Toye, *The Goodbye Book*

The Psychodynamics of Suicide

The psychological model of suicide focuses on the dynamics of an individual's mental and emotional life. Drawing on the theories originated by Sigmund Freud, the psychodynamic model incorporates the role of both unconscious and conscious motivation, and it assumes that an individual's behavior is determined by both past experience and current reality.[28] Unlike the Durkheimian view, which seeks an explanation for suicide in external events, the psychodynamic model focuses on the processes occurring within the mind or personality of the individual.

Among the insights developed from the psychological model of suicide are the following:

1. The *acute* suicidal crisis is of relatively brief duration; that is, it lasts hours or days rather than weeks or months—though it may recur.
2. The suicidal person is likely to be ambivalent about ending his or her life. Plans for self-destruction are generally accompanied by fantasies that rescue or intervention will occur before the fatal act is completed.
3. Most suicidal events are *dyadic*: They involve both the victim and a significant other in some way.

Suicide Note Written by a Married Man, Age 45

My darling,

May her guts rot in hell—I loved her so much.

Henry

The insights made available by the psychodynamic model have been usefully applied in constructing a better understanding of suicide and in devising methods of suicide intervention. For example, an analysis of an individual's dreams may help to assess suicidal intent.[29] In this sense, death dreams may be a manifestation of the need for some transformation within an individual's personality. The psychodynamics of suicide can be understood more completely by looking in greater detail at two of its aspects: aggression and ambivalence.

Aggression

According to the psychodynamic model, suicide involves strong, unconscious hostility combined with a lack of capacity to love others. Under conditions of enormous stress, the intrapsychic pressures impelling a person toward self-destruction increase to the point that they overwhelm the defense mechanisms of the ego, or self. This results in a regression to more primitive ego states, which involve powerful forces of aggression. Whereas murder is aggression turned upon another, suicide is aggression turned upon oneself. In short, suicide is murder in the 180th degree.

Ambivalence

Even with the aggressive forces mobilized, however, the urge toward self-preservation works against the ego's, or self's, acquiescence to its own death. Thus, another psychodynamic process comes into play: *ambivalence*. Analysis of suicidal behavior often reveals the presence of conflicting forces that compete for the greater share of the person's mental energies. At issue is the will to live versus the will to die. Erwin Stengel says, "Most people who commit acts of self-damage with more or less conscious self-destructive intent do not want either to live or to die, but to do both at the same time."[30]

Ambivalence, as it applies to suicidal behavior, can be considered in several ways. First, the person contemplating suicide is likely to harbor simultaneously a wish to live and a wish to die. The balance between these opposing polarities may be delicate, with an otherwise minor incident tipping the scales one way or the other. Ambivalence also refers to situations in which, although one of these forces is stronger than the other, the weaker one nevertheless continues to affect the person's behavior. Stengel says, "Most suicidal acts are manifestations of risk-taking behavior. They are gambles. The danger to life depends on the relationships between self-destructive and life-preserving, contact seeking tendencies, and on a variety of other factors, some of which are outside the control of the individual."

Toward an Integrated Understanding of Suicide

Each of the two major theories of suicide contributes to increased understanding of the patterns of suicidal behavior. Although each model has its roots in a particular methodology, current theories of suicide generally draw upon both to form a comprehensive understanding. For example, taking the integrated approach, it is possible to see how a disrupted or disturbed home environment (the social context) can lead to feelings of abandonment, loneliness, and low self-esteem (psychodynamics), thereby increasing the risk of suicide.

Both models of suicide suggest methods for alleviating the conditions that can lead to suicide. The psychodynamic model points to such factors as low self-esteem; excessive guilt or shame; feelings of isolation, hopelessness, and meaninglessness; a sense of failure or incompetence; and tunnel vision. To counteract these negative influences, this model suggests therapy, emotional support, confidence building, and enhancement of coping skills as deterrents to suicide. The social model, in contrast, calls our attention to membership in groups that are at higher risk of suicide—the elderly, males, Native Americans, and prisoners, among others. Reducing suicide risk means alleviating the stressful experiences that cause individuals within the at-risk groups to choose suicide. In developing an integrated model of suicide, we need to draw on both the sociological and psychological models, as well as the individual situation, to arrive at a comprehensive understanding of a particular suicidal act.

Some Types of Suicide

Many classification schemes have been applied to suicide in attempts to better comprehend its personal and social meanings (see Table 12-4). In this section, we examine more closely some of the "types" of suicide, with the aim of providing a more complete picture of self-destructive behavior.

Suicide as Escape

Suicide is often seen as a means of escape or release from some physical pain or mental anguish. For example, a person with a painful illness may perceive suicide as a way out of suffering. The act of ending one's life in such a circumstance is sometimes termed "rational suicide" because the reasoning used—death will bring release from pain—conforms to normal logic.

Medical problems tend to be viewed as more acceptable reasons for suicide than are psychological problems. In circumstances involving incurable disease, suicide (also termed *euthanasia* in such instances) is viewed by many people as a personal right. This attitude reflects not only on the person who commits suicide but also on his or her family.[31] Whereas suicide is usually

TABLE 12-4   *Meanings of Suicide*

Some Cultural Meanings of Suicide

Suicide is sinful: A crime against nature, a revolt against the preordained order of the universe.

Suicide is criminal: It violates the ties that exist, the social contract between persons in a society.

Suicide is weakness or madness: It reflects limitations or deviancy ("He must have been crazy" or "He couldn't take it").

Suicide is the Great Death, as in *seppuku, suttee,* and other culturally approved forms of ritual suicide.

Suicide is the rational alternative: The outcome of a "balance-sheet" approach that sizes up the situation and determines the best option.

Some Individual Meanings of Suicide

Suicide is reunion with a lost loved one, a way to "join the deceased."

Suicide is rest and refuge: A way out of a burdensome and depressing situation.

Suicide is getting back: A way of expressing resentment and revenge at being rejected or hurt.

Suicide is the penalty for failure: A response to disappointment and frustration at not meeting self-expectations or the expectations of others.

Suicide is a mistake: The attempt was made as a cry for help and was not intended to be fatal, but there was no rescue or intervention and the outcome was death.

Source: Adapted from Robert Kastenbaum, *Death, Society, and Human Experience,* 2d ed. (St. Louis, Mo.: C. V. Mosby, 1981), pp. 239–255.

considered as an act of violence, euthanasia is more likely to be regarded as a benevolent act that ensues from a decision made by the patient and perhaps enacted with the consent of loved ones.

Other forms of seeking escape through suicide result from a destructive logic. In these cases, the victim's self-concept or sense of identity is confused. When this confusion is coupled with problems in relating to others, it can lead to the victim's self-perception as a failure. Suicides of this type are sometimes termed "referred," bringing to mind the analogy of physical pain that is experienced at some distance from its source. An inflammation of the liver may be experienced as pain in the shoulder. Just as this physical phenomenon is characterized as referred pain, so the root causes of referred suicide are likewise only indirectly related to the end result—namely, suicide. The desire to escape from physical pain involves a comparatively straightforward logic between intention and action, but the logic of referred suicide is ambiguous. The decision to end one's life is not based on a dispassionate assessment of the situation, but instead comes out of an overwhelming sense of anguish and confusion about one's options.

Self-concept is an important factor. Not performing up to expectations or according to certain role definitions may provoke a crisis of self-concept that ultimately leads to the desire to escape the unsatisfactory situation. Expectations may be related to something outside the individual ("If I can't be a good

Suicide Note Written by a Single Man, Age 51

Sunday 4:45 PM Here goes

To who it may concern

Though I am about to kick the bucket I am as happy as ever. I am tired of this life so am going over to see the other side.

Good luck to all.

Benjamin P.

enough daughter to please my parents, I give up!"), or they may be related to inward feelings of frustration ("Everybody thinks I'm doing okay, but I feel rotten"). When one's "image" is given excessive importance, a loss of status or identity can be devastating.

The desire to escape may also arise from the loss of meaning in one's life. Despite significant accomplishments, a person may come to feel, "Now what?" The accumulation of successes one after another may seem a Sisyphean effort, a continual struggle for achievement without a corresponding sense of accomplishment. Perhaps one's accomplishments were achieved in the past; there seems nothing more to be gained. Like Alexander the Great, after "conquering the world," there seems nothing more to strive for, no reason to live. Conversely, success may be accompanied by feelings of ennui—"If this is what success is all about, it's not worth the effort." Stress, competition, aggressiveness, and inability to balance conflicting demands can be overwhelming. Being a "super-achiever," or taking on more responsibility than one is comfortable with, can bring on a personal crisis that proves lethal. Low self-esteem coupled with high achievement orientation is a dangerous combination of personality characteristics.[32] The causal chain begins with events that fall short of standards and expectations.[33] A sense of inadequacy and failure makes self-awareness painful, and the individual seeks to escape from this negative sense of self. Drastic measures seem acceptable, with suicide becoming the ultimate step in the effort to find release from self and the world.

Psychotic Suicide and Depression

Psychotic suicide is associated with the impaired logic of a delusional or hallucinatory state of mind related to clinically diagnosed schizophrenia or manic-depressive psychosis. There is no conscious intention to die, but the victim may wish to eradicate the psychic malignancy or punish himself or herself by self-destruction. Treatment of the suicidal impulses requires that one first treat the psychosis.

Although most psychiatrically ill patients do not commit suicide, mental illness—especially severe depression—does place individuals at higher risk for suicide. Depressive disorders affect young people as well as adults.[34] In fact, depression is believed to be a factor in roughly one-half of all suicides. Depressed individuals may act out their depression in harmful, disruptive, or illegal ways, sometimes involving alcohol or drug abuse. Depression is the disorder most commonly associated with deliberate self-poisoning, often by overdosing with drugs available only by prescription.[35]

Major depression is a syndrome that can be triggered by a variety of physical and psychosocial factors; it is a warning sign for suicide that should not be ignored.[36] Differences in family patterns may help to explain why a minority of depressed patients attempt suicide while most do not.[37] Family members or friends often do not realize the depth of an individual's depression or do not wish to admit to the seriousness of the illness.

Subintentional and Chronic Suicide

As defined by Edwin Shneidman, the subintentioned death is "one in which the person plays some partial, covert, subliminal, or unconscious role in hastening his own demise."[38] Some fatalities reported as accidents result from the victim's choosing to take an unnecessary and unwise risk. Such behavior might be called careless or imprudent. A deeper probing into causes, however, shows that accidents are sometimes the end result of a pattern of behavior that conforms to the definition of subintentional suicide. Similarly, homicide investigations sometimes turn up evidence that points to subintentional factors that result in a victim's behaving in ways that provoke his or her death at another's hands.

Besides subintentioned death, Shneidman delineates two other patterns of death-related behaviors: intentioned and unintentioned. Table 12-5 presents an outline of these three patterns. Notice that within each of these categories a person might exhibit a variety of attitudes and behaviors regarding death. As you review this table, ask yourself: Where do I stand on this list? What does that say about my own regard for life and death?

The term *chronic suicide*, coined by Karl Menninger, refers to individuals who choose to destroy themselves by means of drugs, alcohol, reckless living, and the like. Although an individual may find the idea of suicide repugnant or unacceptable, an analysis of his or her life style may suggest the presence of a "death wish." Musician Jim Morrison's death due to a drug overdose is still the subject of debate about whether it was accident or suicide. Although the death of actor James Dean resulted from reckless speeding in his Porsche, an examination of his life style reveals a level of risk-taking associated with chronic or subintentional suicide. Because our laws with respect to suicide evolved from focusing on its "acute" context, we tend to be comparatively insensitive about the incidence of chronic suicide in our society.[39]

Cry for Help

Considered as a *cry for help*, suicide aims to force a change. The suicidal person's situation is such that he or she no longer wishes to continue living in

TABLE 12-5 *Patterns of Death-Related Behavior and Attitudes*

Intentioned Death: Death resulting from the suicide's direct, conscious behavior to bring it about. A variety of attitudes or motives may be operative:

The *death seeker* wishes to end consciousness and commits the suicidal act in such a way that rescue is unlikely.

The *death initiator* expects to die in the near future and wants to choose the time and circumstances of death.

The *death ignorer* believes that death ends only physical existence and that the person continues to exist in another manner.

The *death darer* gambles with death, or, as Shneidman says, "bets his life on a relatively low objective probability that he will survive" (such as by playing Russian roulette).

Subintentioned Death: Death resulting from a person's patterns of management or style of living, although death was not the conscious, direct aim of the person's actions:

The *death chancer,* although in many ways like the death darer, may want higher odds of survival.

The *death hastener* may expedite his or her death by substance abuse (drugs, alcohol, and the like) or by failing to safeguard well-being (for example, by inadequate nutrition or precautions against disease or disregard of available treatments).

The *death facilitator* gives little resistance to death, making it easy for death to occur, as in the deaths of patients whose energies, or "will to live," are low because of their illness.

The *death capitulator* is one who, usually out of a great fear of death, plays a subintentional role in his or her own death, as may a person upon whom a so-called voodoo death has been put, or as may a person who believes that someone admitted to a hospital is bound to die.

The *death experimenter* does not consciously wish to die, but lives on the brink, usually in a "befogged state of consciousness" that may be related to taking drugs in such ways that the person may become comatose or even die with little concern.

Unintentioned Deaths: Death in which the decedent plays no significant causative role. However, various attitudes toward death may shape the experience of dying:

The *death welcomer,* though not hastening death, looks forward to it (as might an aged person who feels unable to manage adequately or satisfactorily).

The *death accepter* is resigned to his or her fate; the style of acceptance may be passive, philosophical, resigned, heroic, realistic, or mature.

The *death postponer* hopes to put death off for as long as possible.

The *death disdainer* feels, in Shneidman's words, "above any involvement in the stopping of the vital processes."

The *death fearer* is fearful, and possibly phobic, about anything related to death; death is something to be fought and hated.

The *death feigner* pretends to be in mortal danger or pretends to perform a suicidal act without being in actual danger, possibly in an attempt to gain attention or to manipulate others.

Source: Adapted from Edwin S. Shneidman, *Deaths of Man* (New York: Quadrangle Books, 1973), pp. 82–90.

it. Generally, the goal is not death but the eradication of some problem; suicide is perceived as a means of accomplishing that goal. Thus, suicidal behavior is a message to the effect that "something has to change in my life; I can't go on living this way." This is typically the situation of a person who becomes suicidal when the normal avenues for expressing frustration are blocked. Much suicidal behavior among young people is of this type.

The "cry for help" is associated with persons who threaten or attempt suicide as opposed to those who actually commit suicide. There is often no history of suicidal behavior, and the lethality of the attempt is generally low. The aim of the behavior is to communicate to significant others how desperate or unhappy the person feels. A suicide attempt says, in effect: "I am deadly serious, and you'd better pay attention!" This message may be directed inwardly to oneself as well as outwardly to others.

In responding to the cry for help, it is important to recognize that a serious problem exists and to make efforts toward increasing communication and proposing remedies. When low-lethality suicidal behavior is met with defensive hostility or with attempts to minimize its seriousness, the suicide risk increases along with the possibility that the next attempt will be lethal.

In studying suicidal behavior, it is useful to make a distinction between *attempted* suicide and the *fait accompli*. According to Evans and Farberow, attempted suicide "refers to behavior directed against the self which results in injury or self-harm, or has strong potential for injury. Intention in the behavior may or may not be to die, or may or may not be to inflict injury or pain on oneself."[40] There may be two fairly distinct populations of individuals who engage in suicidal behavior: (1) *attempters* (who tend toward repeated, but not lethal, attempts) and (2) *completers* (whose first attempt typically results in death). In this view, attempters and completers may have quite different aims with regard to their suicidal acts.[41] Indeed, the suggestion has been made that the study of suicide should focus on attempted suicide as the norm, while viewing completed suicide as a failed behavior in which the individual inappropriately died.[42]

Although there is evidence to support the view that some suicides are meant to result in death and others are not, it should never be assumed that a suicide attempt was meant only as a gesture. Suicidal behavior is life threatening. Psychological autopsies of some suicide victims suggest that they thought the attempt would be stopped short of death, but help did not arrive in time.

Suicide attempts outnumber committed suicides by a significant margin. For the population as a whole, it is estimated that, for every eight suicide attempts, one is lethal. Among adolescents, the ratio between attempts and completions has been estimated as high as two hundred attempts for every completed suicide. In all age groups above age fourteen, females *attempt* suicide more often than do males, while males *kill themselves* more often than do females.[43] (Among children younger than age fourteen, males both attempt and complete suicide more often than do females.) This gender difference may be explained partly by the methods used, with males using

Graffiti

I find a snapshot
buried in my father's drawer.
A picture of the grandfather I never knew.
Small, stooped yet dignified he stands
beside my brother's wicker pram
surrounded by his family.
My mother tells the story, hidden in the past
of the last time she saw him.
She was big with child, and so allowed to sit
while his two daughters served the sons
who gathered at the table.
Grandma who reigned as always at the head
arranged the seating of those sons
not in the order of their age
but of the weekly wage they earned
and without question brought to her.

I learn that you, mild gentle man
never at home in the new language, the new land,
subdued by failure, each passing year withdrew
further into old world memories, and silence.
Rising that evening from the table, as usual
scarcely noticed as you went to lie down
on your narrow bed, there was no sign, no signal.
Only that as you passed, you bent
with a shy unaccustomed show of tenderness
to murmur *"Liebchen"* and to kiss my mother's head.
She tells me that I leaped and struggled in her womb
when from your room you shattered silence
with a shot. Your life exploding
sudden messages across blank walls in bursts of red.

Maude Meehan

more lethal or "aggressive" methods. Females tend to take pills or slash wrists; males tend to use less equivocal means, such as guns. However, the use of aggressive methods by males is only part of the explanation.

Perhaps males consider a failed attempt to be cowardly or unmasculine and thus make a special effort to be successful in their suicidal behavior. In addition to the "suicidal success syndrome" that afflicts males, there is evidence that males are less likely than females to report suicidal thoughts or seek help (such as from crisis intervention centers). By hiding their feelings of depression or hopelessness, males hinder potential efforts at intervention. These gender differences appear to be especially pronounced among young people.

Some people who survive a suicide attempt look upon their continued existence as a second chance or "bonus life." Individuals admitted to intensive care as a result of suicide attempts show a relatively low rate of repeat attempts. The highest rate of repeat suicide attempts is among those who received no treatment for their injuries. Keep in mind that these statistics reflect general patterns of suicidal behavior. They are not a reliable means for predicting the behavior of a particular individual.

Risk Factors Influencing Suicide

Another way to increase our understanding of suicide involves examining the risk factors that influence suicidal behaviors. Generally speaking, these risk factors encompass four broad areas: culture, personality, the individual situation, and biological factors. These risk factors typically are found to overlap to varying degrees when particular instances of suicidal behavior are considered.

Culture

In the area of culture, we consider structural factors that affect members of a particular social group. Such factors include a society's basic attitude toward suicide as well as the nature of that society. For example, suicide intended to end physical suffering related to terminal disease appears to be more acceptable to many people in our society than suicide related to escaping the mental pain of other life problems. Societal messages about the acceptability of various suicidal behaviors can influence the kinds of behavior engaged in by members of a social group.

Many young African Americans consider suicide a weak, cowardly way out of their problems, a view that is also held by many of their elders. The rate of suicide among African Americans is lower than among white Americans, a phenomenon due at least partly to a common perception among African Americans that suicide is a "white thing." In their study of attitudes toward suicide expressed by African Americans, Kevin Early and Ronald Akers observed that religion and family play important roles in "buffering" social forces that might otherwise promote suicide among African Americans. Early and Akers found that suicide is typically viewed as "inherently contradictory to the black experience and a complete denial of black identity and culture."[44]

Kathleen Erwin has written insightfully about the influence of social factors on gay and lesbian suicide.[45] A relatively high rate of psychological distress and suicide among homosexual populations has long been recognized, although explanations have been sought mostly in theories centering on individual psychology. More recently, however, the antecedents of gay and lesbian suicide have been located in terms of a sociocultural model focusing on the impact of social forces that have historically been intolerant and oppressive with respect to homosexuals. Thus, the focus on individual psychology

Suicide Note Written by a Married Man, Age 74

What is a few short years to live in hell. That is all I get around here.

No more I will pay the bills.

No more I will drive the car.

No more I will wash, iron, & mend any clothes.

No more I will have to eat the leftover articles that was cooked the day before.

This is no way to live.

Either is it any way to die.

Her grub I can not eat.

At night I can not sleep.

I married the wrong nag-nag-nag and I lost my life.

W.S.

To the undertaker

We have got plenty money to give me a decent burial. Don't let my wife kid you by saying she has not got any money.

Give this note to the cops.

Give me liberty or give me death.

W.S.

is being balanced by the recognition that social factors are important, if not crucial, in the incidence of homosexual suicide.

The acceptability of violence as a solution to problems is another cultural factor that increases suicide risk. The availability of lethal weapons as well as the prevalence of violence in the media contribute to a sense that violence against oneself is an acceptable alternative when the going gets rough. Easy access to guns is an important factor in suicide among children and young adults. In a 1995 report, Dr. Alex Crosby of the U.S. Centers for Disease Control (CDC) noted that children are increasingly using guns to end their lives instead of methods that might fail. According to the CDC, among persons under age 25 who kill themselves, more than half do so with a gun.[46] The apparent acceptance of violence in our lives can change posturing into deadly deeds.[47]

Likewise, reports of suicide in the modern media are sometimes blamed for triggering more suicides due to "suggestibility"—causing others to imitate the suicidal behavior. The idea that suicide is contagious has a long history. Following the publication of Goethe's *The Sorrows of Young Werther* in 1774, an epidemic of suicide among young people was attributed to the book's influence. However, it is not clear whether, or in what way, attention to suicide in a book, movie, or news report might stimulate an increase in the suicide rate. What is clear is the fact that culture and the social environment do exert a significant influence on the incidence of suicide.

Cultural factors relative to suicide are highlighted in what Brian Barry calls "the balance between pro-life and pro-death forces operating at any given time."[48] Pro-life forces include (1) the belief that problems can promote growth, (2) a perceived ability to solve life problems, (3) a willingness to struggle and suffer if necessary, and (4) a healthy fear of death and its aftermath. In contrast, pro-death forces include (1) the belief that problems are intolerable, (2) a perception that life problems are intractable or unyielding, (3) a sense of entitlement to a rewarding life, and (4) a philosophical stance that sees suicide as a means of obtaining relief. Barry says that individuals in contemporary society, especially young people, have accepted "two fundamental assumptions about life that no previous generation has embraced so massively." First is the belief that we, as human beings, deserve significant levels of fulfillment in our jobs, marriages, and overall lives. The second assumption is that, "rather than adopting a posture of long-suffering acceptance of unalterable circumstances, the responsible thing to do is to live and die on one's own terms." We not only aspire to a good life, but we have become convinced that we are entitled to it. Socially tolerant attitudes toward suicide may also help to remove what has traditionally been a powerful constraint inhibiting people from taking their own lives. The modern emphasis on individual freedom includes the freedom to make irresponsible and costly choices.

Personality

Some people have a "basic optimism" while others have a "basic pessimism"—a phenomenon that can be a deciding factor in some suicides.[49] The way people relate to others, as well as how they relate to their own problems in life, influences the onset of suicidal thoughts. For example, suicidal behavior resulting from the breakup of a romance, especially among young people, is influenced by qualities of personality, with feelings of depression and worthlessness leading to suicidal intent.

An individual's fascination with the "mystique" of death, especially self-willed death, also increases suicide risk. Some suicidal behaviors appear to be related to a "poetic" or "romantic" attraction to death. Following the example of Thomas Chatterton, who killed himself in 1770 at the age of 17, the Romantics thought of death as "the great inspirer" and "great consoler." They made suicide fashionable and felt that "to die by one's own hand was a short and sure way to fame."[50] Death may be seen as a lover to be courted. The poet Sylvia Plath wrote: "I will marry dark death, the thief of the daytime."[51] Do the suicides of such writers as Ernest Hemingway, Anne Sexton, Plath herself, and, more recently, musician Kurt Cobain, reflect a conscious desire to embrace the

Romeo and Juliet also embody another popular misconception: that of the great suicidal passion. It seems that those who die for love usually do so by mistake and ill-luck. It is said that the London police can always distinguish, among the corpses fished out of the Thames, between those who have drowned themselves because of unhappy love affairs and those drowned for debt. The fingers of the lovers are almost invariably lacerated by their attempts to save themselves by clinging to the piers of the bridges. In contrast, the debtors apparently go down like slabs of concrete, apparently without struggle and without afterthought.

A. Alvarez, *The Savage God*

mystery of death, or nonbeing? Or do they result from more commonplace human experiences? Such suicides are characterized by much the same frustrations that can affect anyone. They are not unique to writers or artists. Failure to find meaning in life and problems with relationships are common threads. As someone said: "The death of love evokes the love of death." Low self-esteem, problems with intimate relationships, lack of coping skills, feelings of stagnation, loneliness, despair, hopelessness, and helplessness are among factors related to personality that can contribute to suicidal thoughts and behaviors.

The Individual Situation

The influence of culture and personality creates a unique situation experienced by a particular individual. Environmental factors, including not only the attitudes and social dynamics existing in the broader society but also such particular characteristics as an individual's family patterns and economic situation, create varying degrees of suicide risk. A history of abuse and neglect, conflict in relationships, drug or alcohol abuse, and the availability of firearms or other ready means of self-destruction also influence the degree of risk present in an individual's life. The social environment plays a crucial role. For example, suicide is a leading cause of death for people in jails, with pretrial detainees especially at risk.[52] Among juveniles held in adult detention facilities, the suicide rate is higher than among those held in juvenile detention facilities.[53]

Sociocultural stress appears to be a factor in the comparatively high rate of suicide among some Native American populations. Forced onto reservations, their religions and cultures undermined, and their children placed in schools where non-Indian traditions are taught, the native peoples of North America have undergone severe cultural and economic dislocation. Native Americans may experience feelings of powerlessness and anxiety because of conflicts between their traditional ways and the ways of the contemporary white society. An added burden is experienced by individuals living in cities where support systems, such as family ties and traditional customs, are lacking.

Suicide Note Written by a Single Woman, Age 21

My dearest Andrew,

It seems as if I have been spending all my life apologizing to you for things that happened whether they were my fault or not.

I am enclosing your pin because I want you to think of what you took from me every time you see it.

I don't want you to think I would kill myself over you because you're not worth any emotion at all. It is what you cost me that hurts and nothing can replace it.

Specific life events represent another category of experiences that influence suicidal thoughts and behavior. For example, individuals who have been bereaved as a result of suicide may be especially vulnerable to adverse effects, possibly including an increased risk of committing suicide themselves.[54] People with AIDS are also members of a group that has been described as prone to suicide.[55]

In *crisis suicide,* the typical pattern is that of an adolescent who reaches a point in his or her life involving sudden traumatic changes, such as the loss of a loved one or the loss or threatened loss of status in school. The young person may respond by exhibiting sudden and dramatic changes in behavior, possibly including loss of interest in things that were previously important, hostile and aggressive acts (in a previously placid youngster), or signs of confusion, disorganization, and depression.

The influence of peers can also affect an individual's suicide risk. This phenomenon appears to be especially pronounced among adolescents and young adults. A study of suicide among Micronesian males confirmed the occurrence of an "epidemic-like" increase during a twenty-year period.[56] This period was marked by rapid sociocultural transformation, as traditional styles of living gave way to reliance on a cash economy and modern forms of education, employment, health services, and technology. In studying suicide among Micronesians, investigators found links among suicides, with several suicides occurring among a small circle of friends over several months. There were also cases of suicidal acts in reaction to the suicide of a friend or relative and "suicide pacts" among two or more people. Taken together, these phenomena pointed to the existence of a "suicide subculture" wherein suicide begat suicide. In an environment characterized by a general familiarity with and acceptance of the *idea* of suicide, suicide had become a culturally patterned and partly collective response to personal dilemmas and problems.

Biologic Factors

Recent studies indicate the presence of altered brain neurochemistry in some people who commit suicide.[57] Specifically, biochemical studies of suicide victims and attempters indicate that low levels of serotonin (5-HT) or its neurotransmitter metabolite (5-HIAA) appear to be correlated with suicidal behavior. These findings suggest that such biological markers could be important in assessing risk for suicide. A clearer understanding of the role of serotonin and other neurotransmitter systems could help in the development of comprehensive pharmacologic treatments to reduce suicide risk. However, such neurochemical correlates do not fully explain the timing and type of suicidal behavior, nor do they explain why some aggression is directed outward toward others and some is directed toward the self. Thus, although biochemical factors may have a role in suicide assessment and intervention, environmental and psychosocial factors are likely more important for a comprehensive understanding of suicide risks.

Lifespan Perspectives on Suicide

Statistically, the level of suicide risk changes throughout the lifespan. The motives for suicide also change as human beings encounter a changing constellation of factors that pertain to different periods of development. In this section, we examine some of the specific risks and motives that affect suicidal behaviors throughout the lifespan.

Childhood

Despite a paucity of statistics concerning suicide among young children, many researchers and clinicians believe that suicidal behavior occurs among even very young children. In studying the role of death preoccupation in children ages six to twelve years, Cynthia Pfeffer found that about 12 percent expressed suicidal ideas or actions.[58] Although suicidal behavior appears to be infrequent among school-age children compared with the progressive increases observed among junior high, high school, and college students, suicide among young children is nonetheless of concern.

It is sobering to note that between 1980 and 1991 the suicide rate among children ages ten to fourteen nearly doubled.[59] Among African-American males in this age group, the rate tripled during the same period. With suicide attempts being made (or perhaps *recorded*) at younger ages than in the past, and in light of the fact that suicide risk is higher for people who have made a previous attempt on their lives, those who attempt suicide at a comparatively young age also remain at risk for a longer period of time.

In an early study, five major factors were noted as influencing children's suicide: (1) the desire to escape from a difficult situation; (2) the attempt to assert independence or to punish people who "interfered" with the child; (3) the effort to gain attention and affection; (4) the wish to achieve reunion with a deceased loved one; and (5) spite.[60]

The suicide rate among children might be significantly higher than statistics indicate if accidents were carefully examined for intent. Some childhood deaths resulting from running in front of cars or plastic bag suffocation might

Henry Wallis, Tate Gallery, London

Unable to earn a living by writing and too proud to accept food offered to him by his landlady, this seventeen-year-old killed himself by taking poison. Painted in 1856 by Henry Wallis, The Death of Chatterton *depicts an adolescent suicide that was precipitated by crisis arising out of the developmental transition from child to adult.*

be intentional rather than accidental. However, although young children do engage in suicidal behavior and even kill themselves, labeling a death as suicide is problematic in the case of a young child who may not yet have formulated a mature concept of death.

Adolescence and Young Adulthood

In the United States, suicide is the third leading cause of death among people ages fifteen to twenty-four, following accidents and homicides.[61] Among countries reporting data to the World Health Organization, the rise in overall suicide rates worldwide is due largely to increases among young people.[62] An examination of social indicators suggests that many countries are witnessing a sharp rise in self-destructive behaviors among young people, due primarily to social disruption (or anomie) and depression.

In surveying risk factors for suicide among children and adolescents, Cynthia Pfeffer cites the influence of both early developmental experiences and current environmental situations.[63] Besides aggression and family violence, factors increasing the risk for suicide among youth include depression,

T A B L E *12-6   Risk Factors in Youthful Suicide*

1. Early separation from one's parents
2. Family dissolution, economic hardship, and increased mobility
3. Effect of highly conflicted families or families who are unresponsive to the young person's needs, or who are anomic (not accepting of the usual standards of social conduct) or depressed, alcoholic, and so on
4. Increased social isolation as compared to the support previously provided by the extended family, church, and community
5. Rapidly changing sex roles
6. Increase in relative proportion of young people in the total population, and corresponding increase in competition because of the large youthful cohort population
7. Pressure for achievement and success, perhaps resulting from parental expectations
8. Impact of peer suicides and role models of popular entertainers in terms of "copy cat" suicide
9. Media attention given to suicide, and the influence of self-destructive themes in popular culture, especially in popular song lyrics
10. Sense of lack of control over one's life
11. Low self-esteem and poor self-image
12. Devaluing of emotional expression
13. Lack of effective relationships with peers
14. Easy access to drugs and alcohol

Source: Adapted from William C. Fish and Edith Waldhart-Letzel, "Suicide and Children," *Death Education* 5 (1981): 217–220; Michael Peck, "Youth Suicide," *Death Education* 6 (1982): 29–47; and Judith M. Stillion, Eugene E. McDowell, and Jacque H. May, *Suicide Across the Life Span: Premature Exits* (New York: Hemisphere, 1989), pp. 95–100.

parental suicidal behavior, and family losses. Increased risk is found among youngsters who have recently lost a parent or who suffer from learning disabilities related to hyperactivity, perceptual disorders, or dyslexia. Psychiatric diagnosis, dysfunctional personality traits, and psychosocial problems also increase the risk of suicide.[64] Other characteristics that contribute to increased risk of youthful suicide are listed in Table 12-6. Upheavals in family life during recent decades are viewed as influencing suicidal behavior among the young. Contemporary life styles increase the pressures on all family members. Suicide may seem a way of imposing some control over confusing and upsetting events.

Much youthful suicidal behavior relates to a life style without goals, direction, or substance. Commenting on the values of the home, the family, and parenting, Michael Peck says that many adolescents "describe what might best be called a narcissistic do-your-own-thing upsurge among parents," with the result that youngsters grow up with "little clear-cut guidance, confused or absent values, and a sense of floating along in time without direction."[65] The term "throwaway society" is used by social workers to describe troublesome children who are literally thrown out of their homes by their parents.[66] One social worker calls this phenomenon the "Kleenex mentality," using things and throwing them away.

There may also be a relationship between youthful suicide and the pressures and overcrowding experienced by a large cohort of young people passing through the violence-prone years of childhood. Coupled with lack of employment opportunities and other economic factors, this overcrowding creates significant life style and behavioral changes in the experience of the generation now moving up through young adulthood. The result may be too many young people wanting too many things that are not available, thus increasing their feelings of anonymity and alienation.

Adolescents and young adults seem to be susceptible to an element of "contagion" with respect to suicide whereby one person's suicide triggers another. These so-called *cluster suicides* typically take place within the same locale.[67] Such mutual influencing of one adolescent by another appears to have the greatest impact on individuals who are vulnerable to suicidal thoughts. *Suicide pacts* are a similar phenomenon in that they relate to an arrangement between two or more people who determine to kill themselves at the same time and usually in the same place.[68] In 1987, four teenagers in New Jersey, two boys and two girls, decided to commit suicide together by sitting in a car with the motor running inside a locked garage. Reportedly, they were distraught over the death of a friend. They were discovered dead the next morning. Two days later, another suicide pact took the lives of two teenage girls in Illinois who killed themselves in similar fashion.

Another instance of adolescents entering into a suicide pact involved a boy and girl who reportedly became obsessed with the possibility of reincarnation. They crashed their car into their old junior high school building, causing the boy to be killed instantly. The girl, who apparently had last-second doubts about reincarnation, barely survived by diving under the car's dashboard. As with the "epidemic" suicides among young people in Micronesia, suicide clusters and suicide pacts can be a deadly influence on individuals who are vulnerable to suicidal intentions.

The media is cited by some observers as a factor influencing suicide among young people. Following the movie *The Deerhunter,* which contained a scene depicting soldiers playing Russian roulette with a loaded pistol, there were reports of individuals (mostly males in their teens and early twenties) shooting themselves in the head within a few days of watching the movie.[69] It has been suggested that the media could assist in reducing suicide by promoting coping mechanisms rather than "normalizing" suicide by reporting it.[70]

Alcohol and drug abuse are widely recognized as comprising a deadly link in the chain of self-destruction. Substance abuse among adolescents and young adults is a risk factor for a variety of suicidal behaviors, including suicidal ideation, attempted suicide, and completed suicide.[71] In addition, the data support an association between alcohol intoxication and suicide by firearms. Thus, individuals who engage in substance abuse, particularly those with any type of depressive disorder, are at higher risk for suicidal behavior.

Suicidal behavior sometimes takes place with little planning or forethought about the potential outcome. A person may not fully recognize the danger inherent in his or her self-destructive actions. Such teenage flirtations with death as "playing chicken" may prove to be more than was bargained for. Youth is typically a time of testing the limits. Suicidal behaviors, such as cutting one's wrists or taking a drug overdose, may be engaged in as a means of gaining attention or of expressing frustration without fully recognizing the potential for death. Or, again, suicidal behaviors may be entered into with a lackadaisical attitude about the possible result. Whatever the motive, the outcome can be deadly.

Among older adolescents and young adults, additional risk factors contributing to suicide include depression, separation and divorce, occupational stress, and a sense of hopelessness. This is an age group that is also affected by the AIDS epidemic, which represents yet another risk factor for suicide among those whose lives are touched by the disease.

At present, the most promising approaches for reducing suicide among young people appear to be in two major areas: first, providing treatment for disorders that increase the risk of suicide, such as depression, substance abuse, and family conflict; and, second, targeting prevention efforts at high-risk groups, such as affectively disordered young men who exhibit substance abuse and other antisocial behavior.[72]

Middle Adulthood

Middle age, the period roughly between ages thirty-five and sixty-five, has been termed the "terra incognita" of the human lifespan. Developmentally, this is a period of "generativity," of giving back to society some of the gifts of nurture and sustenance received during earlier periods of life. It is a time of shifting from valuing physical capabilities to valuing wisdom, of building new relationships as old ones are altered or lost, and of gaining greater flexibility. Stillion and her colleagues note that some observers characterize this period as "middlescence," suggesting that middle age may be as turbulent for many adults as the period of adolescence.[73]

This is also a time of coping with the loss of dreams and ambitions, coming to terms with the realization that one may not reach the goal of being a great artist or writer or a company president, or the aim of attaining a perfect marriage or raising perfect children. Factors influencing suicide among the middle-aged include an accumulation of negative life events; affective disorders, especially major depression; and alcoholism.

Late Adulthood

Some of the reasons given for suicide among those in later adulthood (generally defined as people over age sixty-five) are given in Table 12-7. The biological and social changes that accompany old age bring losses that may make life seem less worth living. To some elderly, suicide may appear to be a "rational" option for avoiding severe illness or other hardships of old age.[74] Old age can be a period of increased life satisfaction and ego integrity, or one of dissatisfaction, despair, and disgust.[75]

TABLE *12-7*   *Risk Factors in Late-Adulthood Suicide*

1. Social isolation and loneliness
2. Boredom, depression, sense of uselessness
3. Loss of purpose and meaning in life after retirement and separation from family and friends
4. Financial hardship
5. Multiple losses of loved ones
6. Chronic illness, pain, incapacitation
7. Alcohol abuse and drug dependence
8. Desire to avoid being a "burden" to others or to end one's life with "dignity"

Double suicides (also known as suicide pacts), occur with greatest frequency among the elderly. The typical double suicide involves an older couple with one or both partners physically ill. Heavy alcohol use by one or both partners is also common. Such couples tend to be dependent on each other and isolated from external sources of support. There seems to be a "special chemistry" between couples who commit suicide together, with the more suicidal partner dominant and the more ambivalent partner passive in the relationship.[76]

Contemplating Suicide

Imagine for a moment the progression of thoughts of someone seriously considering suicide. Assume first that in an untenable situation suicide seems the only recourse, or at least an option to be considered further. The next step might involve formulating some means of killing oneself. At this point the means have not been actually acquired, but various possibilities are considered.

Many people have reached this stage—perhaps through mere fantasizing, or perhaps with serious intentions. For some, the shock of recognizing that one is harboring such thoughts is enough to force a decision toward a more life-affirming alternative. For others, the next step toward suicide is taken, a step that greatly increases the level of lethality with regard to suicidal intention.

This stage involves acquiring the means to kill oneself, thus setting into motion the logistics that make suicide a real possibility. As at the earlier steps in this sequence, a change of mind is still possible, and a different solution can be sought. Otherwise, the final step in the suicidal progression comes into play: actually using the means that have been acquired to commit the suicidal act.

These steps toward lethality have been described as occurring in a definite sequence, but to the person involved the process may be experienced as anything but logical and orderly. In actuality, suicide typically involves a complex array of conflicting thoughts and emotions. The predominant experience may be one of confusion. Still, recognizing the particular steps that must be taken to carry out the suicidal act is useful for understanding both the amount

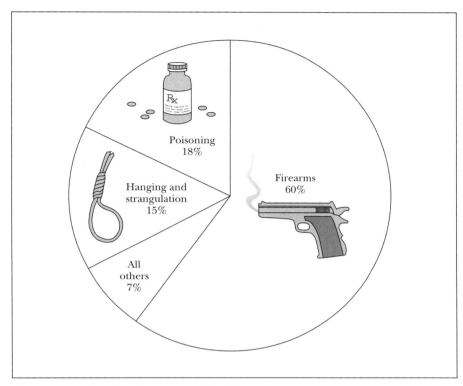

Figure *12-2* *How Americans Commit Suicide*
Source: Bureau of the Census, *Statistical Abstract of the United States 1994,*
p. 100.

of sustained effort involved in completing a suicide and the many decision points at which a change of mind or outside intervention is possible.

Choice of Method

Once a decision is made to commit suicide, a choice must be made concerning the means to be used (see Figure 12-2). Sometimes a particular method of suicide is chosen because of the image it represents to the suicidal individual. One might imagine drowning as a dreamy kind of death, a merging back into the universe. Or one might associate an overdose of sleeping pills with the death of a movie star. Whatever one's image of a particular method, the reality is likely to be quite different. Some persons who overdose on drugs do so expecting a quiet or peaceful death. The actual effects of a drug overdose are usually far from peaceful or serene.

Sometimes a particular method of suicide is chosen for its anticipated impact on survivors. A study of suicide notes found that people using "active" methods of suicide more often communicated that rejection was a critical

Suicide Note Written by a Married Man, Age 45

Dear Claudia:

You win, I can't take it any longer. I know you have been waiting for this to happen. I hope it makes you very happy, this is not an easy thing to do, but I've got to the point where there is nothing to live for, a little bit of kindness from you would of made everything so different, but all that ever interested you was the *dollar.*

It is pretty hard for me to do anything when you are so greedy even with this house you couldn't even be fair with that, well it's all yours now and you won't have to see the Lawyer anymore.

I wish you would give my personal things to Danny, you couldn't get much from selling them anyway, you still have my insurance, it isn't much but it will be enough to take care of my debts and still have a few bucks left.

You always told me that I was the one that made Sharon take her life, in fact you said I killed her, but you know down deep in your heart it was you that made her do what she did, and now you have two deaths to your credit, it should make you feel very proud.

Good By Kid

P.S. Disregard all the mean things I've said in this letter, I have said a lot of things to you I didn't really mean and I hope you get well and wish you the best of everything.

Cathy—don't come in.

Call your mother, she will know what to do.

Love,
Daddy

Cathy don't go in the bedroom.

---

factor in the decision for self-injury.[77] An individual who wants survivors to "really pay for all the grief they caused me" might select a method of suicide that graphically communicates this rage. Someone who did not want to "make a scene" might choose a method imagined as being less shocking to one's survivors.

Experience and familiarity also influence the choice of suicidal method. For example, an experienced hunter, well acquainted with rifles, might be inclined to turn to such a weapon for suicide because of its accessibility and familiarity. Someone who understands the effects of various drugs might use them to concoct a fatal overdose. In short, the choice of suicidal method reflects the experience and state of mind of the person choosing it. It may be a spontaneous choice, with the person using whatever lethal devices are readily at hand. Or it may be the outcome of deliberate thought and even research.

Käthe Kollwitz, Library of Congress

Despair, a common component of many suicides, is starkly depicted in this litho-graph, Nachdenkende Frau, *by Käthe Kollwitz. If the potential victim's warning signals are observed by people who take steps to provide crisis intervention, the suicidal impulse may be thwarted.*

Choosing a method of killing oneself can be likened to making travel arrangements for a cross-country trip. A person wanting to travel from the West Coast to the East Coast must consider the kinds of transportation available—automobile, train, airplane, and so on. Some of these are quite rapid; others are relatively slow and deliberate. For example, once you board an airplane and it lifts off the runway, there is no opportunity to change your mind and disembark before touching down at the scheduled destination. However, someone bicycling from coast to coast has innumerable opportunities to decide on a different destination.

Resume

Razors pain you;
Rivers are damp;
Acids stain you;
And drugs cause cramp.
Guns aren't lawful;
Nooses give;
Gas smells awful;
You might as well live.

Dorothy Parker

Similarly, some methods of committing suicide offer little hope of changing one's mind after the lethal act is initiated. Once the trigger is pulled on a revolver placed next to one's skull, there's virtually no possibility of altering the likelihood of a fatal outcome. However, the would-be suicide who cuts her wrists or takes an overdose of drugs *might* have time to alter an otherwise fatal outcome by seeking medical help. The potential for death, if help is not forthcoming, may be as great as that of the gunshot wound to the head, but there is generally a greater possibility of intervention. Among methods used in the suicidal act, then, there is an order of lethality.

Order of Lethality

The different methods used in suicide attempts are not equivalent in potential lethality. Some methods, as noted, carry a greater statistical risk of lethality than others. A report by the American Medical Association emphasizes the danger of firearms, noting that more than half of all suicides in the United States are committed with guns.[78] In the following listing, eleven methods of attempting suicide are ranked from most to least lethal. Any of these methods is potentially a killer. Ranking is by probability of death from use of the method.[79]

Order of Lethality
1. Gunshot
2. Carbon monoxide
3. Hanging
4. Drowning
5. Plastic bag (suffocation)
6. Impact (from jumping from a high place)
7. Fire
8. Poison
9. Drugs
10. Gas
11. Cutting

Although each method is potentially fatal, how it is applied influences the degree of lethality. For instance, a bullet into the head or the heart is more likely to kill than a gunshot wound to other parts of the body. Likewise, with the least lethal item on this list, cutting, the depth of cut and the location of the wound are significant determinants of the outcome.

Suicide Notes

Suicide notes have been called "cryptic maps of ill-advised journeys."[80] Although it is often assumed that nearly all suicides leave notes behind for their survivors, in fact only about one-fourth of suicides write a final message. As a partial record of the mental state of suicides, such notes are of immense interest to scholars and helping professionals. Imagine yourself in circumstances that would lead to your writing a suicide note. What kinds of things would you want to say in your last words to your survivors?

Actual suicide notes display a variety of messages and intentions. Some notes explain to survivors the decision to commit suicide. Others express anger or blame. Conversely, some notes emphasize that the writer's suicide is "no one's fault." The messages in suicide notes range from sweeping statements of the writer's philosophy or credo regarding suicide to detailed listings of practical chores that will require attention after the writer's death. For example, one note instructs survivors, "The cat needs to go to the vet next Tuesday; don't miss the appointment or you'll be charged double. The car is due for servicing a week from Friday."

Suicide notes may include expressions of love, hate, shame, disgrace, fear of insanity, self-abnegation; feelings of rejection; explanations for the suicidal act or defense of the right to take one's life; disavowal of any survivor's responsibility for the suicide; instructions for distributing the suicide's property and possessions. They typically display dichotomies of logic, hostility toward others mixed with self-blame, the use of particular names and specific instructions to survivors, and a sense of decisiveness about suicide. Many suicide notes convey an intense love-hate ambivalence toward survivors, as expressed succinctly in the following note:

> Dear Betty:
> I hate you.
> Love,
> George

This example of ambivalence also points up the dyadic nature of suicide—here involving husband and wife. Suicide notes provide clues about the intentions and emotions that lead a person to suicide, but they rarely tell the whole story—and they often raise more questions than they answer. The message in a suicide note may come as a surprise to survivors who had no hint of the person's feelings. Suicide notes can have a significant effect on survivors.

Whether the final message is one of affection or blame, survivors have no opportunity to respond. In this sense, suicide represents the ultimate last word.

Suicide Prevention, Intervention, and Postvention

The Los Angeles Suicide Prevention Center, founded in 1958 by Norman L. Farberow and Edwin S. Shneidman, became the prototype for prevention and crisis centers not only in the United States but throughout the world.[81] As Stillion notes:

> The importance of the Los Angeles Suicide Prevention Center cannot be overstated in any history of suicide. The work begun in that center by Shneidman and his associates, and expanded upon later when Shneidman became director of the Suicide Center in the National Institute of Mental Health, changed the nation's view of suicide and suicidal behavior. The most important change was a shift away from seeing suicide as an act committed by an insane person to seeing it as an act committed by a person who felt overwhelming ambivalence toward life.[82]

The ensuing decades have seen a dramatic increase in the number of suicide crisis centers, coupled with the rise of telephone hotlines focusing on suicide prevention among specific groups. For example, during a severe economic crisis affecting American farmers and ranchers, a suicide hotline was established for people in rural areas.[83] The typical suicide prevention center operates as a telephone-answering center with around-the-clock availability to people in crisis. The services provided are mainly designed to serve as a short-term resource for people contemplating suicide. The caller's anonymity is respected, and the caller's expressed need of help is accepted unquestioningly. Staff members—some of them professionals, many of them volunteers who have been given special training—use crisis intervention strategies to reduce the suicidal caller's stress.

Some suicide intervention centers have expanded their services to encompass treatment for a broad range of self-destructive behaviors. For example, the Los Angeles Suicide Prevention Center offers counseling and community services. Low-cost counseling is available for potential suicide victims as well as for survivors of a friend's or relative's suicide. Clinics provide treatment for depression and drug abuse. Community-based programs for former offenders who have been released back into society and for troubled youths have been implemented to help individuals overcome destructive behaviors. The activities of the Los Angeles Suicide Prevention Center exemplify the understanding of suicide as a subset of a larger class of self-destructive behaviors, all of which require attention if tragedy is to be averted.

Prevention

There is little reason to be optimistic about the prospect of preventing suicide, at least in the sense of eliminating it from the repertory of human behaviors. To do so, the sources of human unhappiness and dissatisfaction would have to be eradicated. Efforts to create a social environment conducive

When I was thirteen months old, my mother killed herself. So I eventually learned, as I learned her maiden name, Georgia Saphronia Collier, and where she was born, Sulphur Springs, Arkansas, and how old she was when she ended her life, twenty-nine. (And good lord, writing these words now, all these years afterward, for the first time in memory my eyes have filled with tears of mourning for her. What impenetrable vessel preserved them?) I didn't know my mother, except as infants know. At the beginning of my life the world acquired a hole. That's what I knew, that there was a hole in the world. For me there still is. It's a singularity. In and out of a hole like that, anything goes.

Richard Rhodes, *A Hole in the World:*
An American Boyhood

to the pursuit of happiness inevitably fall short of perfection. Interpersonal problems and social pressures also thwart the achievement of universal happiness and satisfaction. This is not to say that efforts to ameliorate human suffering are unavailing, only that they are inherently limited.

Nevertheless, much can be done to reduce suicide risk. Education is an essential element in any program of suicide prevention. Many programs provide education about suicide to school-age children and adolescents. The lessons to be learned, however, can be applied across the lifespan and include the following key points: First, it is crucial to acknowledge the reality that life is complex and that all of us will inevitably have experiences of disappointment, failure, and loss in our lives. Second, we can learn to deal with such experiences by developing appropriate coping techniques, including the skills of critical thinking. Individuals "who form a habit early of analyzing situations from a variety of perspectives, of asking appropriate questions, and of testing the reality of their own thinking are far less likely to settle easily into the cognitive inflexibility that focuses on suicide as *the* solution."[84] A corollary of such coping skills involves the cultivation of a sense of humor, especially the ability to laugh at oneself and at life's problems, to see the humor in situations. Finally, education can be directed toward learning how to set appropriate and attainable goals. The importance of adequate self-esteem as a preventive against suicide has been stressed repeatedly.[85]

In recent years, a number of school-based suicide awareness and prevention programs have been established.[86] Books about suicide for young people have also become widely available.[87] Nevertheless, much remains to be done, in terms of both fine-tuning present programs and expanding current efforts. For example, some educators make the case that young males require a different kind of suicide awareness program than the one generally provided.[88] Females appear to be more sensitive to suicide and its management, especially with respect to their willingness to seek and accept help when in crisis. Males, however, need to learn how to respond to their own "cries for help," rather than denying them.

Suicide prevention programs must also be expanded to reach the populations at greatest risk. One native Ojibway/Cree community in Ontario, Canada, for example, the Muskrat Dam community, has organized a group known as Helping Hands to confront suicide in a culture that was previously unaffected by it.[89] Patterning its response on traditional Native American spiritual values, the Helping Hands project has as its main objectives the instilling of a sense of value within the youth and general community population, rebuilding the lives of disturbed youth to enable them to proceed with direction and purpose, restoring pride and a sense of well-being within members of the community, motivating young people to lead constructive and productive lives, providing life-skills training that can be applied within the family and community, and helping individuals develop good mechanisms for coping with mental health problems. Programs like this, which are sensitive to the needs of a particular community or segment of the population at risk for suicide, represent a crucial adjunct to conventional methods of suicide prevention.

Intervention

Whereas suicide prevention, strictly defined, aims to eliminate suicide risk, the goal of suicide intervention is to reduce the lethality of the individual suicidal crisis (see Table 12-8). Although many suicide intervention programs are actually named "suicide prevention centers," such programs generally use theories and techniques common to crisis intervention. They emphasize short-term care and treatment for persons who are actively in suicidal crisis, thereby reducing the inherent lethality of suicide.

The cardinal rule in suicide intervention is to *do something*. Intervention means taking threats seriously; watching for clues to suicidal intentions and behaviors; answering cries for help by offering support, understanding, and compassion; confronting the problem by asking questions and being unafraid to discuss suicide with the person in crisis; obtaining professional help to manage the crisis; and offering constructive alternatives to suicide. A key theme of suicide intervention is that talking is a positive step toward resolving the crisis. The emotional support of the suicidal person's family is considered to be essential in limiting the risk that suicidal intentions will be carried through to completion.[90] When family support is inadequate, other sources of support must be sought out and provided.

Postvention

Suicide *postvention*, a term coined by Edwin Shneidman, refers to the assistance given to *all* survivors of suicide, including those who attempt suicide as well as the families, friends, and associates of those who commit suicide. The bereaved survivors of suicide have special needs, for they often experience feelings of guilt and self-blame that need to be confronted. When these feelings are not dealt with or are mismanaged, there is greater likelihood of dysfunctional relationships, emotional problems, and other difficulties in the lives of survivors.

TABLE *12-8* *Two Models of Suicide Intervention*

1. *Crisis-intervention model.* Assumes that feeling suicidal is an acute (time-limited) crisis that will pass. Focuses on keeping the person alive until the crisis is resolved. Emphasizes intervention by others to prevent suicide. Characterized by some as "paternalistic and controlling."

2. *Continuing-therapy model.* Assumes that suicidal thoughts and behavior result from a chronic (long-term) pattern rather than an acute crisis. Suicidality is viewed as part of a person's life style and personality. Focuses on basic therapeutic principles to reframe the suicidal behavior as a problem-solving behavior and to work with it as one would other maladaptive behaviors. Emphasizes the suicidal person's ultimate responsibility for his or her own behavior. Characterized by some as overly "laissez-faire."

Source: Adapted from Joan Pulakos, "Two Models of Suicide Treatment: Evaluation and Recommendations," *American Journal of Psychotherapy* 47, no. 4 (Fall 1993): 603–612.

Helping a Person Who Is in Suicidal Crisis

Warnings that an individual is considering suicide may be communicated in a variety of ways. Evans and Farberow point out that suicidal intent may be expressed in four main ways: (1) *verbal direct* ("I will shoot myself if you leave me"), (2) *verbal indirect* ("A life without love is a life without meaning"), (3) *behavioral direct* (for example, a chronically ill person hoarding pills), and (4) *behavioral indirect*.[91] Among the warning signs that fall under this last category, Evans and Farberow mention:

1. Giving away prized possessions, making a will, or attending to other "final" arrangements
2. Sudden and extreme changes in eating habits or sleep patterns
3. Withdrawal from friends or family, or other major behavioral changes accompanied by depression
4. Changes in school or job performance
5. Personality changes, such as nervousness, outbursts of anger, or apathy about health or appearance
6. Use of drugs or alcohol

The recent suicide of a friend or relative, or a history of previous suicide attempts, should also be seen as a warning sign of potentially increased suicide risk.

A number of commonly held beliefs, or myths, have grown up about suicide and about the kind of person who is likely to commit suicide. Unfortunately, many of these beliefs, being false, are harmful, for they have the effect of depriving the suicidal person of needed help. As you review the listing of fallacies about suicide given in Table 12-9, notice which ones you may have believed or unconsciously incorporated into your assumptions about suicide. According to Charles Neuringer, myths about suicide develop because suicide defies the primary law of nature—survival itself—and raises doubts about the worth of living.[92] By adopting a set of false beliefs about suicide, we avoid

TABLE 12-9   *Myths and Facts About Suicide*

Myth: *People who talk about suicide don't commit suicide.*
 Fact: This fallacy has been called the "grand old myth of suicide," one that excuses the failure to respond to another person's cry for help. Most people who attempt suicide communicate their intentions to others, as hints, direct threats, or self-destructive actions or preparations for suicide. Unfortunately, these cries for help often go unheeded by friends, family members, coworkers, or health care personnel.

Myth: *Improvement in a suicidal person means the risk of suicide has passed.*
 Fact: Improvement may be necessary before a severly depressed person can take the steps necessary to carry out the suicidal intention. Many suicides occur within three to six months following apparent improvement. Thus, an apparently positive change in mood can be a danger signal: Making the decision to carry out the suicidal act can be exhilarating and freeing; the person feels, "Now that I've made the decision, I no longer have to agonize about what I'm going to do." This relief is subject to misinterpretation by others, who may believe the crisis has passed.

Myth: *Once a suicide risk, always a suicide risk.*
 Fact: The peak of suicidal crisis is generally brief. The simultaneous conjunction of the thought of killing oneself, possession of the means to complete the act, and the lack of help or intervention is a more-or-less unusual set of circumstances. If intervention occurs, the suicidal person may well be able to put suicidal thoughts behind and lead a productive life.

Myth: *Suicide is inherited.*
 Fact: Although this fallacy gives suicidal behavior an aura of biological fate, the fact is that suicide does not "run in families," in the sense of being a genetically inherited trait. However, dysfunctional family patterns with respect to problem solving or surviving the suicide of a loved one may create beliefs about suicide that influence a person's subsequent behavior. The fear that one has a greater potential for suicide may create a self-fulfilling prophecy. In this sense, the

facing basic issues about life and death and thereby reduce our discomfort. It is important to separate fact from fallacy if we wish to understand suicide and help the person who is in a suicidal crisis.

If a person says, "I feel like killing myself," that statement should not be taken lightly or brushed aside with the quick response, "Oh, well, you'll probably feel better tomorrow." To the person in crisis, there may seem little hope of a "tomorrow" at all. Pay attention to the message being communicated.

Similarly, responding to a suicidal statement with a provocation—"You wouldn't be capable of committing suicide!"—or with a tone of moral superiority—"I don't want to hear such unhealthy talk!"—can worsen rather than ease the crisis. A response that provides only a litany of the "good reasons" why the person should not commit suicide may also offer little practical assistance to the person in crisis.

More helpful is listening carefully to exactly what the person in crisis is communicating; the tone and context of statements should reveal to the sensitive listener something about the communicator's real intent. Often,

T A B L E *12-9* *(continued)*

suicide of a family member may provide an excuse, or make it easier, to contemplate suicide as a means of escape from a difficult situation.

Myth: *Suicide affects only a specific group or class of people.*

Fact: Suicide is not the "curse of the poor" or "disease of the rich." It occurs among all socioeconomic groups and affects individuals with widely divergent life styles. Social integration is a more important determinant of suicidal behavior than socioeconomic class.

Myth: *Suicidal individuals are insane.*

Fact: Although it is true that some suicides are mentally ill, the planning and carrying out of suicide usually requires careful reasoning and deliberate judgment. Many suicide notes reveal not only ambivalence, but also considerable lucidity about the writer's intentions. Despite its devastating effect on the individual's physical being, suicide can be considered as a defensive act or problem-solving technique to preserve the integrity of the self.

Myth: *Suicidal individuals are fully intent on dying.*

Fact: Actually, most suicides are undecided about continuing to live or ending their lives. In their ambivalence, they may gamble with death, leaving the possibility of rescue to fate. Although some attempters do ultimately commit suicide after previously uncompleted attempts, the majority do not. Thus, a suicide attempt may signal that a person's psychological or interpersonal needs are not being satisfactorily met and a change is desired; it does not necessarily indicate that he or she wants to die.

Myth: *The motive for a particular suicide is clearly evident.*

Fact: People often try to establish a quick "cause" for suicide, attributing it to economic hardship, disappointment in love, or some other immediate condition. Deeper analysis usually uncovers a lengthy sequence of self-destructive behaviors leading up to the act of suicide. The apparent "cause" may be simply the final step of a complex pattern of self-destructive acts.

---

remarks about suicide are made in an offhand manner: "If I don't get that job, I'll kill myself!" Perhaps the remark is a figure of speech, much as in the joking statement, "I'll kill you for that!" There is a tendency to discount such statements in a culture where "talk is cheap," and "actions speak louder than words."[93] Suicidal threats should be taken seriously. To do otherwise is to fall prey to the myth that "talking about suicide means the person will not really go through with it." Knowledge about the patterns of suicidal behavior can help distinguish facts from fallacies. It is also helpful to become acquainted with the crisis intervention resources available in your own community.

Lastly, become aware of your own attitudes about life, death, and suicide. When working with someone who is struggling with suicidal thoughts, it is important to recognize that no one can take *ultimate* responsibility for another human being's decision to end his or her life. This recognition may go against one's inclination to preserve life, yet only so much can be done to assist another person in crisis.

In the short term, it may be feasible to keep someone from taking his or her life. Constant vigilance or some type of custodial care can prevent suicide

Stanley Forman, Boston Herald American

Once a person is this close to the suicidal act, the chance of a successful intervention is usually slight. Fortunately, in this dramatic instance, intervention was successful.

during a brief period of intense suicidal crisis. Over the longer term, however, assuming responsibility for preventing someone else's suicide is likely to be unsuccessful. A terminally ill man dying in great pain said to his wife: "You'd better keep my medication out of reach, because I don't want to keep up this struggle any longer." The wife had to decide whether she could take responsibility for whether he would continue to live with pain or end his life by an overdose. After much soul searching, she concluded that, although she had great compassion for his predicament and did not want him to suffer, she could not assume responsibility for safeguarding his medication, doling out one pill at a time, constantly fearful that he might locate the drugs and attempt suicide anyway.

Not taking responsibility does not mean that one must go to the opposite extreme: "Well, if you're going to kill yourself, then get it over with!" Although there are limits to how much one person can protect another, one can always offer life-affirming support and compassion. A person may seem intent on suicide while hoping for some intervention. It is important to sustain or stimulate that person's desire to live. Plans for self-destruction are likely to proceed apace with fantasies or plans for rescue. The person who is cast in the role of helper in such a drama can affirm the fact that there are choices other than suicide.

One way to help people in crisis is to help them discover what about themselves *can* matter, however small or insignificant it may seem. It is important that something be found that matters *to the person*. Ask the person to think of something he or she has found valuable about himself or herself in the past. Once it has been found, ask the person what the possibilities are of continuing that sense of value into the present. Asking the person what is useful, what he or she needs in order to feel valuable and worthwhile, may be a matter of survival.

Some people do not survive; others can, with assistance from caregivers and commitment from themselves. The sustaining motivation to survive cannot come from without; it has to be generated from within the person's own experience. In the short term, external support can help to ensure survival during the height of crisis. But one should be skeptical of the notion that anyone can sustain, over the long term, another person's will to live.

Suicidal thoughts and behaviors indicate a critical loss of a person's belief that he or she is someone who matters. The feeling that nothing matters, in the sense that one's life is in complete disarray, is not by itself the stimulus for suicide. More important to suicidal thoughts and behaviors is the person's belief that "*I* don't matter." As we have seen, those two streams of thought in combination—the sense that the external situation is unsatisfactory and that one does not matter enough to improve it—can lead to death by suicide. As has been well stated, "Suicide is a permanent solution to what is most likely a temporary problem."[94]

Further Readings

Fred Cutter. *Art and the Wish to Die.* Chicago: Nelson-Hall, 1983.

Kevin E. Early. *Religion and Suicide in the African-American Community.* Westport, Conn.: Greenwood, 1992.

Norman L. Farberow, ed. *Suicide in Different Cultures.* Baltimore: University Park Press, 1975.

Earl A. Grollman. *Suicide: Prevention, Intervention, Postvention,* 2d ed. Boston: Beacon Press, 1988.

Antoon A. Leenaars, ed. *Suicidology: Essays in Honor of Edwin Shneidman.* Northvale, N.J.: Jason Aronson, 1993.

Ronald Maris, ed. *Understanding and Preventing Suicide.* New York: Guilford Press, 1988.

Israel Orbach. *Children Who Don't Want to Live: Understanding and Treating the Suicidal Child.* San Francisco: Jossey-Bass, 1988.

Edwin S. Shneidman. "Some Controversies in Suicidology: Toward a Mentalistic Discipline." *Suicide and Life-Threatening Behavior* 23, no. 4 (Winter 1993): 292–298.

Judith Stillion, Eugene McDowell, and Jacque May. *Suicide Across the Life Span: Premature Exits.* New York: Hemisphere, 1989.

Calling attention to the threat posed by AIDS and other modern encounters with death, this drawing depicts victims embraced by Azrael, the angel of death.

CHAPTER *13*

Risks of Death in the Modern World

*T*he essayist E. B. White said, "To confront death, in any guise, is to identify with the victim and face what is unsettling and sobering."[1] Though we are often insulated from death in modern societies, we nevertheless encounter it in many guises. Mostly, we ignore or give only passing thought to these encounters with death. Seldom do we contemplate death in a way that shakes us emotionally or gives us pause. Yet our environment furnishes us with opportunities for encountering death at almost every turn. In Chapter 1 we saw how the mass media—newspapers, television, movies—as well as art, literature, and music all present images that influence our attitudes toward death. In subsequent chapters we examined other encounters with death, such as life-threatening illness and surviving the deaths of others close to us. Here we look at some of the encounters with death that relate in varying degrees to life in modern societies. Some, such as natural disasters, have been part of human experience since life began; others, such as the nuclear threat, represent a wholly new dimension of death's presence in our lives.

We risk subtle, and sometimes dramatic, encounters with death as we engage in our life's pursuits—on our jobs and in our recreational activities. Fatal accidents and environmental disasters are other experiences in which we face the tragedy of death. Violence and war threaten us not only as persons but also as a society, overshadowing and influencing our plans and activities. Is it surprising that this inventory of potential encounters with death contributes to stress, which becomes yet another potential threat to life?

In 1721, the novelist Daniel Defoe wrote *A Journal of the Plague Year,* a fictional account of the Great Plague of 1665, which had devastated London. Drawing on published accounts and his recollection of tales heard during childhood, he vividly depicted the horror of a plague-stricken city and the terror of its helpless citizens, confronted by a tragedy they could not comprehend. What prompted Defoe to write about a plague that had taken place almost two generations earlier? He knew that a plague again threatened to sweep across Europe, a plague that could cause death and destruction on the scale of the Great Plague of 1665. Defoe wrote to alert a largely indifferent populace to the threat so that precautions could be taken and the catastrophe averted.

Today we no longer fear the Black Death. Yet in a subtle though pervasive way, those of us now living are confronted by a multidimensioned "plague" that is no less threatening than the more easily distinguishable plague of Defoe's time. Writing about the problem of determining the modern threat to our well-being from various risks, Harvey Sapolsky observes: "Although it does not carry a warning label, our political system may be hazardous to our health. It hunts small risks ruthlessly while permitting much bigger ones to exist relatively unmolested."[2] Indifference to the modern forms of plague—excessive risk taking, avoidable accidents, violence, war, environmental pollution, AIDS, and other emerging diseases—only increases the likelihood of a disastrous encounter with death.

Risk Taking

The images communicated by the media and other forms of popular culture influence the kinds of risks we are willing to take in our lives. Risks may accompany the actions we take in pursuit of the "good life." Indeed, all life involves risk, though the degree of risk we are willing to assume is typically subject to our personal choices as to how we live our lives.

Think about your own life. What kinds of risk do you face in your employment, your leisure activities, your style of living in general? Are any of the risks potentially life threatening? Do you take "calculated" risks? Can you exercise choice about assuming these risks, or do some seem to be unavoidable? In some areas of our lives we can exercise considerable choice about the nature and degree of risk that affects us. For example, smoking, drinking, taking drugs, and driving habits typically involve risks that can be controlled. We can also exercise choice in our occupation and recreational activities.

The risks associated with various jobs are sometimes quite dramatic, involving dangers that most people, given a choice, would avoid. Such occupations come readily to mind—explosives expert, high-rise window washer, movie stuntperson, test pilot, as well as police officer and fire fighter, for example. The list could be continued almost indefinitely. We might add

I stared in a horrified trance as a figure appeared, frozen in the air for the briefest moment, its arms outstretched above its head as if in utterly hopeless supplication. Then it continued its relaxed, cart-wheeling descent, with only the thundering crashes attesting to its frightening impacts on the rock. It disappeared into a gully.

"Don't look!" I screamed to my wife, who was, of course, as helplessly trans-fixed as I was. And the sounds continued. After a time, the figure came into view at the base of the gully and continued down the pile of rubble below. My last view of it is frozen in time. The figure's arm was curled easily over its head, and its posture was one of relaxation, of napping. It drifted down that last boulder field like an autumn leaf down a rippling brook. Then it disappeared under the trees, and only the pebbles continued to clatter down the rock. Suddenly it was very, very still.

I looked down to Debby and had to articulate the obvious: "That was a man," I said quietly, numbly.

William G. Higgins, "Groundfall"

scientists and researchers working with hazardous materials, mine workers, electricians, heavy-equipment operators, and farm workers using toxic pesticides. As you add your own examples to this list, notice whether they involve the risk of sudden death (as from an explosion or a fall from a high-rise building) or of long-term exposure to hazardous materials or conditions. Some jobs involve risks that are identified only after many years of continual exposure to the harmful condition.

An occupation may increase the risk of death by increasing the worker's level of stress. No doubt all work involves stress; whether stress becomes a threat to the worker's health, however, depends on both the nature of the work and the worker's attitude. A U.S. government report, *Work in America,* states, "Satisfaction with work appears to be the best predictor of longevity—better than known medical or genetic factors—and various aspects of work account for much, if not most, of the factors associated with heart disease."[3]

The threat of death may also be encountered in our recreational activities and sports: mountain climbing, parachuting, scuba diving, motorcycle racing, and the like. Some people characterize such activities as thrill seeking, though this term suggests motives that some participants in these activities would not ascribe to themselves. Nevertheless, such activities involve an element of risk; the activity presents an opportunity to test limits and develop confidence in one's ability to accept risk and deal positively with fear. Mountain climbers, for instance, accept certain risks because climbing provides both physical conditioning and the aesthetic pleasure of reaching the heights and surveying the expanse of uncluttered nature.

Although mountain climbing involves obvious risks, two different climbers can relate to these risks in vastly different ways. One climber may display an attitude of abandon that could only be characterized as foolhardy or death defying. The other may devote many hours to obtaining instruction, preparing equipment, conditioning for the climb, and asking advice from more experienced climbers before deciding to set foot on a mountain. In short, the risks can be minimized. An activity may be attractive to some persons *because* of its inherent risks, whereas others accept the risks as inseparable from the other attractive features of the activity. When behavior involves doing dangerous things simply for the thrill of it, or as a way to "laugh in the face of death," such behavior may reflect an attempt to deny death or to deny one's fear of death.[4]

No one is immune to risks. At home, on the job, or at play, the risk of death confronts us in one way or another. After a classroom discussion about the risks involved in various activities, one student said, "It seems we're coming around to the point that everything we do involves risks. You could even stab yourself with your knitting needle!" Perhaps, but usually when we consider activities involving risk, we think of pursuits about which there is a direct acknowledgment of the risk. The possibility of falling backward from a rocking chair while knitting strikes most people as less risky than, say, driving a formula race car or embarking on an expedition to the Himalayas.

Sometimes the risks we face are not known. More often, though, we can exercise options that allow us to control or manage the element of risk. What automobile driver has not chosen at some time to drive just a bit faster in order to arrive at the destination sooner? Accident statistics, as well as common sense, tell us that exceeding the speed limit increases the risk. Yet one makes a trade-off; the added risk is exchanged for the expected benefit of arriving at the destination sooner.

A death resulting from a high-risk sport or similar activity may have a special impact on other individuals who engage in the same activity. In addition to the impact upon those who are involved most immediately (for example, people who had rented equipment or given instruction to the deceased), the death also affects the larger community of participants in the sport by challenging "the underlying assumption of the sport that careful, cautious practice insures safety."[5] To cope with this challenge, and with the death itself, rumors may circulate that the deceased failed to take necessary precautions or followed an unwise or ill-considered course of action. These rumors may represent an attempt to fit what has happened into a manageable scheme and to mitigate any feelings of guilt about having been unable to prevent the death. As a means of coping with such a death, this tendency to "blame the victim" may facilitate the resolution of grief and allow other participants to feel comfortable continuing the activity despite the risks.

Accidents

Often, accidents are viewed as happening by "chance" or because of "fate" or "bad luck." From that view, it follows that little if anything can be done to prevent accidents. But the definition of an accident as an event that occurs "by chance or from unknown causes" can be refined, as the dictionary

UPI/Bettmann Newsphotos

To keep from tumbling through space at 125 miles per hour, this mile-high skydiver spreads his arms and legs to control his freefall before opening his parachute. Although risks are ever present in our lives, we expose ourselves to many of them by personal choice.

reflects, to encompass the understanding that an accident may indeed be "unavoidable," or it may result from "carelessness, unawareness, or ignorance." Thus, accidents are typically events over which individuals do have varying degrees of control. For example, suppose a gun is brought into the household. The presence of the gun increases from zero the chance that there may be an accidental firing of the weapon. Of course, such an accident may never happen. But if a gun were *not* in the home, there would be *no* chance of an accidental firing.

In other words, the choices we make affect the probabilities of various kinds of accidents. It is an established fact that drivers who have been drinking tend to take greater risks than do sober drivers. It has also been determined that a driver's judgment and performance are inversely related to the amount of alcohol imbibed, whereas a driver's tendency to overrate his or her driving abilities is directly related to the amount imbibed. The effect of alcohol on driving is evident in the fact that about half of the drivers involved in accidents are under the influence of alcohol.

Are such accidents the result of mere chance or fate? If not, then steps can be taken to reduce the probability of such accidents. The notion that accidents are chance events lessens the probability that steps will be taken to prevent their occurrence. As individuals and as a society, we need to develop a better understanding of accident causes—one that considers such factors as carelessness, lack of awareness, and neglect.

Sometimes—often jocularly—we call certain people *accident prone* because they seem to become involved in accidents much more often than usual. Although there is not sufficient evidence to scientifically define a personality type that would be described as accident prone, certain known factors can affect the type of accident that may occur and the individual's probability of being involved in an accident. Such accident proneness is usually based on factors such as age and experience.

When accidents of all types are considered, adolescent and young adult males are at greatest risk. It is unclear whether the high accident rate for this age group and sex reflects this group's greater willingness to assume risks (to assert masculinity, perhaps?) or cultural attitudes that tend to encourage males more than females to engage in risky activities. Perhaps as we reach the point where as many women as men engage in activities once considered the exclusive province of men, the group at greatest risk may contain as many women as men.

So far we have emphasized intrinsic factors that influence accidents—that is, factors having to do with a person's own physical and mental qualities. Another set of factors—extrinsic factors, or conditions that exist within the environment—also influence the occurrence of accidents. Unsafe conditions present in the environment are sometimes called "accidents waiting to happen." Often such conditions are the result of negligence or of ignorance about the threat they pose to safety. For example, consider a swimming pool that is left unattended and easily accessible to young children; if a toddler happens by and falls into the pool and is drowned, the owner of the pool might be judged negligent.

Typically, unsafe conditions in the environment reflect the attitudes and value systems of the person or group responsible, or of society as a whole. For instance, a landlord who refuses to correct unsafe conditions on a tenant's premises apparently does not value the safety of others. Accidents caused by drunk driving occur because of choices made by both the drinking driver and society. Such neglect is also partly responsible for the numerous fire disasters that occur in the United States. Fire safety remains a serious national problem, though actions could be taken to improve the unsafe conditions that contribute to fire deaths. Despite the threats to health posed by unsafe conditions related to motor vehicles, guns, and so on, experts note that society has failed to take adequate steps to alleviate these major health problems.[6]

**WHEN YOU'RE INSTALLING YOUR
CB BASE STATION OR TV ANTENNA,
TAKE THIS ADVICE OR YOU COULD
BE IN FOR THE SHOCK OF YOUR LIFE!**

1.

When raising any antenna —
either CB or television —
make certain that the antenna
and its support cables or guy wires
cannot fall into or contact power lines.

2.

Never place your ladder next to
electric wires leading to your home.

3.

If you're installing a rotor,
be sure that it won't turn the antenna
around into nearby power lines.
Make sure the power lead is grounded.

4.

Support cables should be
well secured at both ends and
should be insulated according to
manufacturer's instructions.

PG and E

IF YOU GET KILLED
INSTALLING AN ANTENNA,
YOU'LL NEVER FORGIVE YOURSELF

SEE YOU ON THE OTHER SIDE

Figure *13-1* *Antenna Hazard Warning*
The threat of death may be used to warn consumers and employees of risks
to safety. Here, the threat of death is presented with a touch of humor,
being represented as a transition to an angelic state complete with stereotypical harp.

Examples like these could be multiplied many times over in various areas
of environmental health and safety. Indeed, it seems that unsafe conditions are
ubiquitous. It is naive to think that the risks we encounter can be completely
eliminated. Still, in many areas of our lives, risk can be minimized (see Figure
13-1). The lack of attention—perhaps one should say the lack of resolve—to
take the necessary steps toward correcting unsafe conditions prompts the
question: "How negligent must a society be before its 'accidental' deaths are
tantamount to homicide?"[7]

Disasters

Disaster can be defined as a life-threatening event that affects many
people within a relatively brief period of time, bringing sudden and great

misfortune. Disasters result from natural phenomena—floods, earthquakes, and other "acts of God"—as well as from human activities. Included in the latter category would be fires, airplane crashes, chemical spills, and nuclear contamination.

In the United States, the incidence of disasters has increased in recent years. One reason for this increase is that more than half the U.S. population now lives within fifty miles of the coastline, an area that, in the West, is vulnerable to fires, floods, earthquakes, and landslides, and, in the Southeast, is prey to storms, hurricanes, and tornadoes. The growth in population and the rise of industrialization have also brought increased exposure to disasters related to human activities—for example, fires, explosions, and chemical pollution.

These factors have increased the risk of disaster worldwide. Globally, deaths due to natural disasters alone constitute up to 4 percent of the total deaths each year.[8] It is estimated that 2.8 million people were killed by natural events between 1968 and 1988, with the worst disasters—an earthquake at Tangshan city in China and two coastal floods in Bangladesh—each killing more than a quarter of a million people.[9] Floods are the most common and among the most damaging of natural hazards; hundreds of millions of people around the world live on flood plains.

One of the world's worst industrial accidents occurred in 1984 when gaseous methyl isocyanate escaped from Union Carbide's pesticide plant in Bhopal, India, bringing death to 2500 people residing near the plant. The unprecedented magnitude of this accident was followed by what was reported to be the largest human-caused, mass disaster lawsuit ever, with claims totaling more than $100 billion in damages. The accidental contamination of livestock feed with the chemical PBB in Michigan and the emergency shutdown of the nuclear reactor at Three Mile Island are other examples of disasters related to environmental pollution.

In 1986, a nuclear power plant at Chernobyl in the Soviet Union suffered catastrophic failure, releasing radioactivity across a large area of eastern and northern Europe, an accident termed the worst in the history of nuclear power generation. Dangerous levels of radiation contaminated the area surrounding the plant, causing death and serious injury and damaging the food supply. The proliferation of potentially hazardous technologies calls for preventive efforts, to be sure, but also for effective systems of evacuation and disaster relief when such efforts prove inadequate. Although the number of people affected by disasters is increasing, this is an area of death awareness and study that has been mostly neglected. Robert Kastenbaum cites this neglect as an example of "our society's selective attention to death even when it does choose to pay any attention at all."[10]

Reducing the Impact of Disasters

Although communities can decrease the risk of injury and death by taking measures designed to lessen the impact of a potential disaster, the effects of a disaster are difficult to anticipate fully. In September 1985, a devastating earthquake hit Mexico City, without warning, killing almost 10,000 people. Previously, the city had enacted building codes that took into account the possibility of low-frequency earthquake waves associated with the ancient lake beds on which Mexico City is built. But these codes did *not* include a specification for the number of shaking cycles that buildings should be constructed to withstand, a factor that seismologists later determined contributed to the large number of fatalities.

People often allow themselves to risk disaster because of considerations that make the risk acceptable. Employment opportunities, for example, may prove the deciding factor. Also, people who live in areas where disaster is a likely event may rationalize the danger, if they give it any thought at all, as simply "playing the percentages."

Adequate warnings of an impending disaster can save lives. Yet necessary information may be withheld due to greed or political expediency, or simply uncertainty about the nature and extent of the threat, or out of concern about causing panic.

The tragedy that followed the eruption in 1902 of the Mt. Pelee volcano, on the island of Martinique, in the West Indies, is instructive of how information that could warn potential disaster victims is sometimes mismanaged, with disastrous consequences. The officials of the nearby community of St. Pierre were alerted to the likelihood that the volcano would erupt. But, concerned that the population would panic if notified and thus thwart their plans for an upcoming local election, the St. Pierre officials withheld any warning of the danger from the populace. As a result, virtually the entire population of the small community was incinerated. When news of an impending disaster is managed in such a way, it demonstrates what Robert Kastenbaum describes as the "enormously powerful threat [of] a tightly controlled information network."[11] The May 1980 eruption of Mount St. Helens provides an instructive comparison. Even though this eruption was larger, only 60 lives were lost compared with 30,000 casualties resulting from the eruption of Mount Pelee. This dramatic difference is attributable in part to adequate warnings of the hazard and timely establishment of a restricted zone of access.[12]

Even with an adequate warning system and a reliable, efficient information network, however, people do not always respond to such threats in a prudent fashion. Just as some people ignore the risks associated with smoking or drug abuse, individuals may feel they are immune to disaster. Predictions of potential disasters are often met with the response: "I've never been affected before. Why should I start worrying now?" The same attitude is exhibited when people who learn of a chemical spill or a fire nearby decide to travel to the disaster area for a closer look.

Coping with the Aftermath of Disaster

What can be done when disaster strikes? What kind of help is needed in its aftermath? Imagine the situation: People are injured, some are missing, others are dead. Homeless survivors are likely to be in a state of shock and uncertainty about the whereabouts of loved ones and about the future. Each type of disaster, of course, creates particular problems that need attention.

Meeting the immediate needs of survivors—providing food and shelter, caring for medical needs, and restoring vital community services—is essential. Yet even as attention is given to responding to these physical needs, the emotional needs of survivors should not be neglected (see Figure 13-2). Ministering to these needs might include forming a missing persons group to help alleviate the anxieties of survivors worried about the safety of relatives. Locating and caring for the dead is another important aspect of helping survivors cope with the trauma of disaster. The comment of one relief agency worker, "It

Unocal
425 First Street
San Francisco, California 94105-2681
Telephone (415) 362-7600

October 27, 1989

We sincerely hope that you and your family were not seriously affected by the recent earthquake in your area.

We would like to assist our credit card customers whose daily routine has been disrupted by this disaster, by offering additional time to pay their credit card account, if needed.

If we can assist you with special arrangements, just drop us a note in the enclosed postage paid envelope or call toll-free on 1-800-652-1520 and ask for D. Enomoto.

C. B. Evans
General Manager
Credit Card Operations

Figure *13-2* *Disaster Letter from Unocal*
Even a computerized corporate response to the disruption of normal living patterns can assist and comfort survivors as they cope with the devastation wrought by a natural disaster.

doesn't really make too much sense to dig up the dead and then go and bury them again," reveals an unfortunate ignorance of the human emotions that surround disposition of the dead. Perhaps what survivors of a disaster need most is compassion. Although efforts directed toward coping with disaster tend to be focused on the emergency period, the return to financial and emotional stability may take years. Unfortunately, the therapeutic community that comes together to assist in recovery from disaster is usually designed to function for only a brief time, and rapidly dissolves with the end of the emergency period.[13]

Those who come to the aid of the survivors of a disaster may also become "survivors" in the sense that their work of postvention (a term coined in the early 1970s by Edwin Shneidman to denote help given in the aftermath of a disaster) involves an intense encounter with human suffering and tragedy. Consider the experience of a Kansas City doctor who arrived at the scene of the Hyatt Regency Hotel disaster in 1981 to find among the debris bodies chopped in half, decapitated, and maimed. He watched as a critically injured man's leg, trapped under a fallen beam, was amputated with a chain saw. He worked sensitively and professionally as one of the first caregivers to force his way to where the victims were trapped. In the aftermath of the disaster, when things returned more or less to normal, he told officials that he felt the need to spend some time away from reminders of the disaster to cope with his own experience as a survivor. Often, those who provide care and support are themselves given little in the way of support for their own coping needs. The provision of effective care for the survivors of critical incidents or disasters requires a comprehensive approach that includes "predisaster preparedness, early intervention using psychological first aid, and postdisaster treatment" using a range of counseling and therapeutic resources.[14]

When a storm dumped twenty inches of rain in one night on a coastal community in California, residents awoke the next morning to the news that twenty-two people had been killed, more than a hundred families had lost their homes, and another 3000 homes had been severely damaged. Within a few days, an impromptu organization was set up to help survivors deal with the psychological trauma of their losses. Known as Project COPE (Counseling Ordinary People in Emergencies), it provided immediate counseling to disaster victims and coordinated the services of more than a hundred mental health professionals.[15] Counselors found that people who had lost loved ones or property were experiencing grief reactions heightened by the sudden, capricious nature of their losses. Some who had lost only material possessions felt guilty for mourning the loss of property when others had lost family members. Some felt guilty for surviving the disaster. Those made homeless by the storm felt isolated and alone. There were feelings of anger at bureaucratic delay and toward uncooperative insurance companies and government agencies. Many of the victims felt anxious, vulnerable, and depressed. In some cases, old problems reemerged related to personal or relationship issues.

COPE set up programs to respond to each of these problems. Survivors were reassured that their reactions were not unusual and helped to recognize that their grief was legitimate. Victim support groups brought together individuals who could understand and listen to one another's concerns. Counselors helped survivors sort out their priorities so they could begin solving problems created by the disaster. Skills were shared to help victims channel their anger constructively. Emergency crews and relief workers were not left out. It was recognized that individuals who come to the aid of victims (including those who counsel the victims) are also vulnerable to the emotional impact of a disaster. With its comprehensive response to the psychological needs of

James Finley, AP/Wide World Photos

Eight days after a terrorist car bombing killed more than 160 people, the search for victims continues at the Alfred P. Murrah Federal Building in downtown Oklahoma City. The April 1995 bombing focused national attention on deadly violence, as Americans across the country engaged in ceremonies of mourning for victims and their families.

survivors, COPE was cited as a model of providing mental health care to disaster victims. We cannot eliminate the encounter with death that accompanies disaster, but we can take steps to reduce its impact, preserve life, and demonstrate compassion for survivors.

Violence

One of the most potent of our encounters with death, violence can affect our thoughts and actions even though we ourselves have not been victimized. Potentially, if not in actuality, all of us are its unsuspecting victims. Interpersonal violence is now officially recognized as a public health problem, as evidenced by the establishment, at the Centers for Disease Control, of a Violence Epidemiology Branch, an office charged with studying assaultive

When death is unreal, violence also becomes unreal, and human life has no value in and of itself.

Vine Deloria, Jr.

behavior and homicide. In 1992, 22,540 murders occurred in the United States, and roughly half of the victims were under thirty years old.[16] Thirty percent of these murders were related to arguments over money, property, or "romantic" situations, while about 20 percent were related to the commission of a felony. In about two-thirds of all murders, guns were used as the murder weapon.[17] In some urban areas, emergency room physicians report being "besieged with patients whose injuries are identical to wounds incurred by soldiers in Vietnam."[18] These wounds result from semiautomatic "assault weapons" that fire dozens of bullets per minute at several times the velocity of an ordinary pistol: "Organs that would have been merely grazed or even cleanly pierced by a handgun bullet are exploded by assault weapon fire, requiring massive transfusions of blood."

A report by the American Medical Association concludes that firearms injuries and deaths constitute a critical public health issue.[19] "One of the most troubling aspects of handgun violence," according to the AMA report, "is the fact that children very often are the victims of fatal gunshot wounds, self-inflicted either intentionally or accidentally, or received as innocent bystanders in scenes of domestic or street violence." Rap musician Ice-T is among those who have drawn attention to the troubled condition of his hometown, South Central Los Angeles. Gang warfare, he says, is comparable to other wars: The members of gangs are like "veterans from war," and "thousands of people have died on each side of this bloody battlefield."[20] In 1995, the results of the federal government's first nationwide survey of schoolyard violence were released, revealing that more than one in ten of the nation's high school students said they had carried a weapon on school property.[21]

The most threatening of violent acts are those that occur without apparent cause, when the victim is selected seemingly at random, thus heightening anxiety at the possibility that violence could unexpectedly confront anyone. Think about the bystander killed during the commission of a robbery or the victim of what seems a senseless and brutal attack by a mass murderer. A few years ago, in California, a number of murders were committed by someone whom the police dubbed the Trailside Killer, because the killings occurred along several popular woodland trails. A woman who usually jogged every morning along one of these trails expressed feelings of being personally threatened because these violent acts had taken place "so close to home." In an area where she had previously felt safe and secure, she now felt fearful. Although she had no direct experience of the killings, she was nevertheless victimized by the violence because it occurred in her own familiar environment. Rape and other violent crimes against women have prompted some to examine the role of "femicide" as a motivating factor in a "continuum of terror" that all too often results in death.[22]

One woman described a potential encounter with death that began innocently enough when she answered a knock on her door. Recognizing a former schoolmate whom she hadn't seen in a long time, she invited him in and they began to chat. She began to feel somewhat uneasy, though she could not say why. About two months later, she heard on the news that her visitor had been arrested and was subsequently convicted for the brutal murders of several young women. These murders had been committed around the time of his unexpected visit. Recalling the experience, this woman commented, "I sometimes wonder how close we may be to death at times and just not realize it. It seems we really never know."

The possibility of encountering violence seems to be increased by the anonymity and isolation characteristic of much of modern life. Feelings of connectedness to others can generate a sense of safety and security. In small towns and close-knit neighborhoods there is often a community concern that tends to make random violence less likely. The modern landscape, however, seems to provide fewer of such societal mechanisms. Living life in comparative isolation from our neighbors, many of us experience little comfort from the thought that violence might be averted by warnings or that help is available when a threat becomes real.

Some people believe that violence is endemic in American society. The fact that there were often few legal restraints during the great westward expansion gave rise to attitudes that promoted arbitrary justice and encouraged people to do whatever survival seemed to require, be it inside or outside the law. The treatment of Native American people, as well as the history of slavery and prejudice against African Americans, is replete with acts of violence. Combining such historical examples with current statistical analyses of violence leads some to the conclusion that American society has in many ways fostered the notion that violence can solve one's problems.

It takes little investigation, however, to recognize that the use of violence in pursuit of personal or political ends is a phenomenon found worldwide. State-sponsored terrorism, for example, is a historical as well as modern phenomenon that includes not only the mass deaths brought about by Hitler and Stalin, but also the death-dealing actions of innumerable small-group terrorist organizations in many places around the globe. "Terrorists," as Walter Laqueur says, "seek to cause political, social, and economic disruption, and for this purpose frequently engage in planned or indiscriminate murder."[23] Terrorism seems an affront to civilization, an action that occurs outside the boundaries of the social sanctions that we have erected to regulate conduct between individuals and between groups. In this respect, terrorist acts resulting in death are comparable to other acts of homicide that take place between strangers.

This warning sign, prominently displayed at the entrance to a convenience store in Florida, reflects the age-old tactic of deterring potential violence by making a preemptive threat. Although the law-and-order policy exemplified by this warning may be welcomed by individuals who have been victimized by violent acts, such threatening gestures also promote the message that violence is a means of solving problems.

Assessing the Homicidal Act

Community standards of morality and justice play a major role in determining how the act of killing is assessed by a society and by its legal-political-judicial system. As Figure 13-3 illustrates, *homicide*—the killing of one human being by another—is separated into two main categories: criminal and noncriminal. These main categories encompass additional distinctions. For example, an act of homicide is considered excusable or justifiable when a person who kills another is found to have acted within certain legal rights, such as that of self-defense, or when the killing is judged an accident involving no gross negligence.

Thus, although a murder is necessarily a homicide, a homicide is not always a murder. The law has traditionally recognized two main distinctions within the category of *criminal* homicide: murder and manslaughter. Murder is associated with acts carried out with deliberate intention ("malice aforethought"), and the category of first-degree murder is used to designate killings that are carefully planned or that take place in conjunction with other serious crimes, such as rape. Manslaughter, however, is defined as wrongful, unplanned killing, done without malice. An example of *voluntary* manslaughter

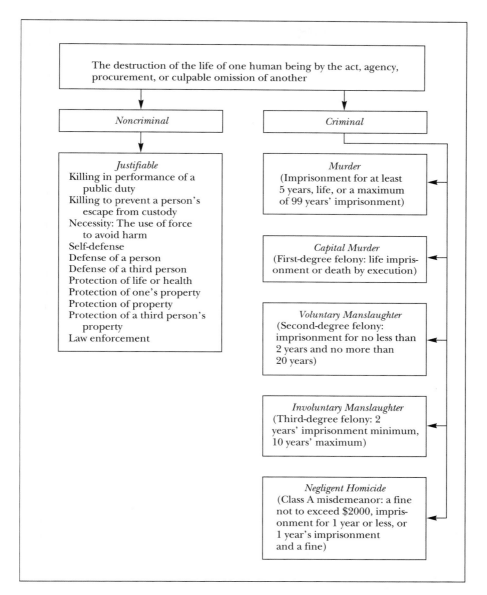

The destruction of the life of one human being by the act, agency, procurement, or culpable omission of another

Noncriminal

Criminal

Justifiable
Killing in performance of a
   public duty
Killing to prevent a person's
   escape from custody
Necessity: The use of force
   to avoid harm
Self-defense
Defense of a person
Defense of a third person
Protection of life or health
Protection of one's property
Protection of property
Protection of a third person's
   property
Law enforcement

Murder
(Imprisonment for at least
5 years, life, or a maximum
of 99 years' imprisonment)

Capital Murder
(First-degree felony: life imprisonment or death by execution)

Voluntary Manslaughter
(Second-degree felony:
imprisonment for no less than
2 years and no more than
20 years)

Involuntary Manslaughter
(Third-degree felony: 2
years' imprisonment minimum,
10 years' maximum)

Negligent Homicide
(Class A misdemeanor: a fine
not to exceed $2000, impris-
onment for 1 year or less, or
1 year's imprisonment
and a fine)

Figure *13-3*   *Schematic View of Texas Homicide Statutes*
Source: Vernon's Texas Codes Annotated: Penal Code, 1974. From Henry
Lundsgaard, *Murder in Space City: A Cultural Analysis of Houston Homicide Pat-*
terns (New York: Oxford University Press, 1977), p. 213.

The deepest grave on earth can never contain the violent death of a single decent soul.

John Nichols, *American Blood*

is that of a person, who after being provoked, kills another person in a fight. Such a person is said to have acted in the heat of passion, without considering the consequences. When homicide results from criminal carelessness but is unintentional, it is termed an act of *involuntary* manslaughter, as in the case of a fatal automobile accident caused by reckless driving or a death caused by gross negligence.

The circumstances surrounding a particular killing, the relationship between the killer and the victim, and the killer's motivation and intention are all considered in determining how an act of homicide is assessed within the American judicial system. In a study by Henry Lundsgaarde of more than 300 killings that occurred in a major American city, it was found that more than half of the suspects were released before reaching trial.[24] To understand why some homicide cases are not brought to trial, it is necessary to look at how the circumstances of a homicidal act influence its investigation and how the judicial processes determine whether an accused killer is brought to trial.

The medical-legal investigation of an act of homicide generally includes three components: (1) an autopsy to determine the official cause of death; (2) a police investigation to ascertain the facts and gather evidence pertinent to the killing; and (3) various judicial and quasi-judicial procedures, carried out by the district attorney's office and the court system, to determine whether there is sufficient cause to bring a case to trial.

Fundamental to this investigation is the acknowledgment that homicide is an interpersonal act. That is, it involves a relationship between the killer and the victim: They may have had close domestic ties, being members of the same family or otherwise related; they may have been friends or associates; or they may have been strangers. In the study conducted by Lundsgaarde, it was found that "the closer, or more intimate, the relationship is between a killer and his victim, the less likely it is that the killer will be severely punished for his act." In other words, killing a stranger was more likely to result in a stiff penalty than was killing a friend or family member.

The response of the criminal justice system to acts of homicide reflects cultural attitudes about killing and what constitutes appropriate punishment. Lundsgaarde says, "What appears so shocking, or understandable, as the case may be, about many killings depends upon our personal understandings of and assumptions about the rules that 'should' and 'ought' to govern a particular kind of relationship."

Basing its standards on cultural attitudes, the criminal justice system in a particular community sets about its task of determining whether an act of

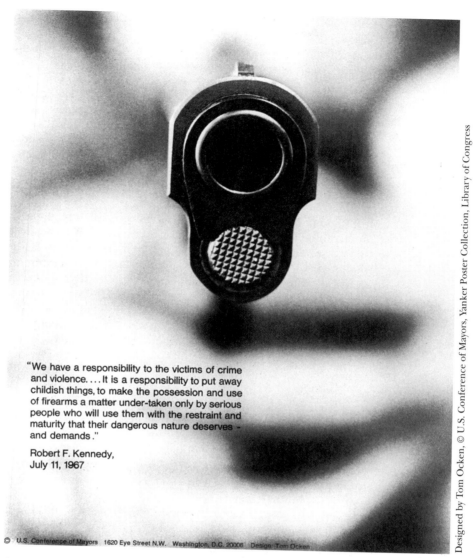

"We have a responsibility to the victims of crime and violence.... It is a responsibility to put away childish things, to make the possession and use of firearms a matter under-taken only by serious people who will use them with the restraint and maturity that their dangerous nature deserves - and demands."

Robert F. Kennedy,
July 11, 1967

© U.S. Conference of Mayors 1620 Eye Street N.W. Washington, D.C. 20006 Design: Tom Ocken

Looking down the barrel of a handgun, the viewer is pointedly confronted by the possibility of death in this poster designed to increase public awareness of the pervasive threat posed by the widespread possession of firearms.

homicide is lawful or unlawful. If lawful, the killer is released and the case is closed. If unlawful, a further determination is made as to whether the killing in question was an act of murder, manslaughter, or negligent homicide—and there are various degrees of criminal intent within each of these categories as well. In making these determinations, the criminal justice system, including the police investigation, takes into account the intention, motivation, and circumstances surrounding the homicide.

What are the cultural assumptions by which an act of homicide is judged? Lundsgaarde's research showed that the legal outcome for a person who kills his wife's lover is quite different from the outcome for a person who combines killing with theft, robbery, or similar criminal or antisocial acts. Society is reluctant to become involved in matters that fall within the domain of the family, even when they involve violence. A close relationship is believed to involve its own set of mutual responsibilities and obligations—its own "code of justice," if you will—that provides social sanctions for acts that occur within the relationship. In contrast, says Lundsgaarde, "The killer who chooses a stranger as his victim overtly threatens the preservation of the social order."

To put it another way, an individual who kills a stranger is not likely to be constrained by personal concern for the victim. Thus, society devotes its attention to acts of homicide that threaten the preservation of law and order within the larger society. Lundsgaarde says: "Intimates form symmetrical social relationships that insulate them within a series of obligations subject to enforcement by social and psychological sanctions. The robber, rapist, killer, or even the self-styled terrorist, is not restrained in his behavior by anything other than criminal sanctions." Killings that occur within the family unit or between persons who know one another tend to be viewed as less of a threat to society at large.

Capital Punishment

Some people believe that violence is "contagious" in modern American society. This reasoning can be developed along several lines: First, it may be that a violent society creates an environment in which psychotic individuals are encouraged to act out their antisocial behaviors in more harmful ways than they might if alternative ways of releasing such potentially violent tendencies were available. Second, each violent incident may spawn others, thus spreading the contagion of violence. Third, some believe that if an act of violence is not properly resolved, it will be repeated. With regard to this last point, a "proper resolution," according to Fredrick Wertham, is "for society to make clear what it wants. Society must say, *No, this we will not tolerate*," and this must be affirmed and upheld by a judicial process that emphasizes accountability for one's acts.[25]

Is capital punishment, then, the strong statement that is needed? In theory at least, capital punishment, which has been termed "planned, timed dying," is supposed to serve a twofold purpose: (1) punish the offender, and (2) deter potential offenders. Although the death penalty has been applied to a wide variety of offenses since ancient times, many political philosophers and social reformers have argued that it is needlessly cruel and overrated as a deterrent to murder. According to Glenn Vernon,

Investigations into the ineffectiveness of the death penalty as a deterrent to murder revealed that some murderers were so busy with other things during the events preceding the murder that they simply did not think of the death penalty, and that others were interacting with their victims in such an extremely emotional manner that the consequences of their murderous acts were not even taken into account.[26]

By the mid-nineteenth century, reforms of the death penalty began to occur in various countries. Today, it is virtually abolished in Western Europe and most of Latin America. In the United States, most capital punishment statutes require that a sentence of death be imposed only after evidence is submitted to establish that "aggravating" or "mitigating" factors were present in the crime. If "aggravating" factors are found and the sentence is death, then the case is reviewed by an appellate court. Apart from certain crimes on which the Supreme Court has not ruled (the most notable being treason), the only capital crime in the United States today is murder.[27] During 1992, 31 people were executed in the United States, all for murder, and, at year's end, nearly 2600 people were under sentence of death.[28] Hanging, electrocution, the gas chamber, and lethal injection have all been used for executing criminals at various times and places in the United States.

Is it inconsistent for society to try to eradicate or prevent murder by itself engaging in killing? It may be that the effect of capital punishment on violence is to increase its frequency, because it reinforces the notion that killing can solve problems. Citing evidence from psychology and behavioral therapy, which emphasizes the beneficial effects of *positive reinforcement,* Kastenbaum and Aisenberg say "there is little evidence to suggest that imposing massive punishment on one individual will 'improve' the behavior of others"; on the contrary, it may serve as positive reinforcement of hostile fantasies and murderous tendencies. The greatest risk for the potential murderer, they contend, is not the risk of execution, "but the risk of being killed by the police, the intended victim, or some bystander."[29]

If capital punishment is not an effective deterrent to murder, then what alternatives are available to society? Comparing our present system with early Anglo-Saxon and English law and with many non-Western legal systems as well, "Modern criminal law has completely transformed the ancient view of homicide as a wrong against a victim and his family to its modern version that views homicide as an offense against the state."[30] In short, the modern tendency is to view crime as a social problem.

The separation of civil and criminal law—more specifically, the separation of personal obligation and criminal liability—essentially eliminates the killer's liability to the *victim as person.* Instead, the liability is viewed as violence against the public at large. Restoring an element of civil liability for violent acts—for example, by some form of victim compensation program—might more effectively deter homicidal behavior and violent crimes than do present arrangements.

Mark Boster, AP/Wide World Photos

These young girls pay a final visit to a slain classmate, who died at age twelve be-
cause of a senseless act of violence. For individuals bereaved as a result of violent
deaths, feelings of grief may be mixed with feelings of dread and fear, a recognition
that death can come at any time and to anyone.

Steps Toward Reducing Violence

Society seems uncertain about how to stem the tide of violence. The judicial system often appears to function arbitrarily. Ambivalence toward the notion that violence between individuals is an acceptable means of solving
problems or achieving goals makes recourse to violence easier to tolerate. The
victim, too, in many cases, may play a crucial role in his or her own demise.
Violence results at least partly from social patterns as well as social problems.
These patterns and problems often reveal the presence of "dysfunctional strategies," factors that increase the likelihood of violence rather than prevent it.

The term *psychic maneuvers* has been used to describe the factors that have
been determined to facilitate murder and other homicidal acts. These factors
are summarized in Table 13-1. You may find it interesting to review this list
three times. First, think about how each of these psychic maneuvers might
function in your own life. Note that they do violence to ourselves and others
even when they function far more subtly than the overt act of homicide.
Second, note how these psychic maneuvers function within society, how they
contribute to antagonisms between individuals and between groups. The third

TABLE *13-1* *Factors Favoring Violence*

Anything that physically or psychologically separates the potential killer from the victim. For example, the use of a gun leads to a concentration on the means (pulling the trigger) rather than the end result (the death of a person). Psychological separation occurs when the victim is perceived as fundamentally different from oneself.

Anything that permits the killer to define murder as something else, such as "making an example of the victim," "making the world safe for democracy," "implementing the final solution," or "exterminating the terrorists."

Anything that fosters perceiving people as objects or as less than human. This happens when victims become "cases," "subjects," or "numbers," as well as when the killing occurs from a distance as with high-altitude bombing or submarine warfare.

Anything that permits one to escape responsibility by blaming someone else: "I was just carrying out orders."

Anything that encourages seeing oneself as debased or worthless: "If I'm treated like a rat, I might as well act like one. What have I got to lose?"

Anything that reduces self-control or that is believed to have this effect: alcohol, mind-altering drugs, hypnotism, mass frenzy, and the like.

Anything that forces a hasty decision or that does not permit time for "cooling off." That is, a situation may force one to decide to shoot or not to shoot with no opportunity for deliberation.

Anything that encourages a person to feel above or outside the law: The notion that rank, prestige, wealth, or the like makes it possible for one to "get away with murder."

Source: Adapted from Robert Kastenbaum and Ruth Aisenberg, *The Psychology of Death: Concise Edition* (New York: Springer, 1976), pp. 291–294.

time, consider how each of these psychic maneuvers represents a dysfunctional strategy that is typically found in the conflicts and wars between nations.

Victims sometimes play a role in encouraging violent acts against themselves. Homicide investigators have found that victims are not always as innocent as might initially be assumed. Consider the example of a husband who has been repeatedly threatened by his angry wife wielding a loaded revolver. His response to this threat is, "Go ahead, you might just as well kill me." What can be said about his role as a victim in such circumstances? Or consider another such incident: A daughter, overhearing her parents arguing, tries to intercede, but is told by her mother, "Never mind, honey, let him kill me." After the daughter leaves the house to seek assistance, her father obtains a revolver from another room and shoots and kills the girl's mother.

Investigators note that, during domestic strife, wives have made statements like, "What are you going to do, big man, kill me?" coupled with dares like, "You haven't got the guts." Kastenbaum and Aisenberg remark that such statements combine "elements of seduction and lethality." They add that, in some instances, there are indications that the victim not only seemed to be "asking for it," but was the one actually responsible for escalating the conflict to the level of physical violence.[31]

While recognizing that victims do sometimes help to bring violence on themselves, we should also be cautious about placing a stigma of blame on

T A B L E 13-2   *Guidelines for Lessening the Potential for Violence*

1. Avoid the use of prejudicial, dehumanizing, or derogatory labels, whether applied to oneself or to others.
2. Avoid or eliminate conditions that underlie dehumanizing perceptions of oneself or others.
3. Promote communication and contact between potential adversaries, emphasizing similarities and common goals rather than differences.
4. Refrain from using physical punishment as the primary means of discipline.
5. Champion the good guys.
6. Teach children that violence is not fun, cute, or smart. Emphasize that they are responsible for their behavior.
7. Identify and foster the human resources that can provide alternatives to violence. For example, promote sharing among children, and encourage them to think before engaging in impulsive and possibly hostile actions against others.
8. Reduce the attractiveness of violence in the mass media.

Source: Adapted from Robert Kastenbaum and Ruth Aisenberg, *The Psychology of Death: Concise Edition* (New York: Springer, 1976), pp. 296–297.

victims indiscriminately. Lula Redmond underscores the fact that labeling victims as bad, careless, seductive, "with the wrong crowd," or as somehow "asking for it" denies the reality that everyone is vulnerable to victimization.[32] Blaming the victim may be a convenient, albeit erroneous, way to overcome one's own sense of vulnerability and thereby regain a sense of personal security. If suitable "explanations" can be found to account for the victim's demise, they might provide convincing evidence that a similar encounter *could never* happen in one's own life. Far more effective than blaming the victim is to understand the factors that favor violence and take steps to reduce their presence in our own lives and throughout society as a whole.

In seeking ways to reduce the level of violence in society, it is useful to consider the factors that tend to *prevent* violent behaviors (see Table 13-2). Even if some individuals apparently have greater potential for violence or aggressive behavior, the manner in which that potential is expressed depends at least partly, and perhaps significantly, on environmental influences.

War

Within the context of ordinary human interaction, our moral as well as legal codes stand in strict opposition to killing. In war, killing is not only acceptable and necessary, but possibly heroic. War abrogates the conventional sanctions against killing by substituting a different set of conventions and rules about moral conduct. The expectation that one will kill and, if necessary, die for one's country is a concomitant of war. As Arnold Toynbee says, "The fundamental postulate of war is that, in war, killing is not murder."[33]

In Dalton Trumbo's classic antiwar novel, *Johnny Got His Gun,* we find a veteran "without arms legs ears eyes nose mouth" who devises a means of communicating with the outside world by "tapping out" messages on his pillow with his head.[34] He asks to be taken outside, where he can become an "educational exhibit" to teach people "all there was to know about war." He thinks to himself, "That would be a great thing to concentrate war in one stump of a body and to show it to people so they could see the difference between a war that's in newspaper headlines and liberty loan drives and a war that is fought out lonesomely in the mud somewhere, a war between a man and a high explosive shell."

The present century has seen not only two major world wars, followed by the unprecedented buildup of armaments that characterized the "cold war," but also innumerable regional conflicts in many areas of the world. Historians believe that 7.5 million Russian troops may have perished during World War II. In recent decades, 58,000 Americans died in Vietnam, while over 400,000 North Vietnamese and Viet Cong died in that conflict. During the Persian Gulf War, while American casualties were few, estimates place the number of Iraqi troops killed at from 40,000 to 100,000.

Genocide, defined as the effort to destroy an entire nation or human group, has also been practiced with dire results during this century.[35] During World War I, the Turkish effort to eradicate Armenians resulted in an estimated 800,000 people killed. Between 1941 and 1945, Nazi Germany exterminated 6 million Jews in the Holocaust and killed another 5 million people who were deemed to be political opponents, mentally ill, retarded, or somehow "genetically inferior." With the coming to power of the Khmer Rouge in Cambodia during the mid-1970s, about 2 million Cambodians died from execution and starvation, an example of "autogenicide," a group killing its own people. Also during the 1970s, the infamous "disappearances" carried out by the military in Argentina resulted in the deaths of as many as 30,000 people. In the aftermath of the Persian Gulf War, early reports indicated that the Iraqi regime led by Saddam Hussein may have killed tens of thousands of the indigenous Kurds in northern Iraq, while causing about 2 million to flee their homes.

Furthermore, chivalrous notions of combat, with mounted men-at-arms meeting gallantly to do battle on an uninhabited hill or plain, have been replaced in modern times by the reality of mass technological warfare. According to figures circulated by the International Red Cross (IRC), nine out of ten casualties in modern warfare are civilians—men, women, and children who simply "got in the way of somebody's war." In the so-called "postwar" period since 1945, says the IRC, at least 20 million people have died in over one hundred conflicts, and another 60 million have been wounded, imprisoned, separated from their families, and forced to flee their homes or their countries.[36] This human misery goes on even as you read these words.

Technological Alienation and Psychic Numbing

When we recall the epic battles of Achilles and Agamemnon, or of the legendary King Arthur and the Knights of the Round Table, or of the samurai

At Buchenwald, near Weimar, Germany, a few of the dead are piled in a yard await-
ing burial following invasion by the Allies. Starvation and disease due to unsanitary
living conditions, as well as the incessant torture of prisoners, caused an average of two
hundred deaths each day at this infamous Nazi concentration camp.

in medieval Japan, we find a sense of warfare as heroic. The enemy was seen as a worthy opponent with whom one was engaged in a "metaphysic of struggle" or a "ritual of purification" that encouraged progress or evolution toward a higher form of life.[37] If this sense of chivalry is now largely absent from warfare, leaving "only the abstract virtue of obedience to duty," it is due in significant measure to technological advances in weaponry. Instead of individual initiative and courage, modern warfare emphasizes bureaucratic cooperation and calculation.

"Technological alienation" has been termed the "most characteristic feature of the twentieth-century war machine."[38] Not until World War I did warfare begin to involve civilians on a large scale. During the Spanish Civil War,

To despise another human being, to wound another human being, to open another human being's body in the name of proving a belief, requires denying those other human beings' essential humanity. Otherwise the wellsprings of compassion, of our profound and bodily identification with one another—all mothers, all fathers, all brothers and sisters and daughters and sons, all lovers and neighbors and friends— would flood the mechanism of alienation that cleaves us apart.

We distance those whom we fear, and we fear them more for their distance. We distance them psychologically by reducing them to epithets: Hun, kike, Jap, kulak, gook, nigger, fascist, liberal, communist, Sandinista, enemy of the people, queer. We distance them physically by refusing to acknowledge their common humanity or to attend their suffering. Only then can we bear to injure or destroy them.

Technology amplifies this effect. Destruction at a distance with projectiles and bombs short-circuits the identification with similarly embodied beings . . . that might otherwise stay our hand.

Richard Rhodes

the world was horrified by the German aerial bombing of the Basque town of Guernica on April 26, 1937, an action that indiscriminately slaughtered civilians of both sexes and of all ages. The distinction between combatants and noncombatants had become blurred, if not erased.

In tallying the dead of World War II, civilian victims outnumbered military casualties. Early warfare had limits: the bow and arrow, the bullet from the gun, the artillery shell. The conventional limits of warfare were radically altered with the advent of the atomic bomb, unleashed on Hiroshima on August 6, 1945. The degree of destruction made possible by modern warfare was exemplified during World War II by the mass deaths in Dresden, Hiroshima, and Nagasaki. Gil Elliot says:

> By the time we reach the atom bomb, the ease of access to target and the instant nature of macro-impact [large-scale destruction] mean that both the choice of city and the identity of the victim have become completely randomized, and human technology has reached a final platform of self-destructiveness. . . . At Hiroshima and Nagasaki, the "city of the dead" is finally transformed from a metaphor into a literal reality.

The characteristic human response to such carnage is one of *psychic numbing*. Exposed to such destruction and death, our self-protective psychological response is to become insensitive, unfeeling. Robert Lifton and Eric Olson observe that "jet pilots who cooly drop bombs on people they never see tend not to feel what goes on at the receiving end."[39] They add that "those of us who watch such bombing on TV undergo a different though not unrelated desensitization."

Confronted by the death-dealing potential of modern weaponry, it is worth remembering the story of Dalton Trumbo's veteran, who asked to be allowed to become a living exhibit of the ravaging, destructive effects of war. His request was denied, the story explains, because "he was a perfect picture of the future and they were afraid to let anyone see what the future was like."

Think for a moment about your responses when you hear or read about war. What kinds of images are evoked when you think about combat, the atomic bomb, the Nazi Holocaust, Hiroshima, Vietnam, or the Persian Gulf War? Reflect on your own personal experiences and the experiences of those close to you. What makes the encounter with death in times of war different from other encounters with death? War is sanctioned by society as a legitimate means of achieving some desired goal—defending the national interest or protecting the homeland. Nevertheless, as Glenn Vernon says, "Confrontation with wartime killing may be one of the most difficult experiences of those who have been taught to avoid killing."[40]

The Conversion of the Warrior

War activates a special set of conventions designed to make it psychologically possible for individuals to go against the grain of what they have learned about right and wrong—to put aside the ordinary rules of moral conduct. As long as the combatant "keeps more or less faithfully to the recognized rules," Toynbee says, "most of humankind have been willing to alter their moral sense in such a way as to regard the killer in war as 'being righteous.'"[41] One of the conventions of warfare, Toynbee points out, is to dress the part. The psychological effect of the soldier's uniform is that it "symbolizes the abrogation of the normal taboo on killing fellow human beings: it replaces this taboo by a duty to kill them." Sam Keen notes that "the job of turning civilians into soldiers involves a liberal use of propaganda and hate training."[42] The enemy must be dehumanized so that he can be killed without guilt. "The problem in military psychology," Keen says, "is how to convert the act of murder into patriotism." As Vernon puts it, "Human behavior is relative to the situation, and given the right situation man can be taught or can learn to kill: whereas given other situations quite different behavior patterns are followed."[43]

Joel Baruch, a Vietnam veteran, writing about his combat experiences, says, "Changes in personality and mood are rooted in the special climate of the combat zone. These mutations evolve in such a wily fashion that the person who undergoes them is not aware of the alterations himself."[44] This is the crux of the matter. The conventions of war are mind- and personality-altering. It is possible to debate the ethical issues involved in war, its demands on citizens, the meaning of patriotism, and so on, arguing whether or not killing in wartime is intrinsically different from what would be defined as murder under other circumstances. The result is the same; the logic, the intention differs.

Here is Baruch's account of his first encounter with death on the battlefield:

The third plane came in, skimming the treetops, engine screeching. Two napalm canisters spun down from the Skyhawk's bomb rack into the tree line, and the plane pulled into a barrel-rolling climb as the red-orange napalm bloomed like an enormous poppy.

"Beautiful! Beautiful!" I said excitedly. "They were right on 'em."

The napalm rolled and boiled up out of the trees, dirty smoke cresting the ball of flame. The enemy mortar fire stopped. Just then, three Viet Cong broke out of the tree line. They ran one behind another down a dike, making for the cover of another tree line nearby. "Get 'em! Get those people. Kill 'em!" I yelled at my machine-gunners, firing my carbine at the running, dark-uniformed figures two hundred yards away. The gunners opened up, walking their fire toward the VC. The bullets made a line of spurts in the rice paddy, then were splattering all around the first enemy soldier, who fell to his knees. Letting out a war whoop, I swung my carbine toward the second man just as a stream of machine-gun tracers slammed into him. I saw him crumple as the first Viet Cong, still on his knees, toppled stiffly over the dike, behind which the third man had taken cover. We could see only the top of his back as he crawled behind the dike. What happened next happened very quickly, but in memory I see it happening with an agonizing slowness. It is a ballet of death between a lone, naked man and a remorseless machine. We are ranging in on the enemy soldier, but cease firing when one of the Skyhawks comes in to strafe the tree line. The nose of the plane is pointing down at a slight angle and there is an orange twinkling as it fires its mini-gun, an aerial cannon that fires explosive 20-mm bullets so rapidly that it sounds like a buzz saw. The rounds, smashing into the tree line and the rice paddy at the incredible rate of one hundred per second, raise a translucent curtain of smoke and spraying water. Through this curtain, we see the Viet Cong behind the dike sitting up with his arms outstretched, in the pose of a man beseeching God. He seems to be pleading for mercy from the screaming mass of technology that is flying no more than one hundred feet above him. But the plane swoops down on him, fires its cannon once more, and blasts him to shreds. As the plane climbs away, I look at the dead men through my binoculars. All that remains of the third Viet Cong are a few scattered piles of bloody rags.

Philip Caputo, *A Rumor of War*

Stone dead, he was. Eyes wide open, staring at nothing. A thin veneer of blood curling at the corner of his lips. Two gaping holes in his chest. Right leg half gone. My first combat fatality. A lifeless body where only moments before a heart beat its customary seventy pumps in one orbit of the minute hand. It is one thing to hear about death; to watch it happen is quite another. I went over to the nearest tree and vomited my guts out.

By his next experience of combat death, however, he questioned whether he was becoming callous and unfeeling: "I was becoming impervious to the death of my fellow soldiers, and, in addition, I was negating the possibility of my own . . . demise.''

Another Vietnam veteran explains:

> Social context is much more important than most people realize. We pretty much live within the boundaries of one social context. If you lived in a different society, you would consider a different set of behaviors as normal. What's bewildering and frightening in the combat situation is how quickly "normal" can change.[45]

Each of us experiences differences in our behavior according to the social context. How we behave among family members is likely to be different from how we behave among strangers or business associates. Sometimes these differences reveal the presence of contradictory values. Usually, such contradictions remain subtle and rarely meet head on. The contradictory values that exist for the soldier in combat, however, require what the veteran just quoted calls

> . . . a much more total schizophrenia. When you're there you don't really remember what it's like to come back into the social context of a society where killing is abhorrent. And, when you come back home, you don't really remember the context of the combat situation, except perhaps in your nightmares.

When a society reflects on its participation in war, it often speaks in terms of patriotism, the heroism of fighting for one's country, the need to defend the things that are held dear. When we listen to the words of those who have lived through combat, however, we often hear a very different kind of value system at work. We hear about individuals fighting for their lives or fighting because they had no alternative. Heroic intentions and patriotic feelings may be the rationale for donning the uniform, but in combat the emphasis is likely to be on survival.[46]

This is an issue that most of us would prefer to avoid. We do not want to hear what combat is really like, the reality of being in a situation where ordinary standards of conduct are turned topsy turvy and killing another human being becomes necessary and accepted behavior. The bravado and heroics of war may fascinate us. The reality is more difficult to face.

As one writer describes it,

> Combat is filled with potential emotional trauma. There's the constant fear of death. The noise and sights and smells, the firing of weapons, watching other human beings die or disappear in a puff of smoke and explosion of fire. There's blood and body bits and screams of pain. People are maimed and killed and some of them may be close friends. It continues hour after hour after hour.[47]

War is dehumanizing and depersonalizing. Lifton and Olson liken Vietnam to Hiroshima in that both events reflected the progression of modern technological warfare, which results in "unseen victims suffering and dying without ever having met their opponents."[48] Despite the extensive reporting

Rites of Passage

... As a psychiatrist who has worked with Vietnam veterans, I know all too well the long-term effects of wartime traumas. Ten and fifteen years after the events, there remain nightmares, fears, depression and, most fundamentally, failures of loving in veterans of combat. The timelessness of the unconscious does not bend to political realities. National treaties mark the beginning, not the end, of the psychic work of mastery.

Primitive societies intuitively knew the value of cultural ceremonies that marked the end of hostilities. Rites of passage were provided for the soldiers and the society to make the transition from the regression of combat to the structure of integrated living. These rituals acknowledged and sanctioned the otherwise forbidden acts of war. They thanked the soldier for his protection, forgave him his crimes and welcomed him back to life.

Our failure to provide such a cleansing for our warriors and ourselves has left our culture struggling for closure. It has as well made the task of intrapsychic mastery so much more difficult for the individual soldier.

Harvey J. Schwartz, M.D.

of war, especially since the time of American involvement in Vietnam, the veteran's experience of it remains incomprehensible to most people.

Coping with the Aftermath of War

The significant losses experienced by veterans are not resolved simply by leaving the combat zone or being discharged from military service. In the aftermath of war, many veterans experience symptoms such as numbness, irritability, depression, difficulties in relationships, and guilt at having survived when others did not. Nightmares and flashbacks to traumatic scenes are also among the protracted reactions to the war experienced by many veterans. Such symptoms have been termed delayed stress syndrome or post-traumatic stress disorder (PTSD). The reactions could also be termed "delayed grief syndrome" or "post-traumatic grief disorder."[49] Known as "shell shock" during World War I and "battle fatigue" during World War II, post-traumatic stress disorder became prominent in the 1970s when many Vietnam veterans experienced postwar readjustment difficulties.

Based on his work counseling individuals suffering from PTSD, psychiatrist Jonathan Shay finds striking parallels between the grief and rage experienced by modern combat veterans and the description in Homer's *Iliad* of similar symptoms experienced by warriors who fought in the Trojan Wars 3,000 years ago.[50] "There have been technological changes," Shay says, "but there have been no changes to the human mind and heart and soul." The chilling atrocities committed by Achilles in a berserk rage following the battlefield death of his friend Patroklos are echoed in modern episodes of grief-driven combat violence like the My Lai massacre during the Vietnam War. One of the lessons to be learned from the *Iliad*, says Shay, is that soldiers should be allowed to grieve: "Snatching bodies off the battlefield in black bags and spiriting them back to stateside mortuaries without permitting comrades to mourn the fallen is profoundly damaging to survivors."

Although psychotherapy, support groups, and other such approaches to healing have been at the center of efforts to treat PTSD, some veterans find solace and renewed self-respect through innovative means of coming to terms with their experiences.[51] On Memorial Day, 1990, a group of Vietnam veterans began a 700-mile walk from Angel Fire, New Mexico, to the Pine Ridge Indian Reservation in South Dakota. At the end of their journey, the veterans (who called themselves "The Last Patrol") were welcomed by several hundred Oglala Sioux and invited to participate in the traditional ceremonies for returning warriors. After participating in the sweat-lodge ceremonies, honoring dances, and smoking the sacred pipe of the Oglala Sioux, one veteran enjoyed one of his few nights of restful sleep after years of nightmares and said, "This is a new life for many of us . . . . [This] was an opportunity to eliminate the things that have tortured us." Other veterans have participated in meditation retreats led by the Vietnamese monk Thich Nhat Hanh. The Buddhist walking meditation reminded some veterans of "walking point" in Vietnam, and traumatic memories surfaced and were discussed during group sessions. One veteran who participated said that the hours of silent meditation with the Vietnamese Buddhists "dissolved his mistrust of the 'enemy.'" Some veterans have visited Vietnam in journeys that conjoin personal pilgrimage and social outreach, especially to the Amerasian children left as outcasts in their own country as a result of the war.

In contrast to the war in Vietnam, the Persian Gulf War was brief, widely supported at home, and regarded as a victory. Yet, no matter what its outcome, combat can leave haunting memories. After the shooting stops and there's peace, the mind must still "sort out and file the almost incomprehensible facts of war."[52] During the Persian Gulf War, one helicopter door gunner told his friends to stop boasting about high Iraqi casualties after he saw dead Iraqi troops for the first time. "It's different when you see their faces, with blood coming out of their wounds," he said.

Places like the Vietnam Veterans' Memorial in Washington provide a point of encounter with this truth and with the healing that can begin as a result. Since its dedication in 1982, the Memorial has become a kind of "wailing wall" for the families and friends of the more than 58,000 whose names are engraved there, as well as for those who served and survived. Many of the visitors have left mementos, ranging from a pair of old cowboy boots first found at the base of the Memorial shortly after its dedication, to childhood teddy bears, baseball caps, newspaper clippings, diaries, and tear-stained letters. One of the first letters was placed by the mother of an Army sergeant whose death had occurred nearly fifteen years before her visit to the Memorial. In the letter, she described finding her son's name for the first time:

> We had been looking for about a half-hour when your father quietly said, "Honey, here it is." As I looked to where his hand was touching the black wall, I saw your name, William R. Stock.
>
> My heart seemed to stop. I felt as though I couldn't breathe. It was like a bad dream. I felt as though I was freezing. My teeth chattered. God, how it hurt.[53]

During the Vietnam war, neither the troops nor their loved ones received much in the way of support or gratitude from society. Efforts have been made since then to distinguish between a much-maligned and unpopular government policy, on the one hand, and the men and women who served in the armed forces, on the other. When troops returned from the Persian Gulf war, they were greeted with a vastly different reception than that given the veterans returning from Vietnam a generation earlier. Mike Marshall, who served two tours of duty in Vietnam, talked about his own experience as compared to the homecoming for his paratrooper son who served in the Persian Gulf:

> I think this reception will be something that he'll remember all his life. And it'll be something I'll always remember. If I had experienced something like this, I wouldn't have the sour taste in my mouth that I do today. All we had was people throwing oranges and tomatoes and stuff at us. I didn't have a town parade or anything. You just kind of drifted back into society. I never really did get a greeting or a handshake or anything like that. I think the American people just wanted to forget it.[54]

The sacrifices made by the families of men and women in the military have often gone unnoticed. In recalling her odyssey as the wife of a Marine Corps officer who served in Vietnam, Marian Novak says: "I watched my husband train for war; I waited thirteen months for him to return from it; and then I waited another fifteen years for him to truly come home."[55] We tend to estimate the cost of a war in terms of the men and women who fought or died in it. Yet, war creates a "phantom army" composed of the spouses, children, parents, and friends who serve invisibly at home.[56] In this sense, the euphemistic term "collateral damage" encompasses not only the civilian deaths that occur in the war zone, but also the emotional pain experienced by individuals and families whose lives are disrupted by the loss of loved ones serving in the armed forces.

Making War, Making Peace

The causes of war have been sought in many areas, including natural human aggression as well as in the role of special interest groups in society. Economics, religion, nationalism, and ideology are also commonly cited. According to Karl von Clausewitz, a nineteenth-century military writer whose *On War* is considered a classic study, war is the continuation of political policy

I grew up during the Depression; everything in the country had stopped; there was no work, the factories were cold and empty. People daydreamed about what this country was going to be like when it got going again—the kind of houses people would live in, the kind of cars they would drive, the kind of vacations they'd take, the kind of clothes they'd wear, and all that—and it was a dream for their descendants. I don't find anybody now who gives a damn about what kind of world their grand-children are going to inherit. . . .

All the ads tell you that your own life is short, enjoy it while you can: buy this right now, start drinking really good wines, just take a really swell vacation, drive a really fast car, do it right now. I think it's much more absorbing to plan a world for our grandchildren, but there are no ads that invite you to do that. In a way, the threat of the Bomb may be a boon to wine merchants, restaurateurs, manufacturers of fancy automobiles, salesmen of condos in Aspen. It's all going to blow up—that's part of the sales message.

Kurt Vonnegut, quoted in *Publishers Weekly*

by other means. Generally speaking, war is defined as a condition of hostile conflict between opposing forces, each of which believes its vital interests are at stake and thus seeks to impose control on the opposing side through the use of force.

Within a comprehensive definition of war, we can distinguish several categories. *Total war* is "war without constraints."[57] It aims to destroy the enemy's forces and involves not only the military combatants, but also the resources and the civilian population of the warring societies. All-out nuclear war is one possible example of total war. The U.S. Civil War and World War II are other examples of total war because of the widespread involvement of noncombatants and the destruction of resources. *Limited war* is concerned less with the destruction of the enemy than with achieving some political or strategic result. It does not significantly affect the daily lives of most of the civilian population. Limited war also refers to situations in which at least one of the principal combatants intentionally places restraints on the use of available weapons or personnel, or limits potential areas of hostilities. Notice that what one side considers "limited war" could be "total war" for the other side.

The third type of warfare is *internal war,* which includes revolutions, insurrections, rebellions, and civil war. Although internal war may be waged by conventional means, it is frequently associated with guerrilla warfare (efforts to harass and disrupt the established government by means of sabotage, assassination, or propaganda).

Why do nations resort to war as a means of solving problems? A number of motives may be related to its onset (see Table 13-3). Whatever the combination

T A B L E *13-3*   *Motives and Needs That Promote Aggression*

1. To gain power or wealth
2. To gain territory or physical dominance, or to get others to adopt one's ideals and values
3. To defend or elevate personal and societal self-concept, self-esteem, or sense of identity
4. To retaliate and do harm after being provoked
5. To achieve personal or national glory
6. To respond to a sense of injustice
7. To act in self-defense
8. To fulfill a sense of duty or responsibility
9. To encourage a sense of personal competence and gain personal power
10. To gain hope for control over events and renewed faith in the future
11. To restore or revitalize the comprehension of self and world following chaos, disorder, or other sudden profound changes
12. To gain a sense of positive social identity by adopting shared ideologies

Source: Adapted from Ervin Staub, *The Roots of Evil: The Origins of Genocide and Other Group Violence* (New York: Cambridge University Press, 1989), pp. 36–43, 249–250.

of needs and motives that characterizes a particular conflict, joining together with others against a common enemy often brings about a sense of connectedness, belongingness, and community within a warring group—qualities that represent yet another need that may be satisfied by going to war. Human beings, it seems, have an innate tendency to divide the world into "us" and "them." Sam Keen says:

> In the beginning we create the enemy. Before the weapon comes the image. We *think* others to death and then invent the battle-axe or the ballistic missiles with which to actually kill them. Propaganda precedes technology. . . . It seems unlikely that we will have any considerable success in controlling warfare unless we come to understand the logic of political paranoia, and the process of creating propaganda that justifies our hostility.[58]

Social systems use propaganda to promote support for national goals. The result can be a uniform definition of events and lack of critical analysis. The media, wittingly or unwittingly, tend to report in ways that support and maintain the social system. When sensationalistic reporting replaces objective appraisal of the facts, truth is one of the first victims. If we see the world and other human beings as hostile, then ambiguous actions may be perceived as threatening. When we act to defend ourselves, others' reactions confirm our initial assumption (see Table 13-4).

The psychological process of projecting onto the enemy qualities that we deny in ourselves does not mean that our images of the enemy are necessarily

TABLE *13-4*   *Faces of the Enemy*

- The enemy as stranger. "Us" versus "Them."
- The enemy as aggressor. "Good" versus "Evil."
- The faceless enemy. "Human beings" versus "Dehumanized barbarians."
- The enemy as enemy of God; war as applied theology. "Holy" versus "Unholy."
- The enemy as barbarian (threat to culture, heathen, pagan).
- The greedy enemy (appetite for empire).
- The enemy as criminal, as committer of atrocities, as torturer (anarchists, terrorists, outlaws).
- The enemy as torturer or sadist.
- The enemy as rapist, desecrator of women and children ("Woman as bait and trophy.")
- The enemy as beast, reptile, insect, germ. (Gives sanctions for extermination.)
- The enemy as death. ("The ultimate threat.")
- The enemy as worthy opponent. ("Heroic warfare or chivalry.") Examples: The epic battles of Achilles and Agamemnon, King Arthur and the Knights of the Round Table, the samurai in medieval Japan.

Source: Adapted from Sam Keen, *Faces of the Enemy: Reflections of the Hostile Imagination* (San Francisco: Harper and Row, 1986).

wrongly placed or that the enemy is innocent. Sometimes the images we hold of the enemy are actually quite realistic. Keen says,

> Short of utopia there are real enemies. It is a luxury of the naive and sheltered to think that right thinking, good intentions, and better communication techniques will turn all enemies into friends. . . . If freedom is the basis of all other human values, then there are times when men and women will have to choose between killing and surrendering their humanity.[59]

We must consider both the individual psyche and social institutions in determining the steps to be taken toward civilizing hostilities (see Table 13-5).

The truism that war and death are intimately linked relates not only to the battlefield loss of life but also, at a deeper level, to the human desire for immortality. Viewed symbolically, war allows us to ritually affirm our own deathlessness by killing the enemy who *is* Death. This idea is reflected in the promise inherent in some religions that warriors who fall in battle go directly to Valhalla or Paradise. "War as the bringer of death," says Keen, "wears the face of horror, but also of ecstasy."[60]

The awareness of death that accompanies combat experience can bring with it appreciation of the fragility of life and a capacity for wonder. A central message of the so-called death awareness movement over the past several decades is that integrating the fact of death into one's life brings a zest for living. A vital society provides opportunities for individuals to fulfill not only basic needs, but also their potential as human beings, including the striving for spirituality or transcendence. Ervin Staub says:

TABLE *13-5*   *Steps Toward Civilizing Hostilities*

1. Replace dehumanizing language with metaphors that dignify the enemy.
2. Become aware of individual and group processes that cause biased perceptions about others, and learn to test perceptions before acting.
3. Create and use strategies to resolve conflict peacefully.
4. Counteract the human tendency to create us/them distinctions by creating "cross-cutting" relations among groups within society and between nations.
5. Limit armaments to reduce the risk of war.
6. Establish mechanisms for dealing with crisis.
7. Exercise restraint about supplying arms or intervening in regional conflicts.
8. Bridge the knowledge gap between adversaries by encouraging exchange programs, tourism, and other forms of direct communication.
9. View war as an "optional" social institution and work toward eliminating the factors—social injustice, poverty, ignorance—that contribute to conflict.
10. Accept responsibility, for better or worse, for the conduct engaged in by one's community or nation.
11. Be aware of the tendency to glorify past wars.
12. Replace the ancient reverence for the warrior and for heroic sacrifice in war with a new ideal of the kindly, compassionate human.
13. Remember that the human species is young and that the past may not be an adequate mirror in which to find an accurate reflection of human possibilities.
14. Keep in mind that the real enemy is the war system itself, which includes both the political and social institutions through which we educate ourselves and our own psychological defense mechanisms.
15. Go beyond the mind set that convinces us *a priori* that war is inevitable and that any hope of a world without war is utopian.
16. Explore options other than war for bringing about the qualities of companionship, bravery, devotion to a worthy cause, and honor.
17. Find positive ways of fulfilling the human potential for transcendence.
18. Implement, as a first necessity, a new vision, a new sense of possibility.

Source: Adapted from Sam Keen, *Faces of the Enemy: Reflections of the Hostile Imagination* (San Francisco: Harper and Row, 1986), pp. 157–168; and Ervan Staub, *The Roots of Evil: The Origins of Genocide and Other Group Violence* (New York: Cambridge University Press, 1989), pp. 255–274.

A vision of the future, ideals that are rooted in the welfare of individual human beings rather than in abstract designs for improving "humanity," small and intermediate goals along the way, commitment and the courage to express ideas in words and actions—all are essential to fulfill an agenda for a world of nonaggression, cooperation, caring, and human connection.[61]

The Nuclear Threat

Since 1945, the growth of the nuclear weapons arsenal has brought about the possibility of an encounter with death of unprecedented proportions. With the notable exception of the atomic bombs dropped on Hiroshima and Nagasaki, this encounter has been more threat than reality. Still, the fact that nuclear weapons might be used, with little or no warning, has shaped our lives

"Disarmament Talks," © 1987 Ralph Steadman, Swann Collection, Library of Congress

in ways both subtle and dramatic. Some believe that the pervasive threat of nuclear war is having a significant effect on the socialization of children.[62] In most societies, war traditionally has served a social function in helping to define the masculine role of "warrior" or protector; now, this historical connection is threatened.[63] With the advent of total war in the early decades of this century and, especially, with nuclear weapons, women and children no longer enjoy the "sanctity of innocence" relative to war's devastating effects.

Our vision of what war would be like if fought with atomic weapons is reflected by its changing portrayal in movies. During the first decade after World War II, the bomb was typically portrayed as an instrument for keeping the peace. Beginning in 1959, however, with Stanley Kramer's *On the Beach,* and continuing to the present with films such as *Dr. Strangelove, Fail Safe, War Games,* and the prime-time television drama *The Day After,* viewers have seen atomic weapons portrayed as something to be feared.

The watershed moment for any discussion of nuclear war must be the bombing of Hiroshima on August 6, 1945.[64] The bomb fell near the center of the city, and its explosive force, heat, and radiation immediately engulfed all of Hiroshima:

> Within a millionth of a second of the atomic bomb explosion over Hiroshima, the temperature of the blast center was several million degrees centigrade. A millisecond later, a 300,000-degree Centigrade sphere formed, sending out a tremendous shock wave. The wave, losing energy as it expanded, was powerful enough to break windows 15 kilometers from the hypocenter.[65]

Besides the physical devastation caused by the bomb, Robert Lifton says, "The most striking psychological feature of this immediate experience was the sense of a sudden and absolute shift from normal existence to an overwhelming encounter with death."[66] A second atomic weapon was used to bomb Nagasaki on August 9, 1945. For the survivors of Hiroshima and Nagasaki, the awesome effects of the atomic bomb initiated "an emotional theme within the victim which remains with him indefinitely: the sense of a more-or-less permanent encounter with death."

The rationale behind the destruction of Hiroshima and Nagasaki with atomic bombs that killed more than 100,000 people and seriously wounded many others remains a source of controversy. While advocates of the bombing contend that it avoided an invasion of the Japanese islands that likely would have resulted in perhaps 1 million casualties and massive civilian damage, others argue that, at best, the bombing only hastened Japanese acceptance of an inevitable defeat. The bombing of Hiroshima and Nagasaki with atomic weapons is also viewed by some as the first act of the ensuing cold war, thereby instigating the tremendous arms buildup of the postwar period. Since the end of World War II, the (former) U.S.S.R., Britain, France, and the People's Republic of China have joined the United States as "nuclear" nations, and a number of other countries have likely acquired nuclear weapons capability, including India, Pakistan, Israel, Libya, Egypt, Syria, South Africa, Argentina, and Brazil.[67] Many fear that terrorists may soon come to possess such weapons. Present stockpiles of nuclear weapons and the possibility of further proliferation are a matter of very real concern to many people despite the apparent end of Cold War hostilities.

Modern weapons technology has progressed to the point where a missile can carry its strategic nuclear warhead a distance of 6000 miles in less than half an hour and hit within a few hundred feet of its target. The hydrogen bomb in today's arsenals is about a thousand times more powerful than the atomic bomb, which itself produces an explosion about a million times more powerful than comparably sized bombs using conventional explosives such as TNT. The impact of even a small or limited nuclear attack would be enormous. More than three decades ago, then-president Dwight Eisenhower called attention to the changed nature of modern warfare. "We are rapidly getting to the point," he said, "that no war can be won."

The potential destructiveness of modern weaponry and its costs—monetary and social—are mind boggling. It is estimated that existing nuclear weapons represent 18,000 megatons of explosive power, the equivalent of 3.5 tons of TNT for every person on the planet; and that, since the end of World War II, expenditures on the global arms race have totaled nearly twice the amount spent for health.[68] Lifton and Olson write:

> Nuclearism is a peculiar, twentieth-century disease of power. We would do well to specify it, trace its roots, and see its connection with other forms of religious and immortalizing expression. It yields a grandiose vision of man's power at a historical time when man's precarious sense of his own immortality makes him particularly vulnerable to such aberrations.[69]

Despite the winds of change that have cooled tensions between the world's superpowers, nuclear warfare remains a threat. Political and military conflicts in many areas of the world, combined with poor economic conditions in many countries, continue to make peace an elusive quarry. In the past few decades, few areas of the world have escaped the impact of war, and the threat to survival represented by nuclear weapons has amounted to a more or less constant encounter with death for five decades.

AIDS and Other Emerging Diseases

Although many people living in modern societies have become complacent about the threat of infectious diseases over the last half-century, the AIDS epidemic may be a harbinger of the emerging diseases that researchers now believe will increasingly threaten the health of human beings worldwide. This threat has been highlighted in a growing number of publications like Richard Preston's *The Hot Zone* and Laurie Garrett's *The Coming Plague*. If the history of AIDS (acquired immune deficiency syndrome) is taken as representative, the social and personal costs of newly emerging diseases will pose devastating consequences for both individuals and societies.

The first cases of AIDS, a disease that destroys the body's natural defenses against infection, were reported in 1981; by early 1982, researchers believed that AIDS was caused by an infectious agent. Discovery of HIV (human immunodeficiency virus) as the cause of AIDS was confirmed in January 1984 by Luc Montagnier at the Pasteur Institute in Paris and by Robert Gallo at the U.S. National Institutes of Health.[70] Late in 1985, the genetic sequence of the virus had been determined and a blood test devised to detect antibodies to HIV.

The presence of opportunistic infections is usually the most prominent and life-threatening manifestation of AIDS. Complications can include fever, diarrhea, severe weight loss, and swollen lymph nodes. People infected with the virus may not be aware of it until symptoms become evident, sometimes years later. Despite efforts by laboratories around the world, no cure or preventive vaccine for AIDS yet exists.

The early response to AIDS by public health agencies was criticized by some as unduly slow, allegedly a result of bias against the affected population, which, at the initial stage of the outbreak, appeared to be mostly homosexual and bisexual men. It soon became evident, however, that AIDS was also appearing among intravenous (IV) drug users, hemophiliacs, and recipients of blood transfusions, and among the sexual partners of those infected with the virus—AIDS was no respecter of people or life styles. Because information about AIDS was sparse or unavailable in the initial period, some health care workers expressed concerns about their own vulnerability to the virus, sometimes resulting in distancing from patients. In some instances, patients with AIDS were placed in rooms far from nurses' stations and told to stay in their rooms. As more was learned about the disease, however, the evidence strongly indicated that AIDS could be transmitted through only three primary routes:

Zoë Lorenz and her daughter Candice are among the many people affected by AIDS. Zoë saw her father die from AIDS, plagued not only by the disease but by the humiliation and shame so often associated with it. Now afflicted with the virus herself, Zoë says, "I have a beautiful four-year-old daughter who has beat the odds and remains HIV negative. So many people have the attitude that I should go off and die somewhere alone. They don't see the tragedy of this child losing her mommy. I don't need to be proud that I have AIDS, but I won't be ashamed that I do. I don't want to feel that I have to tell people I've got cancer or some other acceptable disease."

sexual intercourse (vaginal or anal) with an infected person, exposure to infected blood or blood products, and transmission from an infected mother to her child before or during birth. As hysteria gave way to knowledge, care improved, as did communication between patients and caregivers. The hospice model of caregiving—usually with home care as a major component—has been widely instituted, especially when there is an involved and close community available to sustain the level of care required for most AIDS patients.

The patterns of social response to the early stages of the AIDS outbreak were similar in many respect to the patterns associated with epidemics historically.[71] When confronted by a new disease whose method of transmission is unknown, people typically become anxious or fearful. As more is learned about the disease, panic recedes and more thoughtful measures are implemented. Nevertheless, AIDS and HIV infection remains a tremendous challenge to the health resources of many countries. The World Health Organization (WHO) predicts that 40 million people worldwide will be infected with HIV by the year 2000, and over 5 million will have AIDS.[72] At the personal level, AIDS has caused untold suffering. Many survivors—the friends, neighbors, business associates, and relatives of people who died from AIDS—have experienced multiple losses.

It now seems that AIDS may be the first in a series of diseases threatening societies that until recently seemed to be relatively safe from infectious disease. Rodrick and Deborah Wallace present a compelling argument about some of the factors that may promote the spread of both newly emerging diseases like AIDS and drug-resistant strains of more familiar diseases that were thought to be controlled.[73] They believe that the level of community disruption in many urban neighborhoods is intensifying pathological behaviors and conditions that lead to more rapid spread of infectious diseases, including HIV, drug-resistant strains of tuberculosis, and other contagious diseases that may become increasingly virulent.

Over the past few decades, political abandonment of areas like New York's South Bronx and Los Angeles' South Central has been followed by the loss of municipal services, resulting in a situation that has been characterized as "urban desertification" and "social thanatology."[74] Partly due to inadequate fire protection, burnouts in poor neighborhoods have increased homelessness and other conditions of physical devastation and social disintegration that researchers view as "unprecedented in a modern industrialized state short of the aftermath of total war."[75] In such circumstances, the spread of infectious diseases—both those recently thought to be virtually eradicated, such as tuberculosis, and those for which there is as yet no cure, such as AIDS—becomes a very real and worrisome threat. Ultimately, an entire society can be put at risk as diseases spread from the central cities to the suburbs. To some people living in devastated areas where social services are few, diseases like AIDS appear to be a form of race or class warfare, "a virus created in a government or CIA laboratory in an attempt to 'clean up' a seemingly dirty population."[76]

In 1993, the World Health Organization took the unprecedented step of declaring a global emergency because of a disease.[77] The disease in question was not AIDS, but tuberculosis. It is predicted that 30 million people will die of TB within the next ten years while 90 million will become newly infected with mycobacterium tuberculosis. According to the report, if infectious people are not cured, new infections are expected to spread at a rate of one per second.

This upswing in a disease believed to be under control since the 1940s, when effective drugs were introduced, was blamed on "worldwide medical chaos," resulting in the disease being pushed into the poorer sections of society— particularly inner-city dwellers and the homeless.[78] The reemergence of a disease thought to be largely controlled is affecting not only poor countries; drug-resistant strains of tuberculosis are also spreading in wealthy countries due to migration as well as international business and tourist travel.

In recent years, there have been local epidemics of a wide variety of emerging diseases, including hemorrhagic fevers, Marburg virus, yellow fever, Lassa virus, Ebola virus, Swine Flu and Legionnaires' Disease, cholera, and hantaviruses.[79] Many of these viruses have lain dormant, perhaps for hundreds of years, in remote parts of the world. As the worldwide environment is changed and stressed by human activity, such diseases are emerging as a serious and frightening threat to life and health.

Stress

We see violence, homicide, and war clearly as causes of death. Yet a more subtle condition, stress, can be just as much a threat to our well-being. Many researchers believe that stress plays an important role in such characteristically modern ailments as ulcers, hypertension (high blood pressure), and heart disease. Increased susceptibility to such ailments may result when prolonged stress wears down the body's defenses.

Although the term *stress* in popular usage means different things to different people, it can be defined as the body's reaction to any influence that disturbs its natural equilibrium. In the early 1900s, a Harvard physiologist, Walter Cannon, demonstrated that certain emotional responses to stress, such as fear or rage, prepare the body for what is called the "fight-or-flight" response: intense action designed to return the organism to a state of equilibrium, or homeostasis. Thus, stress results when a situation demands that some adjustment or adaptation be made. This adaptation in turn causes certain physiological changes designed to meet the stressful demand.

All of us experience the alarm reaction as we respond to the changing events of our lives. If the stressor is minor and lasts only briefly, the body's defensive mechanisms subside and functioning quickly returns to normal. If the stressor persists or is more intense, the body's adaptive mechanisms continue to function at an elevated level to resist stress. Eventually, the mechanisms are exhausted and vital functions are depleted. The result may be a lowering of the body's resistance to disease. It is this psychosomatic nature of stress—the ability of emotional and mental states to influence physical changes—that is of particular interest to researchers.

The role of the emotions in influencing health and well-being has received considerable attention in recent years.[80] In his book *The Will to Live,* Arnold Hutschnecker cites clinical observations to support the thesis that the chief cause of death is illness traceable to emotional disorders. Cardiologists

Meyer Friedman and Ray Rosenman established a relationship between certain patterns of behavior and the onset of heart disease, which they reported in their book, *Type A Behavior and Your Heart.* The role of emotional factors in the progress of cancer was dealt with in Lawrence LeShan's *You Can Fight for Your Life.* Oncologist Carl Simonton, in his book *Getting Well Again,* described certain predisposing factors in the development of tumors.

What are some of the common themes in these accounts? They are: loss of sense of purpose in life; inability to express anger or resentment; self-dislike and self-distrust; despairing and hopeless outlook on life; impatience with the pace at which events occur; striving to do more in less time; inability to relax; preoccupation with having, rather than being; inability to forgive; tendency toward self-pity; inability to develop and maintain meaningful relationships; and poor self-image. Taken together, these attitudes and behaviors are characterized by intense stress.

Occupational stress is reportedly claiming the lives of more than 10,000 victims a year in Japan.[81] Mostly men in their prime working years, these victims of *karōshi,* or sudden death from overwork, are found in virtually every occupational category. *Karōshi* is characterized as a buildup of fatigue caused by "long hours of work that clearly exceed all normal physiological limitations," disruptions in an individual's normal daily rhythms (often related to travel or lengthy commutes to and from the job), and other job-related strains placed on workers. In some occupations, the rise of global markets (with their corresponding time differences) has forced workers to conduct business far into the night after the normal day's work has been completed. The incidence of *karōshi* in Japan has been accompanied by a growing recognition that exhaustion induced by chronic overwork can aggravate preexisting health problems and harm even the healthiest person—possibly causing a life-threatening crisis or death.

Stress is a natural part of human existence. Some believe, however, that the nature of stress has changed markedly since the turn of the century. Whereas in earlier times stress was primarily related to such environmental conditions as the need to obtain food, shelter, and warmth, today stress is related to such factors as more complex life styles, rising expectations, and inner discontent. Thus, the psychological factors influencing stress have become predominant.

Table 13-6 shows a rating scale devised by Drs. Thomas Holmes and Richard Rahe to measure the perceived impact of various life-change events in terms of the degree of social readjustment required.[82] Much as a sound of known loudness can be used as a standard against which the intensities of other sounds can be measured, so Holmes and Rahe used marriage—giving it a value of 50—as a standard for evaluating the perceived impact of other life-change events. In their study of subjects representative of a cross section of socioeconomic and demographic groups, Holmes and Rahe found virtual agreement about the relative intensities of various life events. The life events shown in Table 13-6 are listed in decreasing order of intensity as based on the "mean value" comparisons assigned to them by participants in the study. Significantly, Holmes and Rahe found a correlation between the frequency of life-change events and the onset of illness. People who became sick had generally experienced an increasing number of stressful life changes in the preceding year.

Take a few minutes to review the stress scale to determine how many of these events you have experienced during the past year. When a large number of stress-producing events occur within a brief period, or elicit a high level of stress, there is a greater likelihood that stress may become overwhelming. As you review the changes in your own life that required readjustment, would you give them the same ranking as the participants did in the Holmes and Rahe study?

Before 1900, there was comparatively little heart disease. Most researchers date the marked increase in heart disease from the twentieth century, with the greatest increase occurring since the 1940s. Many believe that the epidemic levels of heart disease in developed countries can be traced to the effects of life styles that derive from high technology and affluence. Among the most consequential factors of this life style are cigarette smoking, rich and fatty foods, and physical inactivity. The relationship between life style and the onset of heart disease has been confirmed in findings generated from a study, which began in 1948, of the residents in the small Massachusetts town of Framingham. This important study—officially titled the Framingham Heart Disease Epidemiology Study—has singled out stress as the most pervasive of all risk factors for heart and circulatory disease, noting that stress often influences other risk factors such as cigarette smoking and overeating as well.

Another disease that may be influenced by stress is cancer, which some believe could be more appropriately relabeled one of the "diseases of maladaptation."[83] Although a link between stress and cancer has not been conclusively proved, many believe that the personality type especially prone to cancer is characterized by loneliness, self-containment, and an inability to express emotions.

It is important to recognize that stress does not invariably lead to bodily deterioration and death. Any change is stressful and creates tension within the individual. But the *presence* of stress is less a determinant of potential problems than the manner in which a person *copes* with stress. Understanding how stress works and its effect on the body is the first step toward coping more effectively with it. As Jean Tache says,

> In each one of us lies dormant a primeval man who in certain situations is aroused and imperiously takes command of the personality. Given the ancient problem-solving options available to him—fight or flight, both requiring physical activity—he can hardly come up with satisfactory solutions to modern problems, for they require reflection, negotiation, and compromise.[84]

Hans Selye, perhaps the foremost investigator of stress, advises that people learn how to deal with stress "without distress."[85] How can this be accom-

TABLE *13-6*   *The Social Readjustment Rating Scale*

Life Event	Mean Value
1. Death of spouse	100
2. Divorce	73
3. Marital separation from mate	65
4. Detention in jail or other institution	63
5. Death of a close family member	63
6. Major personal injury or illness	53
7. Marriage	50
8. Being fired at work	47
9. Marital reconciliation with mate	45
10. Retirement from work	45
11. Major change in the health or behavior of a family member	44
12. Pregnancy	40
13. Sexual difficulties	39
14. Gaining a new family member (e.g., through birth, adoption, oldster moving in, etc.)	39
15. Major business readjustment (e.g., merger, reorganization, bankruptcy, etc.)	39
16. Major change in financial state (e.g., a lot worse off or a lot better off than usual)	38
17. Death of a close friend	37
18. Changing to a different line of work	36
19. Major change in the number of arguments with spouse (e.g., either a lot more or a lot less than usual regarding childrearing, personal habits, etc.)	35
20. Taking out a mortgage or loan for a major purchase (e.g., a home, business, etc.)	31
21. Foreclosure on a mortgage or loan	30
22. Major change in responsibilities at work (e.g., promotion, demotion, lateral transfer)	29

plished? First, Selye recommends that each person find the maximum level of stress that he or she is comfortable with, and that situations that exceed this level be avoided when possible. For example, it may be possible to limit the number of stressful changes that occur at a given time in one's life. Also, situations that elicit potentially harmful levels of stress can be managed in such a way that one makes a positive use of stress rather than succumbing to its negative effects. The stress that may accompany taking a test, for example, can be used to generate mental alertness and preparedness rather than anxiety about the outcome.

Regular physical exercise is another means of coping with stress. Physical exertion provides an outlet for the physiological responses associated with the stress encountered in daily life. In addition, relaxation techniques—such as biofeedback and meditation—offer a means of dealing with stress. Finally, the

T A B L E *13-6* *(continued)*

Life Event	Mean Value
23. Son or daughter leaving home (e.g., marriage, attending college, etc.)	29
24. In-law troubles	29
25. Outstanding personal achievement	28
26. Wife beginning or ceasing work outside the home	26
27. Beginning or ceasing formal schooling	26
28. Major change in living conditions (e.g., building a new home, remodeling, deterioration of home or neighborhood)	25
29. Revision of personal habits (dress, manners, association, etc.)	24
30. Troubles with the boss	23
31. Major change in working hours or conditions	20
32. Change in residence	20
33. Changing to a new school	20
34. Major change in usual type and/or amount of recreation	19
35. Major change in church activities (e.g., a lot more or a lot fewer than usual)	19
36. Major change in social activities (e.g., clubs, dancing, movies, visiting, etc.)	18
37. Taking out a mortgage or loan for a lesser purchase (e.g., for a car, TV, freezer, etc.)	17
38. Major change in sleeping habits (a lot more or a lot less sleep, or change in part of day when asleep)	16
39. Major change in number of family get-togethers (e.g., a lot more or a lot fewer than usual)	15
40. Major change in eating habits (a lot more or a lot less food intake, or very different meal hours or surroundings)	15
41. Vacation	13
42. Christmas	12
43. Minor violations of the law (e.g., traffic tickets, jaywalking, disturbing the peace, etc.)	11

Source: T. H. Holmes and R. H. Rahe, "The Social Readjustment Rating Scale," *Journal of Psychosomatic Research,* 11 (1967): 213–218.

symptoms of stress can be a signal that we need to reexamine our patterns of living. These symptoms can be recognized as indicators of personal and social problems that need to be confronted and corrected rather than simply treated with drug therapies or other techniques while the root causes are ignored.

In confronting stress, we must recognize that it involves loss and grief. In the modern era, relentless and rapid change continually transforms the familiar into the new, bringing about a variety of social displacements that affect health and well-being and create occasions for grief. This can be seen in the context of family and community disruptions, work pressures, lack of close social relationships, and inability to relax or enjoy the fruits of one's labor. Rather than mourning these losses, however, we try to adapt to them. To keep pace with modern life, we postpone consideration of our own well-being. We go on living our lives with unresolved, and perhaps unrecognized, losses. How can we get off this unhealthy merry-go-round?

Instead of trying to "manage" stress in order to be more productive, Robert Kugelmann suggests that we give ourselves time and space for experiencing grief and for meditating on death. Such meditations, he says, are really "anti-stress" exercises. They help us mourn and, through mourning, we gain a renewed passion for living. Kugelmann says, "People can love things with intensity to the extent they know the impermanence of things and of themselves."[86] Making room for death awakens us to our life in the flesh. The presence of stress in our lives, then, can be a signal that calls us back to ourselves.

Coping with Risks

Daniel Leviton has coined the term "horrendous death" to describe categories of death that affect large numbers of people.[87] The typical horrendous-type death has its origins in human activity and often involves the motivation to kill, maim, injure, or destroy another human being. Homicide, terrorism, assassination, and genocide are examples of horrendous-type deaths. The first step in eliminating, or at least reducing, such deaths involves confronting the wish to deny the reality of such deaths. Sometimes horrendous-type deaths are treated as an aberration, an anomaly. Yet they involve enormous costs for present as well as future generations.

Look again at Table 13-6, the social readjustment rating scale devised by Holmes and Rahe. Notice that items ranked as most stressful have in common the element of loss: loss of loved ones, relationships, freedom, well-being, self-esteem. Such losses are inherent in the encounters with death discussed in this chapter. Risks of various kinds—accidents, disasters, violence, war, epidemic diseases, and stress—affect us to varying degrees as we go about our daily lives. Sometimes the encounter is subtle; at other times it is overt, calling into action our ability to cope with threat. The failure to find adequate means of coping with these encounters with death and the stress of modern living represents a threat to the survival of the society as well as the individual.

Further Readings

Committee on Trauma Research, National Research Council. *Injury in America: A Continuing Public Health Problem.* Washington, D.C.: National Academy Press, 1985.

Kai Erikson. *A New Species of Trouble: Explorations in Disaster, Trauma, and Community.* New York: W. W. Norton, 1994.

Laurie Garrett. *The Coming Plague: Newly Emerging Diseases in a World Out of Balance.* New York: Farrar, Straus and Giroux, 1994.

Dave Grossman. *On Killing: The Psychological Cost of Learning to Kill in War and Society.* Boston: Little, Brown, 1995.

Albert R. Jonsen and Jeff Stryker, eds. *The Social Impact of AIDS.* Washington, D.C.: National Academy Press, 1993.

Charles Perrow. *Normal Accidents: Living with High Risk Technology.* New York: Basic Books, 1984.

Albert J. Reiss, Jr., and Jeffrey A. Roth, eds. *Understanding and Preventing Violence.* Washington, D.C.: National Academy Press, 1993.

Robert M. Sapolsky. *Why Zebras Don't Get Ulcers: A Guide to Stress, Stress-Related Diseases, and Coping.* New York: W. H. Freeman, 1994.

Jonathan Shay. *Achilles in Vietnam: Combat Trauma and the Undoing of Character.* New York: Atheneum, 1994.

Herbert S. Strean and Lucy Freeman. *Our Wish to Kill: The Murder in All Our Hearts.* New York: St. Martin's Press, 1991.

The corpse placed on the funeral pyre, these men prepare to light the cremation fire. Cremation has been a traditional practice in India, where Hindus believe that "even as the person casts off worn-out clothes and puts on others that are new, so the embodied Self casts off worn-out bodies and enters into others that are new."

CHAPTER 14

Beyond Death/After Life

Death—and then what?

Some people have a ready answer to this perennial question: "When you're dead, you're dead—that's it!" or "You go through a transition and take birth in another body," or "After you die you go to heaven," or "Your body is buried until the end of time when it's resurrected and you live again." Each of these responses reflects a particular understanding of the meaning of human existence. Beliefs about life after death occupy a broad spectrum, from the notion that death spells the end, to the notion that the "soul" or "self" lives on after death in some fashion. Answering the question "What happens after I die?" has occupied the attention of human beings since the dawn of consciousness.

This concern with immortality—that is, the attribute of survival after physical death—is cut from the same cloth as questions about the meaning of life and the corollary, "How, then, should one live?" Responses to these questions reflect a person's values and beliefs about human experience and the nature of reality. Our philosophy of life influences our philosophy of death. Conversely, how we perceive death and what meaning we give it affect the way we live. To someone who holds a well-defined and unequivocal view about the future state of existence following this present life, death might be seen as the "meaning" of the present life. At its most extreme, such a viewpoint might postulate that the *reason* for the present life is some other state of existence. Stephen J. Vicchio points out, however, that

Every time an earth mother smiles over the birth of a child, a spirit mother weeps over the loss of a child.

Ashanti saying

such a view contains a logical fallacy because it fails to address the question of the meaning of *this* life.[1]

Many of us would agree with Socrates that "the unexamined life is not worth living." Such self-investigation includes the discovery of what one believes about death and its consequences. Ambivalence about the issue of survival after death is aptly described in an anecdote related by Bertrand Russell: A woman whose daughter had recently died was asked what she thought had become of her daughter's soul. She replied, "Oh, well, I suppose she is enjoying eternal bliss, but I wish you wouldn't talk about such unpleasant subjects."[2]

Exploring your beliefs about immortality may not result in an easier acceptance of death—nor should it necessarily. After all, the prospect of immortality is not always looked upon favorably.[3] Even so, such an exploration can lead to a more coherent philosophy of life and death, making possible a congruence between hopes and perceptions. In this chapter we explore the meaning of mortality by investigating some of the ways that cultures ancient and modern, Eastern and Western, have answered the question, "What happens after death?" The answers voiced by ancient thinkers as well as the theories put forward by present-day researchers provide grist for the mill of our own contemplation about this ultimate human concern.

Traditional Concepts About Life After Death

The notion that life continues on in some form after death is one of the oldest concepts held by human beings. In some of the earliest known graves, archaeologists have uncovered skeletons that were bound by hands and feet into a fetal position, perhaps indicating beliefs about "rebirth" into other forms of existence following death. We know that in traditional societies death represents a change of status for the deceased, a transition from the land of the living to the land of the dead.

Some form of judgment is a key feature of many beliefs about what follows death. Among the various concepts of afterlife among traditional Hawaiians, for example, was the belief that a person who had offended a god or who had harmed others would suffer eternal punishment.[4] Such an unworthy soul became a wandering spirit, "forever homeless, forever hungry." The ancestor-gods had the power to punish or reward the released spirit, or even to send it back to the body. Misfortune also could result when a person had neither

William Hodges, Bishop Museum

The platform burial of a Tahitian chief is depicted in this drawing by William Hodges, made during Captain Cook's second voyage to the South Pacific in the 1770s.

In a world populated by unseen spirits who could exert their influence for good or evil upon the living, the death of a chief or other important person occasioned a spectacular display of grief, which was presided over by a chief mourner (right). *Usually a priest or close relative of the deceased, the chief mourner wore an elaborate costume of pearl shells and the feathers of tropic birds. Rattling a pearl shell clapper and brandishing a long wooden weapon inset with sharks' teeth, the chief mourner was accompanied by other weapon-carrying men who could strike anyone in their way, thus helping ensure that funeral rites were carried out in a manner that would offend neither the living nor the dead.*

Bishop Museum

loving relatives to care for the corpse nor the guardianship of family ancestor-gods who help souls find their way to the world of spirits. Thus, those who had lived worthily were welcomed into eternity, whereas those who had done misdeeds in life, without repenting for or correcting them, were punished. The reward for living a good life was eternity with those closest to the family-loving Hawaiian: one's own ancestors.

To understand the consciousness from which such a view of immortality arises, the notions of self that have developed in Western cultures during modern times must be put aside momentarily. Against the emphasis on individual identity and the self, imagine a mentality in which group identity is all-encompassing. The family, the clan, the people—these social groups represent the loci of communal consciousness within which the thoughts and actions of the individual are subsumed. Thus, these age-old beliefs convey less concern with individual survival than a desire for the continuation of the community and its common heritage. Having shared in the life of the group, the individual participates in its ultimate destiny, a destiny that can transcend even death.

Jewish Beliefs About Death and Resurrection

Considered as a whole, the books of the Bible do not provide a systematic theology of death or of the afterlife. Death is not ignored, but the biblical literature about it reflects a progression of ideas over a long period of time. The biblical story describes a people whose concerns were focused on a communal destiny. Individuals were seen as actors in the unfolding drama, and its denouement was foretold in the promises made by Yahweh.

As the patriarch Abraham lay dying, his last thoughts were for the continuation of his progeny so that these promises could be realized in the unfolding of history. Abraham's vision is reiterated by the biblical writers in one circumstance after another, as they affirm the destiny of the clan and of the nation of Israel. By contributing to this common destiny, the righteous person never ceased to be part of the continuing story of the people as a whole.

As the expression of Judaic thought changed over time, there were corresponding developments in how mortality and its meaning were understood. In the story of Job's encounter with adversity and death, the human situation is described bleakly: "As a cloud fades away and disappears, so a person who goes down to the grave will not come up from it."[5] This resignation toward death is echoed in the other Wisdom books—including Proverbs, Ecclesiastes, and some of the Psalms—which present the thought of the ancient Hebrew sages on the question of human destiny. Righteous conduct is advised because it leads to harmony in the present life, not because it guarantees future rewards for the individual.

Between the time of Job and the time of the prophets there was gradual change from resignation to hopefulness in the face of death. In the apocalyptic, or visionary, writings of prophets such as Daniel and Ezekiel, we see the

"There is always hope for a tree;
when felled, it can start its life again;
its shoots continue to sprout.
Its roots may be decayed in the earth,
its stump withering in the soil,
but let it scent the water, and it buds,
and puts out branches like a plant new set.
But man? He dies, and lifeless he remains;
man breathes his last, and then where is he?
The waters of the sea may disappear,
all the rivers may run dry or drain away;
but man, once in his resting place, will never rise again.
The heavens will wear away before he wakes,
before he rises from his sleep."

Job 14:7–12, *The Jerusalem Bible*

strands of thought that eventually are woven together in the notions that describe the resurrection of the body. Daniel envisions a future in which the "sleeping" dead will awaken, "some to everlasting life, some to everlasting disgrace."[6]

Hints of this change are also evident in the meanings ascribed over time to the Hebrew word *She'ol*, which in early usage is generally defined as the underworld of the dead, a shadowy realm of disembodied souls. An old story gives an account of necromancy in which King Saul requests the witch of En-dor to summon the spirit of the dead prophet Samuel. Asked by Saul to describe what she sees, the witch of En-dor replies, "I see a ghost [*elohim* = superhuman being] rising up from the earth [*She'ol*]." Later, with further refinement of these concepts, the shadowy underworld of *She'ol* would be divided into two distinct realms: *Gehinom* (hell) and *Pardes* (heaven or paradise).[7]

The idea of the resurrection of the body is an important development in Hebrew thought, and one that influenced Christian theology as well. Stated succinctly, this view of survival after death "consists in the belief that, at the end of time, the bodies of the dead will be resurrected from the grave and reconstituted."[8]

In the main, the evolving doctrine of resurrection did not alter the essential understanding in Hebrew psychology of the human person as an undivided psychophysical entity. Although the breath or spirit was sometimes identified with a "principle of vitality" that is common to all forms of conscious life, no intrinsically immortal element could be distinguished as somehow separate from the whole person. As Wheeler Robinson wrote, "The Hebrew

> For the whole world is the sepulchre of famous men, and it is not the epitaph upon monuments set up in their own land that alone commemorates them, but also in lands not their own there abides in each breast an unwritten memorial of them, planted in the heart rather than graven on stone.
>
> Thucydides, *The Peloponnesian War*

idea of personality is an animated body, and not an incarnated soul."[9] In other words, it is not as if the soul *takes* a body, but rather that the body *has* life. In this understanding of personhood, such concepts as body or soul cannot be abstracted from the essential integrity of the human person. (As we will see, this understanding is quite different from the ancient Greek ideas about the soul surviving the death of the body, ideas that have influenced all subsequent Western thought about death and immortality.)

The consensus expressed by the biblical writers would seem to be: "Our present existence is of God; if there is life hereafter, it will also be God's gift. Thus, what need is there for anxiety about death? What matters is to live righteously and to ensure the well-being and survival of the community." The characteristic theme of Hebraic tradition concerns the importance of faith—faith in the people of Israel as a community with a common destiny, and faith in Yahweh, whose promises will be realized in the unfolding of the divine plan. The enduring concern is that one should not lose sight of the tasks at hand.

Hellenistic Concepts of Immortality

Among the ancient Greeks, or Hellenes, there were differing views about what might follow upon the death of the body. Generally, however, the afterworld was not an attractive prospect. The realm of the dead was usually pictured as a shadowy place, inhabited by bloodless phantoms. It is perhaps not surprising, therefore, that death seems to have elicited feelings of despair.

As with their contemporaries elsewhere, the ancient Greeks did not think about death in the same way many people do today. Rather than focusing on the status of the individual, they were preoccupied with communal concerns. In the Athenian democracy, for instance, what mattered was the survival of the *polis*, the corporate existence of the city-state. Personal immortality became important only to the extent that it affected the survival of the community. Within this context, an individual could hope to achieve social immortality by fulfilling the responsibilities of citizenship—that is, by performing actions directed toward the common good. Because heroic acts are remembered by the community, the hero achieves a renown that extends beyond a single lifetime.

For those who sought more than symbolic immortality, assurances of happiness beyond death could be had by participating in one of the mystery

Speak not smoothly of death, I beseech you, O famous Odysseus. Better by far to remain on earth the thrall of another . . . rather than reign sole king in the realm of bodyless phantoms.

Homer, *The Odyssey*

religions, cults whose origins are clouded in the mists of prehistory. By dedicating themselves to the rites of purification prescribed by the priests of the mystery cult, they could exchange the dire picture of the afterworld for the more promising one of an idyllic future in paradise.

Among the early Greek philosophers, speculation about the afterlife generally conformed to the popular beliefs of their culture. Most conceived of life and death as aspects of an ever-changing, eternal flux. Although they believed that the soul was the vital principle that continued in some fashion after death, they generally did not imagine that the soul would survive as a distinct entity, as the personality or self of a particular individual. To many early Greek thinkers, whatever it was that continued beyond death merged with the stuff of the universe.

Somewhat later, Pythagoras taught that one's conduct during life determined the destiny of the soul after death. Thus, with discipline and purification, one could influence the transmigration of the soul—successive rounds of births and deaths—that led to eventual union with the Divine or Universal Absolute. These beliefs drew upon the Orphic mystery religions of earlier Greece that went back to the ancient cult of Dionysus. The notion that how a person conducted himself or herself in this life could influence the soul's existence in the afterlife contrasted with the predominant view of a rather indistinct immortality in which all participated regardless of their actions. Nevertheless, the ideas expressed by Pythagoras and his followers would eventually find a wider acceptance in somewhat altered form during the pre-Christian era, and the connection between conduct and immortality would be further refined during the early centuries of Christianity.

Become accustomed to the belief that death is nothing to us. For all good and evil consists in sensation, but death is deprivation of sensation. And therefore a right understanding that death is nothing to us makes the mortality of life enjoyable, not because it adds to an infinite span of time, but because it takes away the craving for immortality. For there is nothing terrible in life for the man who has truly comprehended that there is nothing terrible in not living.

Epicurus, *Letter to Menoeceus*

> . . . he who has lived as a true philosopher has reason to be of good cheer when he is about to die, and that after death he may hope to receive the greatest good in the other world. . . . For I deem that the true disciple of philosophy . . . is ever pursuing death and dying; and if this is true, why, having had the desire of death all his life long, should he repine at the arrival of that which he has been always pursuing and desiring?
>
> Plato, *Phaedo*

With Socrates there are signs of a shift from a social immortality predicated on the life of the community to the possibility of personal survival after death. Precisely what Socrates believed in this regard is unclear, although he seems to have favored the notion that the individual soul would survive after the death of the body. On his deathbed, he describes his sense of anticipation at the prospect of communion with the spirits of the great in the afterworld. But, in the *Apology*, he describes death as *either* eternal bliss *or* dreamless sleep.

This concept of immortality of the soul—an idea that pervaded Orphic thought in ancient Greece and that was favored by Pythagoras and Socrates—was further developed in Plato's writings. In the *Phaedo*, he advances a number of "proofs" that the soul is eternal and is released from the body at death. The dualism of body and soul is emphasized, and their respective fates are distinguished from one another: Because it is mortal, the body is subject to corruption; the soul, however, is immortal and not subject to death.

Among Plato's successors, death and the prospect of immortality gained importance. The fact of death as the common fate of all humankind could be used as a reminder of the importance of choosing wisely how to live in the present life. These thoughts are echoed by the Roman Stoic, Marcus Aurelius, who lived in the second century of the present era. "The constant recollection of death," he said, "is the test of human conduct."[10]

Christian Beliefs About the Afterlife

Jesus himself seems to have been little concerned with speculations about the afterlife. Rather, his message focused on the impending arrival of the Kingdom of God and the corresponding need for righteousness. Nevertheless, the ideas of resurrection that had been developing in the Judaic tradition became radically transformed in the minds of early Christians, who proclaimed that death was vanquished by Christ's resurrection. The life, death, and resurrection of Jesus became the new model of reality for Christians. He was the prototype of the salvation from death available to all those who would share in his resurrection. The Kingdom of God described by Jesus was anticipated as a glorious event that would occur in the very near future. Eternal life was, so to speak, just around the corner.

Behold, I show you a mystery; We shall not all sleep, but we shall all be changed. In a moment, in the twinkling of an eye, at the last trump: for the trumpet shall sound, and the dead shall be raised incorruptible, and we shall be changed. For this corruptible must put on incorruption, and this mortal must put on immortality. So when this corruptible shall have put on incorruption, and this mortal shall have put on immortality, then shall be brought to pass the saying that is written, Death is swallowed up in victory. O death, where is thy sting? O grave, where is thy victory?

I Corinthians, 15

With Jesus no longer in their midst, and as the small group of Christians began to reframe their expectations about the chronology of the Kingdom of God, their understanding of resurrection also began to change. In the writings of Paul, there is an attempt to resolve some of these problems of death, afterlife, and the events foretold for the end of time. Resurrection can be understood as a special kind of bodily existence, different from historical existence. But it can also be understood as having a symbolic or spiritual meaning.

The Hellenistic notion of a cosmic dualism was a persistent and pervasive influence on early Christian thought. According to this dualism, the soul was immortal, a part of the human person that existed in a disembodied state after death. During the formative period of the early Church, there was constant interplay between the Hebrew traditions and the intellectual heritage of Greco-Roman culture. Milton Gatch says about this period:

> The notion of resurrection and of the restoration of an elect people continued to be prominent. But the idea of a disembodied afterlife for the soul was also current and led to the conception of some sort of afterlife between the separation and the reunion of soul and body. From a picture of death as the inauguration of a sleep which would last until the divinely instituted resurrection, there emerged a picture of death as the beginning of quiescence for the body and of a continued life for the soul, the nature of which remained more or less undefined.[11]

And so gradually there developed a greater emphasis on the destiny of the individual soul. Correspondingly, there was increasingly greater concern about the consequences of an individual's conduct during life. By the third or fourth century, Church doctrine more or less willingly accommodated the notion that punishment for misconduct could take place during an intermediate period between death and resurrection.[12]

By the thirteenth century, in the writings of Dante and Thomas Aquinas, the original biblical concept is almost completely subordinated to the Greek notion of dualism and its attendant concept of the soul's immortality. The interplay between these contrasting concepts is illustrated by an observation

This scene from Dante's Divine Comedy *shows the guide Charon ferrying worthy souls up the River Styx toward Paradise. Unable to reach the heavenly kingdom, the unworthy, immersed in the river, struggle in despair.*

Go Down, Death—A Funeral Sermon

Weep not, weep not,
She is not dead;
She's resting in the bosom of Jesus.
Heart-broken husband—weep no more;
Grief-stricken son—weep no more;
Left-lonesome daughter—weep no more;
She's only just gone home.

James Weldon Johnson

made by Stephen Vicchio of two tombstone inscriptions, dating from the colonial period, found in New Haven, Connecticut.[13]

On the first tombstone, the inscription reads, "Sleeping, but will someday meet her maker." The second is inscribed, "Gone to his eternal reward." The first inscription reflects an understanding that postulates the resurrection of the body, an event that will occur at some time in the future. The second is based on the concept of the immortality of the soul, which continues to exist even though the body dies. As Vicchio points out, the difference between these two tombstone inscriptions is particularly incongruous when you consider that these two individuals were married to each other and are buried side by side in this New England cemetery. Yet, one of them is "sleeping," while the other is "gone."

In these inscriptions we see a curious example of how such essentially disparate ideas can coexist in time. Today, each of these notions—resurrection and immortality—has its adherents. For some, the distinction is vital. Others give little thought to either the distinction or the necessary logic that follows from each of these conceptual understandings.

Until fairly recent times, most people living in the Western world could find adequate answers to the enigma of death by relying on the teachings of the Christian creeds. In the modern world, however, our understanding of death has been altered radically. The religious consciousness of the Apostle Paul—for whom the subjugation of death was a reality demonstrated by Christ's resurrection—now seems an anachronism to many people. Renee Haynes observed that people brought up in the oldest traditional form of Christianity "will have learned to consider two things from which many of their contemporaries have been conditioned to turn away: the fact of mystery and the fact of death."[14]

The Afterlife in Islamic Tradition

The third of the great religious traditions stemming from the patriarch Abraham is Islam, which has perhaps 900 million adherents worldwide. Like

British Museum

The Egyptian papyrus of Hunefer depicts the Hall of Judgment and the Great Bal-
ance, where the deceased's soul is weighed against the feather of truth. Beneath the
scales, the Devourer of Souls awaits the unjust while Horus is ready to lead the just
to Osiris, the lord of the underworld, and to a pleasurable afterlife.

Judaism and Christianity, Islam shares the Semitic religious heritage of belief
in monotheism, God's revelation through the prophets, ethical responsibility,
and ultimate accountability for one's actions at the Day of Judgment. The word
Islam means "submission to God" and, by extension, being in right relationship with the Divine. The person who adheres to this path is a Muslim, a
"submitter."

The Islamic revelation came through the prophet Muhammad and was
recorded in the Qur'an (perhaps more familiarly spelled phonetically as
"Koran" in the West) over a period of about two decades. About four-fifths
the size of the New Testament, the Qur'an, according to Muslims, "does not
abrogate or nullify, but rather corrects, the version of scripture preserved by
the Jewish and Christian communities."[15] The theological concerns expressed
in the Qur'an are generally the same as those of Judaism and Christianity.
Frithjof Schuon notes that the doctrine of Islam hangs on two statements:
First, "There is no divinity (or reality) outside the only Divinity (or Absolute)"
and, second, "Muhammad is the Envoy (the mouthpiece, intermediary, or
manifestation)."[16]

The happiness of the drop is to
die in the river.

Ghazal of Ghalib

Like the Bible, the Qur'an does not provide a systematic treatment of death, although the subject is not ignored. A basic premise of Qur'anic teaching about death is that God, in his omnipotence, determines the span of a person's life, "he creates man and also causes him to die."[17] Believers naturally owe obedience and gratitude to their creator. Nevertheless, as John Esposito says, "The specter of the Last Judgment, with its eternal reward and punishment, remains a constant reminder of the ultimate consequences of each life."[18] Each individual's moral accountability will ultimately be assessed at the time of the Resurrection and Last Judgment, or Day of Reckoning. The Book of Deeds, wherein are recorded good and bad actions, will be opened and each person will be consigned either to everlasting bliss or everlasting torment. As Huston Smith wrote, "For the Muslim, life on earth is the seedbed of an eternal future."[19]

The vision of the afterlife recorded in the Qur'an is both spiritual and physical. "Since the Last Day will be accompanied by bodily resurrection," says Esposito, "the pleasures of heaven and the pain of hell will be fully experienced."[20] Heaven is described as a paradise of "perpetual peace and bliss with flowing rivers, beautiful gardens, and the enjoyment of one's spouses (multiple marriage partners are permitted in Islam) and beautiful, dark-eyed female companions (*houris*)," and the terrors of hell are described in equally physical terms.

For the believer whose actions demonstrate commitment and faithfulness to the path of Islam, death is a release from the sorrows and troubles of life. When death nears, appropriate passages from the Qur'an may be read to the dying person to facilitate an easy release. After death, the body is laid out with the head in the direction of prayer and a ritual washing is begun—unless the deceased happens to be a martyr, in which case the washing is skipped "in order not to remove traces of blood which are the hallmark of his martyrdom, nor is it necessary to pray for his soul."[21] On hearing of someone's death, it is customary to say, "Allah Karim"—from God we came and to him we shall return.[22]

Among some Muslims, it is believed that, when a person dies and the body is placed in the grave, "two black-faced, blue-eyed angels named Munkar and Nakir visit the grave and interrogate the deceased concerning his beliefs and deeds in life." Depending on the answers given, the deceased, while still in the grave, receives comfort or punishment at the hands of these "two interrogators." Thus, says Alfred Welch, "At a Muslim funeral a mourner may approach a corpse as it is about to be laid in the tomb and whisper instructions for answering these questions."[23] Some Muslims believe that "no one should precede the corpse in the funeral procession because the angels of death go before it."[24] According to orthodox Islamic tradition, the funeral should be conducted without elaborate ceremony with the body laid in a simple, un-marked grave. Some believe the grave should be deep enough for the dead person to sit up without his or her head appearing above ground when it comes time to answer questions at the Last Judgment.

During the last few decades, a resurgence or revivalism of Islam has become increasingly prominent throughout much of the Muslim world. This movement, often termed Islamic fundamentalism, emphasizes religious iden-tity and practice in both individual and community life. Reacting to modern tendencies to separate religion and politics and to offer secular alternatives as the only contemporary option, Islamic revivalism embodies the notion that politics, law, education, social life, and economics are not to be viewed as "secular institutions or areas of life" but as integral to the total and compre-hensive way of life that is Islam.

This concern about the steadily increasing influence of secular and ma-terialistic values is, of course, not limited to Muslims. Many of their "Abra-hamic cousins"—Jews and Christians—are also concerned about "the secular drift and outlook of their societies and its impact on faith and values."[25] We will look at the impact of secularism on our relationship with dying and death later in this chapter.

Death and Immortality in Eastern Religions

The Western approach to experience tends to be dualistic. Experiences are analyzed as being *either* this *or* that. The Western thinker typically makes distinctions, points up contrasts, establishes differences. Within this context, life is opposed to death, death is the enemy of life; life represents affirmation, death negation. Death is "evil," life "good."

In the cultures of the East, however, the characteristic mode of thought emphasizes the integrity of the whole rather than the differences between constituent parts. It seeks the unity that underlies apparently contradictory phenomena. Whereas Western thought distinguishes between "either/or," Eastern thought subsumes such distinctions within a holistic "both/and" approach.

This unitary view of reality is reflected in many of the sacred texts of the East. The *I Ching*, or *Book of Changes*, for instance, postulates a world of expe-rience that is constantly being transformed. Life and death are manifestations of a constantly changing reality. Like the symbol of the *Tao*, these contrasting aspects of reality interpenetrate one another. Death and life are not seen as mutually exclusive opposites, but rather as complementary facets of an underlying process. We see this process in the inexorable cycles of

> Though it will die soon
> The voice of the cicada
> Shows no sign of this.
>
> Bashō

birth, decay, and death. Like a pendulum moving through its arc, the completion of one cycle heralds the beginning of another.

Everything in the phenomenal world exhibits this pattern of constant arising and passing away. Through their observations of this process, the sages of the East developed the concept of reincarnation or transmigration. For some, reincarnation is understood as a physical reality: "I will take birth in another body following the death of my present body." Others shun such a materialist understanding of reincarnation, saying that there is, in fact, no "I" to be reborn. According to this view, what we identify as "I" or "self" is insubstantial, an ever-changing process. In the constant arising and passing away of experience, something is carried over from one state to the next, but this "something" is impersonal and is essentially formless and ineffable.

Hindu Theologies of Death and Rebirth

One of the distinguishing features of Hinduism is the belief in the transmigration of the soul; that is, the passing at death of the soul from one body or being to another. This process is termed *samsara*, which refers to "passing through" a series of incarnational experiences. What links these experiences together is *karma*, which can be roughly defined as the moral law of cause and effect. The thoughts and actions of the past determine the present state of being; and, in turn, present choices influence future states. This karmic process can be interpreted as pertaining to the ever-changing flow of moment-to-moment experience, as well as to the successive rounds of deaths and rebirths. As each moment conditions the next, karma sustains this reincarnational flow of being. In the *Bhagavad-Gita*, Krishna tells Arjuna:

> For death is a certainty for him who has been born,
> and birth is a certainty for him who has died.
> Therefore, for what is unavoidable thou shouldst not grieve.

In his commentary on this passage, Nikhilananda adds, "It is not proper to grieve for beings which are mere combinations of cause and effect."[26]

According to Hinduism, the workings of karma provide only a partial description of reality. Underlying the apparent separateness of individual beings is a unitary reality. Just as the ocean can be imagined as composed of innumerable drops of water, undifferentiated being is manifest in human experience in the form of apparently separate selves. Huston Smith expresses

The cosmic dance of the Hindu deity Shiva, an ever-changing flow of creation and dissolution, embodies the fundamental equilibrium between life and death, the underlying reality behind appearances.

the Hindu perception this way: "Underlying man's personality and animating it is a reservoir of being that never dies, is never exhausted, and is without limit in awareness and bliss. This infinite center of life, this hidden self or *Atman*, is no less than *Brahman*, the Godhead."[27] Our attachment to, or identification with, the concept of "self" as separate and distinct causes us suffering in our present life and perpetuates the endless wheel of births and deaths, the wheel of *karma*.

Hinduism teaches that we can be free of the illusion of separate selfhood, with its attendant pain. Liberation involves the recognition that life and death transcend such mistaken notions of self-identity. The *Bhagavad-Gita* says:

> Worn-out garments are shed by the body:
> Worn-out bodies are shed by the dweller.

Nikhilananda explicates this process: "In the act of giving up the old body or entering into the new body, the real Self does not undergo any change whatsoever. . . . Brahman, through Its inscrutable maya, creates a body, identifies Itself with it, and regards Itself as an individual, or embodied, soul."[28]

To be free of death means letting go of attachments to the phenomenal world, releasing the grasp on the false distinctions of a separate self and its unceasing desires. Death is inescapable, a natural corollary of conditioned existence. What is born passes away. Yet for the person "whose consciousness has become stabilized by the insight that it is the very nature of things to come-to-be and pass-away," there is no "occasion either for rejoicing over birth or grieving over death."[29]

To loosen the bonds of attachment, Hinduism offers various aids in the form of rites and practices that can assist in the awakening to truth. Some of these methods emphasize paying close attention to the processes that surround death. For example, one practice involves attending to the transitory and ever-changing nature of one's own body, observing its inexorable progress toward decay and dissolution, its constant transformation, moment to moment. Another practice involves imagining one's death and the ultimate fate of the body, its return to elemental matter in the grave or on the funeral pyre. Some of these meditation practices occur in the presence of a dead body or at burial or cremation grounds. Death becomes a clear reminder of the ever-changing flow of *karma*, a reminder that there is nothing to hold to, no permanence, no solid self. By confronting one's own mortality, one becomes reoriented toward the transcendent dimensions of reality. The death of the separate self is the letting go of conditioned existence, "the death that conquers death."[30]

The Buddhist Understanding of Death

Zen master Dōgen, founder of the Soto Zen sect in Japan, said, "The thorough clarification of the meaning of birth and death—this is the most important problem of all for Buddhists."[31] Although there is considerable variety in Buddhist practices and beliefs—as there is in the Hinduism that served as the background of Siddhartha Gautama's experience of awakening

Thus shall you think of all this fleeting world:
A star at dawn, a bubble in a stream;
A flash of lightning in a summer cloud.
A phantom, an illusion, a dream.

Buddha,
The Diamond Sutra

to become the Buddha—death holds a central place in the teachings of Buddhism. And although its meaning may be variously interpreted by different sects and schools, the ultimate aim for Buddhists is *nirvana*, which literally means "extinction"—as when a flame goes out if deprived of fuel. It is, says Philip Kapleau, the "unconditioned state beyond birth and death that is reached after all ignorance and craving have been extinguished and all karma, which is the cause of rebirth, has been dissolved."[32]

Buddhism denies the existence of a permanent, unchanging self or substantial soul that transmigrates intact from one life to the next. What we call "self" is simply a process of continuous change. Everything is transitory and impermanent (*anicca*), in continual unease and unrest (*dukkha*), and substanceless (*anatta*). In this view, *karma* is seen as the universal principle of causality that underlies the stream of psychophysical events. Dōgen says, "Life constantly changes, moment by moment, in each of its stages, whether we want it to or not. Without even a moment's pause our karma causes us to transmigrate continuously."[33]

There is no "self" to survive after death or to be reborn, yet *karma* transmigrates to the next moment of arising into being. This transmigration can be likened to impressing a seal onto wax or mud, or to the transfer of energy in a game of billiards when the cue ball strikes the cluster of balls, creating new energy events. Philip Kapleau says: "Rebirth does not involve the transfer of a substance, but the continuation of a process." From the Buddhist perspective, it could be said that there are two kinds of death: continuous and regular. Continuous death is the "passing show" of phenomenal experience, constantly arising and passing away, moment by moment. Regular, or corporeal, death is the physical cessation of vital body functions at the end of a lifetime.

Like Hinduism, Buddhism teaches that it is necessary to renounce the desires and cravings that maintain the delusion of a separate self. When all attachments are dropped, the wheel of *karma*, the incessant round of birth-decay-death, is given no further fuel. How does one awaken to this reality, to *nirvana*? Dōgen says, "Simply understand that birth and death are in themselves nirvana, there being no birth-death to be hated or nirvana to be desired. Then, for the first time you will be freed from birth and death."[34]

The paradox of Dōgen's statement about birth-death and the importance of using death as a means of awakening to truth is echoed in the words of

In the Japanese section of this cemetery on the island of Oahu, graves holding the ashes of deceased members of the community are ornamented with Buddhist symbols of the Wheel of Dharma and the Lotus.

Hakuin, who is known as the reviver of the Rinzai sect, the other great Zen Buddhist lineage in Japan.[35] For those who wish to investigate their true nature, Hakuin advised meditation on the word *shi*, the character for death. To do this, he suggested a *koan* (a teaching question): "After you are dead and cremated, where has the main character [the chief actor or one's "original face"] gone?" Hakuin wrote:

> Among all the teaching and instructions, the word *death* has the most unpleasant and disgusting connotations. Yet if you once suddenly penetrate this "death" koan, you will find that there is no more felicitous teaching than this instruction that serves as the key to the realm in which birth and death are transcended, where the place in which you stand is the Diamond indestructible, and where you have become a divine immortal, unaging and undying. The word *death* is the vital essential that the warrior must first determine for himself.

After-Death States in Tibetan Buddhism

Individuals who by religious persuasion perceive death as an opportunity for awakening are naturally interested in influencing the character of the after-death state and the next incarnation. According to W. Y. Evans-Wentz, "Buddhists and Hindus alike believe that the last thought at the moment of

Before we were born we had no feeling; we were one with the universe. This is called "mind-only," or "essence of mind," or "big mind." After we are separated by birth from this oneness, as the water falling from the waterfall is separated by the wind and rocks, then we have feeling. You have difficulty because you have feeling. You attach to the feeling you have without knowing just how this kind of feeling is created. When you do not realize that you are one with the river, or one with the universe, you have fear. Whether it is separated into drops or not, water is water. Our life and death are the same thing. When we realize this fact we have no fear of death anymore, and we have no actual difficulty in our life.

Shunryu Suzuki, *Zen Mind, Beginner's Mind*

death determines the character of the next incarnation."[36] On this point, the Buddha said: "Rebirth arises from two causes: the last thought of the previous life as its governing principle and the actions of the previous life as its basis. The stopping of the last thought is known as decease; the appearance of the first thought as rebirth."[37] Writings like the *Bardo Thödol*, or *The Tibetan Book of the Dead*, as it is better known in the West, are intended to direct the thought processes of the dying person during the transitional period of life-death-rebirth.

The term *bardo* can be translated as "gap" or "interval of suspension" and is usually taken to mean an intermediate or transitional state between birth and death. Chögyam Trungpa suggests that *bardo* refers not only to the interval after death, but also to "suspension within the living situation."[38] Although the *Bardo Thödol* and similar texts are commonly thought to be designed to be read as a person experiences the process of dying, they actually have a broader application. Such texts can serve as a guide for the living as well as the dying. Chögyam Trungpa says: The *Bardo Thödol* deals with "the principle of birth and death recurring constantly in this life." Indeed, in this view, "the bardo experience is part of our basic psychological make-up."

As to the states described in the *Tibetan Book of the Dead*, they are intermediate states of consciousness. The *Bardo Thödol* offers counsel on how to use these experiences—some terrifying, some benign—to awaken to a more enlightened incarnation. Although acknowledging that these experiences are likely to appear quite real to the *bardo* traveler, the text emphasizes that the deities or demons encountered are simply apparitions, the experiencer's own projections. They do not represent ultimate or transcendent perfection but rather steps on the way. Nevertheless, the period immediately following death is considered to be an especially opportune time for gaining insight. The priest at a Buddhist funeral, for example, speaks directly to the deceased, expounding on the teachings that can awaken the intermediate being to the true nature of existence. Philip Kapleau says, "The funeral and subsequent services thus

> Your essence was not born and will not die. It is neither being nor nonbeing. It is not a void nor does it have form. It experiences neither pleasure nor pain. If you ponder what it is in you that feels the pain of this sickness, and beyond that you do not think or desire or ask anything, and if your mind dissolves like vapour in the sky, then the path to rebirth is blocked and the moment of instant release has come.
>
> Bassui, Zen Buddhist, comforting a dying person

represent literally a 'once in a lifetime' opportunity to awaken the deceased and thereby liberate him from the binding chain of birth-and-death."[39]

Secular Concepts of Immortality

In modern technology-oriented and economics-driven societies—both East and West—traditional beliefs about the purpose of life or the nature of death no longer enjoy the virtually universal acceptance they did when societies and communities were more cohesive, less influenced by ideas and events outside their own domains. For many people, death has been divorced from its mythic and religious connotations. The underpinnings for traditional beliefs no longer carry the same weight in a social milieu that emphasizes empirical verification and the scientific method. Theological or philosophical discussions about the afterlife may seem to resemble the famous debate about the number of dancing angels that will fit on the head of a pin. Yet vestiges of traditional concepts about death and the afterlife remain lodged in the modern consciousness.

The Abrahamic religious traditions—Judaism, Christianity, and Islam—present a linear picture of human history, one that describes a progression of events that begins with creation and eventuates in the resolution of the cosmic story at the end of time. Such an orientation to human experience naturally leads to an interest in eschatologies—pictures of the ultimate state, doctrines of the last things. From the wellsprings of the Judeo-Christian tradition and Hellenistic ideals of progress, Western societies have predominantly framed their beliefs about what happens after death in a historical context that is oriented toward the future. The Western view has been that human beings live a single life; that the soul survives death, perhaps in a disembodied state; that at some future time each soul will be judged; and that, depending on one's conduct during earthly existence, the aftermath will be either hellish torment or heavenly bliss. This view, though it still has many adherents, has been challenged by modernist conceptions of death and its aftermath.

Among the most widespread of the secular alternatives to religion are positivism and humanitarianism. *Positivism*, a doctrine associated with faith in science, reflects the belief that religious or metaphysical modes of knowing are imperfect and inadequate, and that "positive knowledge" must be based on what can be observed in nature and verified by the empirical sciences. *Humanitarianism* is a doctrine or way of life that rejects the supernaturalism of religion and instead centers on human values and interests, stressing self-realization through the use of reason. In the real world, it is not unusual for a person to hold several of these competing world views at the same time, perhaps combining a vague religious faith carried over from childhood with faith in scientific modes of knowing and humanitarian ideals of conduct.

The change that made unbelief an option was influenced, of course, by the ideal of social and scientific progress and by the humanitarian aim of eradicating human suffering. Compassion gained prominence among the "duties of humanity" and was joined with the idea of progress to forge a new moral principle oriented largely toward earthly concerns. Although science and social transformation both played key roles in giving rise to the secular option of not believing in God or at least retiring him "to a private or at best subcultural role," James Turner notes that religion itself bears the major responsibility for this cultural upheaval.[40] As instruction in "life and manners" became the principle purpose of religion, the transcendent concerns that had figured so prominently in the great theological traditions were downplayed, making religion almost solely a moral guide.

New conceptions of knowledge, fostered by the advance of science, focused attention on the problem of verifying religious belief. Capitalist economic development influenced the ways people thought, as well as how they worked. Increasingly, people were becoming "thoroughly enmeshed in the commercial networks of a market economy." Work moved indoors, distancing people from nature's cycles. The effects of this trend were amplified by the regulation of human activities by the clock. Turner says, "Objects of human manufacture enveloped people, separating them from the nature attributed to God's hand," and "even God's time gave way to manmade time." This insulation from nature, as well as the growing sense of control over nature, encroached on the sense of divine activity in nature and helped to push "God's direct presence farther from everyday experience into an intangible spiritual realm."

Findings from anthropology seemed to indicate that religious beliefs were simply an attempt to make sense of the mysteries of nature. Studies in the physiology of the brain apparently reduced the human mind to nothing more mystical than a "grid of electrical nerve impulses." Thus, it became more and more difficult to maintain traditional notions about the soul, immortality, and God. As Turner points out, the "psychic gratifications" that used to be sought in God could now be provided by a "religion of humanity" that embraced science, art, and the worship of nature. Religious leaders were part of this sweeping social and conceptual change as they tried to make peace with modernity "by conceiving God and His purposes in terms as nearly compatible as possible with secular understandings and aims."

Today, despite the option of unbelief, most people still readily affirm their belief in God. A survey completed in 1991 and characterized as "perhaps the

The absolute certainty that death is a complete and definitive and irrevocable annihilation of personal consciousness, a certainty of the same order as our certainty that the three angles of a triangle are equal to two right angles, or contrariwise, the absolute certainty that our personal consciousness continues beyond death in whatever condition (including in such a concept the strange and adventitious additional notion of eternal reward or punishment)—either of these certainties would make our life equally impossible. In the most secret recess of the spirit of the man who believes that death will put an end to his personal consciousness and even to his memory forever, in that inner recess, even without his knowing it perhaps, a shadow hovers, a vague shadow lurks, a shadow of the shadow of uncertainty, and, while he tells himself: "There's nothing for it but to live this passing life, for there is no other!" at the same time he hears, in this most secret recess, his own doubt murmur: "Who knows? . . ." He is not sure he hears aright, but he hears. Likewise, in some recess of the soul of the true believer who has faith in a future life, a muffled voice, the voice of uncertainty, murmurs in his spirit's ear: "Who knows? . . ." Perhaps these voices are no louder than the buzzing of mosquitoes when the wind roars through the trees in the woods; we scarcely make out the humming, and yet, mingled in the uproar of the storm, it can be heard. How, without this uncertainty, could we ever live?

Miguel de Unamuno, *The Tragic Sense of Life*

most detailed religious profile of twentieth-century Americans, found that religion remains a constant point of identification and commonality."[41] According to a 1990 survey of Americans' beliefs about the afterlife, 78 percent reported believing in heaven and 60 percent believing in hell, with the highest percentages of belief in both realms being reported among young adults.[42] Religious ideas and messages continue to play an important role in both individual and social thought. What is different, however, is the lack of a common intellectual life founded in a shared understanding that unifies an entire culture, "a common heritage that underlies our diverse world views."

Assurances about what to expect after death, assurances that were historically part of a community's heritage of shared belief, are now less convincing. For many, perhaps most, people, the idea that immortality signifies an everlasting state of paradisiacal bliss has given way to more modest hopes. As Norman Cousins wrote in his dialogue on immortality, *The Celebration of Life,* one's expectation of the hereafter may be limited merely to "peace of mind" or, even more basically, "to be saved from an eternity in death."[43] Beyond the fact that death, absolute extinction, is unacceptable, the average person may have little concrete notion of what he or she expects of an afterlife state. "Shouldn't your quest for immortality," the docent asks in Cousins' dialogue, "involve more than the mere desire to avoid a shattering blow to your conceit?" Is it really enough, in other words, to wish merely to survive? Isn't non-death, of itself, a rather limited idea?

Within the realm of secular, or nonreligious, answers to the question of immortality, there are various possible responses. The idea of the brotherhood of man, or the essential unity of humankind, may appeal to some as a plausible avenue of immortality. "You live in others; others live in you." The exchange of love and compassion between members of the human community itself assumes a kind of immortality for the person who shares his or her life with others.

Likewise, children represent a form of biological continuity that can be seen as a form of personal immortality. Other "children" that may be construed as conveying immortality on the creator include works of art or contributions to some field of knowledge or technology, as well as heroic or helpful deeds. Notwithstanding the sense of personal continuity that these forms of immortality may bring to the individual, as Robert Lifton and others have pointed out, the modern situation is one in which even the continuity (or, if you like, the immortality) of the human species as a whole cannot be assumed absolutely. The threat of catastrophic evil, whether it takes the form of nuclear annihilation or global environmental disaster, hangs over all our heads like the sword of Damocles. In light of the religious heritage of humankind as well as the more recent changes wrought under the name of secularism, placing our understanding of immortality in the present may serve as a common ground both for those who anticipate a future heavenly state as well as for those who scoff at such notions of a continued existence beyond death.

Near-Death Experiences: At the Threshold of Death

Stories of travel to another world can be found in virtually all cultures. The traveler may be a hero, shaman, prophet, king, or even an ordinary mortal who "passes through the gates of death and returns with a message for the living." Such journeys include the heavenly ascent of the prophet Muhammad and the heavenly visions of Enoch and the Apostle Paul, as well as Gilgamesh's epic adventures to the underworld and the descent of the goddess Inanna. Carol Zaleski identifies three forms of the otherworld journey: (1) the journey to the underworld, (2) the ascent to higher worlds, and (3) the fantastic voyage.[44] The common thread of all such journeys, says Zaleski, is the "story," which is shaped not only by universal laws of symbolic experience, but also by the transitory experiences of a given, local culture.

The publication in 1975 of Raymond Moody's *Life After Life* sparked a renewed interest in otherworld journeys and, specifically, in near-death experiences (NDEs). These stories of people who have come back from the edge of death describe fascinating glimpses of a paranormal, or scientifically unexplainable, order of existence. Some interpret NDEs as indicating that the human personality survives death; others believe that these phenomena are psychological or neurophysiological responses to the stress of facing a life-threatening danger. Despite legitimate questions about how NDEs should be interpreted, we can, nevertheless, be nonjudgmental toward the survivors who report having such experiences.[45]

NDEs: A Composite Picture

Significantly, although researchers differ in their interpretations of near-death experiences, their studies reveal a strikingly similar picture of such phenomena. Let us imagine what might be experienced during an overwhelming encounter with death, resulting perhaps from an accident or from a life-threatening illness or acute medical crisis. Perhaps, almost beyond awareness, you hear a voice saying that you're not going to make it, you're going to die.

It's like a dream, but somehow the experience seems more real than ordinary waking consciousness. Vision and hearing are extremely acute; sensory perceptions are heightened. You experience your thought processes as clear, rational. Yet you no longer seem tied to a body. As you become aware of this feeling of disconnectedness, you notice yourself separate from the body, floating free. From a corner of the room, you look down at the body below and recognize it as your own.

You feel a little lonely, drifting in space, yet there is a sense of calm, a serenity that was rarely if ever experienced in the body. All the usual constructs of time and space seem irrelevant, unreal. As you feel yourself moving farther away from the once-familiar world of your now-dead body, you enter a darkness, a tunnel, some transitional stage in your journey.

At this point you notice a light, more brilliant than any imagined during your earthly existence, beckoning, drawing you onward, its golden hues heralding your approach to the other side.

Now you experience the whole of your previous life in the body, a nearly instantaneous matrix of flashbacks, impressions of your former life, events, places, people: your life reviewed and projected on the transparent screen of consciousness.

You enter the light, glimpsing a world of unimaginable and unspeakable brilliance. A loved one greets you, or perhaps you become aware of Jesus or Moses or another being of ineffable grace. Only now you realize that you cannot enter fully into this light, not yet, not this time.

Dimensions of Near-Death Experiences

For most people who have experienced such phenomena as those encountered in your imaginary journey, the return to the body is a blank. Others report feeling a jolt or becoming aware of pain upon return to consciousness in the body. Many emerge from their experience with a greater appreciation of life, a determination to make better use of the opportunities presented to them. Typically, they feel more self-confident, more able to cope with the vicissitudes of life. Loving relationships become more important and material comforts less important. Researcher Kenneth Ring says that the typical near-death experiencer "has achieved a sense of what is important in life and strives to live in accordance with his understanding of what matters."[46] In some respects, near-death experiences share many features with the "conversion" stories associated with life-changing religious experiences.

Palace of the Doges, Venice

In Hieronymous Bosch's portrayal of the Ascent into the Empyrean—the highest heaven in medieval cosmology—the soul, purged of its impurities, approaches the end of its long journey and union with the Divine.

Our imaginary, composite picture of a near-death experience incorporates a number of elements that are in fact only rarely experienced. Whereas 60 percent of the respondents in Ring's sample experienced feelings of peace and well-being, 37 percent experienced themselves as separate from their bodies, 23 percent experienced the entry into a dark tunnel or transitional stage, 16 percent experienced seeing a bright light, and 10 percent experienced themselves actually entering the light, though only for a "peek" into their unearthly surroundings. Ring found that NDEs resulting from illness were more likely to be complete—to have all of these characteristic core elements—than were NDEs resulting from accidents. However, over half the accident victims experienced panoramic memory, or life review, compared to only 16 percent of the respondents whose experiences were related to illness or attempted suicide.

The *panoramic life review*, in itself an interesting feature of near-death experiences, may consist of vivid, almost instantaneous visions of the person's whole life or "selected highlights" of it.[47] The life review may appear in an orderly sequence, or it may seem to come "all at once." In any case, it apparently occurs without any conscious control or effort by the experiencer. Less frequently, the life review incorporates visions about the future, with experiencers visualizing their death, the reactions of friends and relatives, and events at the funeral.

The encounter with a presence—a feature of NDEs that is commonly related to the "tunnel" experience—usually involves seeing deceased relatives or friends, or sensing some religious presence. Although the presence thus encountered usually appears to involve some representation of the "higher self," in some instances the presence is an entity that seems otherwise.[48] William Serdahely reports the case of an eight-year-old boy who was "comforted by two of his family's pets who had died prior to the incident."[49] Such encounters are sometimes linked to the decision to return, to terminate the experience. Some near-death experiencers believe that the decision to return to the present earthly life is made for them, others that they arrived at this decision themselves. Usually, the decision to return is related in some way to unfinished business or responsibilities that the person believes must be attended to before his or her death.

Although most NDEs include profound feelings of joy, peace, and cosmic unity, some are distressing and frightening.[50] These "hellish" NDEs may include imagery and sounds of torment, and sometimes demonic beings. In some cases, an initial period of terror is followed by peaceful resolution. In other cases, the aftermath of the NDE brings a sense of emptiness and despair. In yet other instances, a benevolent guide accompanies the experiencer through the disconcerting experience. Some NDE researchers postulate that frightening NDEs may be a truncated version of the typically radiant near-death experience; that is, hellish NDEs are *incomplete* NDEs.[51] Another explanation highlights the fact that many saintly persons and mystics—St. Teresa of Avila and St. John of the Cross, to name but two examples—reported frightening visions while engaged in deep prayer or meditation. Thus, the frightening or hellish NDE might be viewed as a "purification experience," a kind of "dark night of the soul," the phrase used by St. John of the Cross to describe his religious experiences. Further investigation into distressing NDEs may expand our understanding of near-death experiences generally.

In broad outline, the description provided in our imaginary near-death experience is typical of reports in the literature. Thus, it is possible to identify four core elements that appear to be characteristic of NDEs: The person (1) hears the news of his or her death; (2) departs from the body; (3) encounters significant others; and (4) returns to the body.

How should the data regarding NDEs be interpreted? What are we to make of these experiences?

Interpreting Near-Death Experiences

Near-death experiences are clearly a fascinating field of inquiry. To some they suggest (or confirm) hoped-for possibilities. Others view NDEs as a fertile field for research into the nature of human consciousness. To yet others, NDEs illustrate the remarkable psychodynamic processes that surface when annihilation of the self is threatened. An important precipitator of the near-death experience is the belief that one is dying—whether or not one is in fact close to death.[52] Although the general features of NDEs tend not to be matters of dispute, such experiences elicit widely divergent interpretations.[53] Some of the major theories devised to explain near-death experiences are listed in Table 14-1.

For early Hawaiians, their observations of *apparent* death, or persons who had "left the body prematurely," were interpreted in accordance with beliefs about the ancestor-gods.[54] On each island, there was a special promontory overlooking the sea; this was the *leina*, or leaping place, of the soul or spirit on its journey to the realm of the ancestors. If, on its way to the *leina*, a soul was met by an ancestor-god and sent back, the body would revive. Otherwise the ancestor-god would lead it safely to and over the *leina*; once beyond that hurdle, the soul was safe with the ancestors. Notice that a specific place was designated as the point of transition between life and death.

For various reasons (often, though not always, having to do with a person's behavior), an ancestor-god might delay a soul's acceptance into eternity. For instance, if a person died before his or her earthly work was done, the ancestor-god conducted the soul back to the body. "Sometimes when it is not yet time to die," reports Mary Pukui, "the relatives [ancestors] stand in the road and make you go back. Then the breath returns to the body with a crowing sound, *o'o-a-moa*." After such a person had been fully restored to life, he or she took a purifying bath and was welcomed back into the family.

Albert Heim, a Swiss geologist and mountain climber, is considered to have been the first investigator to systematically gather data on near-death experiences.[55] Working at the turn of the century, Heim interviewed some thirty skiers and climbers who had been involved in accidents resulting in

TABLE *14-1*   *Theories of the Near-Death Experience*

1. Neuropsychological theories:
    A. *Temporal lobe paroxysm,* or limbic lobe syndrome: Seizurelike neural discharges in the temporal lobe or, more generally, in the limbic system.
    B. *Cerebral anoxia,* or oxygen deprivation: Shortage of oxygen in the brain.
    C. *Endorphin release:* Release of certain neurotransmitters associated with analgesic (pain-killing) effects and a sense of psychological well-being.
    D. *Massive cortical disinhibition:* Loss of control over the random activity of the central nervous system.
    E. *False sight:* Hallucinatory imagery arising from structures in the brain and nervous system.
    F. *Drugs:* Side-effects.
    G. *Sensory deprivation.*
2. Psychological theories:
    A. *Depersonalization:* Psychological detachment from one's body; in this case, a defensive reaction to the perceived threat of death. May be accompanied by hyperalertness.
    B. *Motivated fantasy:* A type of "defensive" fantasy that basically proposes that experiencers have an impression of surviving death because they desire to survive death.
    C. *Archetypes:* Images associated with various elements of the near-death experience are "wired" into the brain as mythological archetypes of our common humanity.
3. Metaphysical theories:
    A. *Soul travel:* Transitional journey of the soul or spirit to another mode of existence or realm of reality (e.g., "heaven"); proof of life after death.
    B. *Psychic vision:* Glimpses into another mode of reality, though not necessarily providing proof of soul-survival after death.

paranormal experiences. Heim's subjects experienced such phenomena as detachment from their bodies and panoramic memory, or life review.

The data compiled by Heim were subsequently interpreted by psychoanalytic pioneer Oskar Pfister, who explained these experiences as being caused by shock and depersonalization in the face of impending death. In other words, when a person's life is threatened, psychological defense mechanisms may come into play, giving rise to the phenomena associated with NDEs. The psychological approach initiated by Pfister continues to be elaborated by a number of present-day researchers, who believe that NDEs can be explained satisfactorily without hypothesizing life after death. Such explanations include suggestions of a possible connection between NDEs and dream states, hallucinations, side effects of pharmacological agents, and various neurophysiological causes.

The psychological model described by Russell Noyes and Roy Kletti posits that defensive reactions lead to depersonalization in the face of mortal danger.[56] Their model is perhaps the most comprehensive explanation of this type offered thus far. According to this model, NDEs can be broken down into three stages: resistance, life review, and transcendence. The first stage, *resistance,*

It is wonderful that five thousand years have now elapsed since the creation of the world, and still it is undecided whether or not there has ever been an instance of the spirit of any person appearing after death. All argument is against it; but all belief is for it.

James Boswell, *Life of Johnson*

involves recognition of the danger, fear of it and struggle against it, and finally acceptance of death as imminent. This acceptance, or surrender, marks the beginning of the second stage, *life review*. As the self is detached from its bodily representation, panoramic memories occur, often in almost simultaneous succession, appearing to encompass a person's entire life. This experience of life review is often related to a sense of affirmation of the meaning of one's existence and its integration into the universal order of things. The third stage, *transcendence*, evolves from the increased detachment from one's individual existence and is marked by an increasingly cosmic or transcendental consciousness replacing the more limited ego- or self-identity.

Experiences such as calm detachment, heightened sensory awareness, panoramic memory or life review, and mystical consciousness represent the ego's protective response when confronted by its own demise. In other words, the threat of death can set into motion various psychological processes that provide an escape for the ego, the experiencing self. Because these processes dissociate the experiencing self from the body, the threat of death is perceived as being a threat only to the *body*, not to the "self" that is doing the perceiving. Although the psychological interpretation of NDEs does not necessarily invalidate their possible spiritual significance, these findings have been used by some to support a reductionist approach that leaves no room for metaphysical interpretation.

In contrast to researchers such as those just discussed, others have followed the lines of inquiry established in the late nineteenth century by parapsychologists. These investigators believe that to adequately understand NDEs one must be willing to go beyond the usual boundaries of scientific inquiry. In short, the researchers must be prepared to accept the possibility, which is not scientifically verifiable, that NDEs are what they seem to be—that is, experiences of states of consciousness that transcend the death of the body. Thus, such researchers tend to accept anecdotal reports of NDEs at face value and try to construct a model of reality that will account for such experiences.

Near-death experiences, they say, teach us that the *appearance* of death is not at all like the *experience* of death. A Gallup poll conducted during the 1980s showed that about two-thirds of all adult Americans answered "yes" to the question, "Do you believe in life after death?"[57] Only one-fifth, however, thought that life after death would be proven scientifically. (About 8 million people have reported near-death experiences.) Of course, those approaching the question of survival after death with their minds already made up in the affirmative have no difficulty finding corroborative evidence. One book on the subject begins with the assertion that "human beings survive physical death," which is supported by accounts of apparitions, hauntings, out-of-body experiences, deathbed visions, resuscitations, possession experiences, reincarnation claims, and mediumistic communications or "accounts from the realm beyond death." It is unlikely that such works accomplish much more than to confirm the preconceptions of the already decided.

A more objective approach is reflected in the work of Karlis Osis and Erlandur Haraldsson, whose cross-cultural studies led them to conclude that the evidence from NDEs strongly suggests life after death.[58] In their view, "Neither medical, nor psychological, nor cultural conditioning can explain away deathbed visions." One of the points put forward in support of this conclusion is the observation that in some deathbed visions there are apparitions that are contrary to the experiencer's expectations. Osis and Haraldsson mention "apparitions of persons the person thought were still living, but who in fact were dead," as well as apparitions that do not conform to cultural stereotypes, as with dying children who are "surprised to see 'angels' without wings."

In the attempt to understand NDEs, two distinct explanations have been offered. The first postulates that near-death experiences indicate survival after death. Death is seen as the transition to another mode of existence. According to this hypothesis, the experiences of incorporeal entities and the glimpses of postmortem states of being result from extrasensory perception of objective phenomena. In other words, NDEs are what they seem to be: experiences of life after death.

The second explanation postulates that death is the destruction of the personality. Near-death experiences are explained as resulting from some dysfunction of the brain or nervous system, or as resulting from the ego's defensive reaction to a life-threatening situation. Thus, what are perceived as visions of an after-death existence actually arise from memories stored in the brain that express the desires, expectations, and fears evoked by an encounter with mortal danger or a threat to the self.

Each explanation offers a model, or representation, of "how the world works." One's own model of reality is likely to cause more favorable treatment of one or the other of these interpretations. Louis Appleby, writing in the *British Medical Journal*, says that all of the explanations put forward to explain NDEs share one attribute: Each requires a form of faith.[59] The explanation that best suits your own perception of how things work is likely to be accepted most readily. There remains, however, another approach to understanding the significance of near-death experiences—namely, the possibility that both propositions are valid: There is life after death and there is also a psychological phenomenon involving various defense mechanisms whereby the personality is radically altered as the transition from one state to the next is negotiated. Carol Zaleski points to the possibility that the various explanations of NDEs, taken together, might result in a comprehensive theory. "We need to find a middle path," she says, "between the extremes of dismissing near-death

"Calvin and Hobbes," drawing by Bill Watterson, © 1990 Universal Press Syndicate

experience as 'nothing but' and embracing it as 'proof.' "[60] In a similar vein, Herman Feifel says:

> What is somewhat disquieting is the claim by some that near-death experiences are evidence for and proof of the existence of an after-life. There may well be life after death, but jumping to that conclusion from reported near-death experiences reflects more a leap of faith than judicious scientific assessment. This in no way minimizes the reality of these occurrences for the people who declare them. I just think that in weighing the evidence in this area we have less far-fetched and more parsimonious interpretations within the canons of science that can explain these phenomena. What strikes me about many of these out-of-body reports is the hunger for meaning and purpose they suggest in this age of faltering faith.[61]

As mentioned earlier, modern society is characterized by a fragmented religious situation. Perhaps, as Zaleski suggests, the near-death experience can serve to "remind us of the need for orientation, the need to have a consecrated cosmos as the setting for a spiritual journey."[62] But, she adds, "it cannot provide the means or material to accomplish this." Thus, however one decides to interpret near-death experiences, gleaning whatever spiritual meaning they might have to convey ultimately throws us "back on our devices, our own partial and provisional solutions."

In considering how to interpret reports of near-death experiences, one should remember that, indeed, these are *near-death* experiences, not, strictly speaking, experiences after death. The reality that such experiences open to investigation may turn out to be much vaster than, and quite different from, what we suppose if we consider them only as glimpses of "another world." Indeed, the matrices for such experiences may lie within the depths of human consciousness. As Charles Garfield states: "If the various Eastern and Western religious traditions and parapsychological disciplines are correct, the period just before physical death is one of maximum receptivity to altered state realities."[63] It should also be noted that many people experience clinical death and, after being resuscitated, simply have nothing to report.

Robert Kastenbaum cautions that one needs to be careful of a too-ready acceptance of the "fantastic voyage" implied by most life-after-death accounts.[64] He says:

> The happily-ever-after theme threatens to draw attention away from the actual situations of the dying persons, their loved ones, and their care givers over the days, weeks, and months preceding death. What happens up to the point of the fabulous transition from life to death recedes into the background. This could not be more unfortunate. The background, after all, is where these people are actually living until death comes.

Finally, three points expressed by Charles Garfield, after extensive work with dying persons, should be considered:[65]

1. Not everyone dies a blissful, accepting death.
2. Context is a powerful variable in such altered-state experiences as those involving hypnosis, meditation, psychedelics, and schizophrenia. It may be that a supportive environment for the dying person is an important factor in determining whether the outcome is a positive altered-state experience for the dying.
3. The "happily ever after" stance toward death may represent a form of denial when what is really needed by the dying is a demonstration of real concern and real caring in their present experience.

Whatever the beliefs that one may hold about life after death, as Garfield says, "Let us have the courage to realize that death often will be a bitter pill to swallow."

Death Themes in Dreams and Psychedelic Experiences

Besides the intimations about what may follow physical death associated with "classic" near-death experiences, fascinating hints about afterlife possibilities have also been communicated through "death dreams" and experiences borne from the use of psychedelic or mind-altering drugs.

Based on an extensive study of death dreams from a Jungian perspective, Marie-Louise von Franz says that, in comparison with near-death experiences, which tend to be schematic and more specifically culture-bound, the death imagery in dreams is richer in graphic detail and more subtle.[66] Among older people, dreams often appear to be psychically preparing them for impending death by symbolically indicating "the end of bodily life and the explicit continuation of psychic life after death." Using the medium of dreams, the unconscious communicates a comforting message—namely, that there *is* an afterlife. Franz argues that such dreams cannot simply be interpreted as "wish-fulfillment" because they also predict the end of physical existence, sometimes quite brutally and unequivocally:

> All of the dreams of people who are facing death indicate that the unconscious . . . prepares consciousness not for a definite end but for a profound

Death and life, usually considered to be irreconcilable opposites, appear to actually be dialectically interrelated. Living fully and with maximum awareness every moment of one's life leads to an accepting and reconciled attitude toward death. Conversely, such an approach to human existence requires that we come to terms with our mortality and the impermanence of existence.

Stanislav Grof and Joan Halifax,
The Human Encounter with Death

transformation and for a kind of continuation of the life process which, however, is unimaginable to everyday consciousness.[67]

Death dreams incorporate a great variety of alchemical and mythological motifs, including themes associated with the growth of vegetation or flowering plants; the divine marriage of the soul with the cosmos; travel through a dark, narrow passageway, or through fire or water, to new birth; sacrifice or transformation of the old body; shifting ego- or soul-identity; and resurrection.

The journey through a dark passageway toward "a light at the end of the tunnel" is a common motif not only in dreams and NDEs, but in numerous mythological traditions. Among the Egyptians, for example, the sun was viewed as the goal of the soul's journey along the pathway of the dead. Indeed, many mythologies embody a comparison of the sun's path with the mystery of life and death. Interpreted psychologically, says von Franz, the sun symbolizes the source of *awareness*, of becoming conscious. "This meaning of life," she says, "also lies behind the widespread custom of lighting candles and letting them burn in mortuary rooms and on tombs and graves," which is a form of "analogy magic through which new life and an awakening to new consciousness is granted to the deceased."[68]

Turning to death imagery in connection with the use of psychedelics, it is interesting to note that, although LSD (lysergic acid diethylamide) was first synthesized in 1938 by the Swiss chemist Albert Hoffman, its chemical action on the brain is still not completely understood.[69] Nevertheless, its amplifying and catalyzing effects on the mind are well-documented. From the earliest studies of LSD, researchers noticed that it activated "unconscious material from various deep levels of the personality."[70] Most notably, it seemed to inaugurate a "shattering encounter" with certain critical aspects of human existence: birth, decay, and death.

This encounter often evokes a profound emotional and philosophical crisis, causing the person taking the drug to question the meaning of existence and his or her values in life. It seems to open up areas of religious and spiritual experience that are intrinsic to the human personality but independent of a person's cultural or religious background.

In the early 1960s, Eric Kast of the Chicago Medical School began pioneering studies of the analgesic effects of LSD and other psychedelic substances on patients suffering intense pain.[71] Besides relieving the symptoms of physical pain and discomfort, LSD therapy also diminished emotional symptoms, such as depression, anxiety, tension, insomnia, and psychological withdrawal. LSD seemed to accomplish these results by altering the patient's learned response to pain—that is, the patient's anticipation of pain based on past experiences. By becoming free of this conditioning, the patient was more oriented to the present and thus able to respond to sensations as they were actually experienced rather than to an image of pain that had grown more and more discomforting over time. Noting that pain is a composite phenomenon that has both a neurophysiological component (the pain sensation) and a psychological component (the pain affect), Stanislav Grof and Joan Halifax conclude that the primary influence of psychedelic therapy seems to be in modifying the psychological component.

Perhaps even more significant than the diminution of pain was the change of attitude toward death and dying among patients. After the psychedelic session, patients typically displayed a diminished fear of death and less anxiety about the life-threatening implications of the illness. According to Grof and Halifax, "Dying persons who had transcendental experiences developed a deep belief in the ultimate unity of all creation; they often experienced themselves as integral parts of it, including their disease and the often painful situations they were facing."[72]

Many patients exhibited a greater responsiveness to their families and their environment. Self-respect and morale were enhanced, and they showed a greater appreciation of the subtleties of everyday life. The fact that LSD induced such transcendental experiences in randomly selected subjects was considered to be strong evidence that "matrices for such experiences exist in the unconscious as a normal constituent of the human personality."[73]

As with the phenomena discussed in connection with near-death experiences, the psychedelic experience typically includes phenomena that are not scientifically explainable. Grof and Halifax point out that persons "unsophisticated in anthropology and mythology experience images, episodes, and even entire thematic sequences that bear a striking resemblance to the descriptions of the posthumous journey of the soul and the death-rebirth mysteries of various cultures."[74] As with near-death experiences, the result is usually a significantly altered outlook with respect to the meaning of life and death. The evidence accumulated through reports of near-death experiences as well as psychedelic experiences have led some researchers to the view that modern science should broaden its perspective on the nature of human consciousness. Stanislav Grof says, "Reality is always larger and more complex than the most elaborate and encompassing theory."[75]

Beliefs About Death: A Wall or a Door?

In the final analysis, then, what shall we believe about personal immortality or the afterlife? Is death's aftermath the joyful and ultimately fulfilling experience it seems to be from reports of near-death experiences? Or are these experiences psychological projections, wish-fulfilling fantasies that mask

Now Let the Weeping Cease (Hymn)

Now let the weeping cease
Let no one mourn again
The love of God will bring you
    peace
There is no end

The Gospel at Colonus

the terror of confronting one's own demise? Furthermore, what shall we say about traditional religious understandings? Do their various concepts of the afterlife have some basis in reality? Or should we adopt a strictly scientific approach to such questions? The two basic philosophical perspectives regarding death and the afterlife can be summarized as follows: Death is either a *wall* or it is a *door*.[76]

In discussing these two views, Clyde Nabe notes that, in the first view, death is seen as the "disorganization of the functional structure of the matter which is a particular human body," and thus is the "cessation of all possibility for the person who dies."[77] In short, death is a *wall*, not a door. In the second perspective, the possibility arises that "what is real need not necessarily be equated with what is material"; thus the dissolution of the body need not be viewed as necessarily resulting in the dissolution of the human person. In other words, death is a *door*, not a wall.

We can imagine many variations on these two basic positions regarding what happens at death. Indeed, the doctrines of various religions and the explanations offered for paranormal experiences of death are just such variations. For example, stating the Christian perspective, we could say that death appears to be a wall, but at some time in the future—at the Resurrection—it turns out to have been a door. The Hindu concept of reincarnation would suggest that death is a door, not a wall. Buddhists might respond that death is both a door and a wall, and is neither. The conventional psychological explanation of NDEs might seem an argument in favor of the position that death is a wall that is experienced as a door. The transpersonal and parapsychologies, however, might suggest that the door and the wall are simply alternative ways of experiencing the same reality.

In promulgating its findings on the assumptions and principles of spiritual care, the Spiritual Care Work Group of the International Work Group on Death, Dying and Bereavement emphasized that "dying is more than a biological occurrence. It is a human, social, and spiritual event."[78] However, "too often the spiritual dimension of patients is neglected." A close relationship between religion and health has existed since ancient times. Only in the comparatively recent past has the spiritual dimension of health care been largely shunted aside in favor of a more mechanistic or scientific model. A number of practitioners, however, are now calling for a revitalized concern with their patients' spiritual health. Clifford Kuhn, for example, posits a comprehensive health model involving body, mind, society/community, and spirituality.[79] It is being increasingly recognized that caregivers need to acknowledge the spiritual component of patient care and provide appropriate resources for those who wish them. In carrying out such aims, it goes without saying that each person's spiritual beliefs and preferences must be respected.[80]

What we believe about death and the afterlife can influence the actions taken when we or others near death. For example, if we adhere to the materialist view, seeing death as a wall, we may insist that life-sustaining efforts be carried out to the end. Conversely, if we conceive of continued consciousness after death, we might prefer that the final hours of life on earth be spent preparing for a transition into another mode of existence. As Nabe says, "How we respond to the death of someone else, and to our own death, is thus dependent on much broader philosophical questions."[81]

Similarly, the bereaved may find solace in their beliefs about what happens after death. The person who views death as the end may feel reassured that the suffering experienced during this life ends at death. Someone else may find comfort in the belief that the personality survives physical death. By understanding our own beliefs about death, says Nabe, we are able to "care more adequately for each other when death—wall or door—comes to those we love."

Further Readings

Carl B. Becker. *Breaking the Circle: Death and the Afterlife in Buddhism.* Carbondale: Southern Illinois University Press, 1993.

Charles Belyea and Steven Tainer. *Dragon's Play: A New Taoist Transmission of the Complete Experience of Human Life.* Berkeley: Great Circle Lifeworks, 1991.

Alan E. Bernstein. *The Formation of Hell: Death and Retribution in the Ancient and Early Christian Worlds.* Ithaca, N.Y.: Cornell University Press, 1993.

John Bowker. *The Meanings of Death.* New York: Cambridge University Press, 1991.

Murray J. Harris. *Raised Immortal: Resurrection and Immortality in the New Testament.* Grand Rapids, Mich.: Eerdmans, 1985.

Kenneth Kramer. *The Sacred Art of Dying: How World Religions Understand Death.* Mahwah, N.J.: Paulist Press, 1988.

Geddes MacGregor. *Images of Afterlife: Beliefs from Antiquity to Modern Times.* New York: Paragon House, 1992.

Ronald W. Neufeldt, ed. *Karma & Rebirth: Post-Classical Developments.* Albany: State University of New York Press, 1986.

Jack Riemer, ed. *Wrestling with an Angel: Jewish Insights on Death and Mourning.* New York: Schocken, 1995.

J. I. Smith and Y. Haddad. *The Islamic Understanding of Death and Resurrection.* Albany: State University of New York Press, 1981.

Carol G. Zaleski. *Otherworld Journeys: Accounts of Near-Death Experiences in Medieval and Modern Times.* New York: Oxford University Press, 1988.

Photojournalist W. Eugene Smith's children appear in his 1946 photo-graph "The Walk to Paradise Garden," the first taken by Smith after two years of inactivity and numerous operations to make him sound again after multiple wounds received in the Pacific during World War II. Smith said he was determined that his first frame successfully "speak of a gentle moment of spirited purity in contrast to the depraved savagery I had raged against with my war photographs."

The Path Ahead:
Personal and Social Choices

Death may be devalued, even denied for a time, but it cannot be eluded. In telling the story of "The Mortal King," a Chinese folk tale, Allan Chinen draws attention to the fact that the human desire for immortality has its own pitfalls. Surveying his realm one day, the King is struck by the awesome thought that someday he will die and lose it all. "I wish we could live forever!" the King exclaims. "That would be wonderful!" Encouraged by his friends, the King fantasizes how great it would be if they were never to grow old and die. Of all his companions, only one refrained from delighting in this prospect. Instead, he bowed to the King and explained, "If we all lived forever as you suggest, why, then, all the great heroes of history would still live among us; compared to them, we would be fit only to plow the fields or be clerks in the provinces."[1]

In our complex relationship with death, we are both survivors and experiencers. In previous chapters we have seen that there can be many different attitudes toward death and dying. Death may be seen as a threat or as a catalyst provoking us to greater awareness and creativity in life. Death may seem the ignominious end to even the best of human accomplishment, or it may be seen as a welcome respite from life's sufferings. Death holds many meanings.

One student in a death and dying class said, "Confronting death has put me in touch with life." Acknowledging the impact of death in our lives can awaken us to the

The Illusion of Order

The world is not an ordered place. It is a chaotic place and random events occur in this chaotic world all the time. We fool ourselves into thinking that the world is an ordered place. That's how we get up in morning and how we go to bed at night, because we are ordering the world in some fashion and it is just an illusion, an illusion that keeps us going. If we didn't pretend that's the way it is, we wouldn't be able to function. We created a nice little world that we work in; we sleep from night to morning and we eat three meals a day. We know about gravity, and we know about the elements, but in fact we don't know anything. The world is just a massive pile of molecules zipping around, knocking into each other. At any time, one of these random events can occur. Earthquakes and floods and other acts of God, being symbols of all that, that all our houses with all of their roofs can be blown off, airplanes could crash into apartment buildings, babies can be taken away from their mothers. A baby that you've waited six years to conceive can go completely wrong inside. It's very, very difficult to go back to an ordered, normal life after this because my illusion of order has been shattered.

Julia

preciousness of life. This insight can lead to a greater appreciation of the relationships in one's life. Learning about death can also bring insights concerning the death of old notions of self, as one grows beyond limiting concepts of "who I am."

Death is inseparable from the whole of human experience. The study of death and dying touches on the past, the present, and the future. It takes account of individual acts as well as customs of entire societies. The study of death and dying leads naturally to the arena of political decision, and it ultimately brings us to choices of an emphatically personal nature. Death education is germane to the sphere of social relationships as well as to the confrontation with mortality that comes in the most private, personal moments of solitude and introspection.

Think about your own relationship to death. What place does death have in your life? What kinds of meanings does death hold for you? Are death and dying compartmentalized in a category all their own, or are they woven into the fabric of human experience?

In this chapter we touch upon some of the ways in which what we learn about death impinges on individual and social experience. Rather than providing answers, our aim will be to stimulate inquiry, to raise questions, to speculate about the path ahead.

The Value of Exploring Death and Dying

Taking a course or reading a book about death and dying offers an opportunity to take death "out of the closet" and examine it from many

I say, "Why should a spirited mortal feel proud, when like a swift, fleet meteor or fast-flying cloud, man passes through life to his rest in the grave?" They've asked me, "How do I feel?" I told them that there's nothing to it; you do things the way they ought to be done. I don't see anything to be proud about. It's pretty difficult for a man to feel proud when knowing as he does the short space of time he's here and all paths, even those of our greatest glory, lead but to the grave. So it is very difficult to feel proud when Death says this. You're here today and gone sometimes today.

"A Very Long Conversation with
James Van Der Zee at the Age of Ninety-One,"
in *The Harlem Book of the Dead*

perspectives. Possibly you are making new choices in your life as a result of your personal exploration of death. Reflecting on the study of death and dying, one student remarked, "The thought of death had always created a lot of fear; now I find that there's something very fascinating about exploring my own feelings about death and the way that society relates to death." Often, the study of death brings insights into past experiences in one's life. One woman said, "I see now what a big part denial and mutual pretense played in my family's experience of death; the subject of death had really been taboo." Another said, "I was surprised to find how many events in my own life had carried the same kind of emotional impact as a death. Divorce, separation, illness, disappointment—all meant coping with grief, loneliness, fear, and sadness in much the same way as when dealing with a death."

As you think about the various topics covered in this book, what do you notice concerning your understanding of death? Has learning about death and dying expanded your perspective or altered your attitude toward death? Do the terms *death* and *dying* elicit the same patterns of thought and emotion as when you began your study?

"When I used to think about my own death," a student remarked, "I used to slam the door, thinking of all the things I still wanted to do in my lifetime. Now, I've become a bit more calm, a bit more balanced about it." Another said, "Before I got involved in studying death, I was really uptight about death and dying, especially my own death, even though I haven't had many personal encounters with death. Now I feel that facing my own death is not as difficult, really, as being a survivor of other people's deaths." For some, investigation of death and dying allows a more accurate perception of what anyone can do to protect or be responsible for another. A parent said, "I've learned something about letting go where my children are concerned. No matter how much you might wish it were otherwise, you can never shield your loved ones from everything."

Responding to this awareness, one student said, "I learned how important it is to appreciate people while you've got them." Becoming aware of death can

I attended your Dealing with Death and Dying class May 10 and 11. You excused me at 1:00, May 11, so that I could go to a function that I needed to attend. I agreed to write notes on an article on cancer to compensate for the class time that I'd miss.

At the same time I was driving home from the class, my Mother was admitted to a Midwestern hospital for internal bleeding due to her accelerated cancerous condition. I left the Bay Area soon after and arrived in Iowa to deal with the reality of death.

Comments on the article don't seem as important to me, now, as some other comments I'd like to make. They concern the necessity of dealing with death and dying.

Had it not been for your class, I would have had more severe problems dealing with all the things death causes us to deal with. The openness of the people in class helped me work through some of the pain I was experiencing as I knew that my Mother didn't have long to live. The class helped me during the time the mortician sat with us and helped us work out the business details, and it helped me through the Midwestern Protestant wake. I was helped as I remembered to make sure that we got what we wanted and were allowed to say good-byes in ways we wanted. I was able to help my family think clearly about the needs they had so that after Mother was removed from us, we would not say "if only."

                                          A student in a Death and Dying class

focus attention on the importance in relationships of taking care of unfinished business, saying the things that need to be said, and not being anxious about those things that do not. As one student expressed it, her study of death and dying had impressed upon her a sense of "the precariousness of life."

Recognizing that the preciousness of the human situation is revealed not only in major changes—such as those brought about by death—but also in the less noticed changes experienced in daily life, one can choose to be attentive to the things and people that are most highly valued. As Thomas Attig points out, coming to terms with our own personal finiteness and mortality can be understood as a grieving process.[2] Such self-mourning is really a lifelong process of coming to terms with impermanence, uncertainty, and vulnerability—qualities that are inherent in being mortal.

As more people willingly confront issues surrounding death and dying, and examine the options for themselves, changes are occurring throughout society. Examples are the establishment of such helping mechanisms as hospices and suicide intervention programs, as well as other support groups that aid individuals and families in crisis. As death is subjected to a less fearful scrutiny, there is movement—individually and as a society—toward gaining knowledge that can be helpful in dealing with death intelligently and compassionately. Think about the personal and social implications of death and dying. Have your previous opinions on such issues as euthanasia, funerals and body disposition, and war been confirmed? Or have they changed as a result of your studies?

For some, the close examination of death brings insights that help to dissipate or resolve long-held feelings of guilt or blame attached to grief about a loved one's death. The encounter with death that comes through study can open up new and creative possibilities that result in an easier, more comfortable relationship with others and with life itself. The study of death and dying can help to put previously unsettling experiences into perspective.

The notions that may be present at the beginning of a personal exploration of death and dying are expressed in the following statement:

> When I first began to recognize the seriousness of death and dying, I fled from it in fear, although I didn't realize what I was doing. Emotionally, it was harder than I had expected. But I learned that people do survive their losses, and I now know why they are called "survivors." I also learned a lot about myself, not all pleasant. A lot of my learning occurred amidst avoidance and trepidation. I thought about things that I had neglected for a long time . . . all my old concepts of death, shadowed in images of hells and old horror movies.

For one man who had felt frustrated, resentful, and guilty about his brother's death twenty years earlier, the study of death provided an opportunity to open up unexpressed and unresolved grief about a number of close family deaths. As the "stored tears" began to be expressed, he summed up the benefit of his exploration of death: "It feels so good to get rid of that ache."

For some, the study of death and dying brings benefits related to professional concerns. One nurse said: "When death occurs on the ward, people often think, 'Oh, well, you're a nurse; it shouldn't bother you.' But it does. . . . I really miss the patient; it's a real loss." A ward clerk in a hospital emergency room described the new and more helpful choices she could use in relating to survivors:

> My desk is in the same area with the survivors of an ER [emergency room] death. I used to feel a pain right in the pit of my stomach, wondering what to say to them. I thought I should be able to comfort them in some way, that I should somehow offer them words of wisdom. But now I don't feel that way. I've learned how important it is to simply listen, to be supportive just by being there, instead of trying to find some words that will magically make it all go away.

Others find the study of death and dying academically intriguing. The avenues of exploration into other cultures or into one's own society opened up through such study can be a rapid means of gaining insight into what is essential about a society's values and concepts. Learning about the meaning of death in feudal Japan, for example, provides the student of Japanese culture an appreciation that goes beyond the usual aesthetic or historic approach to cross-cultural understanding. Concepts about what constitutes a "good" death or about immortality reveal a great deal about the tenor and form of a culture's daily life as well as its highest achievements.

© Carol A. Foote

Culture and individual personality shape our attitudes toward death. What we understand of death and what meanings we ascribe to it become significant to the extent that we construct a meaningful relationship with the experience of death and dying in our lives. This grave marker expresses a memorialization that is consonant with the life styles of both the deceased and her survivors.

Cultural attitudes toward death are reflected in social programs for the aged and medical care of the dying. The willingness of a society to engage in activities that pose risks for the well-being of its citizens also demonstrates something of the consensus with regard to the value of human life. Funeral customs reflect a society's attitudes toward death and intimate relationships.

Investigating a society's relationship with death makes available a wealth of information to the person with an inquiring mind and an interest in discerning the larger patterns of belief and behavior.

New Directions in Death Education

The curricula of death education and standards for measuring outcome are still being defined. A clear sense of continuity and common tradition is still being developed. Although this issue is perhaps most pressing for those in academic settings, it applies as well to persons working as counselors, caregivers, and in other such capacities within communities.

The question of accountability in death education has been difficult to address, partly because such education is conducted in a variety of settings, often with differing methodologies and goals. For example, should the aim of death education be to *alleviate* discomfort and anxiety about dying and death? If acceptance of death is thought to be a superior posture to denial, then we should assess the validity of such notions.[3] Further research is needed to address adequately even some of the fundamental concerns of thanatology.

Robert Fulton has pointed out, for example, that there seems to be a fixation on nineteenth-century hydrostatic models of grief, which postulate a certain volume of grief that must be poured out. The "work" of mourning, Fulton says, is generally conceived of in linear terms, as a step-by-step progression, rather than as a dynamic process of "unraveling the skein of grief."[4] Little is known about how physiological processes of the brain affect the experience of grief. Fulton notes that the "anniversary reaction," for example, a phenomenon commonly experienced by the bereaved, may be a manifestation of the associative nature of brain function. Also requiring further study is a possible link between mourning and creativity.

In striving to improve care of the dying and the bereaved, paternalism may replace advocacy if answers are proposed before the necessary questions have been asked. We should be wary of presuppositions that derive from the caregiver's personal preferences rather than from unbiased and informed appraisal. A caregiver who places a high value on resolving conflicts as part of preparing for endings may unintentionally demand, expect, or wish that his or her patients do the same. Our understanding of the phenomena associated with dying and death can grow only when we take into account the interplay between theory and application in constructing an adequate knowledge base.

Others note that minorities are underrepresented in the resource materials commonly used in death education courses. Observing that one of the larger organizations of professionals in the field "appears to reflect a middle-class white, grassroots movement," Darrell Crase asks the rhetorical question, "Black people do die, don't they?"[5]

Much of the research in thanatology has been concerned with the measurement of attitudes toward death, and, more particularly, death anxiety with its related concepts of fear, threat, and concern in the face of one's own death.

The Past Is Not Dead

Cultures that view birth as a beginning and death as an end can have no sense of a living past. For Mexicans, neither birth nor death is seen to interrupt the continuity of life and neither is considered overly important. Belief in communion with the dead is widespread, not in a psychic or spiritualist sense or as a function of a Christian faith in the afterlife, but simply as an outgrowth of the knowledge that the past is not dead.

Alan Riding,
Distant Neighbors

Robert Neimeyer has stated that more than 760 articles on death anxiety, were published in professional journals between 1955 and 1990.[6] This area of research has been characterized as "the largest area of empirical study in the field of thanatology."[7] Virtually all of this research has used questionnaires to gather data on death anxiety. Since the early 1970s, a number of "death anxiety" and "fear of death" scales have been proposed by various researchers, including Donald Templer, David Lester, John Hoelter, and Robert Neimeyer, to cite several noteworthy examples.[8]

Generally speaking, the findings from this research indicate that death anxiety tends to be higher among females than among males, higher among blacks than among whites, and higher among youth and middle-aged adults than among older people. Religious belief appears to be inversely related to death anxiety; that is, people who characterize themselves as "religious" tend to report less death anxiety than those who do not characterize themselves this way. Individuals who report a greater degree of self-actualization and internal sense of control also report less death anxiety than do their counterparts. The same general finding also applies to people whose orientation to life is one of "living in the present," rather than looking back to the past or ahead to the future.

Despite the bulk of accumulated data, however, there remain significant questions about the research into death anxiety. Robert Neimeyer has summarized these questions as follows:[9] First, what definition of death is implied by the various testing instruments? Second, what are the strengths and limitations of the various instruments that have been used in death anxiety research? Third, based on the answer to the first two questions, what are the implications for future research? And, finally, reviewing the data gathered up to now, what do we really know? As Herman Feifel pointed out in a recent article reviewing the status of research and practice in thanatology:

> Fear of death is not a unitary or monolithic variable. . . . In the face of personal death, the human mind ostensibly operates simultaneously on various levels of reality, or finite provinces of meaning, each of which can be somewhat autonomous. We, therefore, need to be circumspect in accepting at face value the degree of fear of death affirmed at the conscious level.[10]

It's a matter of honor, death. It's your white page, do you see? Or your shame. Either you're worthy of it or you ain't. To accept it, to face it with honor and respect and goodwill, to *earn* it, that is to be brave.

N. Scott Momaday,
The Ancient Child

Robert Kastenbaum recently characterized research into death anxiety as "thanatology's own assembly line."[11] He suggests that part of the appeal of death anxiety research lies in the fact that it "allows the researcher (and the readers, if they so choose) to enjoy the illusion that death has really been studied." Just how the data obtained from death anxiety research should be applied to practical issues in death education, counseling, and care is still largely a matter of uncertainty. If we could reliably state, for example, that physicians with a high degree of death anxiety do less well in relating to dying patients, then that lesson might be applied constructively in the health care setting. For the most part, however, we are not yet in a position to adequately appraise the effects of death anxiety as they impinge on real-world issues. To cite one instance of this problem, consider the fact that some studies indicate that women have higher death anxiety scores than do men. Does this gender difference mean that women are too anxious about death, or that men are not anxious enough?[12] This question is yet to be satisfactorily answered and may be taken as representative of the difficulties in the field of death anxiety research that must be addressed.

There are few signs that practitioners have made much use of either research or theory in their work with patients or with the bereaved. It appears, Kastenbaum says, "that many practitioners in the area of terminal care and bereavement have neither an up-to-date mastery of thanatological research nor a secure grasp of the historical and theoretical dimensions." Completing his portrait of thanatological research, theory, and practice, Kastenbaum concludes that,

> at the worst, perhaps, we have sketched a picture of practitioners who fail to read a literature that wouldn't help them very much anyway. The academicians continue to tread their mills . . . with only each other to amuse, while the practitioners base their services on individual experiences and a grab-bag of unexamined assumptions and "facts" whose veridicality has seldom been tested, let alone established.

Echoing such thoughts, Myra Bluebond-Langner notes that, "while the quantity of research has increased, what more do we actually know? Has progress in thanatology kept pace with publication? What differences have our efforts made in the care of dying patients and their families, and in our own responses to death and impending disasters?"[13] Herman Feifel calls attention

Zen Questions

Men who have seen life and death as . . . an unbroken continuum, the swingings of an eternal pendulum, have been able to move as freely into death as they walked through life.

The Zen masters were so intimately involved with the *whole* of existence that they found overinvolvement with any of its parts, death included, to be a misplaced concern, saying to people who ask about an afterlife, "Why do you want to know what will happen to you after you die? Find out who you are now!"

Philip Kapleau

to the need to "integrate existing knowledge concerning death and grief into our communal and public institutions."[14] Individuals with involvements in the areas of death education, counseling, and care must become active participants in helping to formulate the public policies affecting those areas of concern. Although acknowledging that the field of thanatology (and, by extension, the so-called death awareness movement) has many tasks facing it, Feifel concludes that it already can be credited with a number of contributions to our well-being:

> The [death] movement has been a major force in broadening our grasp of the phenomenology of illness, in helping humanize medical relationships and health care, and in advancing the rights of the dying. It is highpointing values that undergird the vitality of human response to catastrophe and loss. Furthermore, it is contributing to reconstituting the integrity of our splintered wholeness. More important, perhaps, it is sensitizing us to our common humanity, which is all too eroded in the present world. It may be somewhat hyperbolic, but I believe that how we regard death and how we treat the dying and survivors are prime indications of a civilization's intention and target.

Along this line, Robert Fulton and Greg Owen note that the message of palliative care put forward by Elisabeth Kübler-Ross, Cicely Saunders, Mother Teresa of Calcutta, and others also contains a message about "essential religious and spiritual values that extend beyond the immediate goal of care for the dying."[15] The "compassionate acts of service," which the death-awareness movement has encouraged and promoted during the past several decades, are founded on a recognition of the identity and worth of each human being.

As the disciplines of death education, counseling, and care continue to evolve, one of the most persistent calls has been for a global perspective. Although personal experiences related to dying and death are indeed central to thanatological study and practice, the global dimensions of death—war, violence, environmental catastrophe—are increasingly of concern. Dan Leviton and William Wendt have described a conceptual framework that focuses on the reality of death to help improve the quality of civilized life.[16] Using this model, death education may serve not only to aid individuals in their personal confrontations with death, but also to ameliorate the causes of large-scale deaths that are human-caused and unnecessary. Leviton and Wendt use the term "horrendous death" to describe these global confrontations with death, and they define it as

> a form of premature death which is ugly, fashioned by man, without any trace of grace, totally unnecessary, and, as they say of pornography, lacking any redeeming social value. It is that death which is caused by war, homicide, holocaust, terrorism, starvation, and poisoning of the environment.

Benumbed by these categories of horrendous death, most of us tend to deny its presence or feel a sense of hopelessness and loss of control over our own destiny and future. It is this denial, say Leviton and Wendt, that "very much *prevents* worldwide cooperative policy designed to improve the quality of life." Death education, then, can serve a public health function of prevention and intervention in response to potential catastrophe.

The comprehensive nature of the concerns that ought to be addressed within the practice of death education has been eloquently summarized in a document formulated by the International Work Group on Death, Dying, and Bereavement:

> Death, dying, and bereavement are fundamental and pervasive aspects of the human experience. Individuals and societies achieve fullness of living by understanding and appreciating these realities. The absence of such understanding and appreciation may result in unnecessary suffering, loss of dignity, alienation, and diminished quality of living. Therefore, education about death, dying, and bereavement, both formal and informal, is an essential component of the educational process at all levels.[17]

As efforts toward providing education about death continue to mature, it is likely that the vision of a comprehensive role for death education, as reflected in this statement, will serve to guide the creation of diverse forms of death education in the future.

Death in the Future

As we look to the future, what questions about death and dying will increasingly demand our attention both as individuals and as a society? We will continue to see an ever-growing older population. In the United States, it is estimated that the population of people ages sixty-five and over will increase from about 34 million in 1995 to over 60 million by the year 2025.[18] Care of the dying is likely to become big business as corporations expand their role as surrogate caregivers for the aged and dying.

Imagine what death will be like fifty or one hundred years from now. Extrapolate from present realities and current possibilities. Think back over the key issues discussed in previous chapters. What are some of your speculations

> I was sitting by myself. The hotel had cleared. A little old lady came in, so I asked her to sit with me. And she told me her life. She had lived for twelve years in hotels. All she had was in this one little room. She had a daughter. She said her daughter wrote twice a week, but her daughter lived at a distance. She went into quite some detail, and I think it hit me then, harder than it ever had, that some day that might be me!
>
> A student in a Death and Dying class

about what our relationship to death will be by the middle years of the twenty-first century?

For example, imagine the kind of rituals or ceremonies surrounding the dead several decades from now. Writing about the rapid pace of social change among South Pacific societies, Ron Crocombe remarks on the trend in these societies of reducing the time spent on each funeral, marriage, birth, and other such occasion of community celebration, as well as diverting such activities from day to night and weekday to weekend. "Most traditional social rituals took more time than can be spared today," he says, "both because there are many more things to do, and because each person is doing different things."[19]

Although our own value judgments may determine how we spend our time, such decisions are rarely made independently of social norms and practices. For instance, if a work schedule makes it difficult to attend a midweek funeral, we may be reluctant to insist on having time off. As our notions about the use of time change, thereby affecting our attitudes and behaviors relative to death, what kinds of funeral practices and services might evolve to correspond to these changes?

As for disposition of the corpse, will there be enough land to continue the practice of burials? Some have suggested that we may see the substitution of high-rise cemeteries, cities of the dead towering above the landscape of the living. This is already happening in Japan, where burial space in large cities like Tokyo is at a premium. Although it is unlikely that current funeral practices will disappear completely within the foreseeable future, changes in methods of arranging for and conducting last rites will undoubtedly occur as consumers exercise new choices. An example of this change can already be seen in some areas of the country where casket dealers have set up shop to make their wares available to the public independently of conventional funeral establishments.

In coping with the death of a loved one, what types of social services will be available? Few could have foreseen the rapid rise of specialized support groups and activist organizations such as Parents of Murdered Children and Mothers Against Drunk Driving, to name but two of the groups that provide a forum for the issues and a focus for the grief resulting from particular types of bereavement. What other developments in bereavement, grief, and mourning may take place in the coming years?

During an annual cremation ceremony in Bali, young men carry a papier-mâché tiger containing the remains of a villager through the center of town to a temple outside the village, where the actual cremation takes place. On the way, they run, halt abruptly, shout and make noise, and turn the palanquin around and around to confuse the spirit so that it leaves the earthly realm and journeys to the afterworld.

Besides support groups for the bereaved, the recent past also has seen an increased emphasis on counseling or therapy following bereavement. In the future, might there be "grief clinics" available on call for emergencies? Would these clinics—much like present health institutions—send out reminders for patients or clients to come in for a bereavement checkup before the anniversary date of a significant death? Bereavement counseling is already acknowledged for its value, especially when circumstances make coping with a death difficult. Such counseling, however, is not yet widely available, partly due to a persistent belief that coping with grief—regardless of circumstances—should not require outside intervention. In addition, health insurance providers may refuse to reimburse their policyholders for therapy or counseling related to bereavement. With a greater openness in talking about death and acknowledging its place in our lives, the time may not be too far off when professional assistance in dealing with grief is the norm.

What diseases will frighten us and endanger our survival if the currently threatening diseases, such as cancer and heart disease, become matters of routine prevention or cure? What change do you imagine will occur within even as short a period as the next decade? In earlier chapters, we discussed the rapid pace of medical advances in diagnosis and treatment. With new discoveries and techniques, the prognosis for a given disease or category of patients may change from very poor to exceptionally good within the span of a few years. During the same period, however, life-threatening diseases that were previously unrecognized or even nonexistent may present new threats.

As a case in point: Who could have foreseen the frightening implications of AIDS? Virtually nonexistent just a few years ago, this disease has quickly assumed proportions comparable to the great plagues of the Middle Ages in terms of public fear and uncertainty. Individuals, local communities, and society as a whole were caught off guard by the outbreak and unsure about how to respond. To cite one example: When Elisabeth Kübler-Ross proposed a hospice for infants and children with AIDS, the nearby community called an emergency meeting to squelch the proposal. Can we anticipate that new diseases and threats, as yet undescribed and unknown, will cause similar hysteria in the future?

It is difficult to imagine a time when *no* disease or illness will be life-threatening. Yet we have already lived through many technological advances that make possible the sustaining of life beyond any measure conceivable by earlier generations. What technological advances will become commonplace for sustaining life in the coming decades? The future may include "off-the-shelf" replaceable body parts that will sustain life when conventional methods prove futile. In the coming years, organ transplantation may give way to organ substitution. If there is indeed a "bionic" human in our future, what values should guide the use of such innovative, life-sustaining technologies, and who will decide? In Damon Knight's science fiction story, "Masks," a man who has suffered physically devastating injuries is repaired with functional artificial

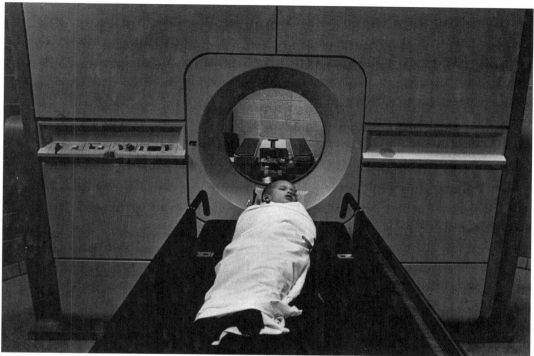

Burton Steele, Times-Picayune

Extrapolating from current medical technologies, we can foresee only faintly the questions and decisions about death and dying that children of the future will face.

body parts.[20] But his mechanically sustained life causes him to question what constitutes a living human being.

Another area of speculation is the development of techniques for accurately predicting the time of a person's death. This theme is explored in Clifford Simak's "Death Scene" and in Robert Heinlein's "Life-Line."[21] Both stories seem to suggest that the moment of one's death may be better left unknown. Although such explorations in speculative fiction are typically located in the future, in a setting different from our own, and often incorporate elements of fantasy, the themes investigated relate directly to present possibilities and current dilemmas of moral choice.

When members of the "baby boom" generation reach retirement age in the first decades of the twenty-first century, what will their lives be like? What changes are likely to occur in the health care system? What will be the quality of life—and of dying? In the story "Golden Acres," Kit Reed envisions a future in which the administrators of an institution for the aged make life-or-death decisions about the aged inmates in order to make room for new arrivals.[22]

Could it be . . . that one reason why the study of death has emerged as one of the dominant concerns of our time is to help us to become globally sensitized to the experience of death precisely because the notion of death on a *planetary scale* now hangs, like the sword of Damocles, over our heads? Could this be the universe's way of "inoculating" us against the fear of death?

Kenneth Ring,
Life at Death

Golden Acres provides everything for its residents except the possibility of living out their lives in the ways they wish. Reed's story focuses on a resident who refuses to acquiesce in society's neglect of its aged members. As the protagonist describes it, Golden Acres is "a vast boneyard." Will that description also apply to the prospects facing the aged members of our own communities?

During the decade of the 1990s, as we approach the end of one millennium and the advent of another, we can expect to encounter a variety of apocalyptic scenarios and perhaps some feelings of trepidation. Prophecies concerning "the end of the world" from ancient traditions around the globe will be dusted off and put forward for our inspection. Nostradamas, writing in the sixteenth century, prophesied that terrible events would occur in the last months before the turning of the millennium. The Bible, according to the view espoused by some readers, speaks of the cataclysmic final battle of Armageddon occurring a generation after the establishment of a Jewish nation-state. Prophecies found in the Buddhist and Hindu traditions, as well as in the Aztec and Hopi traditions, among many others, also suggest the potential for unimaginable upheaval as an accompaniment to the change of millennia.

Cullen Murphy describes a scenario apparently thought to be likely among some astronomers:

> In May of the year 2000 . . . Mercury, Mars, Jupiter, and Saturn will be aligned behind the sun, aimed directly at Earth on the other side. The pull of these planets could, some say, be so intense as to rupture seismic faults and even to cause devastating tsunamis in the planet's underlying magma, the molten rock pulsing in powerful waves beneath the mantle. . . . The geologic disruptions could be so great that they could cause a "wobble" in Earth's rotation and possibly cause a "polar flip," with the planet falling over on its side or turning completely upside down, like an unskilled kayaker.[23]

Scientists, Murphy says, "are unanimous in the view that the result would be a real mess."

Less dramatic, but perhaps no less troublesome for life on planet Earth, are the well-known warnings we have heard concerning the greenhouse effect, acid rain, global warming, holes in the ozone layer, the decimation of the rain

My Death

"Death is our eternal companion,"
Don Juan said with a most serious
air. "It is always to our left, at
an arm's length. . . . It has always been
watching you. It always will until
the day it taps you."

Carlos Castenada

My death
looks exactly like me.
She lives to my left,
at exactly an arm's length.
She has my face, hair, hands;
she ages
as I grow older.

Sometimes, at night,
my death awakens me

or else appears in dreams
I did not write.
Sometimes a sudden wind
blows from nowhere,
& I look left
& see my death.
Alive, I write
with my right hand only.
When I am dead,
I shall write with my left.

But later I will have to write
through others.
I may appear
to future poets
as their deaths.

Erica Jong

forests, and the deaths of species. Many observers believe that "these banner
warnings of planetary trouble" bespeak clear and real dangers that "must in
addressed in an unprecedented, worldwide effort before it is too late."[24] In
addressing these issues, students and practitioners of thanatology have a special responsibility. They have learned from their encounters with dying and
death that life is precious and precarious. The poet Gary Snyder has written:

> The extinction of a species, each one a pilgrim of four billion years of evolution,
> is an irreversible loss. The ending of the lines of so many creatures with whom we
> have traveled this far is an occasion of profound sorrow and grief. Death can be
> accepted and to some degree transformed. But the loss of lineages and all their
> future young is not something to accept. It must be rigorously and intelligently
> resisted.[25]

In working to improve care of the dying and provide comfort for the
bereaved, we must also consider how the insights gained from a study of death
can be compassionately applied to the life of the planet as a whole.

Living with Death and Dying

As you think about the various perspectives covered in your study of death
and dying, take a moment to assess the areas that seem of particular value to
you. What insights have you developed from examining how death is related to
in other cultures? How do the insights gained from study about death and
children relate to your own death experiences as a child or as an adult? What

about your risk-taking behaviors? What aspects of your life style involve risking death? What choices would you make regarding funeral ritual, terminal care, life-sustaining medical technologies? In sum, ask yourself: What have I learned that can be helpful to me as a survivor of others' deaths—and in confronting my own death?

In considering the personal value that is derived from thinking about and exploring the many meanings of death, you may notice that the study of death and dying engages both the cognitive faculties and the emotions. The personal exploration of death also has a rippling effect, extending outward to the social milieu and your relationships with others. What effect does your awareness of death have on the quality of your relationships with family members and friends, or perhaps with the person down the street or at the neighborhood shop? Does an awareness of "the precious precariousness of life" prompt a greater sensitivity toward your own and others' needs and compassion for others? Alfred Killilea says, "Rather than threatening to deprive life of all meaning, death deepens an appreciation of life and the capacity of every person to give life to others."[26]

Humanizing Death and Dying

Many people are encouraged by what they see as the increasing openness about and humanizing of death in American society. There are signs that the circumstances surrounding death are being brought back into the personal control of the individuals and families who are closest to a particular death.

There is some question, however, whether this apparent openness toward death is illusory. When death is accepted as a topic of casual discussion on television talk shows, are we not possibly minimizing or devaluing death, trying to achieve a kind of "death without regrets"? In the urge to humanize death and dying, to accept death, might there also be a more subtle form of denial? Death is not necessarily what it seems to be in our rosy-colored projections and fantasies about the good death.

In one sense, of course, none of us is able to "humanize" death. Death is already an intensely human experience. We can work to balance our fears with openness, our anxieties with trust. We can begin to understand the dynamics of grief, to make room for loss and change in our lives and in the lives of others. Death need not always be seen as something foreign, a foe to be fought valiantly to the bitter end.

But in gaining an easier familiarity with death, we should beware of becoming too casual. We may find we have confronted only our *image* of death, not death itself. There are many signs of an increased casualness toward death in modern society. One example is the increasing number of death notices, bearing the announcement, "No services are planned." Yet few people die without survivors who are affected by the loss. Is death a solitary or a communal event? Can I truly say that my death is "my own"? Or is death an event whose significance ripples outward to touch the lives not only of friends and loved ones, but also the lives of casual acquaintances and even strangers in ways

The contemplation of death and its meaning will determine how we and our children think about and behave toward death in the decades ahead.

little understood? What is the desired balance between the individual and the social connotations of death?

Defining the Good Death

There is no single definition of what constitutes a *good* death. In ancient Greece, to die young, in the fullness of one's creative energies, was considered to be exceptional luck. In our society, however, death at a young age is considered a misfortune; the death of a person just embarking on an independent life or of someone in the prime of life seems a great tragedy.

The good death can be defined in many ways. Take a moment to think about how you might define it. Consider the various factors—age, mode of death, surroundings, and so on—that would enter into your concept of a good death. Is your concept the same for yourself and for others?

Some may question whether there can be any such thing as a good death. "Death is never good," they might say. "It can only cause pain and sadness." More useful, perhaps, is the concept of an *appropriate* death. What makes some deaths seem more appropriate than others? Our answers are influenced by cultural values and by the social context of death. Avery Weisman has

The Angel of Death

The Angel of Death is always with me—
the hard wild flowers of his teeth,
his body like cigar smoke
swaying through a small town jail.

He is the wind that scrapes through our months,
the train wheels grinding over our syllables.
He is the footstep continually pacing through our chests,
the small wound in the soul,
the meteor puncturing the atmosphere.
And sometimes he is merely a quiet between the start of an act
and its completion,
a silence so loud
it shakes you like a tree.

It is only then you look up from the wars,
from the kisses,
from the signing of the business agreements;
It is only then you observe the dimensions
housed in the air of each day,
each moment;

only then you hear the old caressing the cold rims of their sleep,
hear the middle-aged women in love with their pillows
weeping into the gray expanse of each dawn,
where young men, dozing in alleys,
envision their loneliness to be a beautiful girl
and do not know they are part of a young girl's dream,
as she does not know that she is the dream in the sleep
of middle-aged women and old men,
and that all are contained in a gray wind
that scrapes through our months.

enumerated some of the conditions that define an appropriate death in most modern societies.[27]

First, an appropriate death is relatively pain free; suffering is kept to a minimum. The social and emotional needs of the dying person are met to the fullest extent possible. There is no impoverishment of crucial human resources. Within the limits imposed by disabilities, the dying person is free to operate effectively as an individual and to enjoy mobility and independence. In addition, the dying person is able to recognize and resolve, as far as possible, any residual personal and social conflicts. The person is allowed to satisfy his or her wishes in ways that are consistent with the situation and with his or her self-identity and self-esteem.

But soon we forget that the dead sleep in buried cities,
that our hearts contain them in ripe vaults,
We forget that beautiful women dry into parchment
and ball players collapse into ash;
that geography wrinkles and smoothes like the expressions on a face,
and that not even children
can pick the white fruit from the night sky.

And how *could* we laugh while looking at the face
that falls apart like wet tobacco?
How could we wake each morning
to hear the muffled gong beating inside us,
our mouths full of shadows, our rooms filled with a black dust?

Still,
it is humiliating to be born a bottle:
to be filled with air, emptied, filled again;
to be filled with water, emptied, filled again;
and, finally, to be filled with earth.

And yet I am glad that The Angel of Death is always with me:
his footsteps quicken my own,
his silence makes me speak,
his wind freshens the weather of my day.
And it is because of him
I no longer think
that with each beat
my heart
is a planet drowning from within
but an ocean filling for the first time.

Morton Marcus

As death approaches, the dying person is allowed to freely choose to relinquish control over various aspects of his or her life, turning over control to people in whom confidence and trust have been placed. The dying person also may choose to seek out or to relinquish relationships with significant others. In other words, the person chooses a comfortable level of social interaction.

Weisman points out that to achieve an appropriate death we must first rid ourselves of the notion that death is *never* appropriate. This belief, he says, acts as a self-fulfilling prophecy: We shut ourselves off from creating the possibility of a more appropriate death.

For an appropriate death to be possible, the dying person must be protected from needless, dehumanizing, and demeaning procedures. The

Jerry Soloway, UPI/Bettmann Newsphotos

Death can be viewed as a burden or as a blessing. Its meaning changes as circumstances change and as our understanding evolves toward new recognitions of its place in our lives.

person's preferences about pain control and consciousness, and about the extent of solitude or gregarious interaction desired, should be respected. "An appropriate death," Weisman says, "is a death that someone might choose for himself—had he a choice."

The death of Charles Lindbergh reveals many of the features of an appropriate death as defined by Weisman.[28] Lindbergh was diagnosed in 1972 as having lymphoma. Until he died two years later, he continued living an active life, traveling and promoting the cause of conservation. When chemotherapy became ineffective, Lindbergh made arrangements for his eventual burial on his beloved island of Maui, in the Hawaiian islands. As his condition worsened, Lindbergh was hospitalized for several months, but the best efforts of his physicians could not alter the consequences of the disease. Lindbergh then

"Calvin and Hobbes," drawing by Bill Watterson, © 1990 Universal Press Syndicate

instructed that a cabin on Maui be obtained, and he was flown "home to Maui," where, with two nurses, his physician, and his family, he spent the last eight days of his life in the environment he loved.

During this time, he gave instructions for the construction of his grave and for the conduct of his funeral, requesting that people attend in their work clothes. As Dr. Milton Howell, one of Lindbergh's physicians, describes it, "There was time for reminiscing, time for discussion, and time for laughter."

Finally, Lindbergh lapsed into a coma and, twelve hours later, died. In accordance with his wishes, there had been no medical heroics. Dr. Howell says, "Death was another event in his life, as natural as his birth had been in Minnesota more than seventy-two years before."

Postscript and Farewell

Learning about death may have immediate, practical consequences. At the conclusion of a course on death and dying, one student said, "It has helped me and my family in dealing with my mother's serious illness." For others, the practical implications may seem less immediate. Yet, as another student expressed it, "I've gained a lot of useful information which may not be applicable to my life right now, but I know now that information and help is available and I didn't know that before."

Many people find that their explorations have consequences for their life that go beyond their previous notions about death and dying. One student said, "To me, this study has focused on more than just death and dying; it has dealt with ideas and with living, like a class on philosophy." Another student expressed the value of her death explorations as having, "expanded my faith in the resilience of the human spirit." In an article describing the manner in which several individuals faced the prospect of dying, Sandra Bertman concluded: "A common thread in many of the scenarios . . . is connectedness, affinity with all mankind: past, present, alive, dead."[29]

Death education does pertain to the practical and obvious aspects associated with the individual and social encounter with death. But an awareness of death and dying can also bring an added dimension to the experience of living, moment to moment. The remembrance of death can bring us more into the present. It can serve as a reminder of the precious precariousness of life and the value of compassion in the ordinary as well as extraordinary circumstances of human experience.

Further Readings

Norman O. Brown. *Life Against Death: The Psychoanalytical Meaning of History*. 2d ed. Middletown, Conn.: Wesleyan University Press, 1985.

Daniel Callahan. *The Troubled Dream of Life: Living with Mortality*. New York: Simon & Schuster, 1993.

F. Crussi-Gonzalez. *The Day of the Dead and Other Mortal Reflections*. New York: Harcourt, Brace, 1993.

David Feinstein and Peg Elliott Mayo. *Rituals for Living and Dying: From Life's Wounds to a Spiritual Awakening*. San Francisco: HarperCollins, 1990.

Robert Kastenbaum and Beatrice Kastenbaum, eds. *Encyclopedia of Death*. Phoenix: Oryx Press, 1989.

J. Krishnamurti. *On Living and Dying*. San Francisco: HarperCollins, 1992.

Robert A. Neimeyer, ed. *Death Anxiety Handbook: Research, Instrumentation, and Application*. Washington, D.C.: Taylor & Francis, 1993.

Robert G. Stevenson, ed. *Curing Death Ignorance: Teaching Children About Death in Schools*. Philadelphia: Charles Press, 1994.

Tony Walter. *The Revival of Death*. London: Routledge, 1994.

Avery Weisman. *The Coping Capacity: On the Nature of Being Mortal*. New York: Human Sciences, 1984.

E P I L O G U E

It's late. I wonder what Death will look like? A drooling ogre? Perhaps an unblinking skull, the Grim Reaper? A veiled mistress with beckoning arms? The standard forms. Or maybe Death will be a polished young man in a three-piece suit, all smiles and sincerity and confidence. What a disappointment that would be. No, I prefer the scythe—no ambiguity, no surrender . . . no dickering. What's that? . . . I hear him. He's here.

"May I come in?"

I nod. It's the young man who left me two days ago to knock on the doors of his neighbors' homes. "Well . . . ?" My breath is shorter than I thought.

He smiles, looks down at his hands, then at me. "Well, I did as you said. It didn't take long before I realized that I wasn't going to find a household that hadn't been touched by death."

"How many did you go to?"

He covers his mouth with his hand a moment, trying to hide his pride, I guess. "All of them."

"All?"

"Every house . . . I'm very stubborn."

We both smile. My wheezing is worse, and he notices. He shows his concern, and I can see that he understands what is happening.

"You're dying, aren't you, old man?"

I close my eyes in answer. When I open them again, he is at my side.

"Is there someone I should get for you? Your family?"

"Gone."

"Some friend?"

"Gone. All gone . . . except for you." The young man nods, then pulls his chair over next to my own. He takes my hand. I rest a moment. "There is something you must do for me," I wheeze. "When I'm dead, burn this house and everything in it, including me."

613

"Leave nothing behind?"

"This is only a filthy old shack. I'm leaving behind the only thing that anyone really can leave behind . . . the difference I've made in the lives of the people I've met." I squeeze his hand as best I can. He squeezes back. "Oh . . . and this." I try to lift the book in my lap—my book. He sees me struggling, and picks it up for me. "You take this. It's yours." His eyes widen.

"But I don't deserve—"

"There isn't time for that now!" He nods, and lays the book on his lap. Good, that's done. Moments pass. It gets quieter . . . I must close my eyes. I witness again the glory of ten thousand mornings, ten thousand afternoons, ten thousand nights . . . then they, too, fade. All that's left is the sound of our breathing, and the wind. Time slows. Time changes. Where is the scythe? The young man's hand leaves mine and I hear his footsteps recede . . . stop . . . return. He sits down and I feel his hand on mine. He opens my fingers and lays something cool and light in my palm, all lace and limbs . . . the ballerina.

Now I can go.

David Gordon

Notes

C H A P T E R 1

    1. See Ernest Becker, *The Denial of Death* (New York: Free Press, 1973).

    2. See, for example, James J. Farrell, *Inventing the American Way of Death, 1830–1920* (Philadelphia: Temple University Press, 1980); and Martha V. Pike and Janice Gray Armstrong, *A Time to Mourn: Expressions of Grief in Nineteenth Century America* (Stony Brook, N.Y.: The Museums at Stony Brook, 1980).

    3. "Expectation of Life at Birth," *Statistical Abstract of the United States 1994*, 114th ed. (Washington, D.C.: Government Printing Office, 1994), p. 87.

    4. "Deaths by Selected Causes and Characteristics," *Statistical Abstract of the United States 1994*, p. 94.

    5. "Deaths and Death Rates," *Statistical Abstract of the United States 1994*, p. 89.

    6. "Deaths and Death Rates by Selected Causes," *Statistical Abstract of the United States 1994*, p. 93.

    7. S. Jay Olshansky and A. Brian Ault, "The Fourth Stage of the Epidemiologic Transition: The Age of Delayed Degenerative Diseases," *The Millbank Quarterly* 64, no. 3 (1986): 355–391.

    8. "Resident Population by Age," "Live Births, Deaths, Marriages, and Divorces," and "Deaths by Age and Leading Cause," *Statistical Abstract of the United States 1994*, pp. 14, 75, 95.

    9. "Mobility Status of the Population," *Statistical Abstract of the United States 1994*, p. 31.

    10. See, for example, Willard Gaylin, "Faulty Diagnosis: Why Clinton's Health-Care Plan Won't Cure What Ails Us," *Harper's Magazine* (October 1993), p. 63.

    11. Gaylin, "Faulty Diagnosis," p. 59.

    12. Kenneth McLeish, *Key Ideas in Human Thought* (New York: Facts on File, 1993), p. 61.

    13. Marsha McGee, "Faith, Fantasy, and Flowers: A Content Analysis of the American Sympathy Card," *Omega: Journal of Death and Dying* 11 (1980–1981): 27, 29.

    14. Alynn Day Harvey, "Evidence of a Tense Shift in Personal Experience Narratives," *Empirical Studies of the Arts* 4, no. 2 (1986): 151–162.

615

15. Interestingly, the practice of purchasing a coffin in advance of need and using it to store wine, books, or whatever is one that would have been quite acceptable to many people in rural areas of the country during earlier centuries. For example, people living in central Appalachia sometimes used their burial containers for furniture or storage pending the owner's death. James Crissman gives an account of one man using his coffin to store tobacco and liquor and of another man who stored seed corn in his. See James K. Crissman, *Death and Dying in Central Appalachia: Changing Attitudes and Practices* (Urbana: University of Illinois Press, 1994), p. 50.

16. Barry Alan Morris, "The Communal Constraints on Parody: The Symbolic Death of Joe Bob Briggs," *Quarterly Journal of Speech* 73 (1987): 460–473.

17. Mary N. Hall, "Laughing as We Go" (paper presented at the Annual Meeting of the Forum for Death Education and Counseling, Philadelphia, April 1985).

18. See Mary N. Hall and Paula T. Rappe, "Humor and Critical Incident Stress," in *The Path Ahead: Readings in Death and Dying*, ed. Lynne Ann DeSpelder and Albert Lee Strickland (Mountain View, Calif.: Mayfield, 1995), pp. 289–294; adapted from *The Forum: Newsletter of the Association for Death Education and Counseling* 17, no. 5 (September–October 1992): 11–14.

19. See, for example, Ben H. Bagdikian, *The Information Machines: Their Impact on Men and the Media* (New York: Harper and Row, 1971); Clarence R. Wyatt, *Paper Soldiers: The American Press and the Vietnam War* (New York: W. W. Norton, 1983); and Harold Cox, "Mourning Populations: Some Considerations of Historically Comparable Assassinations," *Death Education* 4, no. 2 (1980): 125–138.

20. Robert Kastenbaum, *Death, Society, and Human Experience* (St. Louis: C. V. Mosby, 1977), p. 93.

21. See Wilbur Schramm's quotation in *Newsletter of the International Communication Association* 13, no. 3 (Summer 1985): 8.

22. Jack Lule, "News Strategies and the Death of Huey Newton," in *The Path Ahead,* ed. DeSpelder and Strickland, pp. 33–40; reprinted from *Journalism Quarterly* 70, no. 2 (Summer 1993): 287–299.

23. Staff article, "Why Do They React? Readers Assail Publication of Funeral, Accident Photos," *News Photographer* 36, no. 3 (March 1981): 21–23.

24. John L. Huffman, "Putting Grief in Perspective," *News Photographer* 36, no. 3 (March 1981): 21–22.

25. Sydney H. Schanberg, "Press Can Do Better Covering Personal Tragedy," *Newsday* (February 17, 1989), p. 85.

26. Barbara Hastings, "Interviews Unwelcome by Some in Accident," *Honolulu Star-Bulletin & Advertiser,* April 23, 1989.

27. Michael Arlen, "The Cold, Bright Charms of Immortality," from *The View from Highway 1* (New York: Farrar, Straus & Giroux, 1976), pp. 34–68.

28. Robert Fulton and Greg Owen, "Death and Society in Twentieth Century America," *Omega: Journal of Death and Dying* 18, no. 4 (1987–1988): 379–395.

29. Arlen, "Cold, Bright Charms of Immortality."

30. "Utilization of Selected Media" and "Media Usage," *Statistical Abstract of the United States 1994*, pp. 567, 568.

31. In religious programming, the social topic most often referred to is death—the physical process of dying as well as the emotional process of preparing for death. See Robert Abelman and Kimberly Neuendort, "Themes and Topics in Religious Television Programming," *Review of Religious Research* 29, no. 2 (December 1987): 152–174.

32. George Gerbner, "Death in Prime Time: Notes on the Symbolic Functions of Dying in the Mass Media," *Annals of the American Academy of Political and Social Science* 447 (January 1980): 64–70. See also Fulton and Owen, "Death and Society in Twentieth Century America."

33. George Gerbner, Larry Gross, Nancy Signorielli, and Michael Morgan, "Television's Mean World: Violence Profile No. 14–15," Annenberg School of Communications, University of Pennsylvania (September 1986).

34. Ibid.

35. Roger Ebert, film critic of the Chicago *Sun-Times,* "At the Movies," NBC-TV, September 8, 1985.

36. Bob Thomas, "Natural Born Killers Reviewed," *Associated Press Online* (August 24, 1994).

37. Frederic B. Tate, "Impoverishment of Death Symbolism: The Negative Consequences," *Death Studies* 13, no. 3 (1989): 305–317.

38. See Richard A. Pacholski, "Death Themes in Music: Resources and Research Opportunities for Death Educators," *Death Studies* 10, no. 3 (1986): 239–263.

39. On death and dying themes in the folk music and songs of central Appalachia, see Crissman, *Death and Dying in Central Appalachia,* pp. 156–182.

40. Bruce L. Plopper and M. Ernest Ness, "Death as Portrayed to Adolescents Through Top 40 Rock and Roll Music," *Adolescence* 28, no. 112 (Winter 1993): 793–807.

41. *Associated Press Online* (March 23, 1994).

42. See, for example, Steven Stack, Jim Gundlach, and Jimmie L. Reeves, "The Heavy Metal Subculture and Suicide," *Suicide and Life-Threatening Behavior* 24, no. 1 (Spring 1994): 15–23; Hannelore Wass, M. David Miller, and Robert G. Stevenson, "Factors Affecting Adolescents' Behavior and Attitudes Toward Destructive Rock Lyrics," *Death Studies* 13, no. 3 (1989): 287–303; and Hannelore Wass, Jana L. Raup, Karen Cerullo, Linda G. Martel et al., "Adolescents' Interest in and Views of Destructive Themes in Rock Music," *Omega: Journal of Death and Dying* 19 (1988–1989): 177–186.

43. George S. Kanahele, ed., *Hawaiian Music and Musicians* (Honolulu: University Press of Hawaii, 1979), pp. 53, 56.

44. Marguerite K. Ashford, Bishop Museum, Honolulu, personal communication.

45. See John Hellman, *American Myth and the Legacy of Vietnam* (New York: Columbia University Press, 1986).

46. Alvin H. Rosenfeld, *A Double Dying: Reflections on Holocaust Literature* (Bloomington: Indiana University Press, 1980), p. 12. See also, by Lawrence L. Langer, *Versions of Survival: The Holocaust and the Human Spirit* (Albany: State University of New York Press, 1982) and *Holocaust Testimonies: The Ruins of Memory* (New Haven, Conn.: Yale University Press, 1991); and Terrence Des Pres, *The Survivor: An Anatomy of Life in the Death Camps* (New York: Oxford University Press, 1976).

47. Frederick J. Hoffman, *The Mortal No: Death and the Modern Imagination* (Princeton, N.J.: Princeton University Press, 1964).

48. This theme is explored by Lawrence Langer in *The Age of Atrocity: Death in Modern Literature* (Boston: Beacon Press, 1978).

49. William Ruehlmann, *Saint with a Gun: The Unlawful American Private Eye* (New York: New York University Press, 1984), p. 9.

50. Hoffman, *Mortal No,* p. 312.

51. Jahan Ramazani, *Poetry of Mourning: The Modern Elegy from Hardy to Heaney* (Chicago: University of Chicago Press, 1994), p. 1.

52. Ibid., pp. 1, 361.

53. Richard A. Pacholski, "Death Themes in the Visual Arts: Resources and Research Opportunities for Death Educators," *Death Studies* 10, no. 1 (1986): 59–74.

54. Fritz Eichenberg, *Dance of Death: A Graphic Commentary on the Danse Macabre through the Centuries* (New York: Abbeville, 1983).

55. Paul Johnson, *Enemies of Society* (New York: Atheneum, 1977), p. 221.

56. See Vivian Alpert Thompson, *A Mission in Art: Recent Holocaust Works in America* (Macon, Ga.: Mercer University Press, 1988); and Michael Franklin, "AIDS Iconography and Cultural Transformation: Visual and Artistic Responses to the AIDS Crisis," *The Arts in Psychotherapy* 20, no. 4 (1993): 299–316.

57. Miriam Horn, "The Artists' Diagnosis," *U.S. News & World Report* (March 27, 1989), pp. 62–70.

58. Franklin, "AIDS Iconography and Cultural Transformation."

59. Anita Schorsch, *Mourning Becomes America: Mourning Art in the New Nation* (Philadelphia: Main Street Press, 1976), p. 1.

60. Cindy Ruskin, *The Quilt: Stories from the Names Project* (New York: Pocket Books, 1988).

61. The Vietnam Memorial was designed by Maya Lin; the Names Project was begun in 1987 by Cleve Jones and other activist gay men in San Francisco. On the aesthetic and social implications of these memorials, see Ramazani, *Poetry of Mourning*, pp. 361–365.

62. David E. Stannard, *The Puritan Way of Death: A Study in Religion, Culture, and Social Change* (New York: Oxford University Press, 1977).

63. Robert G. Stevenson, "The Eye of the Beholder: The Media Look at Death Education," *Death Studies* 14 (1990): 161–170.

64. Patrick Vernon Dean, "Is Death Education a 'Nasty Little Secret'? A Call to Break the Alleged Silence," in *The Path Ahead*, ed. DeSpelder and Strickland, pp. 323–326.

65. Robert Kastenbaum, "Reconstructing Death in Postmodern Society," in *The Path Ahead*, ed. DeSpelder and Strickland, p. 8; reprinted from *Omega: Journal of Death and Dying* 27, no. 1 (1993): 75–89.

66. Octavio Paz, *The Labyrinth of Solitude: Life and Thought in Mexico* (New York: Grove Press, 1961), p. 60.

67. Herman Feifel, "Psychology and Death: Meaningful Rediscovery," in *The Path Ahead*, ed. DeSpelder and Strickland, pp. 19–28; reprinted from *American Psychologist* 45 (1990): 537–543.

68. Steven Starker, "Psychologists and Self-Help Books: Attitudes and Prescriptive Practices of Clinicians," *American Journal of Psychotherapy* 63, no. 3 (July 1988): 448–455.

69. Adapted from Kenneth J. Doka, "The Rediscovery of Death: An Analysis of the Emergence of the Death Studies Movement" (paper presented at the Annual Meeting of the Forum for Death Education and Counseling, San Diego, September 1982).

70. Vanderlyn R. Pine, "A Socio-Historical Portrait of Death Education," *Death Education* 1, no. 1 (1977): 57–84; see also, by Pine, "The Age of Maturity for Death Education: A Socio-Historical Portrait of the Era 1976–1985," *Death Studies* 10, no. 3

(1986): 209–231; and Dan Leviton, "The Scope of Death Education," *Death Education* 1, no. 1 (1977): 41–56.

71. Darrell Crase, "Death Education: Its Diversity and Multidisciplinary Focus," *Death Studies* 13, no. 1 (1989): 25–29.

72. Mary Ann Morgan, "Learner-centered Learning in an Undergraduate Interdisciplinary Course About Death," *Death Studies* 11, no. 3 (1987): 183–192.

73. See, for example, Duane Weeks, "Death Education for Aspiring Physicians, Teachers, and Funeral Directors," *Death Studies* 13 (1989): 17–24.

74. On the history and scope of ADEC, see Darrell Crase and Dan Leviton, "Forum for Death Education and Counseling: Its History, Impact, and Future," *Death Studies* 11, no. 5 (1987): 345–359; and Judith M. Stillion, "Association for Death Education and Counseling: An Organization for Our Times and for Our Future," *Death Studies* 13, no. 2 (1989): 191–201.

75. International Work Group on Death, Dying, and Bereavement, "Education about Death, Dying, and Bereavement," in *Statements on Death, Dying, and Bereavement* (London, Ont.: IWG, 1994), pp. 73–92.

76. Hannelore Wass, "Visions in Death Education," in *The Path Ahead*, ed. DeSpelder and Strickland, pp. 327–334; adapted from *Death: Completion and Discovery*, ed. Charles A. Corr and Richard A. Pacholski (Hartford, Conn.: Association for Death Education and Counseling, 1987), pp. 5–16.

77. Robert E. Kavanaugh, *Facing Death* (Los Angeles: Nash, 1972).

78. Kastenbaum, "Reconstructing Death in Postmodern Society," p. 16.

79. "AIDS Top Killer of Young Adults," *Associated Press Online* (January 31, 1995). See also "AIDS Cases Reported" (p. 139) and "AIDS Deaths" (p. 98) in *Statistical Abstract of the United States 1994*.

80. "World AIDS Total: 17 Million," *Associated Press Online* (August 8, 1994).

81. "AIDS Growing Among Minorities," *Associated Press Online* (September 8, 1994).

82. "World AIDS Total" and "WHO: More Young Women Get AIDS," *Associated Press Online* (February 8, 1995).

83. On the political and social response to AIDS, see: Dennis Altman, *AIDS in the Mind of America* (New York: Anchor Press/Doubleday, 1986); Mary Catherine Bateson and Richard Goldsby, *Thinking AIDS: The Social Response to the Biological Threat* (Reading, Mass.: Addison-Wesley, 1988); Inge B. Corless and Mary Pittman-Lindeman, eds., *AIDS: Principles, Practices, and Politics* (New York: Hemisphere, 1989); Douglas Crimp, ed., *AIDS: Cultural Analysis, Cultural Activism* (Cambridge, Mass.: MIT Press, 1988); Institute of Medicine/National Academy of Sciences, *Confronting AIDS: Update 1988* (Washington: National Academy Press, 1988); Eve K. Nichols, *Mobilizing Against AIDS*, rev. ed. (Cambridge, Mass.: Harvard University Press, 1989); Randy Shilts, *And the Band Played On: Politics, People, and the AIDS Epidemic* (New York: Viking Penguin, 1988).

84. "DMV Reverses AIDS Plate Denial," *Associated Press Online* (October 25, 1994).

85. Charles E. Rosenberg, "What Is an Epidemic? AIDS in Historical Perspective," in *The Path Ahead*, ed. DeSpelder and Strickland, pp. 29–32; originally published in *Daedalus: Journal of the American Academy of Arts and Sciences* 118, no. 2 (Spring 1989): 1–17.

86. Vincent Mor, David S. Greer, and Robert Kastenbaum, "The Hospice

Experiment: An Alternative in Terminal Care," in *The Hospice Experiment,* ed. Mor, Greer, and Kastenbaum (Baltimore: Johns Hopkins University Press, 1988), p. 4.

87. Ralph Hingson, Norman A. Scotch, James Sorenson, and Judith P. Swazey, *In Sickness and in Health: Social Dimensions of Medical Care* (St. Louis: C. V. Mosby, 1981), p. 183.

88. Paul Duro, Michael Greenhalgh, Jeremy Musson, and Kenneth McLeish, "Postmodernism," in *Key Ideas in Human Thought,* ed. McLeish, pp. 584–585.

89. Fulton and Owen, "Death and Society in Twentieth Century America."

90. Hingson et al., *In Sickness and in Health,* pp. 184–186.

91. Kathleen B. Bryer, "The Amish Way of Death: A Study of Family Support Systems," *American Psychologist* 34, no. 3 (March 1979): 255–261.

92. Andrew S. Ziner, Department of Sociology, University of North Dakota. Personal communication, May 1994.

CHAPTER 2

1. The use of blood-red oxide to decorate corpses is likely the earliest widespread funeral custom. Red ochre was mined in Africa by the earliest *Homo sapiens;* it appeared in Europe with Neanderthal funeral practices and was used in burials throughout Europe, Africa, Asia, Australia, and the Americas. Imagining the earth as a living organism, hematite is analogous to the blood of Mother Earth. The Christian Eucharist involves a similar symbology: the red wine represents the blood of Christ.

2. William R. LaFleur, *Liquid Life: Abortion and Buddhism in Japan* (Princeton, N.J.: Princeton University Press, 1992), p. 32.

3. Joseph Campbell, "Mythological Themes in Creative Literature and Art," in *Myths, Dreams, and Religion,* ed. Joseph Campbell (Dallas, Tex.: Spring Publications, 1970, 1988), pp. 138–175; see also, by Campbell, *Historical Atlas of World Mythology,* 5 vols. (New York: Harper and Row, 1988, 1989).

4. Hans Abrahamson, *The Origin of Death: Studies in African Mythology* (New York: Arno Press, 1977); Joseph Campbell, *The Masks of God: Primitive Mythology* (New York: Viking Press, 1959); and Jacques Choron, *Death and Western Thought* (New York: Macmillan, 1963).

5. Anita J. Glaze, *Art and Death in a Senufo Village* (Bloomington: Indiana University Press, 1981), pp. 150–151.

6. See, for example, Ndolamb Ngokwey, "Pluralistic Etiological Systems in Their Social Context: A Brazilian Case Study," *Social Science and Medicine* 26, no. 8 (1988): 793–802; and Paul Katz and Faris R. Kirkland, "Traditional Thought and Modern Western Surgery," *Social Science and Medicine* 26, no. 12 (1988): 1175–1181.

7. Ninian Smart, *The Long Search* (Boston: Little, Brown, 1977), p. 231.

8. See, for example, Neville Drury, *The Elements of Shamanism* (Dorset: Element Books, 1989).

9. Mary Kawena Pukui, E. W. Haertig, and Catherine A. Lee, *Nana I Ke Kumu (Look to the Source),* 2 vols. (Honolulu: Hui Hanai; Queen Lili'uokalani Children's Center, 1972). A study conducted in the 1930s found families still tracing their lineage from ancestors who were viewed as spiritual guardians of their descendants, often interceding in very practical ways. See E. S. Craighill Handy and Mary Kawena Pukui, *The Polynesian Family System in Ka-'u, Hawai'i* (Rutland, Vt.: Charles E. Tuttle, 1972).

10. T. H. Gaster, in James Frazer, *The New Golden Bough* (New York: New American Library, 1964), p. 241.

11. Handy and Pukui, *Polynesian Family System in Ka-'u, Hawai'i*, pp. 98–101. About modern practices, Handy and Pukui add: "Today it is just a matter of different relatives 'giving' a name informally; such a name 'given' constitutes a bond, a token of *aloha,* an expression of gratification and mark of pride and esteem."

12. Philippe Ariès, *Western Attitudes Toward Death: From the Middle Ages to the Present* (Baltimore: Johns Hopkins University Press, 1974), and, also by Ariès, *The Hour of Our Death* (New York: Alfred A. Knopf, 1981) and *Images of Man and Death* (Cambridge, Mass.: Harvard University Press, 1985). Except where otherwise noted, material appearing within quotation marks is drawn from Ariès's works. See also T. S. R. Boase, *Death in the Middle Ages: Mortality, Judgment and Remembrance* (New York: McGraw-Hill, 1972); Jacques Choron, *Death and Western Thought* (New York: Macmillan, 1963); Donna C. Kurtz and John Boardman, *Greek Burial Customs* (Ithaca, N.Y.: Cornell University Press, 1971).

13. Charles O. Jackson, "Death Shall Have No Dominion: The Passing of the World of the Dead in America," in *Death and Dying: Views from Many Cultures,* ed. Richard A. Kalish (New York: Baywood, 1980), pp. 47–55.

14. Ian Gentles, "Funeral Customs in Historical Context," *Journal of Palliative Care* 4, no. 3 (1988): 16–20.

15. These paintings, originally in the Cemetery of the Innocents in Paris, were destroyed in the late seventeenth century, but reproductions or copies can be seen in the woodcuts of the Paris printer Guy Marchant. The Flemish artist Hans Holbein the Younger executed a series of drawings on the theme in 1523–1526, depicting the skeletal figure of death surprising victims in the midst of their daily life. In music, the dance of death theme survives in the German *Totentanz,* which dates from the sixteenth century.

16. See, by Robert S. Gottfried, *The Black Death: Natural and Human Disaster in Medieval Europe* (New York: Free Press, 1983) and "Of Rats and Men," *The Sciences* (November–December 1985): 59–61; and Johan Goudsblom, "Public Health and the Civilizing Process," *The Millbank Quarterly* 64, no. 2 (1986): 161–188. See also Lawrence Biemiller, "Plagues: How People Responded to Them in the Past Is Studied by Scholars as a Guide in AIDS Crisis," *Chronicle of Higher Education* 34 (January 27, 1988): A6–A8.

17. See Georges Bataille, *Death and Sensuality: A Study of Eroticism and the Taboo* (New York: Walker and Company, 1962).

18. See Peter Brown, *The Cult of the Saints: Its Rise and Function in Latin Christianity* (Chicago: University of Chicago Press, 1981); and Patrick J. Geary, *Living with the Dead in the Middle Ages* (Ithaca, N.Y.: Cornell University Press, 1994).

19. Rob Kay, *Santa Cruz Sentinel,* March 20, 1983.

20. Frank Gonzalez-Crussi, "Anatomy and Old Lace: An Eighteenth-Century Attitude Toward Death," *The Sciences* (January–February 1988): 48–49.

21. For more on these historical developments, see the following authors: Diana Williams Combs, *Early Gravestone Art in Georgia and South Carolina* (Athens: University of Georgia Press, 1986); James J. Farrell, *Inventing the American Way of Death, 1830–1920* (Philadelphia: Temple University Press, 1980) and "The Dying of Death: Historical Perspectives," *Death Education* 6 (1982): 105–123; Gordon E. Geddes, *Welcome Joy: Death in Puritan New England* (Ann Arbor: UMI Research Press, 1981); David E. Stannard, *The*

Puritan Way of Death: A Study in Religion, Culture, and Social Change (New York: Oxford University Press, 1977) and "Calm Dwellings: The Brief, Sentimental Age of the Rural Cemetery," *American Heritage* 30, no. 5 (August/September 1979): 42–55, and, edited by Stannard, *Death in America* (Philadelphia: University of Pennsylvania Press, 1975); Michael Vovelle, "A Century and One-Half of American Epitaphs (1600–1813): Toward the Study of Collective Attitudes About Death," *Comparative Studies in Society and History* 22, no. 4 (October 1980): 534–547.

22. See, for example, Elisabeth Darby and Nicola Smith, *The Cult of the Prince Consort* (New Haven, Conn.: Yale University Press, 1983); and John Morley, *Death, Heaven, and the Victorians* (Pittsburgh: University of Pittsburgh Press, 1971).

23. Norbert Elias, *The Loneliness of the Dying* (New York: Basil Blackwell, 1985).

24. Herman Feifel, "The Meaning of Death in American Society," in *Death Education: Preparation for Living,* ed. Betty R. Green and Donald P. Irish (Cambridge, Mass.: Schenkman, 1971).

25. On the anthropology of death, see Maurice Bloch and Jonathan Perry, eds., *Death and the Regeneration of Life* (New York: Cambridge University Press, 1982); Loring M. Danforth, *The Death Rituals of Rural Greece* (Princeton, N.J.: Princeton University Press, 1982); Richard Huntington and Peter Metcalf, *Celebrations of Death: The Anthropology of Mortuary Ritual* (New York: Cambridge University Press, 1979); and Johannes Fabian, "How Others Die: Reflections on the Anthropology of Death," *Social Research* 39 (1972): 543–567.

26. Louise B. Halfe, "The Circle: Death and Dying from a Native Perspective," *Journal of Palliative Care* 5, no. 1 (1989): 37–41. See also Paul Radin, *The Road of Life and Death: A Ritual Drama of the American Indians* (Princeton, N.J.: Princeton University Press, 1973).

27. Åke Hultkrantz, *Native Religions of North America: The Power of Visions and Fertility* (New York: Harper and Row, 1987); see also, by Hultkrantz, *The Religions of the American Indians* (Berkeley: University of California Press, 1979) and *The Study of American Indian Religions* (New York: Crossroad, 1983).

28. Jamake Highwater, *The Primal Mind: Vision and Reality in Indian America* (New York: Harper and Row, 1981), p. 165.

29. Joseph E. Trimble and Candace M. Fleming, "Providing Counseling Services for Native American Indians: Client, Counselor, and Community Characteristics," in *Counseling Across Cultures,* 3d ed., ed. Paul B. Pedersen, Juris G. Dragus, Walter J. Lonner, and Joseph E. Trimble (Honolulu: University of Hawaii Press, 1989), pp. 177–204.

30. See, for example, C. E. Schorer, "Two Centuries of Miami Indian Death Customs," *Omega: Journal of Death and Dying* 20 (1989–1990): 75–79; and Carl Waldman, *Atlas of the North American Indian* (New York: Facts on File, 1985).

31. Quoted in Vine Deloria, Jr., *God Is Red* (New York: Dell, 1973), pp. 176–177.

32. Malcolm Margolin, *The Ohlone Way: Indian Life in the San Francisco-Monterey Bay Area* (Berkeley, Calif.: Heyday Books, 1978), pp. 145–149.

33. Concern for the proper disposition of human remains is a major issue for indigenous peoples. See "Human Remains: Contemporary Issues," in *Death Studies* 14 (1990), ed. Glen W. Davidson and Larry W. Zimmerman.

34. David G. Mandelbaum, "Social Uses of Funeral Rites," in *The Meaning of Death,* ed. Herman Feifel (New York: McGraw-Hill, 1959), pp. 189–217.

35. Noel Q. King, *Religions of Africa: A Pilgrimage into Traditional Religions*

(New York: Harper and Row, 1970), pp. 13–14; see also, by King, *Christian and Muslim in Africa* (New York: Harper and Row, 1971), p. 95.

36. King, *Religions of Africa*, p. 68.

37. Kofi Asare Opoku, "African Perspectives on Death and Dying," in *Perspectives on Death and Dying: Cross-Cultural and Multidisciplinary Views*, ed. Arthur Berger et al. (Philadelphia: The Charles Press, 1989), pp. 14–23. See also Dominique Zahan, *The Religion, Spirituality, and Thought of Traditional Africa* (Chicago: University of Chicago Press, 1979).

38. Kwasi Wiredu, "Death and the Afterlife in African Culture," in *Perspectives on Death and Dying*, ed. Berger et al., pp. 24–37.

39. From a story by Robert Dvorchak, *Los Angeles Times* (July 8, 1990).

40. Jack Goody, *Death, Property, and the Ancestors: A Study of the Mortuary Customs of the LoDagaa of West Africa* (Stanford, Calif.: Stanford University Press, 1962).

41. Gillian Feeley-Harnik, "The Political Economy of Death: Communication and Change in Malagasy Colonial History," *American Ethnologist* 11, no. 1 (1984): 1–19.

42. Olatunde Bayo Lawuyi, "Obituary and Ancestral Worship: Analysis of a Contemporary Cultural Form in Nigeria," *Sociological Analysis* 48, no. 4 (1988): 372–379.

43. Miguel León-Portilla, "Those Made Worthy by Divine Sacrifice: The Faith of Ancient Mexico," in *South and Meso-American Native Spirituality: From the Cult of the Feathered Serpent to the Theology of Liberation*, ed. Gary H. Gossen (New York: Crossroad, 1993), pp. 41–64.

44. Octavio Paz, *The Labyrinth of Solitude: Life and Thought in Mexico* (New York: Grove Press, 1961).

45. Jose Antonio Burciaga, "A Day to Laugh at Death," *San Jose Mercury News*, November 1, 1985.

46. See Ignacio Aguilar and Virginia N. Wood, "Therapy Through a Death Ritual," in *Death and Dying: Theory, Research, and Practice*, ed. Larry Bugen (Dubuque, Iowa: William C. Brown, 1979), pp. 131–141; Barbara Brodman, *The Mexican Cult of Death in Myth and Literature* (Gainesville: University of Florida Press, 1976); Patricia Fernández Kelly, "Death in Mexican Folk Culture," *American Quarterly* 26, no. 5 (December 1974): 516–535; Oscar Lewis, *A Death in the Sanchez Family* (New York: Vintage Books, 1970); and Joan Moore, "The Death Culture of Mexico and Mexican Americans," in *Death and Dying: Views from Many Cultures*, ed. Kalish, pp. 72–91.

47. León-Portilla, "Those Made Worthy," p. 56.

48. Judith Strupp Green, "The Days of the Dead in Oaxaca, Mexico: An Historical Inquiry," in *Death and Dying: Views from Many Cultures*, ed. Kalish, pp. 56–71.

49. Glenn Whitney, "Mexico's Day of the Dead Is Actually Very Lively," United Press International story in the *Honolulu Star-Bulletin & Advertiser*, November 1, 1987.

50. Marie Nunez, a caretaker of the village, quoted in Whitney, "Mexico's Day of the Dead."

51. Paz, *Labyrinth of Solitude*.

52. Louise M. Burkhart, "The Cult of the Virgin of Guadalupe in Mexico," in *South and Meso-American Native Spirituality*, ed. Gossen, pp. 198–227.

53. Sources consulted in preparing this section include *A Cultural Dictionary of Japan*, ed. Momoo Yamaguchi and Setsuko Kojima (Tokyo: The Japan Times, 1979); H. Byron Earhart, "Religions of Japan: Many Traditions Within One Sacred Way," in *Religious Traditions of the World*, ed. Earhart (San Francisco: HarperCollins, 1992); Takashi Ishikawa, *Kokoro: The Soul of Japan* (Tokyo: The East Publications, 1986); Hajime

Nakamura, *Ways of Thinking of Eastern Peoples: India, China, Tibet, Japan,* trans. and ed. Philip P. Wiener (Honolulu: University of Hawaii Press, 1964); Sokyo Ono, *Shinto: The Kami Way* (Rutland, Vt.: Charles E. Tuttle, 1962); Ian Reader, *Religion in Contemporary Japan* (Honolulu: University of Hawaii Press, 1991); Robert J. Smith, *Ancestor Worship in Contemporary Japan* (Stanford, Calif.: Stanford University Press, 1974); and Yamaori Tetsuo, "The Metamorphosis of Ancestors," *Japan Quarterly* 33, no. 1 (January–March 1986): 50–53.

54. Dennis Klass, "Ancestor Worship in Japan: Dependence and the Resolution of Grief," *Omega: Journal of Death and Dying* (in press).

55. Reader, *Religion in Contemporary Japan,* p. 7.

56. Ono, *Shinto,* p. 3.

57. Nakamura, *Ways of Thinking,* p. 585.

58. Rev. Shinryo Sakada, Buddhist priest, Jodo Shinshu sect. Personal communication.

59. Nakamura, *Ways of Thinking,* p. 585.

60. Reader, *Religion in Contemporary Japan,* p. 90.

61. Klass, "Ancestor Worship in Japan."

CHAPTER 3

1. Mark W. Speece and Sandor B. Brent, "The Development of Children's Understanding of Death," in *Helping Children Cope with Death and Bereavement,* ed. Charles A. Corr and Donna M. Corr (New York: Springer, in press).

2. Norman Goodman, *Introduction to Sociology* (New York: HarperCollins, 1992), p. 42.

3. Gordon Marshall, ed., *The Concise Oxford Dictionary of Sociology* (New York: Oxford University Press, 1994), p. 104.

4. The authors thank Professor John Williamson, Sociology Department, Boston College, for kindly consenting to review the material covered in this chapter.

5. The authors thank Professor Jack Stevens, Chairman, Social Sciences Division, Cabrillo College, for help in devising figures to illustrate the structural-functionalist approach and symbolic interactionism, and for reviewing the material covered in this chapter.

6. Talcott Parsons, "Death in the Western World," in *Death and Identity,* 3d ed., ed. Robert Fulton and Robert Bendiksen (Philadelphia: The Charles Press, 1993), pp. 72–73.

7. Nancy Scheper-Hughes, "Death Without Weeping: The Violence of Everyday Life in Brazil," in *The Path Ahead: Readings in Death and Dying,* ed. Lynne Ann DeSpelder and Albert Lee Strickland (Mountain View, Calif.: Mayfield, 1995), pp. 41–58; for a more complete account, see Nancy Scheper-Hughes, *Death Without Weeping: The Violence of Everyday Life in Brazil* (Berkeley: University of California Press, 1992).

8. Kathy Charmaz, "Conceptual Approaches to the Study of Death," in *Death and Identity,* 3d ed., ed. Fulton and Bendiksen, pp. 44–45.

9. Robert Blauner, "Death and Social Structure," in *Death and Identity,* rev. ed., ed. Robert Fulton (Bowie, Md.: The Charles Press, 1976), pp. 35–59.

10. Robert Bendiksen, "The Sociology of Death," in *Death and Identity,* rev. ed., ed. Fulton, pp. 59–81.

11. Robert Fulton and Robert Bendiksen, "Introduction," in *Death and Identity,* 3d ed., ed. Fulton and Bendiksen, p. 7.

12. Myra Bluebond-Langner, *The Private Worlds of Dying Children* (Princeton, N.J.: Princeton University Press, 1978), p. 5.

13. Joseph M. Kaufert and John D. O'Neil, "Cultural Mediation of Dying and Grieving Among Native Canadian Patients in Urban Hospitals," in *The Path Ahead,* ed. DeSpelder and Strickland, pp. 59–74; reprinted from *Coping with the Final Tragedy: Cultural Variation in Dying and Grieving,* ed. David R. Counts and Dorothy A. Counts (Amityville, N.Y.: Baywood, 1991), pp. 231–251.

14. Goodman, *Introduction to Sociology,* p. 93.

15. Fulton and Bendiksen, "Introduction," p. 7.

16. Arthur Kleinman, "Problems and Prospects in Comparative Cross-Cultural Medical and Psychiatric Studies," in *Culture and Healing in Asian Societies: Anthropological, Psychiatric, and Public Health Studies,* ed. Arthur Kleinman, Peter Kunstadter, E. Russell Alexander, and James L. Gate (Cambridge, Mass.: Schenkman, 1978), pp. 407–440.

17. See Emily M. Ahern, "Sacred and Secular Medicine in a Taiwan Village: A Study of Cosmological Disorders," in *Culture and Healing in Asian Societies,* ed. Kleinman et al., pp. 17–39; and, in the same source, Katherine Gould-Martin, "Ong-Ia-Kong: The Plague God as Modern Physician," pp. 41–67, as well as E. N. Anderson and Marja L. Anderson, "Folk Dietetics in Two Chinese Communities, and Its Implications for the Study of Chinese Medicine," pp. 69–100. See also Paul U. Unschuld, "Epistemological Issues and Changing Legitimation: Traditional Chinese Medicine in the Twentieth Century," in *Paths to Asian Medical Knowledge,* ed. Charles Leslie and Allan Young (Berkeley: University of California Press, 1992), pp. 44–61; and, by Unschuld, *Medical Ethics in Imperial China: A Study in Historical Anthropology* (Berkeley: University of California Press, 1979).

18. See Judith Farquhar, "Time and Text: Approaching Chinese Medical Practice Through Analysis of a Published Case," in *Paths to Asian Medical Knowledge,* ed. Leslie and Young, pp. 62–73.

19. Wolfgang Stroebe and Margaret Stroebe, "Is Grief Universal? Cultural Variations in the Emotional Reaction to Loss," in *Death and Identity,* 3d ed., ed. Fulton and Bendiksen, p. 181.

20. Greg Owen, Robert Fulton, and Eric Marcusen, "Death at a Distance: A Study of Family Bereavement," in *Death and Identity,* 3d ed., ed. Fulton and Bendiksen, p. 241.

21. Stroebe and Stroebe, "Is Grief Universal?" p. 197.

22. Albert Bandura, *Social Learning Theory* (Englewood Cliffs, N.J.: Prentice-Hall, 1977), pp. 9–10.

23. Ronald L. Akers, *Deviant Behavior: A Social Learning Approach,* 3d ed. (Belmont, Calif.: Wadsworth, 1985), p. 57.

24. The authors thank Professor Ronald L. Akers, Director of the Center for Studies in Criminology and Law at the University of Florida, Gainesville, for help in devising the figure illustrating social learning theory and for making helpful suggestions about the presentation of this theory in the text.

25. Akers, *Deviant Behavior,* p. 5.

26. Glen H. Elder, Jr., Ann Hagell, Laura Rudkin, and Rand D. Conger, "Looking Forward in Troubled Times: The Influence of Social Context on Adolescent Plans and

Orientations," in *Adolescence in Context: The Interplay of Family, School, Peers, and Work in Adjustment,* ed. Rainer K. Silbereisen and Eberhard Todt (New York: Springer-Verlag, 1993), pp. 244–264.

27. Goodman, *Introduction to Sociology,* pp. 84–85.

28. See, for example, Phyllis Silverman, *Widow to Widow* (New York: Springer, 1986); and Scott Campbell and Phyllis Silverman, *Widower: When Men Are Left Alone* (New York: Prentice-Hall, 1987).

29. S. Shirley Feldman and Doreen A. Rosenthal, "Culture Makes a Difference . . . or Does It? A Comparison of Adolescents in Hong Kong, Australia, and the United States," in *Adolescence in Context,* ed. Silbereisen and Todt, pp. 99–124.

30. A. Cordell Perkes and Roberta Schildt, "Death-Related Attitudes of Adolescent Males and Females," *Death Education* 2 (1979): 359–368. For gender differences in adults as well as children, see Judith M. Stillion, *Death and the Sexes: An Examination of Differential Longevity, Attitudes, Behaviors, and Coping Skills* (Washington, D.C.: Hemisphere, 1985).

31. Hedda Sharapan, "'Mister Rogers' Neighborhood': Dealing with Death on a Children's Television Series," *Death Education* 1, no. 1 (1977): 131–136.

32. Martha Wolfenstein and Gilbert Kliman, eds., *Children and the Death of a President: Multi-Disciplinary Studies* (Garden City, N.Y.: Anchor Press/Doubleday, 1965), especially pp. 217–239.

33. "First Graders Paint a Happy Ending," Associated Press story (January 31, 1986); and other newspaper sources.

34. See, for example, Eve Morel, ed., *Fairy Tales and Fables* (New York: Grosset & Dunlap, 1970), pp. 11–13.

35. Ed Young, trans., *Lon Po Po: A Red-Riding Hood Story from China* (New York: Philomel Books, 1989).

36. Kalle Achte, Ritva Fagerstrom, Juha Pentikainen, and Norman L. Farberow, "Themes of Death and Violence in Lullabies of Different Countries," *Omega: Journal of Death and Dying* 20 (1989–1990): 193–204.

37. Reported by Richard Lonetto, *Children's Conceptions of Death* (New York: Springer, 1980), p. 9.

38. Gloria Goldreich, "What Is Death? The Answers in Children's Books—From Fairy Tales to Harsh Reality," *The Hastings Center Report* 7, no. 3 (June 1977): 18–20.

39. David E. Balk and Nancy S. Hogan, "Religion, Spirituality, and Bereaved Adolescents," in *Loss, Threat to Life, and Bereavement: The Child's Perspective,* ed. David W. Adams and Ellie J. Deveau (Amityville, N.Y.: Baywood, in press).

40. Goodman, *Introduction to Sociology,* p. 215.

41. Reed Larson, "Youth Organizations, Hobbies, and Sports as Developmental Contexts," in *Adolescence in Context,* ed. Silbereisen and Todt, pp. 46–65.

42. Ernest Becker, *The Denial of Death* (New York: Free Press, 1973). On the pathological fear of death, see, for example, Vladan Starcevic, "Pathological Fear of Death, Panic Attacks, and Hypochondriasis," *American Journal of Psychoanalysis* 49 (1989): 347–361.

43. For a comprehensive survey of death anxiety research, see Robert A. Neimeyer, ed., *Death Anxiety Handbook: Research, Instrumentation, and Application* (Washington, D.C.: Taylor & Francis, 1993).

44. *Newsweek,* May 5, 1980. See also Roger Rosenblatt, *Children of War* (New York: Anchor/Doubleday, 1983); Claudine Vegh, *I Didn't Say Goodbye: Interviews with the*

Children of the Holocaust (New York: E. P. Dutton, 1985); and Robert Westall, *Children of the Blitz: Memories of Wartime Childhood* (New York: Viking, 1986).

45. James Garbarino, "Challenges We Face in Understanding Children and War: A Personal Essay," in *The Path Ahead*, ed. DeSpelder and Strickland, pp. 169–174; reprinted from *Child Abuse & Neglect* 17, no. 6 (1993): 787–793.

46. Zlata Filipović, "Zlata's Diary: A Child's Life in Sarajevo," in *The Path Ahead*, ed. DeSpelder and Strickland, pp. 175–178; excerpted from *Zlata's Diary: A Child's Life in Sarajevo* (New York: Viking Penguin, 1994).

47. Ice T, "The Killing Fields," in *The Path Ahead*, ed. DeSpelder and Strickland, pp. 179–181; see also *The Ice Opinion* (New York: St. Martin's Press, 1994).

48. See, for example, David J. Schonfeld and Sara Smilansky, "A Cross-Cultural Comparison of Israeli and American Children's Death Concepts," *Death Studies* 13 (1989): 593–604.

49. Ronald Keith Barrett and Lynne Ann DeSpelder, "Ways People Die: The Influence of Environment on a Child's View of Death" (manuscript in preparation).

50. See Gene Stanford and Albert E. Roark, "Seizing the Teachable Moment: Social Learning in the Classroom," *People Watching* 2 (1972): 14–18F; Mary Ryan, "The Teachable Moment: The Washington Center Internship Program," *New Directions for Teaching and Learning* 35 (Fall 1988): 39–47; Noreen M. McAloon, "The Teachable Moment," *Journal of Reading* 36 (October 1992): 150–151; and Patricia Fabiano, "Peer-Based HIV Risk Assessment: A Step-by-Step Guide Through the Teachable Moment," *Journal of American College Health* 41 (May 1993): 297–299.

51. Charles A. Corr, Clyde M. Nabe, and Donna M. Corr, *Death and Dying: Life and Living* (Pacific Grove, Calif.: Brooks/Cole, 1993), p. 457.

52. Lynne Ann DeSpelder and Nathalie Prettyman, *A Guidebook for Teaching Family Living* (Boston: Allyn and Bacon, 1980), pp. 130–134.

53. Goodman, *Introduction to Sociology*, p. 37.

54. David Clark, ed., *The Sociology of Death: Theory, Culture, Practice* (Cambridge, Mass.: Blackwell, 1993), p. 3.

55. David H. Olson and John DeFrain, *Marriage and Family: Diversity and Strengths* (Mountain View, Calif.: Mayfield, 1994), p. 37.

56. Stroebe and Stroebe, "Is Grief Universal?" p. 201. See also M. Eisenbruch, "Cross-Cultural Aspects of Bereavement: Ethnic and Cultural Variations in the Development of Bereavement Practices," *Culture, Medicine, and Psychiatry* 8 (1984): 315–347.

57. See, for example, Ronald Keith Barrett, "Contemporary African-American Funeral Rites and Traditions," in *The Path Ahead*, ed. DeSpelder and Strickland, pp. 80–92.

58. Christopher L. Hayes and Richard A. Kalish, "Death-Related Experiences and Funerary Practices of the Hmong Refugee in the United States," in *The Path Ahead*, ed. DeSpelder and Strickland, pp. 75–79; reprinted from *Omega: Journal of Death and Dying* 18, no. 1 (1987–1988): 63–70.

59. See Philip A. Mellor, "Death in High Modernity: The Contemporary Presence and Absence of Death," in *The Sociology of Death*, ed. Clark, pp. 11–30 (especially pp. 12–13, 18–19). See also, in the same volume, Jane Littlewood, "The Denial of Death and Rites of Passage in Contemporary Societies," pp. 69–84.

60. Eleanor C. Nordyke, *The Peopling of Hawai'i*, 2d ed. (Honolulu: University of Hawaii Press, 1989), p. 1.

61. Patrick Vinton Kirch, *Feathered Gods and Fishhooks: An Introduction to Hawaiian Archeology and Prehistory* (Honolulu: University of Hawaii Press, 1985), p. 298.

62. Interestingly, the term "Asian American" is rarely used in Hawaii; instead, people identify themselves as Chinese, Japanese, or Filipino, or whatever, while at the same time employing the pan-ethnic identity of being a local. Jonathan Okamura says that the notion of "local" represents "the common identity of people of Hawaii and their shared appreciation of the land, peoples, and cultures of the islands." See Jonathan Y. Okamura, "Why There Are No Asian Americans in Hawai'i: The Continuing Significance of Local Identity," *Social Process in Hawaii* 35 (1994): 161–178.

63. See Benjamin B. C. Young, "The Hawaiians," in *People and Cultures of Hawaii: A Psychocultural Profile,* ed. John F. McDermott, Jr., Wen-Shing Tseng, and Thomas W. Maretzki (Honolulu: John A. Burns School of Medicine and University of Hawaii Press, 1980), pp. 5–24.

64. George Hu'eu Sanford Kanahele, *Ku Kanaka, Stand Tall: A Search for Hawaiian Values* (Honolulu: University of Hawaii Press, 1986), p. 182. On the soul after death and realms of the spirits of the dead, see also Donald D. Kilolani Mitchell, *Resource Units in Hawaiian Culture* (Honolulu: The Kamehameha Schools Press, 1982), pp. 84–86.

65. Bob Krauss, "Wails and Prayers for Missing Bones," *Honolulu Advertiser* (March 6, 1994): A1.

66. Nordyke, *The Peopling of Hawaii,* p. 52. See also Walter F. Char, Wen-Shing Tseng, Kwong-Yen Lum, and Jing Hsu, "The Chinese," in *People and Cultures of Hawaii,* ed. McDermott et al., pp. 53–72.

67. Laurence G. Thompson, *Chinese Religion: An Introduction,* 4th ed. (Belmont, Calif.: Wadsworth, 1989), p. 38.

68. Ibid., p. 47.

69. This discussion of contemporary Chinese funeral customs in Hawaii is based on interviews by the authors with Anna Ordenstein and Ken Ordenstein who, along with their Chinese-Hawaiian-Jewish-Portuguese forebears, have provided funeral services to Hawaii residents over the course of five generations. We are grateful for their kind and generous assistance in responding to our request for information about contemporary death practices in Hawaii.

70. Thompson, *Chinese Religion,* p. 23.

71. Terence Rogers and Satoru Izutsu, "The Japanese," in *People and Cultures of Hawaii,* ed. McDermott et al., pp. 73–99; see especially pp. 87ff.

72. John F. McDermott, Jr., "Toward an Interethnic Society," in *People and Cultures of Hawaii,* ed. McDermott et al., p. 231. See also Wayne S. Wooden, *What Price Paradise? Changing Social Patterns in Hawaii* (Washington: University Press of America, 1981).

73. David W. Plath, "Resistance at Forty-Eight: Old-Age Brinksmanship and Japanese Life Course Pathways," in *Aging and Life Course Transitions: An Interdisciplinary Perspective,* ed. Tamara K. Hareven and Kathleen J. Adams (New York: Guilford Press, 1982), pp. 109–125, quote p. 118.

74. McDermott, "Toward an Interethnic Society," pp. 229–230. See also Elvi Whittaker, *The Mainland Haole: The White Experience in Hawaii* (New York: Columbia University Press, 1986).

75. Mary Kawena Pukui and Samuel H. Elbert, *Hawaiian Dictionary,* rev. ed. (Honolulu: University of Hawaii Press, 1986), p. 34.

76. McDermott, "Toward an Interethnic Society," p. 225.

77. Ibid., p. 231.

78. Paul Spickard, quoted in Susan Yim, "Hapa in Hawai'i," *Honolulu* (December 1994), pp. 44–47, 90, 92.

79. Sandor B. Brent and Mark W. Speece, " 'Adult' Conceptualization of

Irreversibility: Implications for the Development of the Concept of Death," *Death Studies* 17 (1993): 203–224.

80. Sandor B. Brent, Mark W. Speece, Chongede Lin, Qi Dong, and Chongming Yang, "The Development of the Concept of Death Among Chinese and U.S. Children 3–17 Years of Age: From Binary to 'Fuzzy' Concepts?" in press.

81. David W. Plath, "Resistance at Forty-Eight," pp. 115–116.

82. Richard A. Kalish and David K. Reynolds, *Death and Ethnicity: A Psychocultural Study* (Los Angeles: Ethel Percy Andrus Gerontology Center, University of Southern California, 1976).

C H A P T E R 4

1. "Hospital Utilization Rates," *Statistical Abstract of the United States 1994,* 114th ed. (Washington, D.C.: Government Printing Office, 1994), p. 128.

2. E. Alison Holman, "Death and the Health Professional: Organization and Defense in Health Care," *Death Studies* 14 (1990): 13–24.

3. See Margaretta K. Bowers et al., *Counseling the Dying* (New York: Thomas Nelson & Sons, 1964).

4. Charles E. Rosenberg, "Institutionalized Ambiguity: Conflict and Continuity in the American Hospital," *Second Opinion* 12 (November 1989): 63–73; see also, by Rosenberg, *The Care of Strangers: The Rise of America's Hospital System* (New York: Basic Books, 1987).

5. "National Health Expenditures," *Statistical Abstract of the United States 1994,* p. 109.

6. See, for example, "Confronting the Crisis in Health Care: An Interview with Arnold Relman," *Bulletin of the Park Ridge Center* (September 1989): 35–42.

7. Rosemary Stevens, *In Sickness and in Wealth: American Hospitals in the Twentieth Century* (New York: Basic Books, 1989), p. 343. See also Gordon K. Douglas, "Ethical Implications of the Revolution in Health Care Finance," in *Health Care and Its Costs,* ed. Walter E. Wiest (Lanham, Md.: University Press of America, 1988); and Victor R. Fuchs, "Has Cost Containment Gone Too Far?" *Millbank Quarterly* 64, no. 3 (1986): 479–488.

8. Peter E. Dans, "The Health Care Revolution: A Preliminary Report from the Front," *Journal of the American Medical Association* 259 (June 17, 1988): 3452–3453.

9. Diana B. Dutton, Thomas A. Preston, and Nancy E. Pfund, *Worse Than the Disease: Pitfalls of Medical Progress* (New York: Cambridge University Press, 1988), p. 4. See also William Ray Arney and Bernard J. Bergen, *Medicine and the Management of Living: Taming the Last Great Beast* (Chicago: University of Chicago Press, 1984); and Stanley Joel Reiser, *Medicine and the Reign of Technology* (New York: Cambridge University Press, 1978).

10. Edward R. Pinckney and Cathey Pinckney, "Unnecessary Measures: Physicians Are Relying Too Heavily on Medical Tests," *The Sciences* 29, no. 1 (January/February 1989): 21–27.

11. Quoted in Paul E. Kalb and David H. Miller, "Utilization Strategies for Intensive Care Units," *Journal of the American Medical Association* 261, no. 16 (1989): 2389–2395.

12. Graham Loomes and Lynda McKenzie, "The Use of QALYs in Health Care Decision Making," *Social Science and Medicine* 28 (1989): 299–308.

13. Daniel Callahan, "The Limits of Medical Progress: A Principle of Symmetry,"

in *The Path Ahead: Readings in Death and Dying,* ed. Lynne Ann DeSpelder and Albert Lee Strickland (Mountain View, Calif.: Mayfield, 1995), pp. 103–105; excerpted from *What Kind of Life: The Limits of Medical Progress* (New York: Simon and Schuster, 1990). See also, by Callahan, "Modernizing Mortality: Medical Progress and the Good Society," *Hastings Center Report* (January–February 1990): 28–32.

14. Elisabeth Kübler-Ross, *On Death and Dying* (New York: Macmillan, 1969), p. 249.

15. Robert Kastenbaum and Ruth Aisenberg, *The Psychology of Death, Concise Edition* (New York: Springer, 1976), p. 179. See also Orville G. Brim, Jr., Howard E. Freeman, Sol Levine, and Norman A. Scotch, eds., *The Dying Patient* (New York: Russell Sage Foundation, 1970); and Richard Schulz and David Alderman, "How the Medical Staff Copes with Dying Patients: A Critical Review," *Omega: Journal of Death and Dying* 7 (1976): 11–21.

16. Jeanne Quint Benoliel, "Health Care Providers and Dying Patients: Critical Issues in Terminal Care," *Omega: Journal of Death and Dying* 18, no. 4 (1987–1988): 341–363.

17. Robert Blauner, "Death and Social Structure," *Psychiatry* 29, no. 4 (November 1966): 378–394. See also Diana Crane, *The Sanctity of Social Life: Physicians' Treatment of Critically Ill Patients* (New York: Russell Sage Foundation, 1975).

18. William M. Buchholz, "Medical Eschatology: Combined Role for Caregiver and Scientist," *American Journal of Hospice Care* (January–February 1985): 22–24.

19. Balfour M. Mount, "Keeping the Mission," in *The Path Ahead,* ed. DeSpelder and Strickland, pp. 125–132; reprinted from *American Journal of Hospice & Palliative Care* 9, no. 5 (September–October 1992): 32–37.

20. "Deaths and Death Rates by Selected Causes," *Statistical Abstract of the United States 1994,* p. 93.

21. Seth B. Golbey, "Critical Cares: Life-Saving Aeromedical Helicopter Services," *AOPA Pilot* 30, no. 4 (April 1987): 39–46, and "Dust Off," pp. 46–48.

22. John Grossman, "Emergency! Emergency!" *Health* 21, no. 7 (July 1989): 76–94.

23. Inge B. Corless, "Settings for Terminal Care," *Omega: Journal of Death and Dying* 18, no. 4 (1987–1988): 319–340.

24. David S. Greer, Vincent Mor, and Robert Kastenbaum, "Concepts, Questions, and Research Priorities," in *The Hospice Experiment,* ed. Mor, Greer, and Kastenbaum (Baltimore: Johns Hopkins University Press, 1988), p. 249.

25. James Luther Adams, "Palliative Care in the Light of Early Christian Concepts," *Journal of Palliative Care* 5, no. 3 (1989): 5–8.

26. Sandol Stoddard, "Hospice in the United States: An Overview," *Journal of Palliative Care* 5, no. 3 (1989): 10–19.

27. See Thelma Ingles, "St. Christopher's Hospice" in *A Hospice Handbook: A New Way to Care for the Dying,* ed. Michael P. Hamilton and Helen F. Reid (Grand Rapids, Mich.: Eerdmans, 1980), pp. 45–56; and William E. Phipps, "The Origin of Hospices/Hospitals," *Death Studies* 12, no. 2 (1988): 91–99.

28. Quoted in Constance Holden, "Hospices for the Dying, Relief from Pain and Fear," in *Hospice Handbook,* ed. Hamilton and Reid, p. 61.

29. Robert W. Buckingham, *The Complete Hospice Guide* (New York: Harper and Row, 1983), pp. 13–15.

30. William M. Lamers, Jr., "Hospice: Enhancing the Quality of Life," in *The Path Ahead,* ed. DeSpelder and Strickland, pp. 116–124; reprinted from *Oncology* 4, no. 5 (May 1990): 121–126.

31. See Charles A. Corr and Donna M. Corr, eds., *Hospice Approaches to Pediatric Care* (New York: Springer, 1985).

32. See Michael A. Patchner and Mark B. Finn, "Volunteers: The Life-Line of Hospice," *Omega: Journal of Death and Dying* 18 (1987–1988): 135–144.

33. Corless, "Settings for Terminal Care," p. 331. See also Josefina B. Magno, "The Hospice Concept of Care: Facing the 1990s," *Death Studies* 14 (1990): 109–119.

34. Barbara McCann, "Hospice Care in the United States: The Struggle for Definition and Survival," *Journal of Palliative Care* 4, no. 1–2 (1988): 16–18.

35. V. David Schwantes and Margaret Ann Smith, *Resource Allocation: The Key to Better Hospital Cost Management* (Minneapolis: Health Initiatives Press, 1994), p. 10.

36. Daniel O. Dugan, "Death and Dying: Emotional, Spiritual, and Ethical Support for Patients and Families," *Journal of Psychosocial Nursing* 25, no. 7 (1987): 21–29.

37. Clive F. Seale, "What Happens in Hospices: A Review of Research Evidence," *Social Science and Medicine* 28, no. 6 (1989): 551–559.

38. Pam Brown, Betty Davies, and Nola Martens, "Families in Supportive Care—Part II: Palliative Care at Home: A Viable Care Setting," *Journal of Palliative Care* 6, no. 3 (1990): 21–27.

39. See, for example, Ted Eidson, ed., *The AIDS Caregiver's Handbook* (New York: St. Martin's Press, 1988); and Leonard J. Martelli, Fran D. Peltz, and William Messina, *When Someone You Know Has AIDS: A Practical Guide* (New York: Crown, 1987).

40. Bart Collopy, Nancy Dubler, and Connie Zuckerman, "The Ethics of Home Care: Autonomy and Accommodation," *Hastings Center Report* (March/April 1990): Supplement.

41. Brown et al., "Palliative Care at Home," p. 24.

42. Mary-Ellen Siegel, "I Can Cope with Cancer," *Cancer News* 38, no. 2 (Spring/Summer 1984): 10–12.

43. See "The Shanti Project: A Community Model of Psychosocial Support for Patients and Families Facing Life-Threatening Illness," in *Psychosocial Care of the Dying Patient,* ed. Charles A. Garfield (New York: McGraw-Hill, 1978), pp. 355–364.

44. Information provided by Frank Ostaseski, director of Zen Hospice Project, and based on the Project's "Mission Statement" and "At a Glance" fact sheet.

45. Frank Ostaseski, "Stories of Lives Lived and Now Ending," *Inquiring Mind: A Journal of the Vipassana Community* 10, no. 2 (Spring 1994): 14–16.

46. Ralph Hingson, Norman A. Scotch, James Sorenson, and Judith P. Swazey, *In Sickness and in Health: Social Dimensions of Medical Care* (St. Louis: C. V. Mosby, 1981), pp. 120, 139–140, 257–265.

47. C. D. Bessinger, "Doctoring: The Philosophic Milieu," *Southern Medical Journal* 81, no. 12 (1988): 1558–1562. See also Edmund D. Pellegrino and David C. Thomasma, *A Philosophical Basis for Medical Practice: Towards a Philosophy and Ethic of the Healing Professions* (New York: Oxford University Press, 1981).

48. Stanley Joel Reiser, "The Era of the Patient: Using the Experience of Illness in Shaping the Missions of Health Care," in *The Path Ahead,* ed. DeSpelder and Strickland, pp. 106–115; reprinted from *JAMA* 269, no. 8 (February 24, 1993): 1012–1017.

49. Clyde Nabe, "Health Care and the Transcendent," *Death Studies* 13 (1989): 557–565.

50. Cited in Bessinger, "Doctoring."

51. Richard B. Gunderman, "Medicine and the Question of Suffering," *Second Opinion* 14 (July 1990): 15–25.

52. For a model of how such discussion can take place, see Ernest Rosenbaum, "Oncology/Hematology and Psychosocial Support of the Cancer Patient," in *Psychosocial Care of the Dying Patient,* ed. Garfield, pp. 169–184.

53. Candace West, *Routine Complications: Troubles with Talk Between Doctors and Patients* (Bloomington: Indiana University Press, 1984).

54. Sandra L. Bertman, Michael D. Wertheimer, and H. Brownell Wheeler, "Humanities in Surgery, a Life-Threatening Situation: Communicating the Diagnosis," *Death Studies* 10 (1986): 431–439.

55. Richard S. Sandor, "On Death and Coding," in *The Path Ahead,* ed. DeSpelder and Strickland, pp. 144–147; reprinted from *Parabola* 28, no. 1 (February 1993): 14–18.

56. See Albert Lee Strickland and Lynne Ann DeSpelder, "Communicating About Death and Dying," in *A Challenge for Living: Dying, Death, and Bereavement,* ed. Inge B. Corless, Barbara B. Germino, and Mary A. Pittman (Boston: Jones and Bartlett, 1995), pp. 37–51.

57. "Tapping Human Potential: An Interview with Norman Cousins," *Second Opinion* 14 (July 1990): 57–71.

58. See, for example, *Foundations of Psychoneuroimmunology,* ed. Steven Locke et al. (New York: Aldine, 1985); and *Psychoneuroimmunology,* ed. Robert Ader, David L. Felten, and Nicholas Cohen (San Diego: Academic Press, 1990).

59. Quoted in Marilee Ivars Donovan and Sandra Girton Pierce, *Cancer Care Nursing* (New York: Appleton-Century-Crofts, 1976), p. 32.

60. Betty Davies, Joanne Chekryn Reimer, and Nola Martens, "Families in Supportive Care—Part I: The Transition of Fading Away: The Nature of the Transition," *Journal of Palliative Care* 6, no. 3 (1990): 12–20.

61. See, for example, David A. Alexander, " 'Stressors' and Difficulties in Dealing with the Terminal Patient," *Journal of Palliative Care* 6, no. 3 (1990): 28–33.

62. C. A. J. McLauchlan, "Handling Distressed Relatives and Breaking Bad News," *British Medical Journal* 301 (November 17, 1990): 1145–1149.

63. See, for example, Egilde P. Seravalli, "The Dying Patient, the Physician, and the Fear of Death," *New England Journal of Medicine* 319 (December 29, 1988): 1728–1730.

64. See Donovan and Pierce, *Cancer Care Nursing.* See also Therese A. Rando, *Grief, Dying, and Death: Clinical Interventions for Caregivers* (Champaign, Ill.: Research Press, 1984).

65. Jeanne Brimigion, "Living with Dying," in *Dealing with Death and Dying* (Nursing Skillbook), 2d ed. (Horsham, Pa.: Intermed Communications, 1980), pp. 91–96.

66. M. L. S. Vachon, W. A. L. Layall, and S. J. J. Freeman, "Measurement and Management of Stress in Health Professionals Working with Advanced Cancer Patients," *Death Education* 1 (1978): 365–369.

67. Jeanette Pickrel, " 'Tell Me Your Story': Using Life Review in Counseling the Terminally Ill," *Death Studies* 13 (1989): 127–135.

68. For additional resources, see Robert Buckman, *I Don't Know What to Say . . . : How to Help and Support Someone Who Is Dying* (Boston: Little, Brown, 1989); David Carroll, *Living with Dying: A Loving Guide for Family and Close Friends* (New York: McGraw-Hill, 1985); Judylaine Fine, *Afraid to Ask: A Book for Families to Share About Cancer* (New York: Lothrop, Lee & Shepard, 1986); Earl Grollman, *In Sickness and in Health: How to Cope When Your Loved One Is Ill* (Boston: Beacon Press, 1987);

Lawrence LeShan, *Cancer as a Turning Point: A Handbook for People with Cancer, Their Families, and Health Professionals* (New York: E. P. Dutton, 1989); and Stephen Levine, *Healing into Life and Death* (Garden City, N.Y.: Anchor Press/Doubleday, 1987).

69. Janmarie Silvera, "Crossing the Border," in *The Path Ahead,* ed. DeSpelder and Strickland, pp. 301–302.

C H A P T E R 5

1. "Deaths and Death Rates by Selected Causes," *Statistical Abstract of the United States 1994,* 114th ed. (Washington, D.C.: Government Printing Office, 1994), p. 93.

2. A. D. Lopez, "Competing Causes of Death: A Review of Recent Trends in Mortality in Industrialized Countries with Special Reference to Cancer," *Annals of the New York Academy of Science* 609 (1990): 58–74.

3. G. P. Sholevar and R. Perkel, "Family Systems Intervention and Physical Illness," *General Hospital Psychiatry* 12 (1990): 363–372.

4. M. E. Koster and J. Bergsma, "Problems and Coping Behavior of Facial Cancer Patients," *Social Science and Medicine* 30 (1990): 569–578.

5. See, for example, D. Welch-McCaffrey, B. Hoffman, S. A. Leigh, L. J. Loescher, and F. L. Meyskens, Jr., "Surviving Adult Cancers: Part 2, Psychosocial Implications," *Annals of Internal Medicine* (1989): 517–524.

6. See Charles A. Garfield, *Stress and Survival: The Emotional Realities of Life-Threatening Illness* (St. Louis: C. V. Mosby, 1979); and Lon G. Nungusser and William D. Bullock, *Notes on Living Until We Say Goodbye: A Personal Guide* (New York: St. Martin's Press, 1988).

7. Elisabeth Kübler-Ross, *On Death and Dying* (New York: Macmillan, 1969). See also Edwin S. Shneidman, "Death Work and the Stages of Dying," in Robert Fulton et al., *Death and Dying: Challenge and Change* (Reading, Mass.: Addison-Wesley, 1978), pp. 181–182.

8. Harold Brodkey, "To My Readers," in *The Path Ahead: Readings in Death and Dying,* ed. Lynne Ann DeSpelder and Albert Lee Strickland (Mountain View, Calif.: Mayfield, 1995), pp. 295–300; reprinted from *The New Yorker* (June 21, 1993).

9. Herman Feifel, "Psychology and Death: Meaningful Rediscovery," in *The Path Ahead,* ed. DeSpelder and Strickland, pp. 19–28; reprinted from *American Psychologist* 45 (April 1990): 537–543.

10. Charles A. Corr, "A Task-Based Approach to Coping with Dying," in *The Path Ahead,* ed. DeSpelder and Strickland, pp. 303–311; reprinted from *Omega: Journal of Death and Dying* 24 (1991–1992): 81–94.

11. Barney G. Glaser and Anselm L. Strauss, *Awareness of Dying* (Chicago: Aldine, 1965).

12. See, for example, Stephanie Matthews Simonton, *The Healing Family: The Simonton Approach for Families Facing Illness* (New York: Bantam, 1984); O. Carl Simonton, Stephanie Matthews Simonton, and James Crieghton, *Getting Well Again: A Step-by-Step Guide to Overcoming Cancer for Patients and Their Families* (Los Angeles: J. P. Tarcher, 1978); O. Carl Simonton and Stephanie Matthews Simonton, "Belief Systems and Management of the Emotional Aspects of Malignancy," *Journal of Transpersonal Psychology* 7 (1975): 29–47; and Dennis T. Jaffe and David E. Bresler, "The Use of Guided Imagery as an Adjunct to Medical Diagnosis and Treatment," *Journal of Humanistic Psychology* 20, no. 4 (Fall 1980): 45–59.

13. Orville Kelly, "Making Today Count," in *Death and Dying: Theory/Research/Practice,* ed. Larry A. Bugen (Dubuque, Iowa: William C. Brown, 1979), pp. 277–283. See also Orville E. Kelly, *Until Tomorrow Comes* (New York: Everest House, 1979).

14. Mickey S. Eisenberg, Lawrence Bergner, Alfred P. Hallstrom, and Richard O. Cummins, "Sudden Cardiac Death," *Scientific American* 254, no. 5 (May 1986): 37–43.

15. Gideon Gil, "The Artificial Heart Juggernaut," *Hastings Center Report* 14, no. 2 (March–April 1989): 24–31.

16. *Carcinomas*—that is, cancers of the skin, mucous membranes, and glandular tissues—are more likely to exhibit metastasis than are *sarcomas*—cancers of the connective tissues such as cartilage, muscle, and bone. Examples of carcinomas include cancers of the skin and breast, as well as cancers of the liver, pancreas, intestines, prostate, and thyroid.

17. Leonard L. Bailey, "Organ Transplantation: A Paradigm of Medical Progress," *Hastings Center Report* (January–February 1990): 24–28.

18. "Organ Transplants and Grafts," *Statistical Abstract of the United States 1994,* p. 131.

19. A description of the psychological issues relative to transplants from a recipient's viewpoint can be found in Robert G. Clouse, "A New Heart in the Face of Old Ethical Problems," *Second Opinion* 12 (November 1989): 13–26. Responses to Clouse's article in the same journal issue are provided by Patricia M. Park, a transplant research nurse, "The Transplant Odyssey," pp. 27–32; George J. Annas, a medical ethicist, "Feeling Good about Recycled Hearts," pp. 33–39; and a transplant-program chaplain, Leslie G. Reimer, "The Power of the Individual's Story," pp. 40–45.

20. See Renee C. Fox and Judith P. Swazey, *The Courage to Fail: A Social View of Organ Transplants and Dialysis* (Chicago: University of Chicago Press, 1974).

21. David K. Reynolds, *A Thousand Waves: A Sensible Life Style for Sensitive People* (New York: Quill/Morrow, 1990).

22. Anson Shupe and Jeffrey K. Hadden, "Symbolic Healing," *Second Opinion* 12 (November 1989): 74–97.

23. Ibid., p. 80. See also Robert Ornstein and David Sobel, *The Healing Brain: Breakthrough Discoveries About How the Brain Keeps Us Healthy* (New York: Simon & Schuster, 1987).

24. "Tapping Human Potential: An Interview with Norman Cousins," *Second Opinion* 14 (July 1990): 57–71. See also Norman Cousins, *Anatomy of an Illness as Perceived by the Patient: Reflections on Healing and Regeneration* (New York: W. W. Norton, 1979).

25. Ross E. Gray and Brian D. Doan, "Heroic Self-healing and Cancer: Clinical Issues for the Health Professions," *Journal of Palliative Care* 6, no. 1 (1990): 32–41.

26. Michael H. Levy, "Pain Control Research in the Terminally Ill," *Omega: Journal of Death and Dying* 18 (1987–1988): 265–279.

27. Linda C. Garro, "Culture, Pain and Cancer," *Journal of Palliative Care* 6, no. 3 (1990): 34–44.

28. See, for example, Pam Brown, Betty Davies, and Nola Martens, "Families in Supportive Care—Part II: Palliative Care at Home: A Viable Care Setting," *Journal of Palliative Care* 6, no. 3 (1990): 21–27.

29. Levy, "Pain Control Research," p. 266.

30. Robert Kastenbaum and Claude Normand, "Deathbed Scenes as Imagined by the Young and Experienced by the Old," *Death Studies* 14 (1990): 201–217.

31. See Barney G. Glaser and Anselm L. Strauss, *Time for Dying* (Chicago: Aldine, 1968). For a brief description of the dying trajectory, see Robert Kastenbaum and

Beatrice Kastenbaum, eds., *Encyclopedia of Death* (Phoenix: Oryx Press, 1989), pp. 275–277.

32. Kastenbaum and Kastenbaum, *Encyclopedia of Death,* pp. 275–276. See also E. Mansell Pattison, *The Experience of Dying* (Englewood Cliffs, N.J.: Prentice-Hall, 1977).

33. Avery D. Weisman, *On Dying and Denying: A Psychiatric Study of Terminality* (New York: Behavioral Publications, 1972). See also Avery D. Weisman, *Coping with Cancer* (New York: McGraw-Hill, 1979).

34. Eric J. Cassell, "Dying in a Technological Society," in *Death Inside Out: The Hastings Center Report,* ed. Peter Steinfels and Robert M. Veatch (New York: Harper and Row, 1974), pp. 43–48. See also David Sudnow, *Passing On: The Social Organization of Dying* (Englewood Cliffs, N.J.: Prentice-Hall, 1967), and the seminal work by Glaser and Strauss, *Awareness of Dying.*

35. Talcott Parsons, *The Social System* (New York: Free Press, 1951). See also Russell Noyes, Jr., and John Clancy, "The Dying Role: Its Relevance to Improved Patient Care," in *Psychiatry* 40 (February 1977): 41–47.

36. Ross E. Gray and Brian D. Doan, "Empowerment and Persons with Cancer: Politics in Cancer Medicine," *Journal of Palliative Care* 6, no. 2 (1990): 33–45.

37. See, for example, Robert J. Baugher, Candice Burger, Roberta Smith, and Kenneth A. Wallston, "A Comparison of Terminally Ill Persons at Various Time Periods to Death," *Omega: Journal of Death and Dying* 20 (1989–1990): 103–155.

38. Allan Kellehear and Terry Lewin, "Farewells by the Dying: A Sociological Study," *Omega: Journal of Death and Dying* 19 (1988–1989): 275–292.

39. Roderick Cosh, "Spiritual Care of the Dying," in *A Challenge for Living: Dying, Death, and Bereavement,* ed. Inge B. Corless, Barbara B. Germino, and Mary A. Pittman (Boston: Jones and Bartlett, 1995), pp. 131–143.

C H A P T E R 6

1. "Organ Transplants and Grafts," *Statistical Abstract of the United States 1994,* 114th ed. (Washington, D.C.: Government Printing Office, 1994), p. 131. See also "Transplants: Are They Worth It?" *Second Opinion* 12 (November 1989): 11.

2. The Hippocratic Oath, named for the ancient Greek physician Hippocrates, has been an enduring guide for the conduct of physicians since the fourth century before the present era. Modified during the twentieth century—most notably by the World Medical Association in its "Declaration of Geneva" (1949)—Hippocratic principles continue to exert a strong moral force in medical practice.

3. Charles L. Sprung, "Changing Attitudes and Practices in Forgoing Life-Sustaining Treatments," *Journal of the American Medical Association* 263 (April 25, 1990): 2211–2215.

4. Edmund D. Pellegrino, "Character, Virtue, and Self-Interest in the Ethics of the Professions," *Journal of Contemporary Health Policy and Law* 5 (Spring 1989): 53–73.

5. Alexander Morgan Capron, "The Burden of Decision," *Hastings Center Report* (May–June 1990): 36–41.

6. The issue of patient autonomy versus medical/social paternalism is highlighted in the experience of Don (Dax) Cowart, whose case has become a classic in the literature of medical ethics. See *Dax's Case: Essays in Medical Ethics and Human Meaning,* ed. Lonnie D. Kliever (Dallas: Southern Methodist University, 1989); and "Symposium on Dax's Case," *Bulletin of the Park Ridge Center* (May 1990): 16–33.

7. James F. Childress, "The Place of Autonomy in Bioethics," *Hastings Center Report* (January–February 1990): 12–17.

8. Marshall B. Kapp, "Medical Empowerment of the Elderly," *Hastings Center Report* (July–August 1989): 5–7.

9. John Hardwig, "What About the Family?" *Hastings Center Report* (March–April 1990): 5–10.

10. Nancy S. Jecker, "The Role of Intimate Others in Medical Decision Making," *Gerontologist* (February 1990): 65–71.

11. The President's Commission for the Study of Ethical Problems in Medicine and Biomedical and Behavioral Research, *Making Health Care Decisions: The Ethical and Legal Implications of Informed Consent in the Patient–Practitioner Relationship;* vol. 1, *Report,* and vol. 3, *Studies on the Foundations of Informed Consent* (Washington, D.C.: Government Printing Office, 1982).

12. Donald Oken, "What to Tell Cancer Patients: A Study of Medical Attitudes," *Journal of the American Medical Association* 175 (1961): 1120–1128.

13. D. H. Novack et al., "Changes in Physician's Attitudes Toward Telling the Cancer Patient," *Journal of the American Medical Association* 241 (March 2, 1979): 897–900.

14. D. H. Novack et al., "Physicians' Attitudes Toward Using Deception to Resolve Difficult Ethical Problems," *Journal of the American Medical Association* 261 (May 26, 1989): 2980–2985.

15. E. A. Green, "Placebo," *Academic American Encyclopedia* on-line (March 1991).

16. David W. Towle, "Medical Ethics," *Academic American Encyclopedia* on-line (March 1991). See also Alan Leslie, "Ethics and Practice of Placebo Therapy," *American Journal of Medicine* 16 (1954): 854–862.

17. Margot L. White and John C. Fletcher, "The Story of Mr. and Mrs. Doe: 'You Can't Tell My Husband He's Dying; It Will Kill Him,'" in *The Path Ahead: Readings in Death and Dying,* ed. Lynne Ann DeSpelder and Albert Lee Strickland (Mountain View, Calif.: Mayfield, 1995), pp. 148–153; reprinted from *The Journal of Clinical Ethics* 1, no. 1 (Spring 1990): 59–62.

18. Howard Brody, "Transparency: Informed Consent in Medical Practice," *Hastings Center Report* (September–October 1989): 5–9.

19. *In the Matter of Karen Quinlan: The Complete Legal Briefs, Court Proceedings and Decisions in the Superior Court of New Jersey* (1975) and *In the Matter of Karen Quinlan, Volume 2: The Complete Briefs, Oral Arguments, and Opinion in the New Jersey Supreme Court* (1976; Arlington, Va.: University Publications of America).

20. Joseph Fletcher, "The Patient's Right to Die," in *Euthanasia and the Right to Die: The Case for Voluntary Euthanasia,* ed. A. B. Downing (London: Peter Owen Ltd., 1969), p. 30; and, also by Fletcher, "The Right to Choose When to Die," *Hemlock Quarterly* 34 (January 1989): 3. See also James Rachels, *The End of Life: Euthanasia and Morality* (New York: Oxford University Press, 1986); and Gretchen L. Johnson, *Voluntary Euthanasia: A Comprehensive Bibliography* (Eugene, Ore.: Hemlock Society, 1987).

21. On the potential value of talking to comatose patients, despite their unresponsiveness and inability to talk back, see John LaPuma, David L. Schiedermayer, Ann E. Gulyas, and Mark Siegler, "Talking to Comatose Patients," *Archives of Neurology* 45 (January 1988): 20–22.

22. Richard M. Gula, "Moral Principles Shaping Public Policy on Euthanasia," *Second Opinion* 14 (July 1990): 73–83. See also Ruth Macklin, *Mortal Choices: Bioethics in Today's World* (New York: Pantheon, 1987); and Robert N. Wennberg, *Terminal*

Choices: Euthanasia, Suicide, and the Right to Die (Grand Rapids, Mich.: William B. Eerdmans, 1989). A brief discussion of how the term *euthanasia* is used by various ethicists can be found in John J. Cole, "Moral Dilemma: To Kill or Allow to Die?" *Death Studies* 13 (1989): 393–406, especially pp. 397–398.

23. On institutional guidelines for terminating treatment, see U.S. Congress, Office of Technology Assessment, *Institutional Protocols for Decisions about Life-Sustaining Treatments—Special Report* (Washington, D.C.: Government Printing Office, 1988); and Hastings Center, *Guidelines on the Termination of Life-Sustaining Treatment and the Care of the Dying* (Bloomington: Indiana University Press, 1988).

24. President's Commission for the Study of Ethical Problems in Medicine and Biomedical and Behavioral Research, *Summing Up: Final Report on Studies of the Ethical and Legal Problems in Medicine and Biomedical and Behavioral Research* (Washington, D.C.: Government Printing Office, March 1983), p. 31. See also the companion volume, *Deciding to Forego Life-Sustaining Treatment: A Report on the Ethical, Medical, and Legal Issues in Treatment Decisions* (Washington, D.C.: Government Printing Office, March 1983).

25. See, for example, Tom Tomlinson and Howard Brody, "Futility and the Ethics of Resuscitation," *Journal of the American Medical Association* 264 (September 12, 1990): 1276–1280; and J. Chris Hackler and F. Charles Hiller, "Family Consent Orders Not to Resuscitate," *Journal of the American Medical Association* 264 (September 12, 1990): 1281–1283.

26. Sprung, "Changing Attitudes and Practices," p. 2214. See also Robert W. Carton, "The Road to Euthanasia," *Journal of the American Medical Association* 263 (April 25, 1990): 2221.

27. "It's Over, Debbie," *Journal of the American Medical Association* 259 (January 8, 1988): 272.

28. David J. Roy, "Euthanasia—Taking a Stand," *Journal of Palliative Care* 6, no. 1 (1990): 3–5. See also Richard M. Gula, "The Virtuous Response to Euthanasia," *Health Progress* 70 (December 1989): 24–27.

29. On euthanasia practices in the Netherlands, see Pieter Admiraal, "Justifiable Active Euthanasia in the Netherlands," in *Euthanasia: The Moral Issues,* ed. Robert M. Baird and Stuart E. Rosenbaum (New York: Prometheus, 1989); Margaret P. Battin, "Euthanasia: The Way We Do It, The Way They Do It," *Journal of Pain and Symptom Management* 6, no. 5 (1991): 298–305; Herbert Hendin, "Seduced by Death: Doctors, Patients, and the Dutch Cure," *Issues in Law and Medicine* 10, no. 2 (1994): 123–168; Nancy S. Jecker, "Physician-Assisted Death in the Netherlands and the United States: Ethical and Cultural Aspects of Health Policy Development," *Journal of the American Geriatrics Society* 42 (1994): 672–678; David C. Thomasma, "The Ethics of Physician-Assisted Suicide," in *Physician-Assisted Death,* ed. James M. Humber, Robert F. Almeder, and Gregg A. Kasting (Totowa, N.J.: Humana Press, 1993), pp. 99–133; G. Van der Wal et al., "Voluntary Active Euthanasia and Physician-Assisted Suicide in Dutch Nursing Homes: Requests and Administration," *Journal of the American Geriatrics Society* 42 (1994): 620–623; and M. A. M. de Wachter, "Active Euthanasia in the Netherlands," *Journal of the American Medical Association* 262 (December 15, 1989): 3316–3319.

Statistics are from a nationwide study in the Netherlands on medical decisions at the end of life. See Paul J. van der Mass, Johannes J. M. van Delden, Loes Pijnenborg, and Casper W. N. Looman, "Euthanasia and Other Medical Decisions Concerning the End of Life," *The Lancet* 338 (September 14, 1991): 669–674; Johannes J. M. van Delden, Loes Pijnenborg, and Paul J. van der Mass, "The Remmelink Study: Two Years

Later," *Hastings Center Report* 23, no. 6 (1993): 24–27; and Loes Pijnenborg, Johannes J. M. van Delden, Jan W. P. F. Kardaun, Jacobus J. Glerum, and Paul J. van der Mass, "Nationwide Study of Decisions Concerning the End of Life in General Practice in the Netherlands," *British Medical Journal* 309 (November 5, 1994): 1209–1212.

30. Neil Macdonald and Balfour Mount, "Controversies in Palliative Care," *Journal of Palliative Care* 4, no. 1–2 (1988): 6–8.

31. Charles J. Dougherty, "The Common Good, Terminal Illness, and Euthanasia," in *The Path Ahead,* ed. DeSpelder and Strickland, pp. 154–164; reprinted from *Issues in Law & Medicine* 9, no. 2 (1993): 151–166.

32. "Florida District Court of Appeals Decides Landmark Case Concerning Life-Sustaining Measures," PR Newswire, April 22, 1986.

33. N. L. Cantor, "The Permanently Unconscious Patient, Non-Feeding, and Euthanasia," *American Journal of Law and Medicine* 15 (1989): 381–437.

34. R. J. Connelly, "The Sentiment Argument for Artificial Feeding of the Dying," *Omega: Journal of Death and Dying* 20 (1989–1990): 229–237. See also Steven H. Miles, "Nourishment and the Ethics of Lament," *Linacre Quarterly* 56 (August 1989): 64–69.

For opposing views on the "bond of human communion" that is maintained by artificially nourishing patients in a persistent vegetative state, see Germain Grisez and Kevin O'Rourke, "Should Nutrition and Hydration Be Provided to Permanently Unconscious and Other Mentally Disabled Persons," *Issues in Law and Medicine* 5 (1989): 165–196.

35. James J. McCartney and Jane Mary Trau, "Cessation of the Artificial Delivery of Food and Fluids: Defining Terminal Illness and Care," *Death Studies* 14 (1990): 435–444.

36. Dena S. Davis, "Old and Thin," *Second Opinion* 15 (November 1990): 26–32; see also, in the same issue, Ronald M. Green, "Old and Thin: A Response," pp. 34–39.

37. Quoted from an article by Joseph F. Sullivan, *New York Times* (June 25, 1987).

38. Background to the Cruzan case and arguments on both sides of the issue can be found in *Hastings Center Report* (January–February 1990): 38–50.

39. Ron Hamel, "The Supreme Court's Decision in the *Cruzan* Case: A Synopsis," *Bulletin of the Park Ridge Center* (September 1990): 18, 20.

40. Ellen Goodman, "Death in the Technological Age," *Los Angeles Times* (December 28, 1990).

41. The Patient Self-Determination Act is discussed in Chapter 9.

42. Case reported in the *Bulletin of the Park Ridge Center* (May 1989): 24–25.

43. For discussion of the legal concept of "personhood" as applied in the Bouvia case, as well as the cases of Hilda Peter (discussed earlier in this section), Claire Conroy, and Paul Brophy, see Edward J. Larson, "Personhood: Current Legal Views," *Second Opinion* 14 (July 1990): 41–53.

44. President's Commission, *Summing Up,* p. 34.

45. Arthur L. Caplan, "Imperiled Newborns," *Hastings Center Report* (December 1987).

46. Marie C. McCormick, "Long-Term Follow-Up of Infants Discharged from Neonatal Intensive Care Units," *Journal of the American Medical Association* 261 (March 24/31, 1989): 1767–1772.

47. Robert McCormick, "To Save or Let Die: The Dilemma of Modern Medicine," in *Ethical Issues in Death and Dying,* ed. Robert F. Weir (New York: Columbia University Press, 1977), pp. 173–184.

48. James M. Gustafson, "Mongolism, Parental Desires, and the Right to Live," in *Ethical Issues in Death and Dying*, ed. Weir, pp. 145–172.

49. President's Commission, *Deciding to Forego Life-Sustaining Treatment*, p. 7.

50. Caplan, "Imperiled Newborns."

51. Douglas N. Walton, *On Defining Death: An Analytic Study of the Concept of Death in Philosophy and Medical Ethics* (Montreal: McGill-Queen's University Press, 1979). Also see Eric Cassell, Leon Kass et al., "Refinements in Criteria for the Determination of Death: An Appraisal," in *Journal of the American Medical Association* 221 (1972): 48–53.

52. When patients continue in a comatose state for longer than a month or so, the condition is described as a "persistent vegetative state" and is usually considered irreversible.

53. Editorial, "Brain Damage and Brain Death," *Lancet* (1974): 342.

54. Clyde M. Nabe, "Presenting Biological Data in a Course on Death and Dying," *Death Education* 5, no. 1 (Spring 1981): 56.

55. Aaron D. Freedman, "Death and Dying," *Academic American Encyclopedia* on-line (March 1991).

56. Nabe, "Presenting Biological Data," p. 53.

57. Robert M. Veatch, *Death, Dying, and the Biological Revolution: Our Last Quest for Responsibility*, rev. ed. (New Haven: Yale University Press, 1989); see also, by Veatch, *A Theory of Medical Ethics* (New York: Basic Books, 1981).

58. Duncan MacDougall, "Hypothesis Concerning Soul Substance Together with Experimental Evidence of the Existence of Such Substance," *Journal of the American Society for Psychical Research* 1, no. 5 (May 1907): 237–244.

59. Karen G. Gervais, "Advancing the Definition of Death: A Philosophical Essay," *Medical Humanities Review* 3 (July 1989): 7–19; see also, by Gervais, *Redefining Death* (New Haven, Conn.: Yale University Press, 1986).

60. Leon R. Kass, "Practicing Ethics: Where's the Action?" *Hastings Center Report* (January–February 1990): 5–12.

61. Lee LaTour, quoted in Andrew Solomon, "A Death of One's Own," *New Yorker* (May 22, 1995), pp. 54–69.

CHAPTER 7

1. Philippe Ariès, "The Reversal of Death: Changes in Attitudes Toward Death in Western Societies," in *Death in America*, ed. David E. Stannard (Philadelphia: University of Pennsylvania Press, 1975), pp. 134–158.

2. Mary Caroline Crawford, *Social Life in Old New England* (Boston: Little, Brown, 1914), p. 461.

3. Terry Tafoya, "The Widow as Butterfly: Treatment of Grief/Depression Among the Sahaptin," unpublished paper.

4. Erich Lindemann, "The Symptomatology and Management of Acute Grief," *American Journal of Psychiatry* 101 (1944): 141–148.

5. J. William Worden, *Grief Counseling and Grief Therapy: A Handbook for the Mental Health Practitioner*, 2d ed. (New York: Springer, 1991), pp. 10–18.

6. Dennis Klass, "Solace and Immortality: Bereaved Parents' Continuing Bond with Their Children," in *The Path Ahead: Readings in Death and Dying*, ed. Lynne Ann DeSpelder and Albert Lee Strickland (Mountain View, Calif.: Mayfield, 1995), pp. 246–259; reprinted from *Death Studies* 17, no. 4 (1993): 343–368.

7. Phyllis R. Silverman, Steven Nickman, and J. William Worden, "Detachment Revisited: The Child's Reconstruction of a Dead Parent," in *The Path Ahead,* ed. DeSpelder and Strickland, pp. 260–270; reprinted from *American Journal of Orthopsychiatry* 62, no. 4 (October 1992): 494–503.

8. David E. Balk and Nancy S. Hogan, "Religion, Spirituality, and Bereaved Adolescents," in *Loss, Threat to Life, and Bereavement: The Child's Perspective,* ed. David W. Adams and Ellie J. Deveau (Amityville, N.Y.: Baywood, in press). See also Nancy Hogan and Lydia DeSantis, "Adolescent Sibling Bereavement: An Ongoing Attachment," *Qualitative Health Research* 2 (1992): 159–177.

9. Margaret Stroebe, Mary M. Gergen, Kenneth J. Gergen, and Wolfgang Stroebe, "Broken Hearts or Broken Bonds: Love and Death in Historical Perspective," in *The Path Ahead,* ed. DeSpelder and Strickland, pp. 231–241; reprinted from *American Psychologist* 47, no. 10 (October 1992): 1205–1212.

10. John D. Kelly, "Grief: Re-forming Life's Story," in *The Path Ahead,* ed. DeSpelder and Strickland, pp. 242–245; reprinted from *Journal of Palliative Care* 8, no. 2 (Summer 1992): 33–35.

11. Sigmund Freud, "Mourning and Melancholia," *Collected Papers,* vol. 4 (New York: Basic Books, 1959), pp. 152–170. Originally published in 1917.

12. In addition to the classic work by Freud, see John Bowlby's three-volume work, *Attachment and Loss* (New York: Basic Books): vol. 1, *Attachment* (1969); vol. 2, *Separation: Anxiety and Anger* (1973); and vol. 3, *Loss: Sadness and Depression* (1982). A summary of Bowlby's stages of mourning can be found in Dale Vincent Hardt's "An Investigation of the Stages of Bereavement," *Omega: Journal of Death and Dying* 9 (1978–1979): 279–285. On inadequacies found in Bowlby's model, see Dennis Klass, "John Bowlby's Model of Grief and the Problem of Identification," *Omega: Journal of Death and Dying* 18 (1987–1988): 13–32.

13. Some believe that the attachments developed by animals for others of their kind, or by domestic pets for their human owners, can result in at least elemental forms of grief (as exhibited through such behaviors as "pining" for a lost home or caretaker) when events occur that threaten or break these bonds of attachment. See, for example, Ute Carson, "Do Animals Grieve?" *Death Studies* 13 (1989): 49–62.

14. Colin Murray Parkes, "Research: Bereavement," *Omega: Journal of Death and Dying* 18, no. 4 (1987–1988): 365–377.

15. Selby C. Jacobs, Thomas R. Kosten, Stanislav V. Kasl, Adrian M. Ostfeld, Lisa Berkman, and Peter Charpentier, "Attachment Theory and Multiple Dimensions of Grief," *Omega: Journal of Death and Dying* 18 (1987–1988): 41–52.

16. Klass, "John Bowlby's Model of Grief," p. 31.

17. This discussion of the phases of grief draws particularly on the following works: Geoffrey Gorer, *Death, Grief, and Mourning in Contemporary Britain* (London: Cresset Press, 1965); Robert E. Kavanaugh, *Facing Death* (Los Angeles: Nash Publishing, 1972), pp. 107–124; Beverly Raphael, *The Anatomy of Bereavement* (New York: Basic Books, 1983), pp. 33–51; and Savine Gross Weizman and Phyllis Kamm, *About Mourning: Support and Guidance for the Bereaved* (New York: Human Sciences Press, 1985), pp. 42–63.

18. Sidney Zisook and Lucy Lyons, "Bereavement and Unresolved Grief in Psychiatric Outpatients," *Omega: Journal of Death and Dying* 20 (1989–1990): 307–322.

19. Sylvia Sherwood, Robert Kastenbaum, John N. Morris, and Susan M. Wright, "The First Months of Bereavement," in *The Hospice Experiment,* ed. Vincent Mor, David S. Greer, and Robert Kastenbaum (Baltimore: Johns Hopkins University Press, 1988), pp. 149–150.

20. Sarah Brabant, "Old Pain or New Pain: A Social Psychological Approach to Recurrent Grief," *Omega: Journal of Death and Dying* 20 (1989–1990): 273–279.

21. Ira O. Glick, Robert S. Weiss, and Colin Murray Parkes, *The First Year of Bereavement* (New York: John Wiley & Sons, 1974), p. viii; see also Colin Murray Parkes and Robert S. Weiss, *Recovery from Bereavement* (New York: Basic Books, 1983).

22. W. D. Rees and S. G. Lutkins, "The Mortality of Bereavement," *British Medical Journal* 4 (1967): 13–16.

23. Arthur C. Carr and Bernard Schoenberg, "Object-Loss and Somatic Symptom Formation," in *Loss and Grief: Psychological Management in Medical Practice,* ed. Bernard Schoenberg et al. (New York: Columbia University Press, 1970), pp. 36–47.

24. See Nicholas R. Hall and Allan L. Goldstein, "Thinking Well: The Chemical Links Between Emotions and Health," *The Sciences* 26, no. 2 (March/April 1986): 34–40. See also Jerome F. Fredrick, "Grief as a Disease Process," *Omega: Journal of Death and Dying* 7 (1976–1977): 297–305; and Edgar N. Jackson, "The Physiology of Crisis," in his *Coping with the Crises of Your Life* (New York: Hawthorne Books, 1974), pp. 48–55.

25. For a review of these studies, see Parkes, "Research: Bereavement."

26. Hans Selye, *The Stress of Life,* rev. ed. (New York: McGraw-Hill, 1976).

27. George L. Engel, "Sudden and Rapid Death During Psychological Stress," *Annals of Internal Medicine* 74 (1971). See also, by Engel, "Emotional Stress and Sudden Death," *Psychology Today,* November 1977.

28. Colin Murray Parkes, "The Broken Heart," in his *Bereavement: Studies of Grief in Adult Life,* 2d ed. (Madison, Conn.: International Universities Press, 1987), p. 37. See also Gerald Epstein, Lawrence Weitz, Howard Roback, and Embry McKee, "Research on Bereavement: A Selective and Critical Review," *Comprehensive Psychiatry* 16 (1975): 537–546.

29. Itzhak Levav, "Second Thoughts on the Lethal Aftermath of a Loss," *Omega: Journal of Death and Dying* 20 (1989–1990): 81–90.

30. Edgar N. Jackson, *Understanding Grief: Its Roots, Dynamics, and Treatment* (Nashville: Abingdon Press, 1957), p. 27; see also, by Jackson, *The Many Faces of Grief* (Nashville: Abingdon Press, 1977). In an interview with the authors, Dr. Jackson described how the death of his young son became the impetus for his studies of grief. In effect, his studies of grief were in part a mechanism for coping with, understanding, and coming to terms with the loss. This is an example of how an individual survivor's value system shapes the means of coping with a loss.

31. Karen S. Pfost, Michael J. Stevens, and Anne B. Wessels, "Relationship of Purpose in Life to Grief Experiences in Response to the Death of a Significant Other," *Death Studies* 13 (1989): 371–378.

32. Richard A. Kalish and David K. Reynolds, *Death and Ethnicity: A Psychocultural Study* (Los Angeles: Ethel Percy Andrus Gerontology Center, University of Southern California, 1976), p. 30.

33. Robert J. Smith, John H. Lingle, Timothy C. Brock, "Reactions to Death as a Function of Perceived Similarity to the Deceased," *Omega: Journal of Death and Dying* 9 (1978–1979): 125–138.

34. Glenn M. Vernon, *Sociology of Death: An Analysis of Death-Related Behavior* (New York: Ronald Press, 1970).

35. Richard M. Leliaert, "Spiritual Side of 'Good Grief': What Happened to Holy Saturday?" *Death Studies* 13 (1989): 103–117.

36. Arlene Sheskin and Samuel E. Wallace, "Differing Bereavements: Suicide, Natural, and Accidental Death," *Omega: Journal of Death and Dying* 7 (1976): 229–242.

37. Yvonne K. Ameche, "A Story of Loss and Survivorship," *Death Studies* 14 (1990): 185–198.

38. Lea Barinbaum, "Death of Young Sons and Husbands," *Omega: Journal of Death and Dying* 7 (1976): 171–175.

39. Bernard Schoenberg, Arthur C. Carr, Austin H. Kutscher, David Peretz, and Ivan K. Goldberg, eds., *Anticipatory Grief* (New York: Columbia University Press, 1974), p. 4. Also see Lindemann, "Acute Grief," p. 141, and Therese A. Rando, *Loss and Anticipatory Grief* (Lexington, Mass.: Lexington Books, 1985).

40. Sherwood, Kastenbaum, Morris, and Wright, "The First Months of Bereavement," p. 150.

41. Francoise M. Reynolds and Peter Cimbolic, "Attitudes Toward Suicide Survivors as a Function of Survivors' Relationship to the Victim," *Omega: Journal of Death and Dying* 19 (1988–1989): 125–133.

42. Gordon Thornton, Katherine D. Whittemore, and Donald U. Robertson, "Evaluation of People Bereaved by Suicide," *Death Studies* 13 (1989): 119–126.

43. Robert G. Dunn and Donna Morrish-Vidners, "The Psychological and Social Experience of Suicide Survivors," *Omega: Journal of Death and Dying* 18 (1987–1988): 175–215; David E. Ness and Cynthia R. Pfeffer, "Sequelae of Bereavement Resulting from Suicide," *American Journal of Psychiatry* 147 (1990): 279–285; Lillian M. Range and Nathan M. Niss, "Long-Term Bereavement from Suicide, Homicide, Accidents, and Natural Deaths," *Death Studies* 14 (1990): 423–433; and Jan Van der Wal, "The Aftermath of Suicide: A Review of Empirical Evidence," *Omega: Journal of Death and Dying* 20 (1989–1990): 149–171.

44. Lula M. Redmond, *Surviving When Someone You Love Was Murdered: A Professional's Guide to Group Therapy for Families and Friends of Murder Victims* (Clearwater, Fla.: Psychological Consultation and Education Services, 1989), pp. 38–39, 46–49, 52–53.

45. See, for example, June S. Church, "The Buffalo Creek Disaster: Extent and Range of Emotional and Behavioral Problems," *Omega: Journal of Death and Dying* 5 (1974): 61–63.

46. Terrence Des Pres, *The Survivor* (New York: Oxford University Press, 1976; Pocket Books, 1977). This is an intense exploration of the survivors of the Holocaust.

47. Robert L. Fulton, "Death, Grief, and Social Recuperation," *Omega: Journal of Death and Dying* 1 (1978): 23–28.

48. Terry Tafoya, "Coyote, Chaos, and Crisis: Counseling the Native American Male," unpublished paper. See also David E. Stannard, *American Holocaust: Columbus and the Conquest of the New World* (New York: Oxford University Press, 1992).

49. Fred Sklar and Shirley F. Hartley, "Close Friends as Survivors: Bereavement Patterns in a 'Hidden' Population, " *Omega: Journal of Death and Dying* 21 (1990): 103–112.

50. Larry A. Bugen, "Human Grief: A Model for Prediction and Intervention," *American Journal of Orthopsychiatry* 47, no. 2 (1977): 196–206.

51. Kenneth J. Doka, "Disenfranchised Grief," paper presented at the Annual Meeting of the Association for Death Education and Counseling, Atlanta, Spring 1986; see also "Disenfranchised Grief," in *The Path Ahead,* ed. DeSpelder and Strickland, pp. 271–275; reprinted from *Disenfranchised Grief: Recognizing Hidden Sorrow,* ed. Kenneth J. Doka (Lexington, Mass.: Lexington Books, 1989).

52. Darlene A. Kloeppel and Sheila Hollins, "Double Handicap: Mental Retardation and Death in the Family," *Death Studies* 13 (1989): 31–38.

53. Vernon, *Sociology of Death*, p. 159.

54. Mary Kawena Pukui, E. W. Haertig, and Catherine A. Lee, *Nana I Ke Kumu* (Look to the Source), vol. 1 (Honolulu: Hui Hanai; Queen Lili'uokalani Children's Center, 1972), pp. 135–136, 141.

55. See Kalish and Reynolds, *Death and Ethnicity: A Psychocultural Study;* and Jean Masamba and Richard A. Kalish, "Death and Bereavement: The Role of the Black Church," *Omega: Journal of Death and Dying* 7 (1976): 23–34.

56. Nissan Rubin, "Social Networks and Mourning: A Comparative Approach," *Omega: Journal of Death and Dying* 21 (1990): 113–127.

57. Onno van der Hart, *Coping with Loss: The Therapeutic Use of Leave-Taking Ritual* (New York: Irvington, 1988); and, also by Van der Hart, "An Imaginary Leave-Taking Ritual in Mourning Therapy: A Brief Communication," *The International Journal of Clinical and Experimental Hypnosis* 36, no. 2 (1988): 63–69.

58. Nancy C. Reeves and Frederic J. Boersma, "The Therapeutic Use of Ritual in Maladaptive Grieving," *Omega: Journal of Death and Dying* 20 (1989–1990): 281–291.

59. Vamik Volkan and C. R. Showalter, "Known Object Loss, Disturbance in Reality Testing, and 'Re-grief' Work as a Method of Brief Psychotherapy," *Psychiatric Quarterly* 42 (1968): 358–374; and Vamik Volkan, "A Study of a Patient's 'Re-grief' Work," *Psychiatric Quarterly* 45 (1971): 255–273.

60. Stephen J. Fleming and Leslie Balmer, "Bereaved Families of Ontario: A Mutual-Help Model for Families Experiencing Death," in *The Path Ahead,* ed. DeSpelder and Strickland, pp. 281–288.

61. Giorgio Di Mola, Marcello Tamburini, and Claude Fusco, "The Role of Volunteers in Alleviating Grief," *Journal of Palliative Care* 6, no. 1 (1990): 6–10.

62. Parkes, "Research: Bereavement."

63. John Schneider, *Stress, Loss, and Grief: Understanding Their Origins and Growth Potential* (Baltimore: University Park Press, 1984), pp. 66–76.

64. Lawrence G. Calhoun and Richard G. Tedeschi, "Positive Aspects of Critical Life Problems: Recollections of Grief," *Omega: Journal of Death and Dying* 29 (1989–1990): 265–272.

65. Julie Fritsch with Sherokee Ilse, *The Anguish of Loss* (Maple Plain, Minn.: Wintergreen Press, 1988).

CHAPTER 8

1. This account draws upon material from the following sources: "Coffins and Sarcophagi," exhibition notes provided by the Metropolitan Museum of Art, New York; Henri Frankfort, *Ancient Egyptian Religion: An Interpretation* (New York: Harper and Row, 1948, 1961); Manfred Lurker, *The Gods and Symbols of Ancient Egypt* (New York: Thames & Hudson, 1980); and Barbara Watterson, *The Gods of Ancient Egypt* (New York: Facts on File, 1984). See also Morris Bierbrier, *The Tomb-Builders of the Ancient Pharaohs* (New York: Charles Scribner's Sons, 1982); John Romer, *Ancient Lives: Daily Life in Egypt of the Pharaohs* (New York: Holt, Rinehart and Winston, 1984); and A. J. Spencer, *Death in Ancient Egypt* (New York: Penguin, 1982).

2. David Sudnow, "Notes on a Sociology of Mourning," *Passing On: The Social Organization of Dying* (Englewood Cliffs, N.J.: Prentice-Hall, 1967), pp. 153–168.

3. Ben H. Bagdikian, *The Information Machines: Their Impact on Men and the Media* (New York: Harper and Row, 1971), pp. 39, 59. Also see Bradley Greenberg, "Diffusion of News of the Kennedy Assassination," *Public Opinion Quarterly* 28, no. 2 (Summer 1964): 225–232.

4. Ronald K. Barrett, "Contemporary African-American Funeral Rites and Tra-

ditions," in *The Path Ahead: Readings in Death and Dying,* ed. Lynne Ann DeSpelder and Albert Lee Strickland (Mountain View, Calif.: Mayfield, 1995), pp. 80–92.

5. J. Z. Young, *Programs of the Brain* (New York: Oxford University Press, 1978), p. 255.

6. John R. Elliott, "Funerary Artifacts in Contemporary America," *Death Studies* 14 (1990): 601–612.

7. Leroy Bowman, *The American Funeral: A Study in Guilt, Extravagance, and Sublimity* (Washington: Public Affairs Press, 1959).

8. Jessica Mitford, *The American Way of Death* (New York: Simon & Schuster, 1963), pp. 16–19.

9. Robert Fulton, "The Funeral and the Funeral Director: A Contemporary Analysis," in *Successful Funeral Service Practice,* ed. Howard C. Raether (Englewood Cliffs, N.J.: Prentice-Hall, 1971), p. 229.

10. Frank Minton, "Clergy Views of Funeral Practice (Part One)," *National Reporter* 4, no. 4 (April 1981): 4.

11. Richard A. Kalish and Helene Goldberg, "Community Attitudes Toward Funeral Directors," *Omega: Journal of Death and Dying* 10, no. 4 (1979–1980): 335–346.

12. Federal Trade Commission, *Compliance Guidelines: Trade Regulation Rule on Funeral Industry Practices* (Washington, D.C., 1984).

13. Vanderlyn Pine, "The Care of the Dead: A Historical Portrait," in *Death and Dying: Challenge and Change,* ed. Robert Fulton et al. (Reading, Mass.: Addison-Wesley, 1978), p. 274. See also, by Pine, *Caretaker of the Dead: The American Funeral Director* (New York: Irvington, 1985).

14. See, for example, Steven D. Rosenbaum and John A. Ballard, "Educating Air Force Mortuary Officers," *Death Studies* 14 (1990): 135–145.

15. Vanderlyn R. Pine, *A Statistical Abstract of Funeral Service Facts and Figures of the United States, 1984 Edition* (Milwaukee: National Funeral Directors Association, 1984), pp. 7, 62. These amounts do not include the cost of an interment receptacle, cemetery or crematory expenses, monument or marker, or items such as clergy honorarium, flowers, additional transportation, burial clothing, or newspaper notices.

16. "Service Industries—Establishments" and "Service Industries—Annual Receipts," *Statistical Abstract of the United States 1994,* 114th ed. (Washington, D.C.: Government Printing Office, 1994), pp. 798, 799.

17. Ronny E. Turner and Charles Edgley, "Death as Theatre: A Dramaturgical Analysis of the American Funeral," *Sociology and Social Research* 60, no. 4 (1976): 377–392; reprinted in *Death and Dying: Theory, Research, and Practice,* ed. Larry A. Bugen (Dubuque, Iowa: William C. Brown, 1979), pp. 191–202.

18. Kenneth V. Iserson, *Death to Dust: What Happens to Dead Bodies?* (Tucson, Ariz.: Galen Press, 1993), p. 314.

19. Ibid., p. 185. For a very detailed description of the process of embalming and other body preparation procedures, see *Death to Dust,* pp. 197–214.

20. Briefly summarized, exceptions to this requirement occur when: (1) state or local law requires embalming; or (2) there are "exigent circumstances," such as: (a) when a family member or other authorized person cannot be contacted despite diligent efforts, and (b) there is no reason to believe the family does not want embalming, and, (c) after the body has been embalmed, the family is notified that no fee will be charged if they choose a funeral that does not require embalming.

21. Casket Manufacturers Association of America, "Nationwide Summary—Estimate of Sales to Funeral Directors, Unit Volume (July–September 1985)." These

sales represent more than 1.8 million casketed deaths out of slightly more than 2 million total deaths occurring in the United States during this period.

22. *Honolulu Star-Bulletin and Advertiser* (June 3, 1984).

23. From a story by Sylvia Wieland Nogaki, *Honolulu Star-Bulletin and Advertiser* (November 26, 1989).

24. Vivian Spiegelman and Robert Kastenbaum, "Pet Rest Memorial: Is Eternity Running Out of Time?" *Omega: Journal of Death and Dying* 21 (1990): 1–13.

25. James M. Weir, "Cremation: Statistics to Year 2000, A Presentation to the Cremation Association of North America," Keystone, Colorado (August 1985), Table 1.

26. See Bruce A. Iverson, "Bodies for Science," *Death Studies* 14 (1990): 577–587; Robert D. Reece and Jesse H. Ziegler, "How a Medical School (Wright State University) Takes Leave of Human Remains," *Death Studies* 14 (1990): 589–600; and Kathleen A. Schotzinger and Elizabeth Kirkley Best, "Closure and the Cadaver Experience: A Memorial Service for Deeded Bodies," *Omega: Journal of Death and Dying* 18 (1987–1988): 217–227.

27. William Lamers, quoted in *Concerning Death: A Practical Guide for the Living,* ed. Earl Grollman (Boston: Beacon Press, 1974), and in *Successful Funeral Service Practice,* ed. Raether.

28. See, for example, Anne Brener, *Mourning and Mitzvah: A Guided Journal for Walking the Mourner's Path Through Grief to Healing* (Woodstock, Vt.: Jewish Lights Publishing, 1993); Paul Irion, *A Manual and Guide for Those Who Conduct a Humanist Funeral Service* (Baltimore: Waverly Press, 1971); and Edgar N. Jackson, *The Christian Funeral: Its Meaning, Its Purpose, and Its Modern Practice* (New York: Channel Press, 1966).

29. Robert Fulton and Greg Owen, "Death and Society in Twentieth Century America," *Omega: Journal of Death and Dying* 18 (1987–1988): 389.

30. Personal communication.

31. Robert Fulton, "Death and the Funeral in Contemporary Society," in *Dying: Facing the Facts,* ed. Hannelore Wass (Washington, D.C.: Hemisphere, 1979), pp. 236–255.

32. E. S. Craighill Handy and Mary Kawena Pukui, *The Polynesian Family System in Ka-'u, Hawai'i* (Rutland, Vt.: Charles E. Tuttle, 1972), p. 157; and Mary Kawena Pukui, E. W. Haertig, and Catherine A. Lee, *Nana I Ke Kumu (Look to the Source),* vol. 1 (Honolulu: Hui Hanai; Queen Lili'uokalani Children's Center, 1972), p. 139.

C H A P T E R 9

1. President's Commission for the Study of Ethical Problems in Medicine and Biomedical and Behavioral Research, *Defining Death: A Report on the Medical, Legal and Ethical Issues in the Determination of Death* (Washington, D.C.: Government Printing Office, July 1981), p. 45.

2. Alexander M. Capron and Leon R. Kass, "A Statutory Definition of the Standards for Determining Human Death: An Appraisal and a Proposal," *University of Pennsylvania Law Review* 121 (1972): 87–118.

3. President's Commission, *Defining Death.*

4. The authors thank Richard G. Polse, Esq., for kindly consenting to review the material covered in this chapter and for providing information and documentation regarding current legislation.

5. Annalisa Pizzarello, "Policy and Attitudes on Advance Directives," *Bulletin*

of the Park Ridge Center (May 1990): 42. Current information about legislation related to advance directives in the various states may be obtained from Choice in Dying, 200 Varick Street, Room 1001, New York, NY 10014; Tel.: (212) 366-5540.

6. George P. Smith III, "Recognizing Personhood and the Right to Die with Dignity," *Journal of Palliative Care* 6, no. 2 (1990): 24–32.

7. Steven H. Miles and Allison August, "Courts, Gender and the 'Right to Die,'" *Law, Medicine and Health Care* 18 (Spring–Summer 1990): 85–95.

8. See Kent W. Davidson et al., "Physicians' Attitudes on Advance Directives," *Journal of the American Medical Association* 262 (November 3, 1989): 2415–2419.

9. S. Van McCrary and Jeffrey R. Botkin, "Hospital Policy on Advance Directives," *Journal of the American Medical Association* 262 (November 3, 1989): 2411–2414.

10. See, for example, Steven H. Miles, "The Case: A Story Found and Lost," *Second Opinion* 15 (November 1990): 55–59, with commentary by Kathryn Montgomery Hunter, pp. 60–87; and Kenneth V. Iserson, "Prehospital DNR Orders," *Hastings Center Report* (November/December 1989): 17–19, with commentary by Fenella Rouse, p. 19.

11. Section 4206 of Public Law 101-508, 101st Congress. The authors thank Senator John C. Danforth of Missouri, a sponsor of this measure, for providing information about its provisions.

12. Leonard Sloane, " '91 Law Says Failing Patients Must Be Told of Their Options," *New York Times* (December 8, 1990), p. 50.

13. Larry R. Churchill, "Trust, Autonomy, and Advance Directives," *Journal of Religion and Health* 28 (Fall 1989): 175–183.

14. Arthur S. Berger, *Dying & Death in Law & Medicine: A Forensic Primer for Health and Legal Professionals* (Westport, Conn.: Praeger, 1993), p. 48.

15. Barbara J. Logue, *Last Rights: Death Control and the Elderly in America* (New York: Lexington Books, 1993), p. 6.

16. John A. Pridonoff, "Introduction," in *Hospice and Hemlock: Retaining Dignity, Integrity, and Self-Respect in End-of-Life Decisions,* ed. Michele A. Trepkowski (Eugene, Ore.: The Hemlock Society, 1993). Further information can be obtained from The Hemlock Society, P.O. Box 11830, Eugene, OR 97440; Tel.: (800) 247-7421.

17. See, for example, Thane Josef Messinger, "A Gentle and Easy Death: From Ancient Greece to Beyond Cruzan Toward a Reasoned Legal Response to the Societal Dilemma of Euthanasia," *Denver University Law Review* 71, no. 1 (1993): 175–251, especially pp. 229–237.

18. See, for example, Robert A. Sedler, "The Constitution and Hastening Inevitable Death," *Hastings Center Report* 23, no. 5 (September–October 1993): 20–25.

19. Rosemary A. Robbins, "Signing an Organ Donor Card: Psychological Factors," *Death Studies* 14 (1990): 219–229.

20. "Organ Transplantation—Questions and Answers" (Rockville, Md.: Division of Organ Transplantation, U.S. Department of Health and Human Services, October 1988).

21. See, for example, Sheila Howard, "How Do I Ask? Requesting Tissue or Organ Donations from Bereaved Families," *Nursing 89* (January 1989): 70–73.

22. David A. Peters, "An Individualistic Approach to Routine Cadaver Organ Removal," *Health Progress* (September 1988): 25–28.

23. David C. Thomasma, "The Quest for Organ Donors: A Theological Response," *Health Progress* (September 1988): 22–24.

24. Robert Fulton and Greg Owen, "Death and Society in Twentieth Century America," *Omega: Journal of Death and Dying* 18 (1987–1988): 388.

25. See, for example, Council on Scientific Affairs and Council on Ethical and Judicial Affairs, "Medical Applications of Fetal Tissue Transplantation," *Journal of the American Medical Association* 263 (January 26, 1990): 565–570; and Richard B. Miller, "On Transplanting Human Fetal Tissue: Presumptive Duties and the Task of Casuistry," *Journal of Medicine and Philosophy* 14 (1989): 617–840.

26. D. Alan Shewmon, "Anencephaly: Selected Medical Aspects," *Hastings Center Report* (October/November 1988): 11–19.

27. Arthur L. Caplan, "Should Foetuses or Infants Be Used as Organ Donors?" *Bioethics* 1 (1987). See also Michael R. Harrison, "Organ Procurement in Children: The Anencephalic Fetus as Donor," *The Lancet* (December 13, 1986); and Task Force for the Determination of Brain Death in Children, "Guidelines for the Determination of Brain Death in Children," *Pediatrics* 80 (1987): 298–300.

28. D. Alan Shewmon, "Commentary on Guidelines for the Determination of Brain Death in Children," *Annals of Neurology* 24 (1988): 780–791. See also D. Alan Shewmon, Alexander M. Capron, Warwick J. Peacock, and Barbara L. Schulman, "The Use of Anencephalic Infants as Organ Sources: A Critique," *Journal of the American Medical Association* 261 (March 24/31, 1989): 1773–1781.

29. Edwin S. Shneidman, "The Death Certificate," in *Deaths of Man* (New York: Quadrangle/The New York Times Book Company, 1973), pp. 121–130.

30. Peter L. Petrakis, "Autopsy," *Academic American Encyclopedia* on-line (March 1991). See also James Adams and Robert D. Mader, *Autopsy* (Ann Arbor: UMI Research Press, 1990); and Ludwig Jurgen, *Current Methods of Autopsy Practice,* 2d ed. (Philadelphia: Saunders, 1979).

31. Clyde Collins Snow, Eric Stover, and Kari Hannibal, "Scientists as Detectives: Investigating Human Rights," *Technology Review* (February/March 1989): 42–51.

32. Jon Yoshishige, "Searching for Answers: Lab Identifies Remains of Soldiers, Civilians," *Honolulu Advertiser* (August 8, 1993): A1, A2.

33. Barton E. Bernstein, "Lawyer and Counselor as an Interdisciplinary Team: Interfacing for the Terminally Ill," *Death Education* 1, no. 3 (Fall 1977): 277–291; and "Lawyer and Therapist as an Interdisciplinary Team; Serving the Terminally Ill," *Death Education* 3, no. 1 (Spring 1979): 11–19.

34. Barton E. Bernstein, "Lawyer and Therapist as an Interdisciplinary Team: Serving the Survivors,"*Death Education* 4, no. 2 (Summer 1980): 179–188.

35. This includes the vital statistics for each family member; military service records and VA (Veterans Administration) number; marriage, divorce, and adoption papers; names, addresses, and phone numbers of relatives and close friends to notify when death occurs, as well as social or professional organizations that should be notified; location of wills and other important documents, including insurance policies, property deeds, and tax returns; names and addresses of attorneys, bank officials, accountants, funeral or cemetery directors, brokers, and mortgage companies; information about notes receivable and accounts outstanding; information regarding funeral plans and wishes for the disposition of the body, including organ donation.

36. Paul Ashley, *You and Your Will: The Planning and Management of Your Estate* (New York: New American Library, 1977), p. 14.

37. Ibid, pp. 76–77.

38. "Life Insurance Companies," *Statistical Abstract of the United States 1994,* 114th ed. (Washington, D.C.: Government Printing Office, 1994), p. 533.

C H A P T E R   10

1. For a review of the literature, see Mark W. Speece and Sandor W. Brent, "Children's Understanding of Death: A Review of Three Components of a Death Concept," *Child Development* 55, no. 5 (October 1984): 1671–1686. For early research on death and children, see Irving E. Alexander and Arthur M. Adlerstein, "Affective Responses to the Concept of Death in a Population of Children and Early Adolescents," *Journal of Genetic Psychology* 93 (1958): 167–177; Sylvia Anthony, *The Discovery of Death in Childhood and After* (New York: Basic Books, 1972); Robert Kastenbaum, "Childhood: The Kingdom Where Creatures Die," *Journal of Clinical Child Psychology* 3 (Summer 1974): 11–13; Maria H. Nagy, "The Child's View of Death," *Journal of Genetic Psychology* 73 (1948): 3–27; Paul Schilder and David Wechsler, "The Attitudes of Children Toward Death," *Journal of Genetic Psychology* 45 (1934): 406–451.

2. Sigal Ironi Hoffman and Sidney Strauss, "The Development of Children's Concepts of Death," *Death Studies* 9 (1985): 469–482.

3. Erik Erikson, *Childhood and Society* (New York: W. W. Norton, 1950).

4. Jean Piaget, *The Child and Reality: Problems of Genetic Psychology,* trans. Arnold Rosin (New York: Grossman Publishers, 1973), and *The Child's Conception of the World* (London: Routledge & Kegan Paul, 1929). See also Mary Ann Spencer Pulaski, *Understanding Piaget: An Introduction to Children's Cognitive Development* (New York: Harper and Row, 1980); Howard E. Gruber and J. Jacques Vonèche, eds., *The Essential Piaget* (New York: Basic Books, 1977); and Hugh Rosen, *Pathway to Piaget: A Guide for Clinicians, Educators, and Developmentalists* (Cherry Hill, N.J.: Postgraduate International, 1977).

5. From a conversation with Jean Piaget in Richard I. Evans, *The Making of Psychology: Discussions with Creative Contributors* (New York: Alfred A. Knopf, 1976), p. 46.

6. Gerald P. Koocher, "Childhood, Death, and Cognitive Development," *Developmental Psychology* 9, no. 3 (1973): 369–375; "Talking with Children About Death," *American Journal of Orthopsychiatry* 44, no. 3 (April 1974): 404–411; and "Conversations with Children About Death," *Journal of Clinical Child Psychology* (Summer 1974): 19–21. Of the children in Koocher's study group, the mean age of those classified as preoperational was 7.4 years; of those who used concrete operations, 10.4 years; and of those who used formal operations, 13.3 years.

7. Helen L. Swain, "Childhood Views of Death," *Death Education* 2, no. 4 (1979): 341–358.

8. See Gregory Rochlin, "How Younger Children View Death and Themselves," in *Explaining Death to Children,* ed. Earl A. Grollman (Boston: Beacon Press, 1967), pp. 51–85.

9. Adah Maurer, "Maturation of Concepts of Death," *British Journal of Medicine and Psychology* 39 (1966): 35–41.

10. For further information about death anxiety, see James B. McCarthy, *Death Anxiety: The Loss of the Self* (New York: Gardner Press, 1980); C. W. Wahl, "The Fear of Death," in *The Meaning of Death,* ed. Herman Feifel (New York: McGraw-Hill, 1959), pp. 16–29; and Martin P. Seligman, *Helplessness: On Depression, Development, and Death* (San Francisco: W. H. Freeman, 1975). See also John Bowlby's classic works on attachment and loss: vol. 1, *Attachment* (1969); vol. 2, *Separation: Anxiety and Anger* (1973); vol. 3, *Loss: Sadness and Depression* (1982) (New York: Basic Books); and, also by Bowlby, *The Making and Breaking of Affectional Bonds* (London: Tavistock, 1979).

11. Mark W. Speece, "Very Young Children's Experiences with and Reactions to Death" (unpublished master's thesis, Wayne State University, 1983).

12. Sandor B. Brent, "Puns, Metaphors, and Misunderstandings in a Two-Year-Old's Conception of Death," *Omega: Journal of Death and Dying* 8 (1977–1978): 285–293. In a subsequent conversation, the father, Dr. Sandor Brent, reported that his son—now an adult—has no recollection of this death-related experience. Dr. Brent believes that the lack of memory regarding this experience indicates a successfully managed event. (Personal communication.)

13. Committee on Trauma Research, National Research Council, *Injury in America: A Continuing Public Health Problem* (Washington, D.C.: National Academy Press, 1985).

14. "Deaths and Death Rates for the 10 Leading Causes of Death in Specified Age Groups: United States, 1992," *Advance Report of Final Mortality Statistics, 1992* (Hyattsville, Md.: National Center for Health Statistics, 1995), p. 23.

15. William G. Bartholome, "Care of the Dying Child: The Demands of Ethics," in *The Path Ahead: Readings in Death and Dying*, ed. Lynne Ann DeSpelder and Albert Lee Strickland (Mountain View, Calif.: Mayfield, 1995), pp. 133–143; reprinted from *Second Opinion* 18, no. 4 (April 1993): 25–39.

16. Myra Bluebond-Langner, *The Private Worlds of Dying Children* (Princeton, N.J.: Princeton University Press, 1978), and "Worlds of Dying Children and Their Well Siblings," *Death Studies* 13 (1989): 1–16.

17. Shirley Steele, ed., *Nursing Care of the Child with Long-Term Illness*, 2d ed. (New York: Appleton-Century-Crofts, 1977), p. 531. See also Jo-Eileen Gyulay, *The Dying Child* (New York: McGraw-Hill, 1978).

18. Sara Dubik-Unruh, "Children of Chaos: Planning for the Emotional Survival of Dying Children of Dying Families," *Journal of Palliative Care* 5, no. 2 (1989): 10–15.

19. Thesi Bergmann and Anna Freud, *Children in the Hospital* (New York: International Universities Press, 1965), pp. 27–28.

20. Donna Juenker, "Child's Perception of His Illness," in *Nursing Care of the Child with Long-Term Illness*, 2d ed., ed. Steele, p. 177.

21. See, for example, Maurice Levy, Ciaran M. Duffy, Pamela Pollock, Elizabeth Budd, Lisa Caulfield, and Gideon Koren, "Home-Based Palliative Care for Children—Part 1: The Institution of a Program," *Journal of Palliative Care* 6, no. 1 (1990): 11–15; Ciaran M. Duffy, Pamela Pollock, Maurice Levy, Elizabeth Budd, Lisa Caulfield, and Gideon Koren, "Home-Based Palliative Care for Children—Part 2: The Benefits of an Established Program," *Journal of Palliative Care* 6, no. 2 (1990): 8–14; D. F. Dufour, "Home or Hospital Care for the Child with End-Stage Cancer: Effects on the Family," *Issues in Comprehensive Pediatric Nursing* 12 (1989): 371–383; Ida M. Martinson, ed., *Home Care for the Dying Child: Professional and Family Perspectives* (Norwalk, Conn.: Appleton-Century-Crofts, 1976); Ida M. Martinson et al., "Home Care for Children Dying of Cancer," *Pediatrics* 62 (1978): 106–113; and D. Gay Moldow, Ida M. Martinson, and Arthur Kohrman, *Home Care for Seriously Ill Children: A Manual for Parents* (Alexandria, Va.: Children's Hospice of Virginia, 1984).

22. A. E. While, "The Needs of Dying Children and Their Families," *Health Visitor* 62, no. 6 (1989): 176–178.

23. See, for example, John E. Schowalter et al., eds., *The Child and Death* (New York: Columbia University Press, 1983); and Hannelore Wass and Charles A. Corr, eds., *Childhood and Death* (Washington, D.C.: Hemisphere, 1984).

24. Jo-Eileen Gyulay, "What Suicide Leaves Behind," *Issues in Comprehensive Pediatric Nursing* 12 (1989): 103–118.

25. Richard Lonetto, *Children's Conceptions of Death* (New York: Springer, 1980), p. 186. This phenomenon is also dealt with in Sylvia Anthony's classic work, *The Discovery of Death in Childhood and After* (New York: Basic Books, 1972).

26. Ute Carson, "A Child Loses a Pet," *Death Education* 3 (1980): 399–404.

27. Jane Brody, "When Your Pet Dies," *Honolulu Star-Bulletin & Advertiser,* December 8, 1985.

28. Randolph Picht, "Fido's Final Resting Place," Associated Press story (January 5, 1986).

29. See William J. Kay, ed., *Pet Loss and Human Bereavement* (Ames: Iowa State University Press, 1984); and Wallace Sife, *The Loss of a Pet* (New York: Howell, 1993).

30. Avery D. Weisman, "Bereavement and Companion Animals," in *The Path Ahead,* ed. DeSpelder and Strickland, pp. 276–280; reprinted from *Omega: Journal of Death and Dying* 22 (1990–1991): 245–248.

31. See, for example, Erna Furman, *A Child's Parent Dies: Studies in Childhood Bereavement* (New Haven, Conn.: Yale University Press, 1974); and Robert A. Furman, "The Child's Reaction to Death in the Family," in *Loss and Grief: Psychological Management in Medical Practice,* ed. Bernard Schoenberg et al. (New York: Columbia University Press, 1970), pp. 70–86.

32. Phyllis R. Silverman, Steven Nickman, and J. William Worden, "Detachment Revisited: The Child's Reconstruction of a Dead Parent," in *The Path Ahead,* ed. DeSpelder and Strickland, pp. 260–270; reprinted from *American Journal of Orthopsychiatry* 62, no. 4 (October 1992): 494–503.

33. Sons and Daughters in Touch can be contacted in care of Friends of the Vietnam Veterans Memorial, 1350 Connecticut Avenue, N.W., Suite 300, Washington, DC 20036. See Al Santoli, "We Never Knew Our Fathers," *Parade* (May 27, 1990), pp. 21–22.

34. For further information on the use of spontaneous drawings, see Robert C. Burns and S. Harvard Kaufman, *Kinetic Family Drawings: An Introduction to Understanding Children Through Kinetic Drawings* (New York: Brunner/Mazel, 1970), and *Actions, Styles and Symbols in Kinetic Family Drawings* (New York: Brunner/Mazel, 1972); Joseph H. DiLeo, *Young Children and Their Drawings* (New York: Brunner/Mazel, 1970), and *Children's Drawings as Diagnostic Aids* (New York: Brunner/Mazel, 1973); and Gregg M. Furth, *The Secret World of Drawings: Healing Through Art* (Boston: Sigo Press, 1988).

35. Barbara Betker McIntyre, "Art Therapy with Bereaved Youth," *Journal of Palliative Care* 6, no. 1 (1990): 16–23.

36. David E. Balk, "Sibling Death, Adolescent Bereavement, and Religion," *Death Studies* 15 (1991): 1–20.

37. John Graham-Pole, Hannelore Wass, Sheila Eyberg, and Luis Chu, "Communicating with Dying Children and Their Siblings: A Retrospective Analysis," *Death Studies* 13 (1989): 465–483; see also S. J. Bendor, "Preventing Psychosocial Impairment in Siblings of Terminally Ill Children," *Hospice Journal* 5 (1989): 151–163; and Linda K. Birenbaum, Michaelle A. Robinson, David S. Phillips, Barbara J. Stewart et al., "The Response of Children to the Dying and Death of a Sibling," *Omega: Journal of Death and Dying* 20 (1989–1990): 213–228.

38. Myra Bluebond-Langner, "Worlds of Dying Children and Their Well Siblings," *Death Studies* 13 (1989): 9.

39. This and the following anecdote from Jo-Eileen Gyulay, *The Dying Child* (New York: McGraw-Hill, 1978), pp. 17–18.

40. Dana Cable, Laurel Cucchi, Faye Lopez, and Terry Martin, "Camp Jamie," *American Journal of Hospice and Palliative Care* 9, no. 5 (1992): 18–21.

41. *HUGS Fact Sheet.* For information, write to "HUGS: Help, Understanding and Group Support for Hawaii's Seriously Ill Children and Their Families," 3636 Kilauea Avenue, Honolulu, HI 96816.

42. Fact Sheet, *Magic Performers of America Club (Magic PAC)*, 1994. For further information about Magic Performers of America Club (Magic PAC), contact Samuel Schoonover, Executive Director, 480 Baker Street, Santa Cruz, CA 95062.

43. Lori S. Wiener, Elizabeth DuPont Spencer, Robert Davidson, and Cynthia Fair, "National Telephone Support Groups: A New Avenue Toward Psychosocial Support for HIV-Infected Children and Their Families," *Social Work with Groups* 16, no. 3 (1993): 55–71.

44. For more information, contact: Sunshine Foundation, 2001 Bridge Street, Philadelphia, PA 19124, Tel.: (215) 535-1413 or (800) 767-1976; Starlight Foundation International, 12424 Wilshire Blvd., Suite 150, Los Angeles, CA 90025, Tel.: (310) 207-5558, Fax (310) 207-2554.

C H A P T E R 11

1. Louis E. LaGrand, "Loss Reactions of College Students: A Descriptive Analysis," *Death Education* 5 (1981): 235–248; see also, by LaGrand, *Coping with Separation and Loss as a Young Adult* (Springfield, Ill.: Charles C. Thomas, 1986).

2. Example from Robert Kastenbaum, *Death, Society, and Human Experience*, 3d ed. (Columbus, Ohio: Charles E. Merrill, 1986), pp. 223ff.

3. Gina Gesser, Paul T. P. Wong, and Gary T. Reker, "Death Attitudes Across the Life-Span: The Development and Validation of the Death Attitude Profile (DAP)," *Omega: Journal of Death and Dying* 18 (1987–1988): 113–128.

4. Russell A. Ward, "Age and Acceptance of Euthanasia," *Journal of Gerontology* 35, no. 3 (May 1980): 428–429.

5. Charles W. Brice, "Mourning Throughout the Life Cycle," *American Journal of Psychoanalysis* 42, no. 4 (1982): 320–321.

6. LaGrand, "Loss Reactions of College Students" and *Coping with Separation and Loss.*

7. Erik H. Erikson, *The Life Cycle Completed: A Review* (New York: W. W. Norton, 1982), p. 67. Neil Salkind says the final psychosocial stage described by Erikson contains mystical elements and has much in common with the state of self-actualization discussed by Abraham Maslow; see Salkind, *Theories of Human Development*, 2d ed. (New York: Wiley, 1985), p. 117.

8. See Stanley Brandes, *Forty: The Age and the Symbol* (Nashville: University of Tennessee Press, 1985).

9. See Harriett Sarnoff Schiff, *The Bereaved Parent* (New York: Crown, 1977).

10. Exhibition note, "Native Peoples," Glenbow Museum, Calgary, Alberta, Canada.

11. Dennis Klass, "Solace and Immortality: Bereaved Parents' Continuing Bond with Their Children," in *The Path Ahead: Readings in Death and Dying*, ed. Lynne Ann DeSpelder and Albert Lee Strickland (Mountain View, Calif.: Mayfield, 1995), pp. 246–259; reprinted from *Death Studies* 17, no. 4 (1993): 343–368. See also Dennis

Klass and Samuel J. Marwit, "Toward a Model of Parental Grief," *Omega: Journal of Death and Dying* 19 (1988–1989): 31–50.

12. Elliott J. Rosen, "Family Therapy in Cases of Interminable Grief for the Loss of a Child," *Omega: Journal of Death and Dying* 19 (1988–1989): 187–202.

13. Kathleen R. Gilbert, "Interactive Grief and Coping in the Marital Dyad," *Death Studies* 13 (1989): 605–626.

14. Cynthia Bach-Hughes and Judith Page-Lieberman, "Fathers Experiencing a Perinatal Loss," *Death Studies* 13 (1989): 537–556.

15. Gilbert, "Interactive Grief and Coping in the Marital Dyad."

16. See, for example, Judy Rollins Bohannon, "Grief Responses of Spouses Following the Death of a Child: A Longitudinal Study," *Omega: Journal of Death and Dying* 22 (1990–1991): 109–121; Nancy Feeley and Laurie N. Gottlieb, "Parents' Coping and Communication Following Their Infant's Death," *Omega: Journal of Death and Dying* 19 (1988–1989): 51–67; and Reiko Schwab, "Paternal and Maternal Coping with the Death of a Child," *Death Studies* 14 (1990): 407–422.

17. "Fetal and Infant Deaths," *Statistical Abstract of the United States 1994,* 114th ed. (Washington, D.C.: Government Printing Office, 1994), p. 91.

18. See Susan Borg and Judith Lasker, *When Pregnancy Fails* (Boston: Beacon Press, 1981); Rochelle Friedman and Bonnie Gradstein, *Surviving Pregnancy Loss* (Boston: Little, Brown, 1982); and J. A. Menke and R. E. McClead, "Perinatal Grief and Mourning," *Advances in Pediatrics* 37 (1990): 261–283.

19. *Dorland's Illustrated Medical Dictionary,* 26th ed. (Philadelphia: Saunders, 1985), p. 828.

20. Ellen Fish Lietar, "Miscarriage," in *Parental Loss of a Child,* ed. Therese A. Rando (Champaign, Ill.: Research Press, 1986), p. 122.

21. *Dorland's Illustrated Medical Dictionary,* 26th ed., pp. 664, 1251.

22. Peter Wingate, *The Penguin Medical Encyclopedia,* 2d ed. (New York: Penguin, 1976), p. 177.

23. Judith A. Savage, *Mourning Unlived Lives: A Psychological Study of Childbearing Loss* (Wilmette, Ill.: Chiron Publications, 1989).

24. Ibid., p. xiii.

25. Ibid., p. 108.

26. Anne C. Smith and Sherry B. Borgers, "Parental Grief: Response to Perinatal Death," *Omega: Journal of Death and Dying* 19 (1988–1989): 203–214.

27. Irwin J. Weinfeld, "An Expanded Perinatal Bereavement Support Committee: A Community-Wide Resource," *Death Studies* 14 (1990): 241–252.

28. Glen W. Davidson, "Death of a Wished-for Child: A Case Study," *Death Education* 1 (1977): 265–275.

29. "Pregnancies by Outcome," *Statistical Abstract of the United States 1994,* p. 84.

30. Larry G. Peppers, "Grief and Elective Abortion: Breaking the Emotional Bond?" *Omega: Journal of Death and Dying* 18 (1987–1988): 1–12.

31. See William R. LaFleur, *Liquid Life: Abortion and Buddhism in Japan* (Princeton, N.J.: Princeton University Press, 1992); Marie Okabe, "Japan Shrine Honors Infants Never Born," *Los Angeles Times* (November 13, 1982); and Tom Ashbrook, "Japanese Temples Exploit Superstitions of Abortion," *Honolulu Star-Bulletin & Advertiser* (October 13, 1985).

32. Kenneth J. Doka, "Disenfranchised Grief" (paper presented at the Annual Meeting of the Association for Death Education and Counseling, Atlanta, Spring 1986); see also, edited by Doka, *Disenfranchised Grief—Recognizing Hidden Sorrow* (Lexington, Mass.: Lexington Books, 1989).

33. John De Frain, Leona Martens, Jan Stork, and Warren Stork, "The Psychological Effects of a Stillbirth on Surviving Family Members," *Omega: Journal of Death and Dying* 22 (1990–1991): 81–108.

34. Jay Ruby, "Portraying the Dead," *Omega: Journal of Death and Dying* 19 (1988–1989): 1–20; and Joy Johnson and S. Marvin Johnson, with James H. Cunningham and Irwin J. Weinfeld, *A Most Important Picture: A Very Tender Manual for Taking Pictures of Stillborn Babies and Infants Who Die* (Omaha: Centering Corp., 1985).

35. De Frain et al., "Psychological Effects of a Stillbirth," p. 87.

36. Beverly Raphael, *The Anatomy of Bereavement* (New York: Basic Books, 1983).

37. Jerome L. Schulman, *Coping with Tragedy: Successfully Facing the Problem of a Seriously Ill Child* (Chicago: Follett, 1976), p. 335.

38. Victor Florian, "Meaning and Purpose in Life of Bereaved Parents Whose Son Fell During Active Military Service," *Omega: Journal of Death and Dying* 20 (1989–1990): 91–102.

39. See, for example, De Frain et al., "Psychological Effects of a Stillbirth," pp. 95–97, 107.

40. Joan Delahanty Douglas, "Patterns of Change Following Parent Death in Midlife Adults," *Omega: Journal of Death and Dying* 22 (1990–1991): 123–137.

41. Marion Osterweis, Fredric Solomon, and Morris Green, eds. *Bereavement: Reactions, Consequences, and Care* (Washington: National Academy Press, 1984), p. 85.

42. Raphael, *Anatomy of Bereavement*.

43. Savine Gross Weizman and Phyllis Kamm, *About Mourning: Support and Guidance for the Bereaved* (New York: Human Sciences, 1985), p. 130. For a personal account of spousal bereavement, see Jill Truman, *Letter to My Husband: Notes about Mourning and Recovery* (New York: Viking Penguin, 1987).

44. Notable studies include Colin Murray Parkes, "The Effects of Bereavement on Physical and Mental Health: A Study of Medical Records of Widows," *British Medical Journal* 1 (1964): 272–279, and "Recent Bereavement as a Cause of Mental Illness," *British Journal of Psychiatry* 110 (1964): 198–204, as well as *Bereavement: Studies of Grief in Adult Life* (New York: International Universities Press, 1972); Ira O. Glick, Robert S. Weiss, and Colin Murray Parkes, *The First Year of Bereavement* (New York: Wiley, 1974), and its follow-up by Colin Murray Parkes and Robert S. Weiss, *Recovery from Bereavement* (New York: Basic Books, 1983); Helena Z. Lopata, *Widowhood in an American City* (Cambridge, Mass.: Schenkman, 1973) and *Women as Widows: Support Systems* (New York: Elsevier, 1979); Paula J. Clayton, "Mortality and Morbidity in the First Year of Widowhood," *Archives of General Psychiatry* 125 (1974): 747–750, and "The Sequelae and Non-Sequelae of Conjugal Bereavement," *American Journal of Psychiatry* 136 (1979): 1530–1543; Herbert H. Hyman, *Of Time and Widowhood: Nationwide Studies of Enduring Effects* (Durham, N.C.: Duke University Press, 1983). See also Margaret S. Stroebe and Wolfgang Stroebe in "Who Participates in Bereavement Research? A Review and Empirical Study," *Omega: Journal of Death and Dying* 20 (1989–1990): 1–29.

45. Brice, "Mourning Throughout the Life Cycle," pp. 320–321.

46. Justine F. Ball, "Widows' Grief: The Impact of Age and Mode of Death," *Omega: Journal of Death and Dying* 7 (1976–1977): 307–333.

47. Paul J. Hershberger and W. Bruce Walsh, "Multiple Role Involvements and the Adjustment to Conjugal Bereavement: An Exploratory Study," *Omega: Journal of Death and Dying* 21 (1990): 91–102. See also Linda J. Solie and Lois J. Fielder, "The Relationship Between Sex Role Identity and a Widow's Adjustment to the Loss of a Spouse," *Omega: Journal of Death and Dying* 18 (1987–1988): 33–40.

48. Judith M. Stillion, *Death and the Sexes: An Examination of Differential Longevity, Attitudes, Behaviors, and Coping Skills* (Washington: Hemisphere, 1985).

49. Ann Bowling, "Who Dies After Widow(er)hood? A Discriminate Analysis," *Omega: Journal of Death and Dying* 19 (1988–1989): 135–153.

50. "Marital Status of the Population," *Statistical Abstract of the United States 1994,* p. 55.

51. See Dale A. Lund, Michael S. Caserta, Jan Van Pelt, and Kathleen A. Gass, "Stability of Social Support Networks After Later-Life Spousal Bereavement," *Death Studies* 14 (1990): 53–73.

52. David M. Bass, Linda S. Noelker, Allen L. Townsend, Gary T. Deimling, "Losing an Aged Relative: Perceptual Differences Between Spouses and Adult Children," *Omega: Journal of Death and Dying* 21 (1990): 21–40.

53. See Phyllis R. Silverman, *Widow to Widow* (New York: Springer, 1986); and, also by Silverman, "Widowhood as the Next Stage in the Life Cycle," in *Widows: North America,* ed. Helena Z. Lopata (Durham, N.C.: Duke University Press, 1987); and "The Widow-to-Widow Program: An Experiment in Preventive Intervention," *Mental Hygiene* 53, no. 3 (1969), a landmark report by Silverman on her work at Harvard Medical School's Laboratory of Community Psychiatry. On mutual support, see also Molly Hill Folken, "Moderating Grief of Widowed People in Talk Groups," *Death Studies* 14 (1990): 171–176.

54. Bernice L. Neugarten, "Growing as Long as We Live," *Second Opinion* 15 (November 1990): 42–51.

55. Robert M. Sapolsky and Caleb E. Finch, "On Growing Old," *The Sciences* 31 (March/April 1991): 30–38.

56. James F. Fries, Lawrence W. Green, and Sol Levine, "Health Promotion and the Compression of Morbidity," *Lancet* (March 4, 1989): 481–483; see also, by Fries, "The Compression of Morbidity," *Millbank Memorial Fund Quarterly* 61 (1983): 397–419.

57. Neugarten, "Growing as Long as We Live."

58. Sandra L. Bertman, "Aging Grace: Treatment of the Aged in the Arts," *Death Studies* 13 (1989): 517–535. See also Pamela T. Amoss and Steven Harrell, eds., *Other Ways of Growing Old: Anthropological Perspectives* (Palo Alto, Calif.: Stanford University Press, 1981); and M. Powell Lawton, Miriam Moss, and Allen Glicksman, "The Quality of the Last Year of Life of Older Persons," *Millbank Quarterly* 68 (1990): 1–28.

59. Daniel Callahan, "Can Old Age Be Given a Public Meaning," *Second Opinion* 15 (November 1990): 12–23.

60. Melvin A. Kimble, "Religion: Friend or Foe of the Aging?" *Second Opinion* 15 (November 1990): 70–81.

61. Robert N. Butler, *Why Survive? Being Old in America* (New York: Harper and Row, 1975).

62. Hannelore Wass, "Aging and Death Education for Elderly Persons," *Educational Gerontology: An International Quarterly* 5 (1980): 79–90.

63. Butler, *Why Survive? Being Old in America.*

64. See Kathleen O'Connor and Joyce Prothero, eds., *The Alzheimer's Caregiver: Strategies of Support* (Seattle: University of Washington Press, 1986).

65. Jon Hendricks and C. Davis Hendricks, *Aging in Mass Society: Myths and Realities* (Cambridge, Mass.: Winthrop, 1977), p. 282. See also Colleen L. Johnson and Leslie A. Grant, *The Nursing Home in American Society* (Baltimore: Johns Hopkins University Press, 1985).

66. See, for example, Colette Brown and Roberta Onzuka-Anderson, eds., *Our Aging Parents: A Practical Guide to Eldercare* (Honolulu: University of Hawaii Press, 1985); and Marty Richards et al., *Choosing a Nursing Home: A Guidebook for Families* (Seattle: University of Washington Press, 1985).

67. Hendricks and Hendricks, *Aging in Mass Society,* pp. 284–285.

C H A P T E R 12

1. Judith M. Stillion, "Premature Exits: Understanding Suicide," in *The Path Ahead: Readings in Death and Dying,* ed. Lynne Ann DeSpelder and Albert Lee Strickland (Mountain View, Calif.: Mayfield, 1995), pp. 182–197.

2. Judith M. Stillion, Eugene E. McDowell, and Jacque H. May, *Suicide Across the Life Span: Premature Exits* (New York: Hemisphere, 1989), p. 1.

3. P. L. McCall, "Adolescent and Elderly White Male Suicide Trends," *Journal of Gerontology* 46 (1991): 43–51.

4. Judith M. Stillion, Hedy White, Pamela J. Edwards, and Eugene E. McDowell, "Ageism and Sexism in Suicide Attitudes," *Death Studies* 13 (1989): 247–261.

5. John L. McIntosh, "Trends in Racial Difference in U.S. Suicide Statistics," *Death Studies* 13 (1989): 275–286.

6. Committee on Cultural Psychiatry, "Suicide and Ethnicity in the United States," *Report: Group for the Advancement of Psychiatry* 128 (1989): 1–131. See also Philip A. May, "A Bibliography on Suicide and Suicide Attempts Among American Indians and Alaska Natives," *Omega: Journal of Death and Dying* 21 (1990): 199–214.

7. Jon B. Ellis and Lillian M. Range, "Characteristics of Suicidal Individuals: A Review," *Death Studies* 13 (1989): 485–500.

8. See, for example, P. W. O'Carroll, "A Consideration of the Validity and Reliability of Suicide Mortality Data," *Suicide and Life-Threatening Behavior* 19 (1989): 1–16.

9. Glen Evans and Norman L. Farberow, eds., *The Encyclopedia of Suicide* (New York: Facts on File, 1988), p. 70.

10. Ezra H. E. Griffith and Carl C. Bell, "Recent Trends in Suicide and Homicide Among Blacks," *Journal of the American Medical Association* 262 (1989): 2265–2269; see also F. M. Baker, "Black Youth Suicide: Literature Review with a Focus on Prevention," *Journal of the National Medical Association* 82 (1990): 495–507.

11. Evans and Farberow, *Encyclopedia of Suicide,* p. 268.

12. Edwin S. Shneidman, "Suicide," in *Death: Current Perspectives,* 2d ed., ed. Shneidman (Mountain View, Calif.: Mayfield, 1980), p. 432.

13. Evans and Farberow, *Encyclopedia of Suicide,* pp. 26, 230–231.

14. James R. P. Ogloff and Randy K. Otto, "Psychological Autopsy: Clinical and Legal Perspectives," *Saint Louis University Law Journal* 37, no. 3 (Spring 1993): 607–646. See also Edwin S. Shneidman, *Clues to Suicide* (New York: McGraw-Hill, 1957); and, by Avery D. Weisman, *The Psychological Autopsy* (New York: Human Sciences Press, 1968), and *The Realization of Death: A Guide for the Psychological Autopsy* (Northvale, N.J.: Aronson, 1974).

15. Thomas J. Young, "Procedures and Problems in Conducting a Psychological Autopsy," *International Journal of Offender Therapy and Comparative Criminology* 36, no. 1 (Spring 1992): 43–52.

16. See Norman Poythress, Randy K. Otto, Jack Darkes, and Laura Starr, "APA's Expert Panel in the Congressional Review of the USS 'Iowa' Incident," *American*

Psychologist 48, no. 1 (January 1993): 8–15; Randy K. Otto, Norman Poythress, Laura Starr, and Jack Darkes, "An Empirical Study of the Reports of APA's Peer Review Panel in the Congressional Review of the U.S.S. IOWA Incident," *Journal of Personality Assessment* 61, no. 3 (December 1993): 425–442; and James R. P. Ogloff and Randy K. Otto, "Psychological Autopsy: Clinical and Legal Perspectives," *Saint Louis University Law Journal* 37, no. 3 (Spring 1993): 607–646.

17. Quoted material from Poythress et al., "APA's Expert Panel."

18. David A. Brent, "The Psychological Autopsy: Methodological Considerations for the Study of Adolescent Suicide," *Suicide and Life-Threatening Behavior* 19 (Spring 1989): 43–57. See also David Shaffer, "The Epidemiology of Teen Suicide: An Examination of Risk Factors," *Journal of Clinical Psychiatry* 49 (September 1988): Supplement, 36–41; and Mohammad Shafi, Shahin Carrigan, J. Russell Whittinghill, and Ann Derrick, "Psychological Autopsy of Completed Suicide in Children and Adolescents," *American Journal of Psychiatry* 142 (1985): 1061–1064.

19. Edwin S. Shneidman, "Perturbation and Lethality as Precursors of Suicide in a Gifted Group," *Suicide and Life-Threatening Behavior* 1 (Spring 1971): 23–45.

20. Emile Durkheim, *Suicide: A Study in Sociology* (New York: Free Press, 1951). Additional material is from Evans and Farberow, *Encyclopedia of Suicide*, pp. xxiii, 11, 14, 102.

21. E. Hunter, "Using a Socio-Historical Frame to Analyze Aboriginal Self-Destructive Behavior," *Australian and New Zealand Journal of Psychiatry* 24 (1990): 191–198.

22. Durkheim, *Suicide*, p. 209.

23. Ronald Maris, "Sociology," in *A Handbook for the Study of Suicide*, ed. Seymour Perlin (New York: Oxford University Press, 1975), pp. 95–96.

24. Norman Farberow, "The History of Suicide," in *Encyclopedia of Suicide*, ed. Evans and Farberow, p. xxiii.

25. See Robert Jay Lifton, Shuichi Kato, and Michael R. Reich, *Six Lives, Six Deaths: Portraits from Modern Japan* (New Haven, Conn.: Yale University Press, 1979); Bernard Millot, *Divine Thunder: The Life and Death of the Kamikazes*, trans. Lowell Bair (New York: McCall, 1971); Jack Seward, *Hara-Kiri: Japanese Ritual Suicide* (Rutland, Vt.: Charles E. Tuttle, 1968). For *seppuku* in its historical context, see Helen Craig McCullough, *The Taiheiki: A Chronicle of Medieval Japan* (Rutland, Vt.: Charles E. Tuttle, 1959, 1979); A. L. Sadler, *The Maker of Modern Japan: The Life of Shogun Tokugawa Ieyasu* (Rutland, Vt.: Charles E. Tuttle, 1937, 1978). On patterns of suicide in modern Japan, see "Japanese Suicide," *The East* 21, no. 5 (October 1985): 46–52.

26. Farberow, "History of Suicide," p. viii.

27. See David Chidester, *Salvation and Suicide: An Interpretation of Jim Jones, the Peoples Temple, and Jonestown* (Bloomington: Indiana University Press, 1988); Jose I. Lasaga, "Death in Jonestown: Techniques of Political Control by a Paranoid Leader," *Suicide and Life-Threatening Behavior* 10, no. 4 (Winter 1980): 210–213; Shiva Naipaul, *Journey to Nowhere: a New World Tragedy* (New York: Simon & Schuster, 1979); James Reston, Jr., *Our Father Who Art in Hell* (New York: Times Books, 1978); and Richard H. Seiden, "Reverend Jones on Suicide," *Suicide and Life-Threatening Behavior* 9, no. 2 (Summer 1979): 116–119.

28. For a discussion of psychoanalytic theory, see Charles Brenner, *An Elementary Textbook of Psychoanalysis*, rev. ed. (Garden City, N.Y.: Anchor Press/Doubleday, 1975).

29. A. L. Evans, "Dreams and Suicidal Behavior," *Crisis* (May 1990): 12–19.

30. Erwin Stengel, "A Matter of Communication," in *On the Nature of Suicide,* ed. Edwin S. Shneidman (San Francisco: Jossey-Bass, 1969), pp. 78–79.

31. Lillian M. Range and Stephen K. Martin, "How Knowledge of Extenuating Circumstances Influences Community Reactions Toward Suicide Victims and Their Bereaved Families," *Omega: Journal of Death and Dying* 21 (1990): 191–198.

32. Richard H. Seiden and Molly Gleiser, "Sex Differences in Suicide Among Chemists," *Omega: Journal of Death and Dying* 21 (1990): 177–189.

33. Roy F. Baumeister, "Suicide as Escape from Self," *Psychological Review* 97 (1990): 90–113.

34. See, for example, Joaquim Puig-Antich, Deborah Goetz, Mark Davies, Thelma Kaplan et al., "A Controlled Family History Study of Prepubertal Major Depressive Disorder," *Archives of General Psychiatry* 46 (1989): 406–418.

35. George Beaumont, "Suicide and Antidepressant Overdosage in General Practice," *British Journal of Psychiatry* (October 1989): Supplement, 27–31.

36. G. D. Tollefson, "Recognition and Treatment of Major Depression," *American Family Physician* 41 (1990): Supplement, 59–66; and A. T. Davis and C. Schrueder, "The Prediction of Suicide," *Medical Journal of Australia* 153 (1990): 552–554.

37. See, for example, Gabor I. Keitner and Ivan W. Miller, "Family Functioning and Major Depression: An Overview," *American Journal of Psychiatry* 147 (1990): 1128–1137.

38. Edwin S. Shneidman, *Deaths of Man* (New York: Quadrangle Books, 1973), pp. 81–90.

39. See, for example, M. A. Fine and R. A. Sansone, "Dilemmas in the Management of Suicidal Behavior in Individuals with Borderline Personality Disorder," *American Journal of Psychotherapy* 44 (1990): 160–171.

40. Evans and Farberow, *Encyclopedia of Suicide,* p. 21.

41. See, for example, Ronald W. Maris, *Pathways to Suicide: A Survey of Self-Destructive Behaviors* (Baltimore: Johns Hopkins University Press, 1981).

42. David Lester, "The Study of Suicide from a Feminist Perspective," *Crisis* 11 (May 1990): 38–43.

43. See Stillion et al., *Suicide Across the Life Span,* p. 69; and James Overholser, Steven Evans, and Anthony Spirito, "Sex Differences and Their Relevance to Primary Prevention of Adolescent Suicide," *Death Studies* 14 (1990): 391–402. See also Silvia Sara Canetto, "She Died for Love and He for Glory: Gender Myths of Suicidal Behavior," *Omega: Journal of Death and Dying* 26, no. 1 (1992–1993): 1–17.

44. Kevin E. Early and Ronald L. Akers, " 'It's a White Thing'—An Exploration of Beliefs About Suicide in the African-American Community," in *The Path Ahead,* ed. DeSpelder and Strickland, pp. 198–210; reprinted from *Deviant Behavior* 14, no. 4 (1993): 277–296.

45. Kathleen Erwin, "Interpreting the Evidence: Competing Paradigms and the Emergence of Lesbian and Gay Suicide as a 'Social Fact,' " in *The Path Ahead,* ed. DeSpelder and Strickland, pp. 211–220; reprinted from *The International Journal of Health Services* 23, no. 3 (1993): 437–453.

46. "Suicide Rates Up Among Young," *Associated Press Online* (April 20, 1995).

47. Richard H. Seiden and Raymond P. Freitas, "Shifting Patterns of Deadly Violence," *Suicide and Life-Threatening Behavior* 10, no. 4 (Winter 1980): 209.

48. Brian Barry, "Suicide: The Ultimate Escape," *Death Studies* 13 (1989): 185–190.

49. Jack D. Douglas, "Suicide," *Academic American Encyclopedia* online (March 1991).

50. Evans and Farberow, *Encyclopedia of Suicide,* p. 240. See also Alfred Alvarez, *The Savage God: A Study of Suicide* (New York: Random House, 1971).

51. On Plath's suicide, see David Lester, "Application of Piotrowski's Dark Shading Hypothesis to Sylvia Plath's Poems Written Before Her Suicide," *Perceptual and Motor Skills* 68 (1989): 122.

52. J. Michael Olivero and James B. Roberts, "Jail Suicide and Legal Redress," *Suicide and Life-Threatening Behavior* 20 (1990): 138–147.

53. John M. Memory, "Juvenile Suicides in Secure Detention Facilities: Correction of Published Rates," *Death Studies* 13 (1989): 455–463.

54. D. E. Ness and C. R. Pfeffer, "Sequelae of Bereavement Resulting from Suicide," *American Journal of Psychiatry* 147 (March 1990): 279–285.

55. See, for example, S. Vomvouras, "Psychiatric Manifestations of AIDS Spectrum Disorders," *Southern Medical Journal* 82 (1989): 352–357.

56. Donald H. Rubinstein, "Epidemic Suicide Among Micronesian Adolescents," *Social Science and Medicine* 17 (1983): 657–665; and "Suicide in Micronesia," in *Culture, Youth and Suicide in the Pacific: Papers from an East-West Center Conference,* ed. Francis X. Hezel, Donald H. Rubinstein, and Geoffrey M. White (Honolulu: Pacific Islands Study Program, University of Hawaii, 1985), pp. 88–111.

57. Representative studies include: K. Y. Little and D. L. Sparks, "Brain Markers and Suicide: Can a Relationship Be Found?" *Journal of Forensic Science* 35 (1990): 1393–1403; J. J. Mann, V. Arango, and M. D. Underwood, "Serotonin and Suicidal Behavior," *Annals of the New York Academy of Science* 600 (1990): 476–484; Lorna Cameron Ricci and Mary M. Wellman, "Monoamines: Biochemical Markers of Suicide?" *Journal of Clinical Psychology* 46 (1990): 106–116; and Michael Stanley and Barbara Stanley, "Postmortem Evidence for Serotonin's Role in Suicide," *Journal of Clinical Psychiatry* 51 (April 1990): Supplement, 22–28.

58. Cynthia R. Pfeffer, "Preoccupations with Death in 'Normal' Children: The Relationship to Suicidal Behavior," *Omega: Journal of Death and Dying* 20 (1989–1990): 205–212.

59. "Suicide Rates by Sex, Race, and Age Group: 1980 to 1991," *Statistical Abstract of the United States 1989,* 114th ed. (Washington, D.C.: Government Printing Office, 1994), p. 101.

60. L. Bender and P. Schilder, "Suicidal Preoccupations and Attempts in Children," *American Journal of Orthopsychiatry* 7 (1937): 225–234.

61. "Deaths and Death Rates for the 10 Leading Causes of Death in Specified Age Groups," *Advance Report of Mortality Statistics, 1992* (Hyattsville, Md.: National Center for Health Statistics, 1995), p. 23.

62. René F. W. Diekstra, "Suicidal Behavior and Depressive Disorders in Adolescents and Young Adults," *Neuropsychobiology* 22 (1989): 194–207.

63. Cynthia R. Pfeffer, "Self-Destructive Behavior in Children and Adolescents," *Psychiatric Clinics of North America* 8, no. 2 (June 1985): 215–226; see also, by Pfeffer, "Assessment of Suicidal Children and Adolescents," *Psychiatric Clinics of North America* 12 (1989): 861–872, and "Studies of Suicidal Preadolescent and Adolescent Inpatients: A Critique of Research Methods, *Suicide and Life-Threatening Behavior* 19 (Spring 1989): 58–77.

64. S. J. Blumenthal, "Youth Suicide: Risk Factors, Assessment, and Treatment of Adolescent and Young Adult Suicidal Patients," *Psychiatric Clinics of North America* 13 (1990): 511–556.

65. Michael Peck, "Youth Suicide," *Death Education* 6 (1982): 29–47.

66. Evans and Farberow, *Encyclopedia of Suicide,* p. 262.

67. See M. S. Gould, S. Wallenstein, and L. Davidson, "Suicide Clusters: A Critical Review," *Suicide and Life-Threatening Behavior* 19 (Spring 1989): 17–29.

68. See R. Milin and A. Turgay, "Adolescent Couple Suicide: Literature Review," *Canadian Journal of Psychiatry* 35 (March 1990): 183–186. Examples cited by Evans and Farberow, *Encyclopedia of Suicide,* pp. 26–27, 72, 254.

69. Evans and Farberow, *Encyclopedia of Suicide,* pp. 83–84.

70. R. D. Goldney, "Suicide: The Role of the Media," *Australian and New Zealand Journal of Psychiatry* 2 (March 1989): 30–34.

71. Frank E. Crumley, "Substance Abuse and Adolescent Suicidal Behavior," *Journal of the American Medical Association* 263 (1990): 3051–3056.

72. B. P. Low and S. F. Andrews, "Adolescent Suicide," *Medical Clinics of North America* 74 (1990): 1251–1264.

73. Stillion et al., *Suicide Across the Life Span,* p. 134.

74. Sidney R. Saul and Shura Saul, "Old People Talk About Suicide: A Discussion About Suicide in a Long-Term Care Facility for Frail and Elderly People," *Omega: Journal of Death and Dying* 19 (1988–1989): 237–251. See also Nancy J. Osgood, Barbara A. Brant, and Aaron A. Lipman, "Patterns of Suicidal Behavior in Long-Term Care Facilities: A Preliminary Report," *Omega: Journal of Death and Dying* 19 (1988–1989): 69–78.

75. Stillion et al., *Suicide Across the Life Span,* p. 163.

76. Ibid., pp. 180–181.

77. Antoon A. Leenaars and David Lester, "The Significance of the Method Chosen for Suicide in Understanding the Psychodynamics of the Suicidal Individual," *Omega: Journal of Death and Dying* 19 (1988–1989): 311–314.

78. American Medical Association Counsel on Scientific Affairs, "Firearms Injuries and Deaths: A Critical Public Health Issue," *Public Health Reports* 104 (March–April 1989): 111–120.

79. Josefina Jayme Card, "Lethality of Suicidal Methods and Suicide Risk: Two Distinct Concepts," in *Omega: Journal of Death and Dying* 5, no. 1 (1974): 37–45.

80. Edwin S. Shneidman, "Self-Destruction: Suicide Notes and Tragic Lives," in *Death: Current Perspectives,* 2d ed., p. 467; and "A Bibliography of Suicide Notes: 1856-1979," in *Suicide and Life-Threatening Behavior* 9, no. 1 (Spring 1979): 57–59. See also Antoon A. Leenaars and David Lester, "What Characteristics of Suicide Notes Are Salient for People to Allow Perception of a Suicide Note as Genuine?" in *Death Studies* 14 (1990): 25–30.

81. Evans and Farberow, *Encyclopedia of Suicide,* p. 187.

82. Stillion et al., *Suicide Across the Life Span,* p. 13.

83. Ralph Beer, "Holding to the Land: A Rancher's Sorrow," *Harper's* (September 1985), p. 62.

84. Stillion et al., *Suicide Across the Life Span,* p. 194.

85. See, for example, Cathie Stivers, "Promotion of Self-Esteem in the Prevention of Suicide," *Death Studies* 14 (1990): 303–327.

86. See Linda Sattem, "Suicide Prevention in Elementary Schools," *Death Studies* 14 (1990): 329–346; Roger Tierney, Richard Ramsey, Bryan Tanney, and William Lang, "Comprehensive School Suicide Prevention Programs," *Death Studies* 14 (1990): 347–370; and Diane Ryerson, "Suicide Awareness Education in Schools: The Development of a Core Program and Subsequent Modifications for Special Populations or Institutions," *Death Studies* 14 (1990): 371–390.

87. See, for example, Jane Mersky Leder, *Dead Serious: A Book for Teenagers About Teenage Suicide* (New York: Atheneum, 1987). Other titles can be found through a search of *Books in Print.*

88. Overholser, Evans, and Spirito, "Sex Differences and Their Relevance," pp. 391–402.

89. Stanley Beardy and Margaret Beardy, "Healing Native Communities Through 'Helping Hands'" (paper presented at the annual meeting of the Association for Death Education and Counseling, Duluth, Minnesota, April 1991).

90. K. D. Atala and R. F. Baxter, "Suicidal Adolescents: How to Help Them Before It's Too Late," *Postgraduate Medicine* 86 (1989): 229–230.

91. Evans and Farberow, *Encyclopedia of Suicide,* pp. 58–59, 63.

92. Charles Neuringer, "The Meaning Behind Popular Myths About Suicide," *Omega: Journal of Death and Dying* 18 (1987–1988): 155–162. See also George Domino, "Popular Misconceptions About Suicide: How Popular Are They?" *Omega: Journal of Death and Dying* 21 (1990): 167–175.

93. See Jack D. Douglas in *The Social Meanings of Suicide* (Princeton, N.J.: Princeton University Press, 1967), pp. 324ff.

94. Stillion et al., *Suicide Across the Life Span,* p. 24.

CHAPTER 13

1. From *Letters of E. B. White,* collected and edited by Dorothy Lobrano Guth (New York: Harper and Row, 1976), p. 558.

2. Harvey M. Sapolsky, "The Politics of Risk," *Daedalus: Journal of the American Academy of Arts and Sciences* 119 (Fall 1990): 83–96.

3. Cited in Daniel M. Berman, *Death on the Job: Occupational Health and Safety Struggles in the United States* (New York: Monthly Review Press, 1978), pp. 179–180.

4. James A. Thorson and F. C. Powell, "To Laugh in the Face of Death: The Games That Lethal People Play," *Omega: Journal of Death and Dying* 21 (1990): 225–239.

5. Kenneth J. Doka, Eric C. Schwartz, and Catherine Schwarz, "Risky Business: Reactions to Death in Hazardous Sports" (paper presented at the Annual Meeting of the Association for Death Education and Counseling, Atlanta, 1986); see also, by the same authors, "Risky Business: Observations on the Nature of Death in Hazardous Sports," *Omega: Journal of Death and Dying* 21 (1990): 215–223.

6. Michael C. Roberts, "Prevention/Promotion in America: Still Spitting on the Sidewalk (Lee Salk Distinguished Service Award Address)," *Journal of Pediatric Psychology* 19, no. 3 (June 1994): 267–281.

7. Robert Kastenbaum and Ruth Aisenberg, *The Psychology of Death: Concise Edition* (New York: Springer, 1976), p. 319.

8. K. David Pijawka, Beverly A. Cuthbertson, and Richard S. Olson, "Coping with Extreme Hazard Events: Emerging Themes in Natural and Technological Disaster Research," *Omega: Journal of Death and Dying* 18 (1987–1988): 281–297.

9. Philip Sarre, "Natural Hazards," in *Key Ideas in Human Thought,* ed. Kenneth McLeish (New York: Facts on File, 1993), pp. 502–504.

10. Robert Kastenbaum, *Death, Society, and Human Experience* (St. Louis: C. V. Mosby, 1977), p. 98.

11. Ibid., p. 103.

12. Robert I. Tilling, U.S. Geological Survey, *Eruptions of Mount St. Helens: Past, Present, and Future* (Washington, D.C.: Government Printing Office, n.d.). See also

Robert D. Brown, Jr., and William J. Kockelman, "Geology for Decisionmakers: Protecting Life, Property, and Resources," *Public Affairs Report* 26, no. 1.

13. Pijawka, Cuthbertson, and Olson, "Coping with Extreme Hazard Events," pp. 291–293.

14. Gail Walker, "Crisis-Care in Critical Incident Debriefing," *Death Studies* 14 (1990): 121–133.

15. Beverly McLeod, "In the Wake of Disaster," *Psychology Today* (October 1984), pp. 54–57.

16. "Murder Victims by Age, Sex, and Race," *Statistical Abstract of the United States 1994,* 114th ed. (Washington, D.C.: Government Printing Office, 1994), p. 201.

17. "Murder—Circumstances and Weapons Used," *Statistical Abstract of the United States 1994,* p. 201.

18. "'Vietnam Style' Triage Techniques Used to Treat Urban Assault Weapon Injuries," *Bulletin of the Park Ridge Center* (May 1989): 11–12.

19. American Medical Association, Council on Scientific Affairs, "Firearms Injuries and Deaths: A Critical Public Health Issue," *Public Health Reports* 104 (1989): 111–120.

20. Ice T, "The Killing Fields," in *The Path Ahead: Readings in Death and Dying,* ed. Lynne Ann DeSpelder and Albert Lee Strickland (Mountain View, Calif.: Mayfield, 1995), pp. 178–181; excerpted from *The Ice Opinion* (New York: St. Martin's Press, 1994).

21. "CDC: School a Hazardous Place," *Associated Press Online* (March 30, 1995).

22. Jane Caputi and Diana E. H. Russell, "'Femicide': Speaking the Unspeakable," *Ms.* (September–October 1990), pp. 34–37. See also Susan Brownmiller, *Against Our Will: Men, Women and Rape* (New York: Simon & Schuster, 1975).

23. Walter Laqueur, *The Age of Terrorism* (Boston: Little, Brown, 1987), p. 72.

24. Henry Lundsgaarde, *Murder in Space City: A Cultural Analysis of Houston Homicide Patterns* (New York: Oxford University Press, 1977). See also Ernest L. Abel, ed., *Homicide: A Bibliography* (Westport, Conn.: Greenwood Press, 1987).

25. Quoted in Kastenbaum and Aisenberg, *Psychology of Death,* pp. 269ff (italics in original).

26. Glenn M. Vernon, *Sociology of Death: An Analysis of Death-Related Behavior* (New York: Ronald Press, 1970).

27. Hugo A. Bedau, "Capital Punishment," *Academic American Encyclopedia Online Edition* (March 1991). See also Hugo A. Bedau, ed., *The Death Penalty in America,* 3d ed. (New York: Oxford University Press, 1982); and Hugo A. Bedau and Chester M. Pierce, eds., *Capital Punishment in the United States* (New York: AMS Press, 1976).

28. "Movement of Prisoners Under Sentence of Death," *Statistical Abstract of the United States 1994,* p. 218.

29. Kastenbaum and Aisenberg, *Psychology of Death,* pp. 95–96, 284–285.

30. Lundsgaarde, *Murder in Space City,* p. 146.

31. Ibid., pp. 281–282.

32. Lula M. Redmond, *Surviving When Someone You Love Was Murdered: A Professional's Guide to Group Grief Therapy for Families and Friends of Murder Victims* (Clearwater, Fla.: Psychological Consultation and Education Services, 1989), p. 37. See also Charles Figley, *Helping Traumatized Families* (San Francisco: Jossey-Bass, 1989).

33. Arnold Toynbee, "Death in War," in *Death and Dying: Challenge and Change,* ed. Robert Fulton et al. (Reading, Mass.: Addison-Wesley, 1978), p. 367.

34. Dalton Trumbo, *Johnny Got His Gun* (New York: Bantam Books, 1970), pp. 214, 224.

35. See Ervin Staub, *The Roots of Evil: The Origins of Genocide and Other Group Violence* (New York: Cambridge University Press, 1989).

36. World Campaign for the Protection of Victims of War, International Red Cross and Red Crescent Movement.

37. Sam Keen, *Faces of the Enemy: Reflections of the Hostile Imagination* (San Francisco: Harper and Row, 1986), p. 71.

38. Gil Elliot, "Agents of Death," in *Death: Current Perspectives,* ed. Edwin S. Shneidman, 3d ed. (Mountain View, Calif.: Mayfield, 1984), pp. 422–440.

39. Robert Jay Lifton and Eric Olson, *Living and Dying* (New York: Praeger, 1974), p. 32.

40. Vernon, *Sociology of Death,* p. 46.

41. Toynbee, "Death in War," p. 367.

42. Keen, *Faces of the Enemy,* p. 12.

43. Vernon, *Sociology of Death,* p. 47.

44. Joel Baruch, "Combat Death," in *Death: Current Perspectives,* ed. Edwin S. Shneidman (Palo Alto, Calif.: Mayfield, 1976), pp. 92–93.

45. Personal communication.

46. See Harvey J. Schwartz, "Fear of the Dead: The Role of Social Ritual in Neutralizing Fantasies from Combat," in *Psychotherapy of the Combat Veteran,* ed. H. J. Schwartz (New York: SP Medical & Scientific Books, 1984), pp. 253–267.

47. Paul Recer, "A Different Johnny," Associated Press wire story (March 3, 1991).

48. Lifton and Olson, *Living and Dying,* p. 24. See also Robert Jay Lifton, *Home from the War: Vietnam Veterans, Neither Victims Nor Executioners* (New York: Basic Books, 1985).

49. See, for example, Harold A. Widdison and Howard G. Salisbury, "The Delayed Stress Syndrome: A Pathological Delayed Grief Reaction?" *Omega: Journal of Death and Dying* 20 (1989–1990): 293–306.

50. Michael Browning, "Homer's 'Iliad' Has Lessons for Vietnam Nightmare," *Honolulu Advertiser* (February 12, 1995): B1, B4. See also Jonathan Shay, *Achilles in Vietnam: Combat Trauma and the Undoing of Character* (New York: Atheneum, 1994).

51. Maja Beckstrom, "Vietnam Vets Find Peace in Healing Ceremonies: Rituals Help End the War Within," *Utne Reader* (March/April 1991): 34–35. See also Rod Kane, *Veteran's Day: A Vietnam Memoir* (New York: Crown, 1989), and Michael Norman, *These Good Men: Friendships Forged from War* (New York: Crown, 1989).

52. Recer, "A Different Johnny."

53. From an account by Barbara Carton, Washington Park Service, in the *Honolulu Star-Bulletin & Advertiser* (August 11, 1985).

54. From an Associated Press wire story, March 9, 1991.

55. Marian Faye Novak, *Lonely Girls with Burning Eyes: A Wife Recalls Her Husband's Journey Home from Vietnam* (Boston: Little, Brown, 1991), p. 3.

56. Susan Fromberg Schaeffer, back cover comment in Novak, *Lonely Girls with Burning Eyes.*

57. Major John I. Alger, "War," *Academic American Encyclopedia Online Edition* (March 1991).

58. Keen, *Faces of the Enemy,* pp. 10–14.

59. Ibid., pp. 180–181.

60. Ibid., p. 137.

61. Staub, *The Roots of Evil,* p. 265.

62. See Jerald Bachman, "High School Seniors View the Military, 1976–1982," *Armed Forces and Society* 10 (1983): 86–94; Robert Fulton and Greg Owen, "Death and Society in Twentieth Century America," *Omega: Journal of Death and Dying* 18, no. 4 (1987–1988): 391; John E. Mack, "Psychosocial Effects of the Nuclear Arms Race," *Bulletin of the Atomic Scientists* 37, no. 4 (April 1981): 19–20; Edwin S. Shneidman, "Megadeath: Children of the Nuclear Family," in *Death and Dying,* ed. Fulton et al., pp. 372–376; and Judith M. Stillion, "Examining the Shadow: Gifted Children Respond to the Nuclear Threat," *Death Studies* 10, no. 1 (1986): 27–41.

63. See, for example, Fulton and Owen, "Death and Society in Twentieth Century America," pp. 390–391; and Sam Keen, *Fire in the Belly: On Being a Man* (New York: Bantam, 1991), p. 46.

64. On the development of the bomb, see Richard Rhodes, *The Making of the Atomic Bomb* (New York: Simon & Schuster, 1987).

65. Joanne Silberner, "Hiroshima and Nagasaki: Thirty-Six Years Later, the Struggle Continues," *Science News* 120, no. 18 (October 31, 1981): 284–287.

66. Robert Jay Lifton, "Psychological Effects of the Atomic Bomb in Hiroshima: The Theme of Death," in *The Threat of Impending Disaster: Contributions to the Psychology of Stress,* ed. George H. Grosser, Henry Wechsler, and Milton Greenblatt (Cambridge, Mass.: MIT Press, 1964), pp. 152–193.

67. Lawrence Badash, "Atomic Bomb" and "Hydrogen Bomb," *Academic American Encyclopedia Online Edition* (March 1991).

68. Ruth Sivard, *World Military and Social Expenditures—1989,* 13th ed. (Washington, D.C.: World Priorities, 1989). See also Christine K. Cassel and Victor W. Sidel, "Prescribing Global Health," *Second Opinion* 10 (March 1989): 126–133.

69. Lifton and Olson, *Living and Dying,* p. 120.

70. Initially Gallo used the term HTLV-III (for human lymphotropic virus); other terms, such as LAV (lymphadenopathy-associated virus) were also used by researchers. HIV is now the official designation.

71. See Charles E. Rosenberg, "What Is an Epidemic? AIDS in Historical Perspective," in *The Path Ahead,* ed. DeSpelder and Strickland, pp. 29–32; see also *Daedalus: Journal of the American Academy of Arts and Sciences* 118, no. 2 (Spring 1989): 1–17.

72. Gill Walt, "Health Care in the Third-World, 1974 to the 1990s," in *Caring for Health: History and Diversity,* ed. Charles Webster, Health and Disease Series, Book 6 (Buckingham, U.K.: Open University Press, 1994), p. 168.

73. Rodrick Wallace and Deborah Wallace, "Inner-City Disease and the Public Health of the Suburbs: The Sociogeographical Dispersion of Point-Source Infection," *Environment and Planning Abstracts* 25 (1993): 1707–1723. See also Rodrick Wallace and Deborah Wallace, "The Coming Crisis of Public Health in the Suburbs," *Millbank Quarterly* 71, no. 4 (1993): 543–564.

74. Rodrick Wallace and John Pittman, "Recurrence of Contagious Urban Desertification and the Social Thanatology of New York City," *Environment and Planning Abstracts* 24 (June 1992): 1–6.

75. Ibid., p. 1.

76. Mitchell Duneier, *Slim's Table: Race, Respectability, and Masculinity* (Chicago: University of Chicago Press, 1992), p. 75.

77. "Report: World Threatened by TB," *Associated Press Online* (March 20, 1995).

78. Rachel Nowak, "WHO Calls for Action Against TB," *Science* 267 (March 24, 1995): 1763.

79. See, for example, Laurie Garrett, *The Coming Plague: Newly Emerging Diseases in a World Out of Balance* (New York: Farrar, Straus and Giroux, 1994).

80. See Arnold A. Hutschnecker, *The Will to Live* (New York: Doubleday, 1954); Meyer Friedman and Ray H. Rosenman, *Type A Behavior and Your Heart* (New York: Alfred A. Knopf, 1974); Lawrence LeShan, *You Can Fight for Your Life* (New York: M. Evans, 1977); and O. Carl Simonton, Stephanie Matthews Simonton, and James Creighton, *Getting Well Again: A Step-by-Step Guide to Overcoming Cancer for Patients and Their Families* (Los Angeles: J. P. Tarcher, 1978).

81. Kawahito Hiroshi, "Death and the Corporate Warrior," *Japan Quarterly* 38 (April–June 1991): 149–157.

82. Thomas H. Holmes and Richard H. Rahe, "The Social Readjustment Rating Scale," *Journal of Psychosomatic Research* 11 (1967): 213–218. See also Richard H. Rahe, "Social Stress and Illness Onset," *Journal of Psychosomatic Research* 8 (1964): 34–43. On life-event scales developed for use in specific populations, as well as general issues in stress research, see Carolyn M. Aldwin, *Stress, Coping, and Development: An Integrative Perspective* (New York: Guilford Press, 1994), pp. 58–60. On stress related to general environmental conditions, see Manfred F. R. Kets de Vries, "Ecological Stress: A Deadly Reminder," *The Psychoanalytic Review* 67, no. 3 (Fall 1980): 389–408.

83. Paul J. Rosch, "Stress and Cancer: A Disease of Maladaptation?" in *Cancer, Stress, and Death,* ed. J. Tache et al. (New York: Plenum, 1979), pp. 211–212.

84. Jean Tache, "Stress as a Cause of Disease," in *Cancer, Stress, and Death,* p. 8.

85. Hans Selye, "Stress Without Distress," in *Stress and Survival: The Emotional Realities of Life-Threatening Illness,* ed. Charles A. Garfield (St. Louis, Mo.: C. V. Mosby, 1979), p. 15. See also, by Selye, *The Stress of Life* (New York: McGraw-Hill, 1976); and "Stress, Cancer, and the Mind," in *Cancer, Stress, and Death,* ed. Tache et al., pp. 11–19. The positive uses of stress are also discussed in an interview with Hans Selye by Laurence Cherry, "On the Real Benefits of Distress," *Psychology Today* (March 1978), pp. 60–70.

86. Robert Kugelmann, *Stress: The Nature and History of Engineered Grief* (Westport, Conn.: Praeger, 1992), p. 178.

87. Daniel Leviton, "Horrendous Death: Improving the Quality of Global Health," in *The Path Ahead,* ed. DeSpelder and Strickland, pp. 165–168; see also, edited by Leviton, *Horrendous Death, Health, and Well-Being* (New York: Hemisphere, 1991).

CHAPTER 14

1. Personal communication.

2. Bertrand Russell, *Unpopular Essays* (New York: Simon & Schuster, 1950), p. 141.

3. See, for example, "The Problem of Immortality," in Jacques Choron, *Death and Modern Man* (New York: Collier Books, 1964).

4. Mary Kawena Pukui, E. W. Haertig, and Catherine A. Lee, *Nana I Ke Kumu (Look to the Source),* vols. 1 and 2 (Honolulu: Hui Hanai; Queen Lili'uokalani Children's Center, 1972). See also E. S. Craighill Handy and Mary Kawena Pukui, *The Polynesian Family System in Ka-'u, Hawai'i* (Rutland, Vt.: Charles E. Tuttle, 1972).

5. Job 7:9, *The Jerusalem Bible.* See also Job 14:7–12.

6. Daniel 12:2, *The Jerusalem Bible.*

7. See Lou H. Silberman in "Death in the Hebrew Bible and Apocalyptic Literature," in *Perspectives on Death,* ed. L. O. Mills (Nashville: Abingdon Press, 1969), pp. 13–32. The "Samuel" story is told in the first book of Samuel (28:3–25).

8. Stephen J. Vicchio, "Against Raising Hope of Raising the Dead: Contra Moody and Kübler-Ross," *Essence: Issues in the Study of Ageing, Dying and Death* 3, no. 2 (1979): 63.

9. H. Wheeler Robinson, "Hebrew Psychology," in *The People and the Book,* ed. Arthur S. Peake (London: Oxford University Press, 1925), pp. 353–382.

10. *The Meditations of Marcus Aurelius,* trans. George Long, *The Harvard Classics,* vol. 2, ed. Charles W. Elliot, pp. 193–301; see especially section II, 5 and 11, pp. 201–202.

11. Milton McC. Gatch, *Death: Meaning and Mortality in Christian Thought and Contemporary Culture* (New York: Seabury Press, 1969), p. 78.

12. See Jacques Le Goff, *The Birth of Purgatory* (Chicago: University of Chicago Press, 1984).

13. Vicchio, "Against Raising Hope," p. 62. See also Gordon E. Geddes, *Welcome Joy: Death in Puritan New England* (Ann Arbor, Mich.: UMI Research Press, 1981); David E. Stannard, *The Puritan Way of Death: A Study of Religion, Culture, and Social Change* (New York: Oxford University Press, 1977), and "Calm Dwellings: The Brief, Sentimental Age of the Rural Cemetery," in *American Heritage* 30 (August–September 1979): 42–56; and, edited by Stannard, *Death in America* (Philadelphia: University of Pennsylvania Press, 1975).

14. Renee Haynes, "Some Christian Imagery." in *Life After Death,* ed. Arnold Toynbee et al. (New York: McGraw-Hill, 1976), pp. 132ff.

15. John L. Esposito, *Islam: The Straight Path* (New York: Oxford University Press, 1988), p. 22.

16. Frithjof Schuon, *Understanding Islam* (Baltimore: Penguin, 1972), p. 16.

17. Alfred T. Welch, "Death and Dying in the Qur'an," in *Religious Encounters with Death: Insights from the History and Anthropology of Religions,* ed. Frank E. Reynolds and Earle H. Waugh (University Park: Pennsylvania State University Press, 1977), p. 184.

18. Esposito, *Islam: The Straight Path,* p. 34.

19. Huston Smith, *The Religions of Man* (New York: New American Library, 1958), p. 215.

20. Esposito, *Islam: The Straight Path,* p. 35.

21. D. S. Roberts, *Islam: A Concise Introduction* (San Francisco: Harper and Row, 1981), p. 128.

22. Abdul Latif Al Hoa, *Islam* (New York: Bookwright Press, 1987), p. 20.

23. Welch, "Death and Dying in the Qur'an," p. 193.

24. Roberts, *Islam: A Concise Introduction,* p. 128.

25. Ibid, p. 202.

26. *Bhagavad-Gita* II.27, trans. Swami Nikhilananda (New York: Ramakrishna-Vivekananda Center, 1952), p. 79.

27. Smith, *Religions of Man,* p. 34.

28. *Bhagavad-Gita* II.22, trans Nikhilananda, p. 77.

29. J. Bruce Long, "Death as a Necessity and a Gift in Hindu Mythology," in *Religious Encounters with Death,* ed. Reynolds and Waugh, p. 92; see also pp. 73–96.

30. This theme is explored by David R. Kinsley in "The 'Death That Conquers

Death': Dying to the World in Medieval Hinduism," *Religious Encounters with Death,* ed. Reynolds and Waugh, pp. 97–108.

31. "The Meaning of Practice-Enlightenment (Sushō-gi)," in *Zen Master Dōgen: An Introduction with Selected Writings,* trans. Yūhō Yokoi (New York/Tokyo: Weatherhill, 1976), p. 58.

32. Philip Kapleau, *Zen: Dawn in the West* (Garden City, N.Y.: Anchor Press/ Doubleday, 1979), p. 296. See also the following works edited by Kapleau: *The Wheel of Death: A Collection of Writings from Zen Buddhist and Other Sources on Death-Rebirth-Dying* (New York: Harper and Row, 1971); and *The Wheel of Life and Death: A Practical and Spiritual Guide* (New York: Doubleday, 1989).

33. "Awakening to the Bodhi-Mind (Hotsu Bodai-shin)," from the Shōbō-Genzō, in *Zen Master Dōgen,* trans. Yokoi, p. 109.

34. "The Meaning of Practice-Enlightenment (Shushō-gi)," in *Zen Master Dōgen,* trans. Yokoi, p. 58.

35. *The Zen Master Hakuin: Selected Writings,* trans. Philip B. Yampolsky (New York: Columbia University Press, 1971).

36. W. Y. Evans-Wentz, *The Tibetan Book of the Dead: or, the After-Death Experiences on the Bardo Plane, According to Lama Kazi Dawa-Samup's English Rendering* (New York: Oxford University Press, 1960).

37. Quoted in Kapleau, *Zen: Dawn in the West,* p. 68.

38. Francesca Fremantle and Chögyam Trungpa, eds., *The Tibetan Book of the Dead: The Great Liberation Through Hearing in the Bardo, by Guru Rinpoche According to Karma Lingpa* (Boulder, Colo.: Shambhala, 1975).

39. Kapleau, *Zen: Dawn in the West,* p. 69. The crucial period is the first forty-nine days following death. Services may be held every day for the first seven days, then once a week thereafter for the remainder of the seven-week period. After that, similar rites are extended into the third year, the seventh year, the thirteenth, and so on, up to fifty years.

40. James Turner, *Without God, Without Creed: The Origins of Unbelief in America* (Baltimore: Johns Hopkins University Press, 1985).

41. David E. Anderson, "Survey Shows Americans a Religious People," United Press International (April 3, 1991).

42. Jeffery L. Sheler, "Hell's Sober Comeback," *U.S. News & World Report* (March 25, 1991), pp. 56–57. See also Daniel J. Klenow and Robert C. Bolin, "Belief in an Afterlife: A National Survey," *Omega: Journal of Death and Dying* 20 (1989–1990): 63–74.

43. Norman Cousins, *The Celebration of Life: A Dialogue on Immortality and Infinity* (New York: Harper and Row, 1974).

44. Carol Zaleski, *Otherworld Journeys: Accounts of Near-Death Experience in Medieval and Modern Times* (New York: Oxford University Press, 1987).

45. Barbara A. Walker, "Health Care Professionals and the Near-Death Experience," *Death Studies* 13 (1989): 63–71. See also Evelyn R. Hayes and Linda D. Waters, "Interdisciplinary Perceptions of the Near-Death Experience: Implications for Professional Education and Practice," *Death Studies* 13 (1989): 443–453.

46. Kenneth Ring, *Life at Death: A Scientific Investigation of the Near-Death Experience* (New York: Coward, McCann, and Geoghegan, 1980), and *Heading Toward Omega: In Search of the Meaning of the Near-Death Experience* (New York: William Morrow, 1984). See also Raymond A. Moody, Jr., *Life After Life,* and its sequel, *Reflections on Life After Life* (various editions); and Elisabeth Kübler-Ross, "Death Does Not Exist," *CoEvolution Quarterly* 14 (Summer 1977): 100–107.

47. H. J. Irwin, *An Introduction to Parapsychology* (Jefferson, N.C.: McFarland, 1989), pp. 188–190.

48. William J. Serdahely, "The Near-Death Experience: Is the Presence Always the Higher Self?" *Omega: Journal of Death and Dying* 18 (1987–1988): 129–134.

49. William J. Serdahely, "A Pediatric Near-Death Experience: Tunnel Variants," *Omega: Journal of Death and Dying* 20 (1989–1990): 55–62. See also William J. Serdahely and Barbara A. Walker, "A Near-Death Experience at Birth," *Death Studies* (1990): 177–183.

50. See Bruce Greyson and Nancy Evans Bush, "Distressing Near-Death Experiences," *Psychiatry* 55 (February 1992): 95–110; P. M. H. Atwater, "Is There a Hell? Surprising Observations About the Near-Death Experience," *Journal of Near-Death Studies* 10, no. 3 (Spring 1992): 149–160; and Kenneth Ring, "Solving the Riddle of Frightening NDEs: Some Testable Hypotheses and a Perspective Based on 'A Course in Miracles,'" *Journal of Near-Death Studies* (in press).

51. See Christopher M. Bache, "A Perinatal Interpretation of Frightening NDEs: A Dialogue with Kenneth Ring," *Journal of Near-Death Studies* (in press).

52. Ian Stevenson, Emily W. Cook, Nicholas McClean-Rice, "Are Persons Reporting 'Near-Death Experiences' Really Near Death? A Study of Medical Records," *Omega: Journal of Death and Dying* 20 (1989–1990): 45–54.

53. An excellent introduction to the main points of view can be found in Stephen J. Vicchio's review article, "Near-Death Experiences: A Critical Review of the Literature and Some Questions for Further Study," *Essence: Issues in the Study of Ageing, Dying and Death* 5, no. 1 (1981): 77–89. Also see James E. Alcock, "Psychology and Near-Death Experiences," *The Skeptical Inquirer* 3, no. 3 (Spring 1979): 25–41; Michael B. Sabom, *Recollections of Death: A Medical Investigation* (New York: Harper and Row, 1981); and Stephen J. Vicchio, "Near-Death Experiences: Some Logical Problems and Questions for Further Study," *Anabiosis: The Journal of the International Association for Near-Death Studies* (1981): 66–87. The history of research into near-death experiences is also traced in Stanislav Grof and Joan Halifax, *The Human Encounter with Death* (New York: E. P. Dutton, 1978), Chapter 7, "Consciousness and the Threshold of Death," pp. 131–157.

54. See Handy and Pukui, *The Polynesian Family System in Ka-'u, Hawai'i;* Donald D. Kilolani Mitchell, *Resource Units in Hawaiian Culture* (Honolulu: Kamehameha Schools Press, 1982); and Pukui et al., *Nana I Ke Kumu (Look to the Source),* vols. 1 and 2.

55. See Roy Kletti and Russell Noyes, Jr., "Mental States in Mortal Danger," which includes a translation of Oskar Pfister's 1930 paper commenting on Heim's observations, in *Essence: Issues in the Study of Ageing, Dying and Death* 5, no. 1 (1981): 5–20.

56. See Russell Noyes, Jr., "Dying and Mystical Consciousness," *Journal of Thanatology* I (1971): 25–41; Russell Noyes, Jr., and Roy Kletti, "Depersonalization in the Face of Life-Threatening Danger: An Interpretation," *Omega: Journal of Death and Dying* 7 (1976): 103–114; Russell Noyes, Jr., and Roy Kletti, "Panoramic Memory: A Response to the Threat of Death," *Omega: Journal of Death and Dying* 8 (1977): 181–194; Russell Noyes, Jr., "Near-Death Experiences: Their Interpretation and Significance," in *Between Life and Death,* ed. Robert Kastenbaum (New York: Springer, 1979), pp. 73–78; and Russell Noyes, Jr., "The Encounter with Life-Threatening Danger: Its Nature and Impact," *Essence: Issues in the Study of Ageing, Dying and Death* 5, no. 1 (1981): 21–32.

57. George Gallup, Jr., *Adventures in Immortality* (New York: McGraw-Hill, 1982).

58. Karlis Osis and Erlendur Haraldsson, "Deathbed Observations of Physicians and Nurses: A Cross-Cultural Survey," in *The Signet Handbook of Parapsychology,* ed.

Martin Ebon (New York: Signet/NAL, 1978); and, by Osis and Haraldsson, *At the Hour of Death* (New York: Avon Books, 1977). See also, by Haraldsson, "Survey of Claimed Encounters with the Dead," *Omega: Journal of Death and Dying* 19 (1988–1989): 103–113.

59. Louis Appleby, *British Medical Journal* 298 (April 15, 1989): 976–977.

60. Zaleski, *Otherworld Journeys.*

61. From a conversation between Herman Feifel and John Morgan, "Humanity Has to Be the Model," *Death Studies* 10 (1986): 1–9.

62. Zaleski, *Otherworld Journeys.*

63. Charles A. Garfield, "The Dying Patient's Concern with 'Life After Death,'" in *Between Life and Death,* ed. Kastenbaum, pp. 52–57.

64. Robert Kastenbaum, "Happily Ever After," in *Between Life and Death,* pp. 17, 19.

65. Garfield, "Dying Patient's Concern with 'Life After Death.'"

66. Marie-Louise von Franz, *On Death and Dreams: A Jungian Interpretation* (Boston: Shambhala, 1986), pp. viii–ix.

67. Ibid., p. 156.

68. Ibid., pp. 66–67.

69. Some evidence suggests that LSD may function by interfering with the transfer of oxygen on the enzymatic level. Anoxia, or diminished levels of oxygen in the bodily tissues, is also frequently found in dying patients as well as in conjunction with certain yogic techniques involving breath control. Thus, the chemical changes caused by anoxia in all these instances may somehow activate certain transpersonal matrices in the unconscious, giving rise to the experiences associated with NDEs, certain yogic states, and LSD sessions. See Stanislav Grof and Joan Halifax, *The Human Encounter with Death* (New York: E. P. Dutton, 1978), pp. 183ff.

70. Stanislav Grof, *Realms of the Human Unconscious: Observations from LSD Research* (New York: E. P. Dutton, 1976).

71. See Stanislav Grof, *LSD Psychotherapy* (Pomona, Calif.: Hunter House, 1980), pp. 252ff; Grof and Halifax, *Human Encounter with Death,* pp. 16ff; and Peter Stafford, *Psychedelics Encyclopedia* (Berkeley, Calif.: And/Or Press, 1977), pp. 23–39.

72. Grof and Halifax, *Human Encounter with Death,* pp. 120–121.

73. Stanislav Grof and Christina Grof, *Beyond Death: The Gates of Consciousness* (New York: Thames and Hudson, 1980), p. 24.

74. Stanislav Grof and Joan Halifax, "Psychedelics and the Experience of Dying," in *Life After Death,* ed. Toynbee et al., pp. 192–193.

75. Grof, *LSD Psychotherapy,* p. 294. On models of human consciousness, see also Seymour Boorstein, ed., *Transpersonal Psychology* (Palo Alto, Calif.: Science and Behavior Books, 1980); Abraham H. Maslow, *The Farther Reaches of Human Nature* (New York: Viking Penguin, 1971); Robert E. Ornstein, ed., *The Nature of Human Consciousness: A Book of Readings* (San Francisco: W. H. Freeman, 1973); Kenneth R. Pelletier and Charles A. Garfield, *Consciousness: East and West* (New York: Harper and Row, 1976); Charles T. Tart, ed., *Transpersonal Psychologies* (New York: Harper and Row, 1975); Roger N. Walsh and Frances Vaughan, eds., *Beyond Ego: Transpersonal Dimensions in Psychology* (Los Angeles: J. P. Tarcher, 1980).

76. The metaphorical presentation of death as door or wall is credited to Herman Feifel, *The Meaning of Death* (New York: McGraw-Hill, 1959), p. xiv.

77. Clyde M. Nabe, "'Seeing As': Death as Door or Wall," in *Priorities in Death Education and Counseling,* ed. Richard A. Pacholski and Charles A. Corr (Arlington, Va.: Forum for Death Education and Counseling, 1982), pp. 161–169.

78. Spiritual Care Work Group, International Work Group on Death, Dying and Bereavement, "Assumptions and Principles of Spiritual Care," *Death Studies* 14 (1990): 75–81.

79. Clifford C. Kuhn, "A Spiritual Inventory of the Medically Ill Patient," *Psychiatric Medicine* 6 (1988): 87–100.

80. See Thomas Attig, "Respecting the Spirituality of the Dying and the Bereaved," in *A Challenge for Living: Dying, Death, and Bereavement,* ed. Inge B. Corless, Barbara B. Germino, and Mary A. Pittman (Boston: Jones and Bartlett, 1995), pp. 177–130.

81. Nabe, " 'Seeing As': Death as Door or Wall."

CHAPTER 15

1. Allan B. Chinen, "The Mortal King," in *The Path Ahead: Readings in Death and Dying,* ed. Lynne Ann DeSpelder and Albert Lee Strickland (Mountain View, Calif.: Mayfield, 1995), pp. 335–336; reprinted from *Once Upon a Midlife: Classic Stories and Mythic Tales to Illuminate the Middle Years* by Allan B. Chinen (Los Angeles: Jeremy P. Tarcher, 1992).

2. Thomas Attig, "Coping with Mortality: An Essay on Self-Mourning," in *The Path Ahead,* ed. De Spelder and Strickland, pp. 337–341; reprinted from *Death Studies* 13, no. 4 (1989): 361–370.

3. J. Eugene Knott and Richard W. Prull, "Death Education: Accountable to Whom? For What?" *Omega: Journal of Death and Dying* 7, no. 2 (1976): 178.

4. Robert Fulton, "Unanticipated Grief" (paper presented at the Annual Meeting of the Forum for Death Education and Counseling, Philadelphia, April 12, 1985).

5. Darrell Crase, "Black People Do Die, Don't They?" *Death Studies* 11, no. 3 (1987): 221–228.

6. Robert A. Neimeyer, "Death Anxiety Research: The State of the Art" (paper presented at the annual meeting of the Association for Death Education and Counseling, Duluth, Minnesota, April 1991).

7. Robert A. Neimeyer and Marlin K. Moore. "Assessing Personal Meanings of Death: Empirical Refinements in the Threat Index," *Death Studies* 13 (1989): 227–245.

8. For an introduction to the literature, see Robert A. Neimeyer and David Van Brunt, "Death Anxiety," in *Dying: Facing the Facts,* 3d ed., ed. Hannelore Wass and Robert A. Neimeyer (Washington, D.C.: Taylor & Francis, 1995), pp. 49–88.

9. Neimeyer, "Death Anxiety Research." See also *Death Anxiety Handbook: Research, Instrumentation, and Application,* ed. Robert A. Neimeyer (Washington, D.C.: Taylor and Francis, 1993).

10. Herman Feifel, "Psychology and Death: Meaningful Rediscovery," in *The Path Ahead,* ed. DeSpelder and Strickland, pp. 19–28; reprinted from *American Psychologist* 45 (April 1990): 537–543.

11. Robert Kastenbaum, "Theory, Research, and Application: Some Critical Issues for Thanatology," *Omega: Journal of Death and Dying* 18, no. 4 (1987–1988): 397–410.

12. Example cited by Kastenbaum, "Theory, Research, and Application," p. 401.

13. Myra Bluebond-Langner, "Wither Thou Goest?" *Omega: Journal of Death and Dying* 18, no. 4 (1987–1988): 257–263.

14. Feifel, "Psychology and Death," p. 27.

15. Robert Fulton and Greg Owen, "Death and Society in Twentieth Century America," *Omega: Journal of Death and Dying* 18, no. 4 (1987–1988): 390.

16. Daniel Leviton and William Wendt, "Death Education: Toward Individual and Global Well-Being," *Death Education* 7 (1983): 369–384; and, edited by Leviton, *Horrendous Death, Health, and Well-Being* (New York: Hemisphere, 1991) and *Horrendous Death and Health: Toward Action* (New York: Hemisphere, 1991). See also Richard A. Pacholski, "Teaching Nuclear Holocaust, the Basic Thanatological Topic," *Death Studies* 13 (1989): 175–183.

17. International Work Group on Death, Dying, and Bereavement, "A Statement of Assumptions and Principles Concerning Education About Death, Dying, and Bereavement," in *Statements on Death, Dying, and Bereavement* (London, Ont.: IWG, 1994). The three documents on death education prepared by this group were originally published in the following journals: *Death Studies* 16 (1991): 59–65 (on education in general), *Omega: Journal of Death and Dying* 23 (1991): 235–239 (on education for professionals in health care and human services), and *The American Journal of Hospice and Palliative Care* 7 (1991): 26–27 (on education for volunteers and nonprofessionals).

18. "Projections of Resident Population by Age, Sex, and Race: 1995 to 2025," *Statistical Abstract of the United States 1994,* 114th ed. (Washington, D.C.: Government Printing Office, 1994), p. 24.

19. Ron Crocombe, *The South Pacific: An Introduction* (Auckland, New Zealand: Longman Paul Ltd., 1983), p. 73.

20. Damon Knight, "Masks," in *A Pocketful of Stars,* ed. Damon Knight (New York: Doubleday, 1971).

21. Clifford Simak, "Death Scene," in *The Worlds of Clifford Simak* (New York: Simon & Schuster, 1960); Robert A. Heinlein, "Life-Line," in *The Man Who Sold the Moon; Harriman and the Escape from the Earth to the Moon!* ed. Heinlein (New York: Shasta Publications, 1950).

22. Kit Reed, "Golden Acres," in *Social Problems Through Science Fiction,* ed. John W. Miestead et al. (New York: St. Martin's Press, 1975).

23. Cullen Murphy, "The Way the World Ends," *The Wilson Quarterly* (Winter 1990): 50–55.

24. See, for example, Jonathan Weiner, *The Next One Hundred Years; Shaping the Fate of Our Living Earth* (New York: Bantam, 1990).

25. Gary Snyder, *The Practice of the Wild: Essays* (San Francisco: North Point Press, 1990), p. 176.

26. Alfred G. Killilea, "The Politics of Being Mortal," in *The Path Ahead,* ed. DeSpelder and Strickland, pp. 342–347; reprinted from *The Politics of Being Mortal* by Alfred G. Killilea (Lexington, University Press of Kentucky, 1988).

27. Avery Weisman, *On Dying and Denying: A Psychiatric Study of Terminality* (New York: Behavioral Publications, 1972), pp. 39–40.

28. This account of Lindbergh's death draws from various sources, including a description by Dr. Milton H. Howell, one of Lindbergh's physicians, reported by Ernest H. Rosenbaum, "The Doctor and the Cancer Patient," in *A Hospice Handbook,* ed. Michael P. Hamilton and Helen F. Reid (Grand Rapids, Mich.: Wm. B. Eerdmans, 1980), pp. 19–43.

29. Sandra L. Bertman, "Bearing the Unbearable: From Loss, the Gain," in *The Path Ahead,* ed. DeSpelder and Strickland, pp. 348–354; reprinted from *Health Values: Achieving High Level Wellness* 7, no. 1 (1982): 24–32.

Credits and Sources

Prologue and Epilogue: Copyright © 1982 by David Gordon. Used by permission.

Page 6: From A. Crosby, "Death in Cades Cove," in *Appalachia: When Yesterday Is Today*, ed. students at the University of Tennessee (Knoxville, 1965), pp. 1–3; quoted in *Death and Dying in Central Appalachia: Changing Attitudes and Practices* by James K. Crissman (Urbana: University of Illinois Press, 1994), p. 27.

Page 12: From the *Los Angeles Times* (December 21, 1990).

Page 13: "Grandmother, When Your Child Died," first published by the California State Poetry Society. Used by permission of Joan Neet George.

Page 17: Reprinted by permission of G. P. Putnam's Sons from *Cruel Shoes* by Steve Martin. Copyright © 1977, 1979 by Steve Martin.

Page 26: "One Tree Hill," music by U2, words by Bono. Copyright © 1987 by U2. All rights administered by Chappell & Co., Inc. All rights reserved.

Page 30: "Buffalo Bill's" is reprinted from *Tulips & Chimneys* by E. E. Cummings, ed. George James Firmage, by permission of Liveright Publishing Corporation and from *Complete Poems 1913–1962*, by permission of Grafton Books. Copyright 1923, 1925 and renewed 1951, 1953 by E. E. Cummings. Copyright © 1973, 1976 by the Trustees for the E. E. Cummings Trust. Copyright © 1973, 1976 by George James Firmage.

Pages 45, 68, 237, and 239: Courtesy of Edward C. and Gail R. Johnson.

Page 50: Illustration copyright © 1982 by Eric Mathes. Courtesy of Eric Mathes.

Page 51: From *Death Customs* by E. Bendann; Knopf, 1930.

Page 52: "When Hare Heard of Death," an excerpt from pp. 23–24 of *The Road of Life and Death: A Ritual Drama of the American Indians* by Paul Radin, Bollingen Series V. Copyright © 1945, renewed 1973, by Princeton University Press. Reprinted by permission of Princeton University Press and Doris Woodward Radin.

Page 53: Aesop's "Eros and Death," reworked by Steve Sanfield, from *Death: An Anthology of Ancient Texts, Songs, Prayers, and Stories*, ed. David Meltzer; North Point Press, 1984.

Page 55: From *Strange Facts About Death* by Webb Garrison. Copyright © 1978 by Webb Garrison. Used by permission of the publisher, Abingdon Press.

Page 60: From *CoEvolution Quarterly* 17 (Spring 1978): 135, "Little Prigs & Sages." Used by permission of CoEvolution Quarterly.

Page 71: Papago song by Juana Manwell. By permission of Smithsonian Institution Press from *Papago Music* by Frances Densmore. Bureau of American Ethnology Bulletin 90. Smithsonian Institution, Washington, D.C. 1929.

Page 71: Dakota song from *The Primal Mind: Vision and Reality in Indian America* by Jamake Highwater; Harper and Row, 1981.

Page 72: "Warrior song" (Omaha; Hethúska Society) from *The Omaha Tribe* by Alice Fletcher and Francis LaFlesche. Bureau of American Ethnology, 27th Report, Smithsonian Institution, 1911.

Page 73: "Burial Oration" (Wintu) from "Wintu Ethnography" by Cora Du Bois, in *University of California Publications in American Archaeology and Ethnology* 36 (1935). Reprinted by permission of the University of California Press.

Page 77: From *Religions of Africa: A Pilgrimage into Traditional Religions* by Noel Q. King; Harper and Row, 1970.

Page 81: From *The Four Seasons: Japanese Haiku Second Series*, trans. Peter Beilenson. Copyright © 1958 by The Peter Pauper Press.

Page 83: Reprinted from *Temple Dusk: Zen Haiku* by Mitsu Suzuki (1992) with permission of Parallax Press, Berkeley, California.

Page 87: From *Japanese Death Poems*, comp. Yoel Hoffman; Charles E. Tuttle, 1986. Reprinted by permission of Charles E. Tuttle, Co., Inc., Tokyo, Japan.

Page 99: From Ruth Walter and Brenda Gameau, "Australia: Its Land, Its People, Its Health Care System, and Unique Health Issues," *Social Work in Health Care* 18, no. 3–4 (1993): 56–57.

Page 103: From *Washing the Stones* by Maude Meehan (Watsonville, Calif.: Papier-mâche Press, 1995). Reprinted by permission of Maude Meehan.

Page 109: From *Journeys Through Bookland*, Volume One, ed. Charles H. Sylvester; Bellows-Reeve Company, Publishers, Chicago, 1922.

Page 110: From *Journeys Through Bookland*, Volume One, ed. Charles H. Sylvester; Bellows-Reeve Company, Publishers, Chicago, 1922.

Page 112: From *After Aztlan: Latino Poets of the Nineties*, ed. Ray González (Boston: David R. Godine, 1992), pp. 143–144. Used by permission.

Page 113: From *The Words* by Jean Paul Sartre; George Braziller, 1964.

Page 116: From *Trinity* by Leon Uris; Doubleday & Company, Inc., 1976.

Page 120 (bottom): Drawing by Dominic Horath created in Mrs. Bronwyn Luffman's classroom at Salesian Sisters School and provided by Linda DaValle. Reprinted by permission of Mary and Frank Horath.

Page 124: "The Shroud" from *Grimms' Tales for Young and Old*, trans. Ralph Manheim. Reprinted by permission of Doubleday & Company, Inc.

Page 146: From the book *To Live Until We Say Good-Bye*. Text by Elisabeth Kübler-Ross, photographs by Mal Warshaw. Copyright © 1978 by Ross Medical Associates, S.C., and Mal Warshaw. Used by permission of the publisher Prentice-Hall, Inc., Englewood Cliffs, N.J.

Page 148: From *Dying and Death: A Clinical Guide for Caregivers*, ed. David Barton. Copyright © 1977 by The Williams and Wilkins Company. Used with permission of The Williams and Wilkins Company and by courtesy of David Barton, M.D.

Pages 152 and 437: © 1995 by Cornelius Eady from *You Don't Miss Your Water* (Henry Holt, 1995); first published in *Pequod*, no. 35 (1993). Reprinted by permission of the author and Henry Holt and Co.

Pages 155 and 231: Used by permission of Elizabeth Bradbury.

Page 159: From *Anatomy of an Illness* by Norman Cousins. Copyright © 1979 by W. W. Norton & Company, Inc.

Page 392: From *The Accident* by Carol and Donald Carrick; Seabury, 1976.

Page 397: Used with permission of Christine and Donovan Longaker.

Page 398: From *A Tropical Childhood and Other Poems* by Edward Lucie-Smith; Copyright © Oxford University Press, 1961. Reprinted by permission of Oxford University Press.

Page 406: From *Winesburg, Ohio* by Sherwood Anderson; Viking Press, 1958.

Page 420: From *Love and Profit: The Art of Caring Leadership* by James A. Autry; William Morrow, 1991. Reprinted by permission of William Morrow & Co., Inc.

Pages 427 and 475: Used by permission of Maude Meehan.

Page 433: From "Psychological Aspects of Sudden Unexpected Death in Infants and Children" by Abraham B. Bergman in *Pediatric Clinics of North America* 21, no. 1 (February 1974).

Page 435: Transcribed by the authors from an inscription at the National Civil Rights Museum in Memphis, Tennessee.

Page 439: From *Alone: Surviving as a Widow* by Elizabeth C. Mooney; G. P. Putnam's Sons, 1981.

Page 444: From *Widow* by Lynn Caine. Copyright © 1974 by Lynn Caine. Used by permission of William Morrow & Co. and Macdonald & Co. (Publishers) Ltd.

Page 446: From *Chipping Bone: Collected Poems* by Maude Meehan; Embers Press, 1985. Courtesy of Maude Meehan.

Page 449: From *Living with Huntington's Disease: A Book for Patients and Families* by Dennis H. Phillips; University of Wisconsin Press, 1982.

Page 451: From *Aging in Mass Society: Myths and Realities* by Jon Hendricks and C. Davis Hendricks; Winthrop, 1977.

Page 457: Edwin Arlington Robinson, "Richard Cory," in *The Children of the Night*. Copyright under the Berne Convention (New York: Charles Scribner's Sons, 1897). Reprinted with the permission of Charles Scribner's Sons.

Page 462: Courtesy of Margaret Macro.

Pages 464, 468, 471, 477, 480, and 488: Suicide notes courtesy of Edwin S. Shneidman.

Page 467: From *The Goodbye Book* by Robert Ramsey and Randall Toye. Copyright © 1979 by Robert Ramsey. Reprinted by permission of Van Nostrand Reinhold Company.

Page 470: Adapted from *Death, Society, and Human Experience*, 2d ed., by Robert J. Kastenbaum (St. Louis: The C. V. Mosby Company, 1981). Used with permission of The C. V. Mosby Company and Robert J. Kastenbaum.

Page 473: Adapted from *Deaths of Man* by Edwin S. Shneidman; Quadrangle Books, 1973. Courtesy of Edwin S. Shneidman.

Page 479: From *The Savage God: A Study of Suicide* by A. Alvarez; Random House, 1972.

Page 490: "Resume" by Dorothy Parker, from *The Portable Dorothy Parker*, revised and enlarged edition, ed. Brendan Gill. Copyright 1926 by Dorothy Parker. Reprinted by permission of Viking Penguin, Inc., and from *The Collected Dorothy Parker* by permission of Gerald Duckworth, Ltd.

Page 493: From *A Hole in the World: An American Boyhood* by Richard Rhodes; Simon & Schuster, 1990.

Page 503: From "Groundfall" by William G. Higgins, in *Sierra* (November–December 1979).

Page 507: Reprinted with the permission of Pacific Gas & Electric Company.

Page 511: Courtesy of the Unocal Corporation.

Page 514: From *Custer Died for Your Sins: An Indian Manifesto* by Vine Deloria, Jr.; Macmillan, 1969.

Page 517: From *Murder in Space City: A Cultural Analysis of Houston Homicide Patterns* by Henry P. Lundsgaarde. Copyright © 1977 by Oxford University Press, Inc. Reprinted by permission.

Page 518: From *American Blood* by John Nichols; Henry Holt, 1987.

Page 527: From "The Flesh Made Word," in *Writing in an Era of Conflict: The National Book Week Lectures* (Washington, D.C.: Library of Congress, 1990), p. 6.

Page 529: From *A Rumor of War* by Philip Caputo. Copyright © 1977 by Philip Caputo. Reprinted by permission of Holt, Rinehart and Winston, Publishers. Used by permission of Macmillan Press, Ltd., London and Basingstoke.

Page 531: Copyright © 1981 New York Times Company. Reprinted by permission. Courtesy of Harvey J. Schwartz, M.D.

Page 534: From *Publishers Weekly* (October 25, 1985). Copyright © by Bowker Magazine Group, Reed Publishing USA. Used by permission.

Page 545: Reprinted with permission from *Journal of Psychosomatic Research* 11 (2): 213–218, T. H. Holmes and R. H. Rahe, "The Social Readjustment Rating Scale." Copyright © 1967, Pergamon Press, Ltd., and Thomas H. Holmes, M.D.

Page 561: From "Go Down Death—a Funeral Sermon," from *God's Trombones* by James Weldon Johnson. Copyright 1927 by Viking Press, Inc. Copyright renewed 1955 by Grace Nail Johnson. Reprinted by permission of Viking Penguin Inc.

Page 563: From *Religious Encounters with Death: Insights from the History and Anthropology of Religions*, ed. Frank E. Reynolds and Earle H. Waugh; Pennsylvania State University Press, 1977.

Page 570: From *Zen Mind, Beginner's Mind* by Shunryu Suzuki (1970). Reprinted by permission of John Weatherhill, Inc.

Page 573: From *Selected Works of Miguel de Unamuno*, Bollingen Series LXXXV, Vol. 4: *The Tragic Sense of Life in Men and Nations*, trans. Anthony Kerrigan. Copyright © 1972 by Princeton University Press.

Page 584: From *The Human Encounter with Death* by Stanislav Grof and Joan Halifax; E. P. Dutton, 1977.

Page 586: From *The Gospel at Colonus*. Music by Bob Telson, lyrics by Lee Breuer.

Page 591: From *Harlem Book of the Dead* by James Van Der Zee; Morgan and Morgan, 1978.

Page 596: From *Distant Neighbors* by Alan Riding; Vintage, 1986.

Page 597: From *The Ancient Child* by N. Scott Momaday; Doubleday, 1989.

Page 598: From *The Wheel of Death: A Collection of Writings from Zen Buddhist and Other Sources on Death, Rebirth, Dying* by Philip Kapleau; Harper and Row, 1971.

Page 604: From *Life at Death* by Kenneth Ring; Coward, McCann & Geoghegan, Inc., 1980.

Page 605: From *At the Edge of the Body* by Erica Jong. Copyright © 1979 by Erica Mann Jong. Reprinted by permission of Henry Holt and Company and the Sterling Lord Agency. Copyright © 1979 by Erica Jong.

Name Index

678

Subject Index